THE NATIONAL ATLAS OF KOREA

NATIONAL GEOGRAPHIC INFORMATION INSTITUTE
MINISTRY OF LAND, TRANSPORT AND MARITIME AFFAIRS

THE NATIONAL ATLAS OF KOREA

Date of Printing: May 2009
Date of Publication: May 2009

Publisher: Hong, Gi-Bum
National Geographic Information Institute (NGII)
Ministry of Land, Transport and Maritime Affairs
587 Worldcup-Gil, Yeongtong-Gu, Suwon-Si, Gyeonggi-Do 443-772
THE REPUBLIC OF KOREA

Phone: +82-31-210-2600
Fax: +82-31-210-2704

You can access to *The National Atlas of Korea* at the homepage of NGII, http://www.ngii.go.kr

9 788993 841039
ISBN 978-89-93841-03-9

FORWARD

*T*he *National Atlas of Korea* comprehensively illustrates the current status of the nation's environment, economy, and society. In order for it to be realized, a system to manage the expansive body of knowledge and most extensive data were needed. Accordingly, the national atlas committee consisting of the four subcommittees of experts worked on the project. As a result, *the National Atlas of Korea* was published in 2007. For the international publicity on the Korea, We have published the concise version of *the National Atlas of Korea*. I hope that *the National Atlas of Korea* will serve as a foundation for the better understanding of the land, environment, society, and culture of Korea.

I would like to extend my gratitude to all the people who were involved in developing this new national atlas, as well as the editorial committee of *the National Atlas of Korea*, for their enormous endeavor, cooperation and support. Especially, I wish to extend my thanks, not only to the members of the National Geographic Information Institute, but also to the Korean Geographic Society who assisted with the preparation for the national atlas.

Hong, Gi-Bum
President of the National Geographic Information Institute
Ministry of Land, Transport and Maritime Affairs
The Republic of Korea

PREFACE

*T*he *National Atlas of Korea* is a collection of maps with geographic information which reflects the nature, environment, history, culture, politics, economy, science and technology of Korea. Korea is now the 11th economic power in the world and this historical publication will support the nation's advancement in the everchanging, competitive world, as well as inform the fields of geography, cartography, mapping, and geographical information science.

The National Atlas of Korea will be a great educational resource for our young generations. Internationally, its wealth of information - the physical and human environment of Korea, the designation of indigenous place names - will inform the international society.

Finally, congratulations on the publication of *the National Atlas of Korea* and many thanks to all the people involved on the behalf of the Korean Geographical Society.

Yongwoo Kwon
President of the Korean Geographical Society

Geography

Location

Korea lies adjacent to China and Japan. The northern border of Korea is formed by the Amnokgang (river) and Dumangang (river), which separate it from Manchuria. A 16-kilometer segment of the Dumangang to the east also serves as a natural border with Russia. The west coast of the Korean Peninsula is bounded by the Korean Bay to the north and the Yellow Sea to the south; the east coast faces the East Sea.

Two hundred kilometers separate the peninsula from eastern China. The shortest distance between Korean and Chinese coasts is 200 kilometers and from the southeastern tip of the peninsula, the nearest point on the Japanese coast is also about 200 kilometers away.

Due to its unique geographical location, Chinese culture filtered into Japan through Korea; a common cultural sphere of Buddhism and Confucianism was thus established between the three countries.

The Korean Peninsula extends about 1,000 kilometers southward from the northeast Asian continental landmass. Roughly 300 kilometers in width, climatic variations are more pronounced along the south-north axis. Differences in vegetation can be seen between the colder north and the warmer south.

The peninsula and all of its associated islands lie between 33°06′43″N and 43°00′42″N parallels and 124°11′04″E and 131°52′22″E meridians. The latitudinal location of Korea is similar to that of the Iberian Peninsula and Greece. The entire peninsula corresponds approximately to the north-south span of the state of California.

The tips of Korean territory

Extreme Points	Places	Coordinates
Northernmost	Yuwonjin, Hamgyeongbuk-do	43°00′42″N
Southernmost	Marado Island, Jeju Special Self-Governing Province	33°06′43″N
Easternmost	Dokdo Island, Gyeongsangbuk-do	131°52′22″E
Westernmost	Maando Island, Pyeonganbuk-do	124°11′04″E

Longitudinally, Korea lies straight north of the Philippines and central Australia. The meridian of 127°30′E passes through the middle of the Korean Peninsula. Korea shares the same standard meridian of 135°E with Japan. Seoul and Tokyo local time is nine hours earlier than Greenwich Mean Time (GMT).

Territory

The total area of the peninsula, including its islands, is 223,170 square kilometers of which about 45 percent (100,032 square kilometers) constitutes the territory of South Korea. The combined territories of South and North Korea are similar to the size of Britain (244,100 square kilometers) and Guyana (215,000 square kilometers). South Korea alone is about the size of Hungary (93,000 square kilometers) and Jordan (97,700 square kilometers).

There are about 3,000 islands belonging to Korea. The islands are located mostly off the west and south coasts; only a handful of them lie off the East Sea. Ulleungdo, the largest island in the East Sea, serves as a major fishery base as does Dokdo. Bigger islands include Jejudo - the largest, Geojedo, Ganghwado, and Namhaedo.

Until the 11th century, the territory of Korea encompassed most of Manchuria. By the 15th century, after repeated conflicts with China, Koreans retreated southward and the Amnokgang (river) and Dumangang (river) became the permanent Sino-Korean border.

At the end of World War II, the peninsula was divided into a northern zone occupied by Soviet forces and a southern zone occupied by U.S. forces. The 38th parallel served as the boundary between the two zones. In 1953, at the end of the Korean War, a new border was fixed at the Demilitarized Zone (DMZ), a 4 kilometer-wide strip of land that runs along the lines of ceasefire from the east to the west coast for a distance of about 241 kilometers.

Administrative Units

There are three administrative tiers in South Korea. The highest tier includes seven metropolitan cities and nine provinces (do). Designated metropolitan cities are those urban areas with a population of over one million. Seoul, the capital of South Korea, is the largest urban center, having 10 million residents. Busan is the second largest city, with a population of over four million. Daegu, Incheon, Gwangju, Daejeon and Ulsan, in descending order, are each home to more than one million people. At the second administrative tier, provinces (do) are subdivided into cities (si) and counties (gun). A city has a population of more than 50,000. A gun consists of one town (eup) and five to ten townships (myeon). Although they are administrative units, provinces (do) also play an important role in the regional identification of the people and many Koreans often identify themselves by the province in which they were born and raised. Metropolitan cities are subdivided into districts (gu). The lowest units are dong in cities and ri in provinces. In the last several decades, South Korea has witnessed the rapid growth of its urban centers. The population of these areas now constitutes over 85 percent of the national total. Urban growth has been particularly spectacular along the Seoul-Busan corridor, the Seoul metropolitan area and the Gyeongsang Province area. By contrast, the southwestern and northeastern regions have sustained a considerable loss in population.

Geographical Regions

Mountain ranges have traditionally served as natural boundary markers between regions. Because these natural boundaries inhibited contacts between peoples living on either side of the range, subtle, and sometimes substantial, regional differences developed in both the spoken language and customs of the people. These regional distinctions also correspond to the traditional administrative divisions set up during the Joseon Dynasty (1392-1910).

The Korean Peninsula is divided into three distinct regions: Central, South and North. These macro regions are divided into three separate geographical spheres, each of which shows particular economic, cultural and physical distinctiveness. In the Central region are the Seoul metropolitan area, Chungcheong and Gangwon provinces; in the South, Gyeongsang, Jeolla and Jeju provinces; and in the North, Pyeongan, Hamgyeong and Hwanghae provinces. The term "northern area" traditionally referred to those regions of Pyeongan and Hamgyeong provinces prior to the division of the peninsula in 1945. The "North" now refers to all the areas north of the Demilitarized Zone, comprising Pyeongan, Hamgyeong, Hwanghae and the northern parts of the Gyeonggi and Gangwon provinces.

The Central Region

This region consists of the Seoul metropolitan area which is part of Gyeonggi Province, Chungcheong Province to the south, and Gangwon province to the east.

The Capital (Seoul / Gyeonggi) Area   This includes Seoul and Incheon, which are encompassed by Gyeonggi-do. The capital area, as the name implies, is the center of all political, economic and cultural activity in South Korea. Clustered around Seoul are also a number of smaller cities, which form a continuous and sprawling urban area. The largest concentration of the nation's industries is in and around Seoul. The capital area is the hub of South Korea's transportation networks, with Gimpo International Airport located on the western outskirts of Seoul, the newly built Incheon International Airport, and railroad networks that connect to all parts of the country. The region serves as South Korea's gateway to the world. Given its strategic importance, the dialect spoken in Seoul is considered to be the nation's standard language.

Chungcheong Area   This region lies between the capital area and the South. Cheongju and Daejeon are the leading urban centers of the region, respectively. Lying just below the capital area, this region consisting of Chungcheongnam-do and Chungcheongbuk-do has been characterized as a southern extension of Seoul; its proximity to the capital has been economically advantageous. New industries have recently mushroomed along the Asanman Bay on the west coast. The region has also profited from transportation and urban services available for Seoul and its vicinity. Chungcheong and Gyeonggi provinces specialize in horticulture and dairy farming to meet the huge demands of the nearby urban centers of the capital area.

Gangwon Area   This region lies to the east of the capital area. The Taebaeksan Mountain range, which runs north-south through the middle of the region, divides the province into eastern coastal and western inland areas. Gangneung, Chuncheon, and Wonju are its leading urban areas. Gangwon-do offers a variety of opportunities for tourism and sports, with its rugged terrain. Mining industries, once a major sector in the regional economy, have recently experienced a drastic decline due to competition from cheaper foreign-imported coal and minerals. The fall of mining industries, coupled with the national trend of rural-to-urban migration, are the major contributing factors for the recent migration out of the region. Gangwon-do, with less than 2 million residents, has now the smallest population of all the mainland provinces.

The South Region

The region includes the Gyeongsang Province, located in the southeast, Jeolla Province in the southwest, and Jejudo province which lies off the south coast.

Gyeongsang Area   This area includes metropolitan cities Busan, Daegu and Ulsan, being encompassed by Gyeongsangbuk-do and Gyeongsangnam-do. Busan and Daegu are the major urban centers of the province, being the second (4 million) and third (2.5 million) largest cities in South Korea.

This region is characterized by the vast basin of the Nakdonggang River and is surrounded by the Sobaeksan mountain ranges. Due to the rugged topography of the surrounding mountains, sub-areas within the region share common cultural traits such as dialect and custom, which are quite distinct from peoples of other regions. The fact that Gyeongsang Province also has another name, "Yeongnam," which literally means "south of the mountain pass," attests to the key role that the mountains have historically played in fostering regional differences between the Korean people.

Gyeongsang Province has one of the largest industrial agglomerations, second only to the capital area, due mainly to the heavy investments in the region by the South Korean government since the 1960s. These heavy industrial facilities of steel, shipbuilding, automobile and petrochemical factories are largely concentrated along the southeast stretch of Pohang, through Ulsan, Busan, Changwon, and Masan. The northern part also has two major clusters of industries around Daegu and Gumi, specializing in textile and electronics.

Jeolla Area Jeolla Province is located southwest of the peninsula and comprises of Jeollabuk-*do* and Jeollanam-*do*. Gwangju, Jeonju, and Naju are their respective centers.

"Honam" is another name for Jeolla Province. The flat fertile lands of the Geumgang and Yeongsangang river basins, as well as the coastal lowlands, have made the region the major granary of the nation. The regional economy has lagged somewhat behind the capital and Gyeongsang regions due to sparse industrial investments made there during the past decades. However, this situation is changing and the region is now experiencing industrial growth in major urban centers like Gwangju and Jeonju, as well as along its western coast. Also, the tidal flats near Gunsan and Mokpo have recently been reclaimed, adding new land for industrial development.

The region is endowed with a very irregular coastline and countless large and small islands, and this unique landscape attracts tourists year-round.

Jejudo Island Area Jejudo is the largest island in Korea located about 140 kilometers south of Mokpo in the South Sea. Its historic isolation from the mainland contributed to the Jejudo peoples' distinct dialect and lifestyle. Of volcanic origin, the island has rugged topography of numerous hills, gorges, and waterfalls. Because of its subtropical climate and the unique lifestyles and customs of its people, tourism is the region's most important industry. The island is also famous for its subtropical fruits such as tangerines, pineapples and bananas. It is also known for its women divers.

The North Region

The northern part of the peninsula is divided into two geographic regions: Pyeongan Province in the northwest and Hamgyeong Province in the northeast. The former with its flatlands is also known as the Gwanseo region while the latter is often referred to as Gwanbuk. Pyeongan Province serves as the major agricultural area of the North. By contrast, Hamgyeong Province, due to its mountainous topography, boasts mining and forestry as its major economic activities. Pyeongyang, the leading urban center in the Pyeongan Province, is the capital of North Korea and Nampo serves as the gateway port to Pyeongyang. Hamheung and Cheongjin are the major cities of Hamgyeong Province.

The third geographical region of the North, Hwanghae Province lies to the south of Pyeongan Province. Once a part of the Central Region prior to the South-North division, Hwanghae Province shares a great many cultural similarities with other west-central regions of the peninsula. Gaeseong is the major city of the region.

Mountains and Hills

Between the Korean Peninsula and Manchuria flow, in opposite directions, lie the two largest rivers of the region, the Amnokgang (river) and Dumangang (river), both originating at Mt. Baekdusan (2,744m), the highest mountain in the region. The peninsula is surrounded by the Yellow Sea, the East Sea, and the South Sea.

Nearly 70 percent of the Korean Peninsula is covered by mountains and hills. Low hills in the southern and the western regions give way gradually to increasingly higher mountains toward the eastern and the northern areas. On the whole, the western and southern slopes of the peninsula are wide with some plains and basins along rivers, while the eastern slope is very steep as high mountains precipitate into the East Sea.

Most of the high mountains are located along the Taebaek mountain range which runs parallel to the east coast, roughly north-to-south. West of this range are the drainage basins of the Hangang and Geumgang rivers. This range extends to the Nangnim range in North Korea, forming the geological and geomorphological backbone of the peninsula and constituting the watershed between the western and eastern slopes of the peninsula. Mt. Nangnimsan (2,184m), Mt. Geumgangsan (1,638m), Mt. Seoraksan (1,708m), and Mt. Taebaeksan (1,567m) are some of the highest peaks along these ranges. Just southwest from the Taebaeksan range is the Sobaeksan range, which culminates in the massive Mt. Jirisan (1,915m). This range was historically a great barrier between the central and southern parts of the peninsula, and also between the eastern and western regions in the south. The Nakdong river basin is thus segregated in southeastern Korea. The Gaemagowon Plateau, the so-called "Roof of Korea," located in the northwestern corner of the peninsula, has an average elevation of about 1,500 meters above sea level.

The landmass of the peninsula is rather stable geologically in spite of its proximity to Japan; it has neither active volcanoes nor strong earthquakes. There are, however, a few dead volcanoes that were formed during the Pleistocene era. Mt. Baekdusan is famous for a large caldera lake, "Cheonji," meaning heavenly tarn. Mt. Hallasan in Jejudo island, the highest mountain in South Korea, was recorded to have had minor volcanic activity in the early 11th century. It has a small crater lake, "Baengnokdam," and there are about 400 parasitic cones in its piedmont.

About two-thirds of the Korean Peninsula is composed of pre-Cambrian metamorphic and granitic rock. Although the distribution of sedimentary rock is very limited, limestone is quite abundant in some regions and a number of limestone caves can be found, some of which are tourist attractions. Among the most famous caves are Gossigul, Gosugul and Seongnyugul, all of which are adorned with stalagmites and stalactites.

Rivers and Plains

Most of major rivers flow into the Yellow Sea and a few into the South Sea, draining the western and southern slopes of the peninsula. Considering its size, Korea has a relatively large number of long rivers, six of them exceeding 400 kilometers. The discharge of rivers fluctuates greatly due to the summer monsoon. In the summertime, rivers swell with heavy rainfall, flooding valley plains every once in a while. In drier seasons, the water level drops and often much of the river bed is exposed. Typhoons, which hit the southern part of the peninsula once every two or three years, also bring heavy rainfall in late summer and early autumn.

In the past, rivers were important for transportation. Historical capitals such as Pyeongyang and Buyeo are located adjacent to major rivers, as is Seoul. After the introduction of railroads and automobiles, however, the importance of rivers for transportation has decreased sharply, and rivers are now used mainly for the irrigation of rice fields and power generation. During the last two decades a number of huge dams have been constructed for flood control, electricity, and irrigation. But these dams have gradually begun to play a major role as reservoirs for piped water supply to large cities and industrial plants as a result of rapid urbanization and industrialization nationwide.

Most farming fields are narrow floodplains developed along rivers, especially in their lower reaches. These plains serve as the major rice-producing lands. Large tidal differences at the mouths of major rivers flowing into the Yellow Sea inhibited the development of deltaic plains, although rivers transport large amounts of sediment during floods. Only the Nakdonggang flowing into the South Sea has a small delta at its mouth. Erosional basins along rivers in areas of granitic rocks have also served as agricultural regions since ancient times. Many large cities such as Chuncheon, Cheongju, and Wonju are located in such basins.

Coasts

Korea has a long coastline divided into the east, west and south coasts. The east coast has small tidal differences, a third of one meter at the most, and a relatively smooth shoreline with few islands offshore. The Taebaek range runs closely along the East Sea. Where mountains protrude from the Taebaeksan range, coasts are rocky in general, but some beaches are found in places into which small streams carry sediment from the high mountains. In many instances, the beaches take the form of sand spits and bars enclosing lagoons, which are notable features of the east coast. Along the coast between Wonsan and Gangneung are located a series of lagoons, including Gyeongpo and Hwajinpo, two famous resorts. The highway connecting Gangneung and Seoul has been expanded recently, reducing the travel time between the central region and the east coast.

The shorelines of the south and west coasts are very irregular with innumerable small peninsulas and bays as well as a large number of islands. The west coast facing the Yellow Sea, which is very shallow, has large tidal ranges, which rise above 10 meters in places. Harbors have been difficult to develop since tidal flats are common coastal features, especially in bays into which rivers discharge sediment during floods. Tidal flats have been reclaimed from ancient times mainly for rice fields, but since the 1970s, the reclamation has grown in magnitude. The Saemangeum Project, the largest such project ever undertaken, seeks to reclaim a total of 40,100 hectares of the flats through the construction of huge dikes, but it faces strong opposition from environmental groups.

The south coast shows a typical ria shoreline, a coastal zone which has been submerged. The length of coastline is nearly eight times longer than its straight-line distance, and its indentation is far greater than that of the west coast. The tidal ranges are relatively small at two to five meters, and tidal flats are not as wide as along the west coast. Although mountains face the sea, there are few beaches and sea cliffs along the mainland coast, as innumerable islands prevent the penetration of waves from offshore. Narrow straits between the mainland and islands are associated with extremely rapid tidal currents. At Uldolmok toward the western end of the south coast, the tidal current reaches up to 13 knots.

People

Koreans are primarily one ethnic family and speak one language. Sharing distinct physical characteristics, they are believed to be descendants of several Mongol tribes that migrated onto the Korean Peninsula from Central Asia.

In the seventh century, the various states of the peninsula were unified for the first time under the Silla Kingdom (57 B.C.-A.D. 935). Homogeneity has enabled Koreans to be relatively free from ethnic conflicts and to maintain a firm solidarity with one another.

As of the end of 2005, Korea's total population was estimated at 48,294,000 with a density of 474 people per square kilometer. The population of North Korea is estimated to be 22,928,040.

Korea saw its population grow by an annual rate of 3 percent during the 1960s, but growth slowed to 2 percent over the next decade. In 2005, the rate stood at 0.44 percent and is expected to further decline to 0.01 percent by 2020.

A notable trend in Korea's demographics is that it is growing older with each passing year. Statistics show that 6.9 percent of the total population of Korea was 65 years or older in 1999, and 9.1 percent was in 2005.

In the 1960s, Korea's population distribution formed a pyramid shape, with a high birth rate and relatively short life expectancy. However, age-group distribution is now shaped more like a bell because of the low birth rate and extended life expectancy. Youths (15 and younger) will make up a decreasing portion of the total, while senior citizens (65 and older) will account for some 15.7 percent of the total by the year 2020.

The nation's rapid industrialization and urbanization in the 1960s and 1970s has been accompanied by continuing migration of rural residents into the cities, particularly Seoul, resulting in heavily populated metropolitan areas. However, in recent years, an increasing number of Seoulites have begun moving to suburban areas.

Population

The registered population of the Republic of Korea as of 2006 was 49,024,737. The population density of the country is 480 persons per square kilometer. As of 2005, the population of North Korea was 24,000,000. Fast population growth was once a serious social problem in the Republic, as in most other developing nations.

Due to successful family planning campaigns and changing attitudes, however, population growth has been curbed remarkably in recent years. The number of people aged 65 and older was up 0.5 percent from 2005 with about 4.56 million, which made up 9.3 percent of the entire population.

Language

Koreans speak and write the same language, which has been a decisive factor in forging their national identity. Koreans have developed several different dialects in addition to the standard used in Seoul. However, the dialects, except for that of Jeju-do Province, are similar enough for native speakers to understand without any major difficulties.

The Korean Alphabet (Hangeul)

Consonants	ㄱ g,k	ㄴ n	ㄷ d,t	ㄹ r,l	ㅁ m	ㅂ b,p	ㅅ s
	ㅇ ng	ㅈ j	ㅊ ch	ㅋ k	ㅌ t	ㅍ p	ㅎ h
Vowels	ㅏ a	ㅑ ya	ㅓ eo	ㅕ yeo	ㅗ o	ㅛ yo	ㅜ u	ㅠ yu	ㅡ eu	ㅣ i

안 녕 하 세 요 (How are you?)
an nyeong ha se yo

Linguistic and ethnological studies have classified the Korean language in the Altaic language family, which includes the Turkic, Mongolic and Tungus-Manchu languages.

The Korean Alphabet, Hangeul, was created under the direction of King Sejong the Great during the 15th century. Before its creation, only a relatively small percentage of the population was literate; few could master the difficult Chinese characters used by the upper class.

In attempting to invent a Korean writing system, King Sejong looked to several writing systems known at the time, such as old Chinese seal characters and Uighur and Mongolian scripts.

The system that Joseon scholars came up with, however, is predominantly based upon phonological studies. Above all, they developed and followed a theory of tripartite division of the syllable into initial, medial and final phonemes, as opposed to the bipartite division of traditional Chinese phonology.

Hangeul, which consists of 10 vowels and 14 consonants, can be combined to form numerous syllabic groupings. It is simple, yet systematic and comprehensive, and is considered one of the most scientific writing systems in the world. Hangeul is easy to learn and write, which has greatly contributed to Korea's high literacy rate and advanced publication industry.

National Flag - Taegeukgi

Korea first felt the need for a national flag as it was preparing to conclude the Korean-American Treaty of Commerce, which was completed on May 22 and signed on June 6, 1882. This was during the 19th year of the reign of King Gojong of the Joseon Kingdom (1392-1910).

Korea adopted a blue and red yin-yang on a white field, a favorite Korean design since ancient times. Thus, the taegeuk design flag became the temporary national flag. Later Korea added eight trigrams combinations of three unbroken and broken bars - around the taegeuk circle and created the taegeukgi, which served as the national colors for a while.

King Gojong appointed Bak Yeoung-hyo as his ambassador to Japan in September 1882. While aboard ship heading for Japan, Bak drew a national flag with a taegeuk circle but included only four trigrams instead of eight, and started using the flag on the 25th of that month. On October 3, Bak reported this change

to King Gojong who formally proclaimed the Taegeukgi as the national flag on March 6, 1883. For some unknown reason, however, he did not have formal instructions published at that time on how to make the flag. In fact, it wasn't till June 29, 1942, that the provisional Korean government in exile enacted a law on the uniform method of making the national flag. The law was promulgated but as the government was in exile, it was not widely known to Koreans at home still under Japanese colonial rule.

Following the founding of the Republic of Korea on August 15, 1948, the government felt that it should codify the method of making the national flag. This prompted the government to form a special commission in January 1949 that issued the provision on the national flag on October 15 of that year. Since then, the Republic of Korea has been using the Taegeukgi as the national flag.

The Meaning of the Taegeukgi

Taegeukgi, the national flag of the Republic of Korea, consists of a blue and red yin-yang circle in the center, one black trigram in each of the four corners, and a white background.

The white background of Taegeukgi symbolizes light and purity and reflects the Korean people's traditional affinity for peace.

The yin-yang circle, divided equally into a blue portion below and a red portion above, represents the dual cosmic forces of yin (blue) and yang (red). It symbolizes universal harmony, in which the passive and the active, the feminine and the masculine, form the whole. The four trigrams of Geon, Gon, Gam, and Li, which surround the yin-yang circle, denote the process of yin and yang going through a series of changes and growth.

Geon (☰), with three solid bars in the upper left-hand corner, denotes "heaven". Gon (☷), with three evenly divided bars in the lower right-hand corner, denotes "earth". Gam (☵), with one evenly divided bar on each side of one solid bar in the upper right-hand corner, denotes "water". And Li (☲), with one solid bar on each side of one evenly divided bar in the lower left-hand corner, denotes "fire".

Collectively, the yin-yang circle and the four trigrams represent universal harmony and unity. Taegeukgi embodies the ideals of all Koreans, who have pursued creativity and prosperity under universal principles and truth.

Therefore, Koreans are dedicated to working harmoniously to carry out the nation's tasks of unifying its people and contributing toward world peace and prosperity.

Source: Korean Culture and Information Service, http://www.korea.net

CONTENTS

Yellow Sea

Jejudo

Ieodo (Ocean Research Station)

East Sea

Ieungdo

Dokdo

THE REPUBLIC OF KOREA

Our country has cultivated a unique culture in its long history and has many time-honored traditions. Despite its territorial division in the 20th century, Korea has achieved remarkable economic and social developments, which have attracted the attention of the world. The nation has gained a central position in trade, and at the same time is growing into an East Asian economic hub.

Immediately following the Korean War, per capita income was a mere USD 67 but, as of 2007, it had reached a high of USD 20,045. The nation's exports also grew from USD 5.5 million in 1962 to USD 371.4 billion in 2006. Major exports consist of capital and technology-intensive products including electronic appliances, automobiles, ships, and semiconductors. Export markets have also diversified, and cover most of the world. Owing to its economic growth, Korea joined the OECD (Organization for Economic Cooperation and Development) in 1996.

Since the 1970s, Korea has participated in various projects in conjunction with international organizations. Private organizations have also engaged in activities of regional development, education, medical aid and refugee assistance in Central Asia, Africa, and other areas. Korea has dispatched UN Peacekeeping Forces to Georgia, India, Pakistan, Afghanistan, Lebanon, Liberia, and Sudan, contributing to the maintenance of world peace.

In 1991, the Republic of Korea (ROK) and the Democratic People's Republic of Korea (DPRK) joined the UN. Our country has also joined other various regional cooperative organizations and, in 2005, the APEC (Asian-Pacific Economic Cooperation) summit meeting was held in Busan.

Geographic Boundary

The territory of Korea consists of a land area with a north-south length of 1,100km. Korea has 3,960 islands, and its total area is 223,170km^2. To the north, Korea is bordered by the Dumangang (Tumen River) and the Amnokgang (Yalu River), along with Russia and China. To the east, the nation is bordered by the East Sea, which is shared with Japan.

Korean territorial waters include the area 12 nautical miles from the mainland, or from the line connecting the islands that are farthest out from the mainland. In the case of Jejudo, Ulleungdo, and Dokdo, territorial waters include the areas within 12 nautical miles from the coastlines. In the Strait of Korea, the territorial waters include only the area within 3 nautical miles from the straight base line. Territorial waters are under exclusive jurisdiction, but the northern waters of Jejudo are an exception.

Territorial History

From the early days, our people lived in the vast areas including Manchuria and the Korean Peninsula. Major states included Gojoseon, Buyeo, Goguryeo, Baekje, and Silla. Our people introduced and conveyed continental cultures to maritime states. At the same time, our people were ceaselessly faced with pressures and challenges from the continental and maritime forces.

Following the unification of the three states by Silla in the 7th century, the displaced people of Goguryeo established Balhae, resulting in the Nambukguk Period (the era of the North and South States), represented by Silla in the south and Balhae in the north. In 926, Balhae was destroyed by Georan (Khitan) and our country lost Manchuria.

In the period of Goryeo, the efforts to recover the northern land continued, and by the end of the Goryeo period (14th century), the territory expanded up to Byeokdong, Ganggye, and Jangjin along the Amnokgang and up to Gapju and Gilju in Hamgyeong Province. In the early Joseon period (15th century), Sagun was established on the west side of the Amnokgang, and Yukjin was installed on the east side of the river.

In the Joseon period, our country was invaded by Japan (1492) and China (1636), but our people did not surrender, choosing instead to fight against the invaders and to defend our territory. In the latter Joseon period, our people began to move to Manchuria and our living area expanded.

In the 20th century, Japan expanded its imperial forces in East Asia and occupied our country for 36 years. Following the liberation from Japanese rule in 1945, our country was divided into North and South along the 38th parallel, leading to the Korean War. After the ceasefire was declared, the age of division began, and it has continued for over 50 years. North and South are coexisting on the Korean Peninsula under heterogeneous social systems, but both are making efforts to overcome the division through the building of mutual trust and the achievement of peaceful coexistence. Despite various difficulties, the two Koreas are expanding personnel and material exchanges through reunions of separated families and summit meetings.

MAP OF KOREA

1 : 4,000,000

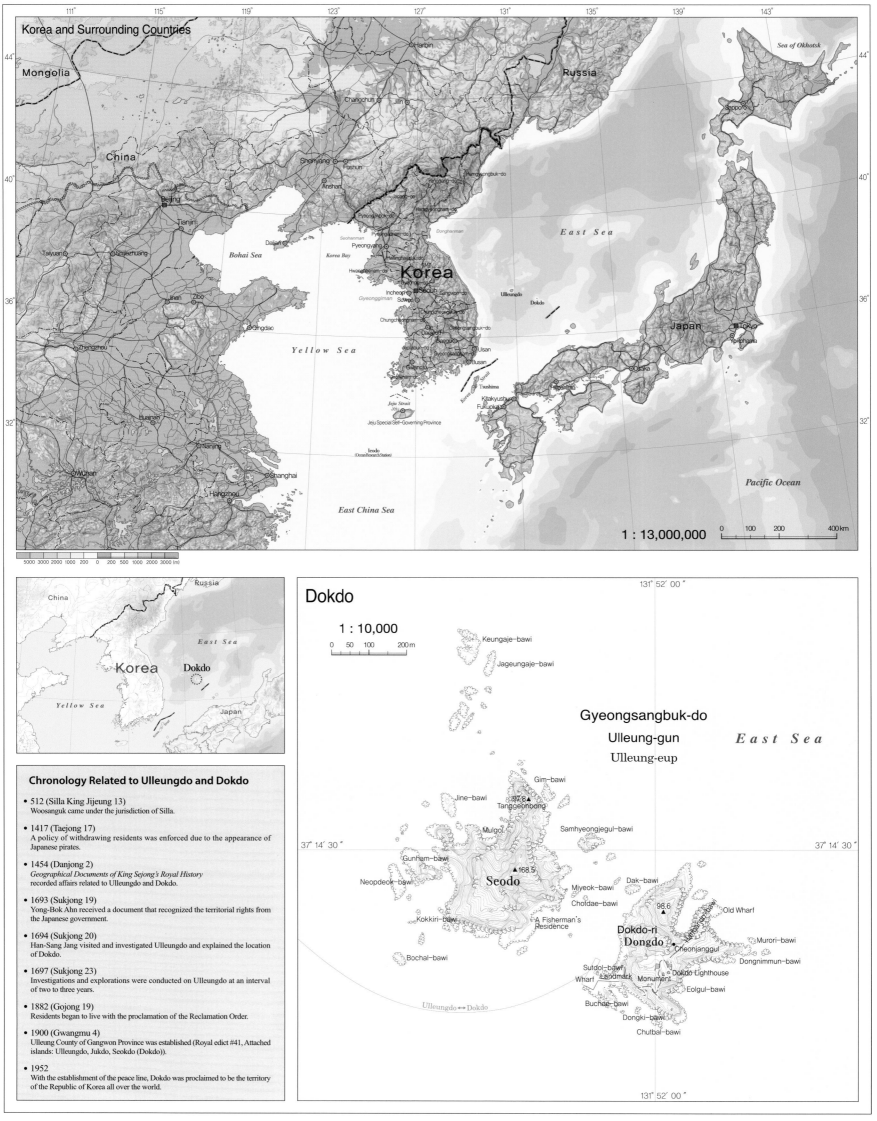

Korea and Surrounding Countries

Mongolia

China

Russia

Sea of Okhotsk

Harbin

Changchun

Jilin

Sapporo

Shenyang

Fushun

Anshan

Hamgyeongbuk-do

Beijing

Pyeongan-do

Hamgyeongnam-do

Tianjin

Pyeongyang

Donghanman

Dalian

E a s t S e a

Taiyuan

Shijiazhuang

Bohai Sea

Korea Bay

Hwanghaebuk-do

Seohanman

Korea

Qingdao

Incheon

Seoul

Gangwon-do

Ulleungdo

Dokdo

Jinan

Zibo

Gyeonggiman

Suwon

Chungcheongnam-do

Gyeongsangbuk-do

Zhengzhou

Daegu

Baegu

Japan

Tokyo

Y e l l o w   S e a

Gwangju

Gyeongsangnam-do

Ulsan

Yokohama

Busan

Huanan

Osaka

Nanjing

Kora Strait

Tsushima

Kitakyushu

Hiroshima

Wuhan

Fukuoka

Jeju Strait

Jeju

Shanghai

Jeju Special Self-Governing Province

Hangzhou

Ieodo
(Ocean Research Station)

Pacific Ocean

East China Sea

1 : 13,000,000

0   100   200   400km

5000 3000 2000 1000 200 0 200 500 1000 2000 3000 (m)

China

Russia

East Sea

Korea

Dokdo

Yellow Sea

Japan

Chronology Related to Ulleungdo and Dokdo

- **512 (Silla King Jijeung 13)**
  Woosanguk came under the jurisdiction of Silla.

- **1417 (Taejong 17)**
  A policy of withdrawing residents was enforced due to the appearance of Japanese pirates.

- **1454 (Danjong 2)**
  Geographical Documents of King Sejong's Royal History recorded affairs related to Ulleungdo and Dokdo.

- **1693 (Sukjong 19)**
  Yong-Bok Ahn received a document that recognized the territorial rights from the Japanese government.

- **1694 (Sukjong 20)**
  Han-Sang Jang visited and investigated Ulleungdo and explained the location of Dokdo.

- **1697 (Sukjong 23)**
  Investigations and explorations were conducted on Ulleungdo at an interval of two to three years.

- **1882 (Gojong 19)**
  Residents began to live with the proclamation of the Reclamation Order.

- **1900 (Gwangmu 4)**
  Ulleung County of Gangwon Province was established (Royal edict #41, Attached islands: Ulleungdo, Jukdo, Seokdo (Dokdo)).

- **1952**
  With the establishment of the peace line, Dokdo was proclaimed to be the territory of Korea all over the world.

Dokdo

1 : 10,000

0 50 100   200m

131° 52' 00"

Keungaje-bawi

Jageungaje-bawi

Gyeongsangbuk-do

Ulleung-gun

Ulleung-eup

E a s t   S e a

Gim-bawi

Jine-bawi

97.8▲
Tanggeonbong

Mulgol

Samhyeongjegul-bawi

37° 14' 30"

37° 14' 30"

Gunham-bawi

▲168.5

Neopdeok-bawi

Seodo

Miyeok-bawi

Dak-bawi

Choldae-bawi

98.6▲

Kokkiri-bawi

A Fisherman's
Residence

Old Wharf

Bochal-bawi

Dokdo-ri
Dongdo

Cheonjanggul

Murori-bawi

Dongnimmun-bawi

Suldol-bawi

Wharf Landmark Monument

Dokdo Lighthouse

Eolgul-bawi

Buchae-bawi

Dongki-bawi

Chutbal-bawi

Ulleungdo ↔ Dokdo

131° 52' 00"

INDEX MAP

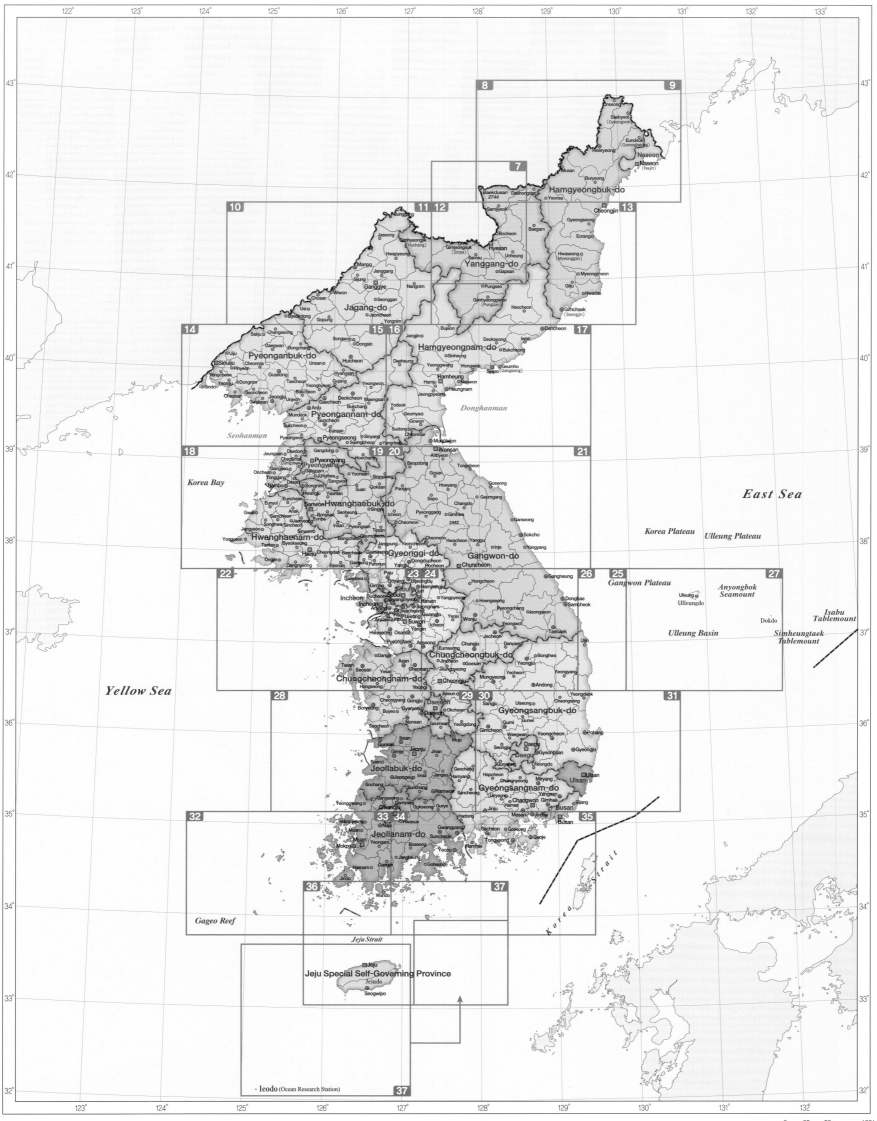

1 : 4,450,000

0   25   50   100 km

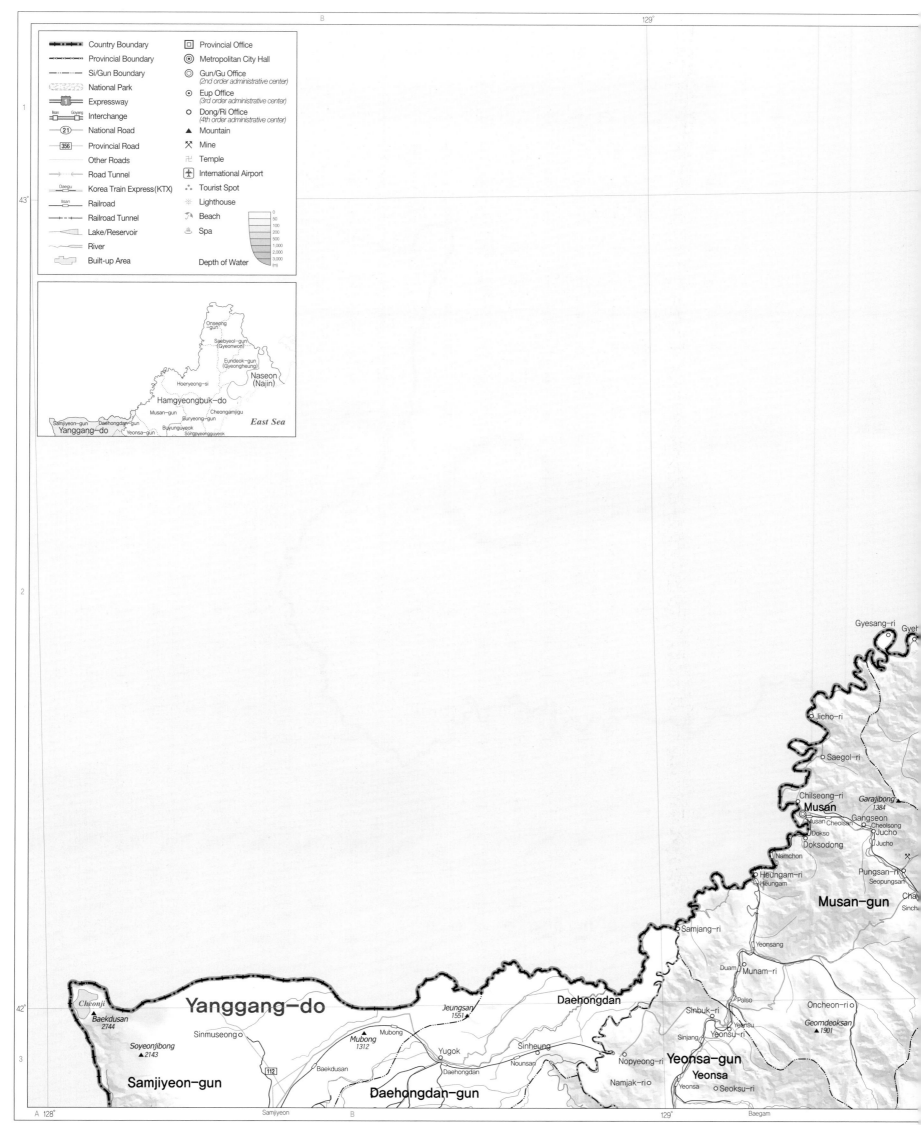

⊢■■■■⊣	Country Boundary	▣	Provincial Office
	Provincial Boundary	◎	Metropolitan City Hall
	Si/Gun Boundary	◉	Gun/Gu Office (2nd order administrative center)
	National Park	⊙	Eup Office (3rd order administrative center)
	Expressway	○	Dong/Ri Office (4th order administrative center)
	Interchange	▲	Mountain
㉑	National Road	✕	Mine
356	Provincial Road	卍	Temple
	Other Roads	✈	International Airport
	Road Tunnel	⠶	Tourist Spot
	Korea Train Express(KTX)	☼	Lighthouse
	Railroad	⚓	Beach
	Railroad Tunnel	♨	Spa
	Lake/Reservoir		
	River		Depth of Water
	Built-up Area		

Onseong -gun
Saebyeol-gun (Gyeonwon)
Eundeok-gun (Gyeongheung)
Hoeryeong-si
Naseon (Najin)
Hamgyeongbuk-do
Musan-gun   Cheongamjigu
Samjiyeon-gun Daehongdan-gun Buryeong-gun East Sea
Yanggang-do   Yeonsa-gun Buryunguyeok
Songpyeongguyeok

Gyesang-ri Gye
Jicho-ri
Saegol-ri
Chilseong-ri *Garajibong 1384*
Musan
Musan Cheolsan Gangseon
Dokso Cheolsong Jucho
Doksodong Jucho
Namchon Pungsan-ri
Heungam-ri Seopungsan
Heungam
Musan-gun Cha
Sinche
Samjang-ri
Yeonsang
Duam Munam-ri
Yanggang-do *Jeungsan 1551* Daehongdan Palso
Oncheon-ri
42° Sinbuk-ri *Geomdeoksan 1901*
Cheonji
Baekdusan 2744 Sinmuseong Sinjang Yeonsu-ri
Mubong 1312 Mubong Yeonsu
Soyeonjibong 2143 Yugok Sinheung Nopyeong-ri **Yeonsa-gun**
Yeonsa
3 Baekdusan Daehongdan Nounsan Yeonsa Seoksu-ri
Samjiyeon-gun 112 Namjak-ri
Daehongdan-gun

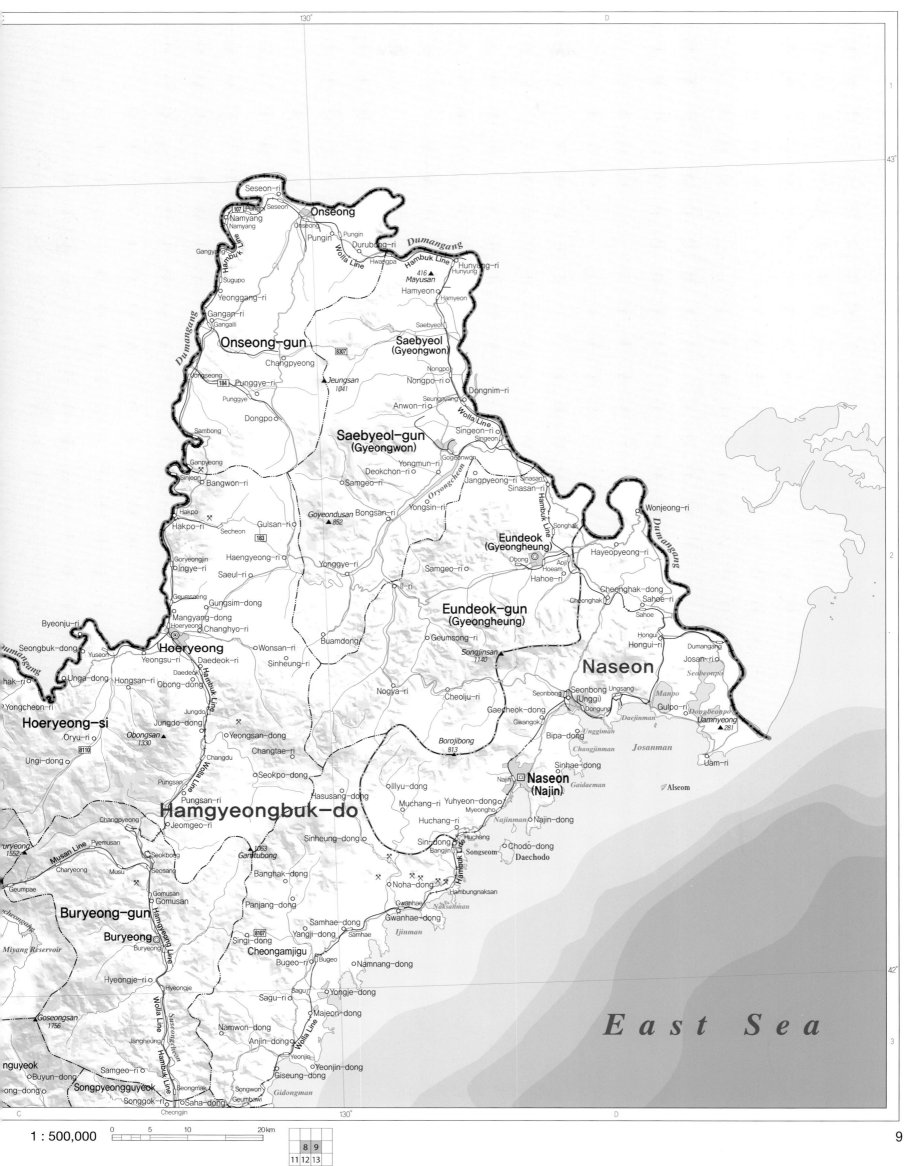

1 : 500,000

0   5   10   20km

East Sea

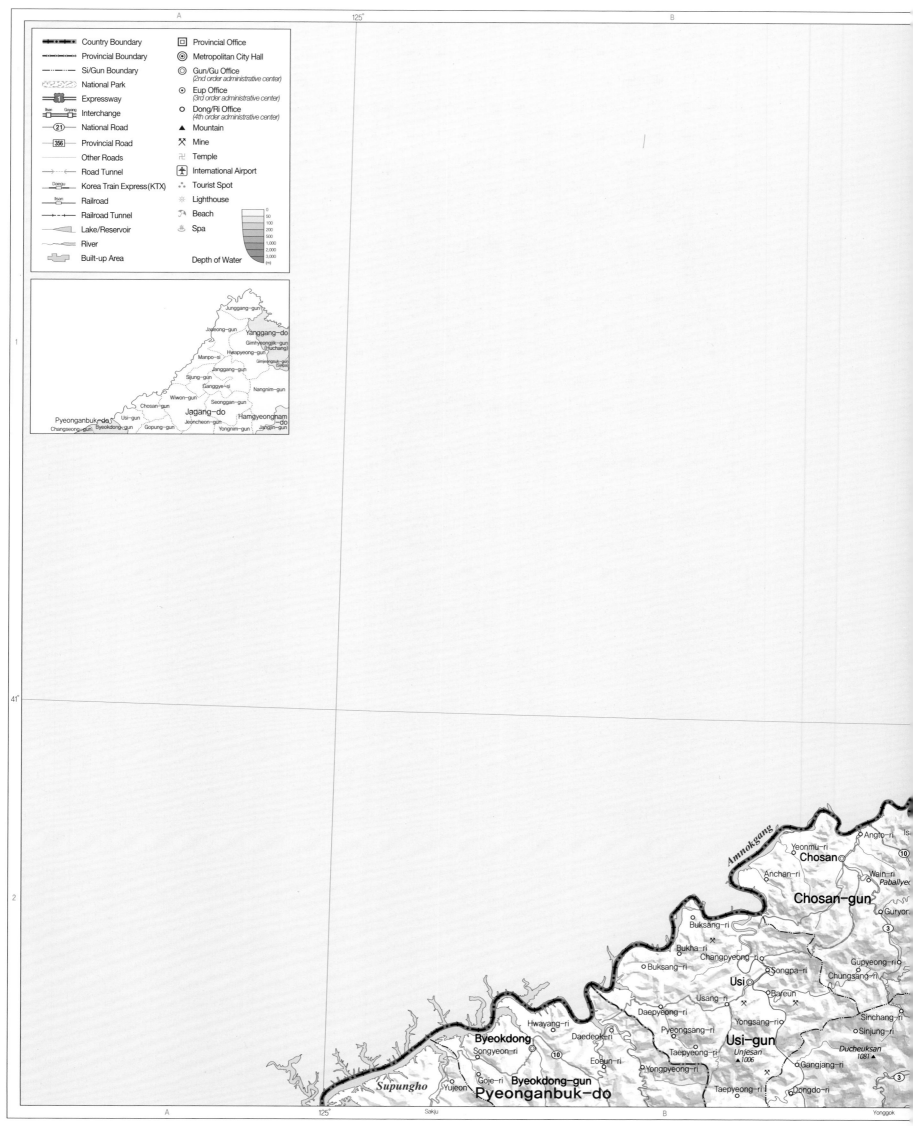

	Country Boundary	⊡	Provincial Office
	Provincial Boundary	◉	Metropolitan City Hall
	Si/Gun Boundary	◎	Gun/Gu Office (2nd order administrative center)
	National Park	⊙	Eup Office (3rd order administrative center)
	Expressway	○	Dong/Ri Office (4th order administrative center)
	Interchange	▲	Mountain
	National Road	⚒	Mine
	Provincial Road	卍	Temple
	Other Roads	✈	International Airport
	Road Tunnel	∴	Tourist Spot
	Korea Train Express (KTX)	☀	Lighthouse
	Railroad		Beach
	Railroad Tunnel		Spa
	Lake/Reservoir		
	River		Depth of Water
	Built-up Area		

Junggang-gun
Jaseong-gun
Yanggang-do
Gimhyeongik-gun (Huchang)
Manpo-si
Hwapyeong-gun
Gimjeongsuk-gun (Seung)
Janggang-gun
Sijung-gun
Ganggye-si
Nangnim-gun
Wiwon-gun
Seonggan-gun
Chosan-gun
Jagang-do
Hamgyeongnam-do
Pyeonganbuk-do
Usi-gun
Jahgin-gun
Changseong-gun
Byeokdong-gun
Gopung-gun
Jeoncheon-gun
Yongnim-gun

Amnokgang
Yeonmu-ri
Angto-ri
Is⌐
Chosan
Anchan-ri
Wain-ri
Paballyec
Chosan-gun
Guryor
Buksang-ri
Bukha-ri
Changpyeong-ri
Songpa-ri
Gupyeong-ri
Buksang-ri
Chungsang-ri
Usi
Bareun
Usang-ri
Daepyeong-ri
Yongsang-ri
Sinchang
Hwayang-ri
Pyeongsang-ri
Sinjung-ri
Byeokdong
Daedeok-ri
Usi-gun
Duchueksan
Songyeon-ri
Eobun-ri
Taepyeong-ri
Unjesan ▲1006
1081 ▲
Yongpyeong-ri
Gangjang-ri
Supungho
Goje-ri **Byeokdong-gun**
Yujeon
Taepyeong-ri
Dongdo-ri
Pyeonganbuk-do

Jungdeok-ri

Junggang
Geonha-ri
Jangheung-ri

Jungjibong
▲1062

Hoha
Osu-ri

Toseong-ri

Junggang-gun

Amnokgang

Yeonpung-ri

Bujeon-ri

10

Ssangdusan
1251

5

Geumchang-ri

**Gimhyeongjik
(Huchang)**

Jaseong-gun

Hakseongsan
1231

Jukjeon-ri
Jukjeon
Duji

Songam-ri

Horye-ri

Daenam-ri

Notan

Najuk-ri

Huchangang

Nolan
Yeonpo

Hoeyang

Muchang-ri
Muchang

Cheonjebong
▲960

Jaseong

Gwanpyeong-ri

Woltan

**Gimhyeongjik-gun
(Huchang)**

Duryusan
1033 ▲

Ipyeong-ri
Jinsong-ri

Hoejung-ri
Yongchul

Jajak-ri

Jaseonggang
Hwapyeong

Hoejung

Yanggang-do

Samgang-ri
Unbong

Okdong
Unbong

Songdeok-ri

Garim-ri

Yusam-ri

65

Songsam

Sinpung-ri

Yanggye-ri
Gasan

Namsa

Wolgibong
1214

Yeoksu-ri

Yangdeok-ri

Manpo Line

Yeonpo-ri

Hambu-ri

Jagang-do

Hwapyeong

Hwangdolbong
1839

Munak

Sadeoksan
1330

Hwapyeong-gun

Bunam-ri

Manpo-si

Myeongsin-ri

Geonsang-ri

Oegwi

Inam-ri

65

Daeheung-ri

Manpo

Manpo

Geonha-ri

Janggang-gun

Byeoro-ri

10

78

Maebawisan
1118

Sinseong-ri

Wonpyeong-ri

65

Heuksu-ri

Garongnyeong
1629

Sijung

Jongpo-ri

Seongjang-ri

5

Gosan-ri

Manpo Line

Jangjagang

Ansang-dong

Yongpo-dong

Sampo-ri

Yeonsang-ri

Jangjagangho

Ssangbu-ri

Janggang

Doga-ri

Insan-ri

Sijung-gun

Ssangbu

Gongbok

Nangnim-gun

Pungcheong-ri

Gokha

78

Hyangha-ri

Seungbang
Oil

Pyeongni
Oil

Jangjagang

Gobo-ri

Pungnyong-ri

Ganggye-si

Ganggye

Seungbanghari

Janghang-ri

Hwangpo
Simnipyeong

Ganggye Line
Jungsinwon

Omandong

Daeheung-ri

Darigol-ri

Hyangyang-ri

Cheonjang-ri

Duheung-ri

Gongin

Ganggye

Gongin-dong

Sangsinwon

Hasinwon

Nangnim

Nangnim

Jangseong-ri

Galjeom-ri

Hyangnaebong
▲1728

Seorubong
1354

5074

Wiwon

Janghang-ri

Chukpo-ri

Seojung-ri

Junggang-ri

Sinyeon-ri

Wiwongang

Yanggang

Sincheong

65

Buk-ri

Nangnimho

Seosang-ri

Yeonhwa-ri

Choam-ri

72

2068

Muchae-ri

Chonggongnyeong

Wiwon-gun

Gwangcheon-ri

Seonggan

Baekja-ri

Oegalbong
2084

Munak-ri

Yukdeoksan
1730

Jungseonggan

Seonggan

Seonggan-gun

Hwangpo-ri

Yongyeon

Oejung

Baegam-ri

Bakdalsan
1817

Daeheungsan
2152

Jungheung-ri

Changdeok-ri

Buheung-ri

Hwaam

Bisambong
▲1833

Unsu-ri

7205

Bukdongsan
1485 ▲

Sinjeok

Soksa-ri

Volmyeong-ri

Mundeok-ri

Sinheung-ri

Galjeon-ri

5

Bangseong-ri

72

Gureumbausan
1599

Sinsang-ri

Memul-ri

pung
Sampyeong-ri

Jeoncheon-gun

Songjeoksan
1970

Jeoncheon
Unsong

Jeoncheon
Dumun-ri

Yongnim-gun

7294

Hamgyeongnam-do

Gopung-gun

Singye-ri

Changpyeong-ri Cheonsan-ri

Yongnim

Daedasan
▲1464

7205

Galcheon-ri

Jangjin-gun

Seomok-ri

Country Boundary	Provincial Office
Provincial Boundary	Metropolitan City Hall
Si/Gun Boundary	Gun/Gu Office (2nd order administrative center)
National Park	Eup Office (3rd order administrative center)
Expressway	Dong/Ri Office (4th order administrative center)
Interchange	Mountain
National Road	Mine
Provincial Road	Temple
Other Roads	International Airport
Road Tunnel	Tourist Spot
Korea Train Express(KTX)	Lighthouse
Railroad	Beach
Railroad Tunnel	Spa
Lake/Reservoir	Depth of Water
River	
Built-up Area	

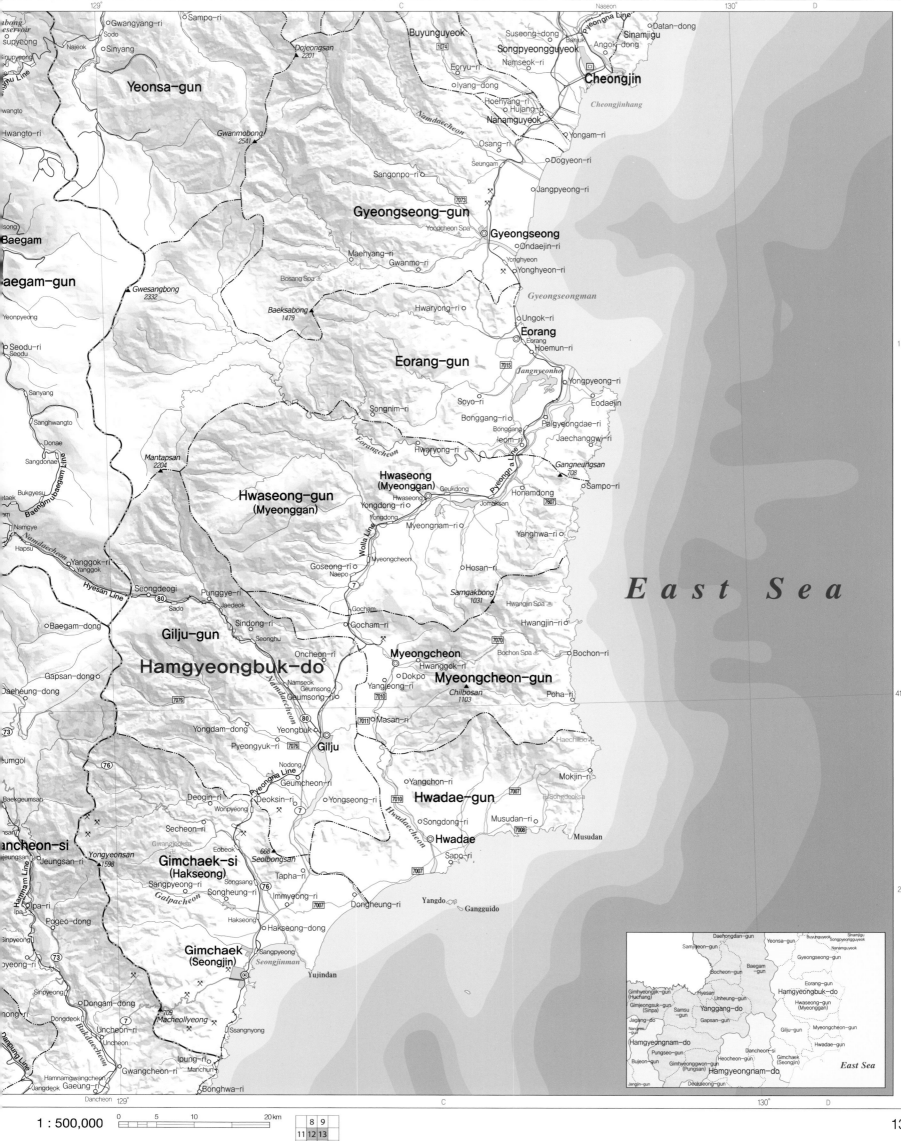

East Sea

Yeonsa-gun

Baegam

Baegam-gun

Gyeongseong-gun

Gyeongseong

Eorang

Eorang-gun

Hwaseong-gun
(Myeonggan)

Hwaseong
(Myeonggan)

Hamgyeongbuk-do

Gilju-gun

Gilju

Myeongcheon

Myeongcheon-gun

Hwadae-gun

Hwadae

Gimchaek-si
(Hakseong)

Gimchaek
(Seongjin)

Cheongjin

Buyunguyeok

Songpyeongguyeok

Nahamguyeok

Sinamjigu

1 : 500,000

13

Country Boundary
Provincial Boundary
Si/Gun Boundary
National Park
Expressway
Interchange
National Road
Provincial Road
Other Roads
Road Tunnel
Korea Train Express(KTX)
Railroad
Railroad Tunnel
Lake/Reservoir
River
Built-up Area

Provincial Office
Metropolitan City Hall
Gun/Gu Office
(2nd order administrative center)
Eup Office
(3rd order administrative center)
Dong/Ri Office
(4th order administrative center)
Mountain
Mine
Temple
International Airport
Tourist Spot
Lighthouse
Beach
Spa

Depth of Water

Yellow Sea

Korea Bay

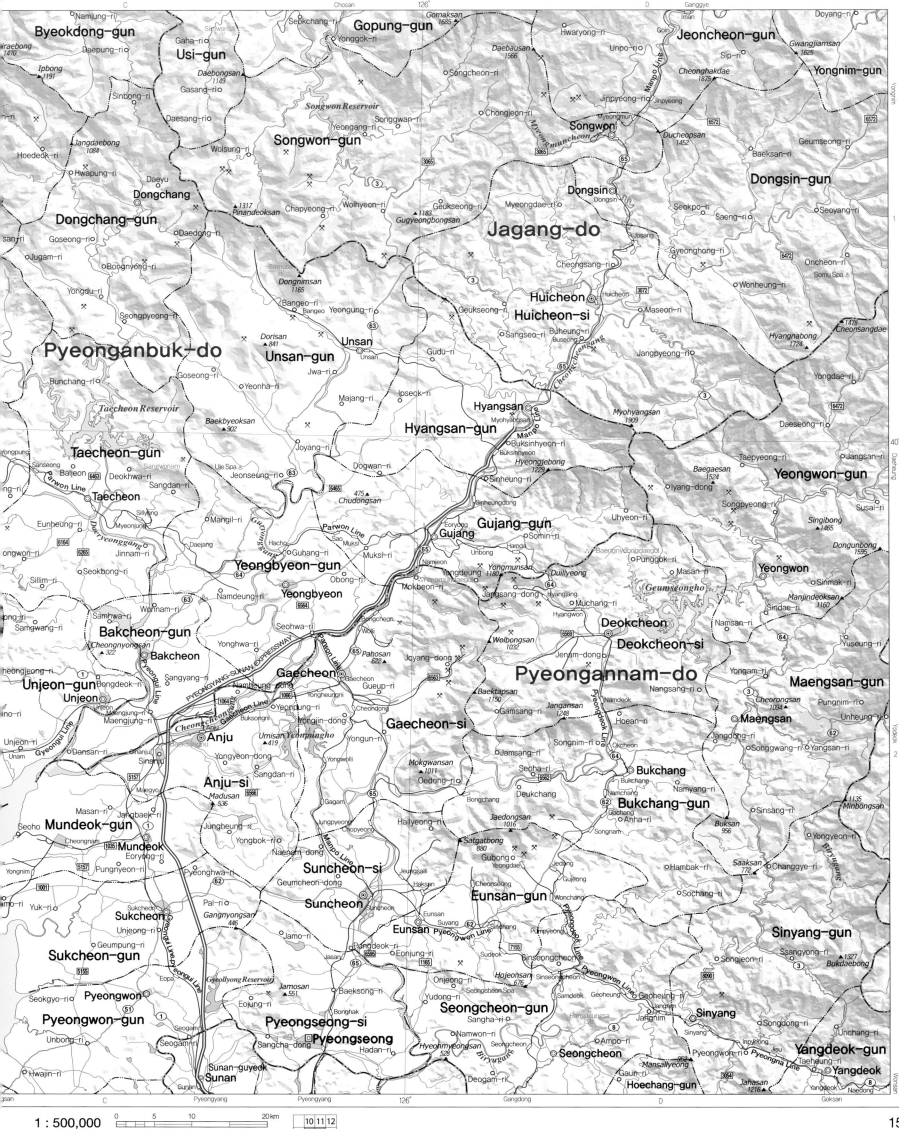

1 : 500,000

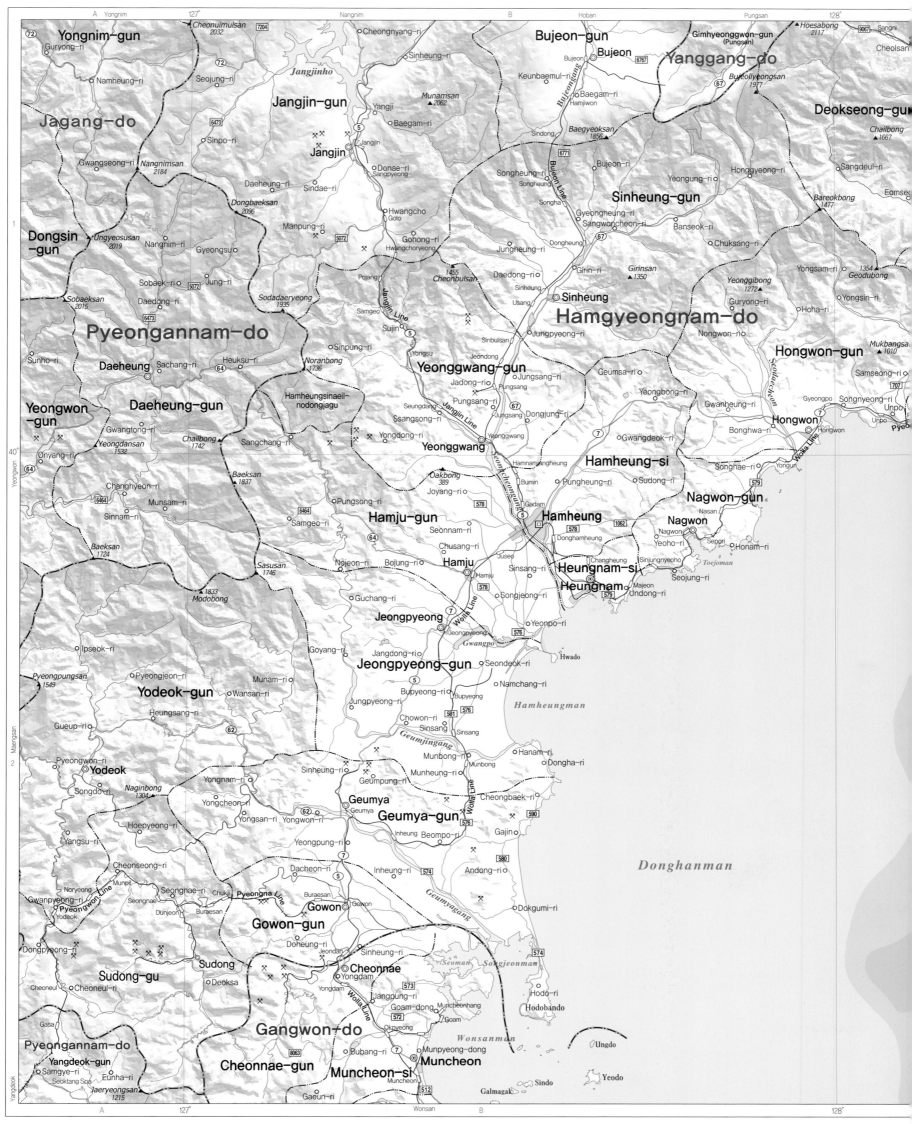

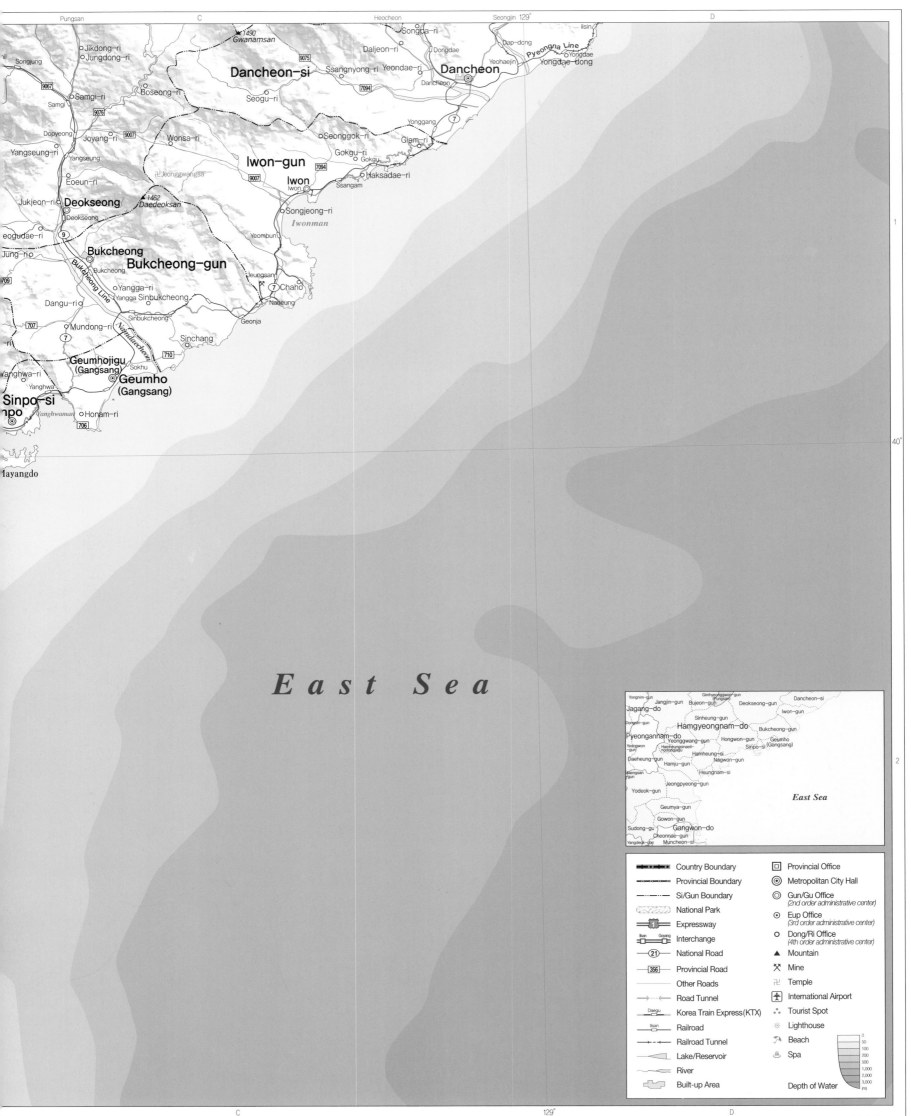

1 : 500,000 0 5 10 20km

BAENGNYEONGDO

	Legend		
Country Boundary		Provincial Office	
Provincial Boundary		Metropolitan City Hall	
Si/Gun Boundary		Gun/Gu Office (2nd order administrative center)	
National Park		Eup Office (3rd order administrative center)	
Expressway		Dong/Ri Office (4th order administrative center)	
Interchange		Mountain	
National Road		Mine	
Provincial Road		Temple	
Other Roads		International Airport	
Road Tunnel		Tourist Spot	
Korea Train Express (KTX)		Lighthouse	
Railroad		Beach	
Railroad Tunnel		Spa	
Lake/Reservoir			
River		Depth of Water	
Built-up Area			

Yellow Sea

Yellow Sea

Pyeongannam-do

Oncheon-gun

Eunyul-gun

Gwail-gun

Songhwa-gun

Samcheon-gun

Jangyeon-gun

Yongyeon-gun

Taetan-gun

Ongjin-gun

Daedongman

Baengnyeongdo

Ongjin-gun

Daecheongdo

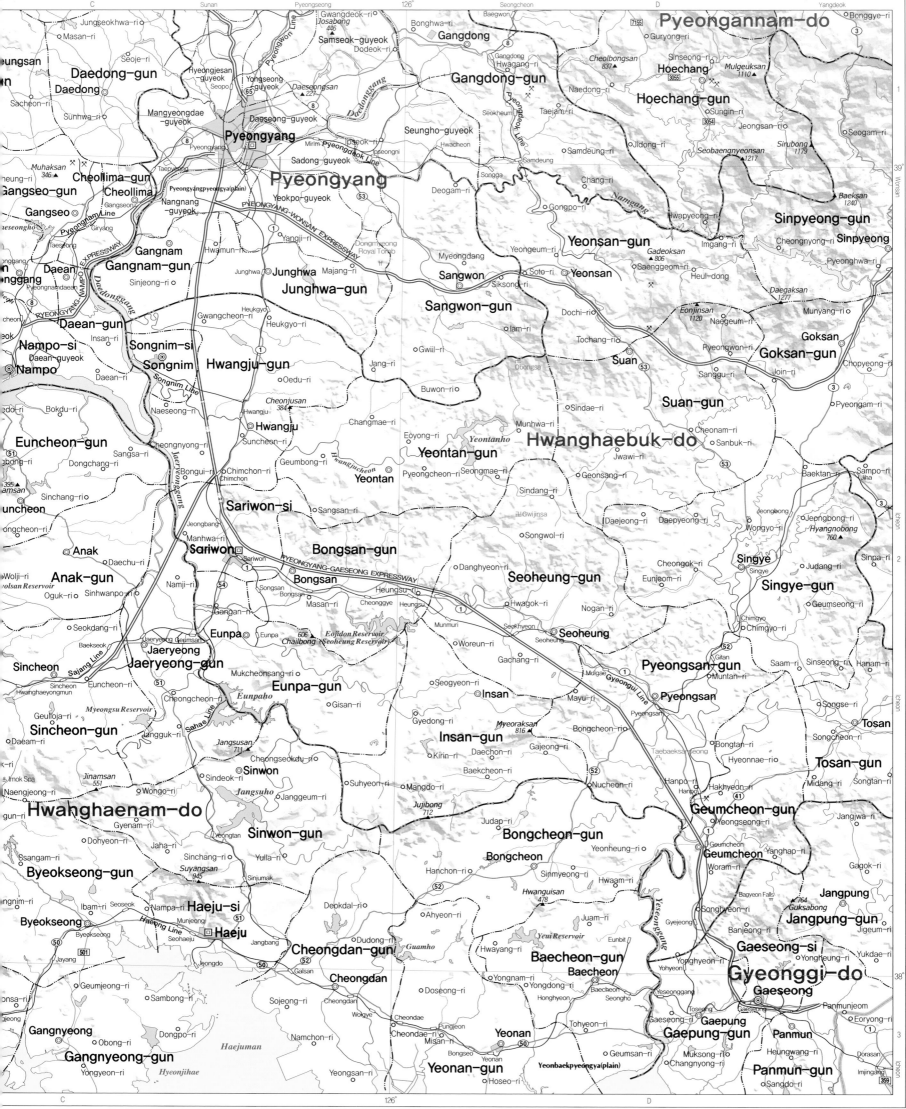

1 : 500,000

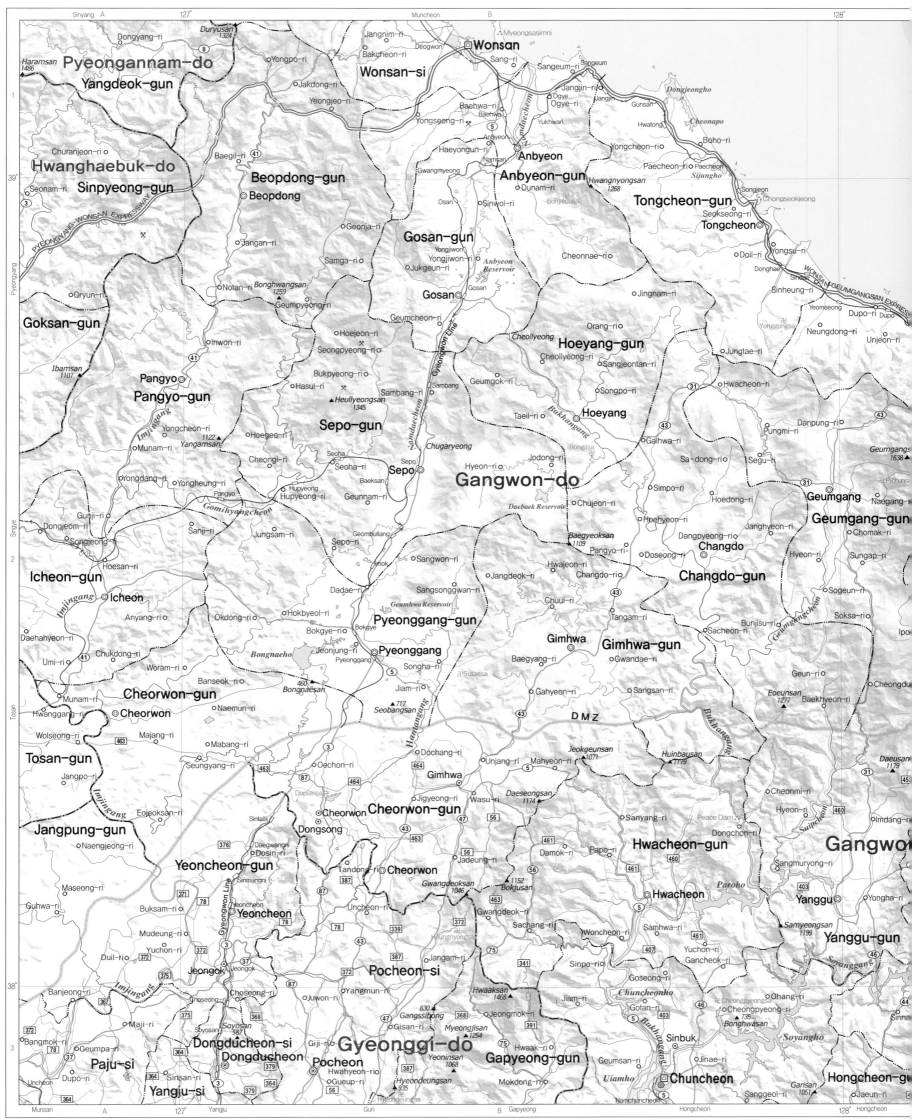

East Sea

ae-ri
Juheom-ri
Yeongjinman
Goseong
ong-ri   Onjeong-ri
Singyesa
yecheon   *Namgang*   Bongsu-ri
Goseong-gun
Wolbisan-ri
Yujeomsa
mga-ri
Sindae-ri   Myeongpa-ri
ndo-ri
Namgang   Daejin-ri   Hwajinpo Beach
Hwajinpo
Geojin
Geonbongsan   Jasan-ri   Geojin Lighthouse
▲908
Goseong-gun   Geonbongsa寺
Goseong
Jangsin-ri   Gonghyeonjin-ri
Hyangnobong   Tapdong-ri   Songjiho Beach
▲1291   426   Oho-ri
n-ri   426   7
Heul-ri   Hagya-ri   Cheongganjeong
Alps Resort   Cheonjin-ri
Seohwa-ri   Ayajin Lighthouse
msan   Cheondo-ri   Misiryeong   Wonam-ri   Sokcho
Yongdae-ri   56   Sokcho Lighthouse
e   453   Cheoksan Spa   Sokcho Beach
Cheongchoho
Sokcho-si
Seoraksan National Park   Jeongam-ri
Wontong-ri   Hangye-ri   Naksansa
O   44   Seoraksan   Naksan Beach
Garibong   1708
▲   Hangyeryeong
46   1519▲   Osaek-ri   Sangpyeong-ri   Yangyang
Osaek Spa   44   Hawangdo-ri
Inje-gun   Jeombongsan   59   Yangyang Int'l Airport
njeon-ri   ▲1424   56   Hajodae Beach
Gwidun-ri   Hagwangjeon
31   418   7
418   Ingu-ri
Hyeon-ri   Yangyang-gun   Eoseongjeon-ri
31   *Bangtaecheon*   Hwangi-ri
ri   Hyeonnam
Bangtaesan   Galcheon-ri   Jumunjin Beach
446   ▲1444   Gachilbong   Eungboksan   65   Jumunjin
Gaeinsan   ▲1240   ▲1360   Jumunjin Lighthouse
Sangnam-ri   Misan-ri   1342   Hongcheon-gun   Gangneung-si
Bangnae-ri
Bangnae   C   Gwangwon   Odaesan   Gangneung   129°

Inset map:
Pyeongannam-do
Yangdeok-gun   Wonsan-si
Hwanghaebuk-do   Anbyeon-gun
Sinpyeong   Gosan-gun   Tongcheon-gun
Goksan-   Beopdong-gun   Changdo-gun
gun
Pangyo-gun   Sepo-gun   Goseong-gun
Gangwon-do   Geumgang-gun
Icheon-gun   Pyeonggang-gun   Gimhwa-gun
Cheorwon-gun   Yanggu-gun   *East Sea*
Cheorwon-si   Yangyang-gun   Sokcho-si
Jangpung-   Hwacheon-gun   Inje-gun
gun   Yeoncheon-gun
Gyeonggi-do   Pocheon-si   Goseong-gun
Pa-   Pocheon-si   Chuncheon-si   Yangyang-gun
ju-si   Gapyeong-gun   Hongcheon-gun   Gangneung-si

Legend:
	Country Boundary
	Provincial Boundary
	Si/Gun Boundary
	National Park
	Expressway
	Interchange
21	National Road
356	Provincial Road
	Other Roads
	Road Tunnel
Daegu	Korea Train Express (KTX)
Ilsan	Railroad
	Railroad Tunnel
	Lake/Reservoir
	River
	Built-up Area

▣	Provincial Office
◎	Metropolitan City Hall
◎	Gun/Gu Office (2nd order administrative center)
⊙	Eup Office (3rd order administrative center)
○	Dong/Ri Office (4th order administrative center)
▲	Mountain
⚒	Mine
卍	Temple
✈	International Airport
∴	Tourist Spot
☼	Lighthouse
⚓	Beach
♨	Spa

Depth of Water
0
50
100
200
500
1,000
2,000
3,000

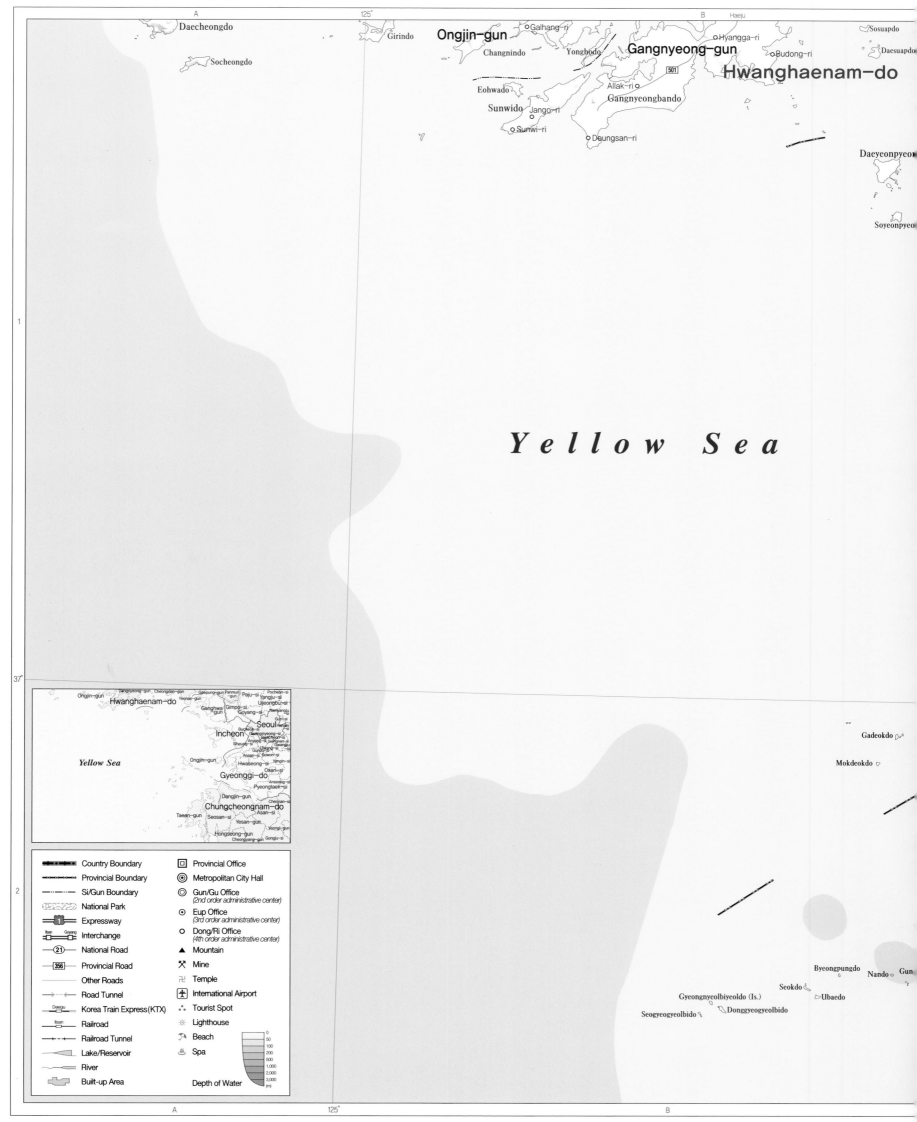

Yellow Sea

Daecheongdo

Socheongdo

Girindo

Ongjin-gun

Changnindo
Yonghodo
Galhang-ri
Hyangga-ri
Gangnyeong-gun
Budong-ri
501
Hwanghaenam-do
Sosuapdo
Daesuapdo

Eohwado
Allak-ri
Gangnyeongbando
Daeyeonpyeo

Sunwido
Jango-ri
Deungsan-ri
Soyeonpyeo

Sunwi-ri

Haeju

125°

A
B

37°

Inset map:

Hwanghaenam-do
Ongjin-gun
Gangnyeong-gun
Cheongdan-gun
Gaepung-gun
Panmun-gun
Paju-si
Pocheon-si
Yangju-si
Uijeongbu-si
Yeoncheon-gun
Ganghwa-gun
Gimpo-si
Goyang-si
Namyangju-si
Seoul
Guri-si
Hanam-si
Incheon
Bucheon-si
Gwangmyeong-si
Siheung-si
Anyang-si
Seongnam-si
Gwangju-si
Gunpo-si
Uiwang-si
Yongin-si
Ongjin-gun
Hwaseong-si
Suwon-si
Yangin-si
Osan-si
Gyeonggi-do
Anseong-si
Pyeongtaek-si
Dangjin-gun
Chungcheongnam-do
Asan-si
Taean-gun
Seosan-si
Yesan-gun
Yongji-si
Hongseong-gun
Cheongyang-gun
Gongju-si

Yellow Sea

Gadeokdo

Mokdeokdo

Byeongpungdo
Nando
Gun
Gyeongnyeolbiyeoldo (Is.)
Seokdo
Ubaedo
Seogyeogyeolbido
Donggyeogyeolbido

Legend

	Country Boundary
	Provincial Boundary
	Si/Gun Boundary
	National Park
1	Expressway
Ilsan Goyang	Interchange
21	National Road
356	Provincial Road
	Other Roads
	Road Tunnel
Daegu	Korea Train Express (KTX)
Ilsan	Railroad
	Railroad Tunnel
	Lake/Reservoir
	River
	Built-up Area

⊡	Provincial Office
◉	Metropolitan City Hall
◎	Gun/Gu Office (2nd order administrative center)
⊙	Eup Office (3rd order administrative center)
○	Dong/Ri Office (4th order administrative center)
▲	Mountain
✕	Mine
卍	Temple
✈	International Airport
∴	Tourist Spot
☀	Lighthouse
🏖	Beach
♨	Spa

Depth of Water
0
50
100
200
500
1,000
2,000
3,000
(m)

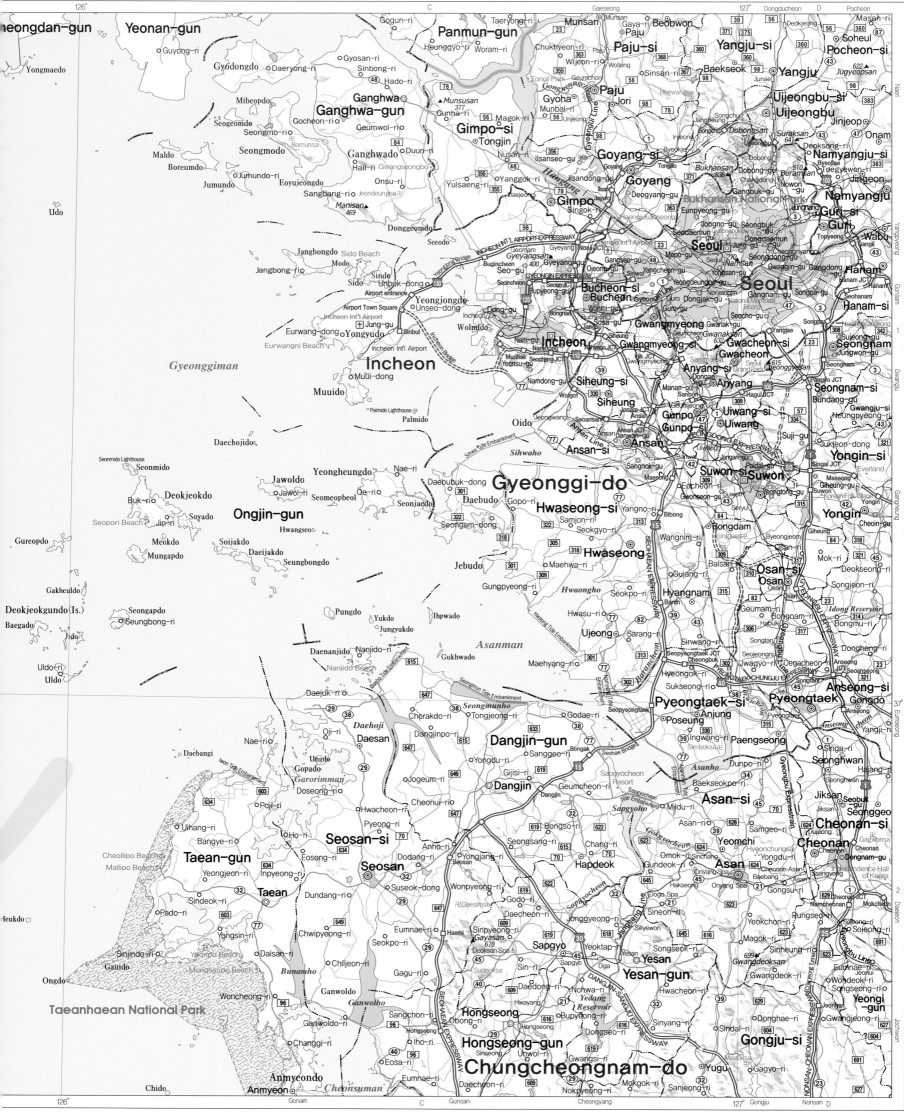

1 : 500,000

0   5   10   20km

18	19	20
22	**23**	**24**
28	29	30

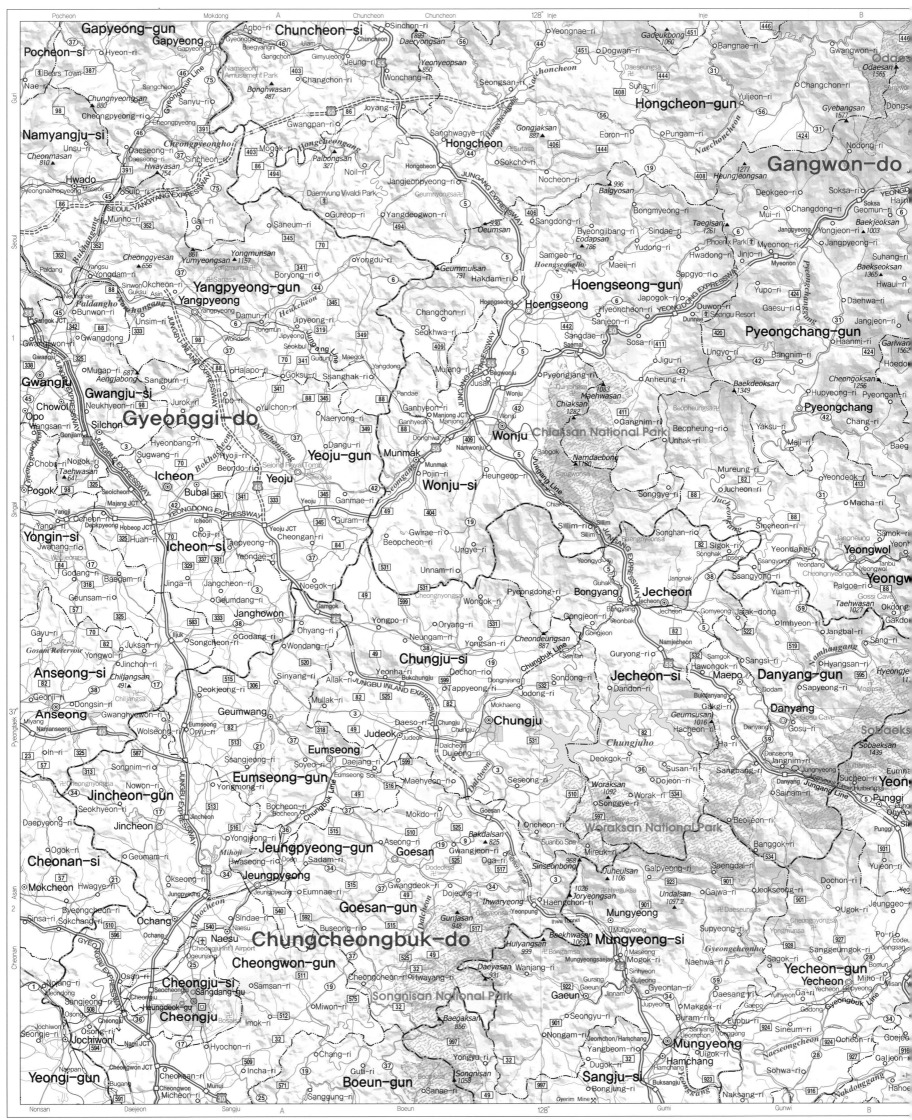

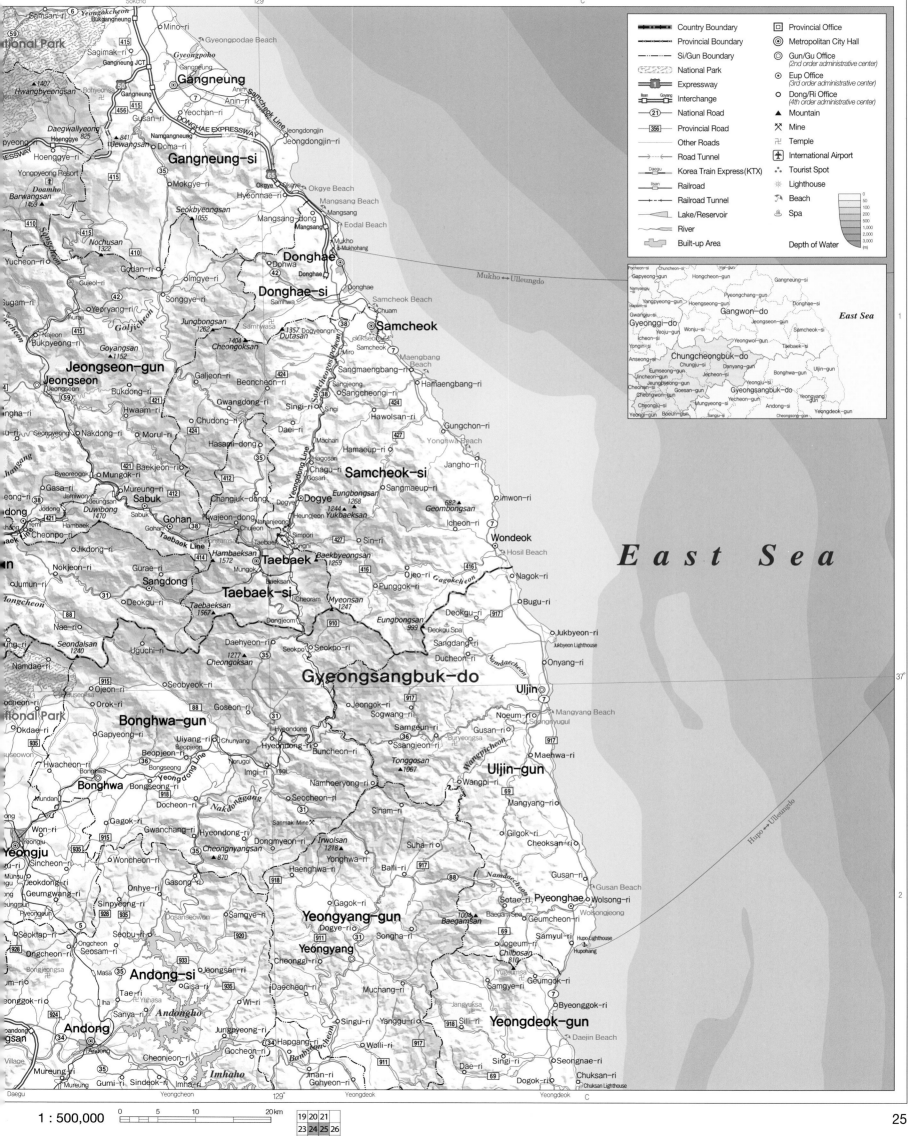

1 : 500,000

0   5   10   20km

19	20	21	
23	24	25	26
28	29	30	31

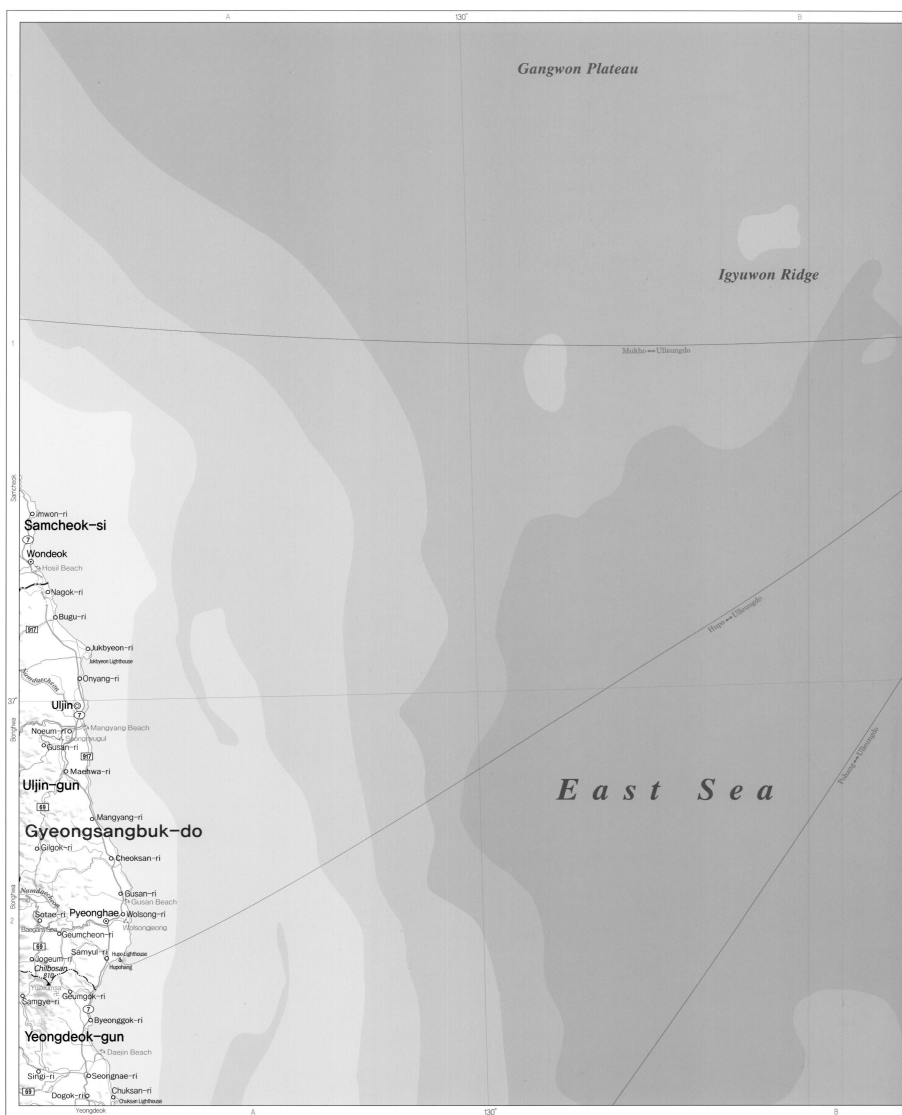

Gangwon Plateau

Igyuwon Ridge

Mukho ↔ Ulleungdo

Samcheok

Hupo ↔ Ulleungdo

1

o imwon-ri
Samcheok-si
⑦
Wondeok
⊙
⚓ Hosil Beach
o Nagok-ri

⑨₁₇
o Bugu-ri

o Jukbyeon-ri
Jukbyeon Lighthouse
o Onyang-ri

Namdaecheon

37
Uljin ◎
⑦
Noeum-ri o
⚓ Mangyang Beach
Seongnyugul
o Gusan-ri
o Maehwa-ri
Uljin-gun
⑥₉
o Mangyang-ri
Gyeongsangbuk-do
o Gilgok-ri
o Cheoksan-ri

Bonghwa

Pohang ↔ Ulleungdo

E a s t   S e a

Namdaecheon
o Gusan-ri
⚓ Gusan Beach
Sotae-ri o **Pyeonghae** o Wolsong-ri
Baegam Spa
o Geumcheon-ri   Wolsongjeong
Samyul-ri o   Hupo Lighthouse
o Jogeum-ri ⚓ Hupohang
Chilbosan
810
Yugeunsa
o Geumgok-ri
Samgye-ri o
⑦
o Byeonggok-ri
Yeongdeok-gun
⚓ Daejin Beach
Singi-ri o   o Seongnae-ri
⑥₉
o Dogok-ri   o Chuksan-ri
Chuksan Lighthouse

Yeongdeok

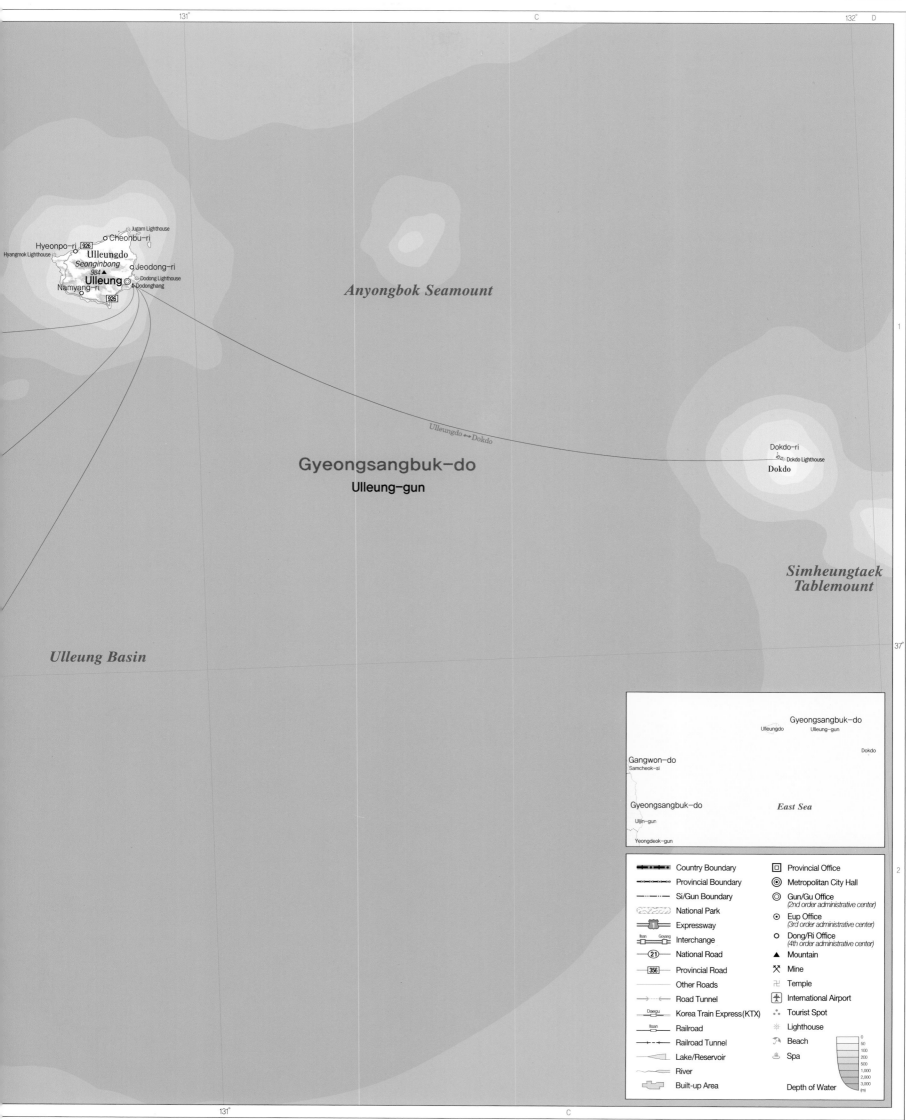

Jugam Lighthouse
○ Cheonbu-ri
Hyeonpo-ri [926]
Hyangmok Lighthouse **Ulleungdo**
Seonginbong
984 ▲ ○ Jeodong-ri
Ulleung ○ ↓ Dodong Lighthouse
Namyang-ri ○ ↓·Dodonghang
[926]

Anyongbok Seamount

Ulleungdo ↔ Dokdo

Dokdo-ri
☆ Dokdo Lighthouse
Dokdo

Gyeongsangbuk-do
Ulleung-gun

Simheungtaek Tablemount

Ulleung Basin

Gyeongsangbuk-do
Ulleungdo   Ulleung-gun

Dokdo
Gangwon-do
Samcheok-si

Gyeongsangbuk-do   *East Sea*

Uljin-gun

Yeongdeok-gun

Country Boundary	▣ Provincial Office
Provincial Boundary	◉ Metropolitan City Hall
Si/Gun Boundary	◎ Gun/Gu Office *(2nd order administrative center)*
National Park	
Expressway	⊙ Eup Office *(3rd order administrative center)*
Interchange	○ Dong/Ri Office *(4th order administrative center)*
(21) National Road	▲ Mountain
(356) Provincial Road	✕ Mine
Other Roads	卍 Temple
Road Tunnel	✈ International Airport
Korea Train Express (KTX)	∴ Tourist Spot
Railroad	☆ Lighthouse
Railroad Tunnel	🏖 Beach
Lake/Reservoir	♨ Spa
River	
Built-up Area	Depth of Water

1 : 500,000   0 5 10 20km

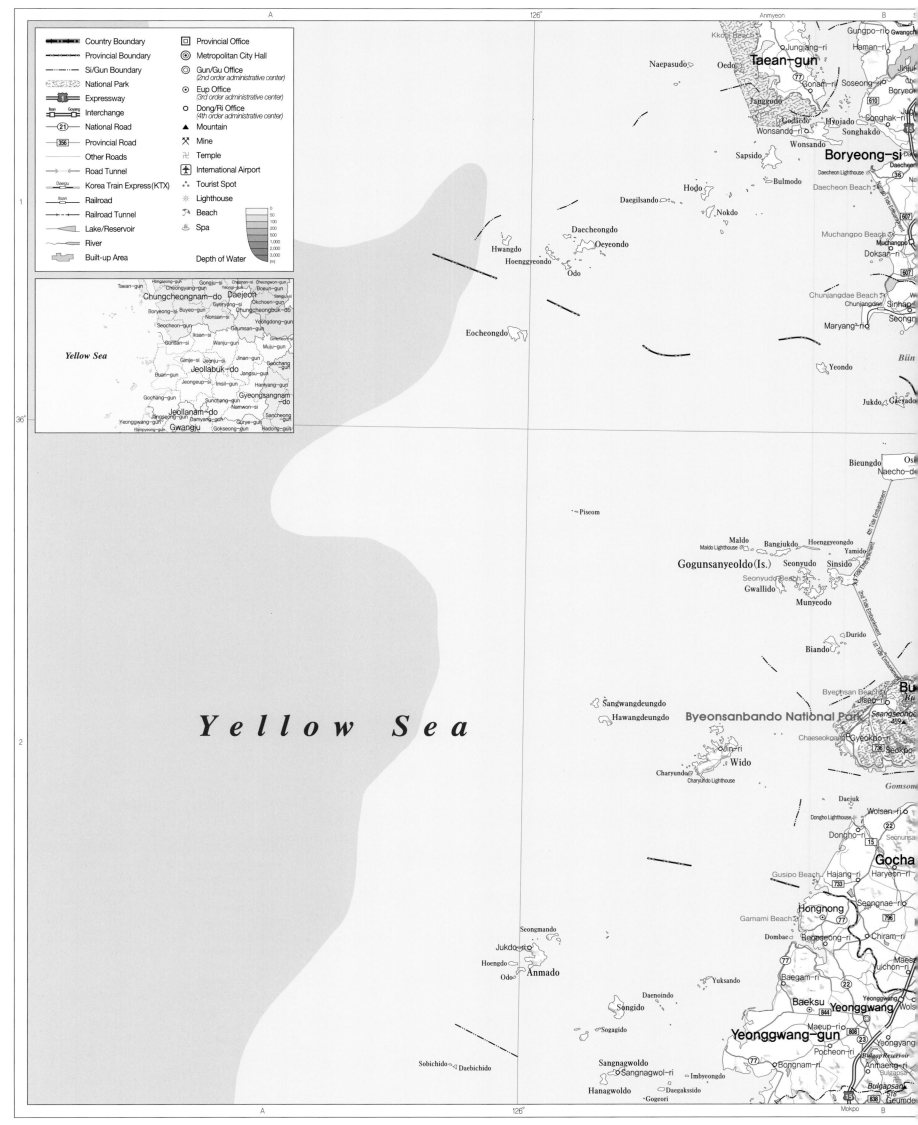

Legend

Country Boundary		▣	Provincial Office
Provincial Boundary		◉	Metropolitan City Hall
Si/Gun Boundary		◎	Gun/Gu Office (2nd order administrative center)
National Park		⊙	Eup Office (3rd order administrative center)
Expressway		○	Dong/Ri Office (4th order administrative center)
Interchange		▲	Mountain
National Road		✕	Mine
Provincial Road		卍	Temple
Other Roads		✚	International Airport
Road Tunnel		∴	Tourist Spot
Korea Train Express(KTX)		☀	Lighthouse
Railroad		⚓	Beach
Railroad Tunnel		♨	Spa
Lake/Reservoir			
River			Depth of Water
Built-up Area			

Yellow Sea

Chungcheongnam-do Daejeon

Jeollabuk-do

Jeollanam-do Gwangju

Yellow Sea

Taean-gun

Boryeong-si

Naepasudo

Hodo

Daegilsando

Nokdo

Daecheongdo

Hwangdo Oeyeondo

Hoenggyeondo Odo

Eocheongdo

Yeondo

Biin

Jukdo Gaeyado

Bieungdo Osi Naecho-do

Piseom

Maldo Bangjukdo Hoenggyeongdo
Maldo Lighthouse Yamido
Gogunsanyeoldo(Is.) Seonyudo Sinsido
Seonyudo Beach
Gwallido Munyeodo

Durido

Biando

Byephsan Beach
Jiseo-ri Bu
Sangwangdeungdo Byeonsanbando National Park Ssangseonbo
Hawangdeungdo Chaeseokgang Gyeokpo
Seokpo

Yellow Sea

Jin-ri Wido
Charyundo
Charyundo Lighthouse

Gomso

Daejuk
Dongho Lighthouse Wolsan-ri
Dongho-ri
Seonunsa

Gusipo Beach Hajang-ri Haryeon-ri

Gocha

Seongmando

Gamami Beach
Jukdo-ri Hongnong Seongnae-ri
Hoengdo Dombae Beopseong-ri Chiram-ri
Odo Anmado

Yuksando

Yeonggwang
Maehu-ri
Baegam-ri
Daenoindo
Songido Baeksu Yeonggwang
Sogagido Maeup-ri Yeongyang
Sangnagwoldo Yeonggwang-gun Pocheon-ri
Sangnagwol-ri Imbyeongdo Anmaeng-ri
Sobichido Daebichido Bongnam-ri
Hanagwoldo Daegakssido Geumde
Gogeori Bulgapsan

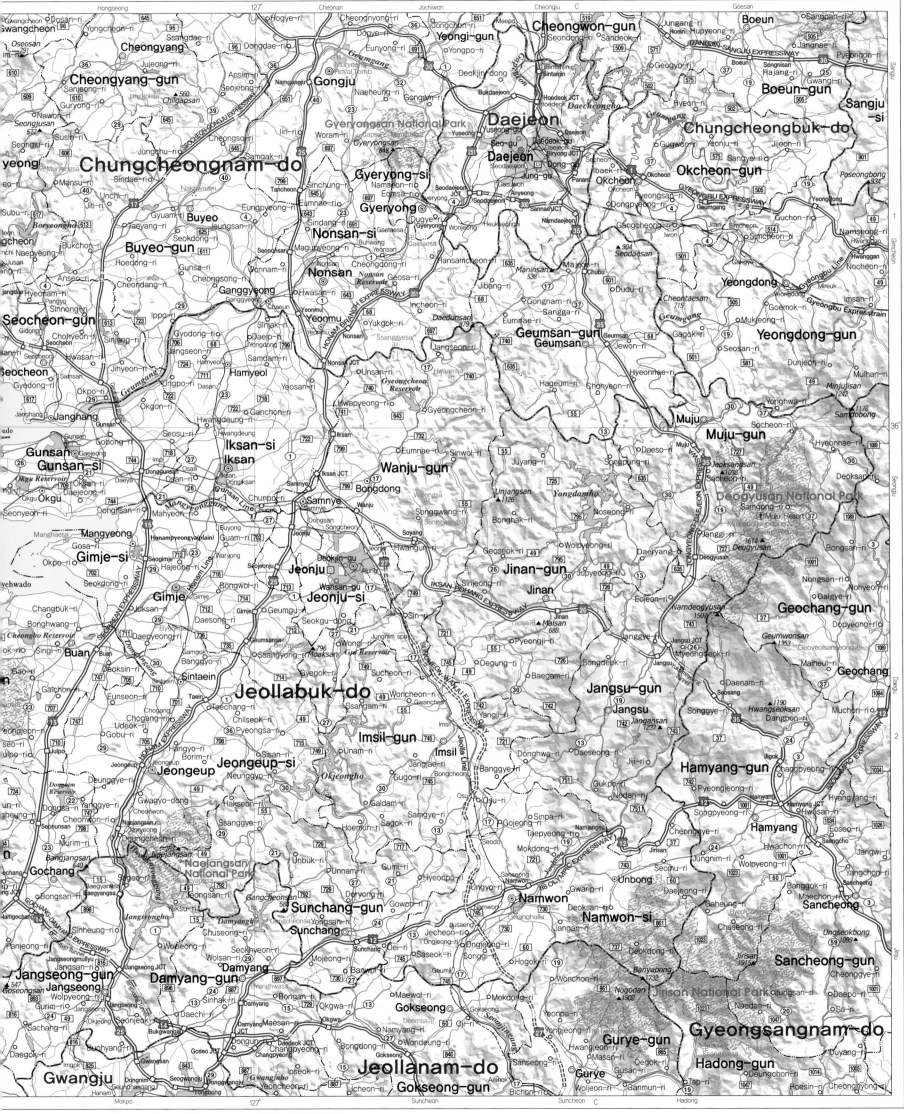

1 : 500,000

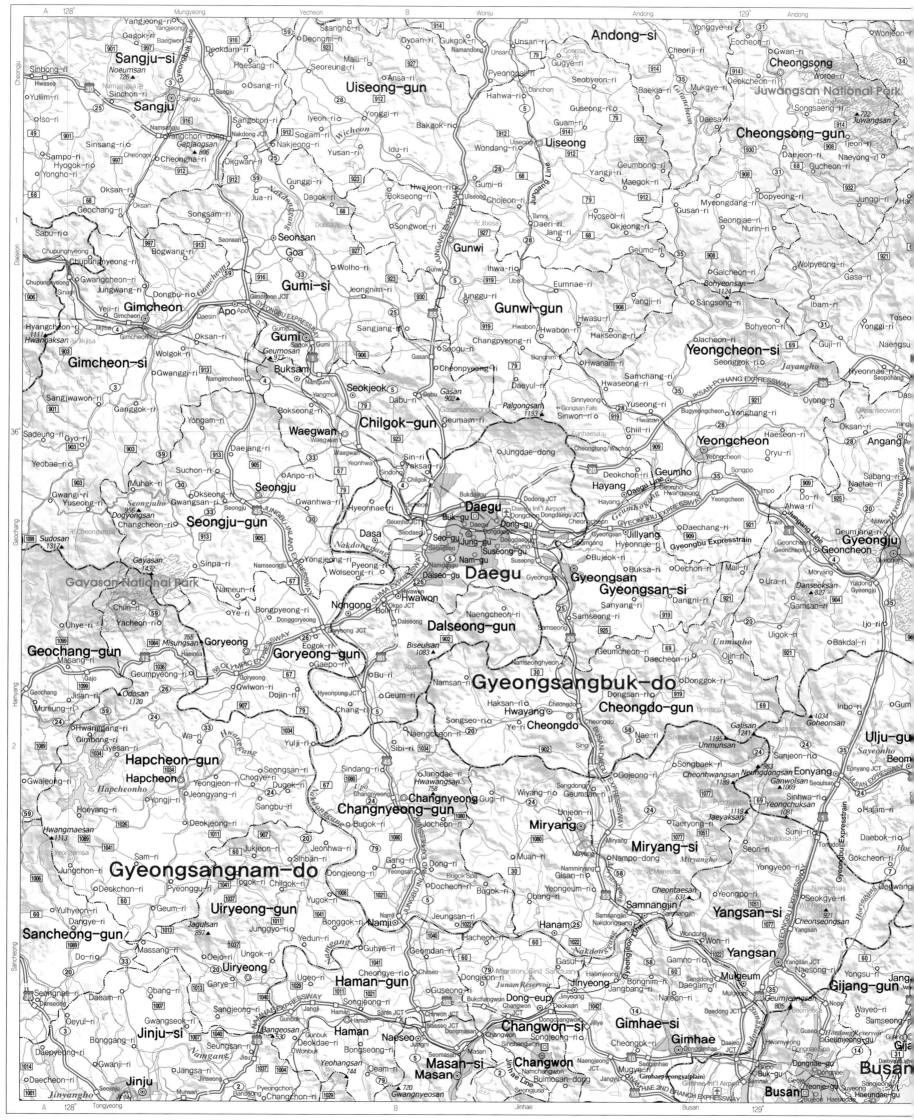

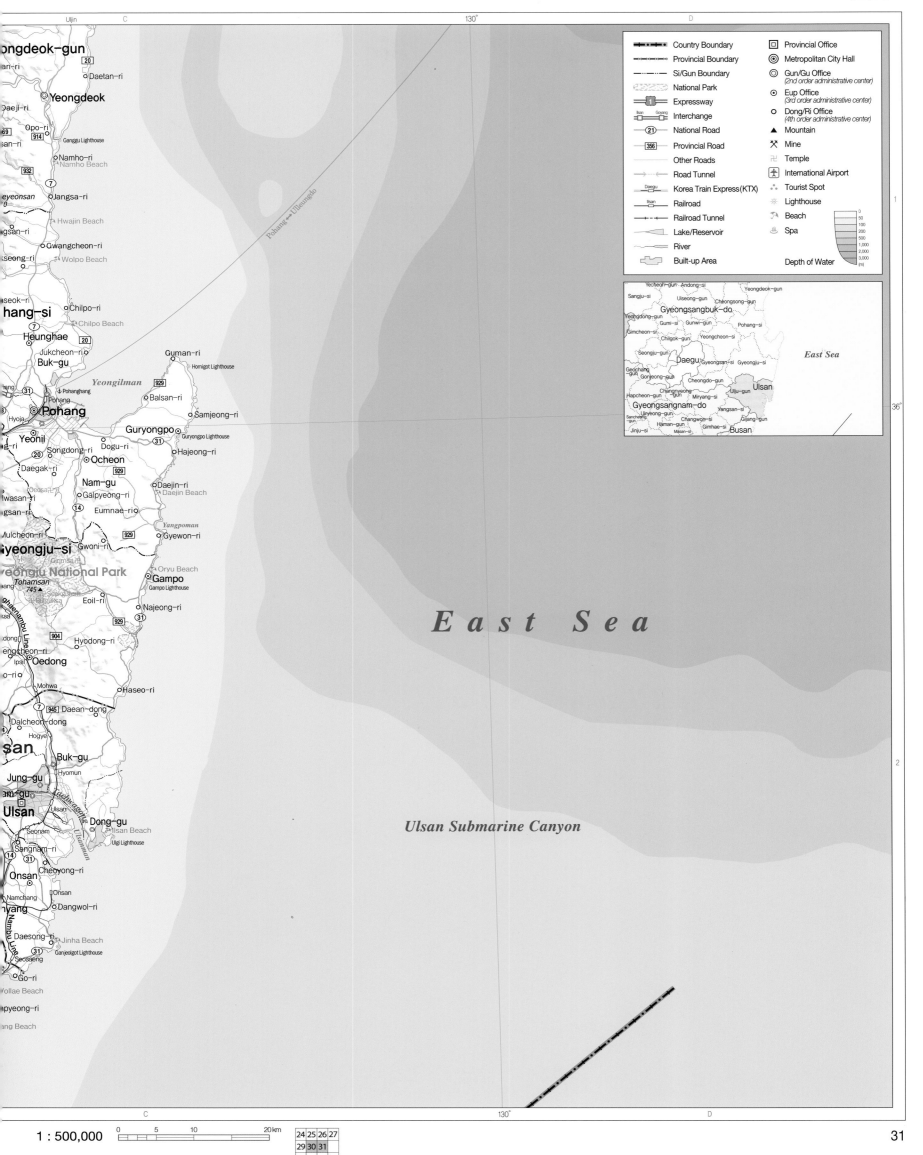

Legend

Country Boundary		Provincial Office	
Provincial Boundary		Metropolitan City Hall	
Si/Gun Boundary		Gun/Gu Office (2nd order administrative center)	
National Park		Eup Office (3rd order administrative center)	
Expressway		Dong/Ri Office (4th order administrative center)	
Interchange		Mountain	
National Road		Mine	
Provincial Road		Temple	
Other Roads		International Airport	
Road Tunnel		Tourist Spot	
Korea Train Express (KTX)		Lighthouse	
Railroad		Beach	
Railroad Tunnel		Spa	
Lake/Reservoir			
River		Depth of Water	
Built-up Area			

East Sea

Gyeongsangbuk-do
Yecheon-gun Andong-si Yeongdeok-gun
Sangju-si Uiseong-gun Cheongsong-gun
Yeongdong-gun Gunwi-gun
Gumi-si Pohang-si
Gimcheon-si Chilgok-gun Yeongcheon-si
Seongju-gun Gyeongsan-si Gyeongju-si
Geochang-gun Daegu
Gonyeong-gun Cheongdo-gun Ulsan
Hapcheon-gun Changnyeong-gun Miryang-si Ulju-gun
Gyeongsangnam-do Yangsan-si
Uiryeong-gun Changwon-si Gijang-gun
Sancheong-gun Haman-gun Gimhae-si
Jinju-si Masan-si Busan

East Sea

E a s t   S e a

Ulsan Submarine Canyon

ongdeok-gun
an-ri
Daetan-ri
Yeongdeok
Daeji-ri
Opo-ri
Namho-ri
Ganggu Lighthouse
Namho Beach
Jangsa-ri
Hwajin Beach
Gwangcheon-ri
Wolpo Beach
seong-ri
seok-ri
Chilpo-ri
hang-si
Chilpo Beach
Heunghae
Jukcheon-ri
Buk-gu
Guman-ri
Homigot Lighthouse
Yeongilman
Pohanghang
Balsan-ri
Pohang
Samjeong-ri
Yeonil
Guryongpo
Songdong-ri
Dogu-ri
Guryongpo Lighthouse
Hajeong-ri
Daegak-ri
Ocheon
Nam-gu
Daejin-ri
Galpyeong-ri
Daejin Beach
Eumnae-rio
Yangpoman
Mulcheon-ri
Gyewon-ri
yeongju-si
Gwoni-ri
Oryu Beach
eongju National Park
Tohamsan
745
Gampo
Gampo Lighthouse
Eoil-ri
Najeong-ri
Hyodong-ri
Oedong
Mohwa
Haseo-ri
Daean-dong
Dalcheon-dong
Hogye
san
Buk-gu
Hyomun
Jung-gu
Dong-gu
am-gu
Ulsan
Ilsan Beach
Seonam
Ulgi Lighthouse
Sangnam-ri
Cheoyong-ri
Onsan
Onsan
Namchang
Dangwol-ri
yang
Daesong-ri
Jinha Beach
Ganjeolgot Lighthouse
Go-ri
Seosaeng
Wollae Beach
apyeong-ri
ang Beach

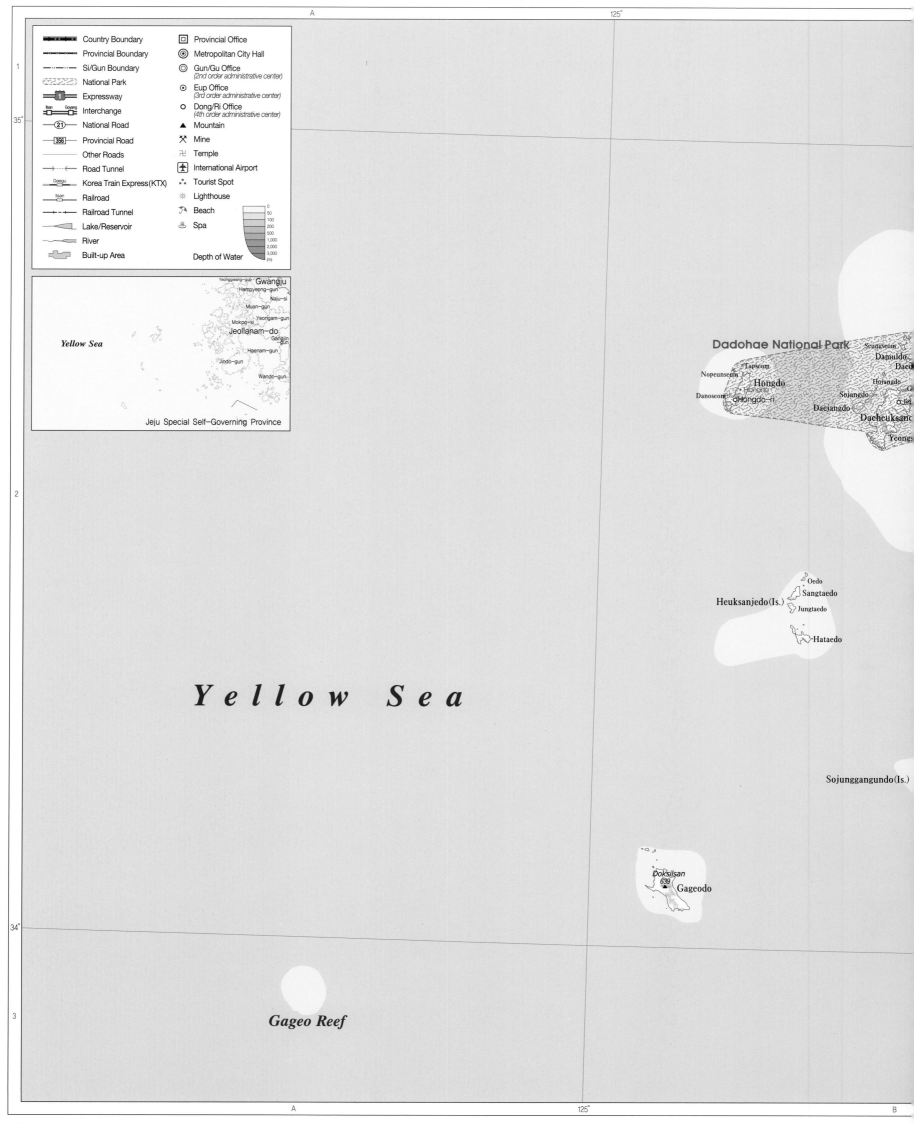

Country Boundary	▣	Provincial Office
Provincial Boundary	◉	Metropolitan City Hall
Si/Gun Boundary	◎	Gun/Gu Office (2nd order administrative center)
National Park	⊙	Eup Office (3rd order administrative center)
Expressway	○	Dong/Ri Office (4th order administrative center)
Interchange	▲	Mountain
National Road	✕	Mine
Provincial Road	卍	Temple
Other Roads	✈	International Airport
Road Tunnel	∴	Tourist Spot
Korea Train Express(KTX)	☀	Lighthouse
Railroad	🏊	Beach
Railroad Tunnel	♨	Spa
Lake/Reservoir		
River		
Built-up Area		Depth of Water

Yellow Sea

Yeonggwang-gun · Gwangju
Hampyeong-gun
Naju-si
Muan-gun
Yeongam-gun
Mokpo-si
Jeollanam-do
Gangjin-gun
Haenam-gun
Jindo-gun
Wando-gun

Jeju Special Self-Governing Province

Dadohae National Park
Seungseom
Damuldo
Daed
Tapseom
Nopeunseom
Hongdo
Horangdo
Danoseom
Hongdo-ri
Sojangdo
Dacjangdo
Daeheuksan
Yeongs

Yellow Sea

Oedo
Sangtaedo
Heuksanjedo(Is.)
Jungtaedo
Hataedo

Sojunggangundo(Is.)

Doksilsan
639
Gageodo

Gageo Reef

B · 126° · Gunsan · Jangseong · C

Dakseom · 808 · Woram-ri
Daejeon-ri · 838
811 · Seokchang-ri · Hampyeong-gun Gwangju
Eouido · Sinjeong-ri · 24 · Samchuk-ri · Seogwangsan-ri
Soheosado · Daecheosado · 805 · Keunpojakdo · Hampyeong · 42
Bunamgundo(Is.) · Norok Lighthouse · 815 · Hyangyo-ri · 825 · Naju Geumidong-ri
Daenorokdo · Daetarido · Gwangsan-ri · Sudo · 818 · 831 · Noan
Jaewondo · Jin-ri · Yangwol-ri · Hampyeong · Donghamnyeong · Najupyeongya(plain) · 801
Bunamdo · Imjado · 24 · Oryu-ri · 60 · Oeban · Woltae-ri · 801 · Naju
Immodo · Galdo · Jido · Mokdong-ri · 815 · Hagyo-ri · Honam Line · Ogang-ri
Saokdo · 805 · Bukmuan · Muan · Dasi
Daechimado · Jeungdo · Anmado · Busado · Muan · Eomda-ri · Naju-si
Jukseok-ri
Yuldo · Seondo · 1 · Dodae-ri · Unsan-ri · 23 · 801 · Geumgok-ri · Deoksan-ri · Oksan-ri
Daecho-ri · Muan Int'l Airport · Sacheon-ri · 23 · 820 · 13
Byeongpungdo · 815 · Yeon-ri · Indong-ri
Hwado · Jangmado · Goiseom · Muan-gun · Dorim-ri · Naedong-ri · 55
Keungjieom · Soakdo · Maehwado · Bogyeong-ri · 825 · Cheongnyong-ri · Heungdeok-ri · 820 · Obong
Jaeundo · Dangsado · Hyojido · 49 · 821 · Yongheung-ri · 23
Guyeong-ri · Aphaedo · 77 · Bokgil-ri · 815 · Naedong-ri · Guhak-ri · 819
Chorando · Garando · Illo · 801 · Unam-ri
Yeokdo · Hakgyo-ri · Illo · 820 · Sinhak-ri
Gidong-ri · Oenseom · 2 · Amtaedo · Maedo · Janggam · Mokpo · 821
Najugundo(Is.) · Chuyeopdo · Singi-ri · Palgeumdo · Imseong-ni · Imseong-ri · Muan · 509
Songtando · Nodaeseom · Geosado · Dado Beach · Mokpo · Muan
Chilbaldo · Chilbal Lighthouse · Usedo · Sangsachido · Eup-ri · Nuldo · Yudalsan · Yeongam-gun · Yeongam
Bigeumdo · Suchido · Eupdong-ri · 805 · Mokpoman · Oedo · Dogap-ri · Wolchulsan · Cheonhwangsa
2 · Gatseom Lighthouse · Anjwado · Oedaldo · Dallido Gohada · Mokpo Lighthouse · Jangcheon-ri · 811 · Wolchulsan National Park
Deoksan-ri · Mokpogu Lighthouse · Heosado · Samho · 835
Dochodo · Sinan-gun · 805 · Wolho-ri · 810 · Yeongsanho · 13 · Geumdang-ri
Gokdo Lighthouse · Oeumokdo · Bakjido · Mangsan-ri · 2 · Dokcheon-ri · 829
Dadohae National Park · Mannyeon-ri · 2 · Chundong-ri · 10 · Songwol-ri
Suhang-ri · Okdo · Banwoldo · Sihado · 22 · Geumhodo · Yeongamho · Pyeong-ri
Daeseom · Busodo · Sihado Lighthouse · 49 · Heukseoksan · 819 · Wolpyeong-ri
Gyeongchido · Jarado · Geumpyeong-ri · 13 · Gangjin
Meongeseom · Jangbyeongdo · Gaedo · Budong-ri · Chosong-ri · Seongrin-ri · 2 · Gangjin
Sanuido · Daeyado · Dochang-ri · Jangsando · Mugo-ri · Geumhoho · 806 · Chunjeon-ri · Gangjin-gun
Uido · Dongsouido · Neungsando · 2 · Makgeumdo · Dongeo-ri · Songseok-ri · 819
Uigundo(Is.) · Sindo · Baegyado · 18 · Hwanae-ri · Jiseok-ri
Jangjaedo · Unggok-ri · Sangtaedo · Namni-ri · Wonho-ri · Haenam · 55
Hauido · Sangtaedong-ri · Pyeongsado · Yuldo · Nokjin-ri · 18 · Godo-ri · Yeongchun-ri · 18
Hataedo · Gosado · Gyomaekdo · Wojin Lighthouse · Haenam-gun · Hangchon-ri · Singi-ri · Gaudo
Byeokpa-ri · Jeunguido · Hanja · 806 · Noguidang · Pyeonghwal-ri · Suyang-ri · 827
803 · Bunto-ri · Osan-ri · Jeolla nam-do · Pyeonghwal-ri
Gasado · Jujido · Yangdeokdo · Jindo · 801 · 77 · Gajwa-ri · Bangchuk-ri · 827
Jangdo · Posan-ri · Jindo-gun · Ilpyeong-ri · 682 · Songcheon-ri
Geumno-ri · 18 · Sangmado · Duryunsan · 55 · Sinwol-ri
Inji-ri · Jindo · Chosa-ri · Anho-ri · Doamman
Seongnamdo · 803 · Seokgyo-ri · Agip Land The Island · Geumhodo · Geumgang-ri · Waryong-ri · Namchang-ri · Gomado · Sahudo
Oebyeongdo · Baegyado · 18 · Jungnim-ri · Songpyeong Beach · Hakga-ri · 13 · Gogeumdo
Naebyeongdo · Okdo · Yeondong-ri · Jeopdo · Mihwangsa · Daldo · Wondong-ri · Jangjwa-ri · Jangdo
Nnrokdo · Sangjodo · Jangjukdo · Eoran · Sanjeong-ri · Samdu-ri · Jangbogo Cheonghaejin Historic Site
Gwansado · Nabaedo · Eoran Lighthouse · 806 · Songho-ri · 77
Jiumokdo · Hapjeong Lighthouse · Sanggujado · Hagujado · Songhori Beach · Baegildo · Wando
Somado · Changyu-ri · Haguja Lighthouse · Songho-ri · Ttangkkeut Tomall · Jungdo-ri · Wando
Geochagundo(Is.) · Hajodo · Eoryong Lighthouse · Eoryongdo · Donghwado
Seogeochado · Jukhangdo · Galmaegiseom · Daejeongdo · Oemogundo(Is.) · Heugildo · Wando-gun
Daemido · Scuido · Dokgeodo · Eoryong · Masakdo · Hoenggando
Witdaeseom · Cheongdeungdo · Dokgeogundo(Is.) · Milmaedo Lighthouse · Iikguldo · Jukuldo · Sinyang-ri · Somodo Lighthouse · Somodo
Jukdo · Gwanmaedo Beach · Donggeochado · Oemodo · Daemodo
Jukdo Lighthouse · Gwanmaedo · Norokdo · Nohwado · Bria-ri · Soando
Maenggoldo · Byeongpungdo · Seoneopdo Lighthouse · Neopdo · Nohwa
Maenggolgundo(Is.) · Dadohae National Park · Meongseom · Bogildo · Buhwang-ri · Yesong-ri · Jinsan-ri · Bulgeumdo
Soangundo(Is.) · Dangsado
Hoenggando · Soando
Dadohae National Park

Jikgudo · Geomeungari
Daeseo-ri · Chuja Lighthouse · Chujagundo(Is.)
Chujado · 1114 · Sinsang-ri

Jeju Special Self-Governing Province

Jeju Strait

1 : 500,000
0 · 5 · 10 · 20km

28	29
32	33	34
36	37

33

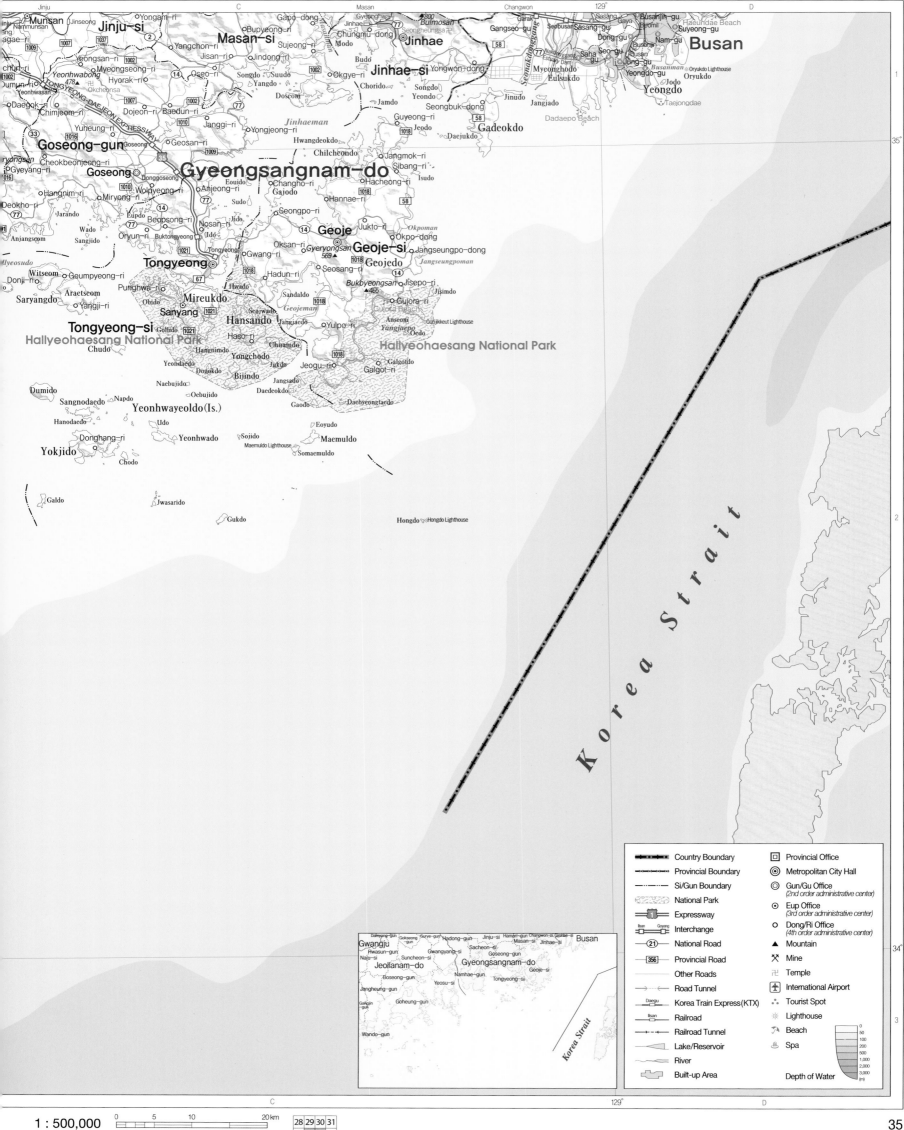

Jinju-si

Masan-si

Jinhae

Jinhae-si

Busan

Goseong-gun

Goseong

Gyeongsangnam-do

Geoje

Geoje-si

Tongyeong

Tongyeong-si

Hallyeohaesang National Park

Mireukdo

Sanyang

Hansando

Hallyeohaesang National Park

Yeonhwayeoldo(Is.)

Yokjido

Korea Strait

Country Boundary	▣	Provincial Office
Provincial Boundary	◎	Metropolitan City Hall
Si/Gun Boundary	◉	Gun/Gu Office *(2nd order administrative center)*
National Park	⊙	Eup Office *(3rd order administrative center)*
Expressway	○	Dong/Ri Office *(4th order administrative center)*
Interchange	▲	Mountain
National Road	✕	Mine
Provincial Road	卍	Temple
Other Roads	✈	International Airport
Road Tunnel	∴	Tourist Spot
Korea Train Express(KTX)	❄	Lighthouse
Railroad	⌇	Beach
Railroad Tunnel	♨	Spa
Lake/Reservoir		
River		Depth of Water
Built-up Area		

Gwangju

Jeollanam-do

Gyeongsangnam-do

Busan

Korea Strait

1 : 500,000

0   5   10   20 km

28	29	30	31
33	34	35
36	37

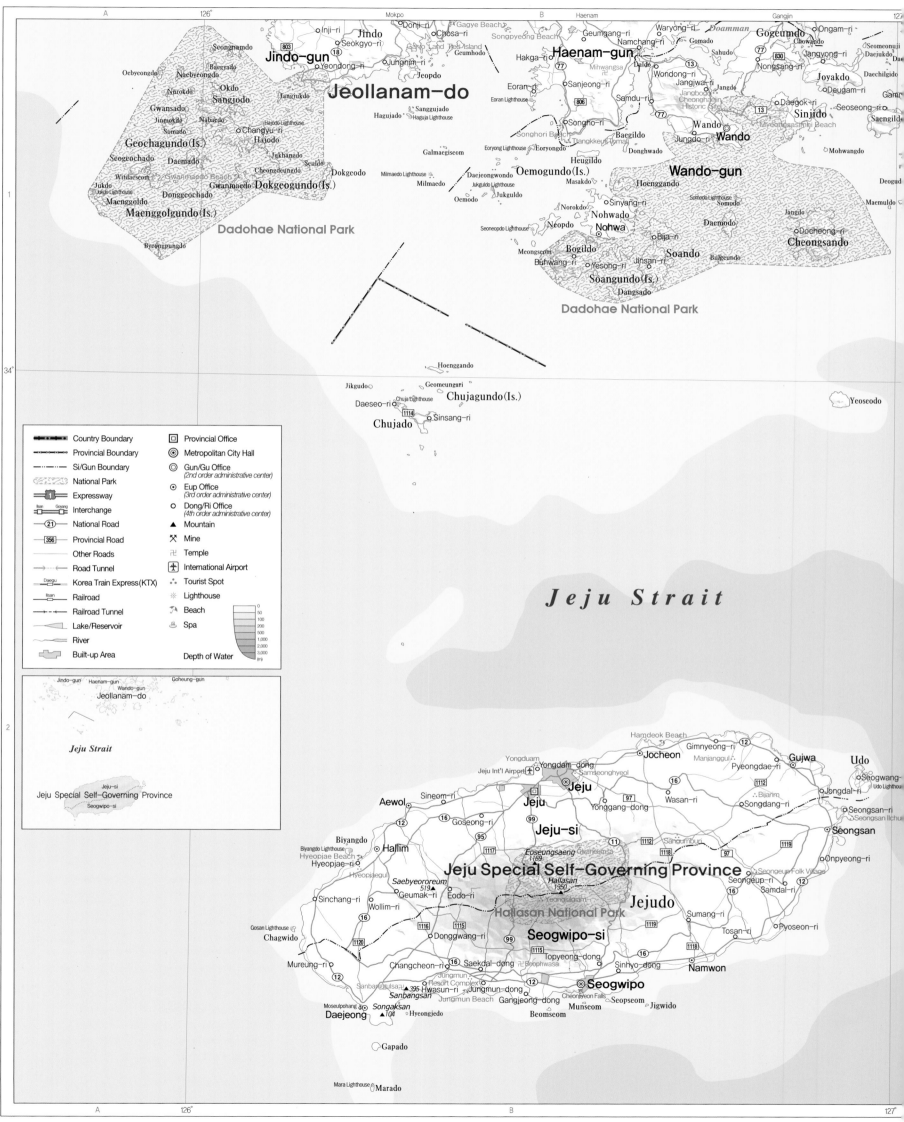

Legend

Country Boundary	
Provincial Boundary	
Si/Gun Boundary	
National Park	
Expressway	
Interchange	
National Road	
Provincial Road	
Other Roads	
Road Tunnel	
Korea Train Express(KTX)	
Railroad	
Railroad Tunnel	
Lake/Reservoir	
River	
Built-up Area	

Provincial Office	
Metropolitan City Hall	
Gun/Gu Office (2nd order administrative center)	
Eup Office (3rd order administrative center)	
Dong/Ri Office (4th order administrative center)	
Mountain	
Mine	
Temple	
International Airport	
Tourist Spot	
Lighthouse	
Beach	
Spa	
Depth of Water	

mdangdo · Geogeumdo
Bigyeongdo
Chungdo
do
Pyeongildo
Geumil Beach
Sorangdo
Darangdo

Ocheon-ri Jukdo Ojjuk-ri
Oecho-ri · Oenarodo

Yeondo-ri Dadohae National Park
Sorido Lighthouse

Dadohae National Park

Muhakdo
Sonjugyeoldo(Is.)
Sonjukdo · Sogeomundo
Sopyeongdo · Gwangdo
Pyeongdo · Galkiseom

Chodogundo(Is.)
Wonda
Hwangjedo Jangdo Chodo

Yeongmando

Dadohae National Park
Mogiseom
Noksan Lighthouse
Dongdo · Daesambudo
Sangbaekdo
Geomundo
Seodo
Geomun-ri Habaekdo
Geomundo Lighthouse

34°

E 125° F 126° G 127° H

Jeju Strait

Hamdeok Beach Gimnyeong-ri
Yongduam 12
Jeju Int'l Airport Jocheon Gujwa Udo
16 Manjanggul Udo Lighthouse
Aewol Wasan-ri
Biyangdo Jeju 112 Seongsan Ilchulbong
Hallim Je'judo Jeju-si 97 Seongsan
Biyangdo Lighthouse 95 Sangumburi 1118
Hyeopjae Beach Hyeopjaegul Hallasan National Park Seongeup-ri
Hallasan 11 1118
Sinchang-ri Geumak-ro Jeju Special Self-Governing Province Pyoseon-ri
Gosan Lighthouse 16 1116 99 Seogwipo-si
Chagwido 1136 Saekdal-dong 1115 12
16 99 Namwon
Sanbanggulsa
Jungmun Beach Resort Complex Seogwipo
Daejeong Jungmun Seopseom Jigwido
Beomseom
Gapado

Mara Lighthouse
Marado

33°

Jeju Int'l Airport ⊕

Ieodo (Ocean Research Station)

Jejudo and Ieodo
1 : 1,000,000
0 5 10 20 km

LANDFORMS

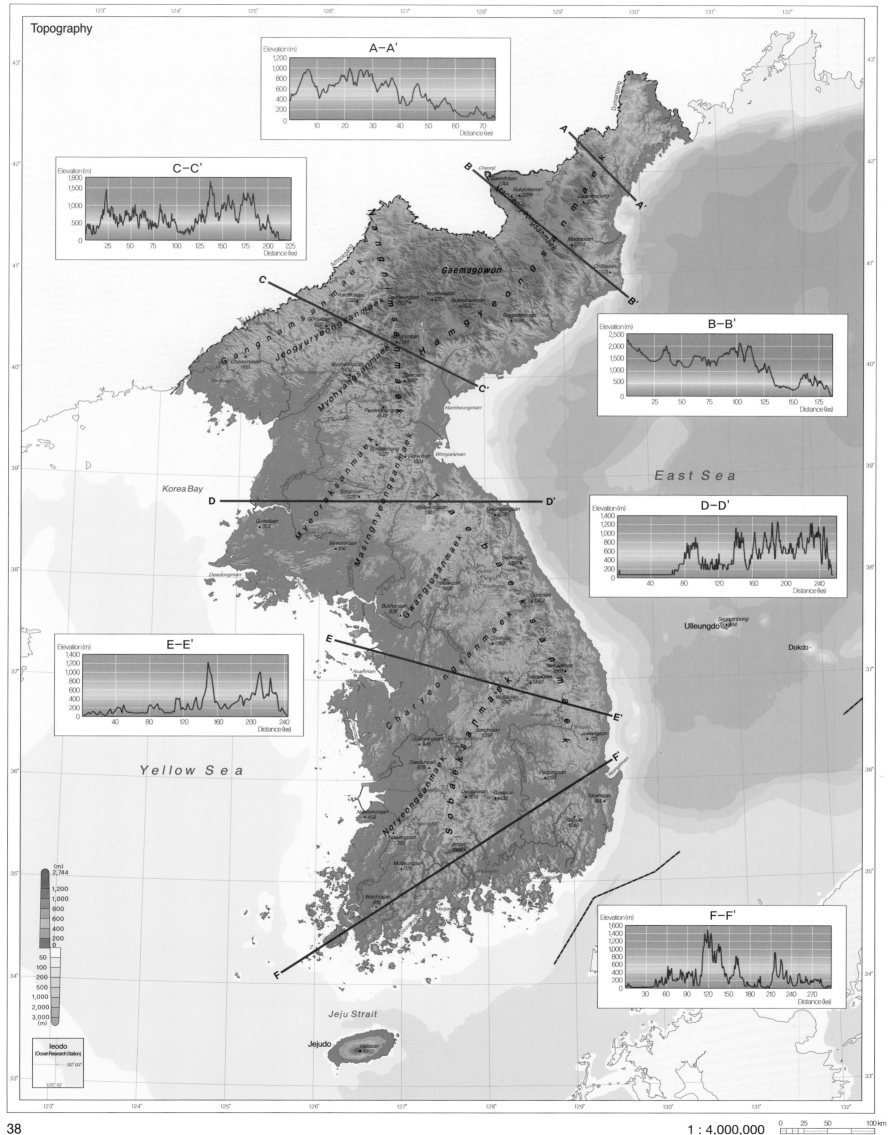

Topography

A–A'

C–C'

B–B'

D–D'

E–E'

F–F'

Gaemagowon

Korea Bay

East Sea

Ulleungdo
Dokdo

Yellow Sea

Jeju Strait

Jejudo
Hallasan
1950

Ieodo
(Ocean Research Station)

1 : 4,000,000

0 25 50 100 km

About 70 percent of the Korean Peninsula is mountainous or hilly. The mean elevation of Korea is 433m and the mean slope angle is 10.4°. The northeastern part is the most rugged area where mountain ranges such as Baekdusan (Baekdu Mountain) rise to over 2,700m in places. The Taebaeksanmaek (Taebaek Mountain Range) rises to over 1,500m on the eastern side of the peninsula and then drops abruptly toward the East Sea with little or no coastal plain. Narrow valleys and plains are located between the hills and mountains in this area. In the central zone, moderately high mountains dominate the landscape. The west and south coasts in the southern half of the country are deeply indented with many islands and harbors. Lowlands are found mainly along the western sides of the peninsula, with some extensive lowlands also in the south. Elevations are generally low, because these mountain ranges have been subjected to long-term erosion with relatively stable tectonic movements. In the low relief region of southwestern Korea, there are abundant 'monadnock' features thought to have been formed by long-term surface erosion.

A profile of central Korea reveals that the eastern side of the Taebaeksanmaek has high relief, while the western flank has widely spaced hills with low relief. These landforms of the entire area are believed to have been formed by asymmetrical tectonic movement centered along the Taebaeksanmaek. This uplift seems to have begun during the middle of the Cenozoic Era after a long period of planation during the Mesozoic Era.

Tectonic Landforms
Korea is a peninsula extending NNW-SSE from the Asian continent toward the Japanese Islands in the western North Pacific Ocean. Because the eastern margin of the Asian continent is often referred as 'The West Pacific Tectonic Zone,' the geological and geomorphological characteristics of Korea are closer to those found in China than in Japan. Due to the lack of significant crustal activity in Korea, there are only a few typical tectonic landforms. There are, however, abundant linear valleys and river channels following faults and other structural features.

Most of the distinctive landforms formed by faults are grabens and fault-line valleys. An example of such a typical structural feature is the Gilju-Myeongcheon graben. This landform was first formed by faulting with subsequent volcanic eruptions during the Pliocene. About 15 hot springs including Jeol spa are found in the feature and the Hamgyeong train route trends along the graben. Chilbosan horst centered at Chilbosan (1,103m) lies at the eastern end of the fault. Representative fault valleys include the Chugaryeong, Bulguksa, and Yangsan tectonic valleys.

Granite Weathering Landforms
Because Korea experiences a temperate climate, chemical weathering is dominant in summer and mechanical processes are more important in winter. In high mountains, physical processes are dominant and locally produce periglacial landforms. The annual average rate of chemical weathering of granite in Korea is estimated to be about 30g/m². This type of weathering mainly occurs during summer due to high temperature and rainfall. In Korea, however, there are many tropical, subtropical, and periglacial features that are widely considered as relict landforms formed under paleo-climatic conditions.

Weathering of granite is a key component in shaping the Korean landscape. The majority of such lithologies in Korea can be divided into two different types: Daebo and Bulguksa granites. Both were intruded during the Jurassic and Cretaceous periods and weathered throughout the Mesozoic and Cenozoic Eras, resulting in thick regolith layers at the surface. The denudation of these materials is the key process in forming typical granitic landforms. In addition, the uplift of the peninsula also plays an important role in the eastern part of Korea. The high rate of uplift caused by the asymmetrical tectonic movement reveals the influence of rock types on relief. In general, granite forms low relief plains or erosion basins, but sedimentary and metamorphic rocks display high relief mountains.

As the deeply weathered regolith is eroded, unweathered bedrock or corestones remain *in situ*. These processes generate various rock features, such as inselbergs and tors. Various weathering pits, including tafoni, gnamma, and grooves are abundant in such rock landscapes.

Fluvial Landforms
The six longest rivers in Korea (Amnokgang, Dumangang, Hangang, Nakdonggang, Daedonggang, and Geumgang) all flow into the Yellow and the South Sea except the Dumangang that enters the East Sea. The tidal range of the Yellow Sea is one of the highest in the world, and the rivers flowing into it are strongly influenced by the large changes in the tides. River channels are usually steep since the water originates at high altitudes. However, the relief ratio of river channels is locally influenced by bedrock types. For example, along the Namhangang, the value is low on Precambrian metamorphic rocks, but relatively high in the limestone regions of the Chosun Super Group.

Along the major rivers in southern Korea, such as Hangang, Nakdonggang, and Geumgang, hills sit close to the channel even at the river mouth. This feature allows most rivers to flow straight. However, there are some incised meanders farther upstream. Cuts caused by active meandering processes are often observed along the channel. The typical landforms generated by such meander cuts are paleo-river channels. Those formed by incised meanders can be observed in the mountainous region in the east, and the other structures formed by free meanders often occur in the western plain region of central Korea. At the lower part of large rivers such as the Amnokgang and Nakdonggang, braided stream channels are often developed. Potholes, waterfalls, and plunge pools are common channel bed landforms, especially at upstream locations. These landforms often become tourist attractions.

Natural levees and backswamps are developed downstream on the major rivers. Backswamps are frequently reclaimed for agriculture with the construction of levees and irrigation canals. These low relief landforms have been used intensively for agriculture, and are now being converted into residential areas with the increase of urbanization. River terraces can be categorized as structural (tectonic movement), climatic (climatic changes) and marine (sea level changes). These landforms are often used to reconstruct the environmental changes during the Pleistocene and Holocene. As flatland is scarce in mountainous areas, the river terraces are used intensively for agriculture. In these regions, residential areas are located between the terraces and steep mountains.

Marine Landforms
Because the Korean Peninsula is surrounded by the sea, it has a long coastline. Although the shoreline of the East Sea is relatively straight and simple, that of the Yellow and the South Sea are complex and irregular with many small islands.

Beaches can be classified according to the texture of their component sediments into sand, gravel, and sand-gravel beaches. Sand beaches are especially common on the East Sea. The constituent materials of sand beaches are determined by the mineral composition of local bedrock; granite produces white-colored quartz-rich sands, while sedimentary and volcanic rocks form dark-colored beaches. Locally, there are some light-colored shell-sand beaches. Rocky coasts are found where mountains and plateaus intersect the sea.

Igneous rocks are located along the coast of volcanic islands including Jejudo (Jeju Island). Typical landforms on rocky coasts are sea-stacks and wave-cut terraces. At the base of sea cliffs, wave action forms sea caves and other erosional features. When a sea cliff collapses due to wave action, gravel beaches may occur locally.

The most typical eolian and marine landforms in Korea are coastal dunes and marine terraces. Predominant north-south seasonal winds have created large-scale coastal dunes on the western coast of the peninsula (e.g. Taeanbando, Anmyeondo, Imjado). Dunes in the Sindu-*ri* are registered as Korean Natural Heritage Feature No. 431. Typical coastal dune subcategories, such as foredunes, dune ridges, swales, and blowouts, are well-developed here. The wave cut terraces or coastal plains were formed due to higher sea level during interglacial periods and were raised by gradual tectonic uplift, which can be observed at Jeongdongjin and Janggigot-Ulsanman along the East Sea. These step-shaped marine terraces indicate repeated tectonic uplifts and are currently registered as Natural Heritage Feature No. 437.

The height above sea level and age of marine terraces indicate the rate of tectonic uplift. Combining various research results, it is calculated that Korea's coast is rising at about 0.1m/1000 years. Thus tectonic movement in Korea is relatively small. There is, however, strong evidence that this rate varies locally.

Plains and Gentle Slope Landforms
Because of its mountainous landscapes, wide areas of low relief are rare in Korea. Relatively large erosional plains occur at the mouths of rivers flowing into the Yellow and South Sea. The typical example is the Honampyeongya (Honam plain), which is located within a erosional basin formed by differential weathering and erosion. Fluvial processes, however, have modified these plains, and they are covered by thick sequences of fluvial sediments primarily laid down during periods of high sea level after the glacial periods. A large part of Honampyeongya is covered by such fluvial sediments, and was intensively reclaimed during the Japanese colonial rule in the early 20th century.

Transitional landforms called 'gentle slopes' between steep mountains and plains are known as pediments or alluvial fans. The morphological shape of these landforms is quite straightforward, but there are some controversies on the process responsible for them. Previously these landforms were defined as pediment-like landforms that were formed by erosion processes of deep weathered granite regoliths. The researcher who supports this explanation argues that these landforms should be called 'gentle erosional slopes' to avoid confusion. Most of these 'gentle erosional slopes' occur at erosional basins which are surrounded by steep mountains. The alluvial fans found on 'gentle slopes' reveal that these landforms were formed under previous dry climatic conditions. However, now they are commonly interpreted as fluvial landforms that were formed by various geomorphological processes. In order to avoid confusion with 'gentle erosional slopes,' some researchers propose that the alluvial fans developed by depositional processes should be called 'fluvial fans.'

Volcanic Landforms
Tectonically the Korean Peninsula is relatively stable, so that there are no active volcanoes. Many relict volcanic landforms, however, can be found throughout Korea, which were formed during the Cenozoic and Mesozoic Eras. There were active volcanic eruptions centered at Gyeongsang basin during the Jurassic Period in the Mesozoic Era. Tuffs and conglomerates found in Gyeongsang Super Group and Yeoncheon Group are evidence for such volcanic activity. Mudeungsan, Juwangsan and Geumseongsan were all formed during this time period. The Pleistocene and Holocene during the Cenozoic Era experienced active volcanic eruptions, which formed typical volcanic landforms in Korea, including Ulleungdo, Dokdo, Jejudo, Baekdusan and lava plateau, and Cheorwon-Pyeonggang lava plateau.

The Hallasan (1,950m) in Jejudo, which is the highest mountain in the southern part of Korea, is a compound volcano surrounded by many parasitic volcanoes called 'Oreum' locally formed during a single eruption. There are around 400 scattered parasitic volcanoes around Jejudo. Baekdusan (2,744m) is the highest mountain in Korea, which is surrounded by a lava plateau whose average height is around 1,600m. The highest peak in Baekdusan is called Janggunbong, and there is a caldera lake called 'Cheonji' at 2,237m high. Ulleungdo is a volcanic mass erupted from ocean bottom 2,200m below current sea level. The highest peak in Ulleungdo is Seonginbong (984m). The height difference between Seonginbong and ocean floor is over 3,000m. Dokdo is another sea volcano formed between 4.6 and 2.5 million years ago. The formation of Dokdo is earlier than Jejudo and Ulleungdo. Only a small tip of Dokdo seamount is exposed above the sea level. The total elevation difference of the Dokdo seamount is 2,068m, which is about 118m higher than the height of Hallasan (1,950m). Cheorwon-Pyeonggang plateau is a typical Quaternary lava plateau formed non-explosively. A similar lava plateau can be found in Singye-Goksan.

Karst Landforms
Karst landforms in Korea are mainly found in the mountainous region underlying Chosun Super Group. Limestone is an important industrial resource used in making cement. The unique landforms generated by the soluble limestone can be found in Yeongwol, Pyeongchang, and Samcheok in Gangwon-*do*, Yecheon in Gyeongsangbuk-*do*, and Danyang in Chungcheongbuk-*do*. Many limestone areas are also scattered in Pyeongannam-*do* and Hwanghae-*do*.

Periglacial Landforms
Because Korea lies in the mid-latitudes, periglacial landforms found in Korea are considered relict landforms that were formed during an earlier glacial period. It is reported, however, that there are some active periglacial landforms on high mountains. Erosion materials over the granite in Daegwallyeong are frequently cited as an example of such activity. Some patterned grounds can be observed at high elevations in Hallasan, Jirisan, and Daegwallyeong. The main controversy on the patterned ground is whether the micro-landforms were formed under previous climatic conditions.

Talus which is commonly called 'Neodeolgang' or 'Neodeolji-dae' is the most typical periglacial landform in Korea. Talus found in mountains is considered a relict geomorphological feature. In addition, block fields and block streams are also considered as relict periglacial landforms. These were originally core stones formed by deep weathering of granites, which were later moved and deposited by periglacial mass movement processes.

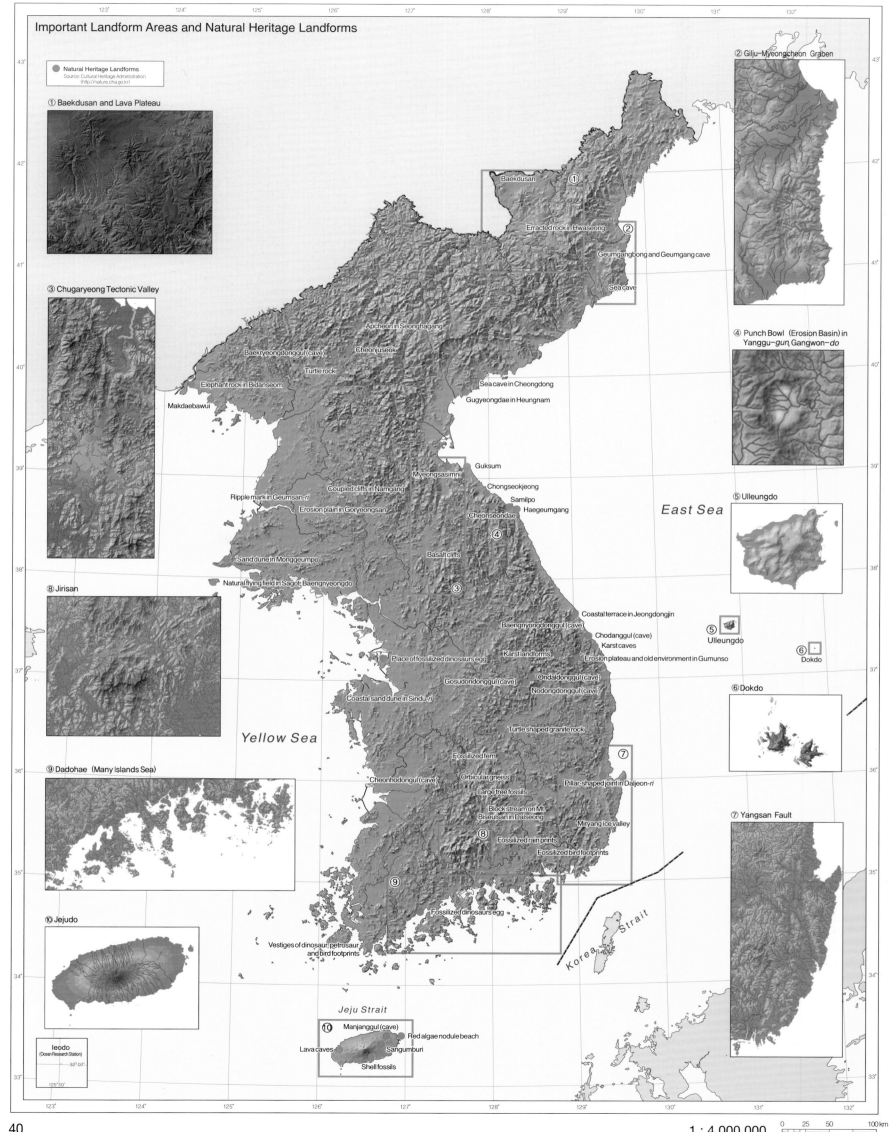

Important Landform Areas and Natural Heritage Landforms

● Natural Heritage Landforms
Source: Cultural Heritage Administration
(http://nature.cha.go.kr)

① Baekdusan and Lava Plateau

② Gilju-Myeongcheon Graben

③ Chugaryeong Tectonic Valley

④ Punch Bowl (Erosion Basin) in Yanggu-*gun*, Gangwon-*do*

⑤ Ulleungdo

⑥ Dokdo

⑦ Yangsan Fault

⑧ Jirisan

⑨ Dadohae (Many Islands Sea)

⑩ Jejudo

Ieodo
(Ocean Research Station)
32° 07'
125° 30'

Baekdusan
①
Erracted rock in Hwaseong ②
Geumgangbong and Geumgang cave
Sea cave

Apcheori in Seonghagang
Cheonjuseok
Baekryeongdonggul (cave)
Turtle rock
Elephant rock in Bidanseom
Makdaebawui
Sea cave in Cheongdong
Gugyeongdae in Heungnam

Guksum
Myeongsasimni
Chongseokjeong
Coupled cliffs in Namgang
Samilpo
Ripple mark in Geumsan-*ri*
Haegeumgang
Erosion plain in Goryeongsan
Cheonseondae
④
Sand dune in Monggeumpo
Basalt cliffs
Natural flying field in Sagot, Baengnyeongdo
③

East Sea

Coastal terrace in Jeongdongjin
Baengnyongdonggul (cave)
Chodanggul (cave)
Karst caves
Karst landforms
Erosion plateau and old environment in Gumunso
⑤
Ulleungdo
⑥
Dokdo

Place of fossilized dinosaurs egg
Gosudondonggul (cave)
Ondaldonggul (cave)
Nodongdonggul (cave)
Coastal sand dune in Sindu-*ri*

Turtle shaped granite rock

Yellow Sea

Fossilized fern
Orbicular gneiss
Cheonhodongul (cave)
Large tree fossils
Block stream on Mt. Biseulsan in Dalseong
⑧
Fossilized rain prints
Fossilized bird footprints
⑦
Pillar-shaped joint in Daljeon-*ri*
Miryang ice valley

⑨

Fossilized dinosaurs egg

Vestiges of dinosaur, petrosaur and bird footprints

Korea Strait

Jeju Strait

⑩ Manjanggul (cave)
Red algae nodule beach
Lava caves
Sangumburi
Shell fossils

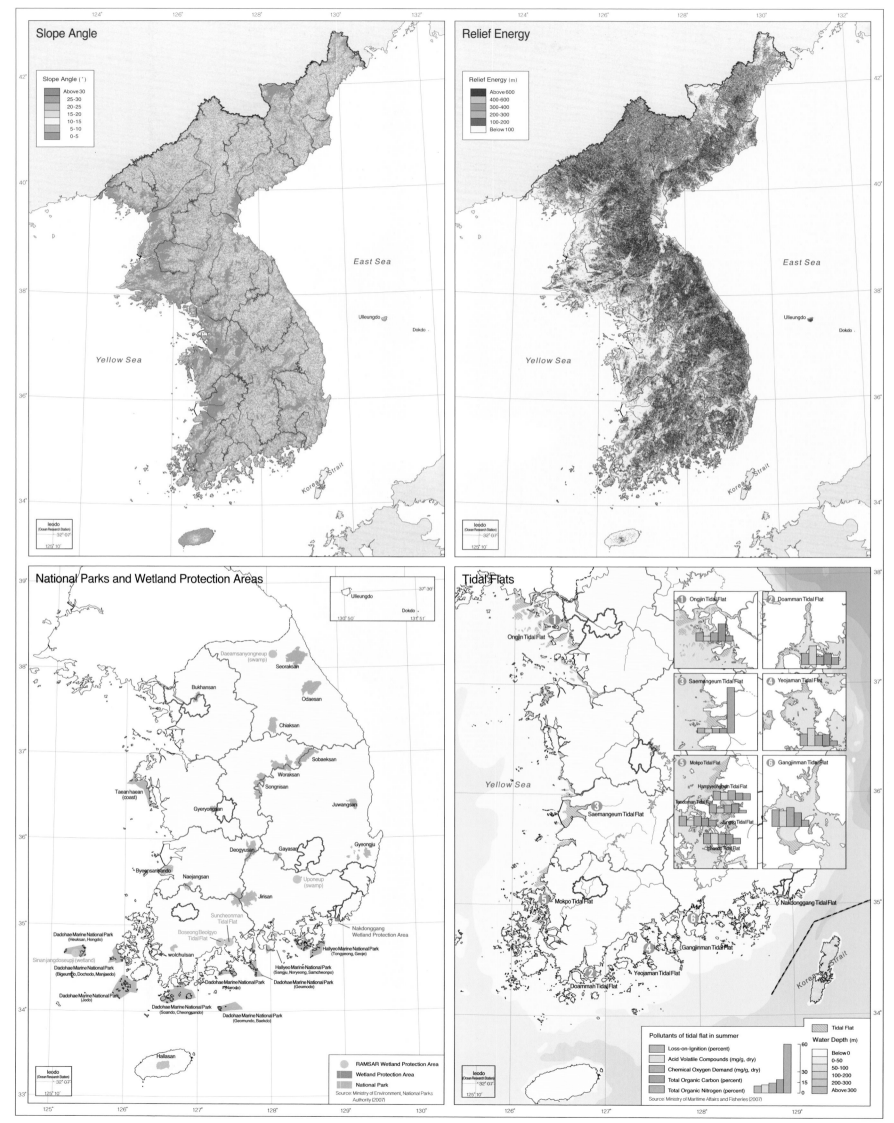

Slope Angle

Slope Angle (°)
- Above 30
- 25-30
- 20-25
- 15-20
- 10-15
- 5-10
- 0-5

East Sea

Yellow Sea

Ulleungdo
Dokdo

Korea Strait

Ieodo
(Ocean Research Station)
32° 07'
125° 10'

Relief Energy

Relief Energy (m)
- Above 600
- 400-600
- 300-400
- 200-300
- 100-200
- Below 100

East Sea

Yellow Sea

Ulleungdo
Dokdo

Korea Strait

Ieodo
(Ocean Research Station)
32° 07'
125° 10'

National Parks and Wetland Protection Areas

Ulleungdo
37° 30'
130° 50'
Dokdo
131° 51'

Daeamsanyongneup (swamp)
Seoraksan
Bukhansan
Odaesan
Chiaksan
Sobaeksan
Woraksan
Songnisan
Taeanhaean (coast)
Gyeryongsan
Juwangsan
Deogyusan
Gayasan
Gyeongju
Byeonsanbando
Naejangsan
Uponeup (swamp)
Jirisan
Suncheonman Tidal Flat
Dadohae Marine National Park (Heuksan, Hongdo)
Boseong Beolgyo Tidal Flat
Hallyeo Marine National Park (Tongyeong, Geoje)
Sinan jangdoseupji (wetland)
wolchulsan
Hallyeo Marine National Park (Sangju, Noryeong, Samcheonpo)
Dadohae Marine National Park (Bigeumdo, Dochodo, Manjaedo)
Nakdonggang Wetland Protection Area
Dadohae Marine National Park (Jeodo)
Dadohae Marine National Park (Narodo)
Dadohae Marine National Park (Geumodo)
Dadohae Marine National Park (Soando, Cheongsando)
Dadohae Marine National Park (Geomundo, Baekdo)
Hallasan

Ieodo
(Ocean Research Station)
32° 07'
125° 10'

RAMSAR Wetland Protection Area
Wetland Protection Area
National Park

Source: Ministry of Environment, National Parks Authority (2007)

Tidal Flats

1 Ongjin Tidal Flat
Ongjin Tidal Flat

2 Doamman Tidal Flat
Doamman Tidal Flat

3 Saemangeum Tidal Flat
Saemangeum Tidal Flat

4 Yeojaman Tidal Flat
Yeojaman Tidal Flat

5 Mokpo Tidal Flat
Mokpo Tidal Flat

6 Gangjinman Tidal Flat
Gangjinman Tidal Flat

Hampyeongman Tidal Flat
Yeodomman Tidal Flat
Jungdo Tidal Flat
Jebado Tidal Flat

Yellow Sea

Nakdonggang Tidal Flat

Korea Strait

Ieodo
(Ocean Research Station)
32° 07'
125° 10'

Tidal Flat

Pollutants of tidal flat in summer
- Loss-on-Ignition (percent)
- Acid Volatile Compounds (mg/g, dry)
- Chemical Oxygen Demand (mg/g, dry)
- Total Organic Carbon (percent)
- Total Organic Nitrogen (percent)

Water Depth (m)
- Below 0
- 0-50
- 50-100
- 100-200
- 200-300
- Above 300

Source: Ministry of Maritime Affairs and Fisheries (2007)

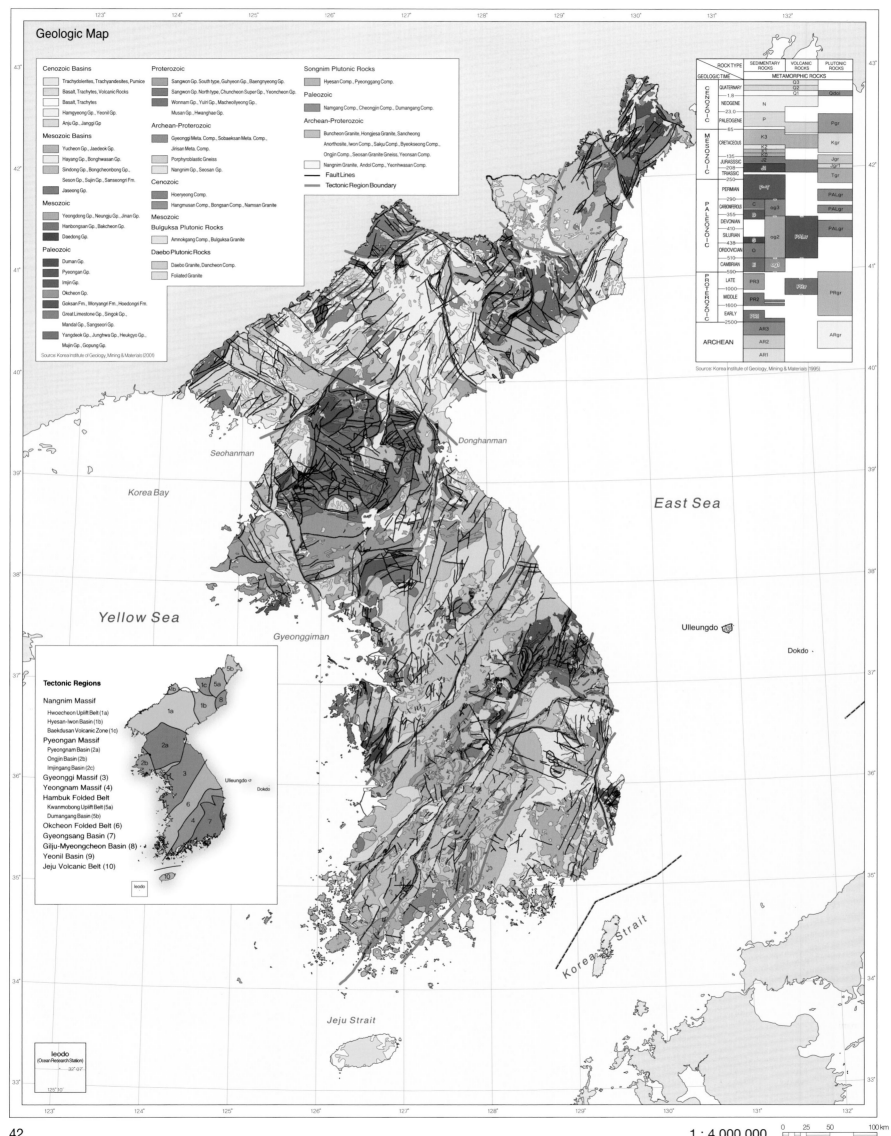

Geologic Map

Cenozoic Basins
- Trachydolerites, Trachyandesites, Pumice
- Basalt, Trachytes, Volcanic Rocks
- Basalt, Trachytes
- Hamgyeong Gp., Yeonil Gp.
- Anju Gp., Janggi Gp

Mesozoic Basins
- Yucheon Gp., Jaedeok Gp.
- Hayang Gp., Bonghwasan Gp.
- Sindong Gp., Bongcheonbong Gp., Seson Gp., Sujin Gp., Sanseongri Fm.
- Jaseong Gp.

Mesozoic
- Yeongdong Gp., Neungju Gp., Jinan Gp.
- Hanbonan Gp., Bakcheon Gp.
- Daedong Gp.

Paleozoic
- Duman Gp.
- Pyeongan Gp.
- Imjin Gp.
- Okcheon Gp.
- Goksan Fm., Woryangri Fm., Hoedongri Fm.
- Great Limestone Gp., Singok Gp., Mandal Gp., Sangseori Gp.
- Yangdeok Gp., Junghwa Gp., Heukgyo Gp., Mujin Gp., Gopung Gp.

Sources: Korea Institute of Geology, Mining & Materials (2001)

Proterozoic
- Sangwon Gp. South type, Guhyeon Gp., Baengnyeong Gp.
- Sangwon Gp. North type, Chuncheon Super Gp., Yeoncheon Gp.
- Wonnam Gp., Yulri Gp., Macheollyeong Gp., Musan Gp., Hwanghae Gp.

Archean-Proterozoic
- Gyeonggi Meta. Comp., Sobaeksan Meta. Comp., Jirisan Meta. Comp.
- Porphyroblastic Gneiss
- Nangnim Gp., Seosan Gp.

Cenozoic
- Hoeryeong Comp.
- Hangmusan Comp., Bongsan Comp., Namsan Granite

Mesozoic

Bulguksa Plutonic Rocks
- Amnokgang Comp., Bulguksa Granite

Daebo Plutonic Rocks
- Daebo Granite, Dancheon Comp.
- Foliated Granite

Songnim Plutonic Rocks
- Hyesan Comp., Pyeonggang Comp.

Paleozoic
- Namgang Comp., Cheongjin Comp., Dumangang Comp.

Archean-Proterozoic
- Buncheon Granite, Hongjesa Granite, Sancheong Anorthosite, Iwon Comp., Sakju Comp., Byeokseong Comp., Ongjin Comp., Seosan Granite Gneiss, Yeonsan Comp.
- Nangnim Granite, Andol Comp., Yecnhwasan Comp.

— Fault Lines

— Tectonic Region Boundary

Tectonic Regions

Nangnim Massif
- Hwoecheon Uplift Belt (1a)
- Hyesan-Iwon Basin (1b)
- Baekdusan Volcanic Zone (1c)

Pyeongan Massif
- Pyeongnam Basin (2a)
- Ongjin Basin (2b)
- Imjingang Basin (2c)

Gyeonggi Massif (3)

Yeongnam Massif (4)

Hambuk Folded Belt
- Kwanmobong Uplift Belt (5a)
- Dumangang Basin (5b)

Okcheon Folded Belt (6)

Gyeongsang Basin (7)

Gilju-Myeongcheon Basin (8)

Yeonil Basin (9)

Jeju Volcanic Belt (10)

Korea Bay
Seohanman
Donghanman
East Sea
Yellow Sea
Gyeonggiman
Ulleungdo
Dokdo
Korea Strait
Jeju Strait

Ieodo
(Ocean Research Station)
32° 07'
125° 10'

Source: Korea Institute of Geology, Mining & Materials (1995)

1 : 4,000,000

0 25 50 100 km

Lying in the continental margin of the eastern Eurasian continent, the Korean Peninsula represents an important tectonic link between the continental blocks of North and South China and the island arcs of Japan. The birth of the peninsula can be traced as early as the middle Archean (ca. 3.5 billion years), as evidenced by the rare occurrence of very old zircon grains in the Precambrian rocks. The peninsula is a composite landmass consisting of three fundamental building blocks that were created largely during the Late Archean to the Early Proterozoic. From north to south, there are the Nangnim, Gyeonggi, and Yeongnam massifs that are divided by two intervening fold-and-thrust belts, the Imjingang, and Okcheon. Despite much uncertainty about their boundaries, the current shape of the Korean Peninsula has been largely created by continental collision among these Precambrian massifs during the Late Paleozoic to the Middle Mesozoic.

Before their amalgamation, two Paleozoic intracratonic basins (e.g., the Pyeongnam Basin in the Nangnim massif and the Taebaeksan Basin in the Yeongnam massif) developed, while late Proterozoic to Paleozoic sedimentary successions in the northern (e.g., Imjingang Basin) and southern (e.g., Okcheon Basin) margins of the Gyeonggi massif developed later. After completion of the continental amalgamation during the early to middle Mesozoic, the tectonic regime in the Korean Peninsula changed from a continental collision system to a continental magmatic arc system. The change in tectonic regime caused not only widespread arc-related magmatism (so-called Daebo granitoids) in the entire peninsula, but also the development of the Cretaceous non-marine Gyeongsang Basin in the southeastern part of the peninsula. The sustained arc system caused a back-arc opening in the East Sea and resulted in transtensional basins (e.g., Gilju-Myeongcheon and Pohang) along the easternmost margin of the peninsula.

All the Precambrian massifs can be divided by lithostratigraphy into (1) the Archean to Early Proterozoic crystalline basements, and (2) the overlying Early to Late Proterozoic supracrustal sequences. The crystalline basements of the massifs are composed largely of unclassified gneiss and schist complexes originating from the amphibolite- to granulite-facies metamorphism of sedimentary and igneous protoliths. In general, orthogneisses are dominant over paragneisses in the Nangnim and Yeongnam massifs, whereas paragneisses are widespread over orthogneisses in the Gyeonggi massif. Because of polycyclic deformation, metamorphism, and igneous activities, detailed stratigraphic relationships are poorly understood in these basements. Although a few of the inherited zircon ages suggest the possible existence of crustal materials as old as the middle Archean (ca. 3.5 billion years), no isotope data indicate that most crustal materials were extracted from mantle during the Late Archean (ca. 2.9 to 2.5 billion years).

All the Archean crustal materials within the massifs experienced terrain-wide metamorphism during ca. 1.9 to 1.7 billion years. It remains unclear how the Archean-aged, discrete bodies are preserved at the present-day exposed level. However, the upper Middle Archean (ca. 2.6 to 2.5 billion years) rocks found in the deeply eroded region between the Nangnim and Gyeonggi massif suggest the possible existence of Archean rocks in the unexposed portions of the massifs. Tectonometamorphic and magmatic events during the early stage of the crustal evolution in the Korean Peninsula are poorly understood but, on the basis of geological and geochronologic evidences, at least two significant orogenic events (e.g., ca. 2.2 to 2.1 billion years and ca. 1.9 to 1.7 billion years) may be responsible for the cratonization of the Korean massifs. These events seem likely to have resulted from crustal thickening orogenies and are usually accompanied by widespread intracrustal granitization, along with anorogenic magmatism (e.g., mangerite-anorthosite complex).

After the cessation of the cratonization possibly during ca. 2.2 to 1.8 billion years, several intramountain basins developed within and around the massifs during the Early to Middle Proterozoic. They produced supracrustal sequences consisting mainly of schists, quartzites, marbles, calc-silicates, and amphibolites, which unconformably overlie the basement rocks. These supracrustal sequences have also suffered greenschist- to amphibolite-facies metamorphism, although the timing of metamorphism has not been determined clearly. They are called the Macheollyeong, Musan, and Hwanghae Groups in the Nangnim massif, the Chuncheon Supergroup in the Gyeonggi massif, and the Wonnam and Yulri groups in the Yeongnam massif.

In addition to these early stage supracrustals, non- to weakly metamorphosed supracrustal sequences, consisting of quartzites, marbles, and siliciclastic, and volcanigenic sediments, have been deposited mainly around the peripheral region of the Nangnim and Gyeonggi massifs. They include the Sangwon Group in the southern part of the Nangnim massif, the Yeoncheon Group, and the lower part of the Okcheon Group in the northern and southern margin of the Gyeonggi massif. During the waning stage of the Precambrian, some extension- or rift-related magmatic events occurred, especially in the Gyeonggi massif.

All the Precambrian massifs in the Korean Peninsula have been united by two of the Phanerozoic fold-and-thrust belts, the Imjingang and Okcheon. The Imjingang belt is an east-trending fold-and-thrust belt, characterized by an occurrence of the Devonian-Carboniferous sequence (Imjin Group), and is underlain unconformably by the Proterozoic Yeoncheon Group. The Imjin Group consists largely of weakly-metamorphosed siliciclastic and carbonate sequences with volcaniclastics, whereas the Yeoncheon Group consists of a lower amphibolite and calc-silicate unit and an upper metasedimentary unit.

The Okcheon belt is a northeast-trending fold-and-thrust belt and can be divided into two zones based on lithology and metamorphic grade: the Okcheon basin to the southwest and the Taebaeksan basin to the northeast. The Okcheon basin consists of non-fossiliferous, low- to medium-grade metasedimentary and metavolcanic rocks whose age has not been well-constrained. Radiometric dating indicates that the Imjingang and Okcheon belts contain both Late Proterozoic (ca. 0.75 billion years) volcaniclastic, and Paleozoic siliciclastic rocks, and have experienced peak metamorphism in the late Permian-early Triassic.

There are two major Paleozoic basins in the Korean Peninsula: the Pyeongnam and Taebaek basins found in the Nangnim massif and the northeastern part of the Okcheon belt. The Paleozoic basins consist mainly of Cambrian-Ordovician (the Hwangju and Chosun Supergroups in the Pyeongan and Taebaek basins, respectively) and Carboniferous-Triassic (Pyeongan Supergroup in both basins) sedimentary sequences. The lower Paleozoic sedimentation ceased from the mid-Ordovician to mid-Carboniferous. This tectonic quiescence is called the 'Great Hiatus,' although few of the Silurian successions have been reported in both basins. The Hwangju and Choseon Supergroups are mainly shallow marine strata in origin and consist predominantly of carbonates with lesser amounts of sandstone and shale, whereas the Pyeongan Supergroup comprises thick clastic successions of marginal marine to nonmarine environments containing economically important coal measures. Minor amounts of the late Paleozoic sequences are also exposed sporadically along the southern margin of the Okcheon belt (Boeun and Hwasun coalfields) and northeastern coast of the peninsula (Tuman system).

Entering the Mesozoic Era, once separated continental blocks, each of which has a distinct history of crustal and basin formations, began to be united into the single continental landmass of the Korean Peninsula via two violent tectonic and magmatic events: the Songrim (late Permian-early Triassic) and Daebo (middle to late Jurassic) Orogenies. The former was largely responsible for the amalgamation of three Precambrian massifs, whereas the latter resulted in the final readjustment of the accreted continental blocks into the shape of the peninsula that we see today. The Songrim Orogeny is contemporary to the Indosinian continental collision event that combined the North China and South China cratons into the Chinese mainland. It influenced widespread crustal thickening and subsequent regional metamorphism in the Gyeonggi massif, as well as two Permo-Triassic fold-and-thrust belts: the Imjingang and Okcheon. At the waning stage of the Songrim Orogeny, several small stocks of syn- to post-orogenic granitoids intruded along the block boundaries. The areal extent of crustal affinity associated with the Chinese cratons and the precise location of the eastward continuation of the Chinese collision belt is, however, still controversial. The end of the Songrim Orogeny is marked by the Daedong Group, deposited mainly along the block boundaries during the late Triassic-early Jurassic.

The Daedong Group consists of nonmarine siliciclastic and lacustrine deposits that were formed in small-scale inland basins, representing deposition in syn-orogenic piggyback basins. They are commonly present in the vicinity of the Daedong River in the Pyeongnam Basin. In South Korea, the Daedong Group occurs in Gimpo, Yeoncheon, Chungnam, and the Mungyeong coalfields. The Daedong Group is an important time-identifier because it temporarily divides the Songrim (late Permian-early Triassic) and the Daebo (early to late Jurassic) Orogenies in the Korean Peninsula.

The Daebo Orogeny, a thrusting event that affected the Daedong Group, was caused when the tectonic environment of the peninsula changed from continental collision to continental magmatic arc during the middle Jurassic. It created an extensive intrusion of granitoids. These granitoids, often called the 'Daebo granitoids,' are in general batholith-size and form several belts (several tens of kilometers in width), trending northeast. They consist mainly of medium- to coarse-grained granite, granodiorite, and tonalite with minor monzonite. These belts represent eroded remnants of an old magmatic arc during the middle to late Jurassic. In the south, these granites are frequently foliated in association with the dextral strike-slip ductile shear zones, collectively called the Honam Shear Zone.

In the early Cretaceous, east-west trending folds and thrusts developed in the mid-southern part of the peninsula, probably due to the oblique (northward) subduction of the Paleo-Pacific Plate. This new plate motion caused sinistral, brittle shearing in a retroarc setting, accompanied by a number of pull-apart (or transtensional) basins within which Cretaceous non-marine sedimentary sequences and volcanics were deposited. These non-marine sedimentary sequences and volcanics were mainly present in the southeastern part (Gyeongsang Supergroup) with subordinate exposures (Eumseong, Gongju, Buyeo, Gyeokpo, Jinan, Yeongdong, Neungju, Hampyeong, and Haenam basins) in the southwest, generally trending northeast to southeast. Small-scale alluvial fans and fluvial channel networks formed in the basin margin and were transitional to ephemeral lacustrine systems under semiarid to arid conditions. During the Cretaceous to early Tertiary, granitic intrusions, usually characterized by stock-sized, and closely associated with contemporaneous volcanic rocks, were also prevalent especially in the Gyeongsang Basin and the central Okcheon Belt. These younger granites, also called Bulguksa granites, were in general fine- to medium-grained, and are composed of granite, granodiorite, and tonalite, together with minor alkali granite. It was noted that there was a stagnant period between the Daebo and Bulguksa magmatism with a gap between 160 and 100 Ma.

Many small Tertiary basins (e.g., Pohang, Gilju-Myeongcheon, and so on) are distributed in several localities as isolated patches, largely along the east coast of the peninsula, in association with the pull-apart opening of the East Sea. In addition, two small Tertiary basins are also found in the western part of the Anju and Sariwon areas. Paleogene and early Miocene sediments are mostly nonmarine, whereas the middle Miocene sediments are marine in origin. Isolated Quaternary volcanic events, as typed in Jejudo and Ulleungdo and Baekdusan, represent intraplate hot spots.

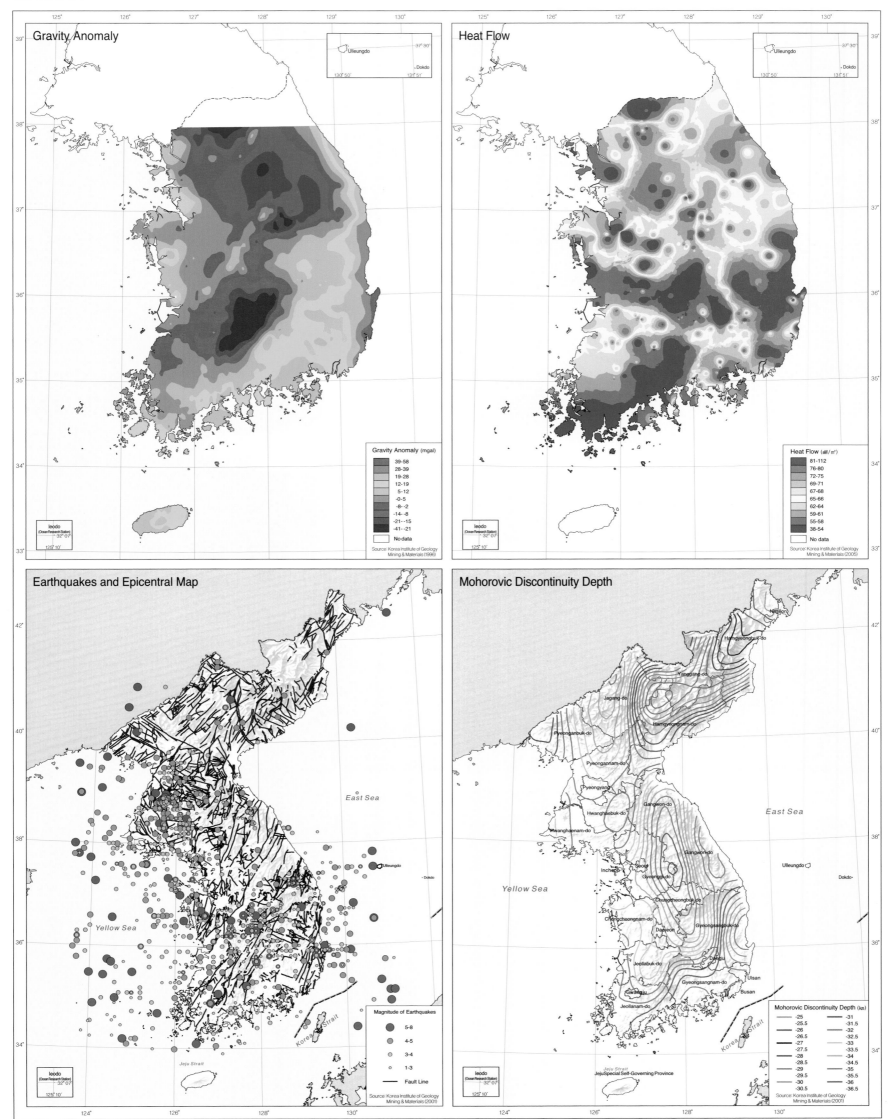

Gravity Anomaly

Gravity Anomaly (mgal)
- 39-58
- 28-39
- 19-28
- 12-19
- 5-12
- -0-5
- -8--2
- -14--8
- -21--15
- -41--21
- No data

Source: Korea Institute of Geology
Mining & Materials (1996)

Heat Flow

Heat Flow (mW/m²)
- 81-112
- 76-80
- 72-75
- 69-71
- 67-68
- 65-66
- 62-64
- 59-61
- 55-58
- 38-54
- No data

Source: Korea Institute of Geology
Mining & Materials (2005)

Earthquakes and Epicentral Map

Magnitude of Earthquakes
- 5-8
- 4-5
- 3-4
- 1-3
- Fault Line

Source: Korea Institute of Geology
Mining & Materials (2001)

Mohorovic Discontinuity Depth

Mohorovic Discontinuity Depth (km)
- -25
- -25.5
- -26
- -26.5
- -27
- -27.5
- -28
- -28.5
- -29
- -29.5
- -30
- -30.5
- -31
- -31.5
- -32
- -32.5
- -33
- -33.5
- -34
- -34.5
- -35
- -35.5
- -36
- -36.5

Source: Korea Institute of Geology
Mining & Materials (2001)

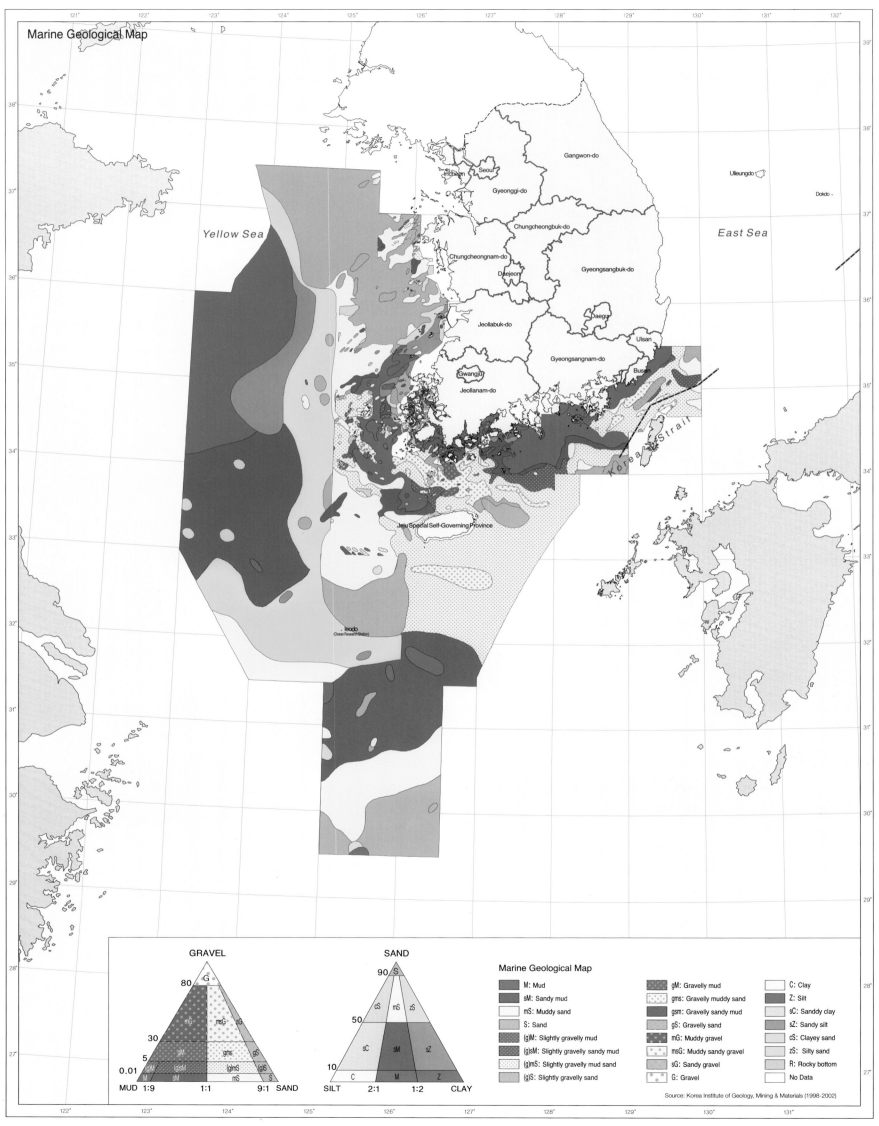

Marine Geological Map

Marine Geological Map

GRAVEL

SAND

M: Mud	gM: Gravelly mud	C: Clay
sM: Sandy mud	gms: Gravelly muddy sand	Z: Silt
mS: Muddy sand	gsm: Gravelly sandy mud	sC: Sanddy clay
S: Sand	gS: Gravelly sand	sZ: Sandy silt
(g)M: Slightly gravelly mud	mG: Muddy gravel	cS: Clayey sand
(g)sM: Slightly gravelly sandy mud	msG: Muddy sandy gravel	zS: Silty sand
(g)mS: Slightly gravelly mud sand	sG: Sandy gravel	R: Rocky bottom
(g)S: Slightly gravelly sand	G: Gravel	No Data

Source: Korea Institute of Geology, Mining & Materials (1998-2002)

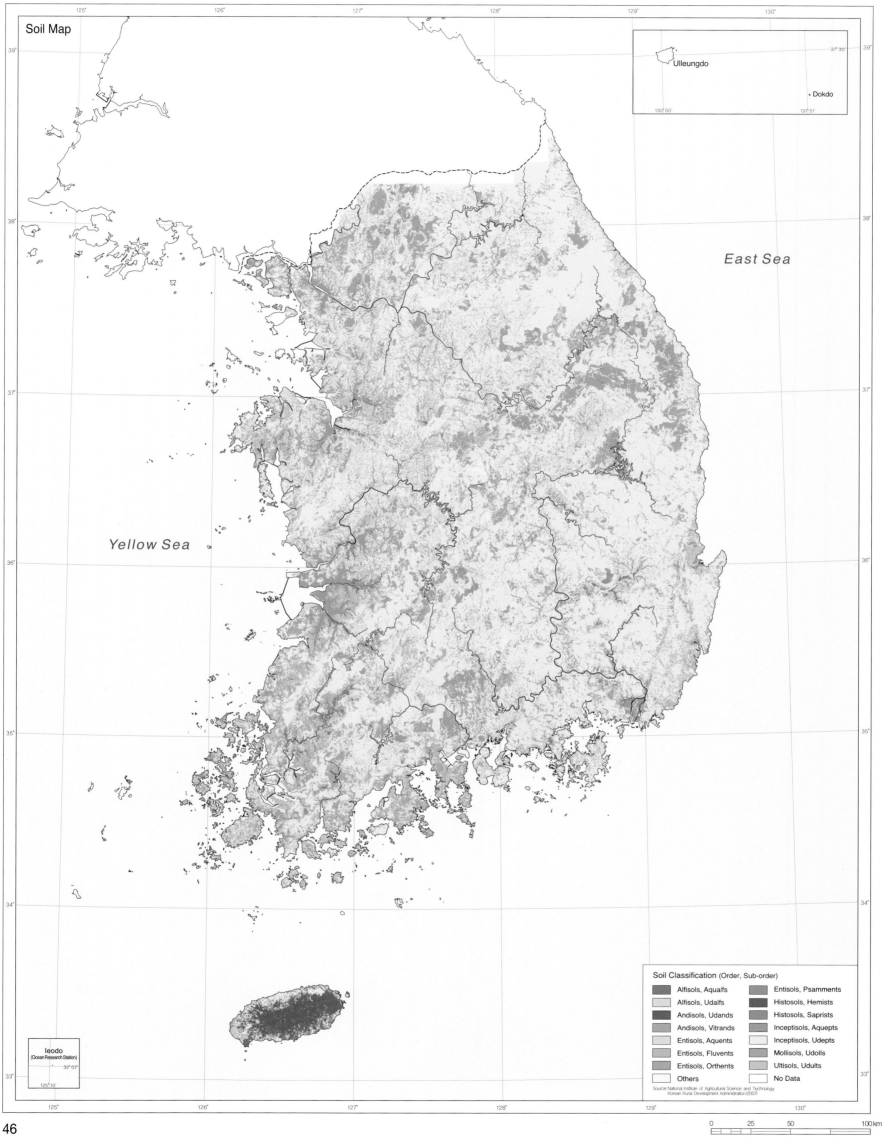

Soil Map

East Sea

Yellow Sea

Ulleungdo

Dokdo

Ieodo
(Ocean Research Station)

Soil Classification (Order, Sub-order)

- Alfisols, Aqualfs
- Alfisols, Udalfs
- Andisols, Udands
- Andisols, Vitrands
- Entisols, Aquents
- Entisols, Fluvents
- Entisols, Orthents
- Others
- Entisols, Psamments
- Histosols, Hemists
- Histosols, Saprists
- Inceptisols, Aquepts
- Inceptisols, Udepts
- Mollisols, Udolls
- Ultisols, Udults
- No Data

Source: National Institute of Agricultural Science and Technology
Korean Rural Development Administration (2007)

0   25   50   100 km

The purpose of a soil map is to delineate the boundaries of different kinds of soils whose characteristics are markedly different due to the various factors affecting soil formation. These factors include climate, parent material, topography, vegetation, and length of time that the soil has been forming. Detailed knowledge of soil characteristics is of great importance for both the use and conservation of soil resources, which are essential for human welfare and the sustainability of ecosystems.

Overview of Soil Forming Factors

Climate: Korea is located in the humid temperate climatic zone affected by the influence of both continental and oceanic air masses. National average annual rainfall is about 1,300mm, ranging from 980mm (Daegu-*si*) to 1,440mm (Jejudo). About 50-60 percent of annual rainfall occurs during the summer months; July to September, with occasional typhoons. During summer, although the ambient temperature is high (mean temperature; 20-25˚C), and crop canopies are thick, the precipitation exceeds the potential evapotranspiration because of concentrated heavy rainfalls. As a result, the base saturation ratio is rather low in the majority of soils. With the exception of soils developed from alkaline rocks containing a large proportion of calcium and/or magnesium carbonates, climate typically produces a low soil pH. Temperatures in spring and autumn are mild (mean temperatures of 10-15˚C) and winter months are rather cold (monthly mean temperature of -5-2˚C), particularly in the central and northern regions. During winter, spring, and autumn, the rainfalls are much smaller than in summer. Despite these seasonal differences, the amount of precipitation and the potential evapotranspiration remain similar all throughout the year because of the lower ambient temperatures in the drier seasons.

Topography: Korea is a mountainous country. More than two-thirds of the country is occupied by mountains with steep slopes. Plains are subdivided into inland plains, coastal plains, and plains in the narrow valleys. The plains have been under intensive use for agricultural production. The high relief of the land coupled with the heavy downpours of rain in summer affects the characteristics of Korean soil profoundly. Erosion of soils has been intensive throughout the country for a long time, particularly where the population density is high. In the past, people in the rural areas relied upon the mountains for their fuel and composts for farming. Exploitation of forest vegetation by the people increased soil erosion to such an extent that there are very few mature soils in the country. Continued erosion has not allowed soil development to occur.

Parent material: The parent materials of Korean soils are part of about ten recognized geologic systems from different geological time series. Dominant rock types include granitic gneiss (32.4%), granite (22.3%), schist (10.3%), and limestone of the Chosun Group (Cambrian-Ordovician: 10.1%). The former three lithologies are present in about 60 percent of the land area and are known as acidic rocks. The fact that the rainfall exceeds the potential evapotranspiration, coupled with the abundance of acidic rocks, results in the wide occurrence of acidic soils in the country. The limestones of the Chosun Group are alkaline, so the soils derived from these rocks tend to be neutral or slightly alkaline. These soils are only found near Gangwon-*do*. Some areas contain sandstone bedrock which results in coarse-textured soils. However, even among soils derived from the same parent rock, textures can vary depending upon the location in the soil catena. Soils developed in higher places tend to

be coarse due to loss of fine particles by erosion. Soils developed at the locations where soil erosion is not severe tend to be fine-textured.

Vegetation: In the past, with the exception of remote areas, forests were heavily used by humans, resulting in extremely low soil fertility. During the last three decades or so, mountains in the country have become green because the exploitation of forests stopped as electricity and fossil fuels became widely available in rural areas. The wide use of chemical fertilizers also contributed to this change. With convenient fertilizers in their hands, farmers did not need to go to mountains to collect the grasses to make compost. If these trends continue, vegetation in the forests may exert a noticeable influence on soil formation in the future. To this point in time, it appears that the influence of vegetation on the characteristics of Korean soils is generally not significant as compared to those of climate, topography, and humans.

Time: Undoubtedly time is a very important factor affecting the characteristics of soils. The older the soil, the more mature the soil. Distinct soil horizons reflect the history of the soil. As mentioned earlier, due to unique rainfall patterns and topographical conditions (e.g. mountains with steep slopes) soils in the highlands are eroded severely, while soils lying in lowlands frequently receive new parent material. Neither of these conditions results in long periods of stability necessary for soils to mature. It follows that, with the exception some locations, time is a minor factor in the development of soils in Korea.

Soil Survey

The importance of soils as the basis for Korean farming was recognized long ago. A book titled *Nong-Sa-Jik-Seol* (Instruction for Agriculture) was published in 1429 during the reign of Great King Sejong. The quality of soils was mentioned in detail, touching upon how and when to plow the lands, how to improve the fertility of barren soils, and even how to test the quality of soil by tasting it. Many books about agriculture were published during the Lee Dynasty, following the example of *Nong-Sa-Jik-Seol*.

In 1959, a survey on soil quality was attempted and some of the results were published as soil maps (1:50,000) for a few areas such as Deajeon, Deaduk, and Suwon. The first modern soil survey was initiated in 1964, when the Korean Government and UNDP/FAO of the United Nations jointly established the Korea Soil Survey Organization and Plant Environment Research Institute (now National Institute of Agricultural Science and Technology) in the Office of Rural Development (now Rural Development Administration) in Suwon. The soil survey was started with a reconnaissance survey, making use of aerial photographs taken during 1964-1967. A detailed soil survey was conducted using the Soil Taxonomy of United States Department of Agriculture (USDA). Now detailed soil maps (1:25,000) for entire country are available in hard copies and highly detailed digital soil maps (1:5,000) are provided on-line for the public.

Soil Distribution and Influence of Anthropogenic Factors on the Soil Quality

When described using the soil taxonomy of the USDA, soils in Korea are classified into seven soil orders which are then further divided into 14 sub-orders. Among those seven soil orders, entisols and inceptisols are dominant. Entisols are the young-

est soils, followed by inceptisols. Alfisols and ultisols are relatively older soils. The working unit of soil classification is the soil series. So far 390 soil series have been identified in Korea. Table 1 summarizes the areal extent of the different soil orders and the number of soil series within them.

Table 1. Major Soil Orders/Sub-orders, and Number of Soil Series

Orders(7)	Sub-Orders (14)	No. of Series(390)	Area (ha)
Inceptisols	Aquepts	77	370,580
	Udepts	133	276,103
Entisols	Aquents	14	657,124
	Fluvents	13	46,896
	Orthents	17	103,730
	Psamments	20	2,041,352
Ultisols	Udults	28	92,064
Alfisols	Aqualfs	7	786,848
	Udalfs	37	4,060,307
Andisols	Udands	39	871,222
	Virands	1	48
Mollisols	Udolls	2	337
Histosols	Saprists	1	309,677
	Hemists	1	5,866

Source: National Institute of Agricultural Science and Technology (NIAST), 2005,
  Achievement and Progress of the Korean Soil Survey,
  Suwon : Rural Development Administration (RDA)

Table 1 shows that the occurrence of younger soils (entisols and inceptisols) is overwhelming. This is a result of the influence of both Korea's unique climate with concentrated rainfalls in summer and rugged topography as characterized by the wide occurrence of highly-sloped mountains. This strongly suggests that, if the soil resources are to be conserved adequately, serious attention must be paid to the development of measures to minimize soil erosion in hilly lands.

In the recent years, as the scope and intensity of human activities altering the nature of soils have been ever increasing, anthropogenic factors have become a major concern. In Korea, while demands for land have increased from various sectors, the per capita land area is very small. Alteration of the nature of soils is occurring due to both agriculture and non-agricultural land use practices. Within agriculture, the alteration of the quality of soils has occurred in two directions, both positively and negatively. The proper use of the adequate amount of fertilizers by a majority of farmers has resulted in an increase in soil fertility levels in open fields. On the other hand, the overuse of manure by protected farms in greenhouses has resulted in degradation of soil quality due to accumulation of undesirable components derived from manure. When this happens, as a means of remedy, some farmers add large quantities of fresh earth collected from the mountain side. Such earth is extremely infertile. This practice is unhealthy because it both destroys the hillside lands and requires farmers to use more manure to grow crops on the infertile earth.

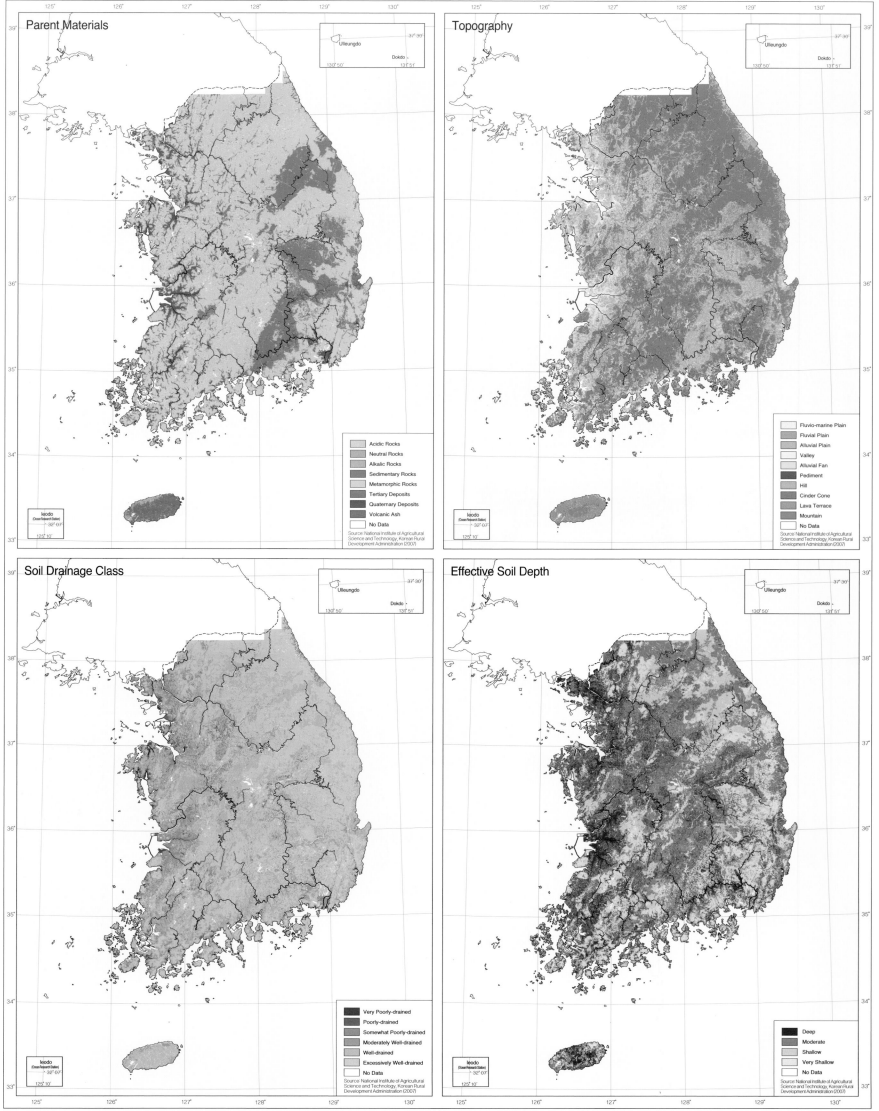

Parent Materials

	Acidic Rocks
	Neutral Rocks
	Alkalic Rocks
	Sedimorphic Rocks
	Metamorphic Rocks
	Tertiary Deposits
	Quaternary Deposits
	Volcanic Ash
	No Data

Source: National Institute of Agricultural
Science and Technology, Korean Rural
Development Administration (2007)

Topography

	Fluvio-marine Plain
	Fluvial Plain
	Alluvial Plain
	Valley
	Alluvial Fan
	Pediment
	Hill
	Cinder Cone
	Lava Terrace
	Mountain
	No Data

Source: National Institute of Agricultural
Science and Technology, Korean Rural
Development Administration (2007)

Soil Drainage Class

	Very Poorly-drained
	Poorly-drained
	Somewhat Poorly-drained
	Moderately Well-drained
	Well-drained
	Excessively Well-drained
	No Data

Source: National Institute of Agricultural
Science and Technology, Korean Rural
Development Administration (2007)

Effective Soil Depth

	Deep
	Moderate
	Shallow
	Very Shallow
	No Data

Source: National Institute of Agricultural
Science and Technology, Korean Rural
Development Administration (2007)

0   25   50   100 km

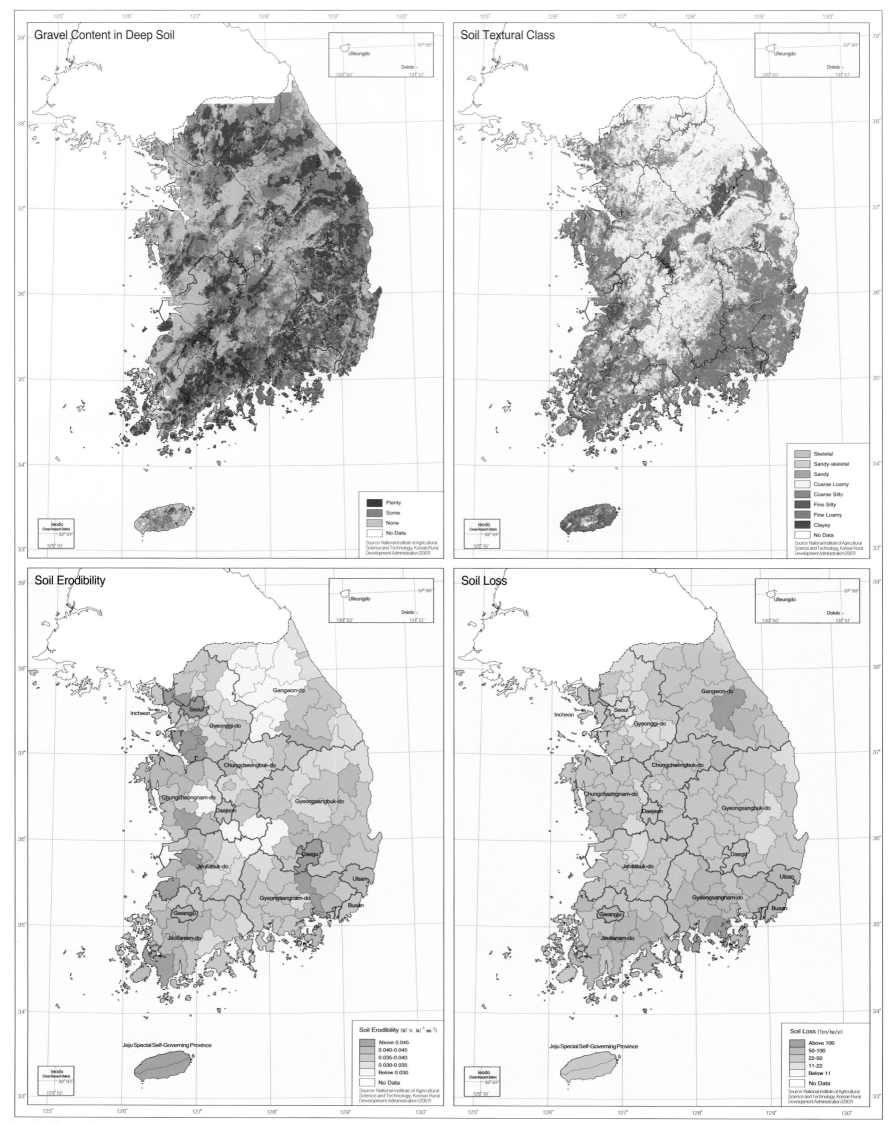

Gravel Content in Deep Soil

Plenty
Some
None
No Data

Source: National Institute of Agricultural Science and Technology, Korean Rural Development Administration (2007)

Soil Textural Class

Skeletal
Sandy-skeletal
Sandy
Coarse Loamy
Coarse Silty
Fine Silty
Fine Loamy
Clayey
No Data

Source: National Institute of Agricultural Science and Technology, Korean Rural Development Administration (2007)

Soil Erodibility

Gangwon-do
Incheon
Seoul
Gyeonggi-do
Chungcheongbuk-do
Chungcheongnam-do
Daejeon
Gyeongsangbuk-do
Daegu
Jeollabuk-do
Ulsan
Gyeongsangnam-do
Busan
Gwangju
Jeollanam-do

Jeju Special Self-Governing Province

Soil Erodibility (MT hr MJ⁻¹ mm⁻¹)
Above 0.045
0.040-0.045
0.035-0.040
0.030-0.035
Below 0.030
No Data

Source: National Institute of Agricultural Science and Technology, Korean Rural Development Administration (2007)

Soil Loss

Gangwon-do
Incheon
Seoul
Gyeonggi-do
Chungcheongbuk-do
Chungcheongnam-do
Daejeon
Gyeongsangbuk-do
Daegu
Jeollabuk-do
Ulsan
Gyeongsangnam-do
Busan
Gwangju
Jeollanam-do

Jeju Special Self-Governing Province

Soil Loss (Ton/ha/yr)
Above 100
50-100
22-50
11-22
Below 11
No Data

Source: National Institute of Agricultural Science and Technology, Korean Rural Development Administration (2007)

Ulleungdo
Dokdo
Ieodo (Ocean Research Station)

0 25 50 100 km

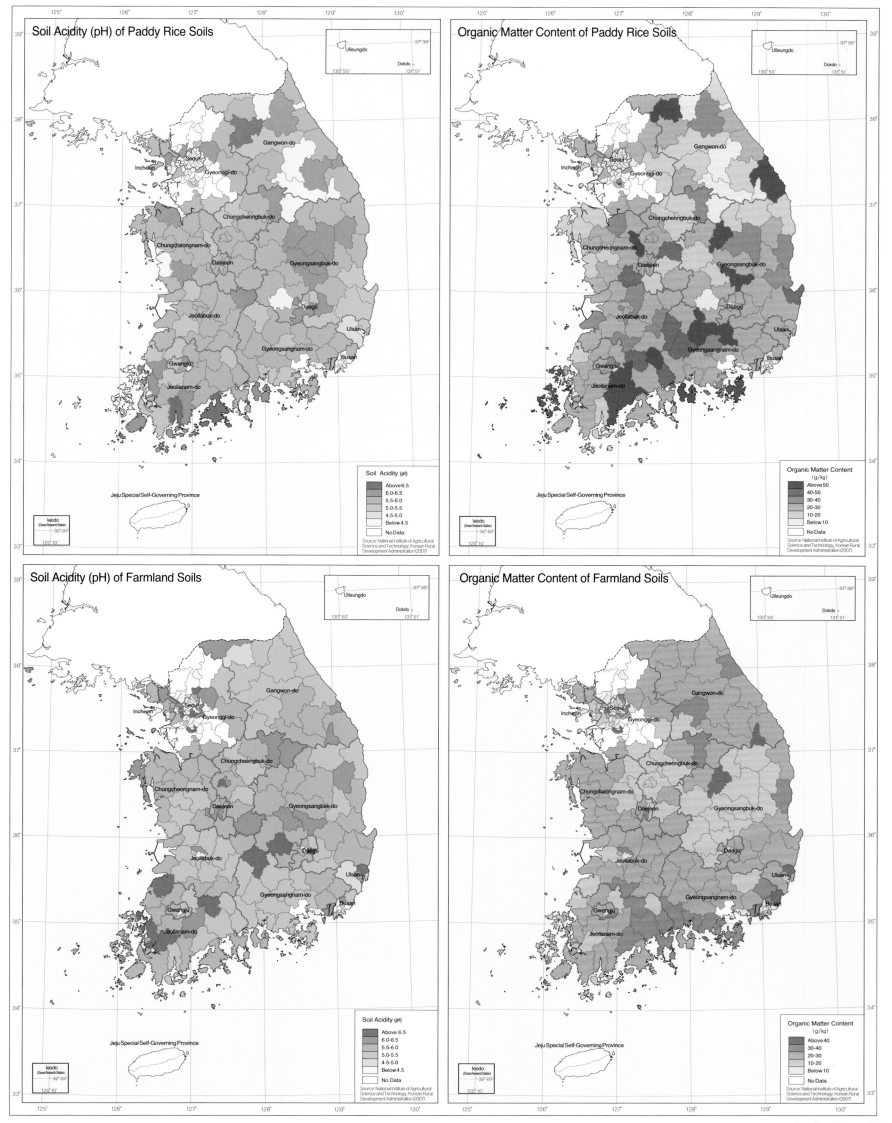

Soil Acidity (pH) of Paddy Rice Soils

Organic Matter Content of Paddy Rice Soils

Soil Acidity (pH) of Farmland Soils

Organic Matter Content of Farmland Soils

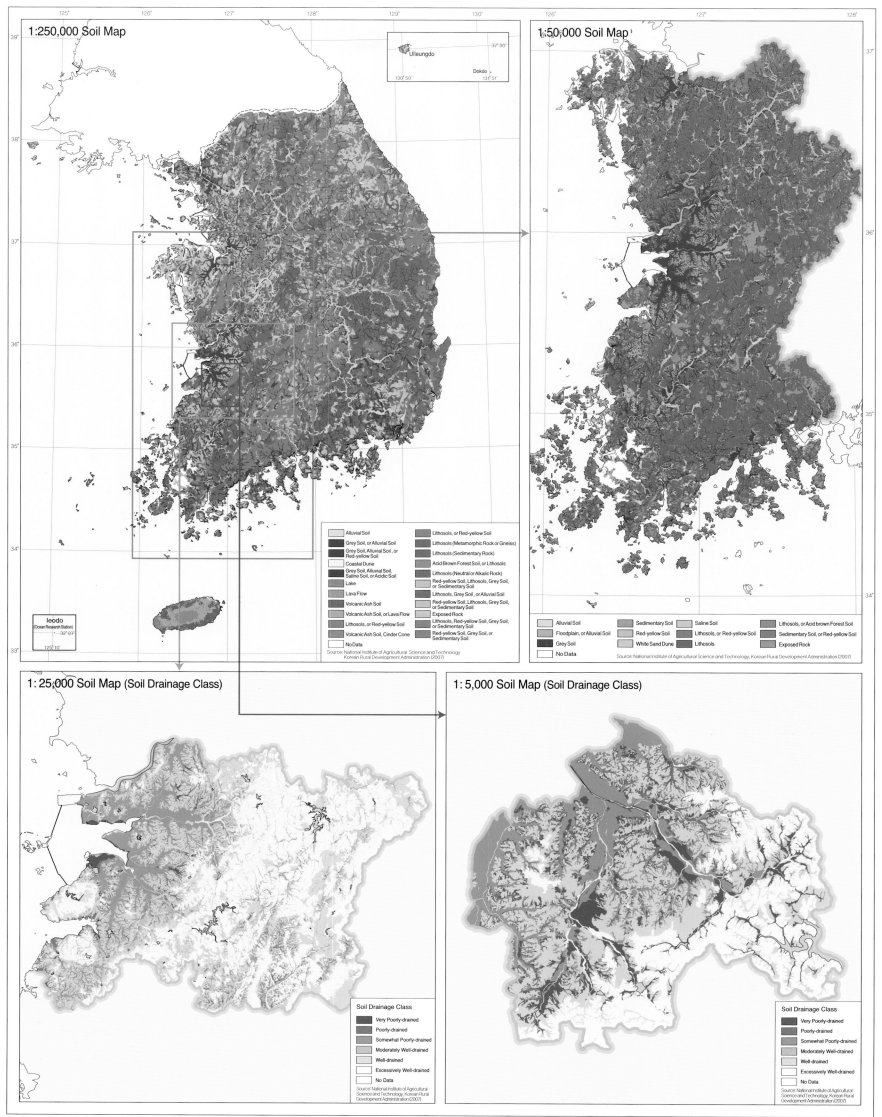

1:250,000 Soil Map

Ulleungdo

Dokdo

Ieodo
(Ocean Research Station)

Alluvial Soil
Grey Soil, or Alluvial Soil
Grey Soil, Alluvial Soil , or Red-yellow Soil
Coastal Dune
Grey Soil, Alluvial Soil, Saline Soil, or Acidic Soil
Lake
Lava Flow
Volcanic Ash Soil
Volcanic Ash Soil, or Lava Flow
Lithosols, or Red-yellow Soil
Volcanic Ash Soil, Cinder Cone

Lithosols, or Red-yellow Soil
Lithosols (Metamorphic Rock or Gneiss)
Lithosols (Sedimentary Rock)
Acid Brown Forest Soil, or Lithosols
Lithosols (Neutral or Alkalic Rock)
Red-yellow Soil, Lithosols, Grey Soil, or Sedimentary Soil
Lithosols, Grey Soil, or Alluvial Soil
Red-yellow Soil, Lithosols, Grey Soil, or Sedimentary Soil
Exposed Rock
Lithosols, Red-yellow Soil, Grey Soil, or Sedimentary Soil
Red-yellow Soil, Grey Soil, or Sedimentary Soil
No Data

Source: National Institute of Agricultural Science and Technology Korean Rural Development Administration (2007)

1:50,000 Soil Map

Alluvial Soil
Floodplain, or Alluvial Soil
Grey Soil
No Data
Sedimentary Soil
Red-yellow Soil
White Sand Dune
Saline Soil
Lithosols, or Red-yellow Soil
Lithosols
Lithosols, or Acid brown Forest Soil
Sedimentary Soil, or Red-yellow Soil
Exposed Rock

Source: National Institute of Agricultural Science and Technology, Korean Rural Development Administration (2007)

1:25,000 Soil Map (Soil Drainage Class)

Soil Drainage Class
Very Poorly-drained
Poorly-drained
Somewhat Poorly-drained
Moderately Well-drained
Well-drained
Excessively Well-drained
No Data

Source: National Institute of Agricultural Science and Technology, Korean Rural Development Administration (2007)

1:5,000 Soil Map (Soil Drainage Class)

Soil Drainage Class
Very Poorly-drained
Poorly-drained
Somewhat Poorly-drained
Moderately Well-drained
Well-drained
Excessively Well-drained
No Data

Source: National Institute of Agricultural Science and Technology, Korean Rural Development Administration (2007)

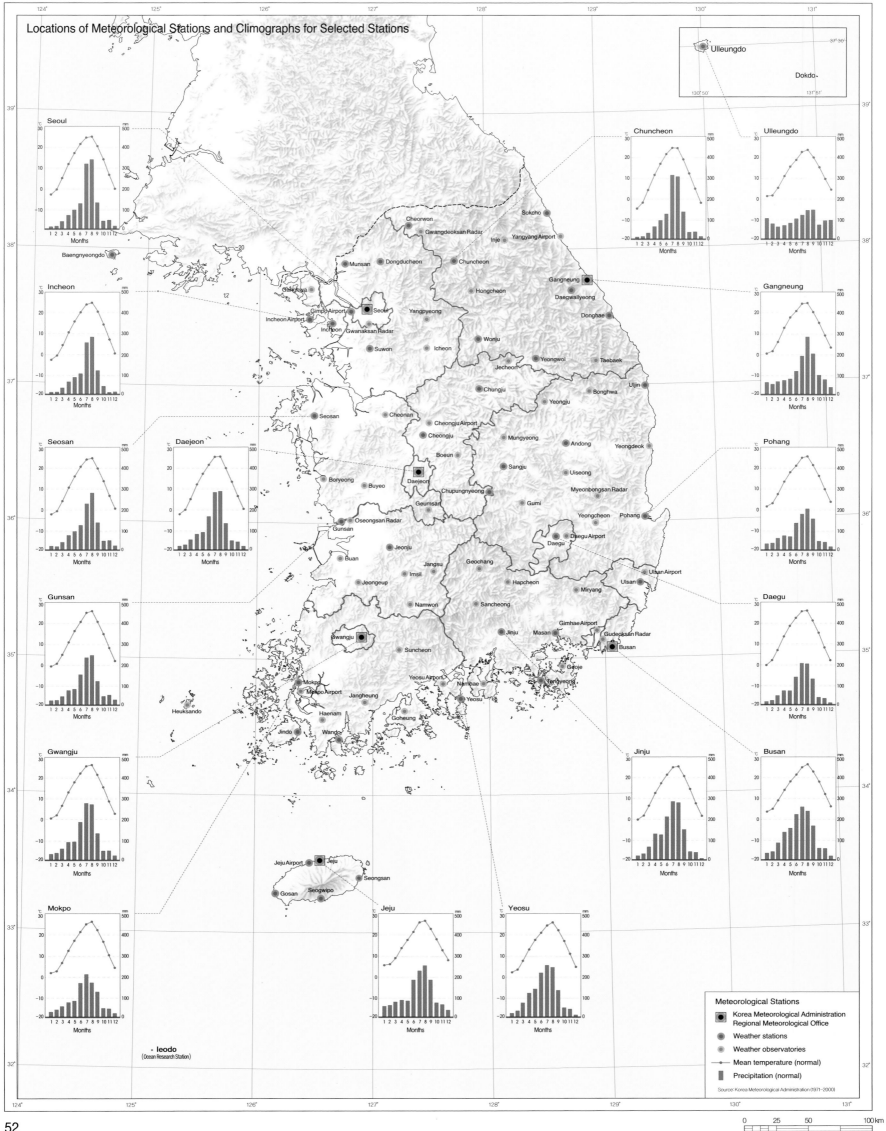

Locations of Meteorological Stations and Climographs for Selected Stations

Meteorological Stations
- Korea Meteorological Administration Regional Meteorological Office
- Weather stations
- Weather observatories
- Mean temperature (normal)
- Precipitation (normal)

Source: Korea Meteorological Administration (1971–2000)

Perhaps the most important climatic feature over the Korean Peninsula is the Asian monsoon system, which is induced by Asian land-Pacific Ocean heat contrast. In winter, cold and dry conditions exist because of the influence of clockwise flow around the eastern side of the Siberian high pressure system, while in summer a warm, moist climate exists owing to the clockwise flow on the western side of the North Pacific high pressure system.

The diversity of regional climates on the Korean Peninsula is due to the long north-south distance and the complicated topography. The adjacency of the northern region to the Eurasian continent, and the proximity of the southern region to the ocean dictates that the regions are strongly affected by both the continent and ocean, respectively. The large extent of mountainous areas also affects local and regional climates. In addition to the obvious impact of elevation changes on temperature, mountains also affect the spatial distribution of precipitation.

Temperature
The spatial distribution of annual mean air temperature generally shows that, owing to the effects of latitude, continentality, topography, and land/sea heating properties, it increases from north to south and is higher in the coastal areas than in the inland areas. Air temperature is lower in the mountain ranges of Taebaek and Sobaek than in the surrounding regions, and higher in regions nearer to the coast. Because of differences in oceanic currents, the coastal areas in the east have higher mean air temperatures than those on the west coast at the same latitude. For instance, the annual mean air temperature in Gangneung is 12.9℃ while that in Incheon is 11.7℃. Daegwallyeong (6.4℃) has the lowest annual mean air temperature in Korea because of high elevations (842.5m). Seogwipo has the highest annual mean air temperature (16.2℃).

During winter Korea is cold due to the Siberian air mass. The spatial pattern of winter air temperature is similar to that of annual mean temperature. The difference in winter temperature between east and west is more pronounced because the Taebaek mountain range prevents the cold, northwesterly seasonal wind from reaching the east coast. The lower seasonal variability of water temperature in the East Sea impacts the temperature difference substantially. For instance, January mean air temperature for Gangneung on the east coast is 0.3℃, while that of Incheon on the west coast is -2.4℃. Daegwallyeong has the lowest January mean air temperature (-7.6℃) in Korea. The mean monthly air temperature is below freezing from December to April at Daegwallyeong, and from December to February in the central areas of Korea. January mean air temperature in most of Jeju is near 6℃, with the highest at Seogwipo (6.6℃). January mean temperature in the southern coastal areas exceeds 2℃.

In summer, the intensity of the Siberian high pressure weakens due to the presence of warmer air caused by increases in solar angle and day length. Instead, the North Pacific high pressure and its associated circulation dominate the summer climate in Korea. August is the month with the highest air temperatures, except in the inland Gaema plateau in North Korea and in its surrounding areas, which experience their highest temperatures in July. Mean air temperatures during summer show less difference between northern and southern regions, and even less between eastern and western regions, in comparison with those during winter. August mean air temperature in most of Jeju-*do* surpasses 26℃, with Seogwipo at 26.6℃ - the highest in the country. August temperatures at Daegu (26.1℃), Jeonju (26.1℃), Gwangju (26.1℃), and Mokpo (26.0℃) also exceed 26℃. By contrast, Daegwallyeong has the lowest August mean air temperature (19.0℃) in South Korea.

The annual temperature range also decreases from north to south. However, the spatial distribution differs from that of the annual air temperature. The annual range is affected more by geographical features than by altitude. For instance, it is greater in the basins between the mountains than it is in the regions near the coast. The annual range of Hongcheon (29.6℃) is the largest in South Korea, while that of Yangpyeong (29.5℃), Wonju (29.3℃), and Cheorwon (29.3℃) is larger than other regions. Notably, Uiseong (28.3℃) in the Yeongnam region has a much larger range than the surrounding regions. These regions have a low winter air temperatures and are located in inland basins. Gosan (19.8℃) in Jeju has the smallest annual temperature range.

Precipitation
Korea is a region of abundant precipitation with an annual mean of about 1,200mm. The regional differences in precipitation are distinct because of the complicated topography. The major producers of precipitation are extratropical cyclones with their trailing fronts, Changma fronts, typhoons, and topographically-enhanced atmospheric lifting. Extratropical cyclones affect the entire peninsula, but the amount of precipitation from such cyclones varies spatially due to differences in the speed and direction of storm movement, and local topographically-affected winds. Precipitation from individual migratory Changma fronts differs regionally, because such fronts typically advance and retreat in a southward and northward direction. Abundant precipitation occurs in areas affected by Changma fronts, but there may be none in the areas that are not influenced by the Changma. Rainfall from typhoons also varies substantially between regions. Typhoons advance from the southwest to the northeast along the Korean Peninsula.

Mean annual precipitation generally increases southward, but the pattern is more complicated than that of annual mean air temperature. The southeastern coast of Jeju-*do* has the most precipitation in Korea, with Seogwipo reporting a mean annual total of 1,850.7mm and Seongsan receiving 1,840.9mm. The areas along the south coast, Jirisan, and the east coast of Gangwon-*do* also have higher annual precipitation than other regions. The annual precipitation in the southern coast areas and Jirisan is 1,400 to 1,800mm, while that in the northern regions of Daegwallyeong and of the east coast of Gangwon-*do* approaches 1,400mm. During summer, the southwesterly winds from the Asian summer monsoon and southeasterly winds from the western edge of the North Pacific high pressure area converge near Korea to create updrafts by the mountains and zones of rainfall. Daegwallyeong and the east coast in northern Gangwon-*do* also experience precipitation during winter due to snowfall caused by the combined effects of northeasterly airflow from the Siberian high pressure and the low temperatures of the Taebaek Mountains. The Yeongnam inland areas, which are surrounded by the Taebaek Mountains to the east, the Sobaek Range to the west, and Unmunsan (1,195m), Cheonhwangsan (1,189m), and Sinbulsan (1,159m) to the south, have the lowest annual precipitation in South Korea, with values slightly higher than 1,000mm.

June through August precipitation represents about 50 to 60 percent of the annual total. These months are characterized by frequent heavy rainfall events in association with Changma fronts, typhoons, and extratropical cyclones. Summer precipitation generally decreases from the coast to the inland regions. The northwestern Yeongseo area including Seoul, Ganghwa, and Cheorwon also has large summer rainfall totals. On the other hand, the east coast and inland areas in Gyeongsangbuk-*do* have smaller totals.

As in much of Asia, winter in Korea (December through February) is a dry season. Winter precipitation averages below 10 percent of the annual total except in islands and coastal areas, but regional differences in the intensity of the dryness do exist. Ulleungdo has the largest precipitation amounts (296.1mm), which is about 25 percent of its annual precipitation. The coastal areas in Gangwon-*do* also experience relatively large winter precipitation.

Because of the overwhelming influence of topography and oceanic moisture sources, snowfall totals differ among regions more widely than most other climatic features. Snowfall in Korea is generally caused by three meteorological mechanisms: the passage of the extratropical cyclone, expansion of the semi-permanent and quasi-stationary Siberian high pressure system, and the passage of migratory high pressure systems. Daegwallyeong has the largest snowfall amounts (243.1cm), with the snow generated by both cyclones and high pressure systems. Snowfall in Ulleungdo (232.8cm) is possible from all three mechanisms.

Wind and other Elements
In summer, southerly winds dominate under the influence of the North-Pacific quasi-stationary, semi-permanent high pressure system. In winter, the prevailing northwesterly winds are caused by the clockwise flow around the eastern side of the quasi-stationary, semi-permanent Siberian high pressure zone over the north-central Asia. However, local topographic effects make this monsoonal flow more complicated. For example, in Gangneung southwesterly winds are dominant during summer and winter, while in Ulleungdo southwesterly and northeasterly winds are dominant in every season.

One feature associated with severe weather is strong wind, which is defined here as wind with mean speed exceeding 13.8ᵐ/s for at least 10 minutes. Winds exceeding 13.8ᵐ/s occur on an average of more than 100 days per year over coastal regions, such as Ulleungdo, Mokpo, Yeosu, and Busan. In inland regions such as Seoul, Chuncheon, Daegu, and Daejeon, the mean number of days with strong wind is less than 10 days per year.

The percentage of possible annual mean sunshine received in Korea (41 to 61 percent) shows larger regional differences. Yeongdeok has the highest percentage of possible sunshine, and the rate on the east coast in Gyeongsang-*do*, and on the west and south coasts is also high. In contrast, the percentage of possible sunshine in Ulleungdo (41 percent) and Jeju is low.

Frequency of Weather Phenomena
The first snow of the season falls around November 5 on average in Daegwallyeong, but in Geoje it occurs near December 30. The mean date of first snowfall in Seoul, Mokpo, and Busan is November 21, November 26, and December 20, respectively. The mean last snowfall occurs around February 19 in Geoje and Busan, March 11 in Mokpo, and March 21 in Seoul, but not until April 19 in Daegwallyeong. Over the mountainous regions the snow season begins early and ends late because of topographic effects. Over the southern coastal region, the snow season begins later and ends earlier, owing to the slow release of energy accumulated during the summer throughout winter.

A heavy snowfall day is defined as a day with a depth of new snowfall exceeding 5cm or higher. Heavy snowfall occurs frequently in January to February when the Siberian high pressure system expands to put Korea on its fringe. The annual mean number of days with heavy snow is the largest (about 15 days) in Ulleungdo.

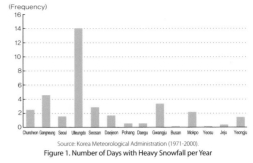
Source: Korea Meteorological Administration (1971-2000).
Figure 1. Number of Days with Heavy Snowfall per Year

The first frost occurs earlier over northern Korea than over the southern region, and earlier over inland locations than coastal regions. The last frost occurs earlier in coastal regions and later in inland locations. In Mokpo, the date of the first frost is as late as November 26 while date of last frost is as early as March 21. By contrast, the earliest date of the first frost occurs over the mountainous Gangwon-*do* region on September 7, with the latest date of last frost on May 30. Over inland regions, the date of the first frost ranges from October 17 to 27, and the date of the last frost ranges from the first to the second ten days of April.

Because cooling factors over mountainous regions are more dominant than in the coastal region, the mean frequency of fog days increases from coastal to mountainous regions. The mean number of days annually with fog in Daegwallyeong is about 120, while over coastal regions only about 20 days per year occur. The spatial distribution of the frequency of freezing days is very similar to that of frost days. The frequency of freezing days increases from coastal to mountainous regions, with less than 80 days annually in the southern coastal region and about 160 days in mountainous regions of Yeongdong.

In Korea, May to June and September to October are the major hail months. The largest average number of days with hail per year occurs in the western coastal region (about 2.8 days). It occurs on about 2.2 days in Seoul and 1.2 days in Busan.

Whangsa frequently occurs in spring because the dry yellow soil can be moved easily by strong winds after snow melts. The number of days with Whangsa varies greatly from year to year, with small regional variability across Korea. The smallest number of days with Whangsa in recent years was less than 5 days in 1997 and 2003 while more than 30 Whangsa days occurred in 2001.

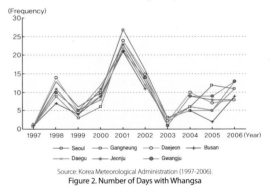
Source: Korea Meteorological Administration (1997-2006).
Figure 2. Number of Days with Whangsa

Although the number of typhoon days varies each year, the mean is about 26 per year. Approximately 70 percent occur from July to October, especially in July, August, and September. Between 1971 and 2000, a total of 102 typhoons affected Korea, with about one per year causing significant damage.

A heavy rainfall is defined as rainfall with totals exceeding 80mm per day. The number of days with heavy rainfall ranges from 1-2 days over central part of Korea and Daegu to 3-4 per year over the southern coastal region, Seoul, and Gyeonggi-*do*. The most extreme values of daily precipitation occur when topographic and meteorological factors both contribute. The largest extreme value of heavy rainfall occurs over Gangneung with 547.4mm per day. The smallest extreme value of heavy rainfall occurs inland of Gyeongsangbuk-*do* with about 160mm per day.

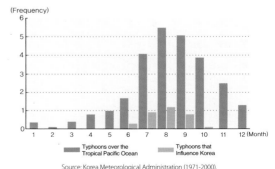
Source: Korea Meteorological Administration (1971-2000).
Figure 3. Monthly Frequency of Typhoon Genesis over the Tropical Pacific Ocean and the Number of Typhoons that Influence Korea

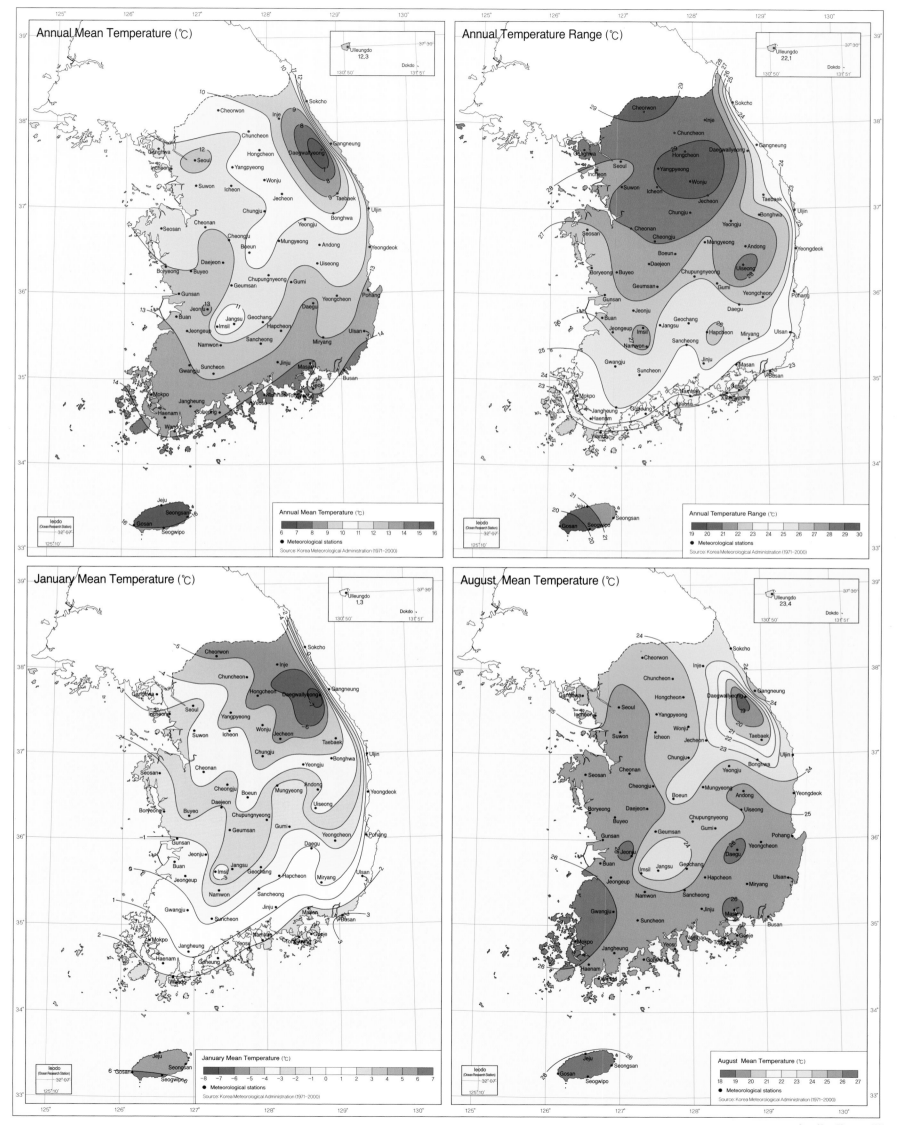

Annual Mean Temperature (℃)

Ulleungdo
12.3
Dokdo

Annual Temperature Range (℃)

Ulleungdo
22.1
Dokdo

January Mean Temperature (℃)

Ulleungdo
1.3
Dokdo

August Mean Temperature (℃)

Ulleungdo
23.4
Dokdo

Annual Mean Temperature (℃)
6 7 8 9 10 11 12 13 14 15 16
● Meteorological stations
Source: Korea Meteorological Administration (1971~2000)

Annual Temperature Range (℃)
19 20 21 22 23 24 25 26 27 28 29 30
● Meteorological stations
Source: Korea Meteorological Administration (1971~2000)

January Mean Temperature (℃)
-8 -7 -6 -5 -4 -3 -2 -1 0 1 2 3 4 5 6 7
● Meteorological stations
Source: Korea Meteorological Administration (1971~2000)

August Mean Temperature (℃)
18 19 20 21 22 23 24 25 26 27
● Meteorological stations
Source: Korea Meteorological Administration (1971~2000)

0 25 50 100 km

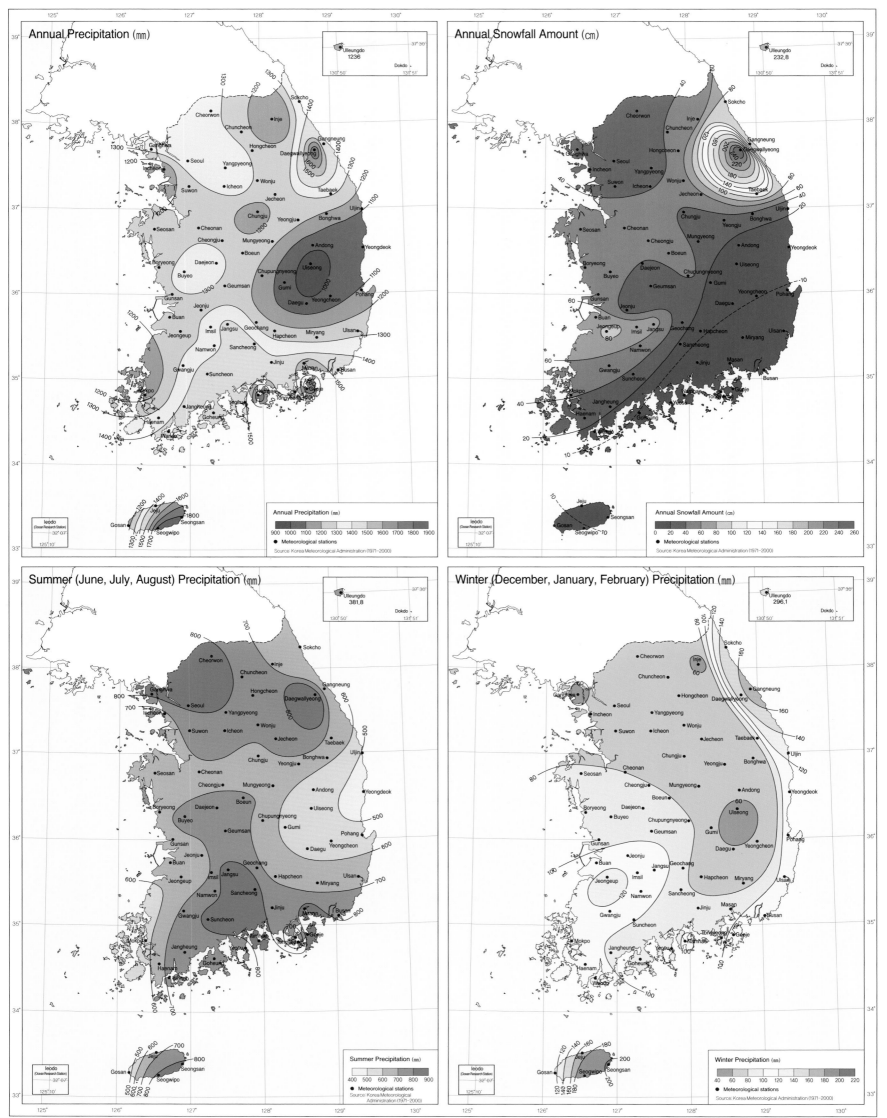

Annual Precipitation (mm)

Summer (June, July, August) Precipitation (mm)

Annual Snowfall Amount (cm)

Winter (December, January, February) Precipitation (mm)

0   25   50   100 km

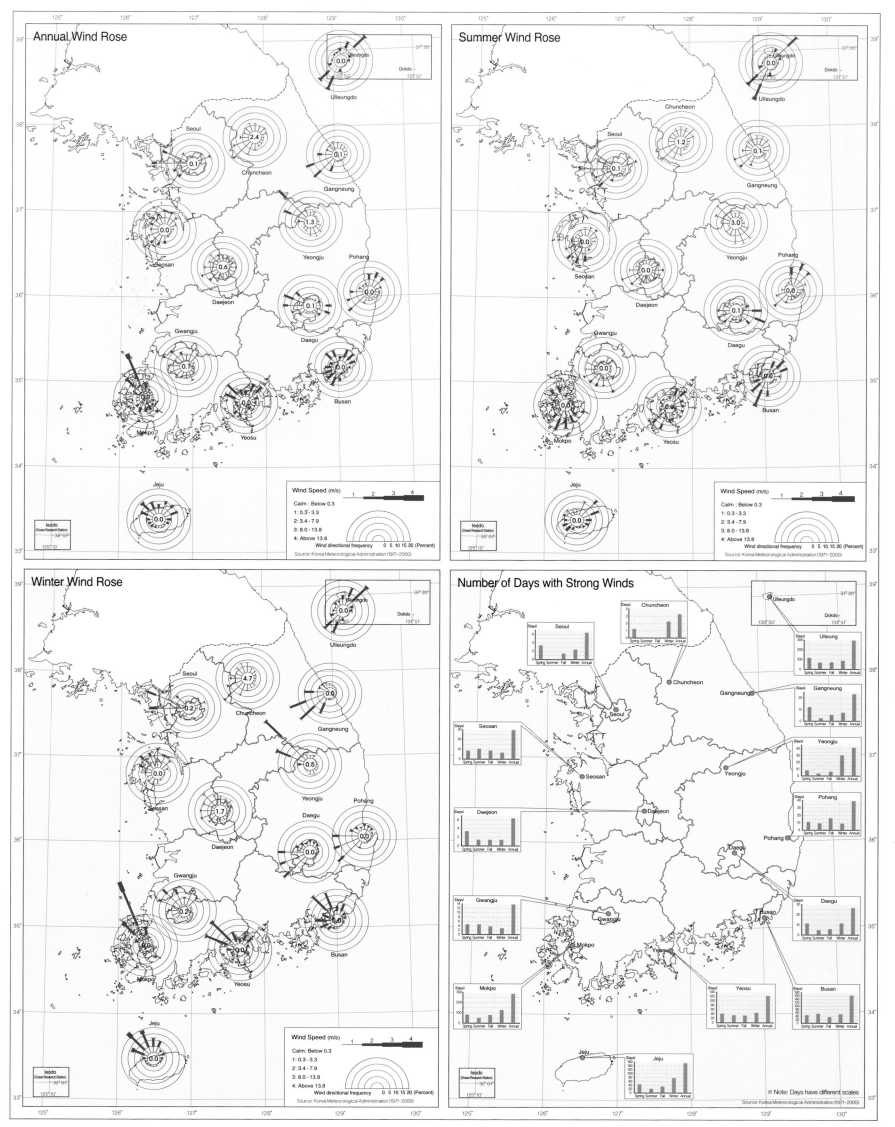

Annual Wind Rose

Summer Wind Rose

Winter Wind Rose

Number of Days with Strong Winds

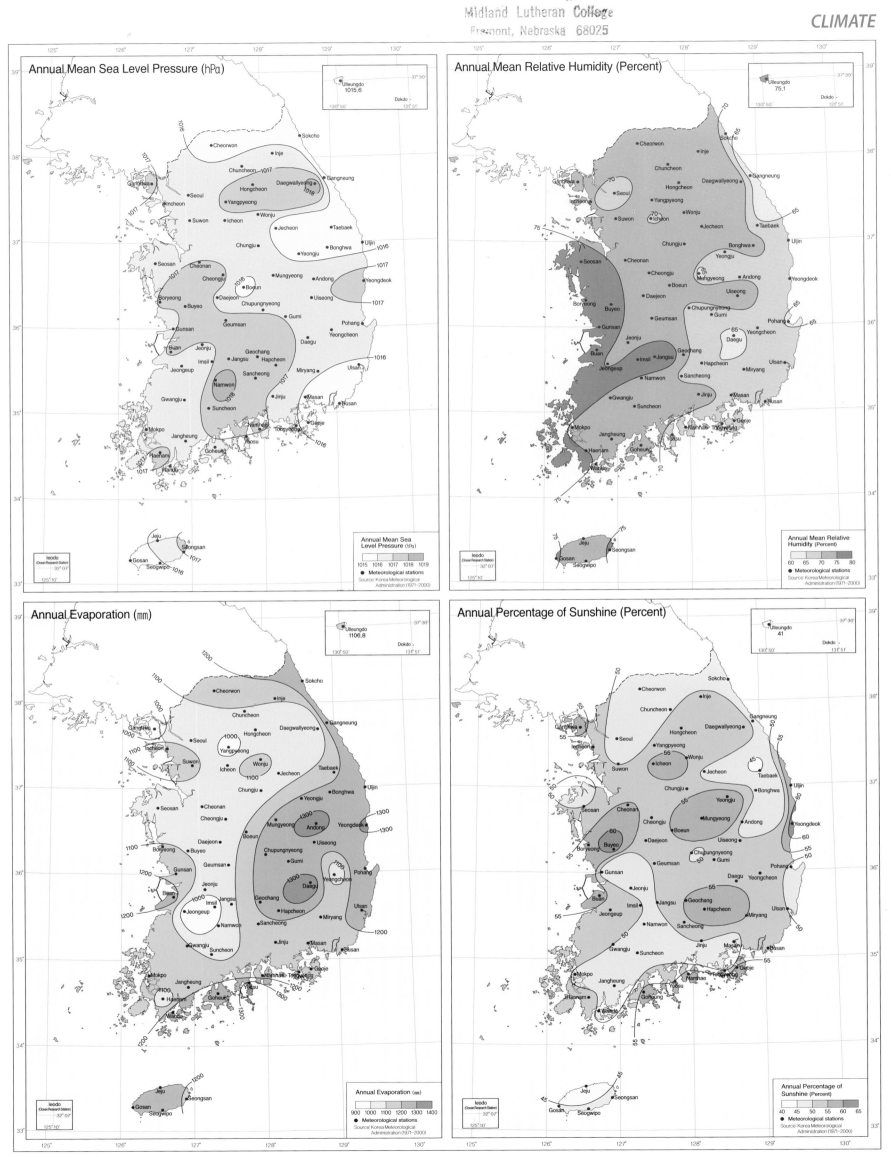

Annual Mean Sea Level Pressure (hPa)

Ulleungdo 1015,6
Dokdo

Annual Mean Sea
Level Pressure (hPa)
1015 1016 1017 1018 1019
● Meteorological stations
Source: Korea Meteorological
Administration (1971~2000)

Ieodo
(Ocean Research Station)
32° 07'
125° 10'

Annual Mean Relative Humidity (Percent)

Ulleungdo 75.1
Dokdo

Annual Mean Relative
Humidity (Percent)
60 65 70 75 80
● Meteorological stations
Source: Korea Meteorological
Administration (1971~2000)

Ieodo
(Ocean Research Station)
32° 07'
125° 10'

Annual Evaporation (mm)

Ulleungdo 1106,8
Dokdo

Annual Evaporation (mm)
900 1000 1100 1200 1300 1400
● Meteorological stations
Source: Korea Meteorological
Administration (1971~2000)

Ieodo
(Ocean Research Station)
32° 07'
125° 10'

Annual Percentage of Sunshine (Percent)

Ulleungdo 41
Dokdo

Annual Percentage of
Sunshine (Percent)
40 45 50 55 60 65
● Meteorological stations
Source: Korea Meteorological
Administration (1971~2000)

Ieodo
(Ocean Research Station)
32° 07'
125° 10'

0   25   50   100 km

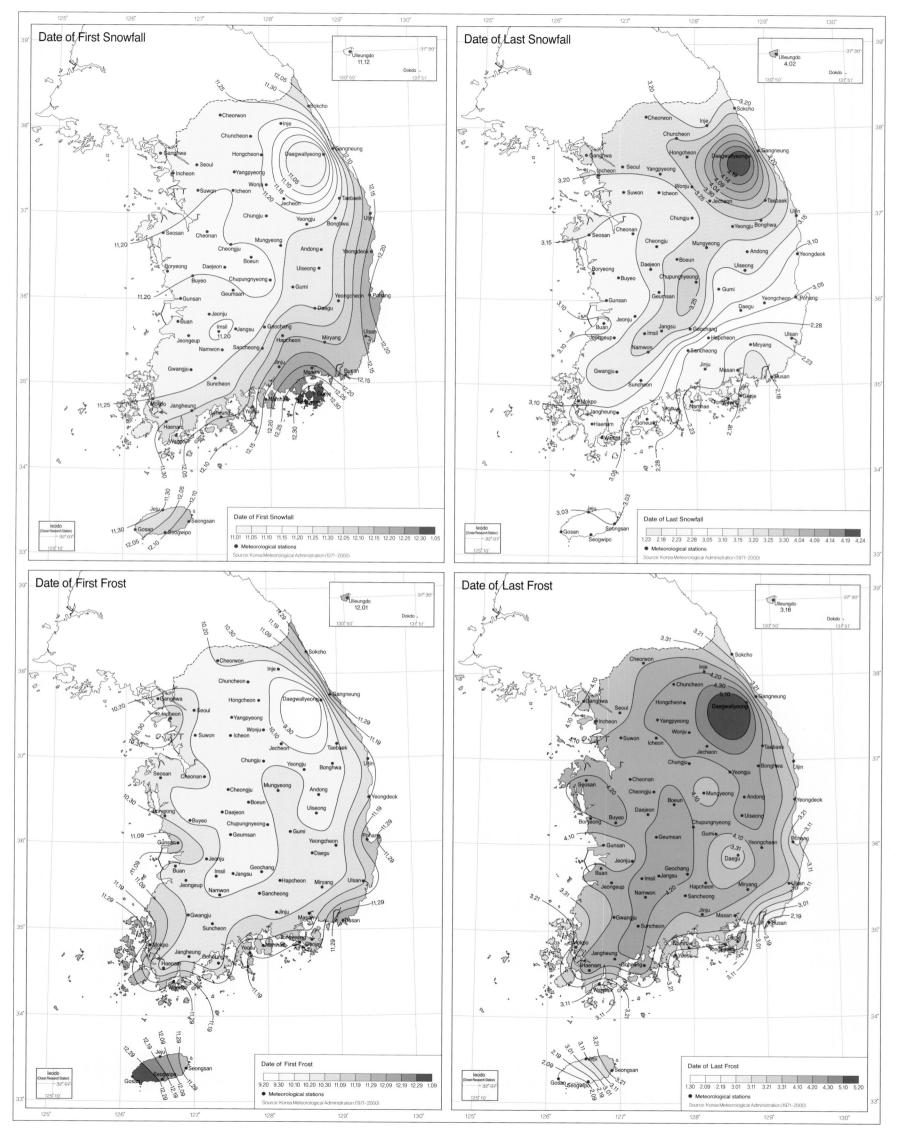

Date of First Snowfall

Date of Last Snowfall

Date of First Frost

Date of Last Frost

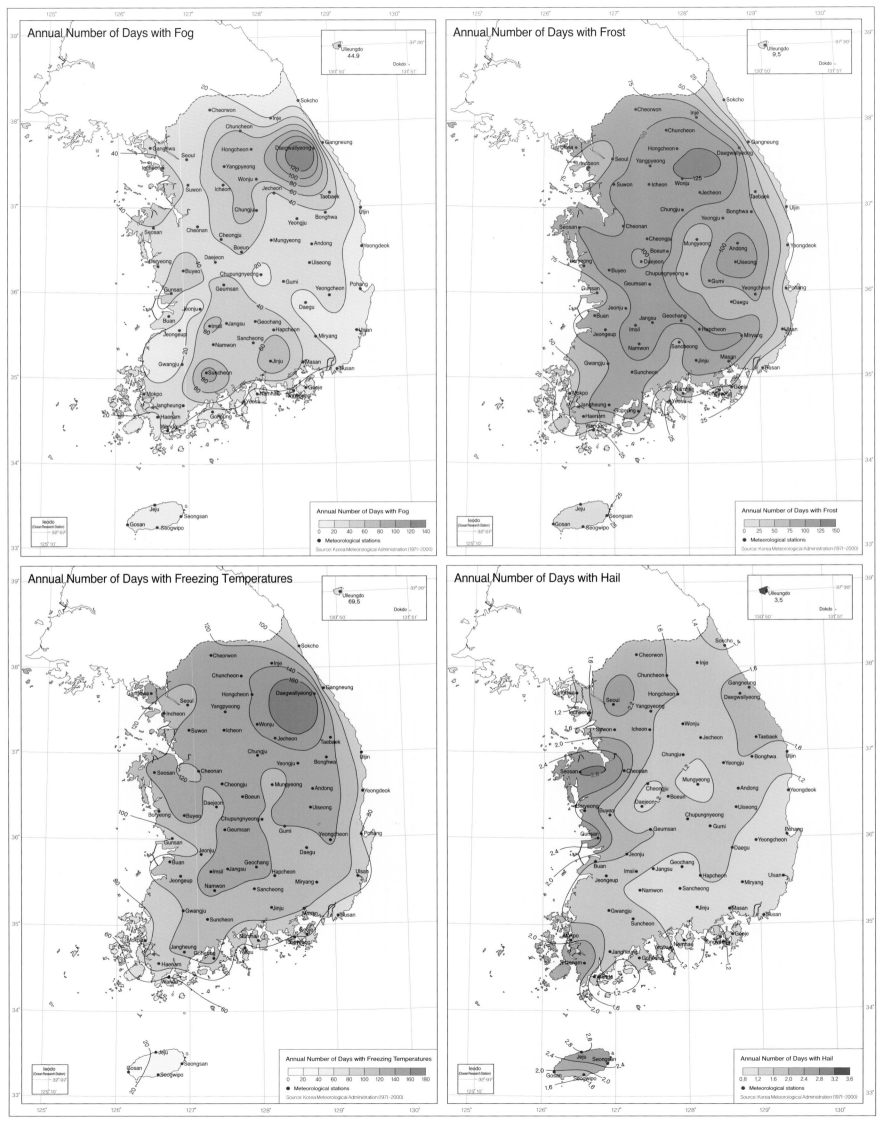

Annual Number of Days with Fog

Ulleungdo
44,9
Dokdo

Ieodo
(Ocean Research Station)

Annual Number of Days with Fog

0 20 40 60 80 100 120 140
● Meteorological stations
Source: Korea Meteorological Administration (1971–2000)

Annual Number of Days with Frost

Ulleungdo
9,5
Dokdo

Ieodo
(Ocean Research Station)

Annual Number of Days with Frost

0 25 50 75 100 125 150
● Meteorological stations
Source: Korea Meteorological Administration (1971–2000)

Annual Number of Days with Freezing Temperatures

Ulleungdo
69,5
Dokdo

Ieodo
(Ocean Research Station)

Annual Number of Days with Freezing Temperatures

0 20 40 60 80 100 120 140 160 180
● Meteorological stations
Source: Korea Meteorological Administration (1971–2000)

Annual Number of Days with Hail

Ulleungdo
3,5
Dokdo

Ieodo
(Ocean Research Station)

Annual Number of Days with Hail

0.8 1.2 1.6 2.0 2.4 2.8 3.2 3.6
● Meteorological stations
Source: Korea Meteorological Administration (1971–2000)

0 25 50 100 km

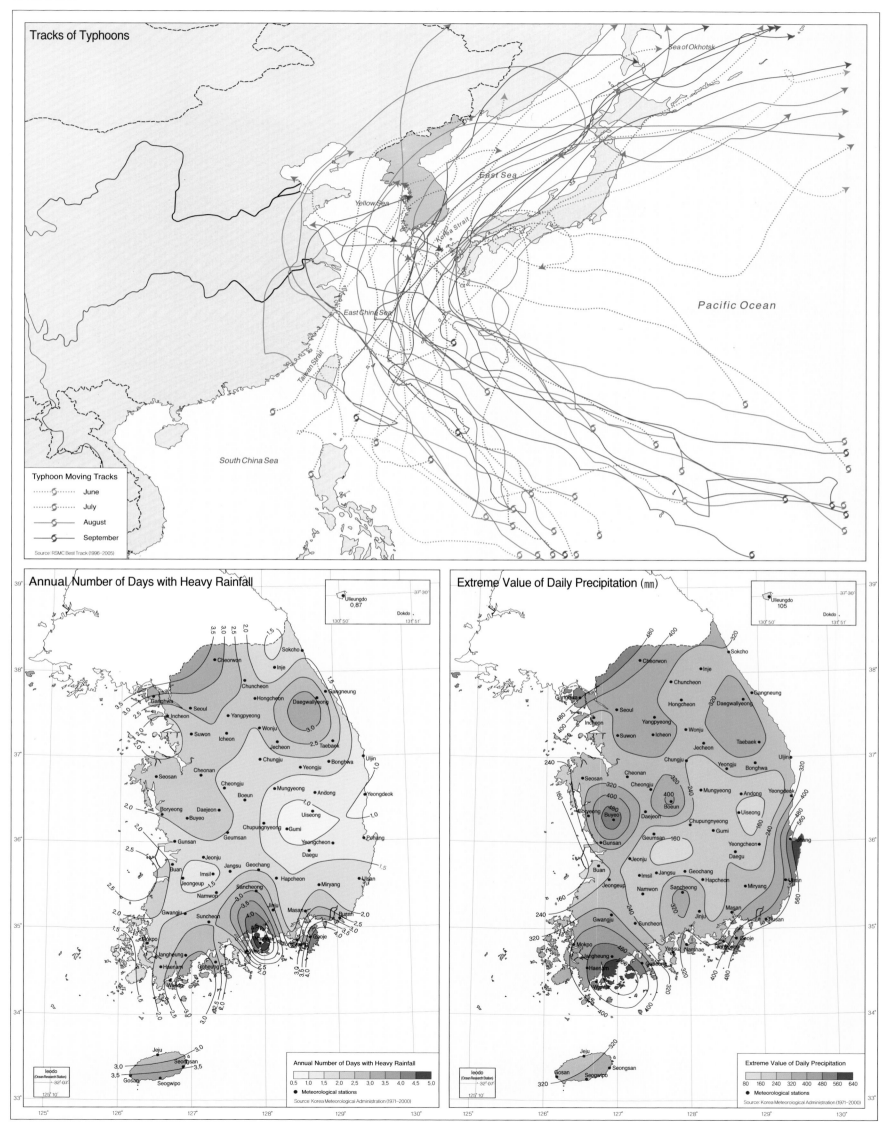

Tracks of Typhoons

East Sea

Sea of Okhotsk

Yellow Sea

Pacific Ocean

Korea Strait

East China Sea

Taiwan Strait

South China Sea

Typhoon Moving Tracks
- June
- July
- August
- September

Source: RSMC Best Track (1996~2005)

Annual Number of Days with Heavy Rainfall

Ulleungdo
0.87

Dokdo

Sokcho
Cheorwon
Inje
Chuncheon
Gangneung
Hongcheon
Daegwallyeong
Ganghwa
Seoul
Yangpyeong
Incheon
Wonju
Suwon
Icheon
Jecheon
Taebaek
Chungju
Bonghwa
Uljin
Cheonan
Yeongju
Seosan
Cheongju
Mungyeong
Andong
Boeun
Yeongdeok
Uiseong
Boryeong
Daejeon
Buyeo
Chupungnyeong
Gumi
Pohang
Geumsan
Yeongcheon
Gunsan
Daegu
Jeonju
Geochang
Buan
Imsil
Jangsu
Hapcheon
Miryang
Jeongeup
Sancheong
Ulsan
Namwon
Jinju
Masan
Gwangju
Suncheon
Busan
Geoje
Mokpo
Jangheung
Goheung
Haenam
Wando

Ieodo
(Ocean Research Station)

Jeju
Seongsan
Gosan
Seogwipo

Annual Number of Days with Heavy Rainfall
0.5 1.0 1.5 2.0 2.5 3.0 3.5 4.0 4.5 5.0
● Meteorological stations

Source: Korea Meteorological Administration (1971~2000)

Extreme Value of Daily Precipitation (㎜)

Ulleungdo
105

Dokdo

Sokcho
Cheorwon
Inje
Chuncheon
Gangneung
Hongcheon
Daegwallyeong
Ganghwa
Seoul
Yangpyeong
Incheon
Wonju
Suwon
Icheon
Jecheon
Taebaek
Chungju
Bonghwa
Uljin
Cheonan
Yeongju
Seosan
Cheongju
Mungyeong
Andong
Boeun
Uiseong
Boryeong
Daejeon
Buyeo
Chupungnyeong
Gumi
Geumsan
Yeongcheon
Gunsan
Daegu
Jeonju
Geochang
Buan
Imsil
Jangsu
Hapcheon
Miryang
Jeongeup
Namwon
Sancheong
Jinju
Masan
Gwangju
Suncheon
Busan
Geoje
Mokpo
Jangheung
Goheung
Haenam
Wando

Ieodo
(Ocean Research Station)

Jeju
Seongsan
Gosan
Seogwipo

Extreme Value of Daily Precipitation
80 160 240 320 400 480 560 640
● Meteorological stations

Source: Korea Meteorological Administration (1971~2000)

0 25 50 100 km

Interannual Variation of Mean Temperature and Total Precipitation

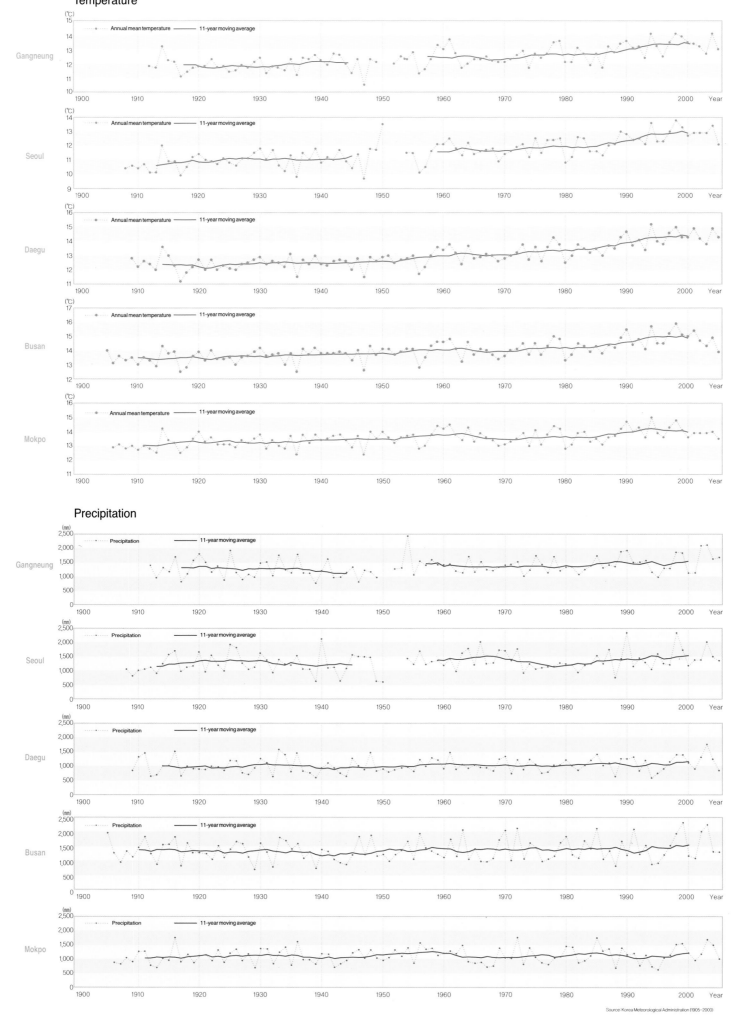

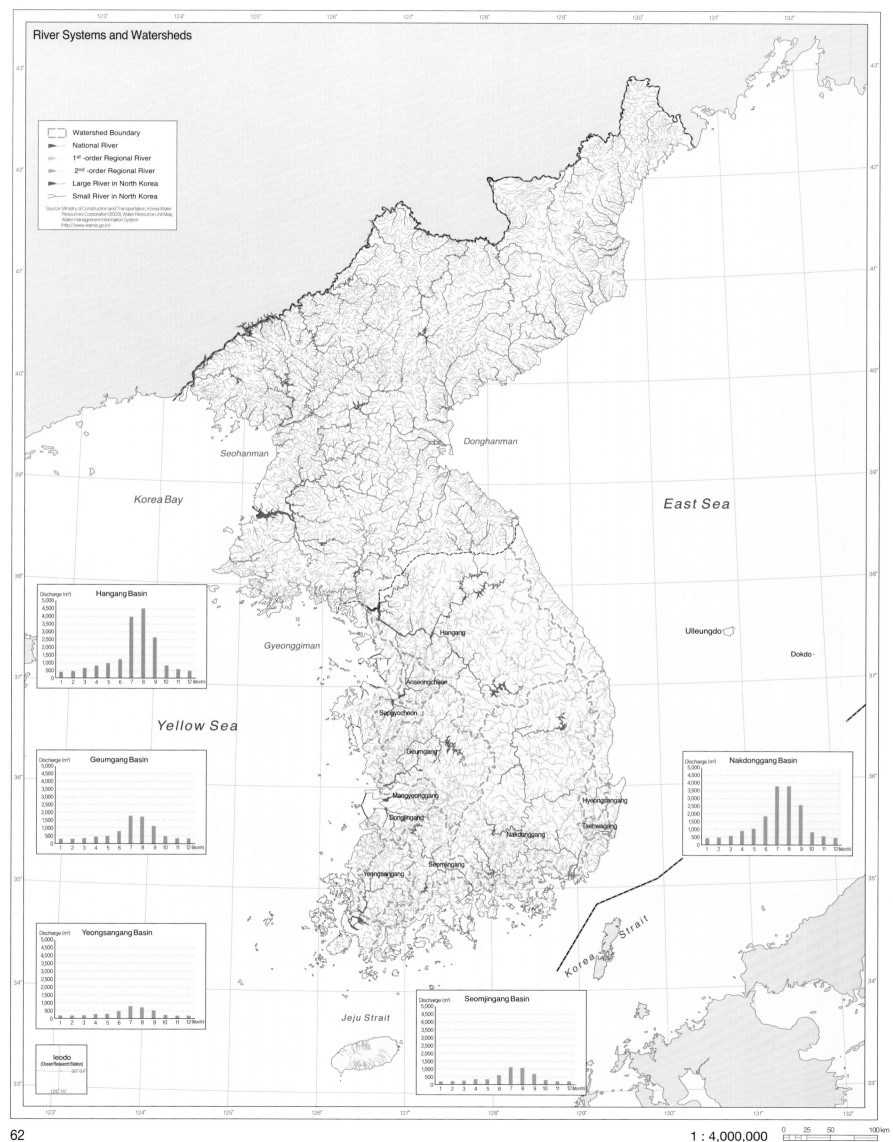

River Systems and Watersheds

Watershed Boundary
National River
1st -order Regional River
2nd -order Regional River
Large River in North Korea
Small River in North Korea

Source: Ministry of Construction and Transportation, Korea Water Resources Corporation (2003), Water Resource Unit Map, Water management Information System (http://www.wamis.go.kr)

Korea Bay

Seohanman

Donghanman

East Sea

Gyeonggiman

Yellow Sea

Hangang

Anseongcheon

Sappyocheon

Geumgang

Mangyeonggang

Dongjingang

Nakdonggang

Hyeongsangang

Taehwagang

Seomjingang

Yeongsangang

Ulleungdo

Dokdo

Jeju Strait

Korea Strait

Hangang Basin
Discharge (m³)

Geumgang Basin
Discharge (m³)

Yeongsangang Basin
Discharge (m³)

Nakdonggang Basin
Discharge (m³)

Seomjingang Basin
Discharge (m³)

Ieodo
(Ocean Research Station)
32° 07'
125° 10'

1 : 4,000,000

0 25 50 100 km

The average annual precipitation in Korea is about 1,245mm. More than 60 percent of the total precipitation is concentrated between June and September, while winter precipitation is less than 10 percent of the total precipitation. The precipitation pattern of Korea is primarily characterized by spring droughts and frequent summer floods. This is primarily caused by localized heavy rains usually associated with stationary fronts, a.k.a. Jangma, and tropical cyclones.

About 70 percent of the Korean Peninsula is mountainous and mainly consists of granite or granite gneiss. In the mountains, the time lags to the peak storm discharge of the streams are usually short because of smaller drainage basins and short, steep reaches, as well as a limited soil water capacity due to thin top soils. Runoff ratios of Korean streams range between 0.45 and 0.65. During the dry season, especially May and early June, significant evapotranspiration reduces soil water content, lowers the groundwater level, and results in an extremely low level of streamflow. Considering this annual precipitation pattern, the Korean government has constructed a number of multipurpose dams and dams for water supplies to prevent drought and to secure the municipal and industrial water needs.

Due to the geological and topographic characteristics, groundwater storage is limited in Korea. Thus, municipal water supplies rely heavily on dams and rivers. The distribution of mountain ranges suggests an overall pattern of regional underground water storage: underground water recharges mainly occur in the eastern mountainous regions and discharges take place in the western plain regions. Abundant groundwater is available in the alluvial layer along the rivers and in a thick zone of weathered bedrock in the western plain region. There is also plenty of groundwater available in the limestone area of the upstream Namhangang and the east coast of Korea. Groundwater is also plentiful in the Gyeongsang Supergroup area in the southeastern part of Korea and Chejudo which is a typical volcanic island and consists of porous basalt. Fluvial aquifers are well developed along the large rivers including the Hangang, Geumgang, Nakdonggang, and Yeongsangang, but these comprise less than 30 percent of South Korea. Excessive groundwater development has caused groundwater salinization in several coastal regions such as Jejudo, Busan, and Incheon.

Rivers

There are five large rivers in South Korea: Hangang, Nakdonggang, Geumgang, Seomjingang, and Yeongsangang; and several mid-to-small size rivers: Anseongcheon, Sapgyocheon, Mangyeonggang, Dongjingang, and Hyeongsangang. The longest river is the Nakdonggang with a length of 506 km. These Korean rivers have been divided into 117 sub-basins for the systematic management of river and water resources. Table 1 shows the important characteristics of major rivers in South Korea. The Hangang has the largest drainage area (35,770 km²) and the greatest river discharge (16 billion m³) which constitutes 26 percent and 28 percent of the nation's total, respectively.

Table 1. Characteristics of Major Rivers in South Korea

River	Drainage Area (km²)	Main River Length (km)	Average Width of the River Basin (km)
Hangang	35,770	494	72.4
Nakdonggang	23,384	506	46.2
Geumgang	9,912	395	25.1
Seomjingang	4,959	224	22.1
Yeongsangang	3,468	138	24.9
Anseongcheon	1,656	76	21.8
Sapgyocheon	1,650	64	25.8
Mangyeonggang	1,504	81	18.6
Dongjingang	1,132	63	17.8
Hyeongsangang	1,124	51	22.0

Source : Water Resources Corporation, 2004.

The topographical characteristics of the Korean Peninsula, such as steep eastern slopes and gentle western slopes, result in a great regional difference in flood potential. There is rapid runoff to the ocean in the east, but frequent flooding in the west. Typical hydrographs of Korean rivers exhibit very short rising limbs with extreme discharges with high peaks, since Korean rivers have relatively small drainage areas and short, steep reaches. The ratio of runoff to the annual average rainfall of 124 billion m³ is about 58 percent, resulting in an annual average river discharge of 72.3 billion m³.

Korean rivers show very high flow variation as shown in Table 2. Seventy-two percent of the annual average river discharge flushes to the ocean during the flooding period, which means 52.2 billion m³ out of 72.3 billion m³ is lost. Generally, only 20.1

billion m³ of water flow through all rivers is used to meet various demands of water annually.

Table 2. Monthly Runoff of Major Rivers

Month \ River	Hangang	Nakdonggang	Geumgang	Seomjingang	Yeongsangang
January	272.6	288.6	179.1	87.1	62.2
February	319.2	328.6	178.5	88.7	65.8
March	520.5	440.4	222.3	120.0	86.2
April	684.9	763.7	322.6	222.5	157.1
May	844.6	913.0	370.5	224.3	173.7
June	1,101.2	1,717.0	660.2	490.4	353.9
July	3,858.5	3,669.2	1,681.9	992.3	669.3
August	4,397.4	3,671.7	1,624.7	970.7	594.2
September	2,512.3	2,452.5	994.9	573.1	398.6
October	699.1	685.8	348.5	170.1	117.8
November	461.9	429.3	225.9	102.2	70.9
December	353.0	319.9	199.0	94.8	70.7
Total	16,025.2	15,679.7	7,008.1	4,136.1	2,820.4

Source : Ministry of Construction, Water Resources Corporation, 2006.

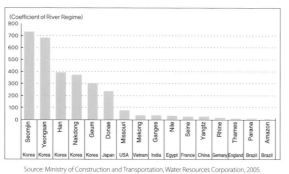

Source: Ministry of Construction and Transportation, Water Resources Corporation, 2005.

Figure 1. Comparison of River Regime Coefficient

The coefficients of the river regime expressed by a ratio of maximum discharge to minimum discharge for Korean rivers usually ranges from 300 to 400, which is far greater than 10 to 30 for major rivers of the world as shown in Figure 1. These river characteristics in Korea cause serious problems in river management, including flood control and water use.

Water Use

The annual potential amount of water resources can be calculated by multiplying the amount of annual precipitation (1,245 mm, average of 1974-2003) with the land area (99,460 km²), a value equivalent to 124 billion m³ in Korea. Actual water use was, however, only 33.7 billion m³ in 2003, as shown in Figure 2.

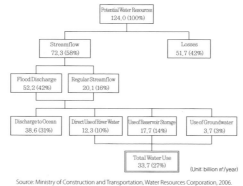

Source: Ministry of Construction and Transportation, Water Resources Corporation, 2006.

Figure 2. Breakdown of Water Resources on Korea (2003)

Figure 2 shows that the regular streamflow is only 20.1 billion m³ after extracting natural losses and flood discharge from the potential water resources, which is far less than the total water use. This gap between water use and regular streamflow has been supplemented by the use of reservoir storage. Within the total water use, 23 percent is for municipal (7.6 billion m³), 8 percent for industrial (2.6 billion m³), and 22 percent for river environment (7.5 billion m³), while the largest portion of it (47 percent) is used for agriculture (160 billion m³) (Figure 3).

In 2003, the amount of water taken from the river was 12.3 billion m³, or 36.5 percent of water demands, while dam reservoirs supplied 17.7 billion m³, which was 52.5 percent of the demand. The remaining 11 percent of the water demand was provided by groundwater in the amount of 3.7 billion m³. Water use in Korea relied largely upon the dam reservoir storage.

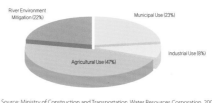

Source: Ministry of Construction and Transportation, Water Resources Corporation, 2006.

Figure 3. Water Demands for all Purposes

Dams

The main purpose of a dam is to stabilize the river discharge to meet the water demand downstream that varies from season to season. The water supply capacity of a dam is generally defined as the maximum amount of water to secure the water supply even during the peak drought season. In 2003, the total water supply capacity of dams was 17.7 billion m³. Fifteen multipurpose dams supplied 10.8 billion m³. Soyanggang Dam and Chungju Dam fall in this category. Sixteen domestic and industrial water supply dams supplied 0.6 billion m³. Yeongcheon Dam and Unmun Dam are in this category. Five estuary barrages supplied 2.2 billion m³. Hydropower generation dams in Hangang Basin supplied 1.3 billion m³. In addition, 17,760 irrigation dams across the country supplied 2.8 billion m³ of water.

As of 2005, 1,214 dams of the approximately 18,000 dams in Korea were categorized as large dams. Large dams are higher than 15 m, or have lengths of at least 2,000 m, or storage capacities of 3 million m³ with heights of 10 to 15 m. Table 3 shows the number of large dams in each watershed and their purpose. Three hundred and ten dams, 25 percent of the total number of dams, are located in the Nakdonggang watershed, 11.3 percent (137 dams) along the Geumgang, 10.7 percent (130 dams) along the Hangang, 8.5 percent (103 dams) and 5.9 percent (72 dams) along the Seomjingang and Yeongsangang, respectively. In terms of the purpose of dams, there are 1,114 dams (91.8%) built for irrigation purposes, 63 dams for municipal and industrial water supplies, 21 for hydropower generation, 14 for multi-purposes, and only one dam for flood control.

Table 3. The Number of Dams in Each Watershed

Purpose	Nationwide	Hangang	Nakdong-gang	Geumgang	Yeongsan-gang	Seomjin-gang	Others
Total	1,214	130	310	137	72	103	462
Multi-purpose	15	3	5	2	-	3	2
Municipal and Industrial Water Supply	63	5	5	4	9	1	39
Hydropower Generation	21	9	7	2	-	1	2
Agricultural	1,114	1112	293	129	63	98	419
Flood Control	1	1	-	-	-	-	-

Source: Ministry of Construction, and Transportation, Water Resources Corporation, 2003, River Statistics of Korea.

Groundwater

Annual groundwater recharge in Korea is estimated at 13-14 billion m³. However, most of the groundwater is discharged as streamflow during the drought season and a poor aquifer condition is the main obstacle to groundwater development. The amount of sustainable groundwater development, which takes the groundwater recharge rate in a drought year of 10-year return period into account, is estimated to be about 11.7 billion m³ per year.

The total usage of groundwater is about 3.7 billion m³ per year, including 1.8 billion m³ (49%) for municipal purposes, 1.7 billion m³ (46%) for agricultural purposes, 0.2 billion m³ (5%) for industrial purposes, and 0.05 billion m³ (1%) for other purposes. Gyeonggi-do, Chungcheong-do and Jeolla-do are the most active areas for groundwater use, since these regions have relatively well-developed aquifer conditions.

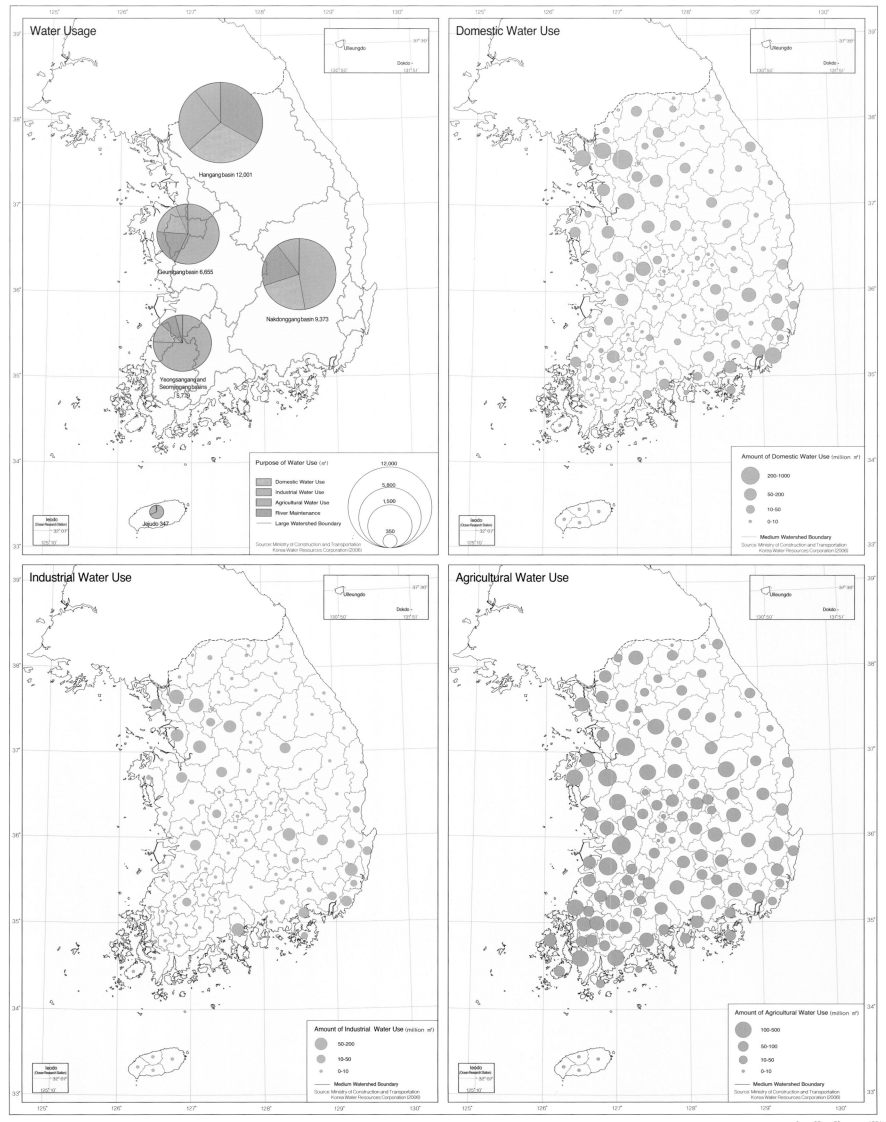

Water Usage

Hangang basin 12,001

Geumgang basin 6,655

Nakdonggang basin 9,373

Yeongsangang and Seomjingang basins 5,779

Jejudo 347

Purpose of Water Use (㎥)

- Domestic Water Use
- Industrial Water Use
- Agricultural Water Use
- River Maintenance
- Large Watershed Boundary

12,000
5,800
1,500
350

leodo (Ocean Research Station) 32° 07'
125° 10'

Source: Ministry of Construction and Transportation
Korea Water Resources Corporation (2006)

Domestic Water Use

Amount of Domestic Water Use (million ㎥)

- 200-1000
- 50-200
- 10-50
- 0-10

Medium Watershed Boundary

leodo (Ocean Research Station) 32° 07'
125° 10'

Source: Ministry of Construction and Transportation
Korea Water Resources Corporation (2006)

Industrial Water Use

Amount of Industrial Water Use (million ㎥)

- 50-200
- 10-50
- 0-10

Medium Watershed Boundary

leodo (Ocean Research Station) 32° 07'
125° 10'

Source: Ministry of Construction and Transportation
Korea Water Resources Corporation (2006)

Agricultural Water Use

Amount of Agricultural Water Use (million ㎥)

- 100-500
- 50-100
- 10-50
- 0-10

Medium Watershed Boundary

leodo (Ocean Research Station) 32° 07'
125° 10'

Source: Ministry of Construction and Transportation
Korea Water Resources Corporation (2006)

Ulleungdo
Dokdo

0 25 50   100 km

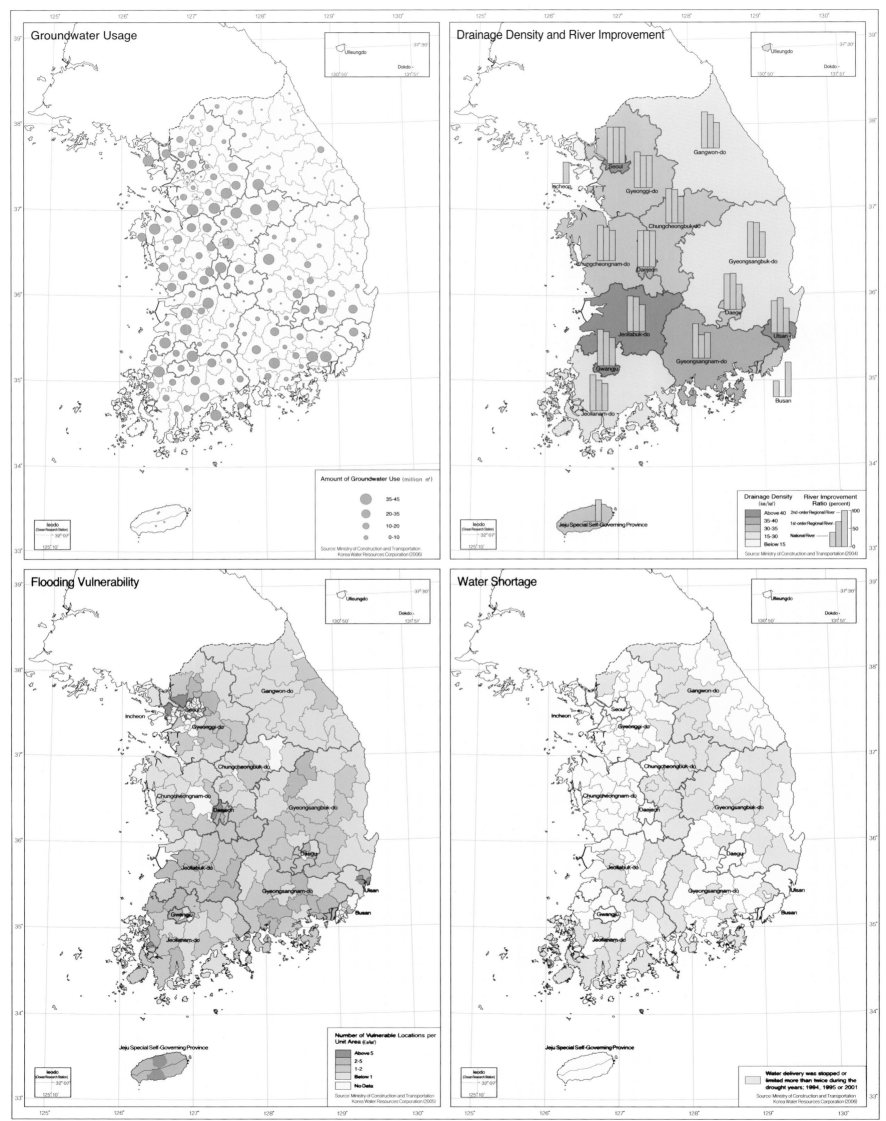

Groundwater Usage

Amount of Groundwater Use (million ㎥)
- 35-45
- 20-35
- 10-20
- 0-10

Source: Ministry of Construction and Transportation,
Korea Water Resources Corporation (2006)

Drainage Density and River Improvement

Incheon
Seoul
Gyeonggi-do
Gangwon-do
Chungcheongbuk-do
Chungcheongnam-do
Daejeon
Gyeongsangbuk-do
Jeollabuk-do
Daegu
Ulsan
Gwangju
Gyeongsangnam-do
Busan
Jeollanam-do

Jeju Special Self-Governing Province

Drainage Density (km/km²)
- Above 40
- 35-40
- 30-35
- 15-30
- Below 15

River Improvement Ratio (percent)
- 2nd-order Regional River
- 1st-order Regional River
- National River
- 100
- 50
- 0

Source: Ministry of Construction and Transportation (2004)

Flooding Vulnerability

Incheon
Seoul
Gyeonggi-do
Gangwon-do
Chungcheongbuk-do
Chungcheongnam-do
Daejeon
Gyeongsangbuk-do
Jeollabuk-do
Daegu
Gyeongsangnam-do
Ulsan
Busan
Gwangju
Jeollanam-do

Jeju Special Self-Governing Province

Number of Vulnerable Locations per Unit Area (EA/km²)
- Above 5
- 2-5
- 1-2
- Below 1
- No Data

Source: Ministry of Construction and Transportation,
Korea Water Resources Corporation (2005)

Water Shortage

Incheon
Seoul
Gyeonggi-do
Gangwon-do
Chungcheongbuk-do
Chungcheongnam-do
Daejeon
Gyeongsangbuk-do
Jeollabuk-do
Daegu
Gyeongsangnam-do
Ulsan
Busan
Gwangju
Jeollanam-do

Jeju Special Self-Governing Province

Water delivery was stopped or limited more than twice during the drought years; 1994, 1995 or 2001

Source: Ministry of Construction and Transportation,
Korea Water Resources Corporation (2006)

0 25 50 100km

65

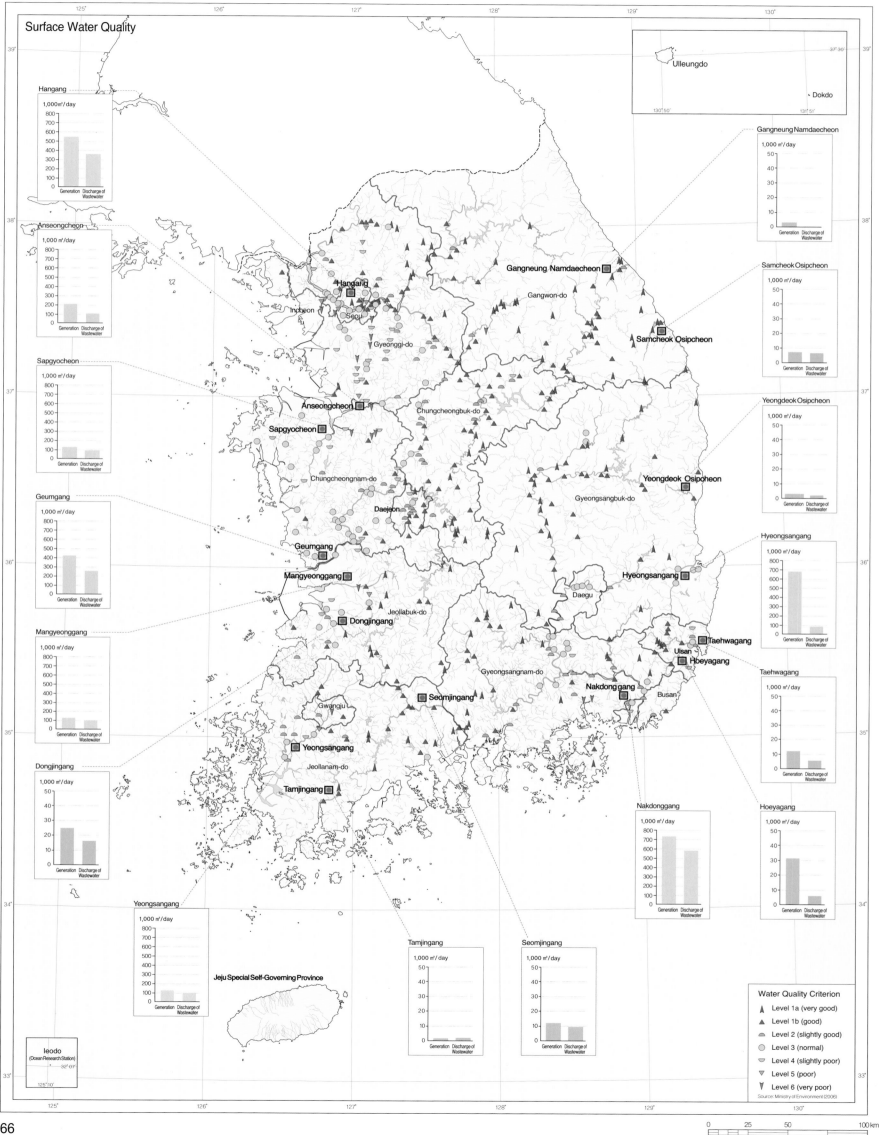

Surface Water Quality

Hangang
1,000 ㎥/day
Generation Discharge of Wastewater

Anseongcheon
1,000 ㎥/day
Generation Discharge of Wastewater

Sapgyocheon
1,000 ㎥/day
Generation Discharge of Wastewater

Geumgang
1,000 ㎥/day
Generation Discharge of Wastewater

Mangyeonggang
1,000 ㎥/day
Generation Discharge of Wastewater

Dongjingang
1,000 ㎥/day
Generation Discharge of Wastewater

Yeongsangang
1,000 ㎥/day
Generation Discharge of Wastewater

Gangneung Namdaecheon
1,000 ㎥/day
Generation Discharge of Wastewater

Samcheok Osipcheon
1,000 ㎥/day
Generation Discharge of Wastewater

Yeongdeok Osipcheon
1,000 ㎥/day
Generation Discharge of Wastewater

Hyeongsangang
1,000 ㎥/day
Generation Discharge of Wastewater

Taehwagang
1,000 ㎥/day
Generation Discharge of Wastewater

Nakdonggang
1,000 ㎥/day
Generation Discharge of Wastewater

Hoeyagang
1,000 ㎥/day
Generation Discharge of Wastewater

Tamjingang
1,000 ㎥/day
Generation Discharge of Wastewater

Seomjingang
1,000 ㎥/day
Generation Discharge of Wastewater

Ulleungdo
Dokdo

Gangneung Namdaecheon
Samcheok Osipcheon
Yeongdeok Osipoheon
Hyeongsangang
Taehwagang
Hoeyagang
Nakdong gang
Seomjingang
Yeongsangang
Tamjingang
Dongjingang
Mangyeonggang
Geumgang
Sapgyocheon
Anseongcheon
Hangang

Incheon
Seoul
Gyeonggi-do
Gangwon-do
Chungcheongbuk-do
Chungcheongnam-do
Daejeon
Gyeongsangbuk-do
Daegu
Jeollabuk-do
Ulsan
Gyeongsangnam-do
Busan
Gwangju
Jeollanam-do

Jeju Special Self-Governing Province

Ieodo
(Ocean Research Station)

Water Quality Criterion
Level 1a (very good)
Level 1b (good)
Level 2 (slightly good)
Level 3 (normal)
Level 4 (slightly poor)
Level 5 (poor)
Level 6 (very poor)
Source: Ministry of Environment (2006)

0 25 50 100 km

Global environmental degradation has accelerated in recent years. Only through the cooperation of the international community and great effort from individual nations can major environmental problems be solved. The United Nations published the eight Millennium Development Goals (MDGs) in October 2000, which should be fulfilled by all the world' countries and all the world' leading development institutions by 2015. The MDGs range from cutting extreme poverty in half to halting the spread of HIV/AIDS and providing universal primary education. The seventh MDG is to ensure environmental sustainability. To achieve the goal, three specific targets are identified: (1) integrate the principles of sustainable development into national policies and programs and reverse the loss of environmental resources, (2) halve the proportion of people without sustainable access to safe drinking water and basic sanitation, and (3) achieve a significant improvement in the lives of at least 100 million slum-dwellers.

In addition, the number of signed or enforced international environmental conventions has continually increased. Among the 52 international environmental conventions, Korea has joined and adopted 47 to date. For example, the Vienna Convention for the Protection of the Ozone Layer was enforced in September 1988 and the Montreal Amendment to the Montreal Protocol was enforced in November 1999. In recent years, Asian dust from the Gobi Desert in China has affected the air quality in Korea, creating an awareness of the importance of international cooperation to reverse environmental degradation.

Surface Water Quality

Korea has a variety of available water resources, including rain water, groundwater, and surface waters from the rivers, lakes, impoundments, and river beds. Ninety-two percent of the water supply consists of surface waters from rivers, lakes, and impoundments. Protection of water resources is very important to obtain a palatable, safe, and abundant water supply. The characteristics of surface water quality show the amount of water pollutant generation and the amount of discharge into the major rivers. Water quality generally depends on the concentration of pollutants and amount of wastewater discharge into a water body. Dilution effects from clean upstream waters and self-purification capacity of the waters may mitigate the problem.

The degree of pollution is generally designated using several water quality variables. The most widely-used measure is biochemical oxygen demand (BOD) - the amount of oxygen (in milligrams per liter) required to decompose the organic matter contained in a sample of water. Previously, water quality criteria of rivers and lakes were divided by BOD using five categories. Recently, the criteria were expanded to consider not only BOD but also the presence of hazardous materials and effects on the ecosystem. Water quality is now divided into seven categories and is explained with terms of 'very good,' 'good,' and 'poor' to aid public understanding. Water quality criteria are used to decide whether water is appropriate for intake. For instance, the supplied water can be potable only with filtration treatment if BOD concentrations of the intake water are lower than 1mg/L.

The Hangang supplies water for approximately ten million people in the Seoul Metropolitan area. BOD concentration is relatively high at Noryangjin and Gayang-*dong* because these areas are located downstream of the Hangang. Similar concentrations of BOD have been maintained since the late 1990s, when a few sewage plants were constructed to relieve pollutant loads into the surface water. The water quality of the upstream Hangang is quite good. However, water quality of downstream water is classified as standard level 3, which means that various efforts should be made to improve it. A nationwide sensor network known as the National Water Environment Information System was built to measure water quality of lakes and rivers continuously and to communicate the information to the public. The information system includes data for 580 rivers and 150 lakes on a real-time basis.

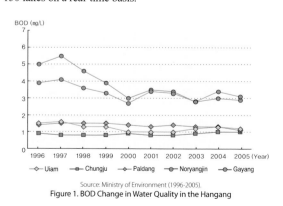

Source: Ministry of Environment (1996-2005).
Figure 1. BOD Change in Water Quality in the Hangang

Environmental Service in Water Supply and Wastewater Treatment

The availability of fresh and clean water is necessary to maintain life and is also closely linked to the modern style of liv-

ing. Water supply services produce potable water from natural water in rivers and lakes. The ratio of people who are supplied water from public drinking water facilities to the total population is used to evaluate the water supply service of a region. The water supply facility includes an intake of raw water, a water delivery system, a treatment plant, and a distribution system. The quality of drinking water is determined at the water treatment plant. About 84.5 percent of Koreans benefitted from the water supply system in 1997 and this ratio increased to 90.7 percent in 2005. However, variation in the ratio across regions is quite substantial. While the ratio is 100 percent for Seoul, it is only 19.1 percent for Haseong-*myeon* and Gimpo-*si* in Gyeonggi-*do*. Although the population of the Haseong-*myeon* region is only 500, an effort should be made to provide clean and safe water to every citizen.

Sewage facilities remove pollutants in wastewater and transfer the output into natural water systems such as rivers and lakes, which ensure the continuous usage of water. Just as waterworks deliver fresh and clean water, sewage works provide conduits to carry away wastewater. Although conduits constructed underground are not easily visible, the sewer system is mandatory to maintain sanitary and healthy conditions in a community. The wastewater contains high concentrations of organic matter, which, if untreated, causes significant harm to natural ecosystems and promotes outbreaks of various water-borne diseases. About 83.5 percent of Koreans (i.e., population in the wastewater works service area divided by the total population) benefited from the sewage system in 2005. However, the disparity between urban and rural areas is wide-88.4 percent for urban and only 35.8 percent for isolated rural areas.

Air Quality

Because of the rapid economic growth in the late 1900s, the air quality of large cities deteriorated significantly and the heat island phenomenon intensified in big cities including the Seoul Metropolitan Area. Numerous efforts have been made to improve air quality. As a result, concentrations of sulfurous acids, one of the major primary pollutants emitted from stacks of industrial factories, were decreased substantially. Data from air quality monitoring stations reveal that SO_2 continuously decreased from 1991. The concentrations of CO show the same trend as SO_2, Since 2000, the concentrations of SO_2, O_3, and NO_2 have remained at a relatively constant value. In some cities such as Gwangju, NO_2 concentration became slightly higher in the 2000s compared to the early 1990s. Nitrogen oxides (NOx), which are generated primarily from vehicle combustion systems, serve as precursor pollutants to the formation of tropospheric ozone, a pollutant which has increased in concentration in recent years. Although ozone in the stratosphere protects us from harmful ultraviolet radiation, in the troposphere it is toxic. In addition, Korea is involved in tackling several international atmospheric environmental issues, such as stratospheric ozone layer depletion, global warming, and Asian dust. Among the most frequently occurring problems in the air quality in recent years are Asian dust events during spring, tremendous increases in concentrations of particulate matter smaller than 2.5 micrometers, and high tropospheric ozone concentrations in the ambient atmosphere. A 2006 report on Korean air quality showed that days affected by Asian dust have increased in frequency and the days with ozone warnings decreased in 2005. For management of air quality, automatic monitoring systems have been installed nationwide, especially for large cities with severe air pollution problems.

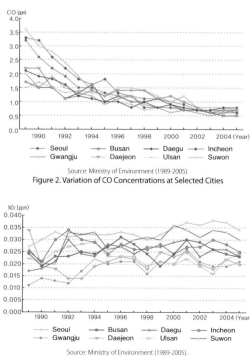

Source: Ministry of Environment (1989-2005).
Figure 2. Variation of CO Concentrations at Selected Cities

Source: Ministry of Environment (1989-2005).
Figure 3. Variation of NO₂ Concentrations at Selected Cities

Waste Treatment and Management

Wastes are defined as unwanted materials produced from everyday life and industrial activities, and can be listed as solid wastes, flammable materials, waste oils, waste acids and alkalis, and animal carcasses. The efficiency of waste disposal can be used as an indicator of national priority for environmental management. People produce various types of wastes during daily activities, including domestic, industrial, and specified wastes. The wastes generated from households are considered to be domestic wastes. Disposal usually occurs in sanitary landfills, by incineration, or through recycling. Disposal in landfills is complicated by the sociological phenomenon known as 'Not in My Back Yard.' Incineration of wastes is often opposed because of hazardous compounds generated during the combustion process. Therefore, recycling of waste is preferable and encouraged. Fortunately, recycling of domestic and industrial wastes was the most frequently-used waste disposal method in recent years, and its role has been increasing continuously. For domestic waste alone, the landfill was the main treatment option in 2001. However, by 2004, the recycling method was used to treat approximately 49 percent of the domestic waste. Waste generation cannot be avoided, so minimizing waste production and increasing waste recycling are major responsibilities of environmental managers.

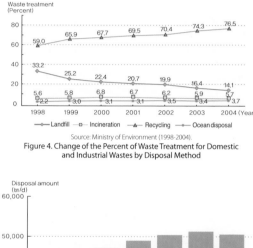

Source: Ministry of Environment (1998-2004).
Figure 4. Change of the Percent of Waste Treatment for Domestic and Industrial Wastes by Disposal Method

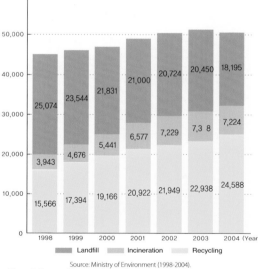

Source: Ministry of Environment (1998-2004).
Figure 5. Change of Amount of Waste by Disposal Method for Domestic Wastes

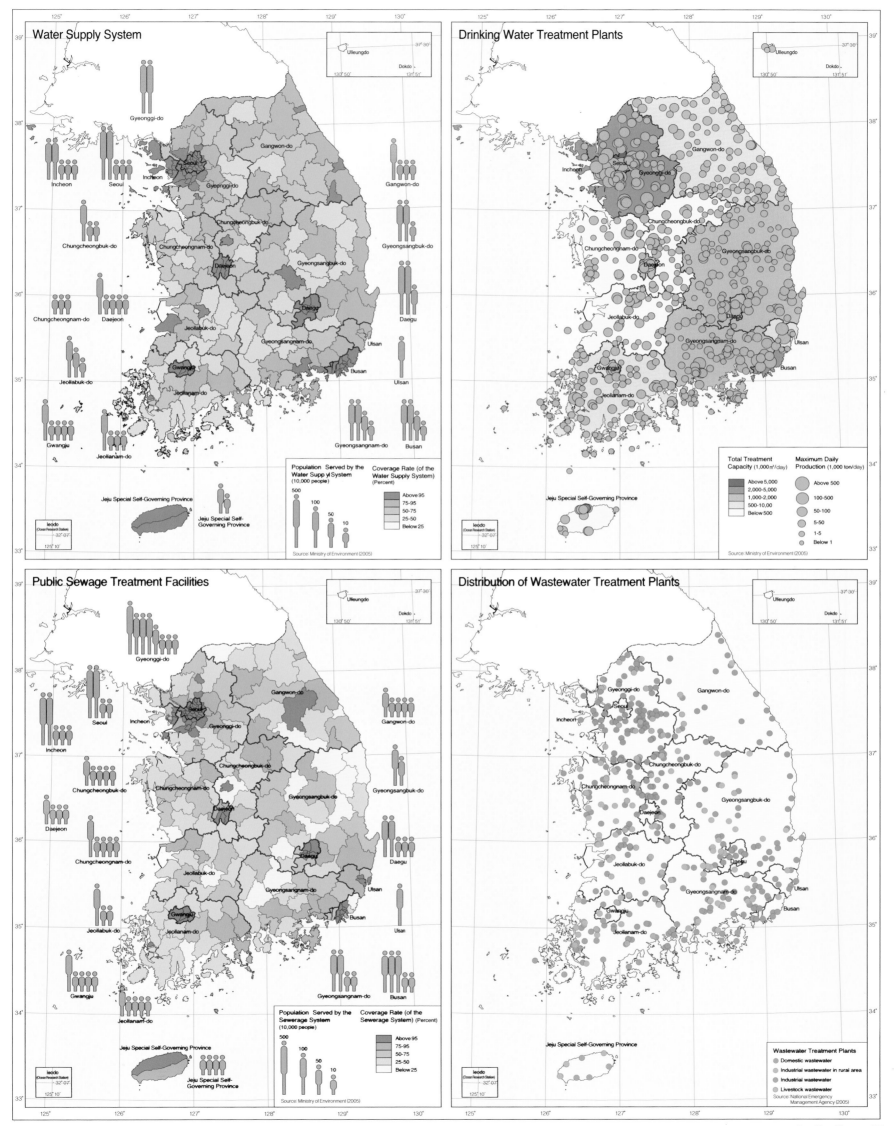

Water Supply System

Population Served by the
Water Supply System
(10,000 people)

500
100
50
10

Coverage Rate (of the
Water Supply System)
(Percent)

Above 95
75-95
50-75
25-50
Below 25

Source: Ministry of Environment (2005)

Drinking Water Treatment Plants

Total Treatment
Capacity (1,000㎥/day)

Above 5,000
2,000-5,000
1,000-2,000
500-10,00
Below 500

Maximum Daily
Production (1,000 ton/day)

Above 500
100-500
50-100
5-50
1-5
Below 1

Source: Ministry of Environment (2005)

Public Sewage Treatment Facilities

Population Served by the
Sewerage System
(10,000 people)

500
100
50
10

Coverage Rate (of the
Sewerage System) (Percent)

Above 95
75-95
50-75
25-50
Below 25

Source: Ministry of Environment (2005)

Distribution of Wastewater Treatment Plants

Wastewater Treatment Plants
Domestic wastewater
Industrial wastewater in rural area
Industrial wastewater
Livestock wastewater

Source: National Emergency
Management Agency (2005)

0   25   50   100 km

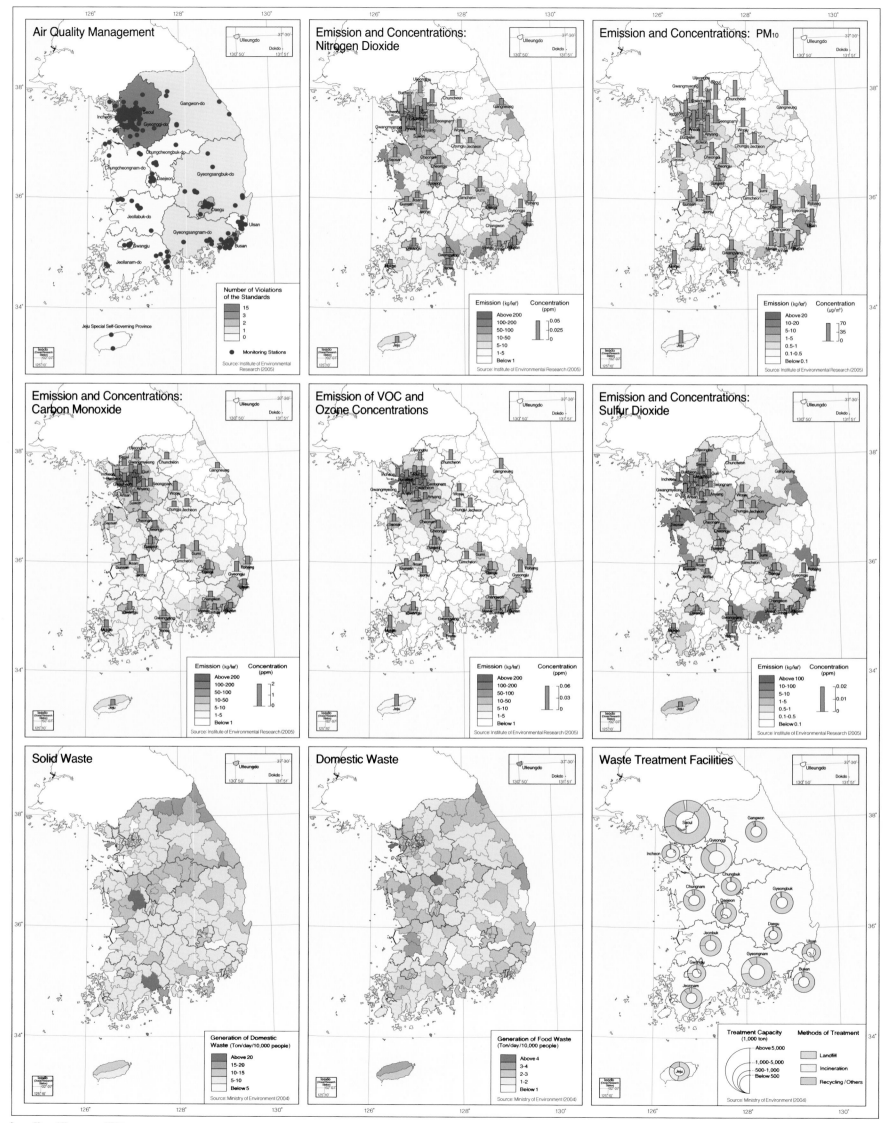

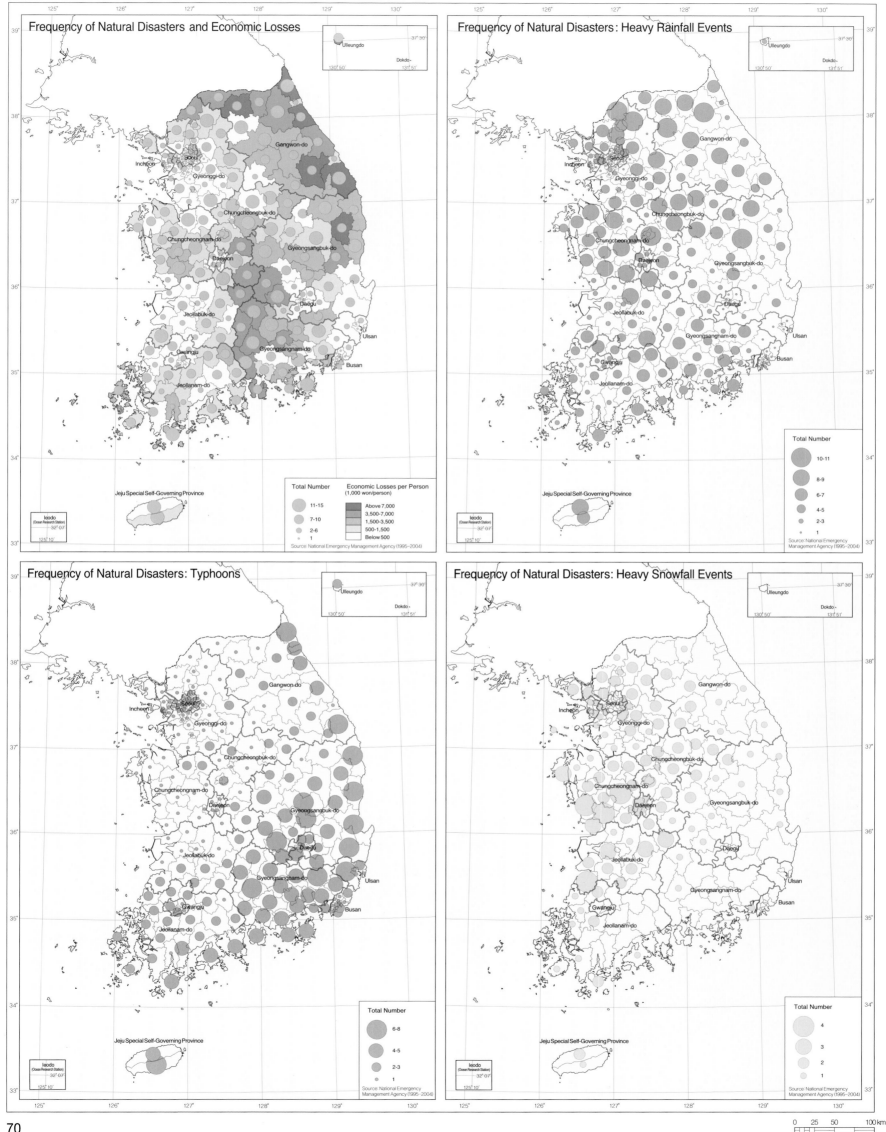

Frequency of Natural Disasters and Economic Losses

Total Number
11-15
7-10
2-6
1

Economic Losses per Person
(1,000 won/person)
Above 7,000
3,500-7,000
1,500-3,500
500-1,500
Below 500
Source: National Emergency Management Agency (1995~2004)

Frequency of Natural Disasters : Heavy Rainfall Events

Total Number
10-11
8-9
6-7
4-5
2-3
1
Source: National Emergency Management Agency (1995~2004)

Frequency of Natural Disasters: Typhoons

Total Number
6-8
4-5
2-3
1
Source: National Emergency Management Agency (1995~2004)

Frequency of Natural Disasters: Heavy Snowfall Events

Total Number
4
3
2
1
Source: National Emergency Management Agency (1995~2004)

0 25 50 100 km

Natural disasters include typhoons, floods, heavy rainfalls, strong winds, landslides, tsunami, heavy snowfalls, droughts, earthquakes, dust storms, and other disasters caused by natural phenomena (Article 2 of Counter-measures against Natural Disasters Act). During the 10-year period from 1995 to 2004, natural disasters caused 1,309 deaths and 19,247.7 billion won of property loss in Korea. Because of the abundant precipitation (about 1,300mm per year) and the hilly and mountainous terrain that covers more than 70 percent of Korea, streams flow rapidly. Therefore, most natural disasters in Korea are caused by hydrometeorological events such as heavy rainfalls and typhoons. The runoff often destabilizes the slopes, causing frequent landslides, in addition to the downstream flood. Such natural disasters are concentrated between June and September when two-thirds of the average annual precipitation falls.

Natural disasters can be exacerbated by human activities. Concrete pavement increases surface runoff at the expense of infiltration and natural drainage, and large-scale deforestation also increases the proportion of precipitation that goes into surface runoff. A general lack of public awareness of the impacts of development on the flood and landslide hazard only increases the damage done by natural disasters.

Some recent examples of such disasters were the devastating heavy rainfall events in Paju-*si*, and Yeoncheon-*gun* of northern Gyeonggi-*do* in July 1996, and in Seoul and the Gyeonggi-*do* in August 1998. Typhoon 'Rusa' in 2002 and 'Maemi' in 2003 made landfall along the eastern and southern coasts of Korea, causing 246 deaths and property losses of 5.1 trillion won for 'Rusa', and 132 deaths and 4.7 trillion won for 'Maemi'.

The damage caused by landslides in Korea is also concentrated in summer when the heavy rainfalls and typhoons occur. Over the past ten years, landslides have caused about 23.4 percent of all natural disaster fatalities in Korea, with about 32 deaths per year.

Snowfalls have caused about 1.7 trillion won in property damage over the 1995 to 2004 10-year period. The highest daily snowfall totals in recent years was 67.9cm in Gangneung and 56.0cm in Daegwallyeong in 1990. While snowfalls pose occasional problems, they occur only sporadically and are less destructive than other meteorologically-driven hazards described above.

Natural Disasters

A total of 1,355 natural disaster events occurred during the 10-year period from 1995 to 2004, with the highest frequencies of 15 events at Andong-*si*. Chuncheon-*si*, Samcheok-*si*, and Sancheong-*gun* experienced 14 occurrences over the same period. On the other hand, only one natural disaster occurred in Jung-*gu*, Seoul, and 27 other areas.

Of the 1,355 events, 836 were caused by heavy rainfall events. The most frequent heavy rainfall events occurred in Cheongwon-*gun* and Andong-*si*, with 11 occurrences each. Yeoncheon-*gun*, Pocheon-*si*, Chuncheon-*si*, and Inje each experienced 10 events. No heavy rainfall events occurred in Jung-*gu* and 20 other areas.

During the same time period, typhoons caused 415 natural disasters in Korea. The most frequently hit areas include Sancheong-*gun*, Goseong-*gun*, Pohang-*si*, and Gyeongju-*si*, with seven typhoon events at each area. Ulju-*gun*, Gunwi-*gun*, Uiseong-*gun*, Yeongdeok-*gun*, Seongju-*gun*, Miryang-*si*, and Sancheong-*gun* each experienced six typhoon events. By contrast, Jung-*gu*, Seoul, and 63 other areas did not experience a typhoon over the 10-year period.

Heavy snowfall events caused 179 disaster events, with Gongju-*si*, Boryeong-*si*, Buyeo-*gun*, and Gochang-*gun* being the most frequently hit areas (four events each). The second-most frequently affected areas were Seocheon-*gun*, Taean-*gun*,

Gimje-*si*, Jinan-*gun*, and Muju-*gun*, which were all hit three times over the same period. On the whole, relatively few areas are hit by heavy snowfalls compared to heavy rainfall events and typhoons.

Natural Disaster Fatalities

A total of 1,309 people, or about 130 persons per year, lost their lives in natural disasters during the 1995-2004 period. Of these, 41 percent resulted from heavy rainfall events, 39 percent from typhoons, and 12 percent from heavy storms during typhoons, respectively. Of the others, five percent were struck by lightning and two percent died in snowstorms.

A total of 584 deaths, or nearly 60 per year, were caused by heavy rainfall-induced flooding. Of these, 35 were in Paju-*si*, 34 in Seogwipo-*si*, 34 in Yangju-*si*, 29 in Sancheong-*gun*, 28 in Namyangju-*si*, and 27 in Dongducheon-*si*. Of the 573 fatalities, or about 60 per year, caused by typhoons, 57 occurred in Gangneung-*si*, with 50, 50, and 48 deaths in Gijang-*gun*, Yeosu-*si*, and Tongyeong-*si*, respectively. Of 246 deaths attributed to 'Rusa,' 53 were in Gangneung-*si*, with 25, 26, and 23 in Sancheong-*gun*, Gimcheon-*si*, and Yangyang-*gun*, respectively. Typhoon 'Maemi' claimed 131 lives.

Fortunately, the number of deaths caused by natural disasters has tended to decrease since 1998. When the largest number of people were killed in recent memory in 1998, 323 deaths were caused by rainstorms, with 57 caused by typhoons, and 1 by other natural disasters. Then, in 2002 when Typhoon 'Rusa' occurred, there were 247 deaths caused by typhoons and 23 caused by rainstorm. In 1995, 158 persons were killed, including 65 by rainstorms and typhoons, 47 directly by typhoons, 31 by windstorms, and 15 by flooding not associated with a rainstorm, respectively. The smallest number of natural disaster-related deaths in recent years occurred in 2004, when nine people were killed by a typhoon and five by rainstorms.

Property Damage Caused by Natural Disasters

Representative types of property damage include embankment and road loss, inundation of farmland, destruction of river structures, burial of homes, and loss of coastal facilities. Accordingly, the property damage caused by natural disasters mainly results from fast river streams and landslides caused by rainstorms or typhoons.

During the 1995 to 2004 period, property losses totaled 19.2 trillion won, or about 2 trillion won per year, in 2004 currency. Yearly damage varied greatly but in general it has increased since 1998, despite the decreasing trend in deaths, with at least 1 trillion won each year since 1998 except 2000.

About 58 percent of the property loss is caused by typhoons, with another 23 percent resulting from non-typhoon-related rainstorms, and an additional 11 percent for rainstorms during typhoons. The leading cause of property loss was rainstorms in 1996, 1997, and 1998, typhoons in 2002 and 2003, rainstorm/typhoon combinations in 1995, 1999, and 2000, heavy snowfalls in 2004, and windstorms/snowfalls in 2001. Over the 1995-2004 period, the most heavily-damaged region was Gangneung-*si*, which was subjected to about 1.7 trillion won of losses, or about 100 billion won per year. The least heavily damaged region was Gunpo-*si* with about 1.2 billion won per year in damage.

Total property damage for the 1995-2004 period caused by rainstorms was 5.3 trillion won, or more than 500 billion won per year. Cheongwon-*gun* had the worst damage at 249.2 billion won, followed by Gimhae-*si* at 221.1 billion and Paju-*si* at 208 billion. On the other hand, Gangdong-*gu*, Seoul, and other 21 regions had no property damage caused by rainstorms during 1995-2004.

Over the same period, total property damage caused by typhoons was 10.2 trillion won, with an average exceeding 1 tril-

lion won each year. The most heavily-damaged area was Gangneung-*si*, where more than 100 billion won per year in damage occurred. Samcheok-*si* was hit nearly as hard, with about 72 billion won per year of property damage. Typhoon 'Rusa' alone caused total property damage of 5.1 trillion won. The most damaged region was Gangneung-*si*, with property damage of 806.4 billion won during the 1995-2004 period, followed by Samcheok-*si* (477.7 billion won), Yangyang-*gun* (427.4 billion won), and Gimcheon-*si* (414.2 billion won). 'Maemi' caused property damage of 4.2 trillion won, with Gangneung-*si* hardest-hit at 233.7 billion won in damage estimates. Other hard-hit areas were Samcheok-*si* (225.1 billion won), Tongyeong-*si* (212.7 billion won), and Yeosu-*si* (198.1 billion won).

Flooded Areas Caused by Natural Disasters

Most natural disaster damage in Korea occurs from summer storms and floods. Total flooded areas for the 1995-2004 period were 578,904ha, or about 60,000ha per year. Fortunately, the areas experiencing flooding have tended to decrease over time in recent years, owing to mitigation efforts such as river projects and pumping facility installations.

Total flooded areas caused by rainstorms were about 2,898,791ha, or 30,000ha each year. 15,925ha of terrain flooded in Paju-*si*, followed by Dangjin-*gun* (12,889ha), Buyeo-*gun* (10,565ha), Cheorwon-*gun* (10,473ha), and Gimpo-*si* (9,418ha). Over the 10-year period, the total area flooded by typhoons was about 95,454ha. There was the inundation of 8,284ha in Jeju, followed by Naju-*si* (8,017ha), Sacheon-*si* (7,473ha), Miryang-*si* (6,943ha), Yeongam-*gun* (5,105ha), and Jinju-*si* (4,535ha). Total flooded areas caused by 'Rusa' were about 30,660ha. 'Rusa' flooded 8,284ha in Jeju, 3,302ha in Sacheon-*si*, and 1,560ha in Gwangyang-*si*. Total flooded areas caused by 'Maemi' were about 35,339ha. 'Maemi' flooded 6,498ha in Miryang-*si* alone, followed by 4,171ha in Sacheon-*si*, and 3,426ha in Changnyeong-*gun*.

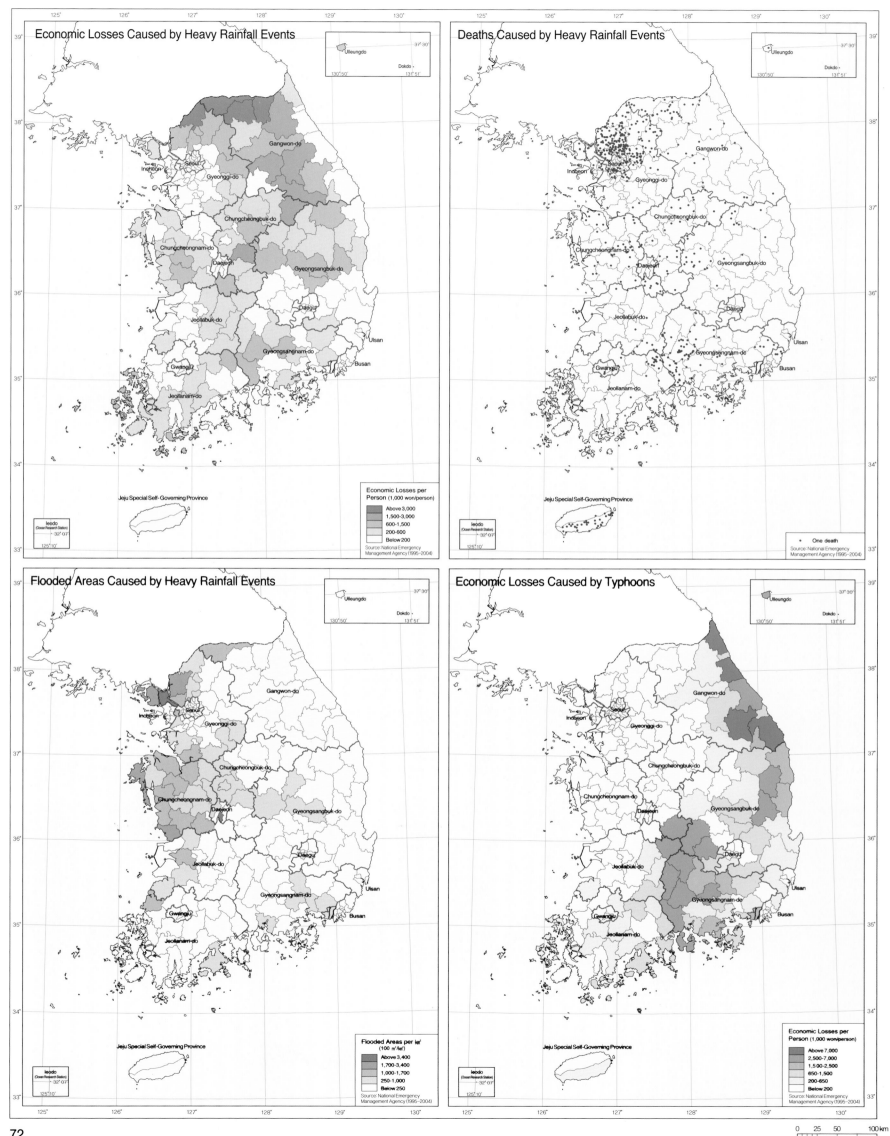

Economic Losses Caused by Heavy Rainfall Events

Deaths Caused by Heavy Rainfall Events

Economic Losses per
Person (1,000 won/person)

Above 3,000
1,500-3,000
600-1,500
200-600
Below 200

Source: National Emergency
Management Agency (1995~2004)

• One death

Source: National Emergency
Management Agency (1995~2004)

Flooded Areas Caused by Heavy Rainfall Events

Economic Losses Caused by Typhoons

Flooded Areas per ㎢
(100 ㎡/㎢)

Above 3,400
1,700-3,400
1,000-1,700
250-1,000
Below 250

Source: National Emergency
Management Agency (1995~2004)

Economic Losses per
Person (1,000 won/person)

Above 7,000
2,500-7,000
1,500-2,500
650-1,500
200-650
Below 200

Source: National Emergency
Management Agency (1995~2004)

0   25   50   100 km

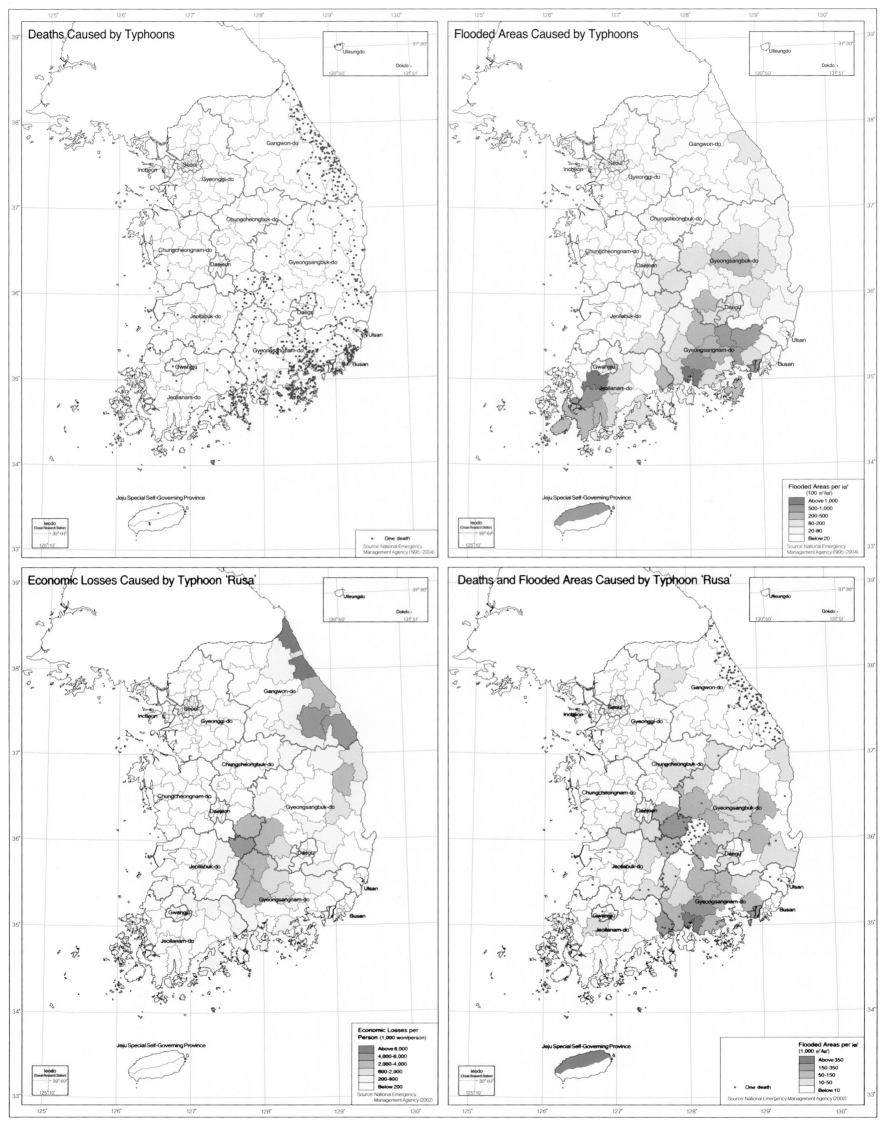

Deaths Caused by Typhoons

Flooded Areas Caused by Typhoons

Flooded Areas per km²
(100 m³/km²)
Above 1,000
500–1,000
200–500
80–200
20–80
Below 20

Source: National Emergency
Management Agency (1995–2004)

One death

Source: National Emergency
Management Agency (1995–2004)

Economic Losses Caused by Typhoon 'Rusa'

Deaths and Flooded Areas Caused by Typhoon 'Rusa'

Economic Losses per
Person (1,000 won/person)
Above 8,000
4,000–8,000
2,000–4,000
800–2,000
200–800
Below 200

Source: National Emergency
Management Agency (2002)

Flooded Areas per km²
(1,000 m³/km²)
Above 350
150–350
50–150
10–50
Below 10

One death

Source: National Emergency
Management Agency (2002)

0 25 50   100 km

FLORA AND VEGETATION

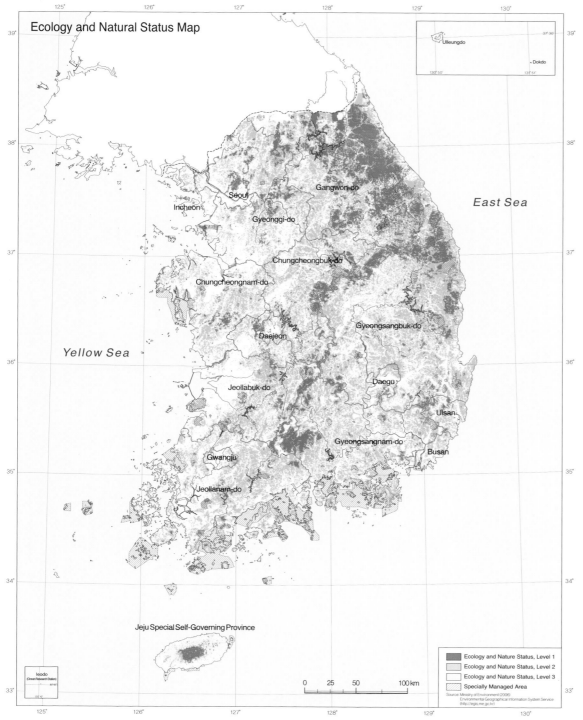

Ecology and Natural Status Map

Biota of Korea consists of 29,828 species, including fauna (18,029 species), flora (8,271 species), and 3,528 species of microorganisms and others. The number of higher plant species is 4,662, including 842 species of monocotyledon, 2,815 species of dicotyledon, and 314 species of ferns and conifers. Korean vascular plants, which are estimated to reach about 4,200 species in total, occupy two percent of the global floristic diversity of vascular plants.

Korean flora are characterized by rich diversity and high ratio of endemic plants, including endemic vascular genera, such as *Pentactina*, *Echinosophora*, *Abeliophyllum*, *Hanabusaya*, and *Megaleranthis*. Endemic plant genera are commonly found on scattered alpine and subalpine belts of northern and southern mountains, transitional zones of northern and southern flora in the central mountain region, remote mountains in the western coast, and isolated islands in the Korea Strait and South Sea, as well as the Yellow Sea.

The high floristic diversity of Korea may be due to several factors. First, the Korean Peninsula extends southward from Northeast Asia to Japan. This geographical characteristic enables Korea to accommodate diverse plants and animals. Second, mountains and hills which occupy more than 70 percent of Korean territory contribute to the diversity. Third, there is a major mountain range that runs from the north to the south, and connects to other mountain chains. Fourth, the presence of 3,400 islands provides a diverse geographical environment which accommodates diverse flora. Fifth, Korea has climatic variability, including the mean annual temperature of 16°C at Jejudo of the South Sea to 5°C at the Gaemagowon in North Korea. The nationwide mean annual precipitation ranges from

1,700mm at the southern coast to 400mm in the northern inland section of Korea. Various climatic zones from warm temperate to boreal climatic zones provide different conditions for diverse plants to grow. Sixth, there is a relatively low frequency of active volcanic and earthquake actions as well as an absence of extensive glacial activities. This secured the survival of the Tertiary flora, along with other conditions, such as very complex lithologic and soil systems. Finally, the Korean Peninsula, which has served as a migration route and refugia during both glacial and interglacial periods, has guaranteed the survival of both northern and southern flora.

Despite of the richness of Korean flora and vegetation, the ecosystem and biodiversity are declining, mainly because of anthropogenic disturbances and destruction. Each year about 67km² of the natural habitat of plants and animals, which occupies 0.1 percent of the Korean territory, has decreased by at least 43 species. For instance, *Cymbidium kanran*, *Aerides japonicum*, *Cypripedium japinicum*, *Ranunculus kazusensis*, *Cotoneaster wilsonii*, and *Diapensia lapponica* var. *obovata* are now endangered. At present, 151 plant and animal species, including 52 plant species are now legally protected.

Phyto-geographic Region

Based on the distribution of 204 evergreen broad-leaved plants, evergreen coniferous plants, and evergreen bamboos at 146 sample sites, eight phyto-geographic regions of the Korean Peninsula have been established by both quantitative and qualitative analyses. The Northern Alpine Region consists of 18 arctic-alpine and alpine evergreen broad-leaved plant species, along with four circumpolar and alpine evergreen coniferous plant species at 11 sample sites. The floristic composition

of this region may be linked to the existence of refugia during the past glacial periods. The segregation of arctic-alpine and alpine species toward the mountaintops (1,500m above sea level in height) might be due to upslope retreat from a former wider range since the Pleistocene.

The North-South Subalpine Region contains 15 northern evergreen coniferous plant species, 10 northern and southern evergreen broad-leaved plant species, and three evergreen bamboos, which covers 21 sites. A wide range of shrub and tree forms in this region, caused by an admixture of arctic-alpine, northern and southern species elements, infers a complex vegetational history along with a diverse present-day habitat condition.

The Midland Mountain Region contains 12 northern evergreen coniferous plant species, four evergreen broad-leaved plant species, and three evergreen bamboos, which covers 16 sites. This region is probably a major inland transitional zone of vegetation between the northern and southern floristic elements.

The Southern Mountain Region includes 15 northern and southern evergreen coniferous plant species, 12 southern evergreen broad-leaved plant species, and six southern evergreen bamboos, which covers 25 sites. The dominance of southern evergreen broad-leaved plant species, evergreen bamboos, and evergreen coniferous plants makes the region 'southern' in character.

The Midwestern Insular Region contains 10 southern evergreen broad-leaved plant species and five northern evergreen coniferous plant species, which covers 11 sites. The admixture of northern and southern floristic elements found within this region suggests that it is an insular transitional zone of vegetation between northern and southern elements.

The Southern Insular Region is comprised of 65 northern and southern evergreen broad-leaved plant species, with eight northern and southern evergreen coniferous plant species and four bamboos, which covers 11 sites. The presence of the largest number of southern evergreen broad-leaved plant species of all the phyto-geographic regions reflects the relatively warm and humid climatic conditions of the present-day. A disjunctive distribution of several arctic-alpine and alpine species, however, seems to indicate comparatively wider distribution for these species during the Pleistocene glaciation through the former land-bridge between the mainland and Jejudo.

The West-South-Eastern Insular and Associated Inland Region includes 28 southern evergreen broad-leaved plants, eight northern and southern evergreen coniferous plants, and five evergreen bamboos in 47 sites. Southern evergreen broad-leaved plants and evergreen bamboos are common in the insular and coastal areas, but northern evergreen coniferous plants occur more frequently in the inland areas.

The North-South Disjunctive Region containing three northern evergreen coniferous plants and two southern evergreen bamboos, comprises four sites. The region is characterized by a high proportion of endemics.

Horizontal Zonation of the Vegetation

Vegetational zonations, which are formed mainly by climate, soil, topography, anthropogenic influence, and other factors, can be classified into horizontal zones and vertical belts. Temperature, which varies with latitude and altitude, is the most important factor for the distribution of vegetational zonation in Korea. Four horizontal vegetation zones (evergreen broad-leaved vegetation zone, deciduous broad-leaved vegetation zone, mixed forests, and evergreen coniferous vegetation zone) can be observed in Korea.

The evergreen broad-leaved vegetation zone is a transitional zone between the tropical and warm temperate region, and is confined to south of 35 degrees north in the inland region and 35-30 degrees north in coastal and insular regions where the mean annual temperature remains over 14℃. In the evergreen broad-leaved vegetation zone, deciduous broad-leaved vegetation normally coexist with each other. Major tree species consist of *Quercus acuta, Quercus glauca, Quercus myrsinaefolia, Castanopsis cuspidata* var. *sieboldii, Cinnamomum camphora, Cinnamomum japonicum, Camellia japonica, Machilus thunbergii, Neolitsea sericea,* and *Euonymus japonica* as well as vines such as *Trachelospermum asiaticum* var. *intermedium, Kadsura japonica, Ficus stipulate,* and *Stauntonia hexaphylla.*

The evergreen broad-leaved vegetation zone includes more than four layers: i.e., a tall tree layer of *Castanopsis cuspidata* var. *sieboldii, Machilus thunbergii, Quercus acuta,* etc., a small tree layer of *Camellia japonica, Ilex integra, Neolitsea sericea,* etc., a shrub layer of shade tolerant *Aucuba japonica, Eurya japonica,* etc., and a herb layer of *Cymbidium goeringii, Liriope platyphylla, Trachelospermum asiaticum* var. *intermedium, Hedera rhombea,* and *Kadsura japonica.* Forests with multiple layers are often regarded as ecologically rich and stable.

Although the evergreen broad-leaved vegetation zone is located at the southern tip of the Korean Peninsula and islands, it is difficult to find evergreen broad-leaved vegetation there, mainly due to the continuous intervention and destruction by human. At present, the actual vegetation of the evergreen broad-leaved vegetation zone is composed of an anthropogenic secondary forest of deciduous broad-leaved trees, a mixed forest of deciduous broad-leaved trees, and evergreen coniferous trees.

The unprecedented presence of a large number of evergreen broad-leaved plants, along with deciduous broad-leaved plants, on the alpine and subalpine belts of both northern and southern parts of Korea needs further discussion in connection to both climate change during the Pleistocene period, and the present environment.

The disjunctive distribution of many arctic-alpine elements, such as *Dryas octopetala* var. *asiatica, Diapensia lapponica* var. *obovata, Empetrum nigrum* var. *japonicum, Ledum palustre* var. *angustum, Oxycoccus microcarpus, Oxycoccus quadripetalus, Phyllodoce coerulea, Vaccinium vitisidaea,* and *Linnaea borealis,* is a glacial relic of the Pleistocene Epoch. Other evergreen broad-leaved plants, for example, *Andromeda polifolia, Ledum palustre* var. *maximum, Rhododendron aureum, Rhododendron brachycarpum,* and others, occur on the alpine belt of northern Korea. These evergreen broad-leaved shrubs show excellent adapted morphological forms, for example, a creeping stem, and narrow, thick, hairy, and revolute leaves, for survival against the hostile alpine environment.

The deciduous broad-leaved vegetation zone occupies latitudes between 35 and 43° N, excluding an alpine belt, and major trees comprising the region are *Acer palmatum, Quercus mongolica, Quercus dentata, Quercus serrata, Quercus aliena, Betula platyphylla* var. *japonica, Zelkova serrata, Styrax japonica, Styrax obassia, Carpinus tschonoskii, Lindera erythrocarpa, Lindera obtusiloba,* and *Acer mono.* The deciduous broad-leaved vegetation zone belongs to the temperate climate region, and is subdivided into three zones on the basis of geographical location and vegetation composition.

Trees of the southern deciduous broad-leaved vegetation zone consist of mainly deciduous trees, such as *Carpinus tschonoskii, Lindera erythrocarpa, Meliosma myriantha, Pourthiaea villosa, Zanthoxylum schinifolium, Acerpalmatum, Sapium japonicum, Platycarya strobilacea,* and *Celtis sinensis,* along with evergreen broad-leaved tree. For instance, *Euonymus japonica, Euonymus fortunei* var. *radicans,* and *Daphniphyl-*

lum macropodum are present. Bamboos, e.g., *Phyllostachys bambusoides* and *Phyllostachys nigra* var. *henonis,* and evergreen coniferous trees, *Pinus densiflora, Pinus thunbergii,* and *Cephalotaxus koreana,* also coexist.

Trees of the central deciduous broad-leaved vegetation zone include *Zelkova serrata, Styrax japonica, Quercus mongolica, Quercus serrata, Quercus aliena, Quercus urticaefolia, Lindera obtusiloba,* and *Betula davurica.,* and grow with evergreen conifers, such as *Juniperus chinensis, Abies holophylla,* and *Pinus densiflora.* Pine is the dominant forest in this region, and mixed forests of *Quercus mongolica* and *Styrax japonica* are also common.

Trees of the northern deciduous broad-leaved vegetation zone contain deciduous trees, such as *Tilia amurensis, Tilia ovalis, Prunus maackii, Acer tegmentosum, Acer tschonoskii* var. *rubripes, Acer ukurunduense, Lonicera chrysanta* var. *crassipes, Betula schmidtii, Quercus mongolica, Corylus heterophylla* var. *thunbergii, Betula costata,* and *Syringa velutina* var. *kamibayashii* along with evergreen conifers, *Abies holophylla* and *Pinus koraiensis,* as well as the deciduous conifer, *Larix gmelinii.*

Mixed forests are more common in natural vegetation, but artificial forests often form single-species forests. Mixed forests are known to be helpful for the maintenance of biodiversity, landscape diversity, environmental conservation, and maintenance of high resistance against climatic change, forest fire, and environmental change. In the past, conifers have been planted for artificial forests. At present, mixed forests of conifers and deciduous broad-leaved trees are normally recommended.

The evergreen coniferous vegetation zone is found in the high plateau and alpine belt of northern Korea, in which the annual mean temperature remains below 5℃ and the January mean temperature is -12℃. Major trees of the evergreen coniferous vegetation zone include the cold-tolerant conifers, such as *Abies holophylla, Abies nephrolepis, Picea jezoensis, Picea koraiensis, Pinus koraiensis, Pinus pumila, Thuja koraiensis,* and *Taxus cuspidata,* and the deciduous conifers, *Larix gmelinii* and *Larix gmelinii* var. *olgensis,* as well as the deciduous broad-leaved trees, e.g., *Betula costata* and *Betula platyphylla.*

Due to extensive development and large scale forest fires, native conifer forests have been destroyed, and several deciduous trees, *Betula platyphylla* var. *japonica, Populus davidiana, Populus maximowiczii,* and *Ulmus davidiana* var. *japonica,* are found along with larch forests.

Vertical Zonation of the Vegetation
Korean mountain vegetation is divided into several zonations based on latitude and altitude. Altitudinal zonations from lowland to the mountaintop are as follows: a hill belt of evergreen broad-leaved trees or deciduous broad-leaved trees, a montane belt of deciduous broad-leaved trees or mixed forests of deciduous broad-leaved trees and evergreen coniferous trees, a subalpine belt of coniferous trees, and an alpine belt of shrubland, grassland, and tundra.

Distinct vegetational and zonal changes can be found at the subalpine belt, in which a forest limit or timberline occurs. The forest limit, from which upslope no commercially valuable timber is produced, normally takes place in a hostile environment, such as areas with low temperature, dry, windy climate, and poor soil conditions.

The transitional belt from the upper boundary of the forest limit to the lower boundary of the tree limit or tree line, where trees are absent, is normally called the subalpine belt. In the subalpine belt, *Abies koreana, Abies nephrolepis, Picea jezoensis,* and cold-tolerant *Pinus* spp. are dominant along with *Betula*

spp., *Andromeda* spp., *Rhododendron* spp., and others.

In the areas above the forest limit, there are alpine landscapes, such as wind-shaped trees, tree limits, krummholz or deformed shapes of dwarf trees, and tree islands, mainly because of the harsh climate, sterile soil, and hostile alpine environment. The area above the lower boundary of the tree limit is called an alpine belt and is normally dominated by arctic-alpine and alpine plants. The isolated occurrence of a large number of arctic-alpine and alpine plants growing on the Korean alpine belt, such as *Diapensia lapponica* var. *obovata, Empetrum nigrum* var. *japonicum, Dryas octopetala* var. *asiatica, Bistorta vivipara* and *Oxyria digyna,* is an indicator of existence of glacial refugia in the Korean Peninsula.

On the basis of height, the life forms of alpine plants are shrubs, and the height is less than 3 meters. The effect of dwarfing and the prostrate growth habit of arctic-alpine and alpine plants are important for the survival in a harsh alpine belt. It enables species to resist desiccation through the reduction of exposed shoots and inflorescence, and mechanical abrasion by wind, snow, ice crystal, and sand. Alpine plants have also coriaceous or leathery leaves, hairs on their leaves, and extensive root systems. These morphological adaptations give arctic-alpine and alpine plants a better chance to survive in a harsh environment.

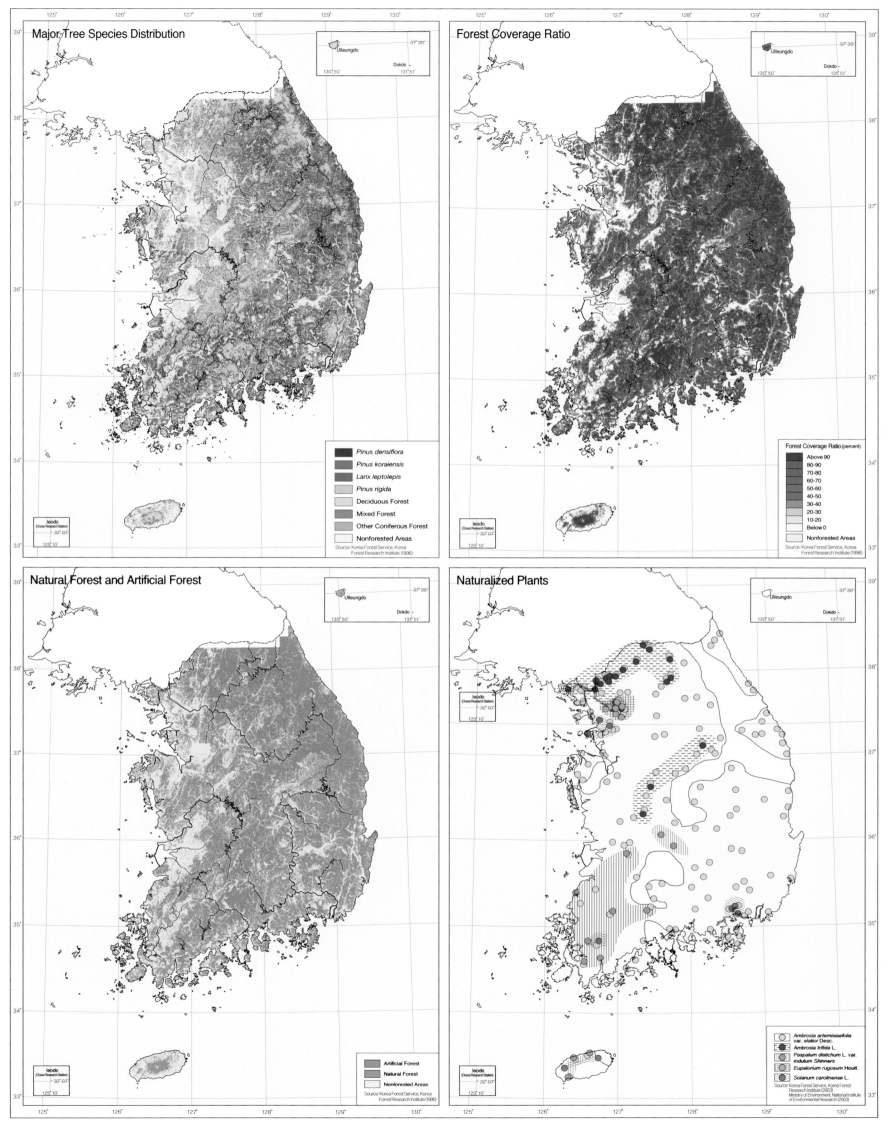

Major Tree Species Distribution

Pinus densiflora
Pinus koraiensis
Larix leptolepis
Pinus rigida
Deciduous Forest
Mixed Forest
Other Coniferous Forest
Nonforested Areas

Source: Korea Forest Service, Korea
Forest Research Institute (1996)

Forest Coverage Ratio

Forest Coverage Ratio (percent)
Above 90
80-90
70-80
60-70
50-60
40-50
30-40
20-30
10-20
Below 0
Nonforested Areas

Source: Korea Forest Service, Korea
Forest Research Institute (1996)

Natural Forest and Artificial Forest

Artificial Forest
Natural Forest
Nonforested Areas

Source: Korea Forest Service, Korea
Forest Research Institute (1996)

Naturalized Plants

Ambrosia artemisiaefolia
var. elatior Desc.
Ambrosia trifida L.
Paspalum distichum L. var.
indutum Shinners
Eupatorium rugosum Houtt.
Solanum carolinense L.

Source: Korea Forest Service, Korea Forest
Research Institute 2003
Ministry of Environment, National Institute
of Environmental Research 2003

0   25   50   100 km

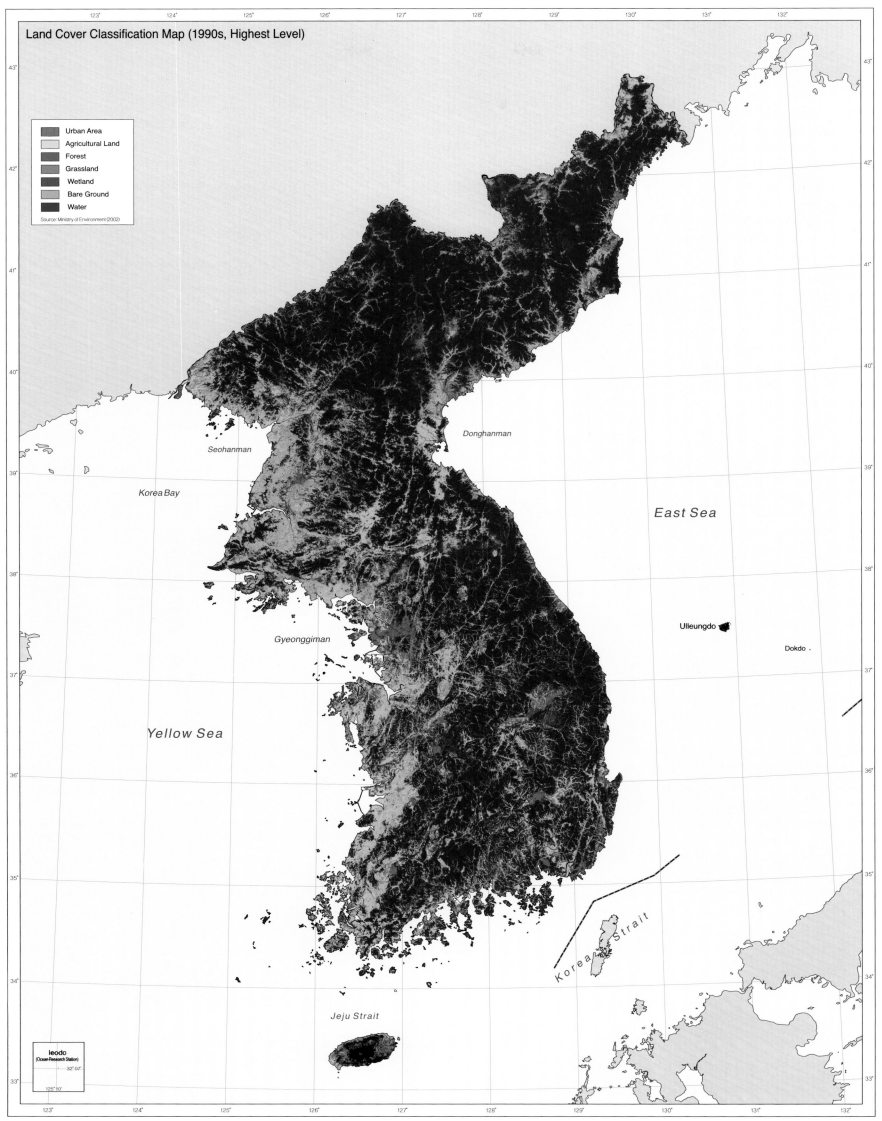

Land Cover Classification Map (1990s, Highest Level)

Urban Area
Agricultural Land
Forest
Grassland
Wetland
Bare Ground
Water

Source: Ministry of Environment (2002)

Donghanman

Seohanman

Korea Bay

East Sea

Ulleungdo

Dokdo

Yellow Sea

Gyeonggiman

Korea Strait

Jeju Strait

Ieodo
(Ocean Research Station)
32° 07'
125° 10'

1 : 4,000,000

0 25 50 100 km

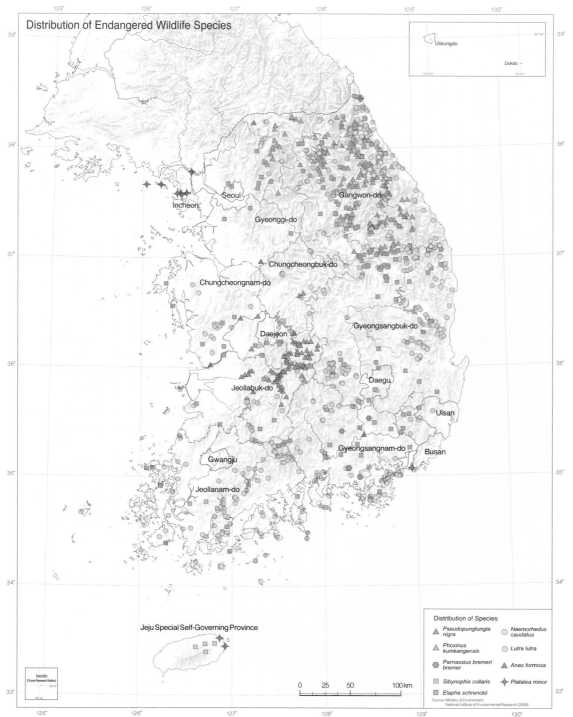

Distribution of Endangered Wildlife Species

Jeju Special Self-Governing Province

Distribution of Species

▲ Pseudopungtungia nigra
▲ Phoxinus kumkangensis
● Parnassius bremeri bremer
□ Sibynophis collaris
■ Elaphe schrenckii
○ Naemorhedus caudatus
○ Lutra lutra
▲ Anas formosa
◆ Platalea minor

Source: Ministry of Environment
National Institute of Environmental Research (2006)

Jejudo, a continental landmass lying 154km off the southwestern coast, was formerly connected to the Korean mainland in the Pleistocene Epoch, but has remained isolated for the past 10,000 years. Ulleungdo is an extinct oceanic volcano lying 145km off the eastern coast of the Korean Peninsula. Due to separation from the mainland, the avian faunas of Jejudo and Ulleungdo are vicariant fauna closely linked to those of the central and southern Japan and China.

To date, 457 species of birds have been recorded in Korea, and additional species are being added by professional ornithologists and amateur bird watchers. Of these, 60 species are permanent residents and about 300 species are migrants. Of the 124 bird species that regularly breed in Korea, 60 are indigenous and 64 are summer visitors. Eighteen species of birds are recorded only in North Korea. Of these, six are boreal residents of the high terrain of Baekdusan and the remaining 12 are vagrants. These include the black grouse (*Tetrao tetrix*), the northern hawk owl (*Surnia ulula*), the lesser spotted woodpecker (*Dendrocopos minor*), the three-toed woodpecker (*Picoides tridactylus*), Jankowski's bunting (*Emberiza jankowskii*), and the alpine accentor (*Prunella collaris*). However, the following three bird species are found only in the lowland areas of South Korea: the Japanese white-eye (*Zosterops japonicus*), the Japanese black wood pigeon (*Columba janthina*), and the russet sparrow (*Passer rutilans*).

Eight types of avian habitats are found in the Korean Peninsula, and each habitat is characterized by a different set of species at different seasons of the year. Typical residents of highland areas are the hazel grouse (*Tetrastes bonasia*), azure-winged magpie (*Cyanopica cyanus*), nutcracker (*Nucifraga caryocatactes*), and several species of tit and woodpecker. Lowland woods account a great number of species at all seasons. The bush warbler (*Cettia diphone*), Chinese grosbeak (*Eophona migratoria*), oriental turtle dove (*Streptopelia orientalis*), grey-headed bunting (*Emberiza fucata*), meadow bunting (*Emberiza cioides*), oriental greenfinch (*Chloris sinica*), jay (*Garrulus glandarius*), red-tailed shrike (*Lanius cristatus*), and common cuckoo (*Cuculus canorus*) are frequent species in this habitat. Much of the western and central regions are cultivated with rice, barley, and other crops. Common birds in this habitat include the ruddy-breasted crake (*Porzana fusca*), stonechat (*Saxicola torquata*), skylark (*Alauda arvensis*), and crested lark (*Galerida cristata*). A great number of buntings occur in agricultural fields during autumn migration. These include the black-faced bunting (*Emberiza spodocephala*), yellow-breasted bunting (*Emberiza aureola*), chestnut bunting (*Emberiza rutila*), Tristram's bunting (*Emberiza tristrami*), meadow bunting (*Emberiza cioides*), and rustic bunting (*Emberiza rustica*).

Coastal areas, beaches, and estuaries are the major habitats for sojourning migratory birds including several species of plover, gulls, geese, ducks, herons, cranes, the dunlin (*Erolia alpina*), red-necked stint (*Erolia ruficollis*), sanderling (*Crocethia alba*), Terek sandpiper (*Xenus cinereus*), and spoon-billed sandpiper (*Eurynorhynchus pygmeus*).

The black-tailed gull (*Larus crassirostris*), common cormorant (*Phalacrocorax carbo*), Temminck's cormorant (*Phalacrocorax capillatus*), pelagic cormorant (*Phalacrocorax pelagicus*) and ancient murrelet (*Synthliboramphus antiquus*) are common breeding birds of rocky cliffs on the coast. The fan-tailed warbler (*Cisticola juncidis*) and fairy pitta (*Pitta brachyura*) occur in the largest island, Jejudo. Another local island bird, the Japanese black wood pigeon (*Columba janthina*), occurs on Ulleungdo and a few islands off the south coast.

There are several kinds of wetland habitats in Korea, and a great diversity of birds is associated with these environments. During winter, many species of duck, grebes, divers, gulls, and murrelets occur on the open sea off the south coast. Small flocks of goosander (*Mergus merganser*), goldeneye (*Bucephala clangula*), and little grebe (*Podiceps ruficollis*) are also found in the areas. The magpie, sparrow, and swallow are major birds of urban areas.

Mammals

Korean mammals are subdivided into a total of eight orders, 27 families, and 124 species. Six of the orders comprising 19 families, and 83 species are terrestrial mammals, whereas two orders comprising 41 species are marine mammals. Among these, 17 species are confined to North Korea. However, a recent survey indicated that three species-the Eurasian lynx (*Lynx*

The Korean Peninsula is bordered along three sides with a highly irregular coastline. There are more than 3,000 islands and islets off the coast, with most of them lying in the southwest. Because of the Korean Peninsula's long north-south extent and topographic complexity, there are broad variations in temperature and rainfall. Such diversified environmental conditions are correlated to the great diversity of wildlife in the country.

The number of wild animal and plant species of Korea is estimated at about 100,000, but currently only 18,118 species have been recorded systematically. These include 124 species of mammals, 457 species of birds, 43 species of reptiles and amphibians, 905 species of fish (709 species of marine fish, 196 species of freshwater fish), 11,853 species of insects, 1,172 species of spiders, and 3,564 species of other invertebrates.

Table 1. Number of Animal Species Native to Korea

(Unit: species)

Animal Group	Taxa	Number of Species
Vertebrates	Mammals	124
	Birds	457
	Reptiles and Amphibians	42
	Fish	905
Invertebrates	Sponges, Bryozoa, Arthroprds	3,564
	Insects	11,853
	Spiders	1,172

Source: Ministry of Environment, National Institute of Environmental Research (2006).

Although Korea has a peninsular connection to the remainder of northeast Asia, it is nevertheless isolated ecologically by three barriers – the high mountain terrain of Baekdusan in the northeast, the Amnokgang River in the northwest, and the Dumangang River in the northeast. These function as geographic

barriers limiting the dispersal of wildlife into Korea from the surrounding regions of China and Russia. As a result, the Korean Peninsula contains a rich assortment of endemic and native species not found naturally anywhere else in the world. Due to the nature of these barriers, a greater proportion of endemic species is found among the freshwater fish and insects than in other animal taxa. Among the vertebrates, fiftynine species of freshwater fish, five species of amphibians, one species of reptile, and two species of mammals are endemic to Korea.

Birds

Although the Korean Peninsula is part of the Palaearctic zoogeographical realm, its fauna consists of a mixture of both Palaearctic (northeast China, Manchuria and Siberia), and Oriental (southern China) taxa. Geographically, the Korean Peninsula is divided into two regions, the northern highlands and the southern lowlands. The northern highland areas are composed of the northeastern portion of the peninsula, the Gaemagowon and adjacent mountains in the north-central part, and extend southward along the high mountain ranges of the east coast to the northern portion of the Taebaksanmaek. The northern portion of the peninsula has an avian fauna more reminiscent of that of Siberia and Manchuria. The southern lowland areas that comprise the remaining portions of Korea not encompassed by the northern highlands include the lowlands of the northwest, and the central and southern parts of the Korean Peninsula. The lowlands are characterized with mild climate, broad-leaved deciduous forests and mixed forests. The avian fauna in these areas is more similar to that of east China and Honsu of Japan.

Two major islands of special interest are Jejudo and Ulleungdo.

lynx), least weasel (*Mustela nivalis*), and Eurasian water shrew (*Neomys fodiens*)-formerly restricted to North Korea but occur in both northern and southern regions. Of the 83 species listed in the Korean Peninsula, 64 species occur in both northern highland and southern lowland areas, and 17 species inhabit only the northern highland areas. The remaining two species occur only on Jejudo.

The communities of Korean mammals are distributed according to habitat characteristics. The following kinds of mammals are typical at the highland environments: the Siberian tiger (*Panthera tigris*), Amur leopard (*Panthera pardus*), Eurasian lynx (*Lynx lynx*), brown bear (*Ursus arctos*), Asiatic black bear (*Ursus thibetanus*), Eurasian badger (*Meles meles*), least weasel (*Mustela nivalis*), yellow-throated marten (*Martes flavigula*), Amur goral (*Nemorhaedus goral*), musk deer (*Moschus moschiferus*), roe deer (*Capreolus pygargus*), Eurasian water shrew (*Neomys fodiens*), and northern pika (*Ochotona hyperborea*). Occurring in mixed coniferous and deciduous forests are the leopard cat (*Prionailurus bengalensis*), red fox (*Vulpus vulpus*), Siberian weasel (*Mustela sibirica*), raccoon dog (*Nyctereutes procyonoides*), wild boar (*Sus scrofa*), red squirrel (*Sciurus vulgaris*), Siberian flying squirrel (*Pteromys volans*), Korean hare (*Lepus coreanus*), and Manchurian (*Amur*) hedgehog (*Erinaceus amurensis*). Lowland environments support a mammalian community that includes a number of species associated with riparian habitats including the Chinese water deer (*Hydropotes inermis*), greater mole (*Mogera robusta*), Siberian chipmunk (*Tamias sibirica*), striped field mouse (*Apodemus agrarius*), Korean field mouse (*Apodemus peninsulae*), reed vole (*Microtus fortis*), Chinese striped hamster (*Cricetulus barabensis*), and the lesser white-toothed shrew (*Crocidura suaveolens*). Streams, rivers, lakes, and coastal areas are the major habitat of Eurasian otter (*Lutra lutra*).

Seventeen species of terrestrial mammals of Jejudo consist dominantly of species that arrived there from the mainland during the Pleistocene. An endemic species-the Jeju striped field mouse (*Apodemus chejuensis*)-and four endemic subspecies, Siberian weasel (*Mustela sibirica quelpartis*), Old World harvest mouse (*Micromys minutus hertigi*), greater horseshoe bat (*Rhinolophus ferrumequinum*), and lesser white-toothed shrew (*Crocidura dsinezumi quelpartis*) are fairly distinct from similar species occurring on the adjacent Korean mainland. The non-volant mammalian fauna of Ulleungdo is composed of only four species which probably were introduced accidentally from the mainland. These include lesser white-toothed shrew (*Crocidura suaveolens*), house mouse (*Mus musculus*), roof rat (*Rattus rattus*), and Norway rat (*Rattus norvegicus*).

Amphibians and Reptiles
Eighteen species of amphibians and 27 species of reptiles have been recorded in Korea. Of these, leatherback turtle (*Dermochelys coriacea*), loggerhead sea turtle (*Caretta caretta*), green turtle (*Chelonia mydas*), slender-necked sea snake (*Hydrophis melanocephalus*), and yellow-bellied sea snake (*Pelamis platurus*) are restricted to marine habitats. Two species of snakes-the Korean beauty snake (*Elaphe taeniura*) and common adder (*Vipera berus*)-occur only in North Korea. Only two species of native freshwater turtles-the Chinese soft-shell turtle or mud slider (*Pelodiscus sinensis*) and Reeve' turtle (*Chinemys reevesii*)-are found in the Korean Peninsula. Eleven snake species have been reported in South Korea including the short-tailed mamushi (*Gloydius brevicaudus*), red-tongue viper (*Gloydius ussuriensis*), short-tailed viper (*Gloydius saxatilis*), Korean rat snake (*Elaphe schrenckii*), cat snake (*Elaphe dione*), red-banded odd-tooth snake (*Dinodon rufozonatus*), Asian keelback snake (*Amphiesma vibakari*), water snake (*Elaphe rufodorsata*), black-headed snake (*Sibynophis collaris*), tape snake (*Zamenis spinalis*), and tiger keelback snake (*Rhabdophis tigrinus*). In addition, three amphibian species-the Suwon treefrog (*Hyla suweonensis*), Gori salamander (*Hynobius yangi*) and Jeju salamander (*Hynobius quelpartensis*)-are endemic species of Korea.

Freshwater Fish
A total of 196 species of freshwater fish are reported in Korea, of which 25 percent (59 species) are considered endemic. Among endemic, families *Cyprinidae* and *Cobitidae* comprise 33 species and 13 species, respectively, and five species only occur in North Korea. Endemism of Korean freshwater fish is very high at 25 percent compared with other taxa because freshwater ecosystems of Korea have been isolated by high mountain terrains of northeast Asia. Consequently, endemic

species have become uniquely adapted to the constraints of local habitats.

Freshwater fish of Korea can be placed in three major biomes. Euryhaline taxa including salmon (*Onchorhynchus keta*), sea rundace (*Tribolodon hakonensis*), river puffer (*Takifugu obscurus*), three-spined stickleback (*Gasterosteus aculeatus*), common mullet (*Mugil cephalus*), and arctic or Japanese lamprey (*Lethenteron [Lampetra] japonica*) inhabit in both freshwaters and the ocean. Among strictly freshwater taxa, the Geumgang fat minnow (*Rhynchocypris kumgangensis*), Amur minnow (*Rhynchocypris steindachneri*), Manchurian trout (*Brachymystax lenok*), torrent catfish (*Liobagrus andersoni*), Korean splendid dace (*Coreoleuciscus splendidus*), black shinner (*Pseudopungtungia nigra*), and the spotted barbel (*Hemibarbus mylodon*) occur only in the upper portions of watersheds, whereas pale chub (*Zacco platypus*), crucian carp (*Carassius auratus*), common carp (*Cyprinus carpio*), striped shinner (*Pungtungia herzi*), and slender bitterling (*Acheilognathus lanceolatus*) are found in the middle portions of watersheds.

Insects
Although 491 families, 4,658 genera, and 11,853 species of insects are recorded in Korea, these figures represent only about 20 percent of an estimated 50,000 insect species in the country. The Order *Hemiptera* contains 596 species; 75 percent of which are from the Palearctic realm, 20 percent from the Oriental realm, and 5 percent are endemic to Korea. Among the Order *Lepidoptera*, 264 species of butterflies have been recorded in Korea, 80 percent of which are Paleartic and only 20 percent are Oriental.

Conservation and Management of Endangered Species
Two Korean ministries are concerned on the management and conservation of wildlife. The authority to list species as endangered is shared by the Cultural Heritage Administration, which is responsible for designation of Natural Monuments, and the Ministry of Environment, which administers the listing of all endangered plants and animals. Designation as a Natural Monument is determined by criteria including historical, natural and scientific value, inherent and international rarity, and aesthetic qualities. Therefore, the designation Natural Monument is interpreted to include the species itself as well as major habitats, breeding area, and migration routes. Species that are currently classified as Natural Monument are musk deer, mountain goral, Russian flying squirrel, Asiatic black bear, Eurasian otter, spotted seal, Hodgson's bat, and 46 species of birds.

The designation 'endangered species' means that a species is in jeopardy of extinction through all or a significant portion of its range due to natural or human-related activities. Currently, 61 species of birds, 22 species of mammals, 2 species of amphibians, 4 species of reptiles and 18 species of freshwater fish have been placed on the endangered list (Table 2).

Table 2. Endangered Species of Wildlife in Korea
(Unit: species)

Taxa	Endangered Species Category I	Endangered Species Category II	Total Numbers of Species
Mammals	12	10	22
Birds	13	48	61
Amphibians and Reptiles	1	5	6
Fish	6	12	18
Insects	5	15	20

Source: Ministry of Environment, National Institute of Environmental Research (2005).

Recovery Plan for Endangered Species
A recovery plan for an endangered species is the process by which the decline of its numbers would be reversed, and threatening factors removed or reduced to ensure long-term survival of animals in the wild. Recovery plans for the Asiatic black bear (*Ursus thibetanus*), musk deer (*Moschus moschiferus*), white stork (*Ciconia boyciana*), black shinner (*Pseudopungtungia nigra*), bullhead torrent catfish (*Liobagrus obesus*), and wind orchid (*Neofinetia falcata*) have been developed. Among these , proposals for the Asiatic black bear and Oriental white stork adopted by the Ministry of Environment were the first official recovery plan for endangered species and have since served as the prototype.

The Asiatic black bear once occupied virtually all mountainous areas from the northeastern and northwestern to the east-central southwestern portions of the Korean Peninsula. Humans played a major role in bringing about the decline of Korea's bear population. Today, the bear has become extremely rare throughout the Korean Peninsula and has been classified as a

Natural Monument since 1982. In 2004, the Ministry of Environment began a translocation program in the Jirisan National Park with the release of six bears received from Russia. Eight bears from North Korea and another six bears from Russia were also released in 2005. More than 50 bears will be released in the park each fall from 2007 through 2012.

The Oriental white stork is listed as a critically endangered species by the International Union for Conservation of Nature (IUCN), and the remnant population is estimated as less than 5,000 individuals in the Amur River basin of Russia. Now in its eleventh year, the recovery plan for the Oriental white stork was initiated in 1996 when two juvenile white storks from Russia and two male storks from Germany, were delivered to the recovery center in Korea. In the following year, two male white storks from Toyooka, Japan, as well as two male and two female white storks from Germany were also received. During the spring of 1999, white stork eggs from Japan hatched, and in April of 2002, the hatchlings were successfully bred in an artificial environment at the recovery center. During the spring of 2003, female and male white storks successfully raised juveniles at the center and prepared for eventual release by exposure training. In the near future, the birds will be transported to their historical habitat where training will continue prior to their release.

Habitat Conservation and Management
Korea has designated areas that are ecologically valuable as protected areas. These areas include national parks, ecosystem and landscape conservation areas, wildlife protection areas, wetland conservation areas, and special island areas (Table 3). Measures are being taken in these areas to prevent further ecological degradation.

Table 3. Types of Protected Areas
(Unit: species)

Type	Area (m²)	No. of Sites
National Parks	6,144	20
Ecosystem and Landscape Conservation Area	293,545	27
Wetland Conservation Areas	186,594	15
Wildlife Protection Areas	1,418	545
Special Islands	10	153

Source: Ministry of Environment, National Institute of Environmental Research (2006).

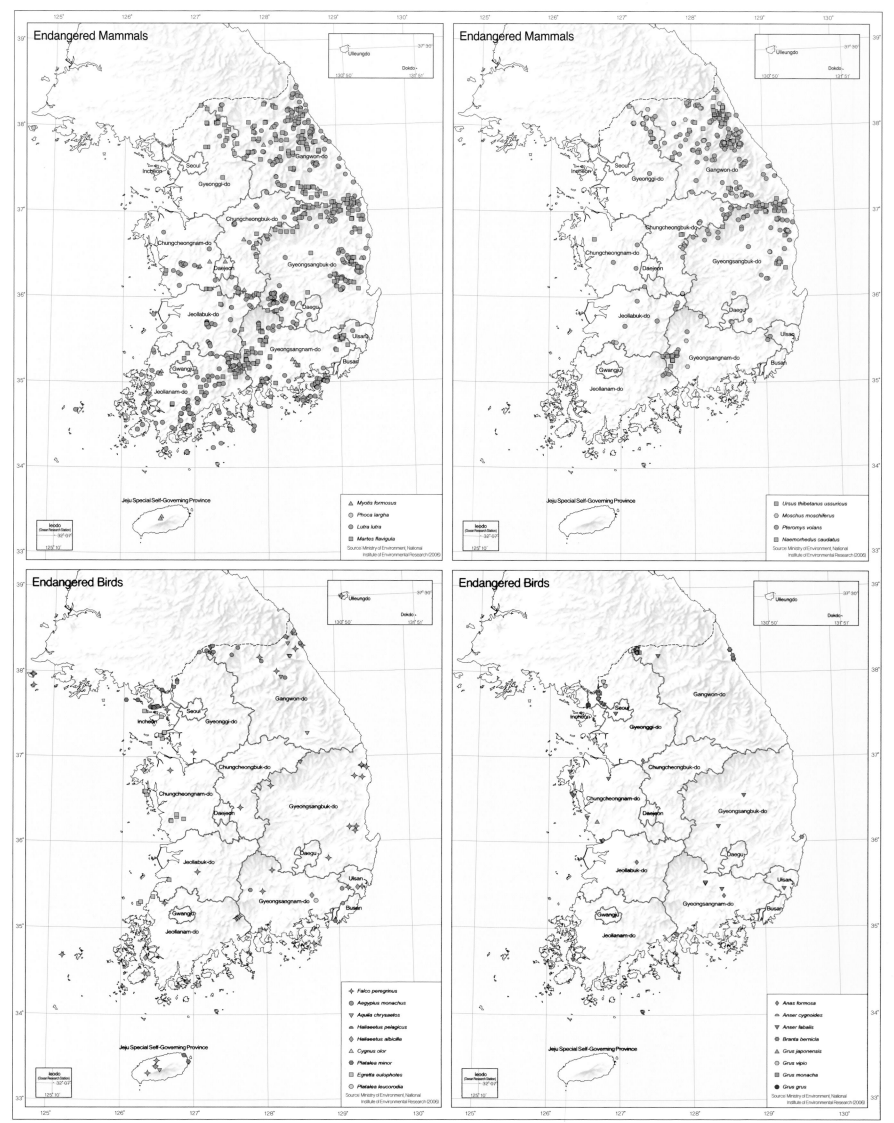

Endangered Mammals

Endangered Mammals

- △ Myotis formosus
- ○ Phoca larpha
- ● Lutra lutra
- ▦ Martes flavigula

Source: Ministry of Environment, National
Institute of Environmental Research (2006)

- ▦ Ursus thibetanus ussuricus
- ● Moschus moschiferus
- ◉ Pteromys volans
- ▦ Naemorhedus caudatus

Source: Ministry of Environment, National
Institute of Environmental Research (2006)

Endangered Birds

Endangered Birds

- ✦ Falco peregrinus
- ● Aegypius monachus
- ▽ Aquila chrysaetos
- ◠ Haliaeetus pelagicus
- ◈ Haliaeetus albicilla
- △ Cygnus olor
- ● Platalea minor
- ▦ Egretta eulophotes
- ○ Platalea leucorodia

Source: Ministry of Environment, National
Institute of Environmental Research (2006)

- ✦ Anas formosa
- ◠ Anser cygnoides
- ▽ Anser fabalis
- ✿ Branta bernicla
- △ Grus japonensis
- ○ Grus vipio
- ▦ Grus monacha
- ● Grus grus

Source: Ministry of Environment, National
Institute of Environmental Research (2006)

0   25   50   100 km

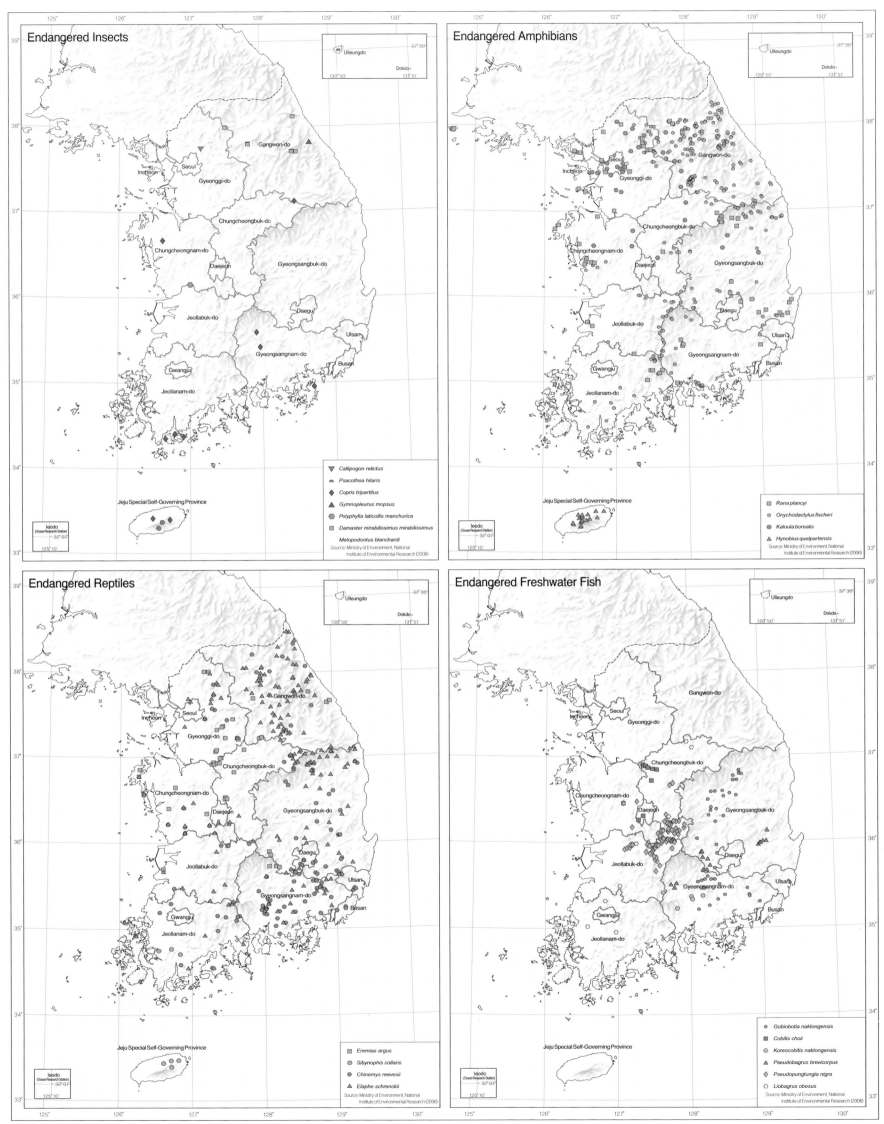

Endangered Insects

Callipogon relictus
Psacothea hilaris
Copris tripartitus
Gymnopleurus mopsus
Polyphylla laticollis manchurica
Damaster mirabilissimus mirabilissimus
Metopodontus blanchardi

Source: Ministry of Environment, National
Institute of Environmental Research (2006)

Endangered Amphibians

Rana plancyi
Onychodactylus fischeri
Kaloula borealis
Hynobius quelpartensis

Source: Ministry of Environment, National
Institute of Environmental Research (2006)

Endangered Reptiles

Eremias argus
Sibynophis collaris
Chinemys reevesii
Elaphe schrenckii

Source: Ministry of Environment, National
Institute of Environmental Research (2006)

Endangered Freshwater Fish

Gobiobotia naktongensis
Cobitis choii
Koreocobitis naktongensis
Pseudobagrus brevicorpus
Pseudopungtungia nigra
Liobagrus obesus

Source: Ministry of Environment, National
Institute of Environmental Research (2006)

0 25 50   100 km

ANIMALS

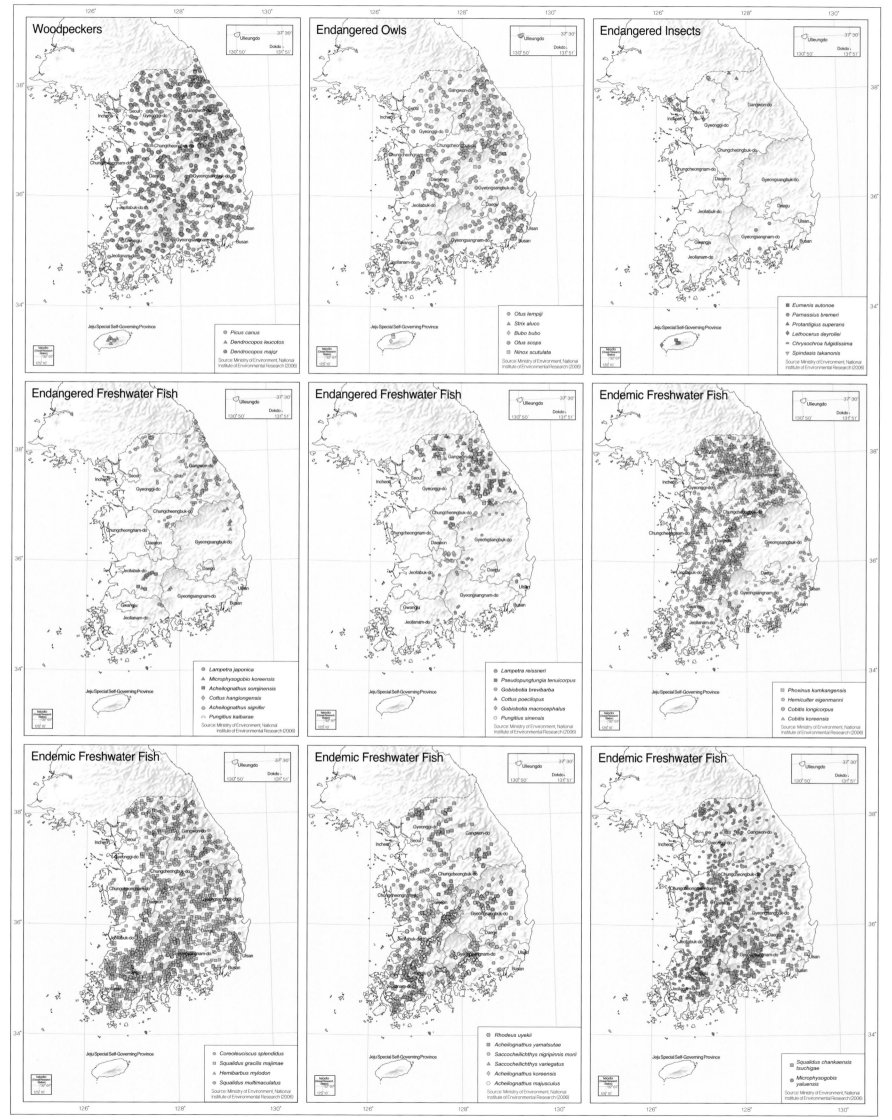

Woodpeckers

Picus canus
Dendrocopos leucotos
Dendrocopos major

Source: Ministry of Environment, National Institute of Environmental Research (2006)

Endangered Owls

Otus lempiji
Strix aluco
Bubo bubo
Otus scops
Ninox scutulata

Source: Ministry of Environment, National Institute of Environmental Research (2006)

Endangered Insects

Eumenis autonoe
Parnassius bremeri
Protantigius superans
Lethocerus deyrollei
Chrysochroa fulgidissima
Spindasis takanonis

Source: Ministry of Environment, National Institute of Environmental Research (2006)

Endangered Freshwater Fish

Lampetra japonica
Microphysogobio koreensis
Acheilognathus somjinensis
Cottus hangiongensis
Acheilognathus signifer
Pungitius kaibarae

Source: Ministry of Environment, National Institute of Environmental Research (2006)

Endangered Freshwater Fish

Lampetra reissneri
Pseudopungtungia tenuicorpus
Gobiobotia brevibarba
Cottus poecilopus
Gobiobotia macrocephalus
Pungitius sinensis

Source: Ministry of Environment, National Institute of Environmental Research (2006)

Endemic Freshwater Fish

Phoxinus kumkangensis
Hemiculter eigenmanni
Cobitis longicorpus
Cobitis koreensis

Source: Ministry of Environment, National Institute of Environmental Research (2006)

Endemic Freshwater Fish

Coreoleuciscus splendidus
Squalidus gracilis majimae
Hemibarbus mylodon
Squalidus multimaculatus

Source: Ministry of Environment, National Institute of Environmental Research (2006)

Endemic Freshwater Fish

Rhodeus uyekii
Acheilognathus yamatsutae
Saccocheilichthys nigripinnis morii
Saccocheilichthys variegatus
Acheilognathus koreensis
Acheilognathus majusculus

Source: Ministry of Environment, National Institute of Environmental Research (2006)

Endemic Freshwater Fish

Squalidus chankaensis tsuchigae
Microphysogobis yalunensis

Source: Ministry of Environment, National Institute of Environmental Research (2006)

0   50   100   200 km

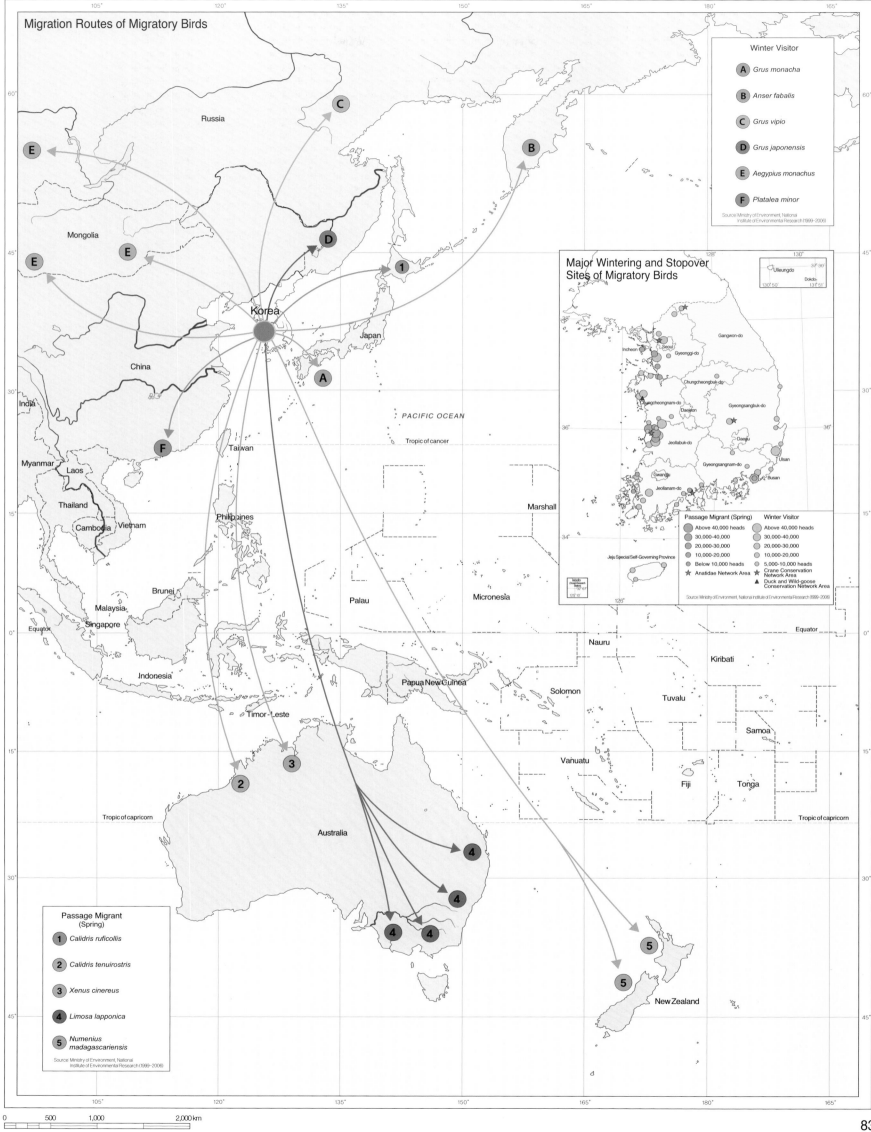

Migration Routes of Migratory Birds

Russia

Mongolia

China

India

Myanmar

Laos

Thailand

Cambodia

Vietnam

Malaysia

Singapore

Indonesia

Philippines

Brunei

Taiwan

Korea

Japan

PACIFIC OCEAN

Tropic of cancer

Brunei

Palau

Micronesia

Marshall

Nauru

Kiribati

Equator

Papua New Guinea

Solomon

Tuvalu

Samoa

Timor-Leste

Vanuatu

Fiji

Tonga

Tropic of capricorn

Australia

New Zealand

Winter Visitor

A *Grus monacha*

B *Anser fabalis*

C *Grus vipio*

D *Grus japonensis*

E *Aegypius monachus*

F *Platalea minor*

Source: Ministry of Environment, National
Institute of Environmental Research (1999–2006)

Major Wintering and Stopover Sites of Migratory Birds

Ulleungdo

Dokdo

Incheon Seoul Gyeonggi-do Gangwon-do

Chungcheongbuk-do

Chungcheongnam-do Daejeon Gyeongsangbuk-do

Jeollabuk-do Daegu

Gyeongsangnam-do Ulsan

Gwangju Busan

Jeollanam-do

Jeju Special Self-Governing Province

Passage Migrant (Spring)
- Above 40,000 heads
- 30,000–40,000
- 20,000–30,000
- 10,000–20,000
- Below 10,000 heads

Winter Visitor
- Above 40,000 heads
- 30,000–40,000
- 20,000–30,000
- 10,000–20,000
- 5,000–10,000 heads

★ Anatidae Network Area
★ Crane Conservation Network Area
▲ Duck and Wild-goose Conservation Network Area

Source: Ministry of Environment, National Institute of Environmental Research (1999–2006)

Passage Migrant (Spring)

1 *Calidris ruficollis*

2 *Calidris tenuirostris*

3 *Xenus cinereus*

4 *Limosa lapponica*

5 *Numenius madagascariensis*

Source: Ministry of Environment, National
Institute of Environmental Research (1999–2006)

0   500   1,000   2,000 km

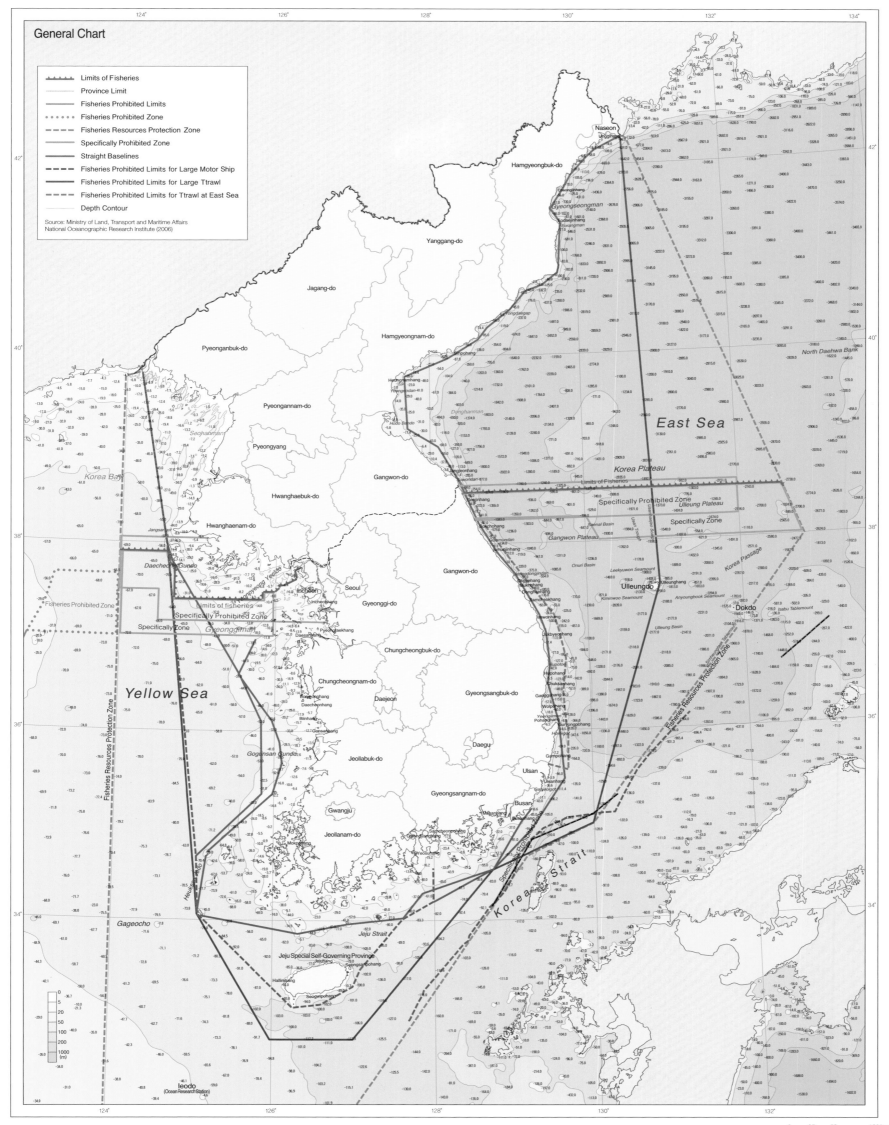

General Chart

Limits of Fisheries
Province Limit
Fisheries Prohibited Limits
Fisheries Prohibited Zone
Fisheries Resources Protection Zone
Specifically Prohibited Zone
Straight Baselines
Fisheries Prohibited Limits for Large Motor Ship
Fisheries Prohibited Limits for Large Ttrawl
Fisheries Prohibited Limits for Ttrawl at East Sea
Depth Contour

Source: Ministry of Land, Transport and Maritime Affairs
National Oceanographic Research Institute (2006)

East Sea

Yellow Sea

Korea Strait

0   25   50   100 km

Located at the gateway of the continent, Korea is a maritime country adjacent to the northwestern North Pacific. It is connected to the Chinese mainland, with three sides surrounded by the East Sea, the South Sea, and the Yellow Sea. Korea is largely separated from the open ocean by Japan and Sakhalin. Oceanographic features including circulation, topography, weather, and climate make the structure of seas in Korea relatively complicated compared to those of other coastal countries. Seas in Korea are affected by seasonally-varying oceanic currents and tides, complicated subsurface topography, and various sea creatures that adapted to such environments.

The maximum depth of the East Sea is over 3,000m. With an average depth of about 1,700m it is as deep as a typical ocean basin. This body of water is surrounded by the Korean Peninsula, the Japanese islands and Sakhalin, and has an area of about one million km^2. At first glance, the East Sea appears to have a simple marine environment because of a relatively straight coastline and a tidal range of less than 30cm. But, the marine environment is complicated by the presence of various currents. It is influenced by the Tsushima Warm Current-a branch of the larger Kuroshio Current of the open ocean-in summer and by the North Korea Cold Current in winter. The East Sea is also occasionally influenced by upwelling of the bottom water from the deep sea. Thus, Samcheok and Ulleungdo are entirely different from each other in biota despite being on the same latitude. Water temperature there falls by 5°C or more across very short distances vertically and laterally. The continental shelf in the East Sea is narrow and less than 200m deep, with only a sporadic appearance around Donghan Bay. The northern half of the East Sea becomes deep and simple bathymetrically from 40°30′ north latitude northward but the southern half is shallow and has a more complicated bathymetry.

The submarine terrain along the coast of the East Sea is dominated by a belt-shaped structure with many banks and troughs along the west coast of the Japanese islands. By contrast, the coast around the Maritime Province of Siberia is very straight and it deepens from narrow continental shelves to the ocean basin where depth reaches 3,000m. The 'Korea Plateau' is a complicated plateau-shaped terrain having a depth of 1,000m adjacent to the sea coast. Daehwa Bank, with a depth between 300 and 500m, is located in the middle of the East Sea, and is northeast of Ulleungdo. It is divided into north and south, with the larger southern portion having dimensions of about 230km long and 55km wide. The waters around Daehwa Bank have abundant nutritious salts because sea water emerges from the bottom of the sea. Also, the water serves as a productive habitat for cuttlefish because of the juxtaposition of the warm current that runs northward and the cold current that runs southward.

The South Sea is less than 150m deep and has a complicated coastline and several oceanic currents that vary seasonally. Water temperature generally remains high, unlike in the Yellow Sea, because it is influenced by the Tsushima Warm Current throughout the year. For these reasons, parts of the South Sea have been designated as a clean zone, characterized by abundant aquatic products because of the influence of the organic matter. Some of the organic matter is washed offshore via overland flow or the Yangtze River in China. Likewise, there is much aquaculture, particularly ascidian farms. The turbidity of the southern coastal waters has increased recently because of the frequent red tides and coastal pollution, but waters surrounding the islands in the open sea are much clearer and support various creatures, including large fishes.

The Yellow Sea opens to the south, and is fed by the Yellow River in China and the Hangang in Korea. It averages 44m deep, with a maximum depth of 103m, and is characterized by complex terrain and strong tides along its wide foreshore. The submarine topography is dominated by a large basin. Near-surface water temperature ranges between 2 and 8°C in winter, and between 24 and 28°C during summer, for a large annual range of 20 to 22°C. However, at depths of 40m and below, the water temperature shows little annual variation. Cold-water fish, such as anglers, skates, and others inhabit these waters, with a large catch around Kamchatka. In summer, warm-water fish including white sharks follow the warm current from the East China Sea. During the last glacial period, when sea level was about 100m lower than at present, the Yellow Sea was part of the mainland.

Oceanic Currents

Several near-surface currents flow in the Korean littoral sea. These include the Tsushima Warm Current, the Korean Donghan Current, the Yellow Sea Warm Current, the North Korea Cold Current, and the Yellow Sea Coastal Compensation Current. On a broader scale, the Korean littoral sea is strongly influenced by the Kuroshio Current that flows northward along the east coast of the Asian continent, from the Pacific east of the Philippines. The Kuroshio is one of the world's strongest surface ocean currents. Another current bifurcates north of Okinawa Island, with the northern branch divided again into the Tsushima Warm Current and Yellow Sea Current.

The Tsushima Warm Current again divides into two branches before entering the East Sea. One branch flows northward along the western coast of the Japanese islands. Another branch flows into the warm East Korean Current along the east coast of Korea. The warm East Korean Current strengthens in summer and weakens in winter. At its maximum strength, it influences the coastal waters of Hamgyeongbuk-*do*.

The Tsushima Warm Current, which runs northward along the continental shelf of the East China Sea, crosses the open sea, flowing 50 to 60 nautical miles west of the Koto Islands between Jeju and Koto. From there it bifurcates into the east and west branches. The western current flows north-northeastward and it again runs northward along the East Sea. The eastern current flows toward the open sea of Gawajiri Headland. Flow velocity near its streamline axis is 30-40cm/s at the surface east of Jeju-*do*, with increasing velocity as it approaches Tsushima Island. Summer velocities are faster and winter velocities are slower than these averages.

A branch of the Liman Current flowing southward from Okhotsk Sea forms the North Korea Cold Current along the coast of Hamgyeongbuk-*do* and Hamgyeongnam-*do*. This current strengthens in the winter and influences southern Gangwon-*do*. In summer, as the water temperatures rise, warm-water fish, such as sauries, anchovies, amberjacks, mackerels, scombroids, and cuttlefish accumulate in the East Sea. These fish migrate northward along warm water between spring and summer, and move southward in autumn as the water temperature falls. The Alaska Pollack is a typical fish that inhabits cold water, and ordinarily moves near the coast of Sokcho.

The Yellow Sea Current, which flows northward west of Jeju-*do*, is relatively weak. It tends to flow into Bohai Bay in summer, but weakens in winter because of the influence of northwesterly winds. Cold currents cannot exist in the Yellow Sea because it is closed by land on its northern edge. The littoral current, which flows southward along the west coast of Korea, reaches its peak intensity in winter because of the influence of northwesterly winds. Yellow corvinas, saurels, brown croakers, anchovies, mackerels, and other fish inhabit the relatively warm waters of the Yellow Sea. Abundant nutritious salts exist in the Yellow Sea because large rivers flow into it from Korea and China. The fry of fishes born in the Yellow Sea spend their developmental period there and move southward in autumn. The South Sea has a high water temperature year-round because of the influence of the Kuroshio Current and has abundant fish, seaweed, and shellfish.

Tides

The tidal range of Korea is remarkable because the relatively shallow Yellow Sea opens toward East China Sea, a part of the North Pacific. The southern part of the Yellow Sea has a tidal range of about 3m, while that at Maenggoldo and the open sea near Mokpo is 2.5 and 4m, respectively. Ranges of about 6m are found near Gunsan, Daecheon, and Yeonpyeong Yeoldo, while 7-m ranges occur around Deokjeokdo and Sindo. Ranges of about 8m are observed around Incheon and Asan. Values fall to about 3m around Baengnyeongdo, before increasing again to about 4.2 and 5.7m around Seokdo and Dasado, respectively. The tidal range of the East Sea is within 0.3m and increases southward to 0.6m and 1.2m around Ulsan and Busan, respectively. The tidal range of the South Sea increases from east to west; it is 2.4, 2.8, and 3.0m around Tongyeong, Samcheonpo, and Wando, respectively. It decreases with distance from the mainland; ranges are about 2.5m around Sorido, Geomundo and Chujado, and only about 2.0m around Maemuldo, Seongsan in Jejudo, and Biyangdo.

Flow velocity of the tide is slower on the east coast than on the west coast, although maximum velocity is near Ulgi in the eastern coast. The tidal current there runs south-southwestward at a speed of 0.6 to 1.9knots, and runs to the East Sea at a speed of 0.9 to 1.4knots. Velocity decreases north of Gyeongsangbuk-*do*. The tide of the South Sea averages 2 to 3knots, but it is much faster in some isolated locations. Along the western coast, the tide is remarkably fast because of the extreme tidal range, and its velocity reaches 5 to 7knots in some places between islands. Jangsangot in Hwanghae-*do*, Sondolmok in Ganghwado, Anheungnyang and Gwanjangmok in Taean Peninsula, and Uldolmok in Usuyeong Peninsula are notorious for violent tides and longshore currents.

Water Temperature and Salinity

Largely because of its shallowness, the surface water temperature of the Yellow Sea is lower than that of the East Sea in winter and is higher in summer. The East Sea averages approximately 5°C in winter near Gangneung and 23°C in summer near Hamheung. An abrupt discontinuity in temperature exists near these areas, however, because of the influence of the Tsushima Warm Current and North Korea Cold Current. The portion of the Yellow Sea and East Sea belonging to North Korea's territorial waters shows a remarkable annual temperature range of approximately 20°C. Ranges are not as large in the East Sea adjacent to Gyeongsangbuk-*do*, and along the south coast.

Surface water temperature adjacent to Boryeong in Chungcheongnam-*do* fluctuates most remarkably. Water temperature around Jeju remains between 18 to 27°C throughout the year because of the influence of the warm Kuroshio Current; subtropical biota can be found around the island because of the consistently warm water year-round. Near the Straits of Korea, water temperature remains at 12 to 15°C. However, water temperatures fall below 10°C around the northwest part, which receives the effect of the Yellow Sea cold water. For this reason, a front develops between the two zones.

The surface of the South Sea generally remains between 25 and 29°C in summer. Waters around the islands from Tongyeong to Yeosu are influenced little by waves, so that warm-water fish are cultivated using enclosing nets. However, the 'red tide' phenomenon can cause large-scale fishkills in this region. August is the most frequent month for red tide, which occurs when the surface water temperature exceeds 25°C. Under such conditions, the influx of domestic sewage and factory wastewater into the sea causes explosive expansion of the population of toxic plankton and the red tide, resulting in the depletion of oxygen or eutrophication of the water body. The red tide disappears after surface water temperature falls below 25°C, decimating the plankton.

Surface water temperature of the East Sea averages 26 to 27°C in the east and 18 to 20°C in the north during summer. In winter, averages are 13 to 14°C in the south, but less than 4°C in the north. The annual range of water temperature is over 20°C in the north and about 13°C in the south. At a depth of 10m, the southern East Sea in summer is at about 15 to 17°C and the northern part is 2°C. A front develops around Jukbyeon and the waters near Ulleungdo, separating waters influenced by warm and cold currents. In winter, temperatures average from 13 to 14°C in the south and 5 to 6°C in the north. During the winter, the Yellow Sea is between 2 and 8°C because of the influence of a continental climate and the shallow waters of the Yellow Sea. In the summer, it warms to 24 to 28°C, for an annual range of 20 to 22°C. At a depth of 50m, water temperatures in winter are about the same as at the surface, but temperatures rise only to 15°C in the warm season. A well-developed thermocline forms at depths between 10 and 30m, with warm surface water flowing northward under the influence of a southwestern wind and colder bottom waters running southward.

Surface salinity of adjacent waters ranges from 27.0 to 34.5‰ on the average, but varies by area and season. The East Sea is more saline than the other water bodies, and the Yellow Sea is the least saline. In the South Sea, the water adjacent to the Kuroshio is more saline than other water. In winter, salinity increases because of the reduced freshwater input from dry mainland Asia. The summer rains reduce the salinity, despite increased evaporation.

Surface salinity in the South Sea begins to increase from autumn until it peaks in April at about 34.5‰. Afterwards, it decreases to below 33.0‰ in August. Values of about 34.5‰ occur around the Tsushima Warm Current in winter, and a salinity front forms between Jeju and the Yangtze River from which Chinese coastal water flows. Values of about 32.2‰ around the Straits of Korea occur in the summer, and a salinity front is distinct between the Kuroshio waters and the continental shelf around the East China Sea.

Salinity of the East Sea may reach 34.5‰ around the Straits of Korea in winter, and falls to 33.0‰ in summer because of lower-salinity water input from the East China Sea and the Yellow Sea. Salinity decreases to 30.0‰ in some places. The annual range of salinity is about 1.5‰ around the area influenced by the Tsushima Warm Current, but it usually remains near 34.1‰ throughout the year under the area of the warm current.

Surface salinity of the Yellow Sea during the winter is about 31.4‰ and 33.2‰ in the north and south respectively. A salinity front forms between the warm current and the cold water of the Yellow Sea. In summer, it is less than 31.0‰ near the coast and between 31.2 and 31.8‰ around the middle, with a salinity front forming between the two areas.

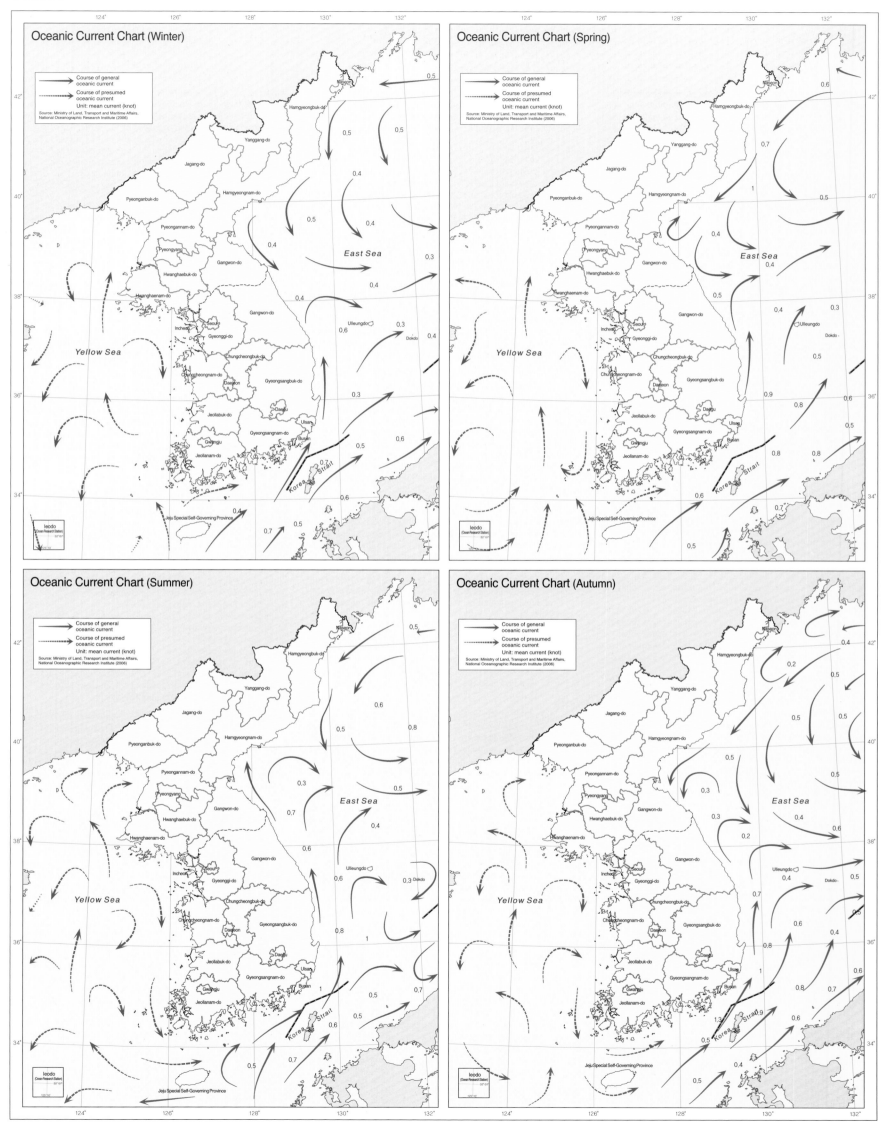

Oceanic Current Chart (Winter)

Oceanic Current Chart (Spring)

Oceanic Current Chart (Summer)

Oceanic Current Chart (Autumn)

0   25   50   100 km

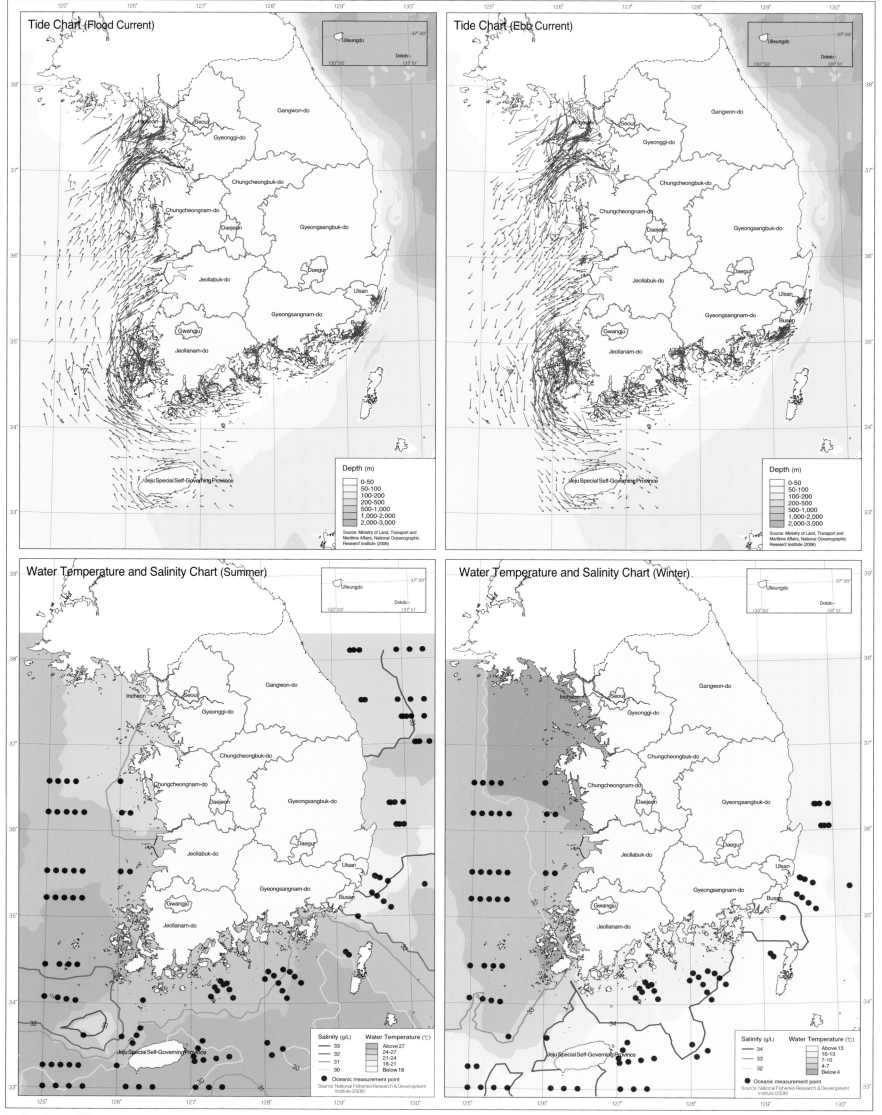

Tide Chart (Flood Current)

Tide Chart (Ebb Current)

Depth (m)
0-50
50-100
100-200
200-500
500-1,000
1,000-2,000
2,000-3,000

Source: Ministry of Land, Transport and
Maritime Affairs, National Oceanographic
Researcf Institute (2006)

Water Temperature and Salinity Chart (Summer)

Water Temperature and Salinity Chart (Winter)

Salinity (g/L)
33
32
31
30

Water Temperature (℃)
Above 27
24-27
21-24
18-21
Below 18

● Oceanic measurement point

Source: National Fisheries Research & Development
Institute (2006)

Salinity (g/L)
34
33
32

Water Temperature (℃)
Above 13
10-13
7-10
4-7
Below 4

● Oceanic measurement point

Source: National Fisheries Research & Development
Institute (2006)

0 25 50   100km

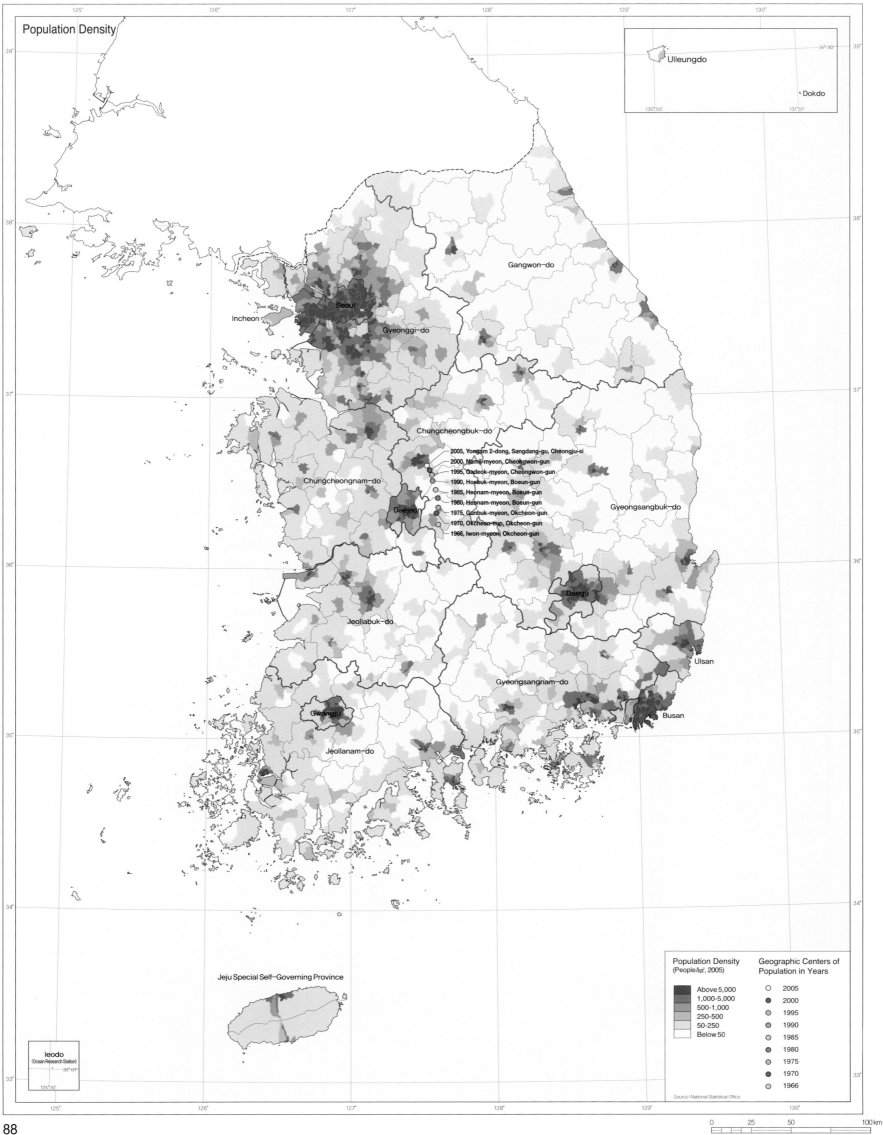

Population Density

Ulleungdo

Dokdo

Gangwon-do

Seoul

Incheon

Gyeonggi-do

Chungcheongbuk-do

2005, Yongam 2-dong, Sangdang-gu, Cheongju-si
2000, Namil-myeon, Cheongwon-gun
1995, Gadeok-myeon, Cheongwon-gun
1990, Hoebuk-myeon, Boeun-gun
1985, Heonam-myeon, Boeun-gun
1980, Heonam-myeon, Boeun-gun
1975, Gunbuk-myeon, Okcheon-gun
1970, Okcheon-eup, Okcheon-gun
1966, Iwon-myeon, Okcheon-gun

Chungcheongnam-do

Daejeon

Gyeongsangbuk-do

Daegu

Jeollabuk-do

Ulsan

Gyeongsangnam-do

Gwangju

Busan

Jeollanam-do

Jeju Special Self-Governing Province

Population Density
(People/㎢, 2005)

	Above 5,000
	1,000–5,000
	500–1,000
	250–500
	50–250
	Below 50

Geographic Centers of
Population in Years

○ 2005
◔ 2000
◑ 1995
◕ 1990
● 1985
● 1980
● 1975
● 1970
● 1966

Source: National Statistical Office

Ieodo
(Ocean Research Station)
32° 07'

125°10'

0   25   50   100 km

The Korean population continued to grow from slightly more than 20 million in 1949, shortly after its liberation from Japanese colonial rule, reaching 30 million in 1970, to over 40 million in 1985, and reaching 47,278,951 in 2005. Gender-wise, the ratio of men to women is almost equal, with the former numbering 23.624 million and the latter 23.655 million. From 1955, the population grew almost 2.2 times over the next 50 years. Within the global population in 2005 (6.465 billion), the Korean population takes up 0.73 percent, making it the 26th most populous country. Korea ranks third in population density after Bangladesh and Taiwan, with 474 persons per km^2.

A close look at the population trend since 1960, when Korea's official population census started, reveals that from 1960 to 1966 the population growth rate was the highest, hitting 2.60 percent per year. After that, the population growth rate of around one to two percent decreased to less than one percent up to 1990, after which it showed a sluggish increase. The average annual population growth rate from 2000 to 2005 was 0.5 percent (see Figure 1).

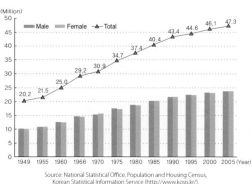

Source: National Statistical Office, Population and Housing Census,
Korean Statistical Information Service (http://www.kosis.kr/).
Figure 1. Population Trend, 1949-2005

An Overview of the Population Distribution

Korea has seen a severe uni-polarized concentration of population in Seoul and the Capital Region since its liberation from Japan at rates almost unprecedented in the world. Also, some major cities have experienced overpopulation, while non-city regions, which take up most of the country's space, have experienced underpopulation.

As for the population distribution per metropolitan city and province (*do*), Gyeonggi-*do* ranks first with 10.4 million, followed by Seoul with 9.8 million (see Table 1). The total population of the Capital Region, consisting of Seoul, Incheon, and Gyeonggi-*do*, is 22.8 million, 48.2 percent of Korea's population. This is a major characteristic of the population distribution in Korea. The percentage of the population in the Capital Region, 23.7 percent in 1966, reached 30 percent in 1975, and 40 percent in 1990. The uni-polarization of the Capital Region seemed to slow down from 1995 to 2000 but its severity increased from 2000 to 2005 (see Figure 2).

Table 1. Total Population by Metropolitan City and Province (*do*) in 2005
(Unit: people, percent)

Areal Units	Population	Proportion	Areal Units	Population	Proportion
The Capital Region*	22,766,850	48.2	Gyeonggi-*do*	10,415,399	22.0
Metropolitan Cities**	22,249,329	47.1	Gangwon-*do*	1,464,559	3.1
Seoul	9,820,171	20.8	Chungcheongbuk-*do*	1,460,453	3.1
Busan	3,523,582	7.5	Chungcheongnam-*do*	1,889,495	4.0
Daegu	2,464,547	5.2	Jeollabuk-*do*	1,784,013	3.8
Incheon	2,531,280	5.4	Jeollanam-*do*	1,819,819	3.8
Gwangju	1,417,716	3.0	Gyeongsangbuk-*do*	2,607,641	5.5
Daejeon	1,442,856	3.1	Gyeongsangnam-*do*	3,056,356	6.5
Ulsan	1,049,177	2.2	Jeju	531,887	1.1

* The Capital Region consists of Seoul, Incheon, and Gyeonggi-*do*.
** Metropolitan cities include Seoul, Busan, Daegu, Incheon, Gwangju, Daejeon, and Ulsan.
Source: National Statistical Office, Population and Housing Census (2005),
Korean Statistical Information Service (http://www.kosis.kr/).

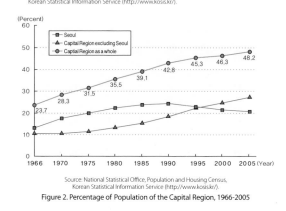

Source: National Statistical Office, Population and Housing Census,
Korean Statistical Information Service (http://www.kosis.kr/).
Figure 2. Percentage of Population of the Capital Region, 1966-2005

The total population of the seven major metropolitan cities, 22.25 million (47.1 percent), is almost equal to the total population of the Capital Region. This verifies that population growth in Korea has been concentrated in major cities. The population size of other cities and provinces is as follows: over three million in Gyeonggi-*do*, Seoul, Busan, and Gyeongsangnam-*do*, two to two and a half million in Gyeongsangbuk-*do*, Incheon and Daegu, one and a half to two million in Chungcheong-

nam-*do*, Jeollanam-*do*, and Jeollabuk-*do*, one to one and a half million for Gangwon-*do*, Chungcheongbuk-*do*, Daejeon, Gwangju, and Ulsan, and about 532 thousand, the smallest amount, in Jeju.

A method used to summarize the overall population distribution is the mapping of the geographic center of population. From 1966 to 2005, the geographic center of population was calculated to express the population distribution based on the population census. The results indicate that the population center since Korea's liberation from Japan has continued to move in the direction of northwest towards the Capital Region. The geographic center moved northward from Yangsan-*myeon*, Yeongdong-*gun* in Chungcheongbuk-*do* in 1949 to Iwon-*myeon*, Okcheon-*gun* in 1966. In 2005, it reached Sangdang-*gu* in Cheongju-*si* in the same province, having moved 56 kilometers northward. The fact that the geographic center gradually moved in the direction of northwest towards Seoul (within Chungcheongbuk-*do*) shows that the share of the Capital Region in the nationwide population distribution has increased. Once the government's balanced regional development policies, bear fruit including construction of the Multifunctional Administrative City (Sejong-*si*), innovation cities and enterprise cities, the locus of the geographic center should change.

Population Density

The most common method to represent the regional distribution of population in relation to land area and other spatial conditions is the population density. It is usually expressed by the population unit per area (people/km²).

Korea's population density in 2005 was 474/km², showing a continued rise along with population growth (see Table 2). As for the population density for each metropolitan city and province, major metropolitan cities had a higher population density than the average, but other regions except for Gyeonggi-*do* had a lower population density than the average. That is, the population density of Gyeonggi-*do* (1,028/km²) is higher than Ulsan (992/km²). Of cities (*si*), counties (*gun*) and district wards (*gu*), Yangcheon-*gu* in Seoul had the highest population density (27,256/km²), while the least populous was Inje-*gun* in Gangwon-*do* (19/km²). Of towns (*eup*), townships (*myeon*), and neighborhoods (*dong*), those with the highest population density had over 70,000/km² and those with the lowest had less than 10/km².

Table 2. Population Density and Population Proximity Index by Metropolitan City and Province (*do*) in 2005
(Unit: people/km², m)

Areal Units	Population Density	Population Proximity Index	Areal Units	Population Density	Population Proximity Index
Nation	474	45.9	Gyeonggi-*do*	1,028	31.2
Metropolitan Cities*	4,161	15.5	Gangwon-*do*	88	106.5
Seoul	16,221	7.9	Chungcheongbuk-*do*	197	71.3
Busan	4,609	14.7	Chungcheongnam-*do*	220	67.5
Daegu	2,786	18.9	Jeollabuk-*do*	221	67.2
Incheon	2,546	19.8	Jeollanam-*do*	151	81.5
Gwangju	2,827	18.8	Gyeongsangbuk-*do*	137	85.4
Daejeon	2,673	19.3	Gyeongsangnam-*do*	291	58.7
Ulsan	992	31.7	Jeju	288	58.9

* Metropolitan cities include Seoul, Busan, Daegu, Incheon, Gwangju, Daejeon, and Ulsan.
Source: National Statistical Office, Population and Housing Census (2005),
Korean Statistical Information Service (http://www.kosis.kr/).

The distribution of population density in 2005 reveals that the first high-density region has formed in the north-south direction in the western part of Korea, from the Capital Region, with Seoul as the center of the northwestern part, to the southwestern region. Second high-density regions are concentrated in the southeastern region, with Busan, Daegu, and Ulsan as the centers, and are smaller in scale than the first. Other high-density areas are mostly administrative and transport centers, and never reach a significance level of concentration. Some minor zones are found along the southern and eastern costal lines, but are still low in concentration and connectivity.

A comparison between the population density in 1980, 1990 and 2000 with that in 2005 reveals that the number of low-density regions (50 to 250/km²) starkly decreased during the period. In 1980, population levels high enough to maintain regional communities were in place, except for mountainous areas in Gangwon-*do*, and some regions and inland mountainous areas in Gyeongsangbuk-*do*. However, continued rural-to-urban migration, a rapid decline of fertility, and an aging population in rural areas characterizes most of the land, except for major cities and some plains, low-density regions with less than 50 people. In most of these regions, an actual disintegration of communities is taking place. Overpopulation in some major cities and stark population gaps in most rural areas are an offshoot of not only social, but also regional divides in Korea.

The population proximity index is another way to express the population distribution. Assuming that the intra-regional population is equally distributed, it refers to an average distance (meters) to the neighboring person. It is calculated using the formula: $\sqrt{land\ area(m^2)/population}$. Areas with high population densities have smaller population proximity indices, while those with low population densities have higher indices. In 2005, Korea's overall population proximity index was about 45.9 meters. As for Seoul, which has the highest density, its proximity index is only 7.9 meters, but as for Gangwon-*do*, with the smallest population density, the index is 106.5 meters (see Table 2).

Population Growth

Five stages describe Korea's modern demographic transition. The first stage is the traditional high stationary period (prior to 1910) when the population grew at a gradual pace due to high birth rates and high death rates. For 500 years during the Joseon period, the average population growth rate is estimated at merely around 0.2 percent. The second stage is the early expanding period (from 1910 to 1945) where the population rapidly increased due to high birth rates and lower death rates. This is the result of the spread of healthcare, medical systems, and medicines from the West, which started to be adopted from the late Joseon period. The third stage is the unstable population growth period (from 1945 to 1960) in which rapid social transitions including Korea's liberation from Japanese colonial rule, the North-South divide and the Korean War, led to societal population increases and a baby boom in the aftermath of the war. From 1945 to 1950, the average population growth rate is reported to have been 6.1 percent due to large-scale return migration and people taking refuge from the war. In addition, the "baby boom" led to the natural population growth rate expanding to 28.7 percent from 1955 to 1960. The fourth stage is the late expanding period (from 1960 to 1985) where the high-level fertility of the previous stage started to suddenly plummet and the mortality continued to decline. The average population growth rate hovered around 3.0 percent from 1960 to 1966, but plummeted to 1.6 percent from 1980 to 1985. The fifth stage is the low-stationary period (from 1985 to present) in which the fertility rapidly shrunk with stable death rates and sluggish population growth. In addition, all the stages of the demographic transition have been completed, and Korea has reached the stable stage of advanced countries. Population increases entered a stable stage starting 1990, and the population growth rate from 2000 to 2005, on average, was 0.5 percent (see Table 3).

Table 3. Annual Population Growth Rate by Metropolitan City and Province (*do*) 1985-2005
(Unit: percent)

Areal Units	Annual Population Growth Rates*				
	1985-1990	1990-1995	1995-2000	2000-2005	Entire Period (1985-2005)
Nation	1.4	0.5	0.7	0.5	0.8
The Capital Region**	3.3	1.7	1.1	1.3	1.8
Metropolitan Cities***	2.2	0.5	0.0	0.0	0.7
Seoul	1.9	-0.7	-0.7	-0.2	0.1
Busan	1.5	-0.2	-0.8	-0.8	-0.1
Daegu	1.9	1.1	0.3	-0.1	0.8
Incheon	4.9	3.7	1.4	0.4	2.6
Gwangju	1.8	2.0	1.5	0.9	1.5
Daejeon	2.2	3.9	1.5	1.1	2.1
Ulsan	3.8	3.7	1.0	0.7	2.3
Gyeonggi-*do*	5.3	4.8	3.3	3.0	4.1
Gangwon-*do*	-1.7	-1.5	0.3	-0.3	-0.8
Chungcheongbuk-*do*	0.0	0.1	1.0	-0.1	0.2
Chungcheongnam-*do*	-0.4	-2.6	0.9	0.5	-0.4
Jeollabuk-*do*	-1.2	-1.7	-0.1	-1.2	-1.0
Jeollanam-*do*	-1.5	-3.8	-0.7	-1.8	-2.0
Gyeongsangbuk-*do*	-1.1	-0.7	0.4	-0.9	-0.6
Gyeongsangnam-*do*	0.2	0.5	0.7	0.5	0.5
Jeju	1.0	-0.4	0.3	0.7	0.4

* Calculated based on the 2005 administrative boundaries.
** The Capital Region consists of Seoul, Incheon, and Gyeonggi-*do*.
*** Metropolitan cities include Seoul, Busan, Daegu, Incheon, Gwangju, Daejeon, and Ulsan.
Source: National Statistical Office, Population and Housing Census,
Korean Statistical Information Service (http://www.kosis.kr/).

A comparison of population growth rate maps for each metropolitan city and province (*do*) for the periods 1995 to 2000 and 2000 to 2005 reveals a clear difference. During 1995 to 2000, regions with population increases were sparsely located, and those with stark population decreases were few in numbers. However, from 2000 to 2005, the population concentration in the Capital Region intensified. As for the spatial distribution from 1995 to 2000, metropolitanization in the Capital Region stood out, with most of the population growth taking place in most regions in the Capital Region except for Seoul and the northern part of the Chungcheong region. Furthermore, areas around Busan and Daegu showed high population growth.

As for 2000 to 2005, the population concentration was distinctive due to continued construction of new cities in the Capital Region. Except for Gimhae-*si* (5.4 percent) in Gyeongsangnam-*do*, all the cities and counties with over five percent population growth rates were in the Capital Region. Such a weakened population concentration in the Capital Region and the re-concentration since then are clearly evident given the proportion of the Capital Region in the overall population growth. From 1990 to 1995, the proportion of the population growth in the Capital Region was 133.8 percent. This implies that the number of increased populations in the Capital Region was 33.8 percent larger than the nationwide figure, meaning population reduction took place to the same extent in the non-Capital Region. This number dropped to 76.3 from 1995 to 2000, a lower figure than 93.4 from 1985 to 1990. However, the proportion increased to 123.6 during the period 2000 to 2005, showing a re-intensification of the population concentration in the Capital Region since 2000.

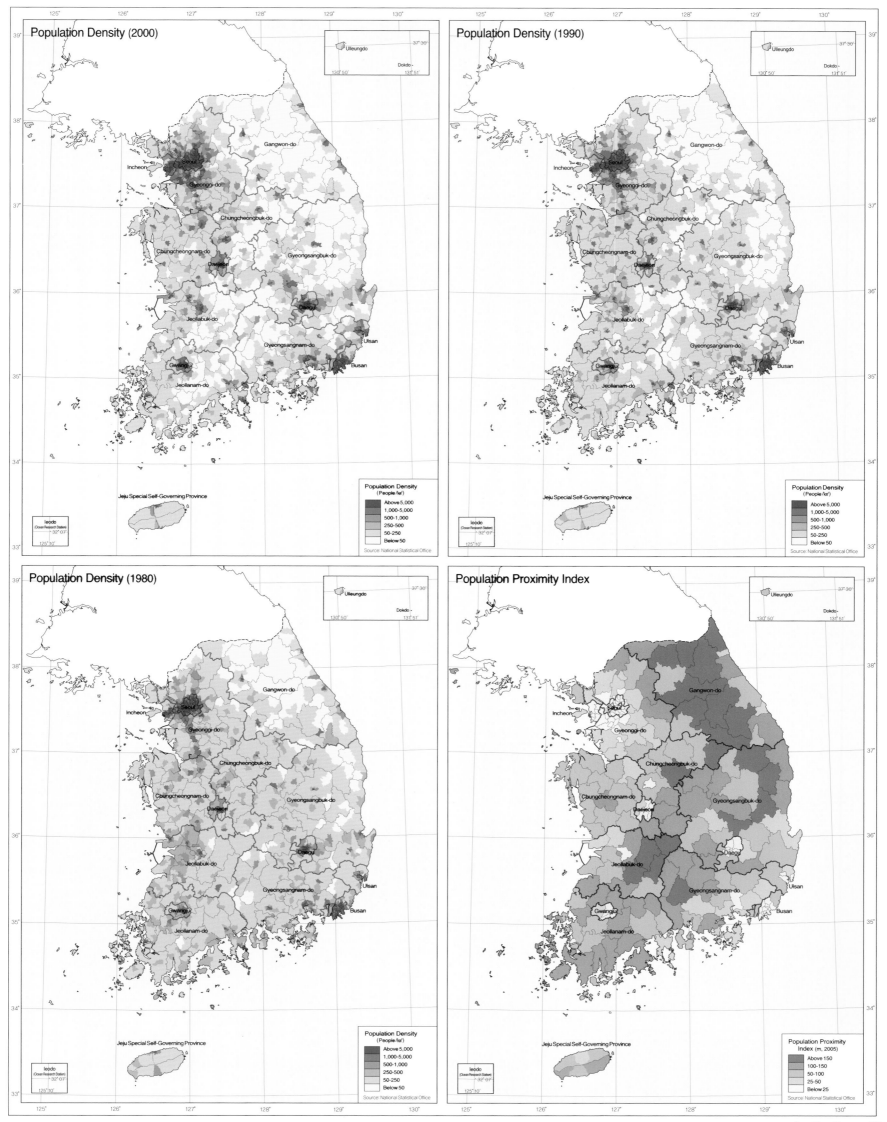

Population Density (2000)

Population Density (1990)

Population Density (1980)

Population Proximity Index

Population Density
(People /㎢)
Above 5,000
1,000-5,000
500-1,000
250-500
50-250
Below 50
Source: National Statistical Office

Population Proximity
Index (m, 2005)
Above 150
100-150
50-100
25-50
Below 25
Source: National Statistical Office

0   25   50   100 km

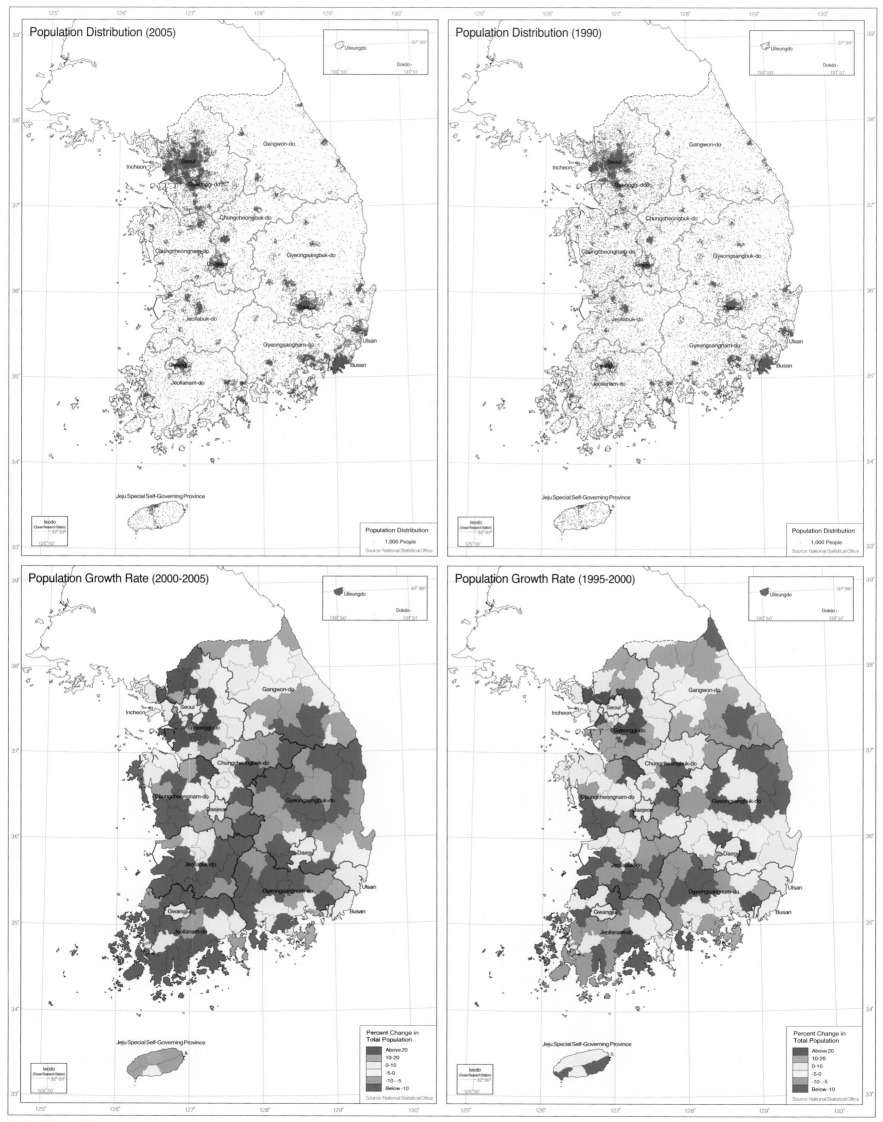

Population Distribution (2005)

Population Distribution (1990)

Population Distribution
· 1,000 People
Source: National Statistical Office

Population Growth Rate (2000-2005)

Population Growth Rate (1995-2000)

Percent Change in
Total Population
Above 20
10-20
0-10
-5-0
-10 - -5
Below -10
Source: National Statistical Office

0 25 50   100 km

Total Fertility Rate

Ulleungdo

Dokdo

Gangwon-do

Seoul

Incheon

Gyeonggi-do

Chungcheongbuk-do

Chungcheongnam-do

Daejeon

Gyeongsangbuk-do

Jeollabuk-do

Daegu

Ulsan

Gyeongsangnam-do

Gwangju

Busan

Jeollanam-do

Jeju Special Self-Governing Province

Ieodo
(Ocean Research Station)

Total Fertility
Rate (2005)

Above 1.5
1.3-1.5
1.1-1.3
1.0-1.1
Below 1.0

Source: National Statistical Office

0   25   50   100 km

VITAL STATISTICS

Vital statistics refer to data of events that could change the population structure in a region, and constitute the backbone of knowledge for crucial decision making in various public spheres such as the economy, social concerns, education and health. In a broad sense, vital statistics encompass all kinds of dynamic events occurring in a population, but in general, they consist of births, deaths, marriages, and divorces. Vital statistics, unlike those gathered in a population census, are obtained by official registration systems.

Birth and Death

The fertility level of Korea is one of the lowest among the OECD countries. TFR (Total Fertility Rate), the average number of children born to a woman over her lifetime (usually aged 15-49), was as low as 1.08 in 2005. This figure is lower than the world average, 2.55, estimated for 2005-2010 by the United Nations, and, in fact, is one of the lowest in the world. Annual TFRs were stable at around 6 up to the 1960s; but the figures have dramatically decreased since the early 1970s. In 1974, the TFR dropped to the sub-4 (3.81) range for the first time and then rapidly decreased to 2.65 in 1978 and 1.76 in 1984 (see Figure 1). Up until the late 1990s, the trend remained flat with a small fluctuation between 1.4 and 1.8, but a sharp drop occurred again beginning in 2000, showing an absolute decline of 0.39 for the five years from 2000-2005. This low fertility trend will result in decreases in births in the short run, and will cause various problems relating to a labor deficit and an aging population in the long run.

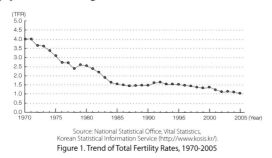

Source: National Statistical Office, Vital Statistics,
Korean Statistical Information Service (http://www.kosis.kr/).
Figure 1. Trend of Total Fertility Rates, 1970-2005

The spatial distribution of regional TFRs at the city(*si*)-county(*gun*)-district(*gu*) level shows that there is a significant geographical variation in the fertility level. As for TFRs by metropolitan city and province (*do*) in 2005, Busan (0.88), Seoul (0.92), and Daegu (0.99) reported less than 1, while Jeju-*do*, Jeollanam-*do* and Chungcheongnam-*do* more than 1.2, which is reflective of the urban-rural divide. A temporal trend is evident; all the metropolitan cities and provinces (*do*) showed a high level of fertility in 1997, over 1.3, but have experienced a sharp drop since 2000.

The CBR (Crude Birth Rate) and CDR (Crude Death Rate) determine RNI (Rate of Natural Increase) and are directly related to population changes in a region. The CBR, the number of births per 1,000 persons per year, has rapidly decreased from 31.2 in 1970, to 15.4 in 1990, and to 9.0 in 2005 (see Figure 2). The CDR gradually decreased from 8.0 in 1970, to 5.8 in 1990, and to 5.0 in 2005. Since the decreasing trend is sharper in the CBR than in CDR, the gap of the two measures has been reduced. Also, as the difference between the CBR and CDR defines the RNI, the population growth rate in Korea has effectively decreased unless international migration is considered. The RNI dropped from 23.2 in 1970 to 9.7 in 1986, stood stable at 10+ during the first half of the 1990s, and dropped rapidly again from 1997, reaching 4.0 in 2005. This trend can be accounted for by the flattened CDR and the sharply decreasing CBR since the late 1990s. Korea's RNI of 4.0 is much lower than the world average, 11.7, estimated for 2005-2010 by the United Nations, but is still slightly higher than the average of the most developed countries. The spatial pattern of the RNI is reflective of those of the CBR and CDR; Gyeonggi-*do* reported the highest value (6.3) and Jeollanam-*do*, did the lowest (-0.2).

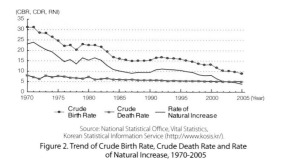

Source: National Statistical Office, Vital Statistics,
Korean Statistical Information Service (http://www.kosis.kr/).
Figure 2. Trend of Crude Birth Rate, Crude Death Rate and Rate of Natural Increase, 1970-2005

Marriage and Divorce

Marriage-related statistics are relatively more versatile year to year than other vital statistics in the sense that they are sensitive in a socio-economic context. The serial trend of the CMR (Crude Marriage Rate), the number of marriages per 1,000 persons per year, can be characterized by an increase during the 1970s, stabilizing around 9 up until the financial crisis of 1997, followed by a decrease, reaching 6.5 in 2005 (see Figure 3). The sharp drop since the late 1990s is associated with the popularization of later marriages, and attitudinal and conceptual changes of marriage, including an increasing preference for single-life. The CDR (Crude Divorce Rate) has gradually increased since 1970; in 1985, it exceeded 1 for the first time, hit 2 in 1997, and reached its apex at 3.5 in 2003. However, a decreasing trend has recently been observed; the CDR in 2005 was 2.6, a decrease of 0.9 in only two years.

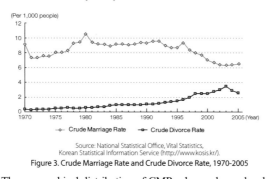

Source: National Statistical Office, Vital Statistics,
Korean Statistical Information Service (http://www.kosis.kr/).
Figure 3. Crude Marriage Rate and Crude Divorce Rate, 1970-2005

The geographical distribution of CMRs show a lower level of spatial variation in comparison with other vital indices. As for the CMR by metropolitan city and province (*do*) in 2005, Seoul (7.0) and Gyeonggi-*do* (6.8) reported the highest rates, while Jeollanam-*do* (5.1), Busan (5.2) and Daegu (5.2) showed the lowest values.

MIGRATION

Migration refers to the interregional movement of the population, which is reported in the migration statistics based on all resident address changes. Migration brings changes to the population distribution across regions, which in turn becomes a factor in subsequent population movements. Recent geographic patterns of migration are examined using the migration statistics data reporting residence address changes over administrative boundaries in 2005.

Two kinds of indices are employed to portray the geographic patterns of migration. One group of indices is introduced to capture migration patterns by region, such as total migrants, inward- and outward-migrants, total migration rate, net migration rate and the demographic effectiveness of migration. The other group of measures and statistics is employed to examine interregional migration patterns, such as ones indicating whether regions are receiving or sending migrants to or from similar regions, their major origins or destinations, and the regional distribution of inward or outward-migrants to or from the Capital Region and major metropolitan cities.

Migration Patterns by Region

The regional pattern of migration can be examined via the distribution of the total number of migrants, including inward- and outward-migrants. Overall, large cities and the Capital Region in particular tend to be the origin and destination of population movements. The regional distribution of total migrants follows the population size of the regions. The ratio of inward and outward-migrants is half and half, while the ratio of outward-migrants is higher in many counties (*gun*) of Gyeongsangbuk-*do*, Jeollanam-*do*, and Jeollabuk-*do*. The ratio of inward-migrants is higher in the cities of Gyeonggi-*do*, reflecting rural outward-migration and the suburbanization of Seoul.

The net migration rate reveals the effects of migration on the population size in a region. A population increase, or positive rate, is found in the Capital Region and most metropolitan cities except Daejeon; a population decrease, or negative rate, is found in most other regions. This indicates that the areas with decreased populations are concentrated in a few urban areas. In fact, there are 68 areas which have experienced a population increase, whereas 166 areas have seen their populations decline among the 234 city(*si*)-county(*gun*)-district(*gu*) units (see Figure 4).

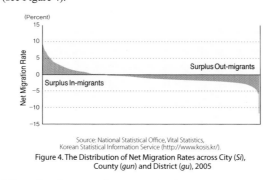

Source: National Statistical Office, Vital Statistics,
Korean Statistical Information Service (http://www.kosis.kr/).
Figure 4. The Distribution of Net Migration Rates across City (*Si*), County (*gun*) and District (*gu*), 2005

Migration Patterns between Regions

The interregional pattern of migration examined in the distribution of inward-migrants from the Capital Region and metropolitan cities reveals that the Capital Region has a relatively even distribution across regions (see Figure 5). Metropolitan cities, however, reveal biased reliance, especially Daegu and Gwangju, which draw more than 50 percent of their migrants from nearby areas. Busan is similar, but lower in its reliance; Daejeon draws its largest proportion of migrants from the Capital Region, followed by nearby areas. The outward-migrants of the Capital Region distribute somewhat evenly across regions, whereas the metropolitan cities reveal a biased distribution similar to the case of inward-migrants. The regional distribution suggests differences across regions and between inward and outward-migration as shown in Figure 5. The Capital Region and Daejeon have a relatively even distribution across regions; other cities are biased across regions, but more in terms of inward-migrants from nearby areas.

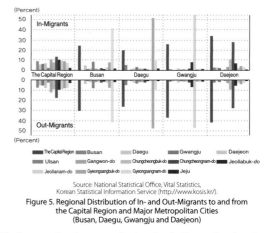

Source: National Statistical Office, Vital Statistics,
Korean Statistical Information Service (http://www.kosis.kr/).
Figure 5. Regional Distribution of In- and Out-Migrants to and from the Capital Region and Major Metropolitan Cities (Busan, Daegu, Gwangju and Daejeon)

The inter-regional pattern of migration indicates that Seoul and other metropolitan cities have their own migration field close to provincial administrative boundaries as major destinations and origins. As expected, Seoul has the largest migration field when it comes to receiving hierarchical migration from other major destination cities, and when sending migrants to nearby Gyeonggi-*do* and Gangwon-*do* or further to the northern part of Chungcheongnam-*do* and Chungcheongbuk-*do*. Other large cities have migration fields similar to their administrative boundaries. The regional distributions of migration flows for the metropolitan cities reveal established migration fields in contiguous areas similar to the above except for the Capital Region, which has the whole nation as a migration field, and Daejeon, which has inter-migration with the Capital Region. The higher regional concentration in terms of inward-migration compared to that of outward-migration indicates that metropolitan cities receive migrants from nearby and send them to more diverse areas.

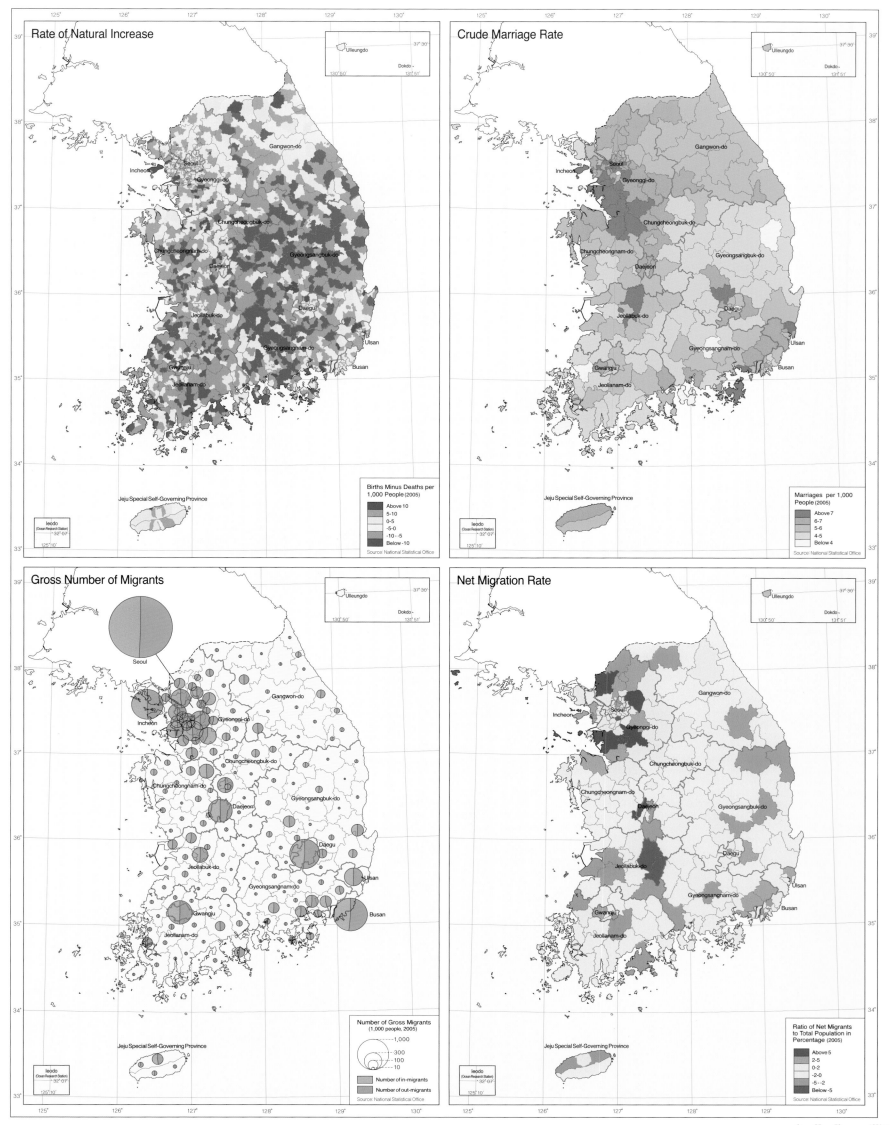

Rate of Natural Increase

Births Minus Deaths per
1,000 People (2005)

- Above 10
- 5-10
- 0-5
- -5-0
- -10--5
- Below -10

Source: National Statistical Office

Crude Marriage Rate

Marriages per 1,000
People (2005)

- Above 7
- 6-7
- 5-6
- 4-5
- Below 4

Source: National Statistical Office

Gross Number of Migrants

Number of Gross Migrants
(1,000 people, 2005)

- 1,000
- 300
- 100
- 10

- Number of in-migrants
- Number of out-migrants

Source: National Statistical Office

Net Migration Rate

Ratio of Net Migrants
to Total Population in
Percentage (2005)

- Above 5
- 2-5
- 0-2
- -2-0
- -5--2
- Below -5

Source: National Statistical Office

0 25 50   100 km

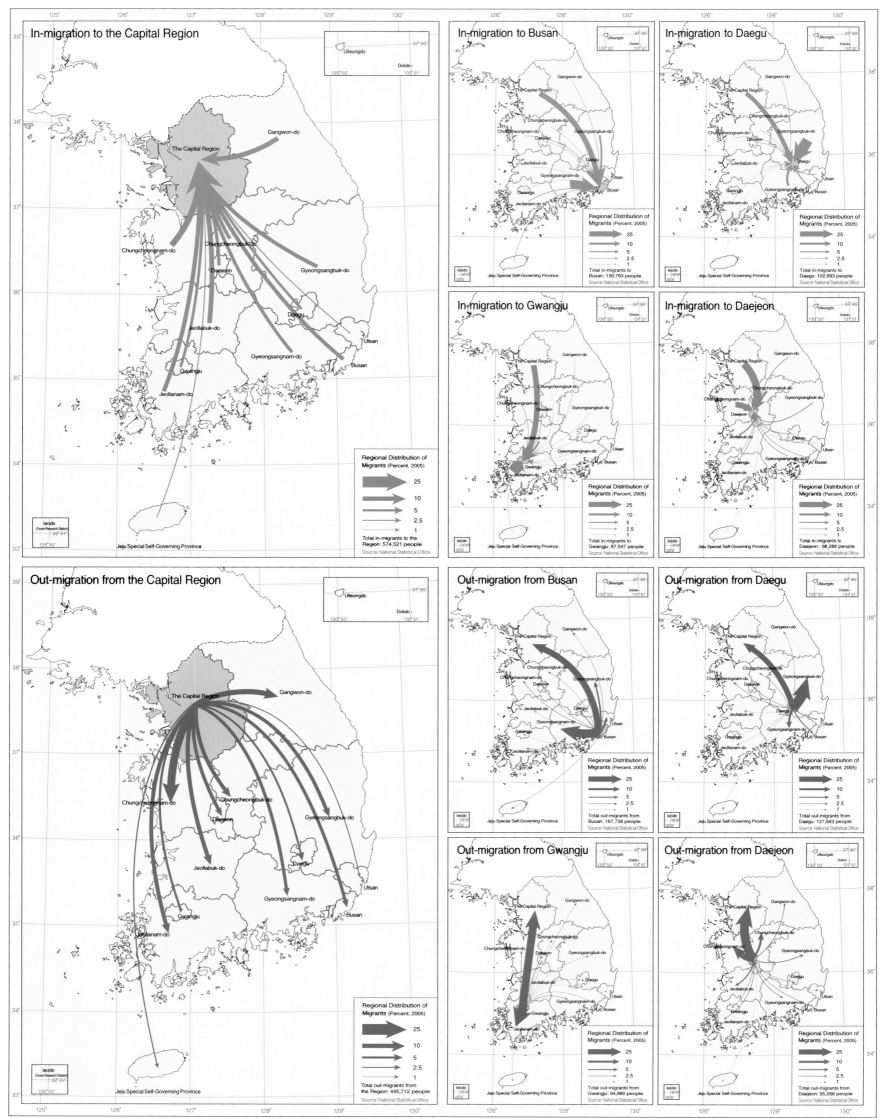

Classification of the Population Pyramid

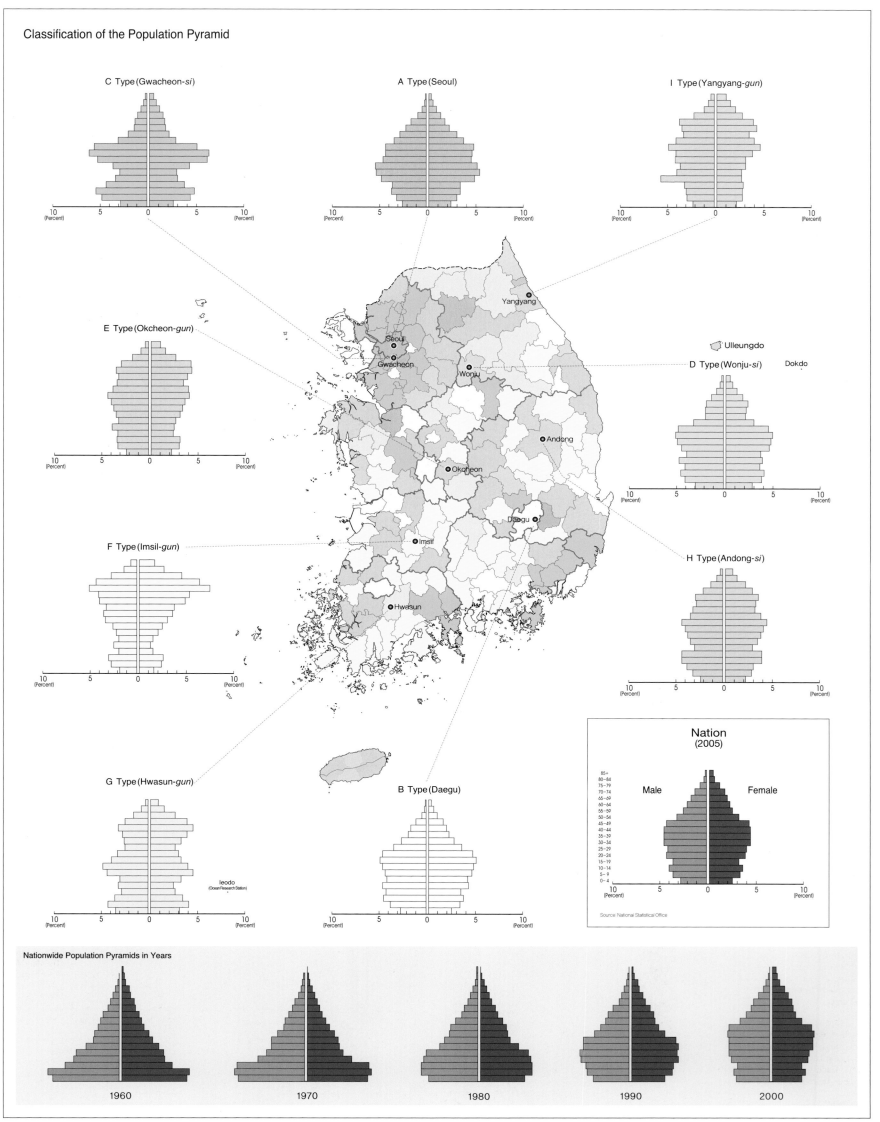

C Type (Gwacheon-*si*)

A Type (Seoul)

I Type (Yangyang-*gun*)

E Type (Okcheon-*gun*)

D Type (Wonju-*si*)

F Type (Imsil-*gun*)

H Type (Andong-*si*)

G Type (Hwasun-*gun*)

B Type (Daegu)

Nation (2005)

Male   Female

Source: National Statistical Office

Nationwide Population Pyramids in Years

1960   1970   1980   1990   2000

The population structure changes according to the social and economical situation of its region, which is significantly affected by the birthrate, death rate, and migration patterns. Generally, there are three types of population structures, which include demographic structure based on sex and age, sociological structure based on marriage, size of households, education, and religion, and finally, economic structure based on occupation and industry classification.

DEMOGRAPHIC STRUCTURE OF POPULATION

Population Structure by Gender

The sex ratio, the most basic population feature with a direct effect on actual fertility, is defined as the number of males per 100 females. In the 2005 census, South Korea's sex ratio was 99.53 ((23,624,000/23,655,000) × 100). It indicates that there are 99.53 males for every 100 females.

Before Independence, the sex ratio was over 100, meaning there was a surplus of males in South Korea, but the ratio began to decrease because of the Korean War, when a number of men were killed in battle, falling to 100.1 in 1955. However, it increased to 101.5 in 1966, which can be explained by the tendency to prefer sons to daughters. Nevertheless, the ratio gradually dropped when the national family planning program was initiated, and since 1980 a balance between the number of men and women has generally been maintained. The sex ratio in 2000 was 100.7, but by 2005 it had fallen to 99.5.

The national sex ratio follows a natural trend, whereas the ratios in cities and rural areas show a big difference driven by social influence, especially caused by inward and outward migration. The ratios for neighborhoods (*dong*) and towns (*eup*) are 99.8 and 101.1, respectively, showing similar numbers of men and women, but in townships (*myeon*) the ratio is 96.5, indicating a surplus of women. Meanwhile, for sex ratios based on age, the ratio of the younger age groups, particularly of a marriageable age, between *myeon* and *dong* regions shows the greatest difference (see Figure 1). This phenomenon can be explained by the outward-migration of young women from rural areas to cities.

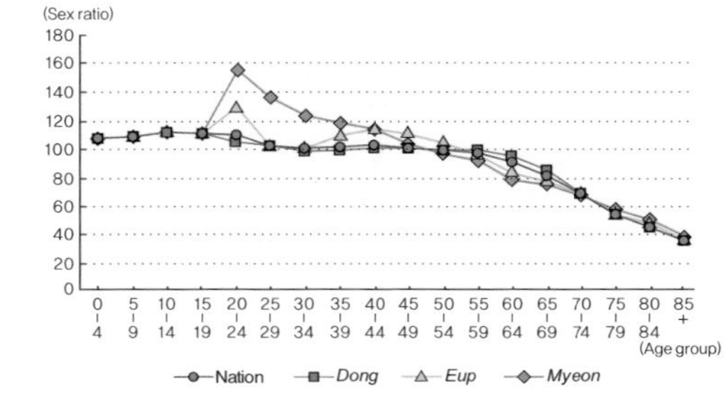

Source: National Statistical Office, Population and Housing Census (2005)
Korean Statistical Information Service (http://www.kosis.kr/).

Figure 1. Sex Ratio between Age Groups by Neighborhood (*dong*), Town (*eup*), and Township (*myeon*), 2005

Population Structure by Age

Since the socio-economic behaviors in which human beings engage vary widely depending on their age, the age distribution is very important. However, since the age data of the population is provided in one-year intervals, it is difficult to grasp the characteristics of the population. Therefore, the age distribution data are analyzed by three different methods as follows.

The median age method uses a single index to understand the age characteristics of a population, and is often used rather than the mean age because of an asymmetry in age distribution. All individuals gradually get older, but the median age in a certain society may become higher or lower. When birth and death rates fall, the population age increases, or the median age rises, while it decreases (or the median age falls) when birth and death rates rise. Generally, a society with a 30-or-higher median age is called an "aging" society.

On the whole, as a society modernizes, the median age rises due to a declining birth rate. Hence, the median age is sometimes used as an index to roughly understand the level of modernization and the transition stage of a population in a given society. As for South Korea, the median age was 21.7 years in 1980, but it rose consistently, to 23.7 in 1985, to 27 in 1990, to 32 in 2000, and to 35 years in 2005, showing that the country has become an aging society. In regional terms, the median age for *dong* is 34 years, for *eup* it is 35.8, and for *myeon* it is 46.5 years. These figures show that more elderly people live in more rural areas.

The range of the age distribution in a certain society is divided into three age groups. In other words, it is classified into three categories, the young age group (aged between 0-14), the adult age group (aged 15-64), and the old age group (aged 65 and older). Each group's proportion to the total population is used to understand the age structure.

The proportion of the old age group has increased along with economic development and modernization. While the proportion of the young age group dropped from 42.9 percent in 1960 to 19.1 percent in 2005, that of the old age group increased from 3.3 percent in 1960 to 9.3 percent in 2005 (see Figure 2). The decrease for the young age group and the increase for the old age group is mostly due to the increase in the average life span, a lower birth rate and a relatively lower death rate in accordance with national family planning, modernization, and industrialization.

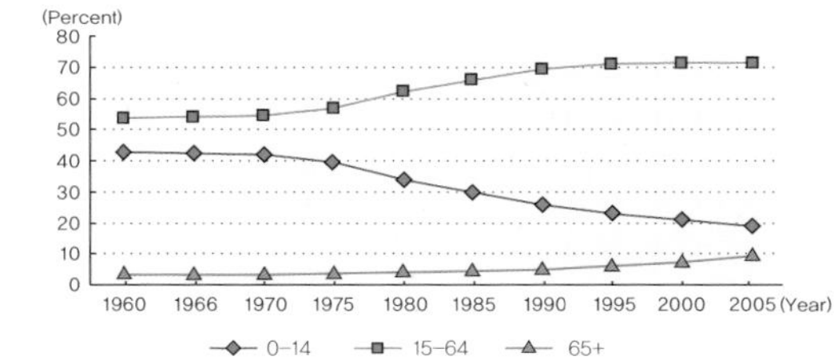

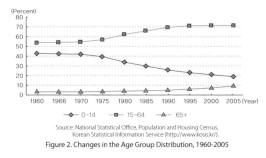

Source: National Statistical Office, Population and Housing Census,
Korean Statistical Information Service (http://www.kosis.kr/).

Figure 2. Changes in the Age Group Distribution, 1960-2005

With economic development and modernization underway, the shapes of national population pyramids have changed due to the continuous decline in fertility rates. In 1960, the population pyramid showed a classical pyramid shape composed of high birth and death rates, but since the late 1980s it has shifted into a spindle type of structure marked by low birth and low death rates. However, the shapes of population pyramids for individual cities and counties can be very different because of massive population movements from rural areas to cities, and differences in labor force demands according to the economic base of each region.

ECONOMIC STRUCTURE OF POPULATION

Dependency Ratio

The relationship between the population of youth and elderly groups, the members of which are mostly non-productive consumers, and the population of working age groups is very important in economic aspects. Therefore, the dependency ratio can be applied as an index of economic structure. The dependent population is largely divided into two groups. That is, one group of the young population from age 0-14 and the other group aged 65 and older, both of which are generally too young or too old to engage in productive economic activities. The population of working age people in the 15-64 age group is defined simply by the age range regardless of actual participation in economic activities.

The dependency ratio is often divided into two parts, called the youth dependency ratio and the elderly dependency ratio. Hence, the total dependency ratio is the proportion of nonproductive population to the productive population and can also be calculated by adding the elderly dependency ratio and the youth dependency ratio.

In 1960, the total dependency ratio was 86, with an elderly dependency ratio of 6 and a relatively high youth dependency ratio of 80. Since then, the total dependency ratio has gradually decreased as the birth rate has declined due to economic development and national family planning. The dependency ratio dropped considerably from 84 in 1970 to 60.5 in 1980, and steadily declined from 52.1 in 1985, to 40.6 in 1995 and to 39.7 in 2005. Particularly, the youth dependency ratio in 2005 was 26.7, which was much lower than in 1960, but the elderly dependency ratio increased gradually, reaching 13.0 in 2005.

Table 1. Changes in Dependency Ratio in Urban and Rural Areas, 1960-2005

Classification	1960	1970	1980	1990	2000	2005
Total Dependency Ratio						
Nation	86.0	83.3	60.5	44.2	39.4	39.7
Urban	77.9	67.0	53.9	42.7	37.0	36.4
Rural	89.4	90.6	70.3	48.5	50.0	55.7
Child Dependency Ratio						
Nation	79.9	77.2	54.3	37.0	29.2	26.7
Urban	74.0	63.1	49.9	37.6	29.5	26.7
Rural	82.4	85.9	60.8	35.1	28.0	26.7
Elderly Dependency Ratio						
Nation	6.0	6.1	6.2	7.2	10.2	13.0
Urban	3.9	3.9	3.9	3.9	7.5	9.8
Rural	7.1	7.7	9.6	9.6	22.0	28.9

Source : National Statistical Office, Population and Housing Census,
Korean Statistical Information Service (http://Kosis.kr/).

Population Structure by Industry

Industry types can be classified by the level of development and the degree of technological advancement. Among twenty industries, based on the revised industrial classification system, the one engaging the largest portion of the population as of 2005 was the manufacturing industry, which accounted for about 20 percent, followed by the wholesale and retail trades, and agriculture and fisheries. Nevertheless, the ratio of the population working in these traditional industries has declined, and the ratio working in new industries, such as business services, personal services, education, and public services, has increased. This shift reflects the gradual change from hardware-based industries to software-based industries.

In the case of metropolitan areas, there is a greater portion of the population engaged in higher-level services (fourth industry), such as producer and business services. However, there is also a higher ratio of the population engaged in consumer services and retail trade in small towns. When the industrial structures of special cities and provinces are compared, special cities like Seoul, Busan, Gwangju, and Daejeon have a relatively high proportion of higher-level industries, indicating tertiary economization. On the other hand, provinces like Chungcheongnam-*do* and Jeollanam-*do* show a relatively higher proportion of the population engaged in agriculture, forestry or fisheries.

SOCIAL STRUCTURE OF POPULATION

Population Structure by Educational Level

Educational attainment is a barometer indicating the cultural level of a certain region. A society's average education level and its distribution are regarded as very important indexes to estimate the level of welfare and the qualitative characteristics of a population in a society.

As for the non-attendance ratio, an index of the average education level in Korea, it significantly decreased from 40 percent in 1960 to 20 percent in 1970, and reached 8 percent in 1990 and 5.3 percent in 2005. People with academic backgrounds of university level or higher numbered about 10,496,000 (34.3 percent) in 2005. Seoul accounted for 30 percent of all graduates from a four-year or higher college program, and cities like Seongnam-*si* and Goyang-*si* have about 2 million graduates. Some remote mountain counties (*gun*) located in Jeollabuk-*do*, Jeollanam-*do*, Gyeonsangbuk-*do*, and Gyeongsangnam-*do* have no more than 1,000 graduates.

The average number of schooling years, computed using a target population of age 30 and above, was 11.01 years in 2005, corresponding to the second year of high school. However, there was a steady increase from 9.67 years in 1995 and to 10.24 years in 2000. In the meantime, when average schooling years for the population of age 6 and older are compared between cities (*si*), counties (*gun*), and districts (*gu*), Seocho-*gu* and Kangnam-*gu* in Seoul report a little bit more than 13 years, and the other districts (*gu*) in Seoul report at least 11 years. However, in the case of the inland rural areas of Jeollabuk-*do*, Jeollanam-*do*, Gyeongsangbuk-*do*, and Gyeongsangnam-*do*, the average number of schooling years only reaches 6-7 years.

Population Structure by Religion

The religious population gradually grew and reached about 25 million in 2005, accounting for 53.1 percent of the total population, which was about a 2.4 percent increase compared to 1995. As for the distribution based on specific religions, the Buddhist population accounts for about 22.8 percent, which is the largest portion of the total population, followed by Christians (Protestants) with 18.3 percent, and Catholics with 10.9 percent. For the religious population by sex, the ratio of religious males is 49.7 percent and that of religious females is 56.4 percent. Among age groups, the 50-60 age group shows the highest proportion of religious males, and for the female population, the 60-70 age group shows the highest ratio.

International Marriage

Since marriage directly affects the fertility rate and reflects social changes very well, it receives a lot of attention vis-a-vis the social structure of a population. Particularly, international marriage draws the most attention because it usually occurs between people with significantly different traditions, values, and languages. Also, international marriages bring with them challenges related to the social adaptation of non-Korean married immigrants and the next generation of multi-ethnic children.

The international marriage rate in 2005 was about 13.6 percent, meaning approximately 13 out of 100 Koreans married foreigners that year. In rural areas, the international marriage rate reached as high as 27.4 percent, about one out of four. Hence, Korea has become a more multi-ethnic and multi-cultural society.

The regions with a relatively higher rate of international marriage are mostly located in remote mountain villages or typical agricultural areas. In particular, the regions with more than 30 percent foreign wives are usually in farming communities where there are more unmarried men.

POPULATION STRUCTURE

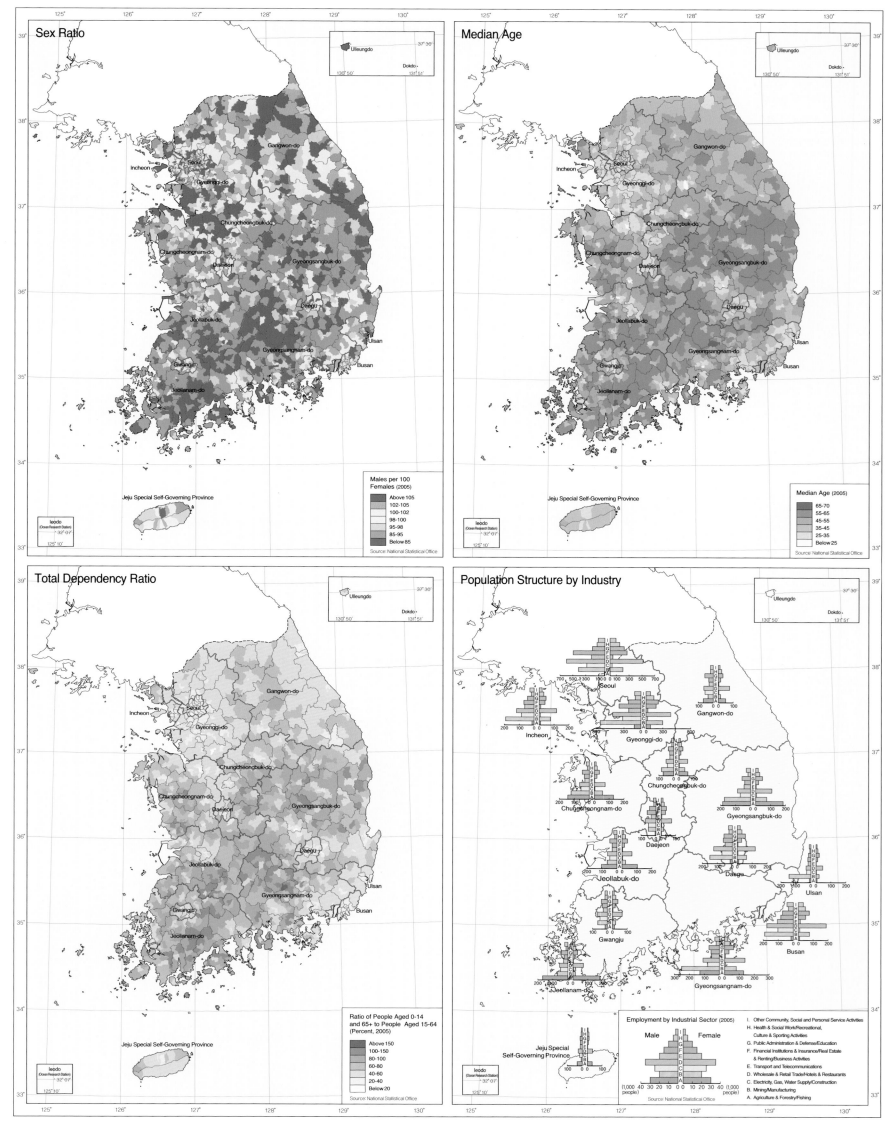

Sex Ratio

Males per 100 Females (2005)
- Above 105
- 102-105
- 100-102
- 98-100
- 95-98
- 85-95
- Below 85

Jeju Special Self-Governing Province

Ieodo (Ocean Research Station)

Source: National Statistical Office

Median Age

Median Age (2005)
- 65-70
- 55-65
- 45-55
- 35-45
- 25-35
- Below 25

Jeju Special Self-Governing Province

Ieodo (Ocean Research Station)

Source: National Statistical Office

Total Dependency Ratio

Ratio of People Aged 0-14 and 65+ to People Aged 15-64 (Percent, 2005)
- Above 150
- 100-150
- 80-100
- 60-80
- 40-60
- 20-40
- Below 20

Jeju Special Self-Governing Province

Ieodo (Ocean Research Station)

Source: National Statistical Office

Population Structure by Industry

Employment by Industrial Sector (2005)

Male | Female

(1,000 people) 40 30 20 10 0 0 10 20 30 40 (1,000 people)

I. Other Community, Social and Personal Service Activities
H. Health & Social Work/Recreational, Culture & Sporting Activities
G. Public Administration & Defense/Education
F. Financial Institutions & Insurance/Real Estate & Renting/Business Activities
E. Transport and Telecommunications
D. Wholesale & Retail Trade/Hotels & Restaurants
C. Electricity, Gas, Water Supply/Construction
B. Mining/Manufacturing
A. Agriculture & Forestry/Fishing

Jeju Special Self-Governing Province

Ieodo (Ocean Research Station)

Source: National Statistical Office

0 25 50 100 km

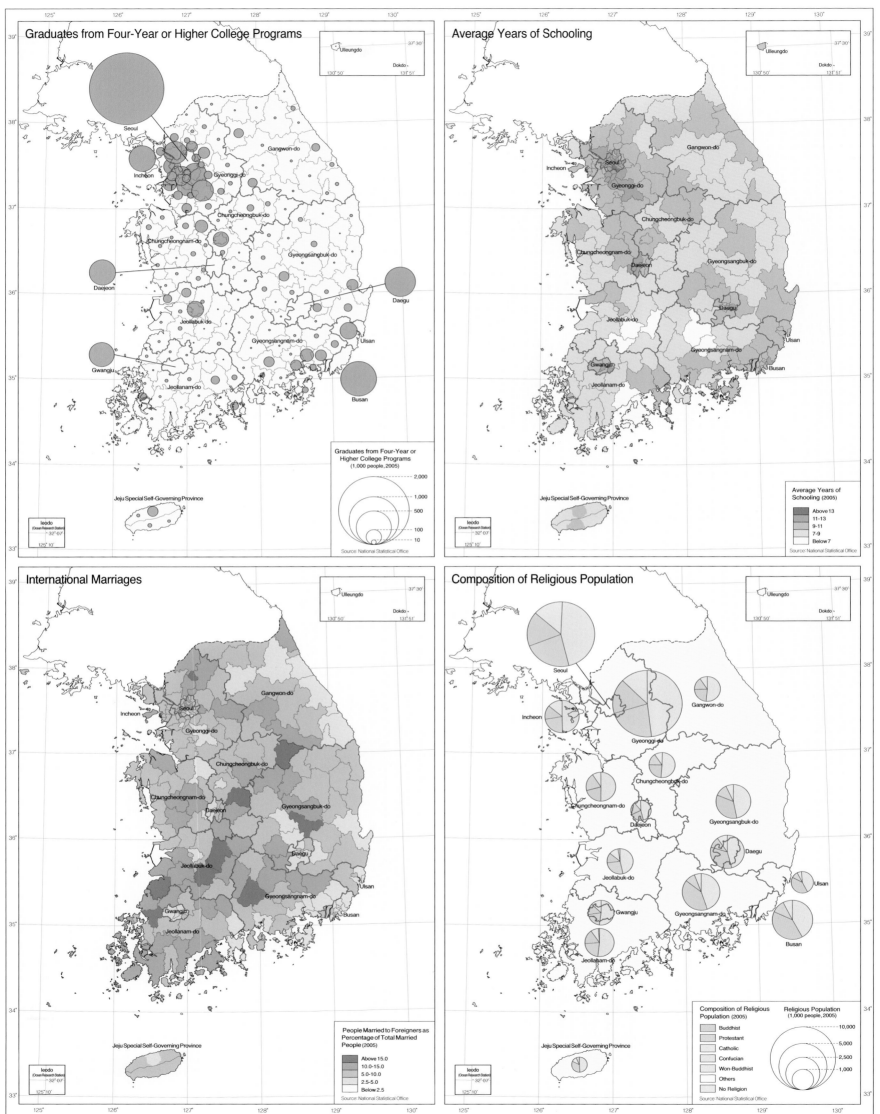

Graduates from Four-Year or Higher College Programs

Average Years of Schooling

Graduates from Four-Year or Higher College Programs (1,000 people, 2005)
2,000
1,000
500
100
10
Source: National Statistical Office

Average Years of Schooling (2005)
Above 13
11-13
9-11
7-9
Below 7
Source: National Statistical Office

International Marriages

Composition of Religious Population

People Married to Foreigners as Percentage of Total Married People (2005)
Above 15.0
10.0-15.0
5.0-10.0
2.5-5.0
Below 2.5
Source: National Statistical Office

Composition of Religious Population (2005)
Buddhist
Protestant
Catholic
Confucian
Won-Buddhist
Others
No Religion

Religious Population (1,000 people, 2005)
10,000
5,000
2,500
1,000
Source: National Statistical Office

HOUSEHOLD AND HOUSING

Average Number of People per Household

Ulleungdo

Dokdo

Gangwon-do

Seoul

Incheon

Gyeonggi-do

Chungcheongbuk-do

Chungcheongnam-do

Daejeon

Gyeongsangbuk-do

Jeollabuk-do

Daegu

Gyeongsangnam-do

Ulsan

Gwangju

Busan

Jeollanam-do

Jeju Special Self-Governing Province

Ieodo
(Ocean Research Station)

Average Number of People
per Household (2005)

Above 3.0
2.7-3.0
2.4-2.7
Below 2.4

Source: National Statistical Office

0   25   50   100 km

The fundamental unit of a modern society is the household. The household, as an essential demographic concept, is usually defined as people 'living together in a physical living environment,' and is mainly based not only on primary relationships such as blood, marriage, and adoption (called a 'relative household'), but also on secondary relationships, mainly the sharing of a physical living space among non-related people ('non-relative household'). The most important and fundamental is the relative household, which can be categorized into one-, two-, three- and other-generation types. The household's composition and characteristics reflect the basic structure of a society.

The house as a dwelling unit also represents characteristics of a society. That is, it reflects not only the economic characteristics of a society as it is the fundamental component of people's lives, but also the main index for residential characteristics. In this part, we will review changes in the number of households, characteristics of households by generation, characteristics of the heads of households, one-person households, the residential type and characteristics of housing, and the state of housing supply by period.

Changes in Households
Since the 1980s, the total number of households rapidly increased from about 8 million in 1980, to 10 million in 1990, and to 16 million in 2005 (see Figure 1). During this period (1980-2005), the total number of households doubled, and the proportion in the Capital Region rapidly increased from 36.6 percent in 1980 to 47.1 percent in 2005, which reflects the high concentration of households in the Capital Region. On the other hand, during the same period, the average number of people per household decreased from 4.55 in 1980, to 3.71 in 1990, and to 2.88 in 2005. The main reason for this was the major shift to the two-generation household in the Korean society and the significant increase in one-person households due to several social factors such as divorce, separation by death, and an increasing number of people choosing to remain single.

In terms of the spatial distribution of the average number of people per household, there are higher values in metropolitan cities and the Capital Region, but lower values in rural areas. With the shift toward urbanization, a significant portion of the population in rural areas, especially the younger generation, rapidly migrated toward metropolitan cities and the Capital Region, which resulted in a lower number of households in rural areas and a higher number in metropolitan cities and the Capital Region. Another reason for this is that housing prices in urban regions have been relatively higher than in rural areas, which has led to different opportunities for purchasing large-sized housing units and choices in the independence level of householders.

The change in the spatial pattern of the household number by region is similar to that of the average number of people per household. The household number rapidly decreased in the metropolitan cities, and the Capital Region, while there was a lower increasing rate of households or even a decrease in rural regions. Related to the above, the absolute number of households in rural areas decreased due to urbanization.

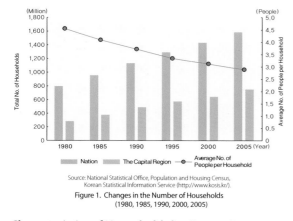

Source: National Statistical Office, Population and Housing Census,
Korean Statistical Information Service (http://www.kosis.kr/).
Figure 1. Changes in the Number of Households
(1980, 1985, 1990, 2000, 2005)

Characteristics of Households by Generation
There are significant spatial patterns for households by generation: one-generation, two-generation, and three-or-more generation households (see Table 1). In household composition by generation, the two-generation households account for more than 50 percent, and one-person and one-generation households account for 20.0 percent, and 16.2 percent, respectively, while three-or-more generation households comprise a relatively lower proportion. In the spatial distribution, the rate of two-generation households is higher in the metropolitan cities and the Capital Region, while the rate of one-generation households is relatively higher in provinces (*do*) and the non-Capital Region.

Table 1. Regional Differences of Households by Generation, 2005   (Unit: household, percent)

	Total Households	Proportions of Household Types by Generation					
		One Generation	Two Generation	Three Generation	Four Generation	One Person	Other
Nation	15,887,128	16.2	55.4	6.9	0.1	20.0	1.4
Metropolitan Cities	7,411,926	14.1	58.7	6.6	0.1	19.3	1.2
Provinces (*do*)	8,475,202	18.1	52.6	7.1	0.1	20.5	1.6
The Capital Region	7,462,090	14.1	58.9	7.0	0.1	18.5	1.4
Non-Capital Region	8,425,038	18.1	52.4	6.8	0.1	21.3	1.4

Source: National Statistical Office, Population and Housing Census (2005),
Korean Statistical Information Service (http://www.kosis.kr/)

When we examine the spatial pattern of one-generation households, such as couples without children or relatives, and the heads of households living with their relatives, the non-Capital Region shows a higher proportion than the Capital Region, and rural areas in provinces than metropolitan cities. On the other hand, two-generation households has a higher proportion in metropolitan cities, especially Daegu and Busan, and the Capital Region, but lower proportions in the inland regions of Jeollanam-*do*, Jeollabuk-*do* and Gyeongsangnam-*do*, and the whole of Gyeongsangbuk-*do*. This can be explained by a decrease in the number of multi-generation households in rural areas due to separation and the outward-migration of the young population toward urban regions. Conversely, the rate of three-or-more generation households is higher in the north-eastern part of the Capital Region, parts of Gangwon-*do*, Chungcheongnam-*do*, Chungcheongbuk-*do*, and Jeju-*do*, which are typically rural areas in Korea.

Characteristics of Heads of Households
There has been a continued increase in one-person households both in number and proportion (see Figure 2). The rate of one-person households is relatively higher in rural areas, especially Gyeongsangnam-*do* and Gyeongsangbuk-*do*, inland areas of Jeollanam-*do* and Jeollabuk-*do*, and Gangwon-*do*, than in metropolitan cities and the Capital Region. The general tendency of the spatial pattern of one-person households indicates that the majority of the young are in metropolitan cities and that the aged are in rural areas.

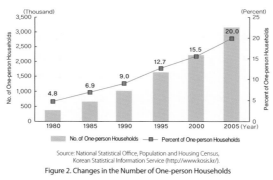

Source: National Statistical Office, Population and Housing Census,
Korean Statistical Information Service (http://www.kosis.kr/).
Figure 2. Changes in the Number of One-person Households

Characteristics of Housing
With the trend of a growing population, the housing supply has increased in response to the increase in demand. The housing supply has rapidly increased since the 1980s, with about 5 million housing units in 1980, over 7 million in 1990, and over 10 million in 2000. This trend brought the rate of housing supply to 71.2 percent in 1980, 86 percent in 1995, and to over 100 percent in 2005. Even though the rate of housing supply is currently over 100 percent, there are still spatial mismatches between supply and demand in local housing markets in terms of spatial distribution. The major portion of the housing supply has been concentrated in metropolitan cities and the Capital Region, but due to the relatively higher housing demand with an increasing population in these regions, the rate is relatively lower than in rural regions and the non-Capital Region.

In terms of the type of living quarters, the proportion of detached dwellings was traditionally high, but in recent years the proportion of apartments has increased, since most housing units supplied recently have been of the apartment type, and not detached dwelling. That is, the rate of detached dwelling units was about 95 percent in the 1970s, but 47 percent in 1995, and 32.2 percent in 2005, while the rate of apartments was 37 percent in 1995 and 52.7 percent in 2005. There is also a spatial mismatch for the provision of new apartments, which means there is a higher concentration of new apartments in metropolitan cities and the Capital Region.

Table 2. Housing Supply by Type   (Unit: housing, percent)

	Year	Total Housing Units Built	Proportions of Household Types by Generation			
			Detached dwelling	Apartment	Row house	Apartment unit in a private house
Nation	1997	596,435	8.9	81.3	3.2	6.6
	2000	433,488	8.0	76.5	2.4	13.1
	2005	463,641	6.0	89.6	1.0	3.4
The Capital Region	1997	229,370	6.6	77.9	6.0	9.5
	2000	240,985	4.0	75.3	2.4	18.2
	2005	197,901	2.9	91.8	0.9	4.4
Non-Capital Region	1997	367,065	10.3	83.4	1.5	4.8
	2000	192,503	13.1	78.0	2.3	6.7
	2005	265,740	8.3	88.0	1.1	2.7
Metropolitan Cities	1997	209,073	7.0	78.0	4.3	10.7
	2000	186,252	4.7	73.0	1.9	20.3
	2005	177,496	3.2	90.3	0.7	5.8

Source: National Statistical Office, Population and Housing Census (2005),
Korean Statistical Information Service (http://www.kosis.kr/).

The rate of apartments is highest in metropolitan cities and the Capital Region, while detached-dwelling residences have a higher concentration in the non-Capital Region and traditional rural regions, especially the traditional sub-regions of Jeolllanam-*do*, Jeollabuk-*do*, Gyeongsangnam-*do*, and Gyeongsangbuk-*do*.

In terms of housing characteristics, the average number of rooms per household has tended to increase over time, from 2.32 in 1970, to 3.09 in 1995, and to 3.39 in 2000. The average number of rooms per household is higher in rural areas such as Jeolllanam-*do* and Gyeongsangnam-*do* than in the metropolitan cities. The residential area per person also increased from 19.8 square meters in 2000 to 22.8 in 2005, and is presently higher in rural areas rather than in the metropolitan cities.

The amount of housing supply since 2000 has differed significantly by region. A huge concentration of the housing supply is in the Capital Region, Busan, Daegu, and Daejeon, which means a spatial mismatch between housing demand and supply. For this reason, some regions have an excess of housing units, while other regions still suffer from housing deficits. In the case of the over-supplied regions, some existing housing units remain empty. In this respect, there is a higher rate of empty housing units in major parts of Gangwon-*do*, while there is a relatively low rate in the metro regions.

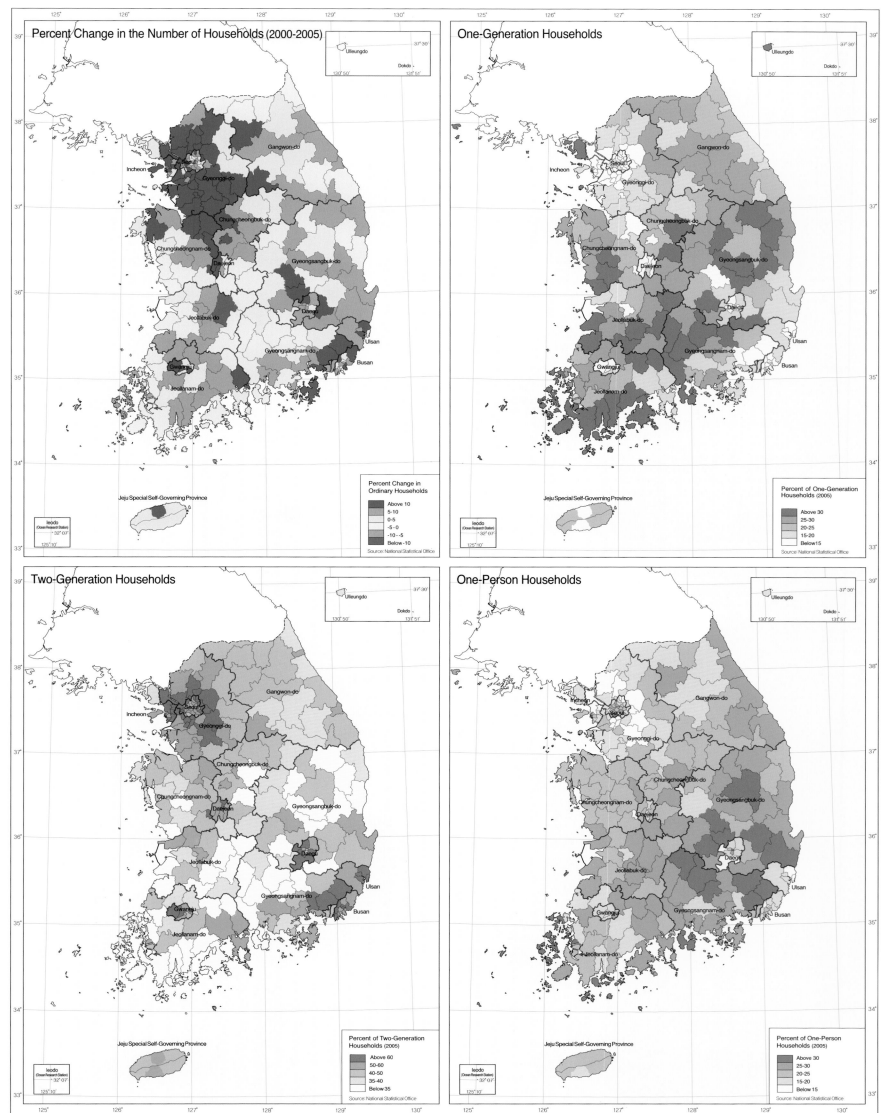

Percent Change in the Number of Households (2000-2005)

Percent Change in
Ordinary Households

Above 10
5-10
0-5
-5 - 0
-10 - -5
Below -10

Source: National Statistical Office

One-Generation Households

Percent of One-Generation
Households (2005)

Above 30
25-30
20-25
15-20
Below 15

Source: National Statistical Office

Two-Generation Households

Percent of Two-Generation
Households (2005)

Above 60
50-60
40-50
35-40
Below 35

Source: National Statistical Office

One-Person Households

Percent of One-Person
Households (2005)

Above 30
25-30
20-25
15-20
Below 15

Source: National Statistical Office

0   25   50   100 km

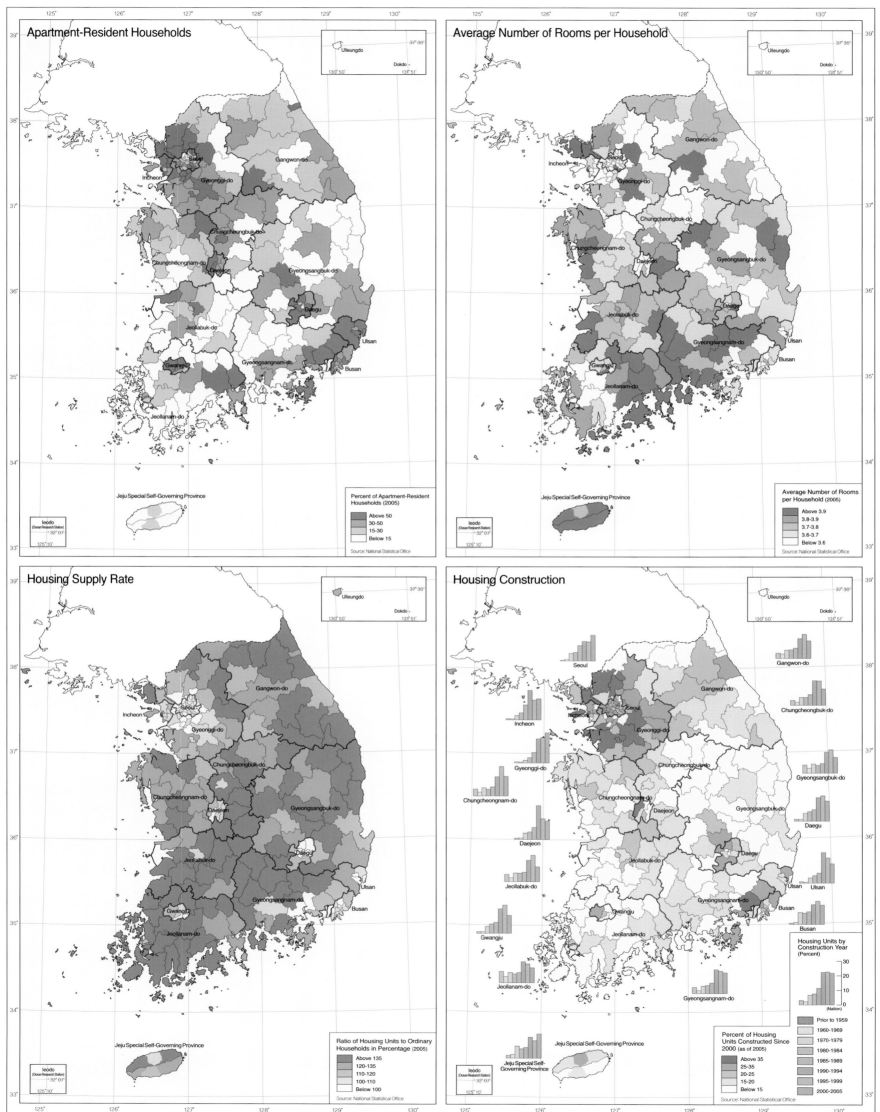

Apartment-Resident Households

Percent of Apartment-Resident Households (2005)

- Above 50
- 30-50
- 15-30
- Below 15

Jeju Special Self-Governing Province

Ieodo (Ocean Research Station)

Source: National Statistical Office

Average Number of Rooms per Household

Average Number of Rooms per Household (2005)

- Above 3.9
- 3.8-3.9
- 3.7-3.8
- 3.6-3.7
- Below 3.6

Jeju Special Self-Governing Province

Ieodo (Ocean Research Station)

Source: National Statistical Office

Housing Supply Rate

Ratio of Housing Units to Ordinary Households in Percentage (2005)

- Above 135
- 120-135
- 110-120
- 100-110
- Below 100

Jeju Special Self-Governing Province

Ieodo (Ocean Research Station)

Source: National Statistical Office

Housing Construction

Housing Units by Construction Year (Percent)

(Nation)

- Prior to 1959
- 1960-1969
- 1970-1979
- 1980-1984
- 1985-1989
- 1990-1994
- 1995-1999
- 2000-2005

Percent of Housing Units Constructed Since 2000 (as of 2005)

- Above 35
- 25-35
- 20-25
- 15-20
- Below 15

Jeju Special Self-Governing Province

Ieodo (Ocean Research Station)

Source: National Statistical Office

0 25 50 100 km

CULTURE AND TOURISM

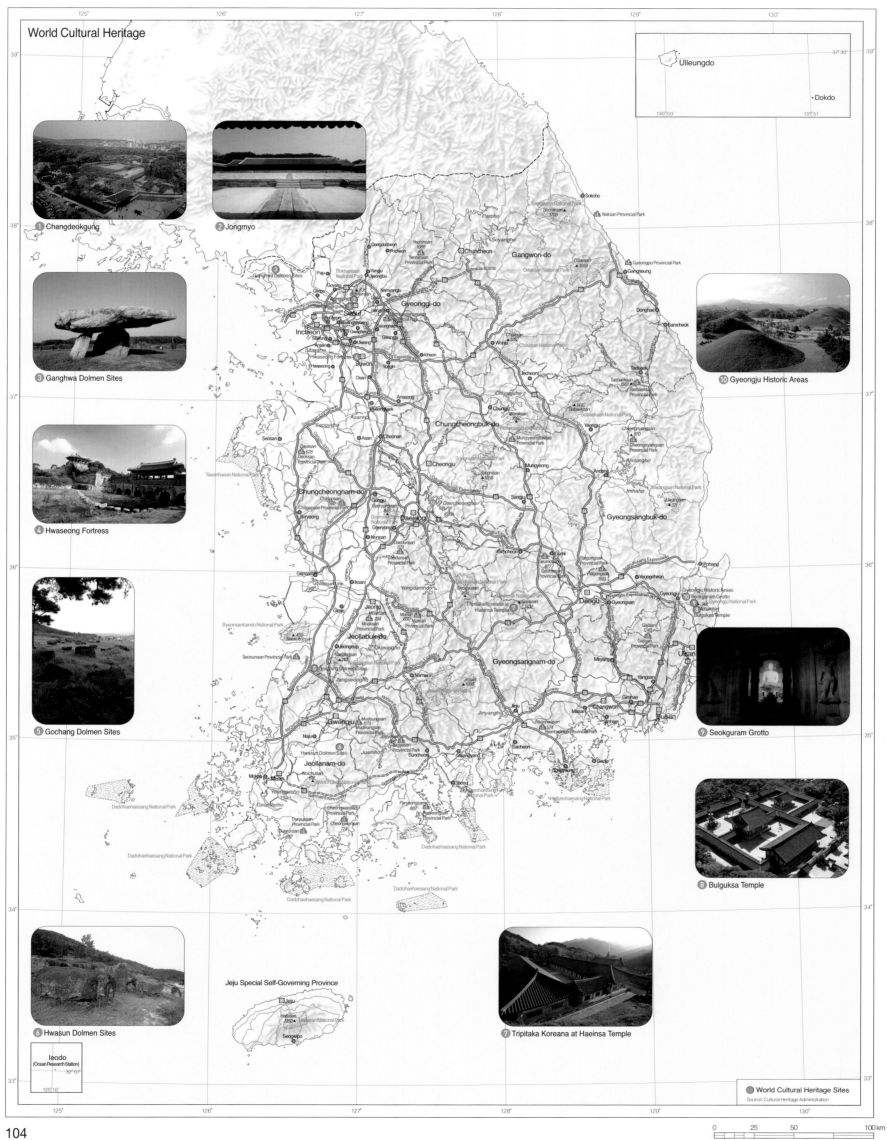

World Cultural Heritage

① Changdeokgung
② Jongmyo
③ Ganghwa Dolmen Sites
④ Hwaseong Fortress
⑤ Gochang Dolmen Sites
⑥ Hwasun Dolmen Sites
⑦ Tripitaka Koreana at Haeinsa Temple
⑧ Bulguksa Temple
⑨ Seokguram Grotto
⑩ Gyeongju Historic Areas

Jeju Special Self-Governing Province

Ieodo
(Ocean Research Station)
32°07'
125°10'

● World Cultural Heritage Sites
Source: Cultural Heritage Administration

0   25   50   100 km

The Growth of Leisure in Time and Expenditure

The development of culture and tourism industries is closely associated with the growth of time and money spent on leisure activities. Leisure time is related to the decrease of time spent on labor activities. Since the mid-1980s, labor time has decreased approximately by 6 hours, from 51.6 hours per week in 1980 to 45.7 hours per week in 2004. The average monthly working days have also decreased by 1 day, from 24.6 days in 1980, to 23.6 days in 2004 (see Figure 1).

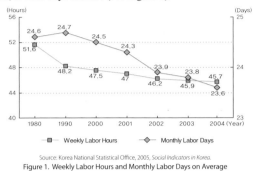

Source: Korea National Statistical Office, 2005, *Social Indicators in Korea.*

Figure 1. Weekly Labor Hours and Monthly Labor Days on Average

According to the *Survey Report on Cultural Enjoyment*, 50.1 percent of a sample population of 3,000 reported that daily leisure hours spent on weekends or holidays in 2006 were more than 5 hours on average. Differences in leisure time were not so dramatic among large cities, medium and small cities, and rural areas. People in large cities, however, spent a little more time on leisure activities than people in the other two regional settings (see Figure 2).

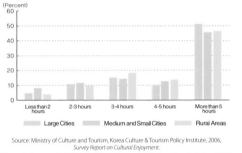

Source: Ministry of Culture and Tourism, Korea Culture & Tourism Policy Institute, 2006, *Survey Report on Cultural Enjoyment.*

Figure 2. Average Daily Leisure Hours Spent on Weekends or Holidays, 2006

Another important indicator is the increase of expenditures on leisure activities along with the increase of income and leisure hours. The amount of expenditures per capita on leisure, as shown in Table 1, has greatly increased, from 636,000 won in 1980, to 8,334,000 won in 2004. Table 2 shows the composition of domestic expenditure. Expenditure on services has increased from 34.9 percent in 1980 to 58.1 percent in 2004, and consisted of approximately 60 percent of total expenditures, while expenditures on goods, such as durable, semi-durable, and non-durable goods, decreased over time. Such an increase of expenditure on services can include the growth of expenditures on culture and tourism-related activities.

Table 1. Private Final Consumption Expenditures

(Unit: billion won, percent, thousand won)

Year	Private Final Consumption Expenditure	As Percent of GDP	Final Consumption Expenditure per capita
1980	24,250.6	62.5	636
1990	94,968.0	50.9	2,215
2000	312,300.5	54.0	6,644
2001	343,416.6	55.2	7,252
2002	381,063.0	55.7	8,003
2003	389,177.2	53.7	8,133
2004	400,696.5	51.5	8,334

Source: Korea National Statistical Office, 2005, *Social Indicators in Korea.*

Table 2. Composition of Domestic Consumption Expenditure by Type of Goods

(Unit: billion won, percent)

Year	Domestic Consumption Expenditure	Type of Goods			
		Durable Goods	Semi-durable Goods	Non-durable Goods	Services
1980	24,077.3	3.0	12.4	49.7	34.9
1990	93,535.0	10.2	8.6	35.1	46.0
2000	305,796.2	9.3	7.0	30.3	53.4
2001	335,391.0	9.0	6.6	29.5	54.9
2002	368,882.8	8.8	6.9	28.5	55.8
2003	376,221.3	7.3	6.6	28.5	57.6
2004	386,113.4	6.4	6.3	29.5	58.1

Source: Korea National Statistical Office, 2005, *Social Indicators in Korea.*

In 2006, monthly consumption expenditures on leisure per household, according to the *Survey Report on Cultural Enjoyment*, showed that 43.1 percent of the total sample households spent less than 100,000 won, 20.2 percent spent 100,000-150,000 won, 12.3 percent spent 150,000-200,000 won, and 1.3 percent spent more than 500,000 won. When regional differences of expenditure are explored among large cities, medium and small cities, and rural areas, those who spent less than 100,000 won on leisure comprised 35 percent in large cities, but 54.5 percent in rural areas. Those who spent more than 500,000 won on leisure accounted for 1.6 percent of total households in large cities, but only a mere 0.7 percent in rural areas. In brief, urban residents more actively participate in, and spend more money on, leisure activities than rural residents.

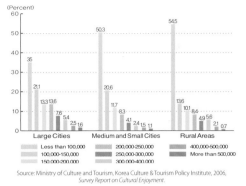

Source: Ministry of Culture and Tourism, Korea Culture & Tourism Policy Institute, 2006, *Survey Report on Cultural Enjoyment.*

Figure 3. Monthly Consumption Expenditures on Leisure Per Household, 2006

Cultural Heritage

In this section, cultural resources will be explored, focusing on cultural heritage in terms of characteristics of their geographical distribution and usage.

Cultural heritage sites in Korea are mapped with respect to UNESCO World Heritage. There are 4 types of State-designated Heritage: National Treasures, Treasures, Historic Sites, and Natural Monuments. Korea is home to 10 UNESCO World Heritage sites, which include Changdeokgung (Jongno-gu, Seoul), Jongmyo (Jongno-gu, Seoul), Hwaseong (Suwon-si, Gyeonggi-do), Tripitaka Koreana at Haeinsa Temple (Hapcheon-gun, Gyeongsangnam-do), Bulguksa Temple (Gyeongju-si, Gyeongsangbuk-do), Seokguram (Gyeongju-si, Gyeongsangbuk-do), Gyeongju Historic Areas (Gyeongju-si, Gyeongsangbuk-do), Ganghwa Dolmen Sites (Ganghwa-gun, Incheon), Gochang Dolmen Sites (Gochang-gun, Jeollabuk-do), and Hwasun Dolmen Sites (Hwasun-gun, Jeollanam-do). Regarding the geographical distribution of UNESCO World Heritage sites in Korea, 50 percent of such sites are concentrated in Gyeongju-si and Seoul: the former was the capital city of the ancient Silla Kingdom, and the latter has been the capital city since the Joseon Dynasty.

National Treasures refer to heritage of a rare and significant value in terms of human culture, and Korea has approximately 300 National Treasures as of 2005. The geographical pattern of National Treasures by metropolitan city and province (*do*) shows spatial concentrations in three major areas, all of which used to be capital cities of past dynasties. Among the National Treasures, 50 percent are located in Seoul, the capital city since the Joseon Dynasty, 17 percent are in Gyeongsangbuk-do, which contains Gyeongju-si, and 9 percent are in Chungcheongnam-do, which contains Gongju-si and Buyeo-gun. By contrast, National Treasures are relatively scarce in areas located far away from past capitals, such as Jeju-do (0 percent), Jeollabuk-do (2 percent), and Gangwon-do (3 percent).

There are 1,400 Treasures in Korea as of 2005. The geographical distribution of Treasures by metropolitan city and province (*do*) shows a much weaker spatial concentration compared to that of National Treasures. Treasures are found the most in Seoul (29 percent), followed by Gyeongsangbuk-do (18 percent), Gyeonggi-do (10 percent), and Jeollanam-do (9 percent). Gyeonggi-do and Jeollanam-do have more Treasures than National Treasures, and these are largely found in Chungcheongnam-do. Jeju-do (0.2 percent) and Gangwon-do (4 percent) have the fewest treasures.

Historic Sites refer to places and facilities of great historic and academic values that are especially commemorable, such as prehistoric sites, fortresses, ancient tombs, kiln sites, dolmens, temple sites and shell mounds. Korea has 460 Historic Sites as of 2005. The geographical distribution of Historic Sites shows that most of them are located in Gyeongsangbuk-do, which includes Gyeongju-si (21 percent), whereas the largest number of both National Treasures and Treasures are located in Seoul. Seoul (15 percent) also has the second most Historic Sites, followed by Gyeonggi-do (13 percent). The fewest Historic Sites as well as Treasures are found in Jeju-do (1 percent) and Gangwon-do (3 percent).

Natural Monuments refer to animals, plants, minerals, caves, geological features, biological products and special natural phenomena, carrying great historic, cultural, scientific, aesthetic or academic value, through which the history of a nation and/or the secrets to the creation of the earth can be identified or revealed. There are approximately 460 Natural Monuments in Korea as of 2005. Unlike National Treasures, Treasures, and Historic Sites, Natural Monuments are affected more by natural environmental conditions than by historical or cultural factors. The geographical distribution of Natural Monuments indicates that most are located in Gyeongsangbuk-do (18 percent), followed by Jeollanam-do (14 percent), Jeju-do (12 percent), Gyeongsangnam-do (11 percent), and Gangwon-do (11 percent). Jeju-do and Gangwon-do take relatively higher ranks in terms of Natural Monuments compared to their ranks in terms of National Treasures, Treasures, and Historic Sites. By contrast, Seoul has the least number of Natural Treasures (3 percent).

Cultural and Tourism Industries : Amount and Distribution

The development of cultural and tourism industries, induced by the increasing demand for culture-related products, is important to note. The cultural industry, including publications, comics, films, animation, and digital education and information services, are highly geographically concentrated in Seoul (64.4 percent of the total cultural industry), followed by six metropolitan cities (13.7 percent) and Gyeonggi-do (10.2 percent). Such distinct spatial concentrations in the Capital Region and large cities are due to the strong preferences of cultural industries to locations with highly-skilled human resources, cultural resources, and consumers.

The characteristics of the tourism industry in Korea can be examined in terms of the number and geographic distribution of tourism sites, accommodation facilities, and tourists. Tourism sites can be classified into local festivals, special tourist zones, tourist resorts, and designated tourist attractions. Local festivals allow us to identify characteristics of the cultural industries and tourist attractions of regions that host festivals. In 2006, the city where the largest number of local festivals were held was Busan, followed by Jeju-si in Jeju-do, Daegu, Incheon, Ulsan, Gangneung-si in Gangwon-do, Seogwipo-si in Jeju-do, and Seoul, in descending order. Except for the metropolitan cities, festivals are held in regions with rich cultural and tourism resources such as Jeju-si and Seogwipo-si in Jeju-do, and Gangneung-si in Gangwon-do. Festivals are subdivided into 4 categories in terms of their purpose and nature: culture/art, tourism/specialty, tradition/folk, and other festivals. Tourism/specialty festivals, which promote and market tourism and special products, are the most popular type, and account for 310 out of the 725 total festivals. Culture/art festivals are the second most popular type (230 events). Festivals held in counties (*gun*) are mostly characterized as tourism and specialty festivals. This implies that local festivals are used as a useful means for stimulating the local economy through regional natural tourism resources and specialty marketing. Meanwhile, local festival participation rates in 2006 were reported to be much higher in rural areas than for large cities or medium and small cities.

Special Tourist Zones (STZs) are areas which are designated to be intensively developed into tourist-friendly regional areas with the necessary ingredients to attract foreign tourists, including legal services, high-grade services, and public information services. With a focus on foreign tourists, large shopping districts in Seoul have been developed in Jongno, Dongdaemun Fashion Town, Myeongdong, Namdaemun, and Bukchang, as well as in shopping districts surrounding the U.S. Army bases in Itaewon, Dongducheon, and Songtan in Pyeongtaek-si. The remaining 17 STZs, except Gyeongju, are mainly dependent on natural features such as mountains, hot springs, and valleys. Tourist resorts are areas designated to be comprehensively developed with facilities to serve tourists' various needs associated with sightseeing and recreation. Twelve tourist resorts, except Gyeongju Bomun tourist resort and Andong where the cultural landscapes are major tourist attractions, are designated owing to their natural landscapes such as seas, mountains, and spas. Five tourist resorts out of 14 are located in Gangwon-do, which has beautiful natural landscapes.

Designated tourist attractions are areas designated by law that have natural or cultural tourist attractions with basic facilities. As of 2006, Korea has a total of 225 designated tourist attractions distributed relatively evenly across the nation. In terms of the types of tourist attractions, Gangwon-do, with its natural features, has the most designated tourist attractions (39), Jeju-do, also abundant in unique landscapes, has 19 designated tourist attractions, which is a lot considering its size. By contrast, Gyeonggi-do has a relatively small number of sites with 14.

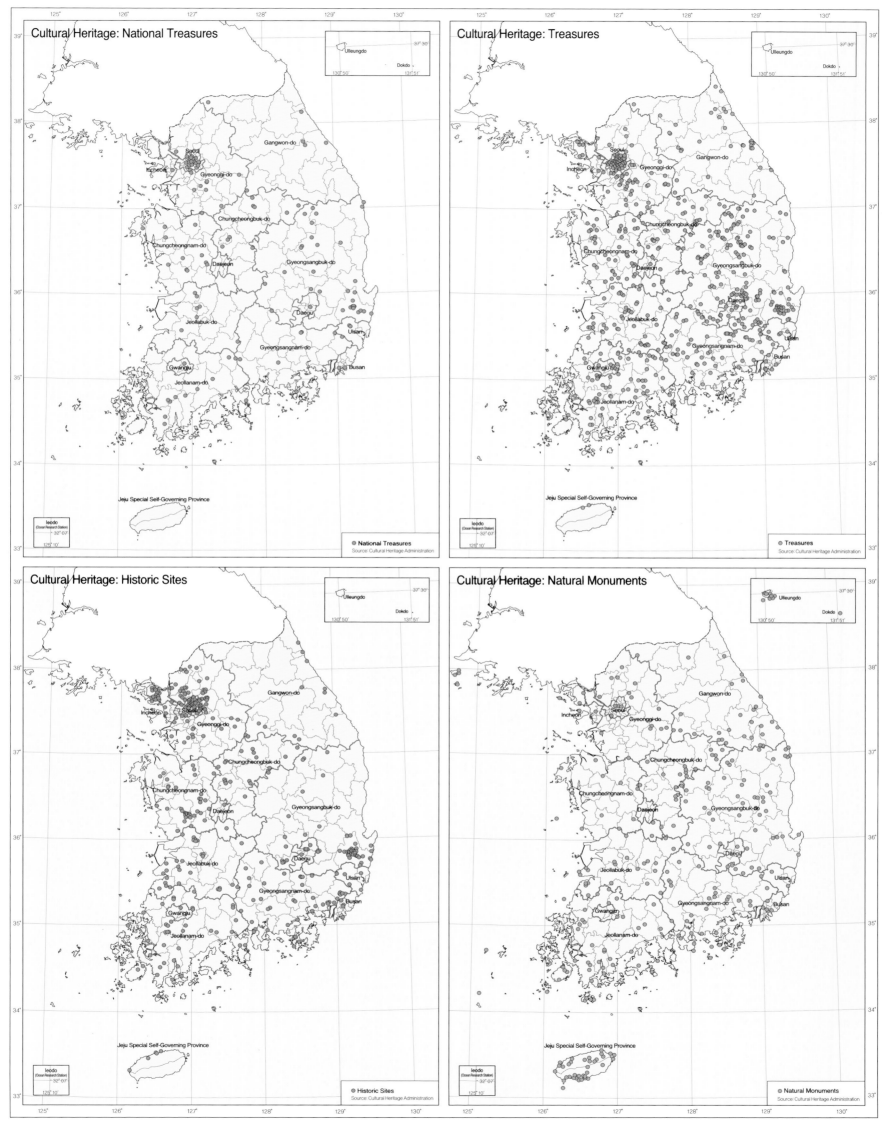

Cultural Heritage: National Treasures

● National Treasures
Source: Cultural Heritage Administration

Cultural Heritage: Treasures

● Treasures
Source: Cultural Heritage Administration

Cultural Heritage: Historic Sites

● Historic Sites
Source: Cultural Heritage Administration

Cultural Heritage: Natural Monuments

● Natural Monuments
Source: Cultural Heritage Administration

0 25 50 100 km

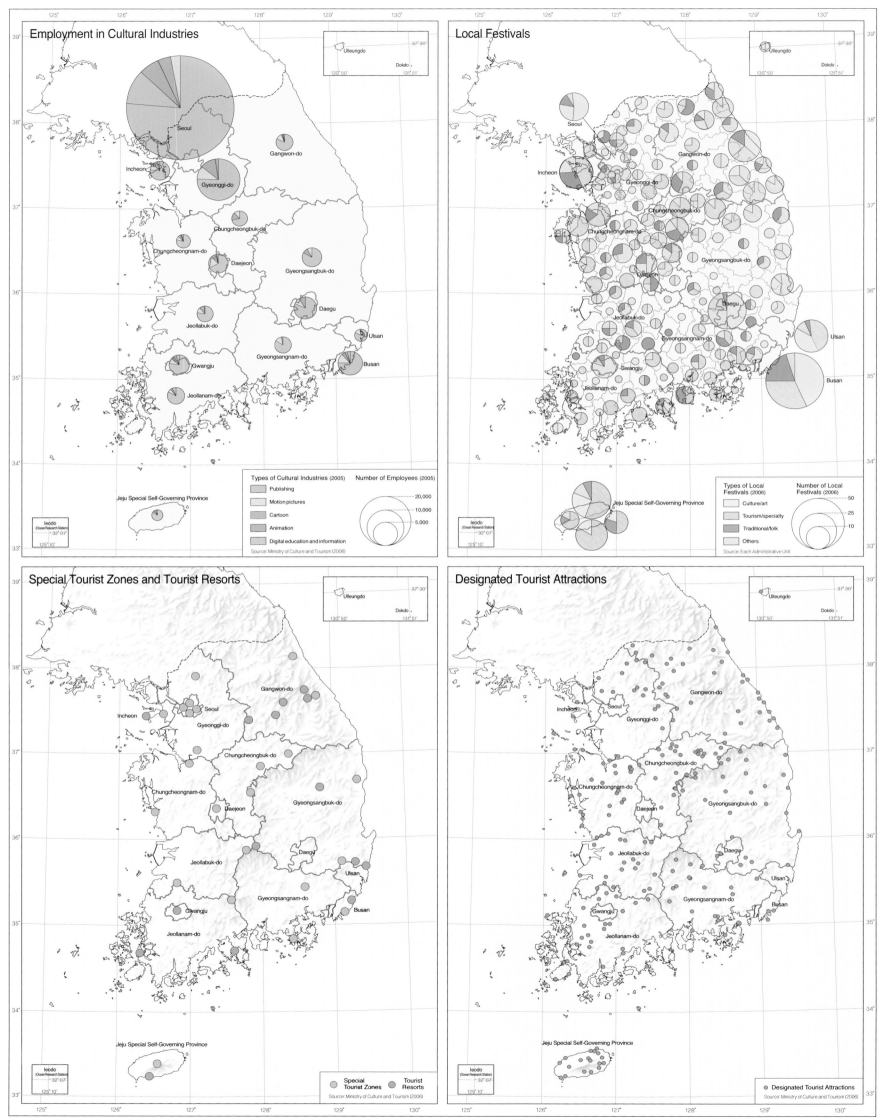

Employment in Cultural Industries

Local Festivals

Types of Cultural Industries (2005)
- Publishing
- Motion pictures
- Cartoon
- Animation
- Digital education and information

Number of Employees (2005)
- 20,000
- 10,000
- 5,000

Source: Ministry of Culture and Tourism (2006)

Types of Local Festivals (2006)
- Culture/art
- Tourism/specialty
- Traditional/folk
- Others

Number of Local Festivals (2006)
- 50
- 25
- 10

Source: Each Administrative Unit

Special Tourist Zones and Tourist Resorts

Designated Tourist Attractions

- Special Tourist Zones
- Tourist Resorts

Source: Ministry of Culture and Tourism (2006)

- Designated Tourist Attractions

Source: Ministry of Culture and Tourism (2006)

Jeju Special Self-Governing Province

Ieodo
(Ocean Research Station)

0 25 50 100 km

Urban and Rural Areas

Ulleungdo

Dokdo

Seoul

Incheon

Gangwon-do

Gyeonggi-do

Chungcheongbuk-do

Chungcheongnam-do

Daejeon

Gyeongsangbuk-do

Jeollabuk-do

Daegu

Ulsan

Gyeongsangnam-do

Busan

Gwangju

Jeollanam-do

Jeju Special Self-Governing Province

Ieodo
(Ocean Research Station)

Categories of Administrative
Units (2005)

Dongs (Urban Areas)

Eups (Rural Centers)

Myeons (Rural Areas)

Source: National Statistical Office
(as of December 31, 2005)

0   25   50   100 km

Urbanity and Rurality

Looking at the overall nation in terms of urban and rural concentrations is essential to get a picture of a country's settlement system. One of the ways to identify urban areas is the differentiation of the administrative system. At the smallest administrative area level, Korea is divided into 3,573 *dongs* or *eups* or *myeons*, which are well reflective of different urbanity levels; *dongs* tend to be very much urban, while *myeons* are mostly rural, with *eups* between the two as transitional zones. As of 2005, there are 2,163 *dongs* (60.5 percent), 210 *eups* (5.9 percent), and 1,200 *myeons* (33.6 percent). Population-wise, 81.5 percent of the total population resides in *dongs*, 8.3 percent in *eups* and the remainder of 10.2 percent in *myeons*. Given that *dongs* takes up much less space than *myeons* (see the urban and rural region map), the population density in *dongs* is significantly higher than that in *myeons*.

A close look at the major metropolitan cities reveals that Seoul, Gwangju and Daejeon are all composed of *dongs*, while Busan, Daegu, Incheon and Ulsan have *dong* populations of 97.9 percent, 93.9 percent, 97.2 percent, and 84.2 percent, respectively. As for provinces (*do*), the proportion of population residing in *dongs* is starkly lower than that of the metropolitan cities, with that of Chungcheongnam-*do* and Jeollanam-*do* being merely 37.3 percent and 43.5 percent, respectively. However, Gyeonggi-*do* is highest at the provincial level, reaching 82.7 percent, similar to Ulsan. Given that it was 67.4 percent in 1990, the urban population has increased at a rapid pace. As the concept of urban-rural integrative cities was introduced, even at the city (*si*) and county (*gun*) levels, urbanization rates have been diverse.

Urbanization rates refer to the percentage of the urban population whose value might differ if only *dongs* were considered as urban areas or *eups* were also included in the calculation. The changes of urbanization rates throughout the nation are as follows (see Figure 1): they rapidly rose until the 1980s, and have gradually declined since then. This shows that in terms of the urbanization curve, Korea has entered the terminal stage from the acceleration stage. As of 2005, Korea's urbanization rates were 81.5 percent in only considering *dongs*, and 89.8 percent when including *eups*.

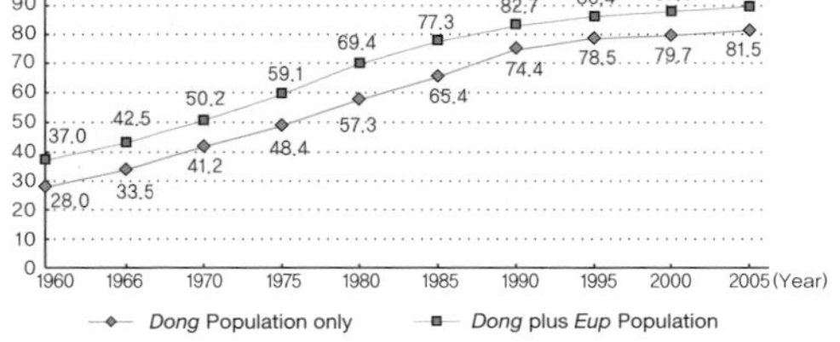

Source: National Statistical Office, Population and Housing Census, Korean Statistical Information Service (http://www.kosis.kr/).

Figure 1. Trend in Urbanization Rates, 1960-2005

The urban system in a country can be most easily described when urban locations and populations are simultaneously given on a map. In the mid-1990s, as the concept of urban-rural integrative cities was adopted, the system of central places in Korea faced a change in form. That is, many rural central places included in the county unit came to belong to the adjacent city boundaries, becoming a part of urban-rural integrative cities. A comparison of the geographical distribution of the urban population size in 2005 and 1990 reveals that the enlargement of the Capital Region and the growth of port cities in the Southeast Industrial Belt are outstanding, a hint that the two regions are connected along the Seoul-Busan axis. Also, the growth of Daejon, Cheongju-*si* and other cities in the Chungcheong Region, as well as cities in the Jeolla Region including Gwangju, Jeonju-*si*, and Mokpo-*si* is evident.

As of 2005, the population size of major metropolitan cities is as follows: Seoul (9.8 million) and Busan (3.5 million) surpassed three million; Incheon and Daegu was about 2.5 million; Daejeon and Gwangju were about 1.4 million; and Ulsan about 1.05 million. Of the 77 general cities, those whose populations top 500,000 include Suwon-*si* (1,044 thousand), Seongnam-*si* (935 thousand), Goyang-*si* (867 thousand), Bucheon-*si* (839 thousand), Yongin-*si* (690 thousand), Ansan-*si* (682 thousand), Cheongju-*si* (643 thousand), Jeonju-*si* (623 thousand), Anyang-*si* (612 thousand), Cheonan-*si* (522 thousand), and Changwon-*si* (502 thousand). Nine of the 18 cities whose populations amount to over 500,000, including the major metropolitan cities, are located in the Capital Region, showing the severity of the population concentration there. The most populous towns (*eup*) included in counties are Hwasun-*eup*, Hwasun-*gun* in Jeollanam-*do* (43 thousand), while eight of the least populous *eups* have less than 5,000.

Land-value variation is another indicator used to grasp the dynamic features of urbanity and rurality. Regions with high land-value growth rates in cities imply that the utilization value of urban land has been boosted. Those with a high land-value rate in rural areas imply that a rapid conversion from rural to urban land usage has taken place. Such dynamism in the land-value growth is closely linked to the artificial land development taking place in the national territory, including the construction of new cities. The annual land-value variation rate reflects the growth rate of the land value for a given year, and is calculated by comparing land-values of standard parcels at the beginning of the year and the end of the year by region.

Recently, the digital divide is spotlighted as an indicator differentiating urban and rural areas. The urban and rural digital divide has been greatly eased thanks to various policies, including the establishment and operation of "information villages." However, in terms of accessibility to information communications devices, usage capacity and utilization extent, rural regions still lag behind urban ones. The information advancement level among the general public nationwide versus farmers and fishers in 2006 (see Figure 2) was 50.2 as a comprehensive index covering all sectors. This implies that the information advancement level of farmers and fishers is almost half of that of the general public nationwide. Sector-wise, accessibility of IT infrastructure including computers and Internet was 30.5, a significant advancement. However, in terms of the capacity (computer and Internet usage capability) and qualitative usage (utilization of information infrastructure), it was still high - 70.9 and 68.7, respectively.

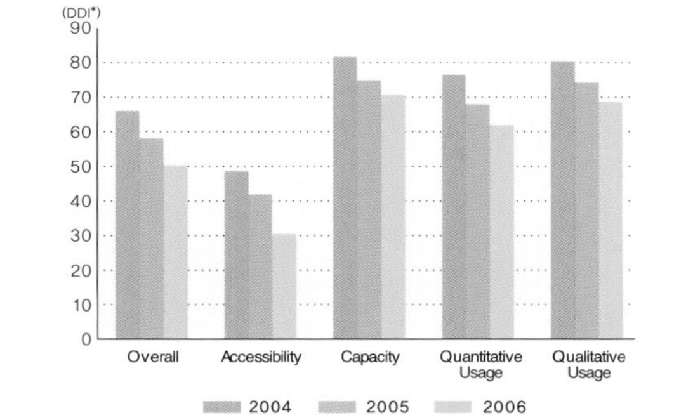

*Digital Divide Index (DDI) refers to differences in information advancement level between a particular group of people and all the people in a nation, and a value closer 100 means a more serious digital divide.

Source: Korean Agency for Digital Opportunity & Promotion, *2006 Digital Divide Index and Survey*.

Figure 2. Digital Divide Index for People in Rural Areas

An urban and rural digital divide per metropolitan city and province also stands out. According to the Internet usage rate as of 2006, major metropolitan cities showed over 70 percent of usage rates, including Ulsan (83.6 percent), Gyeonggi-*do* (79.7 percent), Incheon (79.2 percent), Gwangju (78.7 percent), and Seoul (78.1 percent). By contrast, many provinces including Jeollanam-*do* (63.4 percent), Gyeongsangbuk-*do* (65.1 percent), and Chungcheongnam-*do* (65.1 percent) had less than 70 percent usuage rates. In addition, computer usage rates were high in major metropolitan cities, including Ulsan (85.6 percent), Gwangju (80.3 percent), Gyeonggi (80.1 percent), and Seoul (78.9 percent), a contrast to Gyeongsangbuk-*do* (64.6 percent), Jeollanam-*do* (65.0 percent), and Chungcheongnam-*do* (65.6 percent). As of 2000, the digital divide at the city-county-district level was diverse, even within the same metropolitan cities and provinces.

Commuting Patterns

Commuting patterns are critical for understanding intra-regional interactions and the system of central places. As of 2005, Korea's commuting population amounted to 61.3 percent of those aged 12 and older, or 24.2 million

By looking at the main flow of commuting between cities (*si*), counties (*gun*) and districts (*gu*) in each region, major directions of spatial interaction can be explored and dynamic aspects of urban life can be captured. When considering commuting flows surpassing 10,000 alone, spatial interaction within each major metropolitan city appears. In particular, the number of commuters from Songpa-*gu* and Gwanak-*gu* to Gangnam-*gu* in Seoul, from Seo-*gu* to Yuseong-*gu* in Daejeon, and from Jung-*gu* to Nam-*gu* in Ulsan surpassed 30,000. In particular, Gangnam-*gu* is the nation's biggest commuting destination with over 500,000 people. In the Capital Region, intra-city flows are dominant. For example, the flows from Suwon-*si* to Hwasung-*si* and Yongin-*si*, from Yongin-*si* to Seongnam-*si*, and from Ansan-*si* to Siheung-*si* stand out. Outside the Capital Region, the number of commuters from Masan-*si* to Changwon-*si* and from Cheongju-*si* to Cheongwon-*gun* surpasses 30,000.

Urban areas are places where various human activities take place in an intense manner, so a relationship between the nighttime population and daytime population reveals each area's urban centrality. The Daytime Population Index refers to the daytime population divided by the nighttime population represented as a percentage. The fact that the index is above 100 means that commuting-induced in-flows are greater in numbers than out-flows, implying a higher centrality of daytime activities. As for the Daytime Population Index for each metropolitan city and province (*do*) as of 2005 (see Figure 3), Seoul showed the highest figure of 105.8. In the six major metropolitan cities except for Ulsan, the number of outflows is high, with an index of less than 100. As for provinces (*do*), Gyeonggi-*do* alone showed a low index due to great out-flows toward Seoul and Incheon. As for other provinces (*do*), they absorbed out-flows from adjacent metropolitan cities, and had an index of above 100.

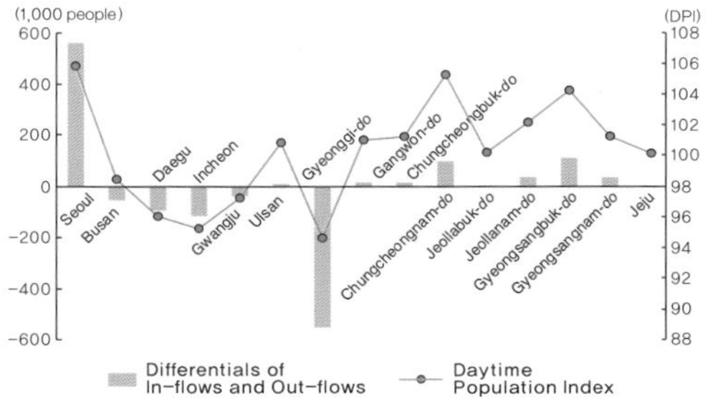

Source: National Statistical Office, Population and Housing Census (2005), Korean Statistical Information Service (http://www.kosis.kr/).

Figure 3. In- and Out-flows and Daytime Population Index by Metropolitan Cities and Provinces (*do*)

A close look at the cities (*si*), counties (*gun*) and districts (*gu*) whose Daytime Population Index surpassed 130 over time (see Table 1) reveals several points. The region with the highest index in all years was Jung-*gu* in Seoul, an exclusive daytime activity center. In addition, trends from 1995 to 2000 and from 2000 to 2005 show contrasts. That is, in the former period, the overall Daytime Population Index decreased, while it increased in the latter period. Furthermore, in the Capital Region, Gangnam-*gu* in Seoul was continuously on the rise, and outside the Capital Region, Gangseo-*gu* in Busan skyrocketed.

Table 1. Cities or Districts over 130 in Daytime Population Index (1995, 2000, 2005)

1995		2000		2005	
City or District	Daytime Population Index	City or District	Daytime Population Index	City or District	Daytime Population Index
Jung-*gu*, Seoul	394.9	Jung-*gu*, Seoul	292.0	Jung-*gu*, Seoul	353.9
Jung-*gu*, Busan	249.0	Jongno-*gu*, Seoul	215.7	Jongno-*gu*, Seoul	251.0
Jongno-*gu*, Seoul	243.8	Jung-*gu*, Busan	190.5	Gangseo-*gu*, Busan	213.3
Jung-*gu*, Incheon	191.0	Jung-*gu*, Daegu	168.1	Jung-*gu*, Busan	197.3
Jung-*gu*, Daegu	167.5	Gangnam-*gu*, Seoul	166.4	Jung-*gu*, Daegu	186.1
Gangnam-*gu*, Seoul	160.1	Jung-*gu*, Incheon	144.5	Gangnam-*gu*, Seoul	181.7
Yeongdeungpo-*gu*, Seoul	150.5	Dong-*gu*, Gwangju	140.5	Jung-*gu*, Incheon	171.5
Dong-*gu*, Gwangju	140.4	Yeongdeungpo-*gu*, Seoul	137.9	Dong-*gu*, Gwangju	140.1
Gyeongsan-*si*, Gyeongsangbuk-*do*	135.8	Gangseo-*gu*, Busan	133.4	Seocho-*gu*, Seoul	139.8
Yongsan-*gu*, Seoul	134.6	Yongsan-*gu*, Seoul	130.7	Yongsan-*gu*, Seoul	133.8
Yuseong-*gu*, Daejeon	134.4			Yeongdeungpo-*gu*, Seoul	132.8

Source: National Statistical Office, Population and Housing Census (2005), Korean Statistical Information Service (http://www.kosis.kr/).

The fact that the areas with high scores in the Daytime Population Index are mostly districts (*gu*) in major metropolitan cities shows that the higher the centrality of employment, the higher the Daytime Population Index.

Land Value Distribution within Large Cities

Land value results from the value evaluation of certain points within a city. Land value reflects urban functional differentiation and nodal structures, and is most widely used in examining the internal structure of a city.

The land value in Seoul is not only the highest, compared to other major metropolitan cities, but is also outstanding in terms of areal differentiation within Seoul. The most expensive land parcel is found in Chungmuro 1(il)-ga-*dong* in Jung-*gu*, and 19 out of the top 20 most expensive *dongs* are located in Jung-*gu* and Jongro-*gu*. However, the land value of the commercial and business districts around Samseong-*dong*, Yeoksam-*dong*, and Daechi-*dong* in Gangnam-*gu*, and Seocho-*dong* in Seocho-*gu* is also very high, so it can be said that at least two CBDs (central business districts) exist in Seoul. Also, Changcheon-*dong* and Daehyun-*dong* in Seodaemun-*gu* also possess a high land value, having outstanding centrality among city sub-centers.

The highest land value in Busan is found in Bujeon-*dong* in Busanjin-*gu*, where Seomyeon Rotary is located. However, other top 10 *dongs* are all located in Jung-*gu*. In particular, the district around Changseon-*dong*, Nampo-*dong* and Gwangbok-*dong* belong to a traditional CBD. Busan, due to topographical influences and other related urbanization characteristics, has many sub-centers. The area with the highest land value in Daegu is located in Dongseongro 2(i)-ga-*dong* in Jung-*gu*, and 25 of the top 30 *dongs* are all located in Jung-*gu*. As for Incheon, Bupyeong-*dong* in Bupyeong-*gu* recorded the highest land value. The top 10 *dongs* are scattered not only in Jung-*gu*, the traditional center, but also in Nam-*gu*, Namdong-*gu* and Bupyeong-*gu*. The highest land value in Gwangju came from Chungjangro 2(i)-ga-*dong* in Dong-*gu*, where top 10 *dongs* are all located. In Daegeon, the area with the highest land value is located in Eunhaeng-*dong* in Jung-*gu*, and some *dongs* adjacent to it in Jung-*gu* and Dong-*gu* also showed a high land value. However, concerning the top 10 *dongs*, some in Seo-*gu* and Yuseong-*gu* are included, indicating a primitive form of multi-nucleation. As for Ulsan, the highest land value level is somewhat low compared to other major metropolitan cities, and, centering on Samsan-*dong* in Nam-*gu*, a high land value nucleus exists around Jung-*gu* and Nam-*gu*.

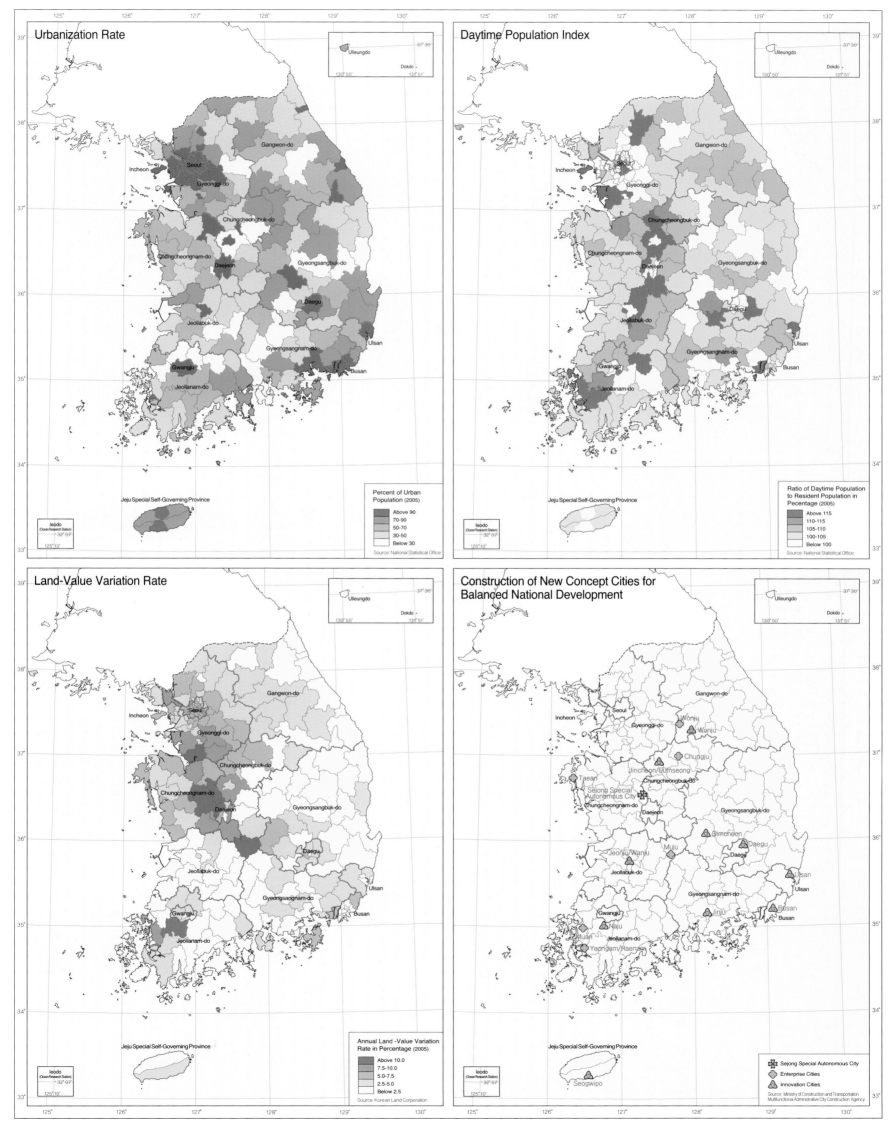

Urbanization Rate

Percent of Urban
Population (2005)

- Above 90
- 70-90
- 50-70
- 30-50
- Below 30

Source: National Statistical Office

Daytime Population Index

Ratio of Daytime Population
to Resident Population in
Percentage (2005)

- Above 115
- 110-115
- 105-110
- 100-105
- Below 100

Source: National Statistical Office

Land-Value Variation Rate

Annual Land-Value Variation
Rate in Percentage (2005)

- Above 10.0
- 7.5-10.0
- 5.0-7.5
- 2.5-5.0
- Below 2.5

Source: Korean Land Corporation

Construction of New Concept Cities for Balanced National Development

- Sejong Special Autonomous City
- Enterprise Cities
- Innovation Cities

Source: Ministry of Construction and Transportation
Multifunctional Administrative City Construction Agency

0 25 50 100 km

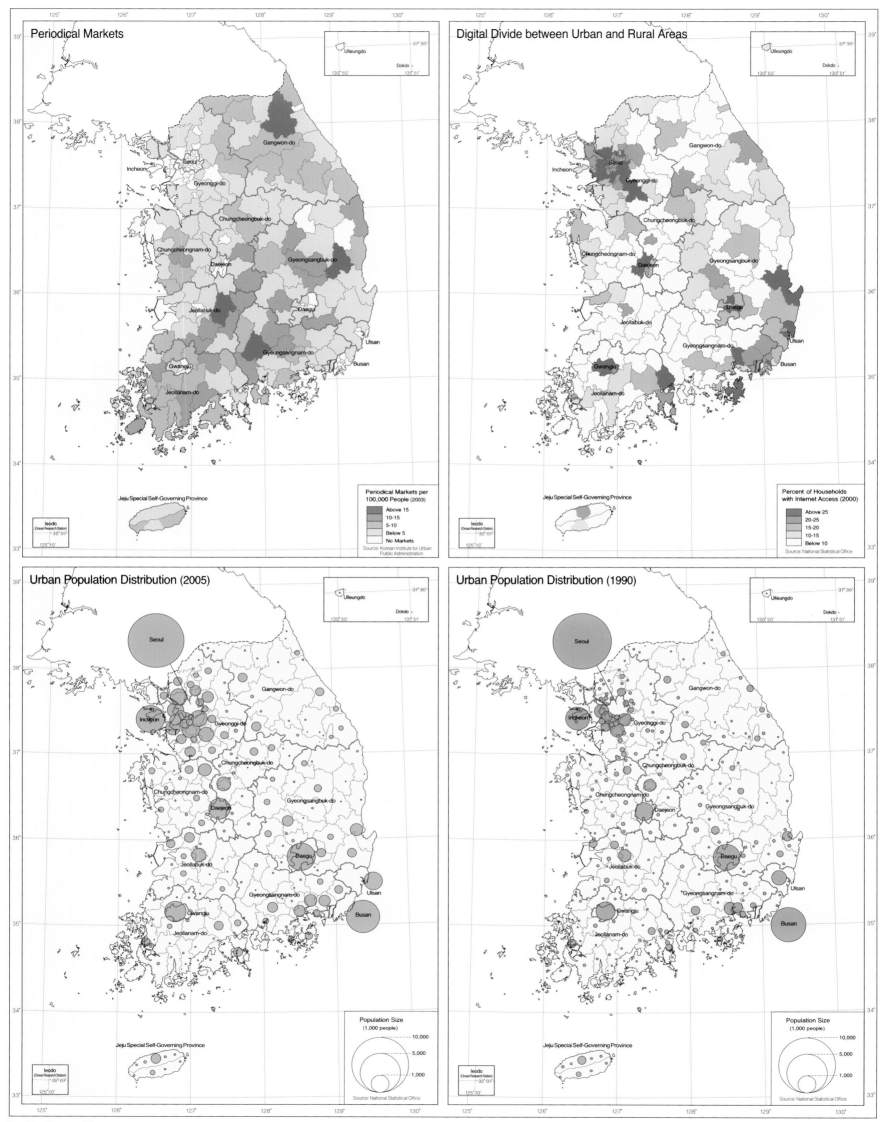

Periodical Markets

Periodical Markets per
100,000 People (2003)
Above 15
10-15
5-10
Below 5
No Markets

Source: Korean Institute for Urban
Public Administration

Digital Divide between Urban and Rural Areas

Percent of Households
with Internet Access (2000)
Above 25
20-25
15-20
10-15
Below 10

Source: National Statistical Office

Urban Population Distribution (2005)

Population Size
(1,000 people)
10,000
5,000
1,000

Source: National Statistical Office

Urban Population Distribution (1990)

Population Size
(1,000 people)
10,000
5,000
1,000

Source: National Statistical Office

0   25   50   100 km

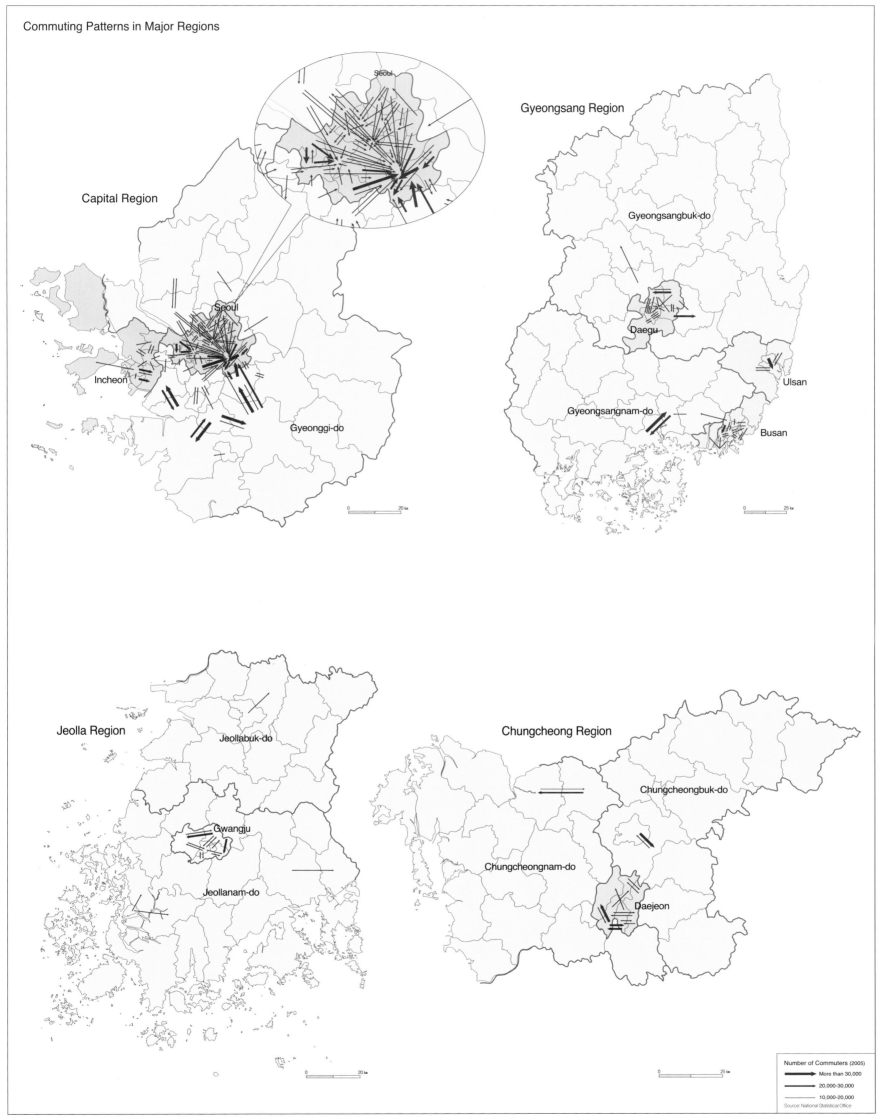

Commuting Patterns in Major Regions

Capital Region

Seoul

Seoul

Incheon

Gyeonggi-do

Gyeongsang Region

Gyeongsangbuk-do

Daegu

Ulsan

Gyeongsangnam-do

Busan

Jeolla Region

Jeollabuk-do

Gwangju

Jeollanam-do

Chungcheong Region

Chungcheongbuk-do

Chungcheongnam-do

Daejeon

Number of Commuters (2005)

More than 30,000

20,000-30,000

10,000-20,000

Source: National Statistical Office

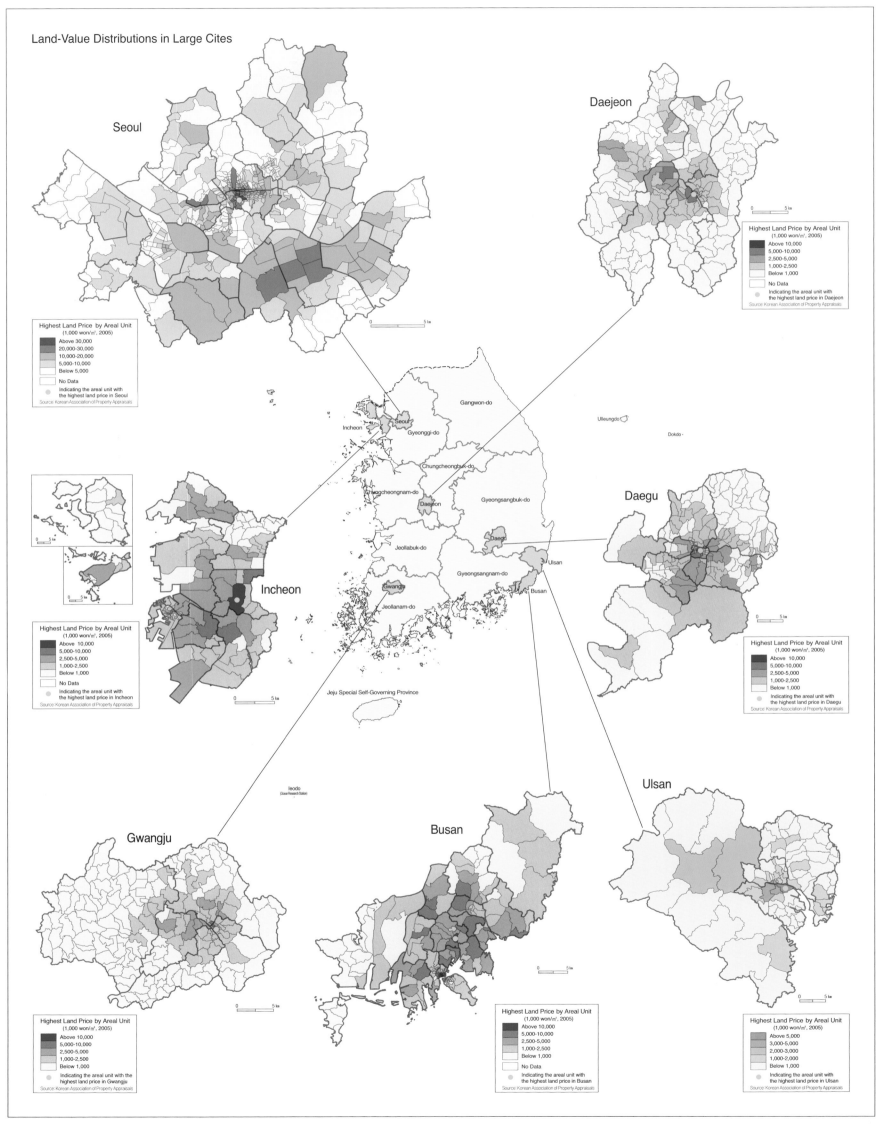

Land-Value Distributions in Large Cites

Seoul

Highest Land Price by Areal Unit
(1,000 won/m², 2005)
Above 30,000
20,000-30,000
10,000-20,000
5,000-10,000
Below 5,000
No Data
Indicating the areal unit with
the highest land price in Seoul
Source: Korean Association of Property Appraisals

Daejeon

Highest Land Price by Areal Unit
(1,000 won/m², 2005)
Above 10,000
5,000-10,000
2,500-5,000
1,000-2,500
Below 1,000
No Data
Indicating the areal unit with
the highest land price in Daejeon
Source: Korean Association of Property Appraisals

Incheon

Highest Land Price by Areal Unit
(1,000 won/m², 2005)
Above 10,000
5,000-10,000
2,500-5,000
1,000-2,500
Below 1,000
No Data
Indicating the areal unit with
the highest land price in Incheon
Source: Korean Association of Property Appraisals

Daegu

Highest Land Price by Areal Unit
(1,000 won/m², 2005)
Above 10,000
5,000-10,000
2,500-5,000
1,000-2,500
Below 1,000
Indicating the areal unit with
the highest land price in Daegu
Source: Korean Association of Property Appraisals

Gwangju

Highest Land Price by Areal Unit
(1,000 won/m², 2005)
Above 10,000
5,000-10,000
2,500-5,000
1,000-2,500
Below 1,000
Indicating the areal unit with the
highest land price in Gwangju
Source: Korean Association of Property Appraisals

Busan

Highest Land Price by Areal Unit
(1,000 won/m², 2005)
Above 10,000
5,000-10,000
2,500-5,000
1,000-2,500
Below 1,000
No Data
Indicating the areal unit with
the highest land price in Busan
Source: Korean Association of Property Appraisals

Ulsan

Highest Land Price by Areal Unit
(1,000 won/m², 2005)
Above 5,000
3,000-5,000
2,000-3,000
1,000-2,000
Below 1,000
Indicating the areal unit with
the highest land price in Ulsan
Source: Korean Association of Property Appraisals

Gangwon-do
Incheon
Seoul
Gyeonggi-do
Ulleungdo
Dokdo
Chungcheongbuk-do
Chungcheongnam-do
Daejeon
Gyeongsangbuk-do
Daegu
Ulsan
Jeollabuk-do
Gyeongsangnam-do
Busan
Gwangju
Jeollanam-do
Jeju Special Self-Governing Province
Ieodo
(Ocean Research Station)

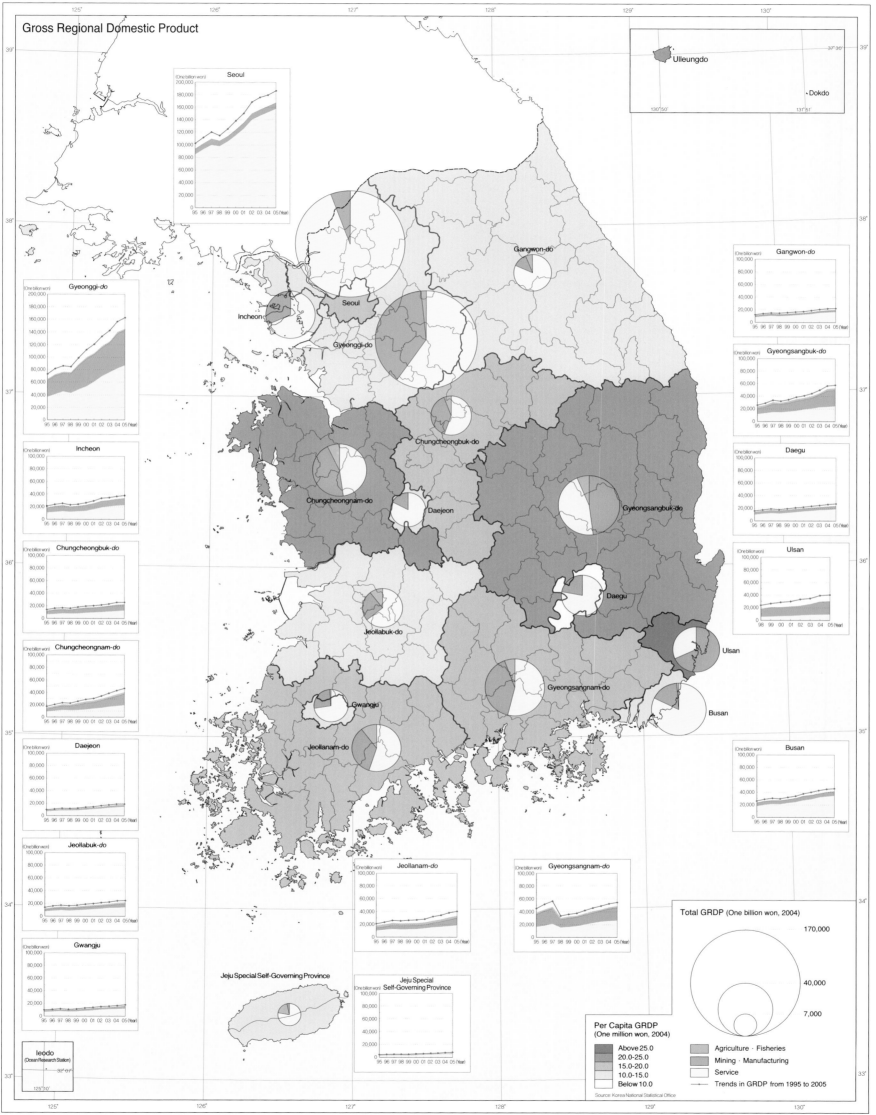

Gross Regional Domestic Product

Seoul
(One billion won)
200,000
180,000
160,000
140,000
120,000
100,000
80,000
60,000
40,000
20,000
95 96 97 98 99 00 01 02 03 04 05 (Year)

Gyeonggi-do
(One billion won)
200,000
180,000
160,000
140,000
120,000
100,000
80,000
60,000
40,000
20,000
95 96 97 98 99 00 01 02 03 04 05 (Year)

Incheon
(One billion won)
100,000
80,000
60,000
40,000
20,000
0
95 96 97 98 99 00 01 02 03 04 05 (Year)

Chungcheongbuk-do
(One billion won)
100,000
80,000
60,000
40,000
20,000
0
95 96 97 98 99 00 01 02 03 04 05 (Year)

Chungcheongnam-do
(One billion won)
100,000
80,000
60,000
40,000
20,000
0
95 96 97 98 99 00 01 02 03 04 05 (Year)

Daejeon
(One billion won)
100,000
80,000
60,000
40,000
20,000
0
95 96 97 98 99 00 01 02 03 04 05 (Year)

Jeollabuk-do
(One billion won)
100,000
80,000
60,000
40,000
20,000
0
95 96 97 98 99 00 01 02 03 04 05 (Year)

Gwangju
(One billion won)
100,000
80,000
60,000
40,000
20,000
0
95 96 97 98 99 00 01 02 03 04 05 (Year)

Ieodo
(Ocean Research Station)

Jeju Special Self-Governing Province

Gangwon-do
(One billion won)
100,000
80,000
60,000
40,000
20,000
95 96 97 98 99 00 01 02 03 04 05 (Year)

Gyeongsangbuk-do
(One billion won)
100,000
80,000
60,000
40,000
20,000
95 96 97 98 99 00 01 02 03 04 05 (Year)

Daegu
(One billion won)
100,000
80,000
60,000
40,000
20,000
95 96 97 98 99 00 01 02 03 04 05 (Year)

Ulsan
(One billion won)
100,000
80,000
60,000
40,000
20,000
98 99 00 01 02 03 04 05 (Year)

Busan
(One billion won)
100,000
80,000
60,000
40,000
20,000
95 96 97 98 99 00 01 02 03 04 05 (Year)

Jeollanam-do
(One billion won)
100,000
80,000
60,000
40,000
20,000
0
95 96 97 98 99 00 01 02 03 04 05 (Year)

Gyeongsangnam-do
(One billion won)
100,000
80,000
60,000
40,000
20,000
0
95 96 97 98 99 00 01 02 03 04 05 (Year)

Jeju Special
Self-Governing Province
(One billion won)
100,000
80,000
60,000
40,000
20,000
95 96 97 98 99 00 01 02 03 04 05 (Year)

Ulleungdo
Dokdo

Seoul
Incheon
Gyeonggi-do
Gangwon-do
Chungcheongbuk-do
Chungcheongnam-do
Daejeon
Gyeongsangbuk-do
Daegu
Jeollabuk-do
Ulsan
Gyeongsangnam-do
Busan
Gwangju
Jeollanam-do

Total GRDP (One billion won, 2004)
170,000
40,000
7,000

Per Capita GRDP
(One million won, 2004)
Above 25.0
20.0-25.0
15.0-20.0
10.0-15.0
Below 10.0

Agriculture · Fisheries
Mining · Manufacturing
Service
Trends in GRDP from 1995 to 2005

Source: Korea National Statistical Office

0 25 50 100 km

Characteristics of a regional economy can be understood through statistically available economic indicators such as gross regional domestic product, local finance, international trade and research & development activities. Amongst these indicators, gross regional domestic product and per capita gross regional domestic product are most conventionally used to show characteristics and changes in the regional economy.

Gross Regional Domestic Product (GRDP) is one of the ways to measure the size of a regional economy. The GRDP of a region is defined as the market value of all finished goods and services produced within a region in a given period of time. It is also considered as the sum of value added at every stage of production of all finished goods and services produced within a region in a given period of time. The most common approach to measuring and understanding GRDP is the expenditure method:

GRDP = consumption+investment+local government spending
+(exports-imports)

"Gross", meaning the depreciation of capital stock, is not included. With depreciation and net investment used instead of gross investment, the indicator becomes the net domestic product. The total of consumption and investment in this equation is the expenditure on finished goods and services. The exports-minus-imports part of the equation (often called cumulative exports) then adjusts this by subtracting the part of this expenditure not produced domestically (the imports), and then adding the domestic portion (the exports).

The general characteristics of industrial structure and economic activities in each region of Korea can be illustrated on the basis of GRDP and per capita GRDP. In 2004, the national total amount of nominal GRDP was 787.8 trillion won, which shows an increase of 7.7 percent (56.2 trillion won) over the previous year. The three highest regions in terms of GRDP are Seoul (23.1 percent), Gyeonggi-do (19.9 percent), and Gyeongsangbuk-do (7.2 percent), while the lowest regions are Jeju Special Self-Governing Province (0.9 percent), Gwangju (2.1 percent), and Daejeon (2.4 percent). The highest three regions account for 50.2 percent of the national total GRDP, which means there is an excessive concentration in the capital region.

In addition to this, there is a great deal of regional disparity revealed in the rate of growth in GRDP compared to the previous year. Gyeongsangbuk-do (14.2 percent), Ulsan (12.2 percent), and Gyeonggi-do (10.4 percent) are the regions that show the highest rate of growth in GRDP. In contrast, Daegu (3.6 percent), Seoul (3.7 percent), and Jeju Special Self-governing Province (3.9 percent) are the regions that display the lowest rate of growth in GRDP.

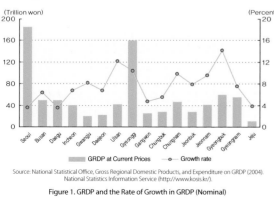

Figure 1. GRDP and the Rate of Growth in GRDP (Nominal)

Source: National Statistical Office, Gross Regional Domestic Products, and Expenditure on GRDP (2004). National Statistics Information Service (http://www.kosis.kr/).

As the capital region, including Seoul, Incheon and Gyeonggi-do, accounts for 47.7 percent of the national total GRDP, it also

shows a decrease of 0.4 percent compared to the previous year. The reason for this is that the ratio of Seoul to the national total GRDP decreased to 23.1 percent in 2004 from 24.0 percent in 2003. Likewise, it shows that the ratio of the capital region to total GRDP is lower than the ratio of the capital region's population to the national total population.

Table 1. Comparison between the Capital Region and the Non-capital Region in the Component Ratio of GRDP

	Ratio of GRDP (Percent)			Ratio of Population (Percent)		
	2003	2004	Growth Rate	2003	2004	Growth Rate
Capital Region	48.1	47.7	-0.4%	47.5	47.9	0.4%
Seoul	24.0	23.1	-0.9%	20.9	2.8	-0.1%
Incheon	4.7	4.7	0.0%	5.4	5.4	0.0%
Gyeonggi-do	19.4	19.9	0.5%	21.2	21.7	0.5%
Non-Capital Region	51.9	52.3	0.4%	52.1	52.1	-0.4%

Source: National Statistical Office, 2005, *The Estimation of Future Population by Region.*

The ratio of the seven metropolitan cities (Seoul, Busan, Daegu, Incheon, Gwangju, Daejeon and Ulsan) to the national total GRDP accounts for 46.2 percent, which shows a decrease of 0.9 percent from the previous year (47.1 percent). In detail, Ulsan shows an increase of 0.2 percent, while Seoul, Daegu and Busan show a drop of 0.9 percent, 0.1 percent and 0.1 percent, respectively. The component ratio of GRDP in the seven metropolitan cities is slightly lower than the component ratio of their population (1.1 percent).

Table 2. Comparison between Metropolitan Cities and the Provinces in the Component Ratio of GRDP

	Ratio of GRDP (Percent)			Ratio of Population (Percent)		
	2003	2004	Growth Rate	2003	2004	Growth Rate
Metropolitan cities	47.1	46.2	-0.9%	47.4	47.3	-0.1%
Provinces	52.9	53.8	0.9%	52.6	52.7	0.1%

Source: National Statistical Office, 2005, *The Estimation of Future Population by Region.*

Following figure 2 illustrates the growth rate of GRDP and presents changes in the development of the regional economy. On the basis of the year 2004, the real GRDP shows a decrease in the finance & insurance industry and the wholesale & retail industry, but an increase in the manufacturing, transportation, and construction industries. Gyeonggi-do had the highest real GRDP by virtue of the growth in its manufacturing, transportation, and construction industries., Gangwon-do had the lowest real GRDP, which was caused by decreases in the construction and manufacturing industries. The three highest regions in terms of GRDP growth rates were Gyeonggi-do (9.8 percent), Chungcheongnam-do (9.3 percent), and Ulsan (9.0 percent), while the lowest regions were Gangwon-do (0.1 percent), Jeju Special Self-governing Province (0.6 percent), and Daegu (0.8 percent).

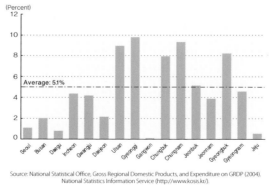

Source: National Statistical Office, Gross Regional Domestic Products, and Expenditure on GRDP (2004). National Statistics Information Service (http://www.kosis.kr/).

Figure 2. The Growth Rate of GRDP (at 2000 prices)

Table 3 illustrates the ratio of individual industries to a region's overall industry, which reflects the characteristics of industrial structure by region. The highest three regions by ratio for the agriculture, forestry and fisheries sector were Jeollanam-do (16.2

percent), Gyeongsangbuk-do (14.4 percent), and Chungcheongnam-do (13.2 percent). The lowest three regions by ratio for the mining and manufacturing sectors were Gyeonggi-do (27.5 percent), Gyeongsangbuk-do (12.6 percent), and Ulsan (10.1 percent). The capital region accounted for 37.6 percent, which was a decrease of 1.1 percent from the previous year as a result of a decrease in the ratio for Seoul and Incheon. The ratio of the seven metropolitan cities accounted for 29.3 percent, decrease of 1.4 percent from the previous year, which was a result of a decrease in the ratio of Seoul, Busan and Incheon. However, the ratio of the capital region (54.1 percent) grew slightly (0.2 percent) from the previous year.

Table 3 also shows the ratio of private consumption expenditure to GRDP. In 2004, the nominal final consumption expenditure showed an increase of 3.5 percent over the previous year. The scale of final consumption expenditure was the highest in Seoul, Gyeonggi-do and Busan. These regions accounted for 51.3 percent of the national total final consumption expenditure (slightly larger than the ratio of population). In the ratio of private consumption expenditure, the capital region accounted for 51.2 percent, while the seven metropolitan cities accounted for 51.1 percent.

Table 3. Comparison between the Capital Region and the Non-capital Region in the Component Ratio of Private Consumption Expenditure

	Ratio of Consumption Expenditure (Percent)			Ratio of Population (Percent)		
	2003	2004	Growth Rate	2003	2004	Growth Rate
Capital Region	51.1	51.2	0.1%	47.5	47.9	0.4%
Metropolitan cities	51.1	51.1	-0.4%	47.4	47.3	-0.1%

Source: National Statistical Office, 2005, *The Estimation of Future Population by Region.*

Figure 4 illustrates the level of per capita GRDP and private consumption expenditure by region. In terms of the level of per capita GRDP (national average = 100), Ulsan (217.7), Chungcheongnam-do (138.7), and Gyeongsangbuk-do (129.1) were the highest regions in order, while Daegu (60.7), Gwangju (71.9), and Busan (77.0) were the lowest regions in order. Together with this, the levels of per capita private consumption expenditure (national average = 100) were highest in Seoul and Busan, while Jeollanam-do and Chungcheongbuk-do had the lowest levels.

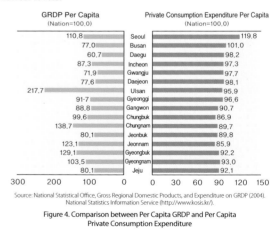

Source: National Statistical Office, Gross Regional Domestic Products, and Expenditure on GRDP (2004). National Statistical Information Service (http://www.kosis.kr/).

Figure 4. Comparison between Per Capita GRDP and Per Capita Private Consumption Expenditure

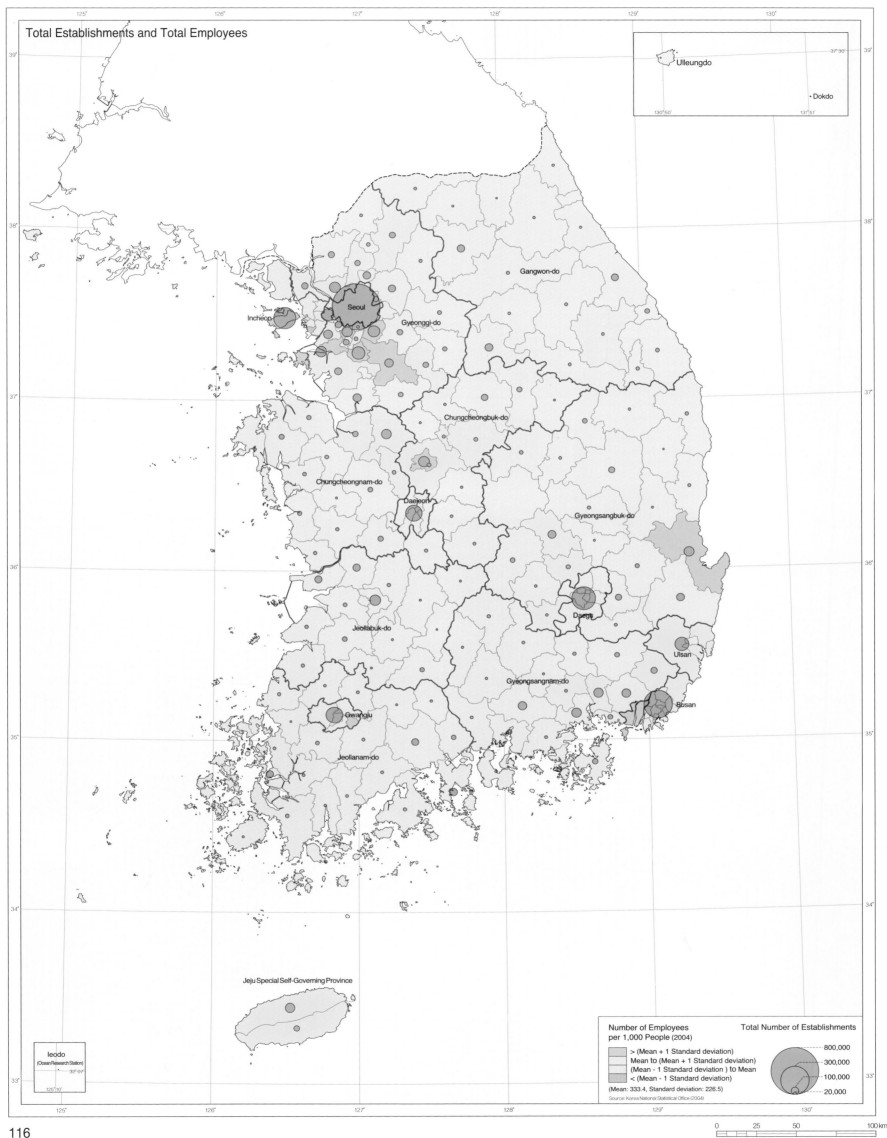

Total Establishments and Total Employees

Ulleungdo

Dokdo

Gangwon-do

Seoul

Incheon

Gyeonggi-do

Chungcheongbuk-do

Chungcheongnam-do

Daejeon

Gyeongsangbuk-do

Jeollabuk-do

Daegu

Ulsan

Gyeongsangnam-do

Busan

Gwangju

Jeollanam-do

Jeju Special Self-Governing Province

Ieodo
(Ocean Research Station)

Number of Employees
per 1,000 People (2004)

> (Mean + 1 Standard deviation)
Mean to (Mean + 1 Standard deviation)
(Mean - 1 Standard deviation) to Mean
< (Mean - 1 Standard deviation)
(Mean: 333.4, Standard deviation: 226.5)
Source: Korea National Statistical Office (2004)

Total Number of Establishments

800,000
300,000
100,000
20,000

0   25   50   100 km

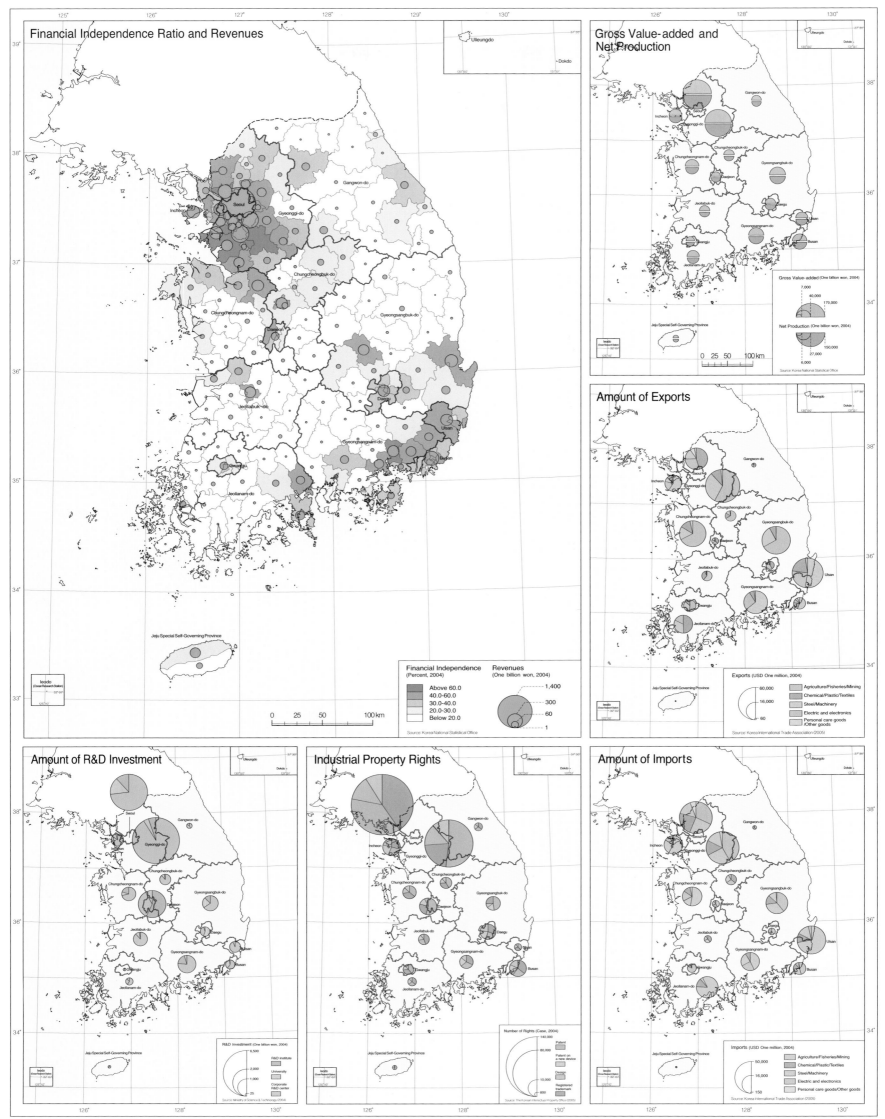

Financial Independence Ratio and Revenues

Gross Value-added and Net Production

Gross Value-added (One billion won, 2004)
7,000
40,000
170,000

Net Production (One billion won, 2004)
150,000
27,000
6,000

0 25 50 100 km

Source: Korea National Statistical Office

Amount of Exports

Exports (USD One million, 2004)
60,000
16,000
60

Agriculture/Fisheries/Mining
Chemical/Plastic/Textiles
Steel/Machinery
Electric and electronics
Personal care goods /Other goods

Source: Korea International Trade Association (2005)

Financial Independence (Percent, 2004)

Above 60.0
40.0-60.0
30.0-40.0
20.0-30.0
Below 20.0

Revenues (One billion won, 2004)
1,400
300
60
1

0 25 50 100 km

Source: Korea National Statistical Office

Amount of R&D Investment

R&D Investment (One billion won, 2004)
6,500
2,000
1,000
25

R&D institute
University
Corporate R&D center

Source: Ministry of Science & Technology (2004)

Industrial Property Rights

Number of Rights (Case, 2004)
140,000
80,000
10,000
800

Patent
Patent on a new device
Design
Registered trademark

Source: The Korean Intellectual Property Office (2005)

Amount of Imports

Imports (USD One million, 2004)
50,000
16,000
150

Agriculture/Fisheries/Mining
Chemical/Plastic/Textiles
Steel/Machinery
Electric and electronics
Personal care goods/Other goods

Source: Korea International Trade Association (2005)

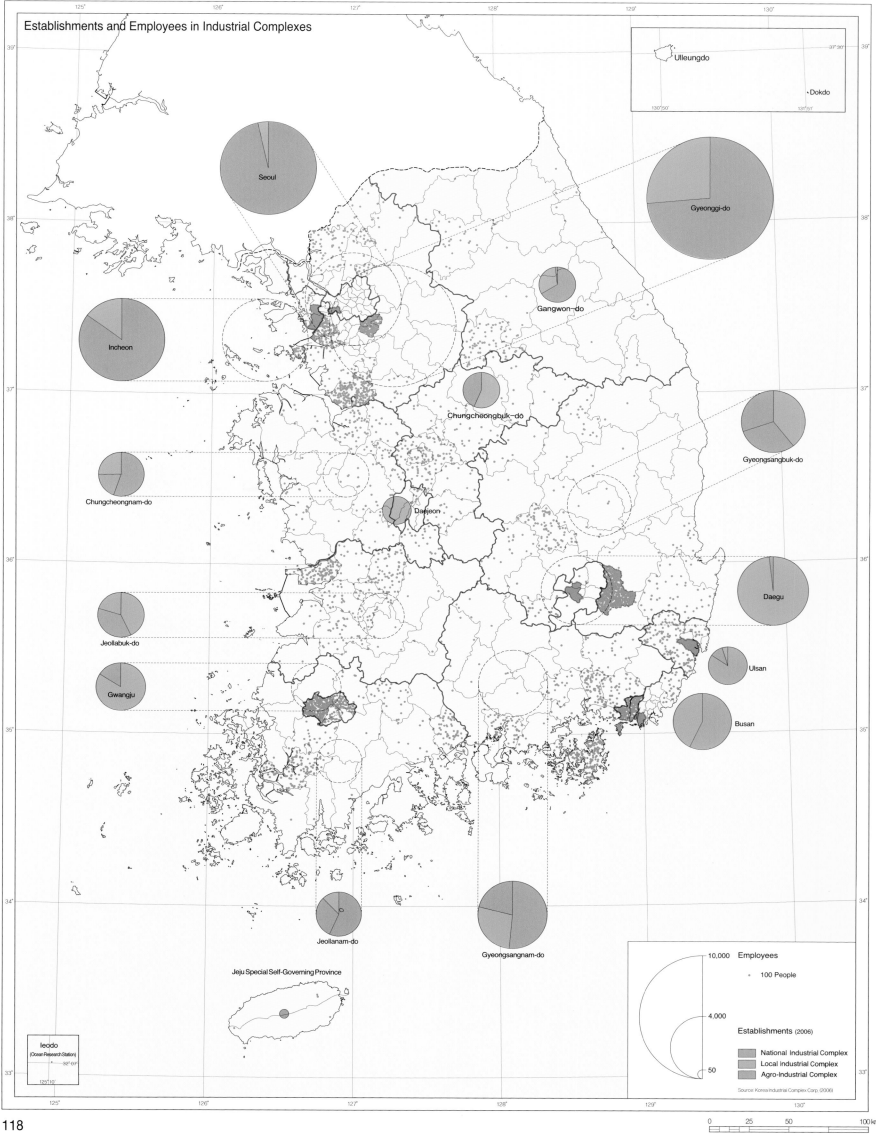

Establishments and Employees in Industrial Complexes

Ulleungdo

Dokdo

Seoul

Gyeonggi-do

Gangwon-do

Incheon

Chungcheongbuk-do

Gyeongsangbuk-do

Chungcheongnam-do

Daejeon

Daegu

Jeollabuk-do

Ulsan

Gwangju

Busan

Jeollanam-do

Gyeongsangnam-do

Jeju Special Self-Governing Province

Ieodo
(Ocean Research Station)

125°10'

32°07'

10,000   Employees

•   100 People

4,000

Establishments (2006)

50

National Industrial Complex

Local Industrial Complex

Agro-Industrial Complex

Source: Korea Industrial Complex Corp. (2006)

0   25   50   100 km

Industrial Infrastructure

The construction of industrial complexes, which has played a significant role in the rapid industrialization of Korea since the 1960s, continues today. Among various advantages of the industrial complexes, their construction can first reduce the initial investment costs to firms by providing industrial estates with better infrastructure, tax incentives and financial assistance. Second, they can benefit the production activities of firms through, for example, promoting synergistic effects through the agglomeration of similar firms and activities. Third, at the national scale they can reduce social and environmental costs by increasing land use efficiency with the grouping of manufacturing units. Therefore, the construction of these complexes has been used as a major tool in Korea's national industrial location policy.

Industrial complexes are classified into national, local and agro-industrial complexes according to the agent of designation and type of development. National, local and agro-industrial complexes are designated and developed by the minister of construction and transportation, metropolitan mayors, county leaders and district leaders, respectively. Local industrial complexes are further classified into general industrial complexes and urban high-tech industrial complexes. Additionally, Korea has venture enterprise exclusive complexes, cultural industrial complexes, software promotion complexes, and industrial technology complexes for promoting knowledge-cultural-IT industries as well.

In 2005, the total number of industrial complexes in Korea was 578, an increase of 90 from 2001 (Figure 1). These industrial complexes can be broken down as: 30 national, 211 local and 337 agro-industrial. The major contributor to this growth in the number of complexes was local complexes (55 establishments). The total area of the industrial complexes has reached 696 millionm², of which national complexes account for 58.8 percent.

Table 1. General Conditions of Industrial Complexes (2005)

Division	Establishment (Unit)	Area (1,000m²)	Lots Sold (percent)
National Industrial Complex	30	409,201	98.2
Local Industrial Complex	211	239,757	93.8
Agro-Industrial Complex	337	47,421	98.0
Total	578	696,379	96.6

Source: Korea Industrial Complex Corporation, 2005, *Statistics of Industrial Complexes in Korea.* Industry-University-Research Integrated Information Network (http://www.e-cluster.net/).

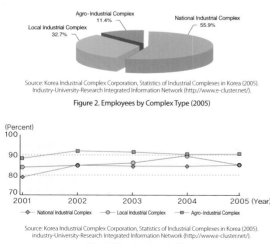

Source: Korea Industrial Complex Corporation, Statistics of Industrial Complexes in Korea (2005). Industry-University-Research Integrated Information Network (http://www.e-cluster.net/).

Figure 1. Changing Number of Industrial Complexes

By the end of 2005, the number of total establishments in the complexes had reached 42,393 with total employment of 1.2 million persons. These national complexes accounted for the largest share in terms of both establishments and employees, whereas agro-industrial complexes, although most numerous, were the smallest in size (Figure 2). The actual operation rate of industrial establishments serves as a better indicator than just the number for regional economies. In 2005, agro-industrial complexes had the highest operation rate at 90.6 percent, whereas local and national complexes operated at a rate of 85.3 percent and 85.2 percent, respectively. However, in terms of change, the national industrial complexes have shown a steady increase since 2001 (Figure 3).

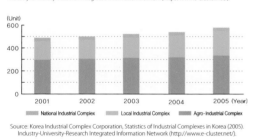

Source: Korea Industrial Complex Corporation, Statistics of Industrial Complexes in Korea (2005). Industry-University-Research Integrated Information Network (http://www.e-cluster.net/).

Figure 2. Employees by Complex Type (2005)

Source: Korea Industrial Complex Corporation, Statistics of Industrial Complexes in Korea (2005). Industry-University-Research Integrated Information Network (http://www.e-cluster.net/).

Figure 3. Changing Operation Rates

The industrial complex has played an important role in manufacturing production and exports in Korea. Looking at the changing share of the complex in the manufacturing sector during the 1996-2005 period, the share of the establishments located in industrial complexes increased from 17.5 percent to 36.2 percent and the number of employees increased by 7.8 percent. In addition, the share of the output also increased from 43.7 percent to 53.2 percent, all of which demonstrates the ever-increasing importance of the industrial complex to the Korean economy.

Table 2. Share of Industrial Complex by Establishment, Employees, and Output

Division	1996			2005		
	Establishment (Unit)	Employee (1,000 people)	Output (Billion won)	Establishment (Unit)	Employee (1,000 people)	Output (Billion won)
Ind. complex	16,965 (17.5%)	999 (34.5%)	175,508 (43.7%)	42,393 (36.2%)	1,216 (42.2%)	453,069 (53.2%)
Manufacturing	97,144	2,898	401,953	177,205	2,866	851,789

Source: Korea Industrial Complex Corporation, 2006, *Statistics of Industrial Complex in Korea.* Industry-University-Research Integrated Information Network (http://www.e-cluster.net/). Cho, H. Y., 2002, The Current Conditions of Industrial Complexes and Policy Tasks in Korea *Industrial Location*, 9 in Korea.

The total output of industrial complexes in 2005 amounted to 453 trillion won, which was an increase of 10.9 percent over the previous year. The share of the national industrial complexes in terms of output was as high as 68 percent. In the meantime, the industrial complex also played a remarkable role in the area of exports, which has been a driving force for the Korean economy. By 2005, total exports from the complexes had reached USD 189.1 billion, with the national complexes accounting for USD 140.1 billion, almost 75 percent of Korea's total export value.

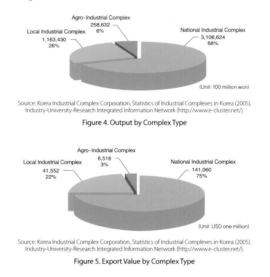

Source: Korea Industrial Complex Corporation, Statistics of Industrial Complexes in Korea (2005). Industry-University-Research Integrated Information Network (http://www.e-cluster.net/).

Figure 4. Output by Complex Type

Figure 5. Export Value by Complex Type

Exports from the industrial complexes have shown remarkable growth since 2000, with the exports of 2005 almost doubling those of 2001. Obviously, exports from the national complexes provided a major contribution to this growth with an increase of USD 69.1 billion in exports during the given period.

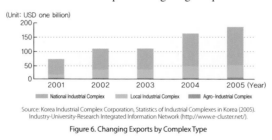

Source: Korea Industrial Complex Corporation, Statistics of Industrial Complexes in Korea (2005). Industry-University-Research Integrated Information Network (http://www.e-cluster.net/).

Figure 6. Changing Exports by Complex Type

Energy

In terms of energy supply in Korea, coal and hydraulic power, even though domestically produced, account for as little as 3.1 percent of total energy supply, while the majority (96 percent as of the end of 2005) of the energy supply has to be imported. Overseas energy imports to Korea increased with the rapid growth of the national GDP and income level. Crude oil accounts for the biggest share, even though LNG has recently shown fast growth. As a consequence, Korea ranks the 4th in oil imports and the 8th in natural gas imports worldwide, with energy imports accounting for as much as 25.5 percent of total imports to Korea in 2005.

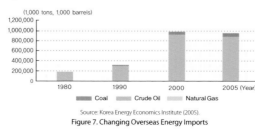

Source: Korea Energy Economics Institute (2005).

Figure 7. Changing Overseas Energy Imports

Korea ranks 10th in the world in terms of total energy consumption and 7th in terms of oil usage in 2005. Total energy consumption in 2005 reached 228.6 million TOE with oil accounting for the largest share at 44.4 percent and coal, atomic power and natural gas accounting for 24.0 percent, 16.1 percent and 13.3 percent, respectively. In addition, in terms of the total energy consumption structure, the shares of coal and oil have decreased, whereas the shares of atomic power and natural gas have increased, transforming the very structure of energy consumption in Korea.

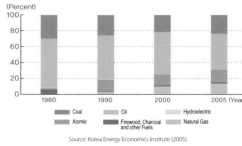

Source: Korea Energy Economics Institute (2005).

Figure 8. Changing Energy Consumption Structure

Coal is mostly consumed in the industrial sector in Korea with the domestic and commercial sectors accounting for only 4.8 percent. This results from both decreasing domestic and commercial consumption and ever-increasing industrial consumption. In the meantime, in terms of oil consumption, the industrial sector accounts for more than half (52.6 percent), followed by the transportation sector (36.2 percent) and the domestic and commercial sectors (9.8 percent).

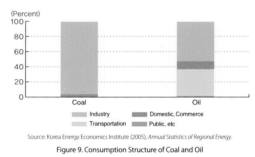

Source: Korea Energy Economics Institute (2005), *Annual Statistics of Regional Energy.*

Figure 9. Consumption Structure of Coal and Oil

Total electricity use in Korea in 2005 reached 364.6 trillion watts, which was 9.8 times consumption levels in 1980. In terms of electricity generation, steam power accounts for the highest share (57.4 percent), followed by atomic power (40.3 percent). In terms of electricity consumption, about half (50.2 percent) is consumed in the industrial sector, with the domestic and commercial sector and the public and other sectors accounting for 42.8 percent and 6.2 percent, respectively.

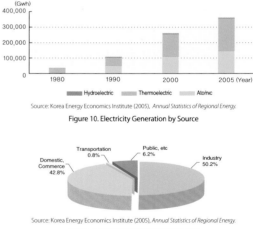

Source: Korea Energy Economics Institute (2005), *Annual Statistics of Regional Energy.*

Figure 10. Electricity Generation by Source

Figure 11. Electricity Consumption by Use

New renewable energies used in Korea only amounted to 4 million TOE in 2005, which is quite low compared to the use of other types of energies. The majority of the new renewables consumed comes from waste incineration heat (93.6 percent). Other energies such as biomass, small hydraulic power and solar heat were all minimally in use.

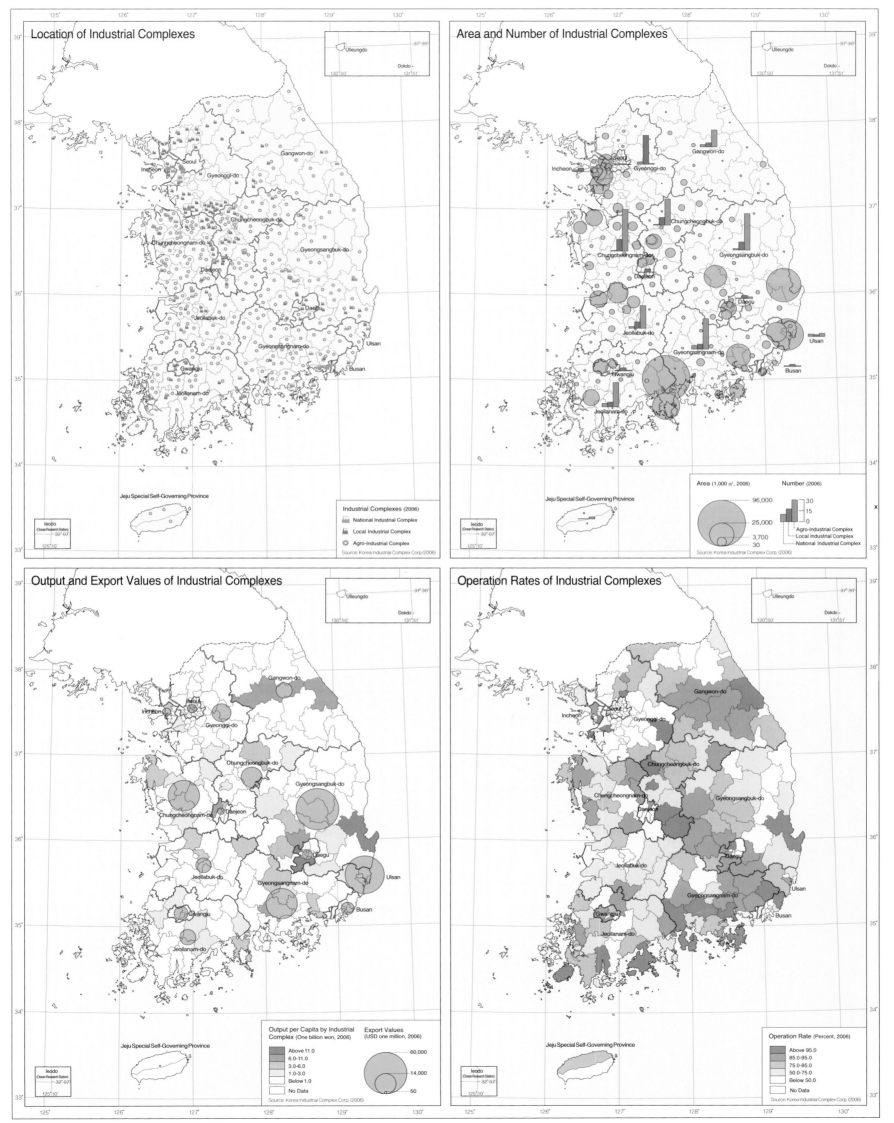

Location of Industrial Complexes

Industrial Complexes (2006)
- National Industrial Complex
- Local Industrial Complex
- Agro-Industrial Complex

Source: Korea Industrial Complex Corp. (2006)

Area and Number of Industrial Complexes

Area (1,000 m², 2006)
- 96,000
- 25,000
- 3,700
- 30

Number (2006)
- 30
- 15
- 0
- Agro-Industrial Complex
- Local Industrial Complex
- National Industrial Complex

Source: Korea Industrial Complex Corp. (2006)

Output and Export Values of Industrial Complexes

Output per Capita by Industrial Complex (One billion won, 2006)
- Above 11.0
- 6.0–11.0
- 3.0–6.0
- 1.0–3.0
- Below 1.0
- No Data

Export Values (USD one million, 2006)
- 60,000
- 14,000
- 50

Source: Korea Industrial Complex Corp. (2006)

Operation Rates of Industrial Complexes

Operation Rate (Percent, 2006)
- Above 95.0
- 85.0–95.0
- 75.0–85.0
- 50.0–75.0
- Below 50.0
- No Data

Source: Korea Industrial Complex Corp. (2006)

0   25   50   100 km

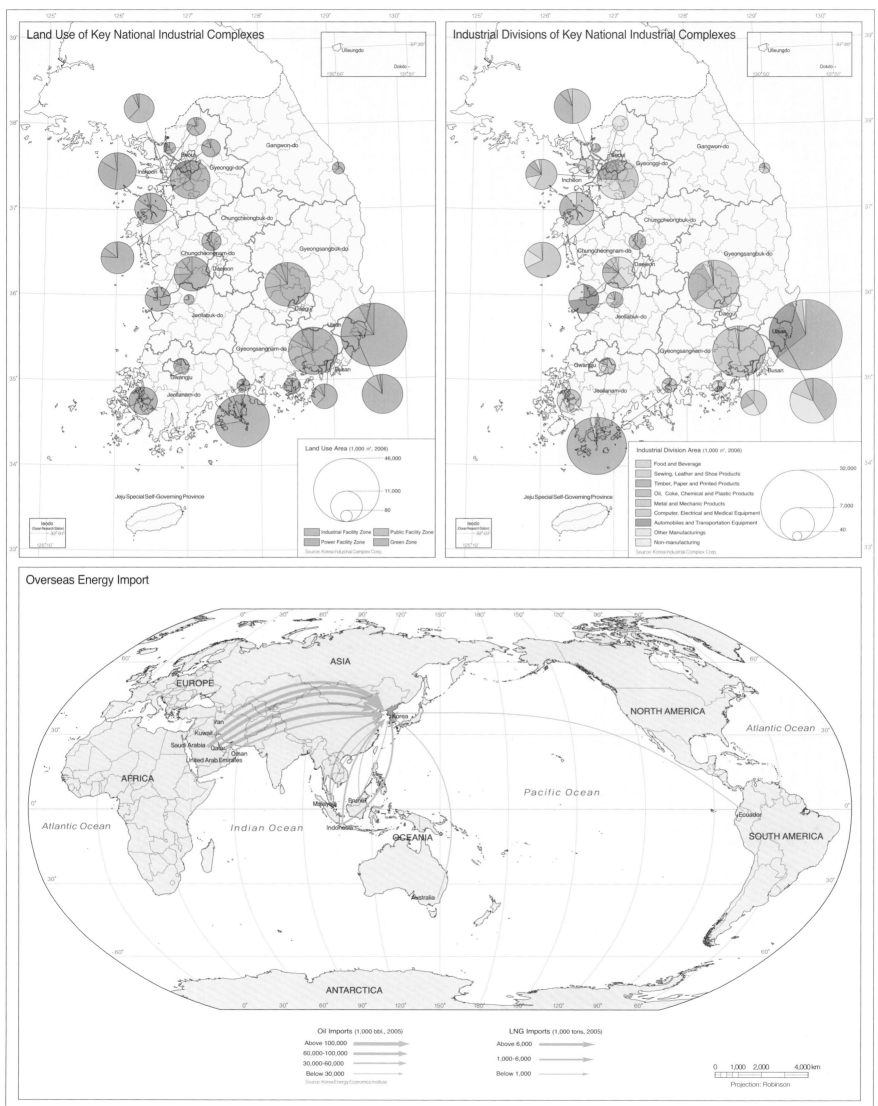

Land Use of Key National Industrial Complexes

Ulleungdo
Dokdo

Gangwon-do
Seoul
Incheon
Gyeonggi-do
Chungcheongbuk-do
Chungcheongnam-do
Daejeon
Gyeongsangbuk-do
Daegu
Ulsan
Jeollabuk-do
Gyeongsangnam-do
Busan
Gwangju
Jeollanam-do

Land Use Area (1,000 m², 2006)
46,000
11,000
80

Jeju Special Self-Governing Province

Ieodo
(Ocean Research Station)

| Industrial Facility Zone | Public Facility Zone |
| Power Facility Zone | Green Zone |

Source: Korea Industrial Complex Corp.

Industrial Divisions of Key National Industrial Complexes

Ulleungdo
Dokdo

Gangwon-do
Seoul
Incheon
Gyeonggi-do
Chungcheongbuk-do
Chungcheongnam-do
Daejeon
Gyeongsangbuk-do
Daegu
Ulsan
Jeollabuk-do
Gyeongsangnam-do
Busan
Gwangju
Jeollanam-do

Industrial Division Area (1,000 m², 2006)
32,000
7,000
40

Jeju Special Self-Governing Province

Ieodo
(Ocean Research Station)

- Food and Beverage
- Sewing, Leather and Shoe Products
- Timber, Paper and Printed Products
- Oil, Coke, Chemical and Plastic Products
- Metal and Mechanic Products
- Computer, Electrical and Medical Equipment
- Automobiles and Transportation Equipment
- Other Manufacturings
- Non-manufacturing

Source: Korea Industrial Complex Corp.

Overseas Energy Import

ASIA
EUROPE
NORTH AMERICA
Atlantic Ocean
Iran
Kuwait
Saudi Arabia
Qatar
Oman
United Arab Emirates
Korea
AFRICA
Pacific Ocean
Malaysia
Brunei
Indian Ocean
Indonesia
OCEANIA
Ecuador
SOUTH AMERICA
Atlantic Ocean
Australia
ANTARCTICA

Oil Imports (1,000 bbl., 2005)
Above 100,000
60,000-100,000
30,000-60,000
Below 30,000

Source: Korea Energy Economics Institute

LNG Imports (1,000 tons, 2005)
Above 6,000
1,000-6,000
Below 1,000

0 1,000 2,000 4,000 km

Projection: Robinson

121

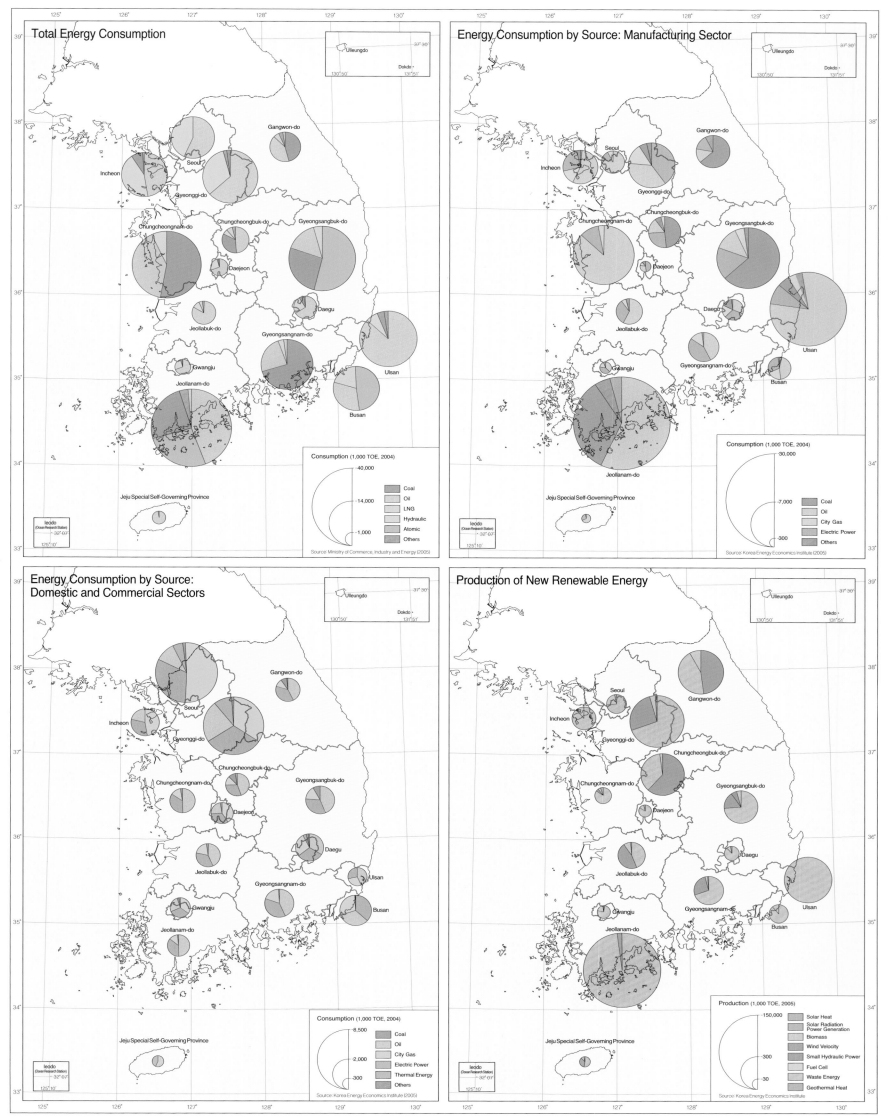

Total Energy Consumption

Energy Consumption by Source: Manufacturing Sector

Consumption (1,000 TOE, 2004)
- 40,000
- 14,000
- 1,000

- Coal
- Oil
- LNG
- Hydraulic
- Atomic
- Others

Source: Ministry of Commerce, Industry and Energy (2005)

Consumption (1,000 TOE, 2004)
- 30,000
- 7,000
- 300

- Coal
- Oil
- City Gas
- Electric Power
- Others

Source: Korea Energy Economics Institute (2005)

Energy Consumption by Source:
Domestic and Commercial Sectors

Production of New Renewable Energy

Consumption (1,000 TOE, 2004)
- 8,500
- 2,000
- 300

- Coal
- Oil
- City Gas
- Electric Power
- Thermal Energy
- Others

Source: Korea Energy Economics Institute (2005)

Production (1,000 TOE, 2005)
- 150,000
- 300
- 30

- Solar Heat
- Solar Radiation Power Generation
- Biomass
- Wind Velocity
- Small Hydraulic Power
- Fuel Cell
- Waste Energy
- Geothermal Heat

Source: Korea Energy Economics Institute

0 25 50 100 km

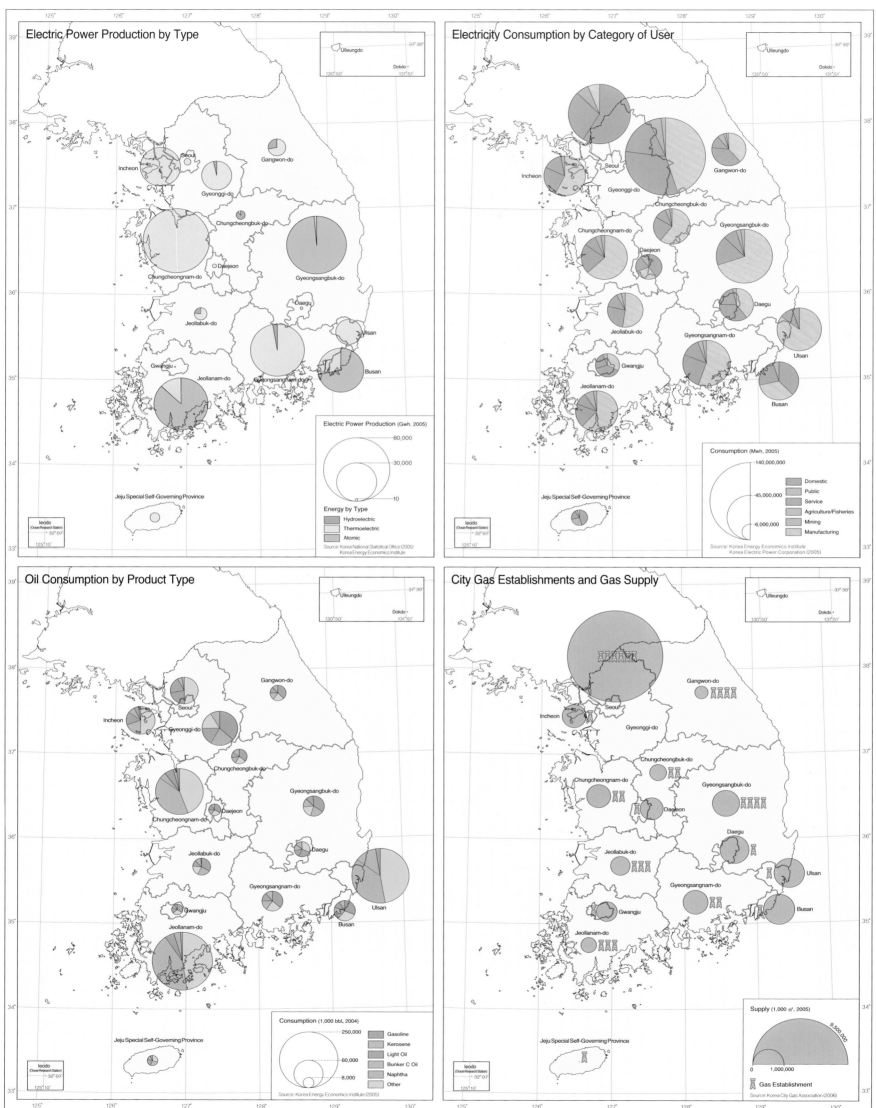

Electric Power Production by Type

Electric Power Production (Gwh, 2005)
- 80,000
- 30,000
- 10

Energy by Type
- Hydroelectric
- Thermoelectric
- Atomic

Source: Korea National Statistical Office (2005)
Korea Energy Economics Institute

Electricity Consumption by Category of User

Consumption (Mwh, 2005)
- 140,000,000
- 45,000,000
- 6,000,000

- Domestic
- Public
- Service
- Agriculture/Fisheries
- Mining
- Manufacturing

Source: Korea Energy Economics Institute
Korea Electric Power Corporation (2005)

Oil Consumption by Product Type

Consumption (1,000 bbl, 2004)
- 250,000
- 60,000
- 8,000

- Gasoline
- Kerosene
- Light Oil
- Bunker C Oil
- Naphtha
- Other

Source: Korea Energy Economics Institute (2005)

City Gas Establishments and Gas Supply

Supply (1,000 m², 2005)
- 9,500,000
- 1,000,000
- 0

⚡ Gas Establishment

Source: Korea City Gas Association (2006)

0 25 50   100 km

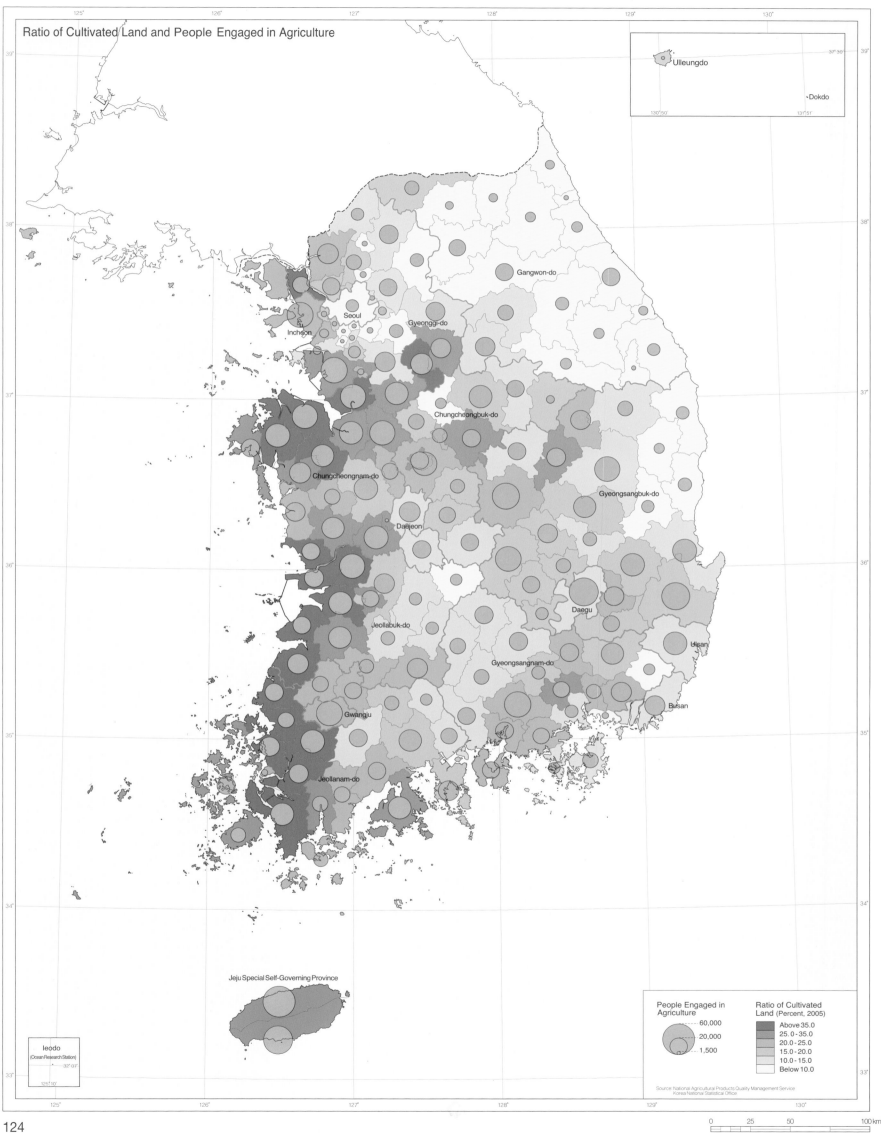

Ratio of Cultivated Land and People Engaged in Agriculture

Ulleungdo

Dokdo

Gangwon-do

Seoul

Incheon

Gyeonggi-do

Chungcheongbuk-do

Chungcheongnam-do

Daejeon

Gyeongsangbuk-do

Jeollabuk-do

Daegu

Gyeongsangnam-do

Ulsan

Gwangju

Busan

Jeollanam-do

Jeju Special Self-Governing Province

Ieodo
(Ocean Research Station)

People Engaged in
Agriculture

- 60,000
- 20,000
- 1,500

Ratio of Cultivated
Land (Percent, 2005)

- Above 35.0
- 25.0 - 35.0
- 20.0 - 25.0
- 15.0 - 20.0
- 10.0 - 15.0
- Below 10.0

Source: National Agricultural Products Quality Management Service
Korea National Statistical Office

0   25   50   100 km

Primary Industries

In the last half century, the rapid growth of the Korean economy has not only advanced structural changes among the primary secondary and tertiary industries, but has also had a significant influence on internal structural changes to the primary industry. The production proportion occupied by the primary industry compared to all industries was approximately 60 percent in 1950, 47.9 percent in 1960, 28.4 percent in 1970, 16.6 percent in 1980, and 8.1 percent in 1990, and it continued to decline to below 5.0 percent by 2000. The characteristics of each category of primary industry are as follows:

Agriculture

The farming population in Korea has been diminishing since the 1960s as the majority of the population has changed occupations to the manufacturing and service sectors given the influence of urbanization and industrialization. As shown in Table 1 and Table 2, the farming population went from 14.9 million in the early 1960s to 3.4 million in 2005, and the average farming household went from 6.2 in the early 1960s to 2.7 in 2005. Such decreases caused some adjustments to the composition of farming households. As for business conditions for the composition of farming households, the number of full-time farming households decreased by an annualized 1.7 percent every year for 40 years, going from 90 percent in the early 1960s to 65 percent in early 2000. As for the cultivated acreage per farming household, those with less than 2.0ha of land have decreased in the last 50 years, those with larger than 2.0ha of land have increased, and those with larger than 3.0ha of land have also increased, showing that large-scale farming households are expanding. In conjunction with this expansion, the cultivated acreage per farming household increased from 136.5ha in 2000 to 143.3ha in 2005, resulting in an 8.4 percent increase.

Table 1. The Change of Farming Households and Farming Population in Korea

Contents / Year*	Farm Households (Million Household)	Farm Households Composition(Percent)		Farm Households Composition by Size of Cultivated Land (Percent)					Farmhouse Population (Million people)	Average People in Farm Household (people)
		Full-time	Part-time	Smaller than 0.5ha	0.5-1.0ha	1.0-2.0ha	2.0-3.0ha	Larger than 3.0ha		
1950-53	2.22	89.1	10.9	44.2	34.8	16.6	4.2	0.1	12.9	5.8
1960-63	2.40	90.9	9.1	41.2	32.0	20.7	5.9	0.3	14.9	6.2
1970-73	2.46	85.1	14.9	36.0	31.6	26.1	4.8	1.5	14.7	6.0
1980-83	2.01	81.5	18.5	31.1	36.3	27.3	4.1	1.2	9.7	4.8
1990-93	1.65	63.4	36.6	29.7	30.3	29.3	7.5	3.1	5.7	3.5
2000-03	1.30	65.6	11.4	35.7	26.8	23.9	7.5	6.1	3.9	2.8

*Average for selected years
Source: Ministry of Agriculture and Forestry, *Agriculture and Frestry Statistical Yearbook*.

Table 2. Farming Households and Cultivated Land (2000-2005) (Unit: people, ha)

Year	Farming Households	Farming Population	Area of Cultivated Land	Average Area of Cultivated Land by Farming Household
2000	1,383,468	4,031,065	1,888,765	136.5
2002	1,353,687	3,933,250	1,876,142	138.6
2001	1,280,462	3,590,523	1,862,622	145.5
2003	1,264,431	3,530,102	1,845,994	146.0
2004	1,240,406	3,414,551	1,835,634	148.0
2005	1,272,908	3,433,573	1,824,039	143.3

Source: National Statistical Office, *Korea Statistical Yearbook*.

Comparing the production structure of Korean farm products and total agricultural production, the production proportion of sowing to stock-breeding, which was about 90:10 in the early 1950s, changed to 70:30 in the early 2000s, illustrating an expansion in stockbreeding and a contraction in sowing. The proportion of rice to total agricultural production, however, is still relatively high. Hence, the production variations of rice influence the entire agricultural production totals. The production of grains other than rice expanded until the late 1960s, but declined noticeably after that. The production proportion of grains, which accounted for 11 percent in the 1960s, fell to 1 percent in the early 2000s. The production of beans decreased from the late 1970s, and the production of potatoes decreased from the early 1960s, but has recently begun to increase. In the meantime, vegetables and fruits experienced the opposite trend, with an annual production growth of 4.1 percent and 6.4 percent, respectively. In the early 2000s, the production proportions of fruits and vegetables rose to 13 percent and 26 percent, respectively, constituting about 37 percent of total production.

The total cultivation area of farm products is continuously decreasing, and these decreases are occurring across all crop types. From the years 2000 to 2005, especially, the cultivation area of rice grains decreased by 92,000ha. The cultivation areas of each type of farm product are as follows: grains (64.1 percent), vegetables (12.5 percent), fruit orchards (7.8 percent), and greenhouse crops (5.3 percent).

The production proportion of rice, the staple food for Koreans, occupies over 85 percent of total food grains. However, rice consumption has been continuously decreasing due to a better understanding of health, and an increased consumption of substitute foods, such as fruits and vegetables. The annual rice consumption per person in Korea has been on the decline, with per person consumption levels of 112.7kg in 1960, 136.4kg in 1970, 132.4kg in 1980, 119.6kg in 1990, 93.6kg in 2000, and 80.7kg in 2005. Consequently, the cultivation area for rice in the past 10 years has decreased continuously. The production output of rice rises and falls every year depending on the weather conditions, but the overall trend is a decrease. The production outputs of rice for each province (*do*) are not consistent in their rankings, but usually Jeollanam-*do* has the highest production, and Jeju Special Self -Governing Province has the lowest production.

Table 3. Cultivated Area by Crops (Unit: 1,000 ha)

Year	Total	Food Crops (Rice)	Vegetables	Orchards	Greenhouse Crops	Speciality Crops	Others
2000	2.098.0	1,316.5 (1072.4)	295.8	169.4	105.8	92.1	118.5
2002	2,098.3	1,332.8 (1083.1)	279.9	163.3	101.8	94.0	117.5
2001	2,019.7	1,298.8 (1053.2)	251.4	162.5	97.6	94.5	114.9
2003	1,935.8	1,234.3 (1016.0)	244.6	158.6	100.3	84.6	113.4
2004	1,940.6	1,230.9 (1001.2)	255.0	152.6	104.3	75.5	122.3
2005	1,921.0	1,231.8 (979.7)	239.6	149.8	100.9	76.8	122.2

Source: Ministry of Agriculture and Forestry, *Crops Statistics*.

The consumption of vegetables in Korea has grown considerably due to changes in eating habits, so the production proportion of vegetables has increased significantly. The utilization of farmland to total cultivated acreage, which was 3.9 percent in the 1960s increased to 12.5 percent in 2005. The cultivation acreage for vegetables reached 374,000ha in 1995 and 282,000ha in 2005, constituting about 18 percent of total cultivated acreage of food. The most highly produced vegetables in Korea are green vegetables, including Korean cabbage, spinach, and lettuce, root vegetables, including icicle radish and carrots, fruits and fruit vegetables, including Korean melon, watermelon, cucumbers, tomatoes, and strawberries, and seasoning vegetables including hot pepper, garlic, green onions, onions, and ginger. In 2005, the production proportions of each vegetable type were: green vegetables (31.7 percent), fruit vegetables (27.3 percent), seasoning vegetables (25.7 percent), and root vegetables (15.3 percent). The rankings of cultivated acreage of vegetables are, in order, Korean cabbage, garlic, icicle radish, watermelon, green onion, and onion.

The cultivated acreage of fruit trees in Korea, which was 20,000ha in 1955, increased to 176,000ha by the end of the 1990s. However, the acreage gradually decreased to 155,000ha by 2005, yet this figure is still seven times larger than the acreage of orchards in the 1950s. Meanwhile, the production output for fruit increased to 2,593,000 tons in 2005 from 117,000 tons in 1955. The most significant fruit trees in Korea and their production rankings for 2005 were tangerines, Korean pears, grapes, apples, persimmons, and peaches. The acreage ranking in 2005 was apples, persimmons, grapes, Korean pears, tangerines, and peaches. Gyeongsangbuk-*do* (province) cultivated the most fruit trees, constituting 31.4 percent of total national production and 32.7 percent of total cultivated acreage.

In 2005, the annual income per farm household was 30,503,000 a 5.2 percent (1,502,000) increase from the year before. This increase was due to a 3.6 percent and a 35.7 percent growth in non-farming and transfer incomes, respectively. The weight of farming income came out to 38.7 percent.

The majority of all Korean land, approximately 70 percent, is mountainous. In 2005, the acreage of mountains and forests totaled 6,390,000ha, with component ratios of 23.2 percent for state forests and 76.8 percent for private forests. The accumulation of forest trees per 1ha has been increased, from 9.5m^3 in 1960, to 10.4m^3 in 1970, to 22.2m^3 in 1980, to 38.5m^3 in 1990, to 63.4m^3 in 2000, and to79.2m^3 in 2005. The demand for domestically produced wood has reduced drastically due to the importation of foreign lumber. Presently, the Korean wood processing industry is heavily dependent on the importation of lumber. Because it has not been long since the start of artificial forestation, Korea imports 94 percent of its annual wood consumption of 27,000,000m^3 from Indonesia, Malaysia, the Philippines, and New Zealand. Unlike before, the Korean wood processing industry is currently producing high value-added products such as plywood, boards, sawn wood, wooden housing, charcoal, and wood vinegar. Korea firms are anticipating a higher demand in the future for these products because of their environmentally-friendly characteristics.

There are a variety of harvestable products from mountains and forests, the most important being nuts, such as chestnuts and pine nuts.

Mushrooms, originally a product of the mountains, are classified as a forest product, but nowadays most of them are raised indoors. The growing number of mushroom producing districts are distributed fairly evenly throughout the nation.

The ranking of Korea's fish catch lingered around 15th worldwide until the late 1960s and rose to 7th in the world in 1973. Since 2000, however, Korea has maintained the 10th spot. This index indicates that Korea is one of the most prominent fishing nations in the world. The fishing population of Korea was over 800,000 in 1960 and 1,477,000 in 1967, but has been decreasing ever since, falling to a mere 220,000 in 2005. The number of fishing households, which totaled 242,000 in 1967, dropped to 79,000 in 2005, and the number of fishery workers was one third of that of 1970. However, the ratio of full-time fishery households has been continuously increased from 1980 to 2000. The regional distribution of fishing households has rank in the following order: Jeollanam-*do* (33.0 percent), Gyeongsangnam-*do* (17.3 percent), and Chungcheongnam-*do* (11.6 percent).

As for the output for each fishery sector, general offshore fisheries occupied over 95 percent in the 1960s but that figure fell to reduced to 40 percent in 2005. On the other hand deep sea fisheries, which accounted for only 0.1 percent in the 1960s, increased to over 20 percent in 2005. Also, the shallow water breeding industry showed rapid growth from the 1960s, occupying 38.4 percent in 2005. The inland waters fisheries are very low in production and have shown little change. In 2005, the annual income per fishing household was 28,028,000, and the fishing income was 11,950,000, constituting about 42.6 percent of total income.

Mining Industry

There are about 300 kinds of minerals found in Korea, of which 140 are useful. However, only 20 different minerals are mined, and only a few of them are high in reserve. The conditions of domestically endowed mineral resources vary depending on the mineral types and regions. The minerals extracted as underground resources are classified into metallic and non-metallic minerals. Among the metallic minerals, iron, manganese, tungsten, molybdenum, lead, and zinc are scattered throughout the Taebaeksanmaek area (Samcheok-*si*, Taebaek-*si*, and Yangyang-*gun* of Gangwon-*do*), copper is dispersed throughout the Taebaek Mountain area as well as across Gyeongsangnam-*do* and Gyeongsangbuk-*do*. and gold and silver are dispersed throughout the nation; however due to their scarce reserves, Korea is dependent mostly on imports.

Representative resources of non-metallic minerals are limestone, kaolin, and coal. Limestone can be extracted from Yeongwol-*gun*, Gangneung-*si*, Donghae-*si*, and Samcheok-*si* in Gangwon-*do*, Danyang-*gun* and Jecheon-*si* in Chungcheongbuk-*do*, Mungyeong-*si* in Gyeongsangbuk-*do*, and Jangseong-*gun* in Jeollanam-*do*. Production has been continuously increasing with the development of the cement industry. Kaolin and agalmatolite are dispersed evenly throughout Gyeongsangnam-*do* and Gyeongsangbuk-*do*, and silicon dioxide and feldspar can be mostly found anywhere in the nation. Reserves of limestone, silicon dioxide, zeolite, and feldspar are abundant in Korea, completely satisfying all domestic demand.

Fossil resources found in Korea include anthracite coal, lignite coal, and peat, but they are undeveloped due to poor reserve conditions and economic inefficiency. The majority of coal extracted in Korea is anthracite coal, and it is mostly buried in the Pyeongan layers formed during the Paleozoic and Mesozoic eras. Anthracite coal is dispersed throughout Gangwon-*do*, Chungcheongnam-*do*, Chungcheongbuk-*do*, Jeollanam-*do*, Jeollabuk-*do*, and Gyeonggi-*do*, but over half of the coal reserves are buried in the Samcheok-*si* and Jeongseon-*gun* coalfields in the Taebaeksanmeak area. The coal industry is gradually contracting due to people's preference for clean fuels and the government's enforcement of coal industry rationalization policies.

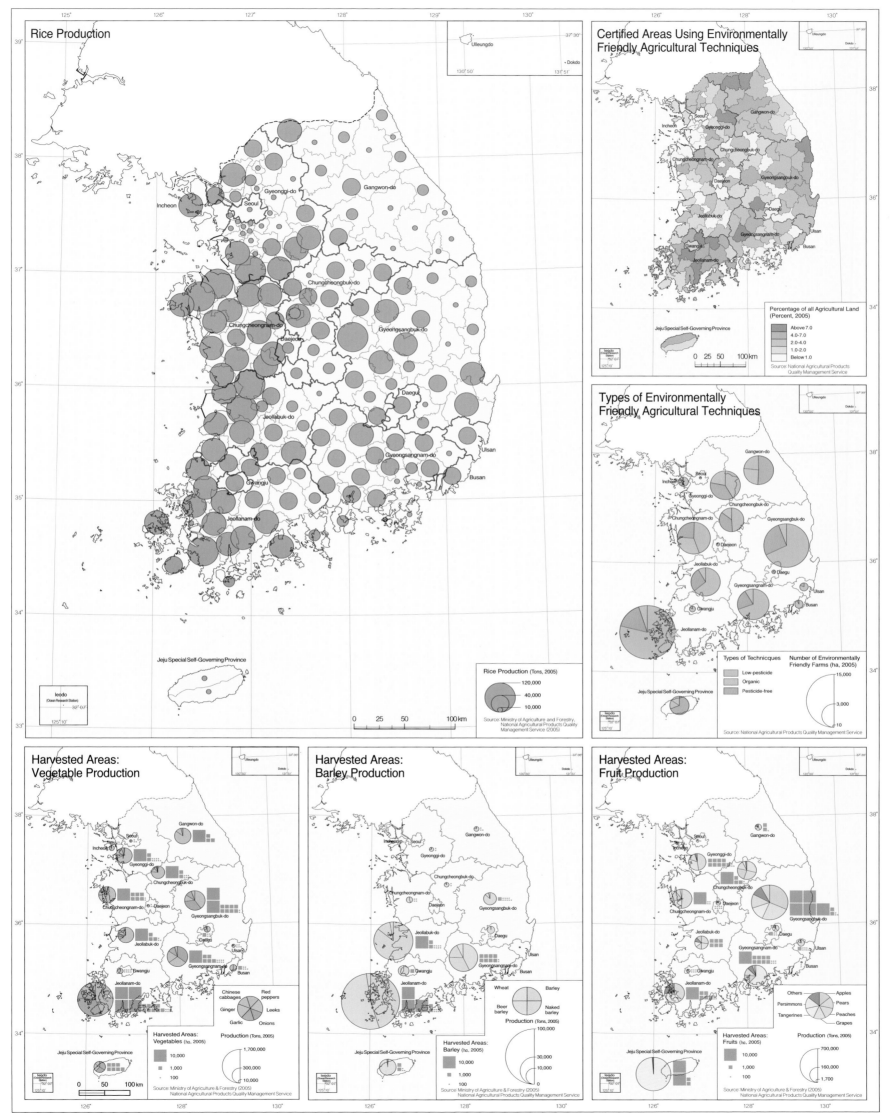

Rice Production

Certified Areas Using Environmentally Friendly Agricultural Techniques

Percentage of all Agricultural Land (Percent, 2005)
Above 7.0
4.0-7.0
2.0-4.0
1.0-2.0
Below 1.0

Source: National Agricultural Products Quality Management Service

Types of Environmentally Friendly Agricultural Techniques

Rice Production (Tons, 2005)
120,000
40,000
10,000

Source: Ministry of Agriculture and Forestry, National Agricultural Products Quality Management Service (2005)

Types of Technicques
Low-pesticide
Organic
Pesticide-free

Number of Environmentally Friendly Farms (ha, 2005)
15,000
3,000
10

Source: National Agricultural Products Quality Management Service

Harvested Areas: Vegetable Production

Chinese cabbages
Red peppers
Ginger
Leeks
Garlic
Onions

Harvested Areas: Vegetables (ha, 2005)
10,000
1,000
100

Production (Tons, 2005)
1,700,000
300,000
10,000

Source: Ministry of Agriculture & Forestry (2005) National Agricultural Products Quality Management Service

Harvested Areas: Barley Production

Wheat
Barley
Beer barley
Naked barley

Harvested Areas: Barley (ha, 2005)
10,000
1,000
100

Production (Tons, 2005)
100,000
30,000
10,000
0

Source: Ministry of Agriculture & Forestry (2005) National Agricultural Products Quality Management Service

Harvested Areas: Fruit Production

Others
Apples
Persimmons
Pears
Tangerines
Peaches
Grapes

Harvested Areas: Fruits (ha, 2005)
10,000
1,000
100

Production (Tons, 2005)
700,000
160,000
1,700

Source: Ministry of Agriculture & Forestry (2005) National Agricultural Products Quality Management Service

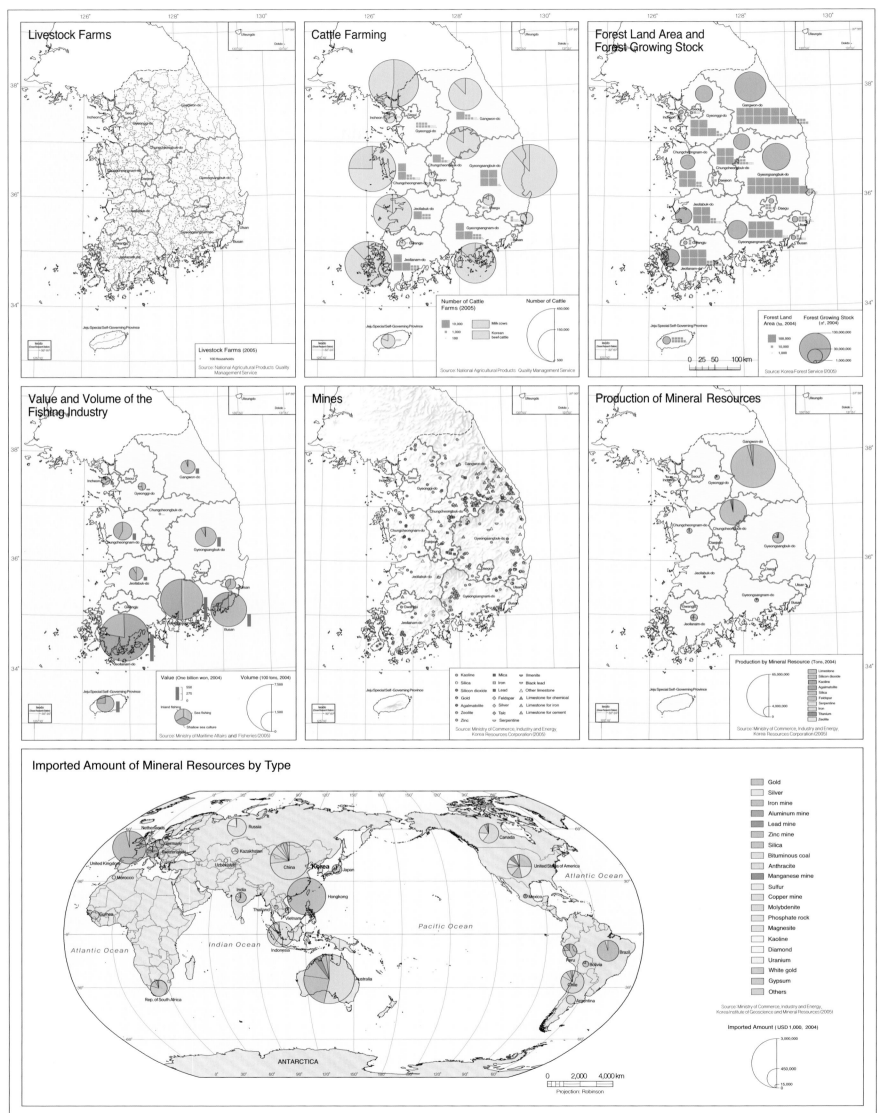

Livestock Farms

Livestock Farms (2005)
· 100 Households
Source: National Agricultural Products Quality Management Service

Cattle Farming

Number of Cattle Farms (2005)
■ 10,000
□ 1,000
· 100

Number of Cattle
450,000
150,000
Milk cows
Korean beef cattle
500

Source: National Agricultural Products Quality Management Service

Forest Land Area and Forest Growing Stock

Forest Land Area (ha, 2004)
■ 100,000
■ 10,000
· 1,000

Forest Growing Stock (m³, 2004)
130,000,000
30,000,000
1,000,000

0 25 50 100 km

Source: Korea Forest Service (2005)

Value and Volume of the Fishing Industry

Value (One billion won, 2004)
550
275
0
Inland fishing
Sea fishing
Shallow sea culture

Volume (100 tons, 2004)
7,500
1,500

Source: Ministry of Maritime Affairs and Fisheries (2005)

Mines

⊙ Kaoline   ■ Mica   ▽ Ilmenite
○ Silica   ■ Iron   ▼ Black lead
□ Silicon dioxide ■ Lead   △ Other limestone
● Gold   ◇ Feldspar   △ Limestone for chemical
● Agalmatolite ◇ Silver   △ Limestone for iron
● Zeolite   ◇ Talc   △ Limestone for cement
● Zinc   ◆ Serpentine

Source: Ministry of Commerce, Industry and Energy,
Korea Resources Corporation (2005)

Production of Mineral Resources

Production by Mineral Resource (Tone, 2004)
65,000,000

4,000,000

Limestone
Silicon dioxide
Kaoline
Agalmatolite
Silica
Feldspar
Serpentine
Iron
Titanium
Zeolite

Source: Ministry of Commerce, Industry and Energy,
Korea Resources Corporation (2005)

Imported Amount of Mineral Resources by Type

Gold
Silver
Iron mine
Aluminum mine
Lead mine
Zinc mine
Silica
Bituminous coal
Anthracite
Manganese mine
Sulfur
Copper mine
Molybdenite
Phosphate rock
Magnesite
Kaoline
Diamond
Uranium
White gold
Gypsum
Others

Source: Ministry of Commerce, Industry and Energy,
Korea Institute of Geoscience and Mineral Resources (2005)

Imported Amount (USD 1,000, 2004)
3,000,000
450,000
15,000

0 2,000 4,000 km

Projection: Robinson

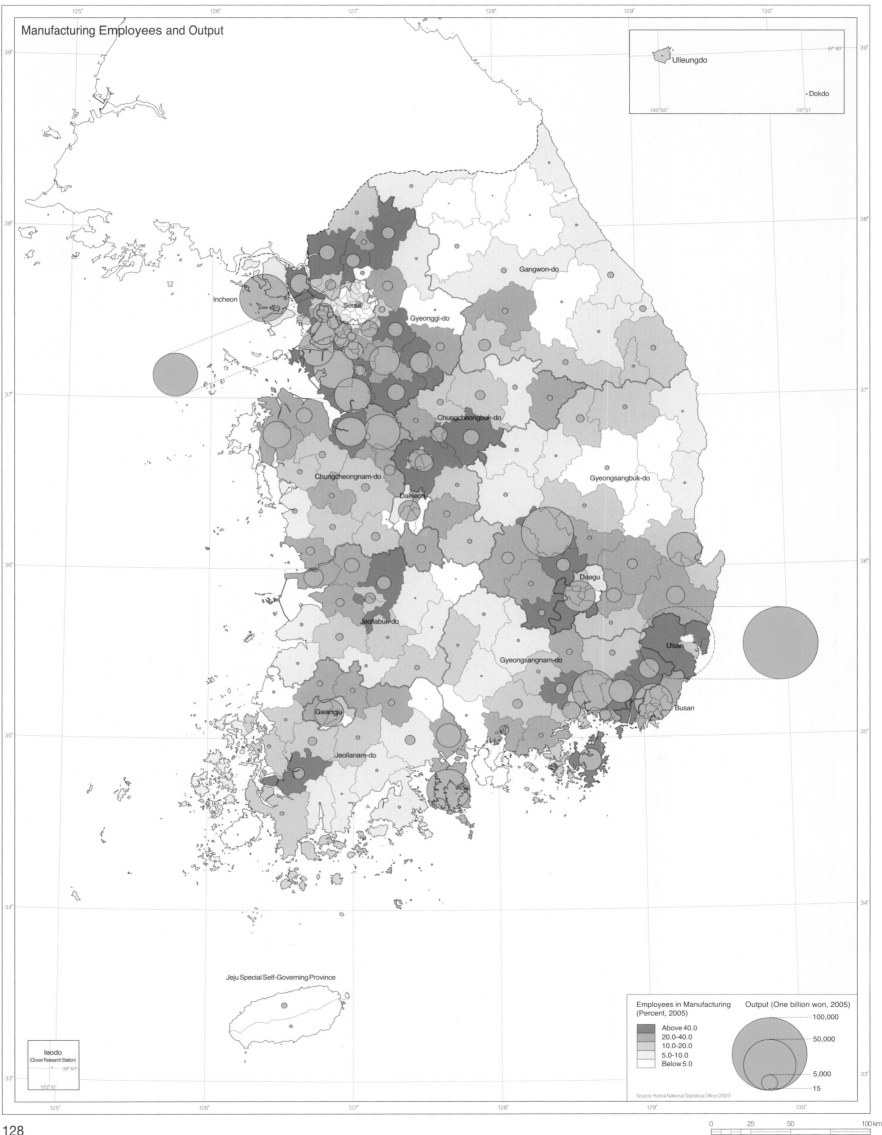

Manufacturing Employees and Output

Ulleungdo

Dokdo

Incheon

Seoul

Gangwon-do

Gyeonggi-do

Chungcheongbuk-do

Chungcheongnam-do

Daejeon

Gyeongsangbuk-do

Jeollabuk-do

Daegu

Gyeongsangnam-do

Ulsan

Busan

Gwangju

Jeollanam-do

Jeju Special Self-Governing Province

Ieodo
(Ocean Research Station)

32°67'

125°10'

**Employees in Manufacturing
(Percent, 2005)**

Above 40.0
20.0-40.0
10.0-20.0
5.0-10.0
Below 5.0

Output (One billion won, 2005)

100,000

50,000

5,000

15

Source: Korea National Statistical Office (2007)

0   25   50   100 km

Korean manufacturing industries have experienced very rapid growth since the 1960s. Leading industries in Korea transformed from labor-intensive industries in the 1960s and the early 1970s, to heavy industries and mass-production systems in the late 1970s and 1980s, followed by technology-intensive industries in the 1990s, and knowledge-intensive industries in the 21st century. As for the changes in the shares of the various economic sectors, service industries have grown gradually. Manufacturing experienced deindustrialization in the 1980s and the early 1990s, and has been in the process of reindustrialization since the IMF bailout program of 1997-1998. The share of manufacturing in real GDP increased slightly from 27 percent in 1975, sustained a share of around 30 percent in the 1980s and 1990s, and increased again after 1997.

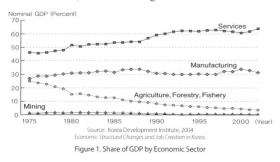

Figure 1. Share of GDP by Economic Sector

Manufacturing has been concentrated in the capital region, Seoul, Incheon, and Gyeonggi-do. Seoul has played a critical leading role in the changes of the industrial structure of Korea during the last four decades, because new industries, initially developed and concentrated in Seoul at first, spread to nearby Gyeonggi-do and then to other provincial areas. There has been a significant spatial division of labor between Seoul and provincial areas in the progress of the changes. Engineering services, software industries, design and advertising industries have been concentrated mostly in Seoul. Along with these businesses has come the agglomeration of economic control functions. Due to the leading role of Seoul in the introduction of new industries and the spatial division of labor, the spatial disparity between the Capital Region and the rest of the country has been a key issue for policy makers.

There have been significant structural changes in Seoul's manufacturing industries since the 1980s. Seoul has specialized in apparel & clothing, publishing & printing, and the information and fashion industries, while other Capital Regions have specialized in knowledge-intensive industries such as the electrical and electronic industries. More than three quarters of Seoul's manufacturing industries consist of apparel & clothing, fabricated metals, and publishing & printing industries. At the same time, the share of producer services such as R&D, engineering, and marketing has increased very rapidly.

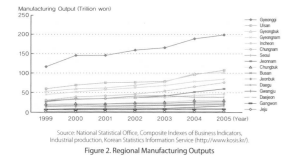

Figure 2. Regional Manufacturing Outputs

The most distinct characteristics of the structural changes to Korean manufacturing industries concerns the size of the firms. Since the 1990s, excluding the IMF bailout program period of 1997-8, the number of establishments has grown steadily. On the other hand, employment decreased or remained stagnant. Furthermore, the share of small firms (companies employing between 5-19 people) has increased gradually, but the number of medium-and-large-sized firms (companies employing more than 100 people) has decreased.

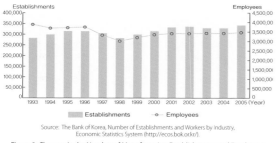

Figure 3. Changes in the Number of Manufacturing Establishments and Employees

The performance of major manufacturing industries has been marked by remarkable progress. The electrical and electronics and the motor vehicle industries have recorded strong growth, and chemical and machinery industries have shown a relatively constant increase. The apparel and clothing industry, which experienced rapid growth in the 1960s and the 1970s, has decreased in size relative to overall Korean manufacturing production. The share of the apparel and clothing industry fell to 4 percent in 2002, compared to a 28 percent share in 1975. At the same time, the share of the electrical and electronics industry and the motor vehicle industry increased to 35 percent and 13 percent, respectively, by 2002 from 5 percent and 4 percent in 1975.

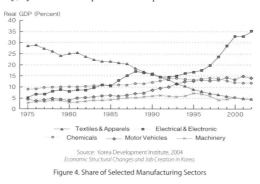

Figure 4. Share of Selected Manufacturing Sectors

The main Korean manufacturing industries are the IT and ship building industries. Ship building tonnage increased from 10 million G/T in 2000 to 18 million G/T in 2005, a near two-fold growth in just 5 years. The production of mobile phones experienced a radical expansion from 4.7 million produced in 1995 to 202 million produced in 2005, marking a 43-fold growth. One dramatic contrast in manufacturing production is the manufacture of television products. While the production of picture tube TVs decreased swiftly, the production of flat panel display TVs continuously increased from 2000.

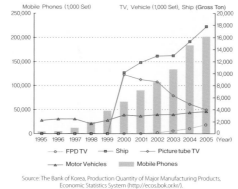

Figure 5. Outputs of Selected Manufacturing Products

The progress of IT industries in Korea has been magnificent. The production of information and communications devices expanded from 111 trillion won in 2000 to 166 trillion won in 2005. Also, revenues from information and communications services and software and computer-related services expanded from 32 trillion won and 11 trillion won in 2000 to 47 trillion won and 22 trillion won in 2005, respectively. This progress implies that the IT industries have contributed to the competitiveness and growth of Korean manufacturing.

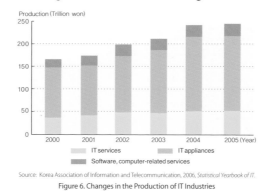

Figure 6. Changes in the Production of IT Industries

The productivity of Korean manufacturing has risen constantly and at a relatively rapid rate. Looking at the manufacturing industries as a whole, the productivity indices increased from 13.7 in 1980, to 42.9 in 1990, and to 148.1 in 2005 (year 2000 =100). The productivity level for light industries such as apparel and clothing, leather and luggage, footwear, and the furniture industries all increased steadily in the 1980s, reaching a local peak in the late 1980s, and has since slowly decreased. Heavy

industries, such as electrical and electronics, machinery and equipment, metal and IT, have shown a brisk increase since the 1990s. The leather, luggage, and footwear industries showed a productivity level of 197.8 in 1980, peaked at 480.3 in 1988, and then plummeted to 58.6 in 2006. In contrast, the productivity of electronic components, radio and TV, and communications equipments increased from merely 1.4 in 1980 to 11.0 in 1990, and reached 323.1 in 2006, which marked the highest growth rate among all Korean manufacturing industries.

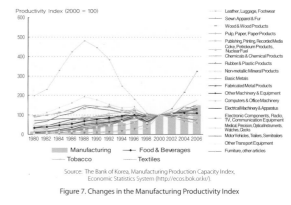

Figure 7. Changes in the Manufacturing Productivity Index

Korean R&D investment increased steadily beginning in the year 2000, reaching 10 trillion won in 2003, except for the period of the IMF bailout program of 1997-1998. The share of R&D investment as a percentage of revenues for large firms is generally higher than that of small-and-medium-sized firms. The share of R&D investments for high-tech industries, such as electronic components, radio and TV and communications equipment, accounted for a very large proportion, 43.8 percent, while highly competitive industries, such as pharmaceuticals, computers and office machinery, medical, precision and optical instruments, and aircraft parts and accessories, showed a relatively low proportion at 14.9 percent.

Korean manufacturing industries have experienced radical structural changes toward the high-tech and highly-competitive industries. In 2004, the Korean government launched an innovative industrial cluster promotion policy in order to support industry-university-research institution networking, R&D capacity. The government localized business services to boost local buzz, and deepened social capital in the industrial complexes located outside the Capital regions. These cluster policies aim both to enhance manufacturing competitiveness and to contribute to balanced regional development.

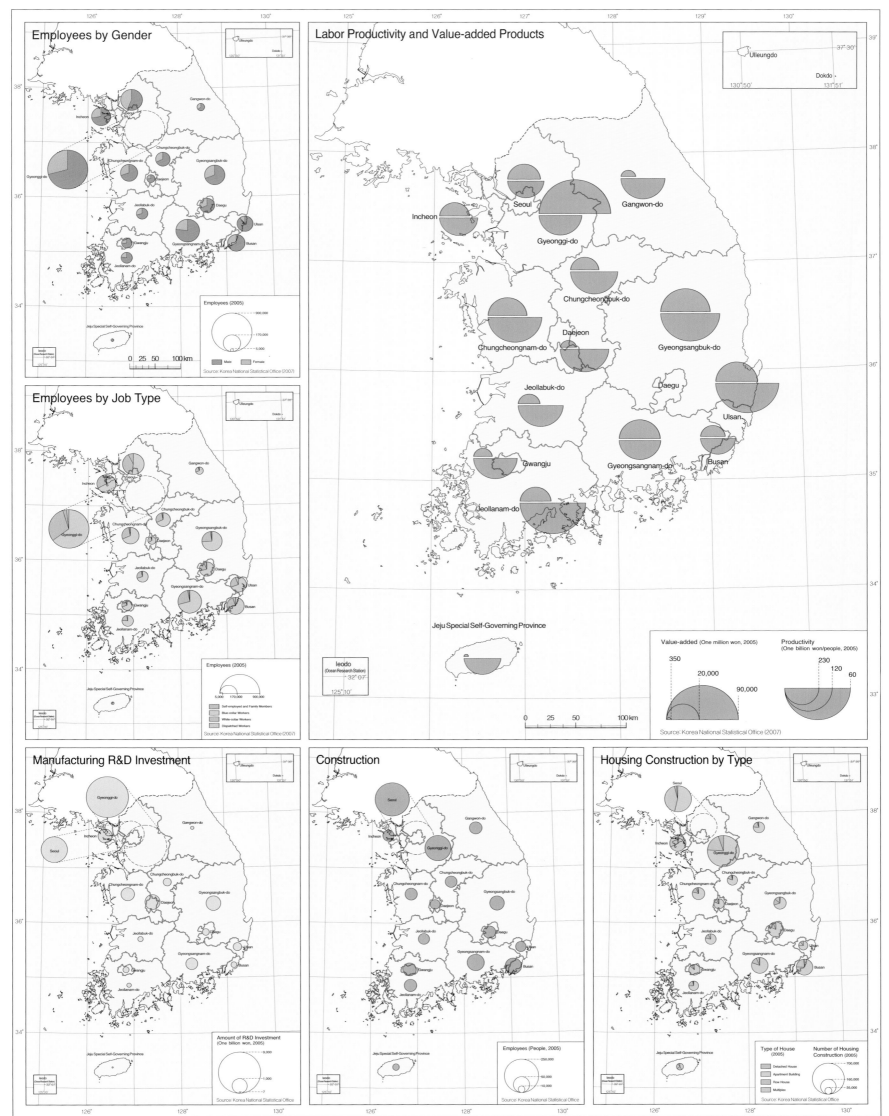

Employees by Gender

Employees (2005)
900,000
170,000
5,000

Male Female

0 25 50 100 km

Source: Korea National Statistical Office (2007)

Employees by Job Type

Employees (2005)
5,000 170,000 900,000

Self-employed and Family Members
Blue-collar Workers
White-collar Workers
Dispatched Workers

Source: Korea National Statistical Office (2007)

Labor Productivity and Value-added Products

Ulleungdo
Dokdo

Seoul
Incheon
Gyeonggi-do
Gangwon-do

Chungcheongbuk-do
Daejeon
Chungcheongnam-do
Gyeongsangbuk-do

Jeollabuk-do
Daegu
Ulsan

Gwangju
Gyeongsangnam-do
Busan

Jeollanam-do

Jeju Special Self-Governing Province

Ieodo
(Ocean Research Station)

Value-added (One million won, 2005)
350
20,000
90,000

Productivity
(One billion won/people, 2005)
230
120
60

Source: Korea National Statistical Office (2007)

0 25 50 100 km

Manufacturing R&D Investment

Gyeonggi-do
Seoul
Incheon
Gangwon-do

Chungcheongnam-do
Chungcheongbuk-do
Gyeongsangbuk-do
Daejeon

Jeollabuk-do
Daegu
Gwangju
Ulsan
Busan

Gyeongsangnam-do

Jeollanam-do

Jeju Special Self-Governing Province

Amount of R&D Investment
(One billion won, 2005)
9,000
1,000
7

Source: Korea National Statistical Office

Construction

Seoul
Incheon
Gangwon-do
Gyeonggi-do

Chungcheongnam-do
Chungcheongbuk-do
Daejeon
Gyeongsangbuk-do

Jeollabuk-do
Daegu
Gyeongsangnam-do
Ulsan
Gwangju
Busan

Jeollanam-do

Jeju Special Self-Governing Province

Employees (People, 2005)
250,000
50,000
10,000

Source: Korea National Statistical Office

Housing Construction by Type

Seoul
Incheon
Gangwon-do
Gyeonggi-do

Chungcheongnam-do
Daejeon
Gyeongsangbuk-do

Jeollabuk-do
Daegu
Gyeongsangnam-do
Busan

Jeollanam-do

Jeju Special Self-Governing Province

Type of House (2005)
Detached House
Apartment Building
Row House
Multiplex

Number of Housing Construction (2005)
700,000
160,000
35,000

Source: Korea National Statistical Office

130

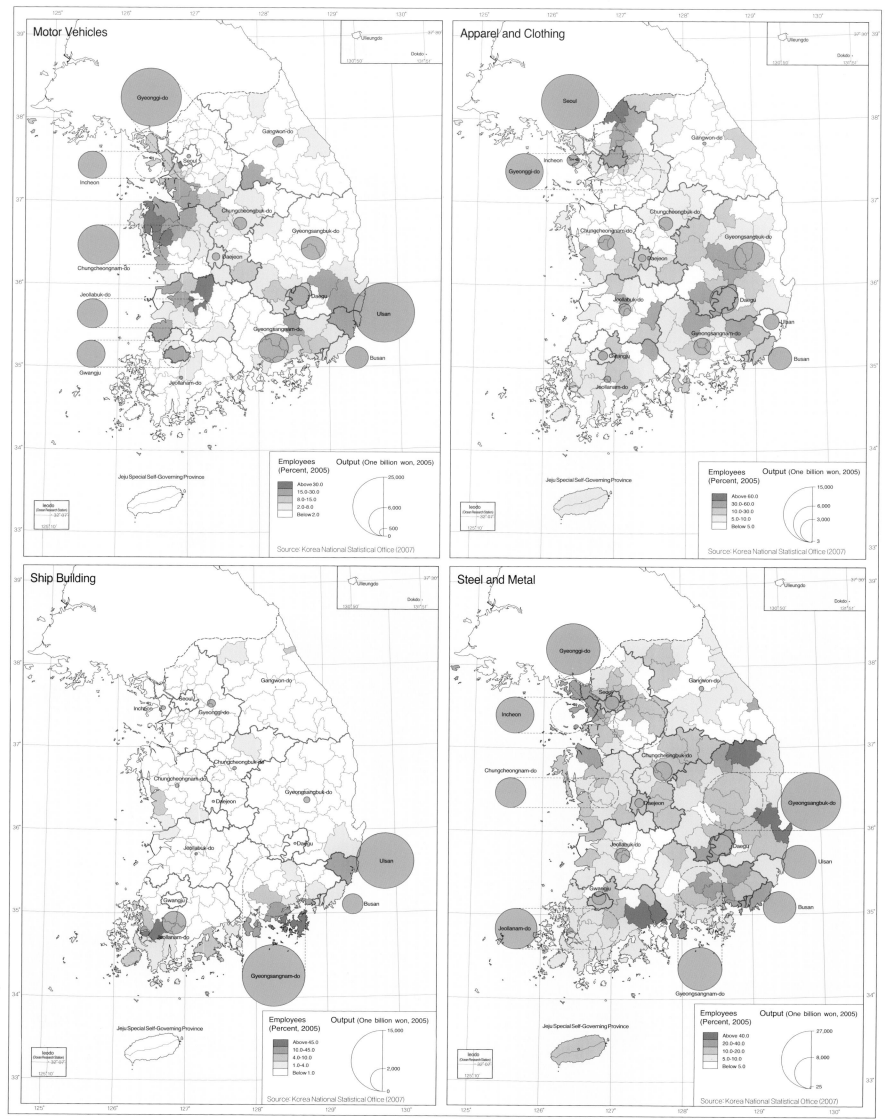

Motor Vehicles

Gyeonggi-do

Gangwon-do

Incheon

Seoul

Chungcheongbuk-do

Gyeongsangbuk-do

Chungcheongnam-do

Daejeon

Jeollabuk-do

Daegu

Ulsan

Gyeongsangnam-do

Gwangju

Busan

Jeollanam-do

Jeju Special Self-Governing Province

Ieodo
(Ocean Research Station)

Employees
(Percent, 2005)

Above 30.0
15.0-30.0
8.0-15.0
2.0-8.0
Below 2.0

Output (One billion won, 2005)

25,000
6,000
500
0

Source: Korea National Statistical Office (2007)

Apparel and Clothing

Seoul

Gangwon-do

Incheon

Gyeonggi-do

Chungcheongbuk-do

Chungcheongnam-do

Gyeongsangbuk-do

Daejeon

Jeollabuk-do

Daegu

Ulsan

Gyeongsangnam-do

Gwangju

Busan

Jeollanam-do

Jeju Special Self-Governing Province

Ieodo
(Ocean Research Station)

Employees
(Percent, 2005)

Above 60.0
30.0-60.0
10.0-30.0
5.0-10.0
Below 5.0

Output (One billion won, 2005)

15,000
6,000
3,000
3

Source: Korea National Statistical Office (2007)

Ship Building

Seoul

Gangwon-do

Incheon

Gyeonggi-do

Chungcheongbuk-do

Chungcheongnam-do

Gyeongsangbuk-do

Daejeon

Jeollabuk-do

Daegu

Ulsan

Busan

Gwangju

Jeollanam-do

Gyeongsangnam-do

Jeju Special Self-Governing Province

Ieodo
(Ocean Research Station)

Employees
(Percent, 2005)

Above 45.0
10.0-45.0
4.0-10.0
1.0-4.0
Below 1.0

Output (One billion won, 2005)

15,000
2,000
0

Source: Korea National Statistical Office (2007)

Steel and Metal

Gyeonggi-do

Seoul

Gangwon-do

Incheon

Chungcheongbuk-do

Chungcheongnam-do

Gyeongsangbuk-do

Daejeon

Jeollabuk-do

Daegu

Ulsan

Gwangju

Busan

Jeollanam-do

Gyeongsangnam-do

Jeju Special Self-Governing Province

Ieodo
(Ocean Research Station)

Employees
(Percent, 2005)

Above 40.0
20.0-40.0
10.0-20.0
5.0-10.0
Below 5.0

Output (One billion won, 2005)

27,000
8,000
25

Source: Korea National Statistical Office (2007)

0 25 50 100 km

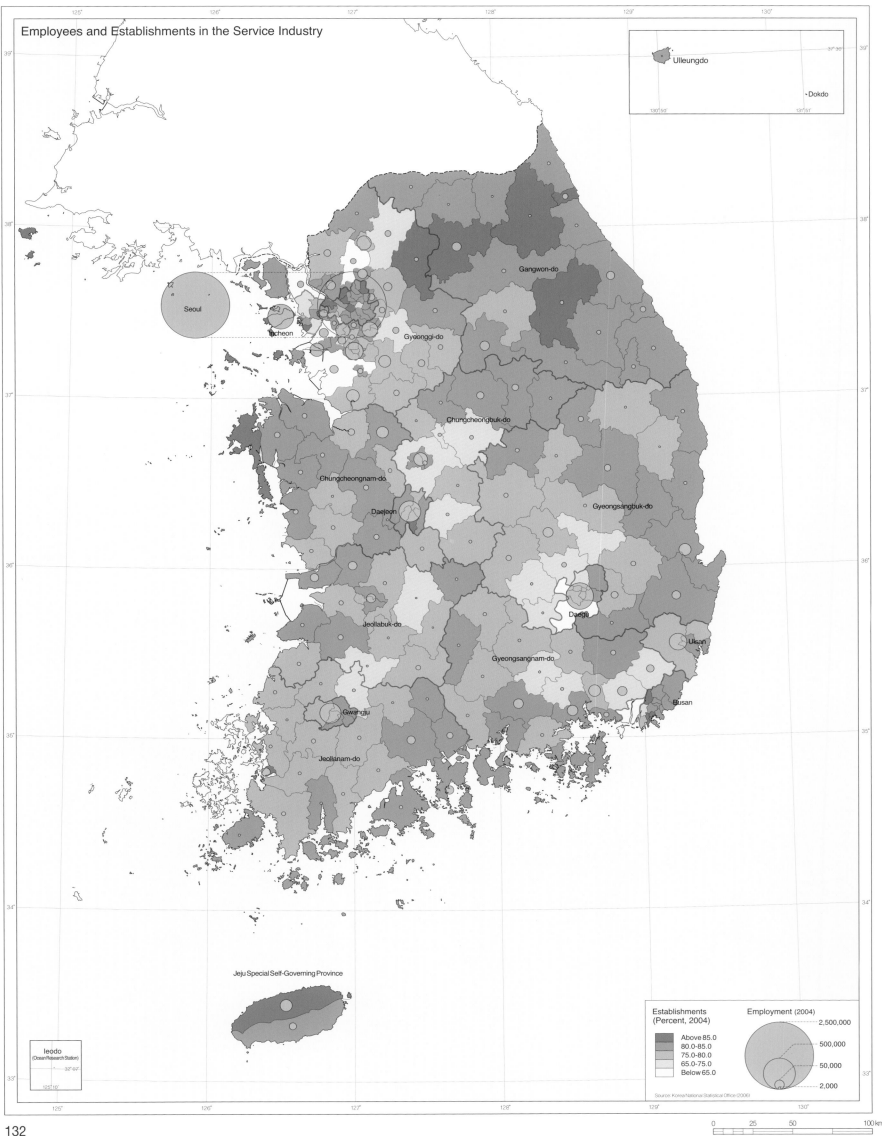

Employees and Establishments in the Service Industry

Ulleungdo

Dokdo

Gangwon-do

Seoul

Incheon

Gyeonggi-do

Chungcheongbuk-do

Chungcheongnam-do

Daejeon

Gyeongsangbuk-do

Jeollabuk-do

Daegu

Ulsan

Gyeongsangnam-do

Gwangju

Busan

Jeollanam-do

Jeju Special Self-Governing Province

Ieodo
(Ocean Research Station)

Establishments
(Percent, 2004)

Above 85.0
80.0-85.0
75.0-80.0
65.0-75.0
Below 65.0

Employment (2004)

2,500,000

500,000

50,000

2,000

Source: Korea National Statistical Office (2006)

0   25   50   100 km

The service industry is difficult to define because it includes different activities. It becomes even more difficult to define as developed economies and living standards demand more specific, diversified services beyond the traditional activities that help support manufacturing and consumers.

Widely classified, the service industry refers to the tertiary industrial activities. That is, it follows the concept of helping or facilitating primary and secondary economic activities. The common practical perspective sees service as "the activities not directly related to producing materials," which is the definition accepted by the OECD. It considers the service industry as supporting the primary and secondary industries. The service industry in the Korean Standard Industrial Classification is subdivided into 14 categories such as wholesale and retail, eating and lodging places, transportation, communication, finance, etc (Table 1).

Table 1. Levels and Categories of Korean Standard Industrial Classification of Services

Level 1: Sections	Level 2: Divisions	Level 3: Groups
G. Wholesale, Retail Trade	50. Automobile, Fuel Retail	
H. Hotels and Restaurants	55. Hotels and Restaurants	551. Hotels
		552. Restaurants
I. Transportation	60. Land Transportation, Pipelines	
J. Communication	64. Communication	641. Postal Service
		642. Telecommunication
K. Banking, Insurance	65. Banks	
	66. Insurance and Pension	
L. Real Estate, Renting	70. Real Estate	
M. Business Service	74. Professional, Technical Services	741. Legal, Accounting
		742. Market Research, Management Consultancy
N. Public Administration	76. Public Administration, Defense	
O. Education	80. Education	
P. Health and Social Work Activities	85. Human Health	
Q. Entertainment, Cultural, Sports Activities	87. Motion Picture, Broadcasting, Performing Arts	871. Motion Picture Producing
R. Other Public Administration, Social, and Personal Services	90. Sewage, Refuse Disposal	
S. Households	95. Services of Households	
T. International, Foreign Organizations	99. International, Foreign Organizations	

Source: National Statistical Office, 2000, *Korean Standard Industrial classification*.

Nowadays, the service industry has become more important in a service-dominant economy. The service industry has increased in proportion over the manufacturing industry, which has dwindled since the 1970s (Figure 1). Since 1988, over 50 percent have been employed in the service industry, but that employment number has since risen to more than 60 percent, and the industry has accounted for more than 50 percent of gross domestic product since 1995. The industrial structure, in terms of percentage of the gross domestic product for 2006, shows Service at 57.5 percent, Mining and Manufacturing at 28.2 percent, Construction at 9.1 percent, and Agriculture, Forestry, and Fisheries at 3.2 percent.

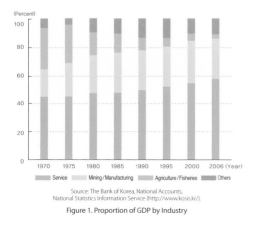

Source: The Bank of Korea, National Accounts,
National Statistics Information Service (http://www.kosis.kr/).

Figure 1. Proportion of GDP by Industry

The importance of the service industry lies in its close relationship to the daily activities of people as well as to its role in facilitating the activities of manufacturing and other industries. The growth rate of the service industry in Korea had been very low compared to that of manufacturing during the 1970s (Figure 2). However, the growth rate of the service industry moved closer to that of manufacturing during the 1980s and had a greater than 7 percent annual average growth rate from the 1980s to the 1990s (Table 2). In particular, producer services, including communication, finance and insurance, business services, real estate and renting, have been major contributors to the service sector's growth. This is largely the result of the rapid growth of knowledge-intensive services, such as information and communication, and an increase in service outsourcing for work efficiency. Traditional services such as wholesale and retail, and hotels and restaurants, been growing slowly since 2000.

Source: The Bank of Korea, National Accounts,
National Statistics Information Service (http://www.kosis.kr/).

Figure 2. Growth Rate of the Service Industry

Table 2. Annual Growth Rate of the Service Industry by Sector, 2000-2006

	2000	2001	2002	2003	2004	2005	2006
Wholesale and Retail Trade	9.5	6.1	7.7	-1.7	-1.0	1.9	4.0
Hotels and Restaurants	8.2	7.4	9.4	0.5	-0.7	0.3	2.1
Transportation	7.5	2.8	7.7	2.9	6.2	4.2	6.3
Communication	21.7	19.0	7.5	2.3	5.8	4.1	2.8
Banking and Insurance	2.4	1.0	7.8	0.5	0.1	7.3	7.9
Real Estate and Renting	11.0	8.2	12.6	1.7	-6.3	8.5	10.2
Business Services	10.7	6.8	16.7	5.4	1.9	2.8	5.9
Education Services	12.4	9.4	6.4	3.5	1.6	0.7	2.3
Health and Social Work	-6.2	-3.1	10.2	0.6	5.0	7.3	10.0
Recreational, Cultural and Sporting Activities	27.1	11.3	3.8	0.2	-3.3	3.0	2.5
Other Social and Personal Services	5.9	6.9	6.0	-0.4	-10	1.9	3.8
Total	8.8	6.1	2.8	1.6	1.9	3.4	4.2

Source: National Statistical Office, Service industry,
National Statistics Information Service (http://www.kosis.kr/).

Productivity growth in services is one-fifth that of manufacturing. A higher proportion of the service industry is still taken up by low value-added sectors such as wholesale and retail, and hotels and restaurants. These productivity and value-added aspects have kept the Korean service industry in its early stage of development. However, the amount of electronic commerce has been increasing very rapidly along with the development of information and communication technology. The total amount of electronic commerce was 358,450 billion won in 2005, with a rapid annual growth rate of 30 percent since 2002 (Table 3). The revenues for cyber shopping malls grew at a 25 percent annual rate, reaching 10 trillion won in 2005. Among the types of electronic commerce, business-to-business(B2B), a fast growing activity, accounted for 89 percent in the amount of 319 trillion won; business-to-government(B2G) took 8.1 percent in the amount of 29 trillion won, and business-to-consumer(B2C) took in 2.2 percent in the amount of 7.9 trillion won (Figure 3).

Table 3. Amounts of Electronic Commerce and Cyber Shopping Mall Trade

(Unit: billion won)

	2002	2003	2004	2005
Electronic Commerce	177,809	235,025	214,079	358,451
Cyber Shopping Mall	6,030	7,055	7,768	10,676

Source: National Statistical Office, Service industry,
National Statistics Information Service (http://www.kosis.kr/).

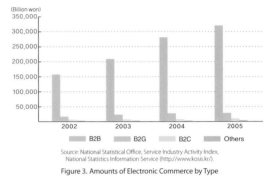

Source: National Statistical Office, Service Industry Activity Index,
National Statistics Information Service (http://www.kosis.kr/).

Figure 3. Amounts of Electronic Commerce by Type

Since the service industry consists of activities linking producers and consumers, it operates on a relatively small scale, and demand is widely distributed across regions. Larger populations and economic activities, however, require more service establishments. To present the geographical distribution of the service industry, a series of 17 maps are drawn: one for the overall coverage of the service industry in employment and establishments, and 16 for the detailed service sectors of Wholesale and Retail(G), Hotels and Restaurants(H), Transportation(I), Communication(J), Banking and Insurance(K), Business Services(M), Personal Services(R) and their activities. Data used are from the 2004 Census on Basic Characteristics of Establishments compiled by the National Statistical Office.

Most maps reveal that the employment and establishments of service sector businesses are concentrated in the highly-populated large cities, in particular the Capital Region. Such a concentration is more prominent in service activities such as large-sized general retail stores. Seoul has overwhelming concentrations in trade for both wholesale and retail. Hotels and restaurants and the number of retail establishments per 1,000 people are less concentrated than other service sectors. Transportation, communication, banking and insurance, business services, and personal services reveal similar concentrated patterns in large cities and the Capital Region. Prominent concentrations are found in business services including data processing and computer operation(M72), research and development(M73), professional and scientific(M74), and business consultancy(M75). Personal services activities tend to be dispersed along with the demands of individual consumers.

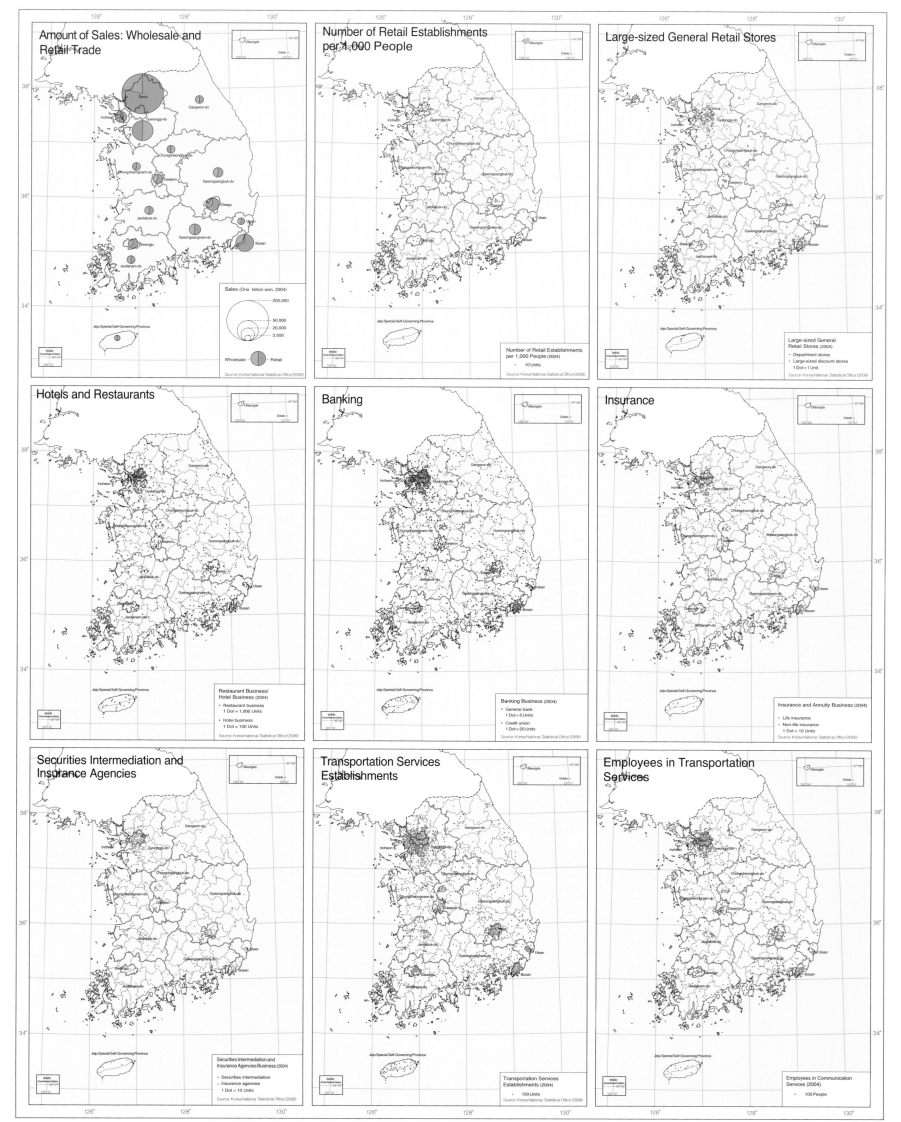

Amount of Sales: Wholesale and Retail Trade

Sales (One billion won, 2004)
200,000
50,000
20,000
3,500
Wholesale · Retail

Source: Korea National Statistical Office (2006)

Number of Retail Establishments per 1,000 People

Number of Retail Establishments per 1,000 People (2004)
· 10 Units

Source: Korea National Statistical Office (2006)

Large-sized General Retail Stores

Large-sized General Retail Stores (2004)
· Department stores
· Large-sized discount stores
1 Dot = 1 Unit

Source: Korea National Statistical Office (2006)

Hotels and Restaurants

Restaurant Business/ Hotel Business (2004)
· Restaurant business
1 Dot = 1,000 Units
· Hotel business
1 Dot = 100 Units

Source: Korea National Statistical Office (2006)

Banking

Banking Business (2004)
· General bank
1 Dot = 5 Units
· Credit union
1 Dot = 20 Units

Source: Korea National Statistical Office (2006)

Insurance

Insurance and Annuity Business (2004)
· Life insurance
· Non-life insurance
1 Dot = 10 Units

Source: Korea National Statistical Office (2006)

Securities Intermediation and Insurance Agencies

Securities Intermediation and Insurance Agencies Business (2004)
· Securities intermediation
· Insurance agencies
1 Dot = 10 Units

Source: Korea National Statistical Office (2006)

Transportation Services Establishments

Transportation Services Establishments (2004)
· 100 Units

Source: Korea National Statistical Office (2006)

Employees in Transportation Services

Employees in Communication Services (2004)
· 100 People

0   50   100   200 km

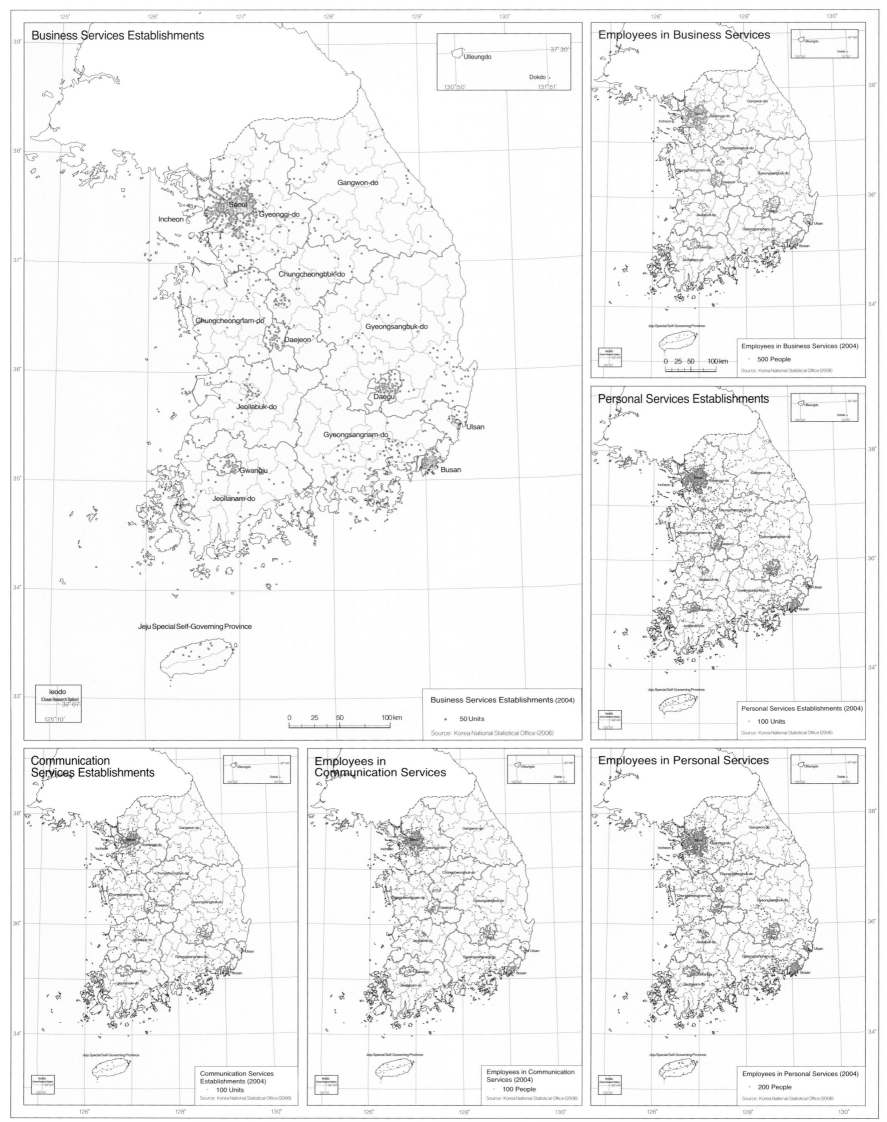

Business Services Establishments

Ulleungdo

Dokdo

Gangwon-do

Seoul

Incheon Gyeonggi-do

Chungcheongbuk-do

Chungcheongnam-do

Daejeon Gyeongsangbuk-do

Jeollabuk-do Daegu

Jeollabuk-do

Gyeongsangnam-do Ulsan

Gwangju Busan

Jeollanam-do

Jeju Special Self-Governing Province

Ieodo
(Ocean Research Station)

Business Services Establishments (2004)
• 50 Units
Source: Korea National Statistical Office (2006)

Employees in Business Services

Employees in Business Services (2004)
0 25 50 100 km
• 500 People
Source: Korea National Statistical Office (2006)

Personal Services Establishments

Personal Services Establishments (2004)
• 100 Units
Source: Korea National Statistical Office (2006)

Communication Services Establishments

Communication Services Establishments (2004)
• 100 Units
Source: Korea National Statistical Office (2006)

Employees in Communication Services

Employees in Communication Services (2004)
• 100 People
Source: Korea National Statistical Office (2006)

Employees in Personal Services

Employees in Personal Services (2004)
• 200 People
Source: Korea National Statistical Office (2006)

135

Transportation Networks

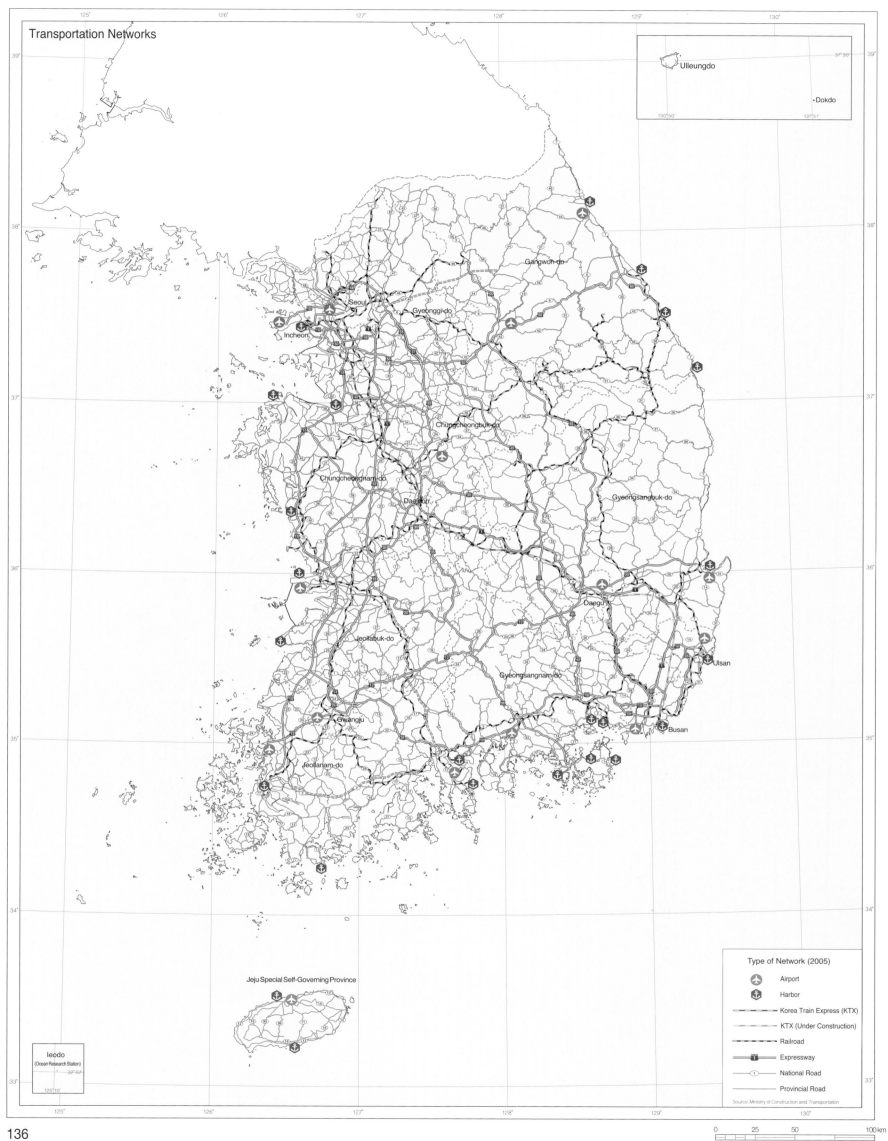

Ulleungdo

·Dokdo

Gangwon-do

Seoul

Gyeonggi-do

Incheon

Chungcheongbuk-do

Chungcheongnam-do

Daejeon

Gyeongsangbuk-do

Jeollabuk-do

Daegu

Gyeongsangnam-do

Ulsan

Gwangju

Busan

Jeollanam-do

Jeju Special Self-Governing Province

Ieodo
(Ocean Research Station)

Type of Network (2005)

✈	Airport
⬢	Harbor
	Korea Train Express (KTX)
	KTX (Under Construction)
	Railroad
▮	Expressway
	National Road
	Provincial Road

Source: Ministry of Construction and Transportation

0   25   50   100 km

Since the 1960s transportation and communication (TC) in Korea have developed dramatically along with the rapid economic growth achieved through an export-led industrialization policy. At the regional level, the development of TC gave rise to uneven spatial development as the structure of regional growth focused upon the metropolitan area and the Seoul-Busan axis. This means that the TC developed accumulatively on the basis of economic demand at the regional level. Before presenting this development on a map, it would be helpful to examine flows of the development of TC to understand the basis of this sectors's rapid development.

Modern transportation in Korea started with the railroad, which was constructed in the period of imperialist Japan for the purpose of the invasion and plundering of Korea. After the railroad construction rights were transferred from UN allied forces to the Korean government in 1955, the government began the modernization of railroad transportation. The diesel locomotive and electric railway were introduced along with the construction of the first multi-trackage railway and a high-speed railroad later in 2004. In the case of road transportation, development started with the construction of the Seoul-Busan expressway in the 1970s. Since the late 1980s, due to the increase in the number of cars and associated demand on the roads, continuous construction and the improvement of existing roads have been implemented. For example, the lack of a traffic network on the east-west axis due to natural constraints was one of the most difficult factors. However, by constructing flyovers and tunnels to overcome constraints such as the lofty and steep passes Daegwallyeong and Misiryeong, convenience of transportation and economic efficiency increased.

Water and marine transportation in Korea have relatively long traditions. However, with the emergence of more economical means of transportation domestically, water and marine transportation have been more predominantly used to transport commodities overseas. Therefore, main trading ports were established at places with favorable locational conditions to facilitate exports and imports. The reason large trading ports are mainly located on the south and east coast is related to economic factors. There has been a high rate of dependence on imports of raw materials in the heavy industry, and the economy grew based on export-led development since the 1970s.

The important infrastructure supporting air transportation is the airport. Korea established the Army Field Airdrome (currently, Yeouido Park) at Yeouido, Siheung-*gun*, Gyeonggi-*do* in 1916. This airport moved to Gimpo in 1958. At present, there are 18 airports in Korea, 7 of which are located at Incheon, Gimpo, Jeju, Gimhae, Cheongju, Daegu and Yangyang.

The development of information and communication (IC), the so-called 'soft infrastructure' causes high ripple effects by networking the existing social overhead capital (SOC) with a new type of IC-based SOC. Therefore, the importance of the IC-based infrastructure, which is the basis of the IC industry, increases dramatically. In the 19th century, the communication technology, which started from ground and marine transportation and the development of telegraph technology changed spatially by overcoming temporal and spatial constraints. Along with the transition from an industrial to an information based society, each country has established main national telecommunication networks and applied its communication infrastructure to urban development since the late 1980s.

Within this context, since the late 1980s, Korea has restructured its telecommunication services three times in order to cope with the development of communication technology, the diversification of communication demands, pressures to open the telecommunication market, and the changing situations of the telecommunication industry. After a change from a monopolistic system of public enterprise to a competitive system in the Korean information and communication industry, the production scale increased sharply from 18.4 trillion won in 1991 to 187 trillion won in 2002. The main trends of each sector in transportation and communication are discussed in the following paragraphs.

With respect to the present status of transportation in Korea, the freight volume of domestic traffic increased from 50 million tons in 1966 to 687.5 million tons in 2005. The freight volume of international traffic increased 8.4 million tons in 1966 to 757.5 million tons in 2005 (Table 1). Along with these sharp increases in freight volume, the transportation infrastructure in Korea has developed continuously since the 1990s (Table 2). In particular, consistent investment in the construction of transportation infrastructure has been conducted since 1994. The Korean government established the 20-year National Transportation Network Plan for the country (2000-2019), and through this plan, presented the long-term direction of main national transportation networks. The main contents of the plan are as follows: (1) the establishment of an efficient transport structure among different transport modes, (2) the construction of cross stripe-shaped highway networks for the improvement of mobility and the accessibility of the main inland transportation networks, (3) the construction of X-shaped high-speed railway networks running through the Korean Peninsula, (4) the implementation of the Northeast Asia hub strategies, and (5) the establishment of continent-connecting transportation networks. In terms of the expansion of national transportation establishments (2000-2019), the government has invested 186 trillion won in roads, 94 trillion won in railroads, 37 trillion won in ports, and 4 trillion won in distribution facilities. Throughout the implementation of the "20-year National Transportation Network Plan (2000-2019)", Korea expects to undertake the expansion of its transportation infrastructure, the improvement of traffic congestion costs, the establishment of an interconnected transportation system, and the increase of the passenger transport share through rail use.

Table 1. The Change of Freight Traffic by Mode of Transportation

(Unit: 1,000 tons)

	Domestic Freight Traffic	Railway	Road	Marine Transportation	Air Transportation	International Freight Traffic	Marine Transportation	Air Transportation
1966	50,888	24,064	24,528	2,295	1	8,442	8,435	7
1970	104,219	31,551	61,775	10,888	5	22,310	22,284	56
1975	139,103	42,758	84,527	11,812	6	45,226	45,128	98
1980	172,777	49,008	104,526	19,230	13	94,226	94,035	191
1985	238,292	55,346	148,700	34,179	67	133,344	133,010	333
1990	337,145	57,922	215,125	63,915	183	220,558	219,781	777
1995	595,272	57,469	408,368	129,112	323	405,714	404,424	1,291
2000	676,315	45,240	496,174	134,467	434	571,549	569,599	1,949
2005	687,451	41,669	526,000	119,410	372	757,553	754,936	2,617

Source: Ministry of Construction and Transportation, Korea Statistical Information Service (http://www.kosis.kr/).

Table 2. The Growth of Transportation Infrastructure

Transportation Infrastructure	1990	2004
Length of Minimum 4 Lane-wide Road (㎞)	4,823	18,290
Length of Multi-tracked Railway (㎞)	847	1,315
Cargo Handling Capacity of Seaport (1 million tons per annum)	190	501
Airport Operating Capacity (1,000 per annum)	1,331	2,012

Source: Ministry of Construction and Transportation, 2006, *Construction Transportation Whitepaper*.

Examining the mode of transportation for domestic traffic, as shown in Table 1, the current share of transportation is uneven. In terms of passengers and freight, the transport mode with the highest share of transportation is the roads, that is to say, the road transportation using cars, trucks, and two-wheeled vehicles. With respect to the share of transportation for passenger transportation, the road shared 90 percent before the 1980s when the subway was activated. However, the share of passenger transportation utilizing the subway increased beginning in the 1980s, and the road's share fell to 74 percent by 2005 (Figure 1). Korea opened line number 1 from Seoul Station to Cheongnyangni station (7.8㎞) in 1974. Since then, subway use in Korea has increased gradually. There are 9 lines in Seoul, 3 lines in Busan, 1 line in Incheon, 1 line in Daejeon, 2 lines in Daegu, and 1 line in Gwangju. Its share of transportation was 17 percent in 2005. With regard to the share of freight transportation, the road shared 40 percent of the total in 1966 and 36 percent in 2005 (Figure 2).

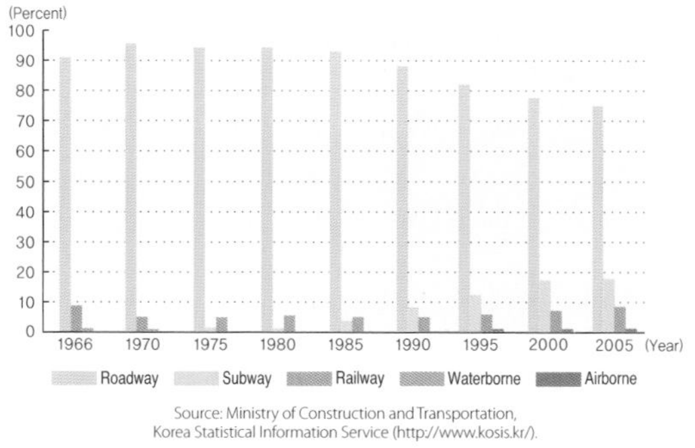

Source: Ministry of Construction and Transportation, Korea Statistical Information Service (http://www.kosis.kr/).

Figure 1. Transition of Share of Passenger Transportation by Mode (1966-2005)

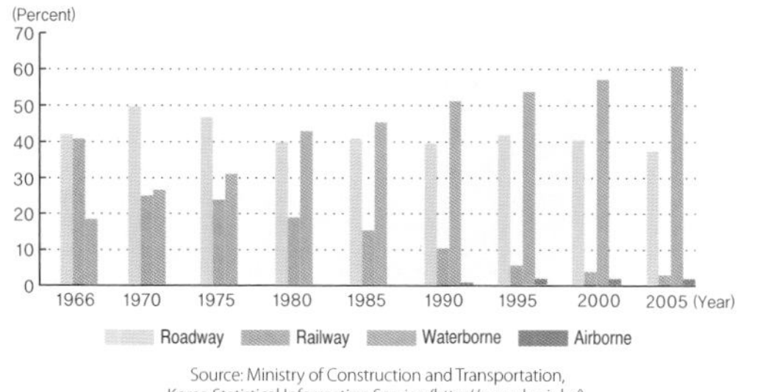

Source: Ministry of Construction and Transportation, Korea Statistical Information Service (http://www.kosis.kr/).

Figure 2. Transition of Share of Freight Transportation by Mode (1966-2005)

With respect to the share of international transportation by mode of transportation, and comparing air transportation with marine transportation, the volume of air transportation increased gradually from 1966 to 2005 (Table 3).

Table 3. Transition of Proportions of Volume of Marine Transportation to Air Transportation

	Air Transportation	Marine Transportation
1966	1	1,205
1970	1	857
1975	1	460
1980	1	492
1985	1	399
1990	1	283
1995	1	313
2000	1	292
2005	1	288

Note: Proportion of volume of marine transportation assuming that volume of air transportation is '1'
Source: Ministry of Construction and Transportation, Korea Statistical Information Service (http://www.kosis.kr/).

Trends in Korea's information infrastructure were identified in two reports: the 2006 Information White Paper by the National Information Society Agency, and the Information Index in Korea published by the ITU (International Telecommunication Union). The importance of the communications industry in Korea rose from 22nd place (1993) to 3rd place (2002) over the course of roughly 10 years. In the short-term, the competitiveness of the information and communication services in Korea increased sharply. Broadband internet service subscribers ranked in the 4th place. With respect to the number of personal computers in use, it ranked in the 16th place.

Such rapid development of the information and communication (IC) related industries in Korea is linked to industrial ripple effects to a large degree. For example, examining establishments the IC industry, the number of information technology (IT) services, establishment increased from 1,382 in 1993, to 5,477 in 2002, and up to 2,422 in 2004. In software and computer related services, establishments increased from 527 in 1993 to 5,601 in 2002, then decreased to 4,875 in 2004. In IT equipment the number of establishments increased dramatically, from 3,402 in 1993, to 7,121 in 2002, to 8,436 in 2004.

We present here 11 maps related to transportation and communication in Korea: an overall view of transportation in Korea, maps of roads, railways, airports and trading ports, and then maps on communication in Korea such as the diffusion rate of personal computer and internet service by household, the diffusion rate of wireless internet services, the possession of communication equipments and services, and information and communication networks in Korea.

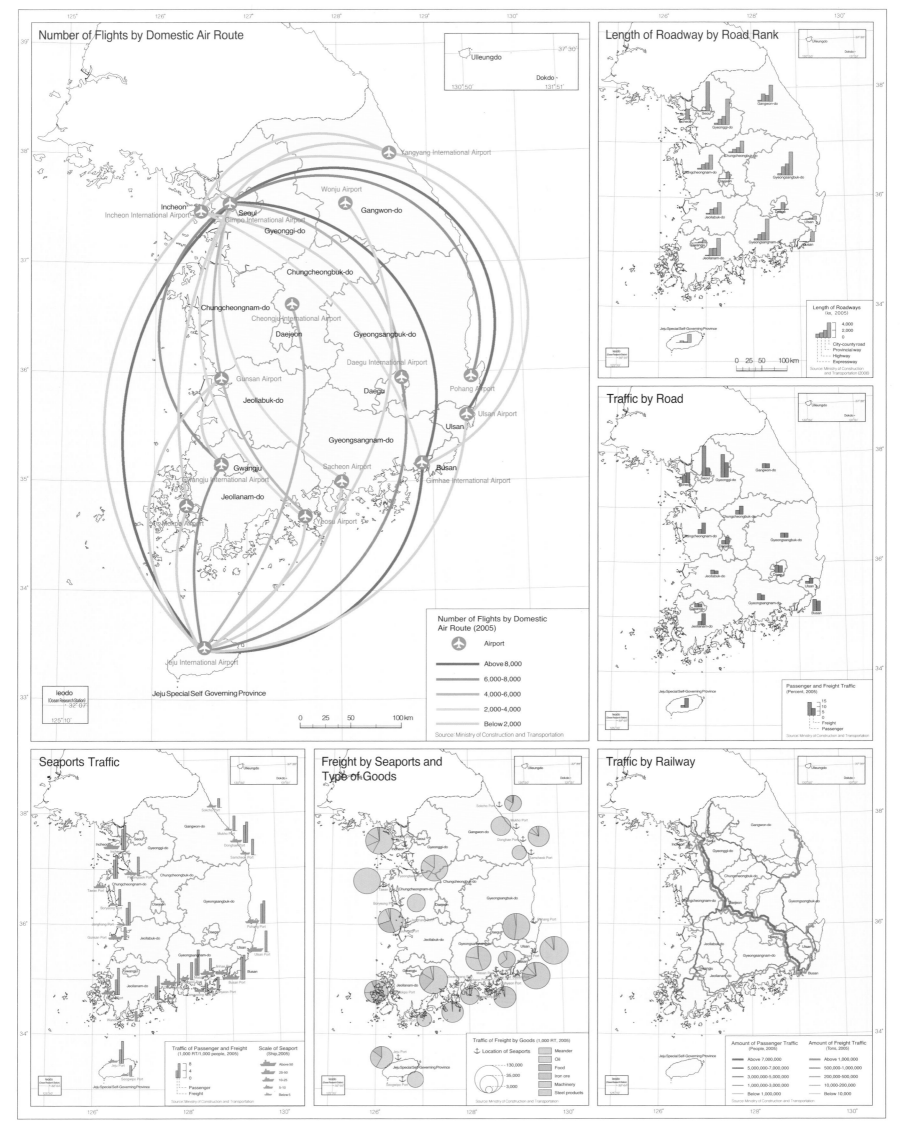

Number of Flights by Domestic Air Route

Ulleungdo

Dokdo

Yangyang International Airport

Wonju Airport

Gangwon-do

Incheon
Incheon International Airport

Seoul
Gimpo International Airport

Gyeonggi-do

Chungcheongbuk-do

Chungcheongnam-do

Cheongju International Airport

Daejeon

Gyeongsangbuk-do

Daegu International Airport

Gunsan Airport

Jeollabuk-do

Daegu

Pohang Airport

Ulsan Airport

Ulsan

Gyeongsangnam-do

Gwangju
Gwangju International Airport

Sacheon Airport

Busan
Gimhae International Airport

Jeollanam-do

Mokpo Airport

Yeosu Airport

Jeju International Airport

Jeju Special Self Governing Province

Ieodo
(Ocean Research Station)
32° 07'
125°10'

Number of Flights by Domestic Air Route (2005)

✈ Airport

Above 8,000
6,000-8,000
4,000-6,000
2,000-4,000
Below 2,000

0 25 50 100km

Source: Ministry of Construction and Transportation

Length of Roadway by Road Rank

Ulleungdo

Dokdo

Gangwon-do

Chungcheongbuk-do

Gyeongsangbuk-do

Ulsan

Jeollabuk-do

Gyeongsangnam-do

Jeju Special Self-Governing Province

Length of Roadways (km, 2005)

4,000
2,000
0

City-county road
Provincial way
Highway
Expressway

0 25 50 100km

Source: Ministry of Construction and Transportation (2006)

Traffic by Road

Ulleungdo

Dokdo

Gangwon-do

Seoul

Gyeonggi-do

Chungcheongbuk-do

Chungcheongnam-do

Gyeongsangbuk-do

Ulsan

Jeollabuk-do

Gyeongsangnam-do

Busan

Jeollanam-do

Jeju Special Self-Governing Province

Passenger and Freight Traffic (Percent, 2005)

15
10
5
0

Freight
Passenger

Source: Ministry of Construction and Transportation

Seaports Traffic

Ulleungdo

Dokdo

Sokcho Port

Gangwon-do

Mukho Port

Donghae Port

Incheon

Gyeonggi-do

Samcheok Port

Pyeongtaek Port

Chungcheongnam-do

Taean Port

Boryeong Port

Gyeongsangbuk-do

Janghang Port

Pohang Port

Gunsan Port

Jeollabuk-do

Ulsan Port

Gwangju

Gyeongsangnam-do

Busan Port

Jeollanam-do

Gwangyang Port

Wando Port

Jeju Port

Seogwipo Port

Jeju Special Self Governing Province

Traffic of Passenger and Freight (1,000 RT/1,000 people, 2005)

8
4
0

Passenger
Freight

Scale of Seaport (Ship, 2005)

Above 50
25-50
10-25
5-10
Below 5

Source: Ministry of Construction and Transportation

Freight by Seaports and Type of Goods

Ulleungdo

Dokdo

Sokcho Port

Mukho Port

Gangwon-do

Donghae Port

Gyeonggi-do

Samcheok Port

Pyeongtaek Port

Taean Port

Chungcheongnam-do

Boryeong Port

Chungcheongbuk-do

Gyeongsangbuk-do

Pohang Port

Jeollabuk-do

Ulsan

Gwangju

Gyeongsangnam-do

Busan Port

Jeollanam-do

Gwangyang Port

Jeju Port

Seogwipo Port

Jeju Special Self Governing Province

Traffic of Freight by Goods (1,000 RT, 2005)

⚓ Location of Seaports

Meander
Oil
Food
Iron ore
Machinery
Steel products

130,000
3,000

Source: Ministry of Construction and Transportation

Traffic by Railway

Ulleungdo

Dokdo

Gangwon-do

Gyeonggi-do

Chungcheongbuk-do

Cheonan

Gyeongsangbuk-do

Jeollabuk-do

Gyeongsangnam-do

Busan

Amount of Passenger Traffic (People, 2005)

Above 7,000,000
5,000,000-7,000,000
3,000,000-5,000,000
1,000,000-3,000,000
Below 1,000,000

Amount of Freight Traffic (Tons, 2005)

Above 1,000,000
500,000-1,000,000
200,000-500,000
10,000-200,000
Below 10,000

Source: Ministry of Construction and Transportation

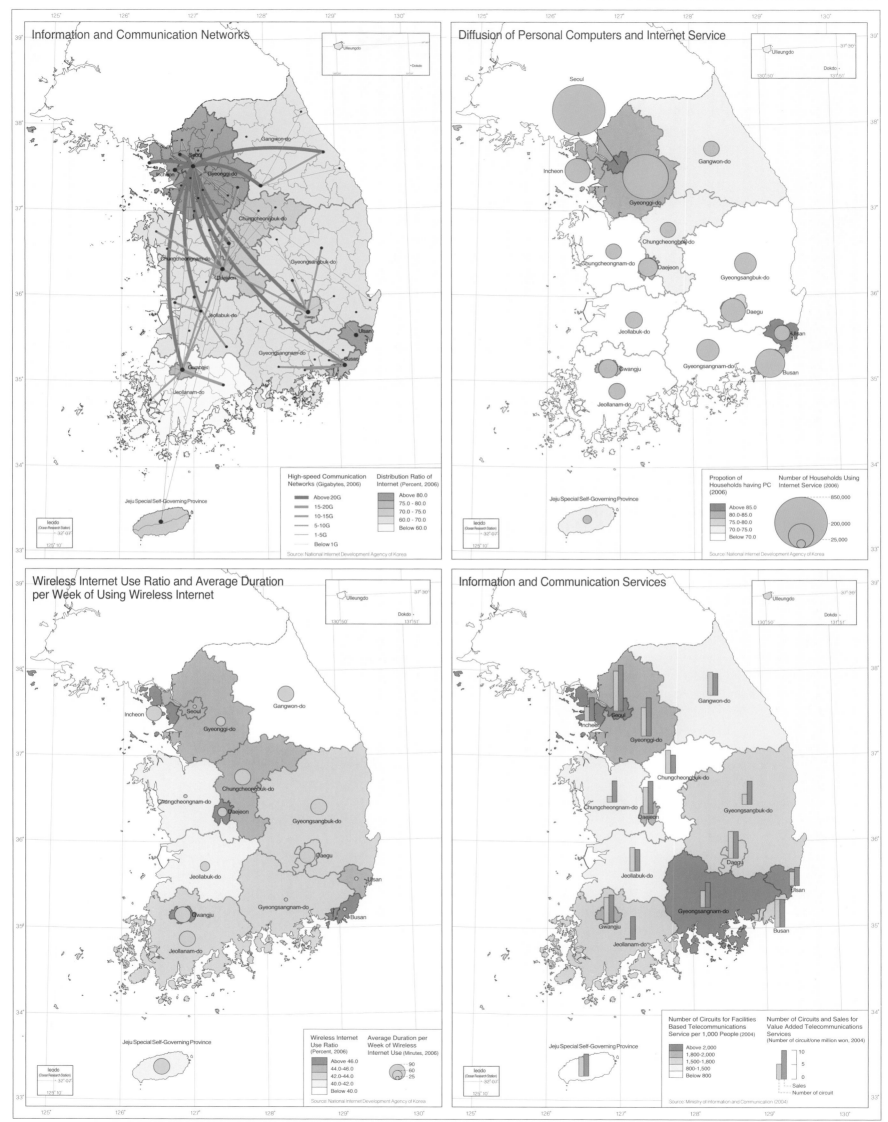

Information and Communication Networks

High-speed Communication Networks (Gigabytes, 2006)
- Above 20G
- 15-20G
- 10-15G
- 5-10G
- 1-5G
- Below 1G

Distribution Ratio of Internet (Percent, 2006)
- Above 80.0
- 75.0 - 80.0
- 70.0 - 75.0
- 60.0 - 70.0
- Below 60.0

Source: National Internet Development Agency of Korea

Diffusion of Personal Computers and Internet Service

Propotion of Households having PC (2006)
- Above 85.0
- 80.0-85.0
- 75.0-80.0
- 70.0-75.0
- Below 70.0

Number of Households Using Internet Service (2006)
- 850,000
- 200,000
- 25,000

Source: National Internet Development Agency of Korea

Wireless Internet Use Ratio and Average Duration per Week of Using Wireless Internet

Wireless Internet Use Ratio (Percent, 2006)
- Above 46.0
- 44.0-46.0
- 42.0-44.0
- 40.0-42.0
- Below 40.0

Average Duration per Week of Wireless Internet Use (Minutes, 2006)
- 90
- 60
- 25

Source: National Internet Development Agency of Korea

Information and Communication Services

Number of Circuits for Facilities Based Telecommunications Service per 1,000 People (2004)
- Above 2,000
- 1,800-2,000
- 1,500-1,800
- 800-1,500
- Below 800

Number of Circuits and Sales for Value Added Telecommunications Services (Number of circuit/one million won, 2004)
- 10
- 5
- 0
- Sales
- Number of circuit

Source: Ministry of Information and Communication (2004)

0   25   50   100 km

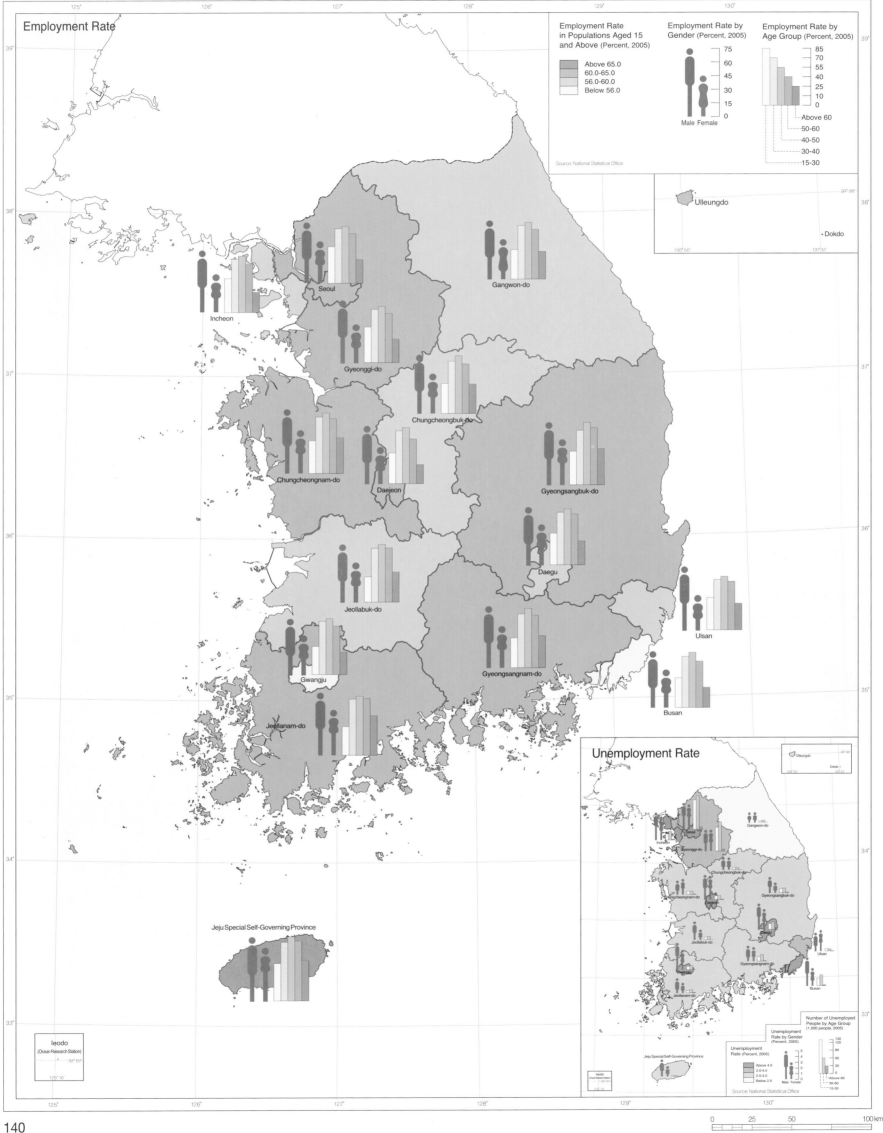

Employment Rate

Employment Rate in Populations Aged 15 and Above (Percent, 2005)
- Above 65.0
- 60.0-65.0
- 56.0-60.0
- Below 56.0

Employment Rate by Gender (Percent, 2005)
75
60
45
30
15
Male Female

Employment Rate by Age Group (Percent, 2005)
85
70
55
40
25
10
0
- Above 60
- 50-60
- 40-50
- 30-40
- 15-30

Source: National Statistical Office

Ulleungdo

Dokdo

Incheon

Seoul

Gangwon-do

Gyeonggi-do

Chungcheongbuk-do

Chungcheongnam-do

Daejeon

Gyeongsangbuk-do

Jeollabuk-do

Daegu

Ulsan

Gwangju

Gyeongsangnam-do

Busan

Jeollanam-do

Jeju Special Self-Governing Province

Ieodo
(Ocean Research Station)

Unemployment Rate

Ulleungdo

Dokdo

Incheon

Gangwon-do

Gyeonggi-do

Chungcheongbuk-do

Chungcheongnam-do

Gyeongsangbuk-do

Jeollabuk-do

Daegu

Ulsan

Gyeongsangnam-do

Busan

Jeollanam-do

Jeju Special Self-Governing Province

Unemployment Rate (Percent, 2005)
- Above 4.0
- 3.0-4.0
- 2.0-3.0
- Below 2.0

Unemployment Rate by Gender (Percent, 2005)
5
4
3
2
1
Male Female

Number of Unemployed People by Age Group (1,000 people, 2005)
130
120
90
60
30
0
- Above 60
- 50-60
- 15-30

Source: National Statistical Office

0   25   50   100 km

Key indicators of labor statistics such as employment structure, income level, and industrial relations reveal the characteristics of working people in Korea.

Employment Structure

Recent trends in Korea's employment structure can be understood in terms of the labor force participation rate, the composition of employed people, and the unemployment rate. The labor force participation rate (LFPR) is estimated by dividing the economically active population by the working age population (people over 15 years of age). The economically active population denotes people over 15 years old who can and intend to provide labor for the production of commodities and services. As demonstrated in Figure 1, the LFPR increased from 59.0 percent in 1980 to 61.9 percent in 2005. While the LFPR of women grew from 42.8 percent to 50.0 percent between 1980 and 2005, that of men declined from 76.4 percent to 74.4 percent during the same period. This notable increase of female participation in the labor force over the past 25 years is attributed to the expansion of women's education and rights, and improved access to childcare. By contrast, the decrease of male labor force participation is attributed to the rapid evolution of an aging society over this same period. Regarding the geographical dispersion of the LFPR, Jeju Special Self-Governing Province (70.0%) recorded the highest levels for both men and women, followed by Seoul, Chungcheongnam-do, Jeollanam-do, Gyeongsangbuk-do, and Gyeongsangnam-do. On the other hand, Busan (58.3%) recorded the lowest level, while Gangwon-do, Gwangju, Jeollabuk-do, Ulsan, Daegu, and Incheon also recorded levels below the national LFPR average of 61.9 percent.

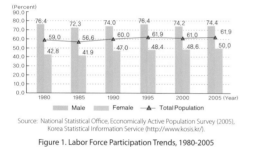

Figure 1. Labor Force Participation Trends, 1980-2005

Examination of the composition of employment by industry, occupation and employment status indicates recent trends in these areas. Total employment grew from 15.0 million workers in 1985 to 22.9 million workers in 2005. Regarding employment by industry, as illustrated in Figure 2, during the period from 1985-2005, the proportion of workers engaged in the agriculture and fishery sector decreased from 24.9 percent to 7.9 percent, while that engaged in manufacturing and mining dropped by 5.8 percent (from 24.4% to 18.6%). In contrast, the proportion of workers in the business-personal-public service sectors tripled (from 13.0% to 39.4%), and that of retails-wholesale-restaurant-hotel sectors grew from 22.6 percent to 25.4 percent. As such, the changing industrial structure of employment illustrates the drastic transformation in Korea over the past 20 years toward a 'de-industrialized' or 'service economy'.

The period of 1985-2005, as shown in Figure 3, witnessed a sharp increase in the share of professional-technician-managerial workers (tripling from 7.3% to 20.9%), followed by a slight increase in clerical workers (growing from 11.5% to 14.3%). The sustained growth of professional-technician-managerial and clerical jobs may be associated with the expansion of a highly educated working population and the development of a knowledge-based economy in Korea. Over this period, the proportion of workers employed in the agriculture-fishery and production sectors declined by 17.1 percent and 2.4 percent respectively, which further reflects the industrial restructuring taking place in these sectors.

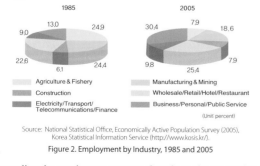

Figure 2. Employment by Industry, 1985 and 2005

Regarding the employment status of workers, the proportion of non-wage workers, such as self-employed workers and family

workers, decreased from 45.6 percent in 1986 to 33.6 percent in 2005. During this same period, the share of wage-workers grew from 54.4 percent to 66.4 percent. When classifying wage workers according to the type of employment contract (permanent workers, temporary workers, and daily workers), the share of permanent workers remained steady at 52-53 percent during the 1986-2005 period. The share of temporary workers increased from 29.3 percent in 1986 to 33.3 percent in 2005, whereas that of daily workers declined proportionally.

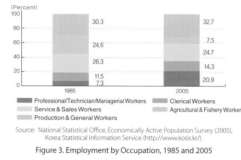

Figure 3. Employment by Occupation, 1985 and 2005

Geographically, the majority of the workforce in 2005 was distributed in Gyeonggi-do (22.1%) and Seoul (21.4%), while Jeju Special Self-Governing Province contributed the lowest (1.2%) share of employment. The share of the Capital Region, including Seoul, Incheon, and Gyeonggi-do, accounted for 48.7 percent of total employment; the Youngnam region, comprised of Busan, Daegu, Ulsan, Gyeongsangbuk-do, and Gyeongsangnam-do, accounted for 26.9 percent. The Honam region (Gwangju, Jeollabuk-do, and Jeollanam-do) and the Chungcheong region (Daejeon, Chungcheongbuk-do, and Chungcheongnam-do) accounted for 10.4 percent and 9.9 percent, respectively, of total employment during 2005.

The unemployment rate in Korea during the 1980s and 1990s stayed at a very low level compared to Western countries owing to the sustained economic growth of the country. In particular, Korea showed full employment (an unemployment rate below 3%) before the 1997 economic crisis. As displayed in Figure 4, the unemployment rate, which was at a level of 6 percent in the early 1980s, continued to decline from the middle of the 1980s, where it remained at a level of 2.1-2.4 percent during the early- and mid- 1990s. It soared to over 4 percent in the late 1990s, and fell to a level of 3 percent at the beginning of the new millennium. In looking at the breakdown of the unemployment rate by gender, fewer women were employed in the workforce than men. This fact is associated with the low labor force participation of women, whose work has usually supplemented family income in Korea. In 2005, large cities, except for Ulsan, exceeded the nation-wide unemployment rate, while provinces remained below the national average. Seoul showed the highest (4.8%) unemployment rate among large cities, and Gangwon, also having a low labor force participation rate, had the lowest unemployment (1.8%) among the provinces.

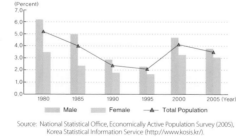

Figure 4. Changes in Unemployment Rate by Gender

Wage Level

Wages have increased over 10 percent annually since the mid-1980s owing to sustained economic growth. This increase is estimated through calculating basic pay, extra work allowances, and bonuses. Although wages were cut during the 1998 economic crisis, between 1985 and 2005 the nominal wage increased in the manufacturing sector and industrial sector (excluding agriculture), climbing to 11.8 percent and 10.9 percent, respectively. As shown in Table 1, real wages, reflecting the offset of consumer price increases, grew annually by 5.9 percent in all industries, and by 6.8 percent in manufacturing, demonstrating the steady enhancement of workers' living standards.

Table 1. Average Wage Increases between 1985 and 2005 (Unit: Percent)

	All Industries except Agriculture	Manufacturing
Nominal Wage Increases	10.9	11.8
Real Wage Increases	5.9	6.8

Source: Ministry of Labor (MOLAB: http://www.molab.go.kr), 1986-2006, Yearbook of Labor Statistics.

When estimating the monthly income of workers employed at establishments having over five employees, and organized by geographic region, only Seoul, Ulsan, Daejeon, and Jeollanam-do exceeded the national average monthly income (1.872 million Won). In particular, there is a wide gap between Seoul, which has the highest average monthly income (2.157 million Won), and Jeollabuk-do, which has the lowest average monthly income (1.581 million Won). Korea relied upon long working hours during its era of economic development. However, since democratization in 1987, and under collective pressure from workers, the government reduced the statutory work hours. The statutory working hours were reduced from 48 hours per week to 44 hours in 1989, and were further shortened to 40 hours in 2003. Due to the improvement of workers' living standards and the extension of their leisure activities as well as the reduction of statutory working hours, the weekly working hours declined from 51.9 to 45.1 in all industries (except agriculture) and from 53.8 to 46.9 in manufacturing during the 1985-2005 period (see Figure 5). Nonetheless, workers in Korea are still working longer working hours than workers in advanced Western countries; 5 hours or more of extra work in addition to the 40 statutory working hours is still prevalent. In 2005, workers in Incheon, Daegu, Gyeonggi-do, Gangwon-do, Chungcheongnam-do, Chungcheongbuk-do, Gyeongsangnam-do, Gyeongsangbuk-do worked above the national average for monthly working hours (195.9), whereas in Seoul, Daejeon, Gwangju, Ulsan, Jeollanam-do, and Jeollabuk-do workers worked below the average. A wide gap of 25.7 hours exists between the region with the shortest working hours (182.6 hours in Seoul) and the region with the longest working hours (208.3 hours in Gyeongsangnam-do).

Gwangju, Ulsan, Jeollanam-do, and Jeollabuk-do workers worked below the average. A wide gap of 25.7 hours exists between the region with the shortest working hours (182.6 hours in Seoul) and the region with the longest working hours (208.3 hours in Gyeongsangnam-do).

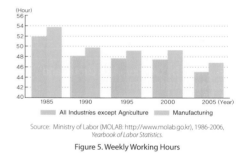

Figure 5. Weekly Working Hours

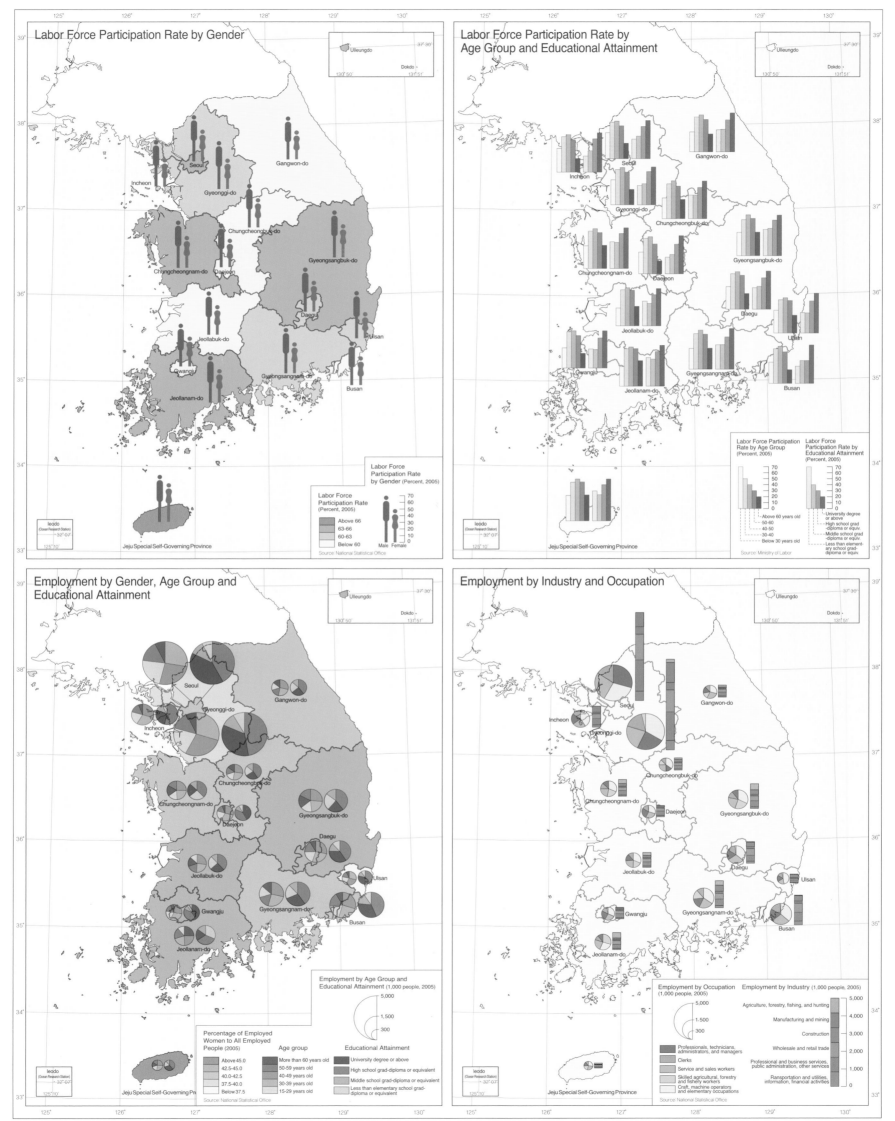

Labor Force Participation Rate by Gender

Labor Force Participation Rate by Gender (Percent, 2005)

Labor Force Participation Rate (Percent, 2005)
- Above 66
- 63-66
- 60-63
- Below 60

Male Female

Source: National Statistical Office

Labor Force Participation Rate by Age Group and Educational Attainment

Labor Force Participation Rate by Age Group (Percent, 2005)

Labor Force Participation Rate by Educational Attainment (Percent, 2005)

- Above 60 years old
- 50-60
- 40-50
- 30-40
- Below 30 years old

- University degree or above
- High school grad-diploma or equiv.
- Middle school grad-diploma or equiv.
- Less than elementary school grad-diploma or equiv.

Source: Ministry of Labor

Employment by Gender, Age Group and Educational Attainment

Employment by Age Group and Educational Attainment (1,000 people, 2005)

- 5,000
- 1,500
- 300

Percentage of Employed Women to All Employed People (2005)
- Above 45.0
- 42.5-45.0
- 40.0-42.5
- 37.5-40.0
- Below 37.5

Age group
- More than 60 years old
- 50-59 years old
- 40-49 years old
- 30-39 years old
- 15-29 years old

Educational Attainment
- University degree or above
- High school grad-diploma or equivalent
- Middle school grad-diploma or equivalent
- Less than elementary school grad-diploma or equivalent

Source: National Statistical Office

Employment by Industry and Occupation

Employment by Occupation (1,000 people, 2005)
- 5,000
- 1,500
- 300

Employment by Industry (1,000 people, 2005)

- Professionals, technicians, administrators, and managers
- Clerks
- Service and sales workers
- Skilled agricultural, forestry and fishery workers
- Craft, machine operators and elementary occupations

- Agriculture, forestry, fishing, and hunting
- Manufacturing and mining
- Construction
- Wholesale and retail trade
- Professional and business services, public administration, other services
- Transportation and utilities, information, financial activities

- 5,000
- 4,000
- 3,000
- 2,000
- 1,000
- 0

Source: National Statistical Office

0 25 50 100 km

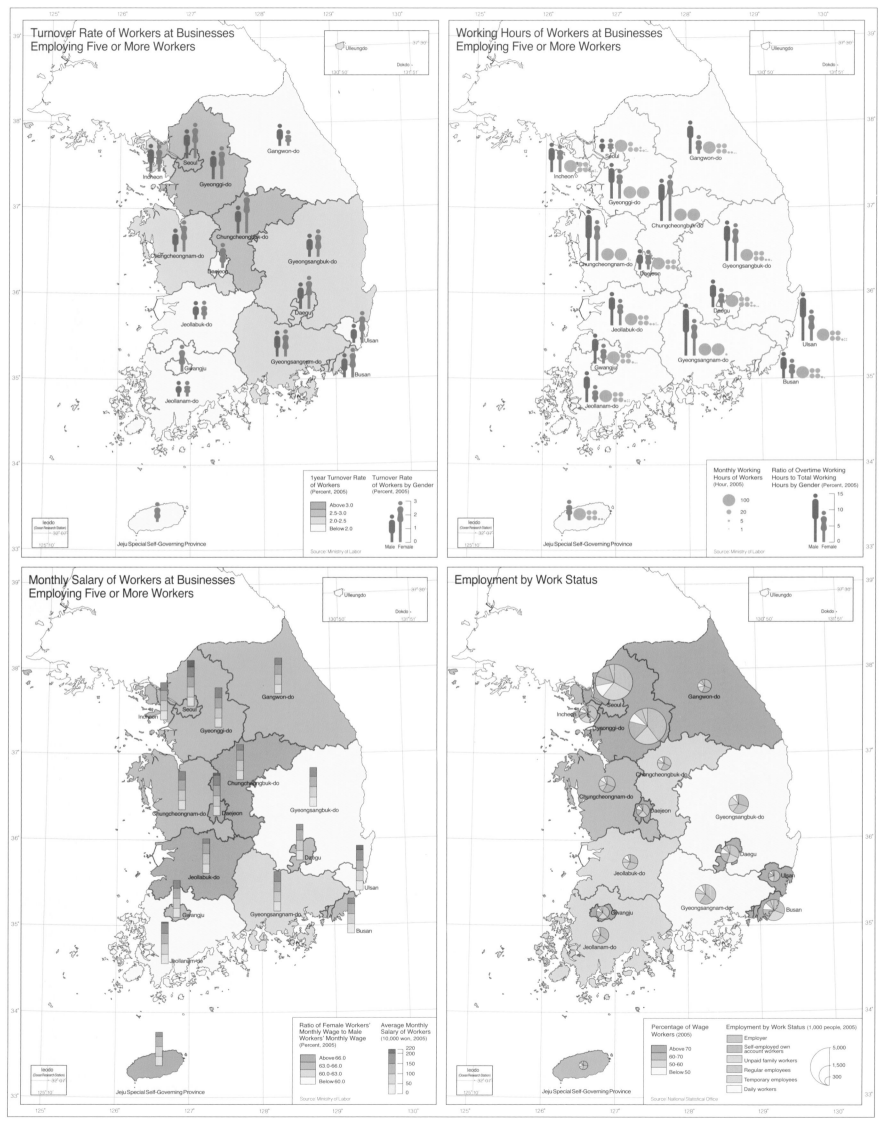

Turnover Rate of Workers at Businesses Employing Five or More Workers

1year Turnover Rate of Workers (Percent, 2005)
Turnover Rate of Workers by Gender (Percent, 2005)

Above 3.0
2.5-3.0
2.0-2.5
Below 2.0

Source: Ministry of Labor

Working Hours of Workers at Businesses Employing Five or More Workers

Monthly Working Hours of Workers (Hour, 2005)
Ratio of Overtime Working Hours to Total Working Hours by Gender (Percent, 2005)

100
20
5
1

Source: Ministry of Labor

Monthly Salary of Workers at Businesses Employing Five or More Workers

Ratio of Female Workers' Monthly Wage to Male Workers' Monthly Wage (Percent, 2005)
Average Monthly Salary of Workers (10,000 won, 2005)

Above 66.0
63.0-66.0
60.0-63.0
Below 60.0

220
200
150
100
50
0

Source: Ministry of Labor

Employment by Work Status

Percentage of Wage Workers (2005)
Employment by Work Status (1,000 people, 2005)

Above 70
60-70
50-60
Below 50

Employer
Self-employed own account workers
Unpaid family workers
Regular employees
Temporary employees
Daily workers

5,000
1,500
300

Source: National Statistical Office

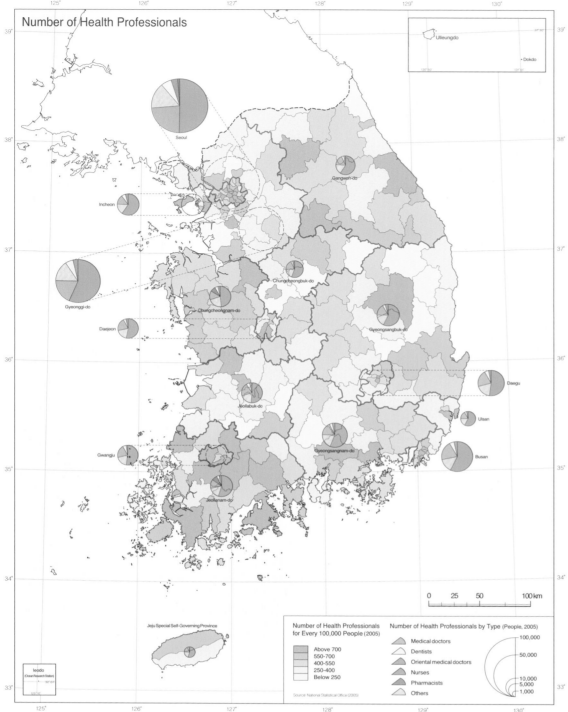

Number of Health Professionals

Jeju Special Self-Governing Province

Ieodo
(Ocean Research Station)

Number of Health Professionals for Every 100,000 People (2005)
Above 700
550-700
400-550
250-400
Below 250

Number of Health Professionals by Type (People, 2005)

- Medical doctors
- Dentists
- Oriental medical doctors
- Nurses
- Pharmacists
- Others

100,000
50,000
10,000
5,000
1,000

Source: National Statistical Office (2005)

Public Health Policy

Public Health Expenditure as a percentage of National Health Expenditure was 49.4 percent in 2003. This was lower than other developed countries except for the United States (44.4%) (see Figure 4). In order to maintain National Health Expenditure at an appropriate level, the percentage of Public Health Expenditure should be increased.

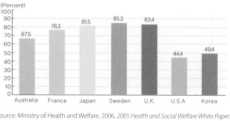

Source: Ministry of Health and Welfare, 2006, 2005 Health and Social Welfare White Paper.

Figure 4. Public Health Expenditure as a Percentage of National Health Expenditure (2003)

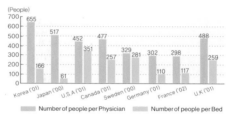

Source: Ministry of Health and Welfare, 2006, 2005 Health and Social Welfare White Paper.

Figure 5. Indicators of the Health Supply

In order to see regional differences in the health supply, we can refer to the number of health professionals per 100,000 people at the local level in 2005. Jung-*gu* in Daegu and Jongno-*gu* in Seoul recorded the greatest number of health professionals. In contrast, Ongjin-*gun* in Incheon and Yeongyang-*gun* in Gyeongsangbuk-*do* recorded the lowest number of health professionals per population unit. In terms of the number of beds per 100,000 people, Jung-*gu* in Daegu has the highest level of beds per 100,000 people, with 3,290 beds.

National Health Status

In Korea, people consume an average of 8.6 liters of alcohol per year, a level that is lower than that of the 29 OECD countries (see Figure 6). However, heavy drinking rates and the alcohol-related death rate were at very high levels. Furthermore, alcohol consumption per person has been gradually increasing in recent years. Thus, this increase is reflected in the number of alcohol-use disorders in the 18 to 64 age group - about 2.21 million, or about 8.6 percent of total population.

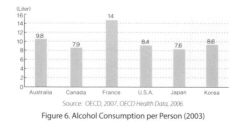

Source: OECD, 2007, OECD Health Data, 2006.

Figure 6. Alcohol Consumption per Person (2003)

The proportion of alcohol drinkers ranged from 79.8 percent in Ulsan to 63.3 percent in Jeollanam-*do* and 65.5 percent in Jeollabuk-*do*. These levels were relatively lower than other cities or provinces. In terms of the proportion of alcohol drinkers

Social Expenditure

Social Expenditure as a percentage of Gross Domestic Product (GDP) in Korea increased from 4.25 percent in 1990 to 8.7 percent in 2003. However, the percentage of expenditure in Korea was still lower than that of other developed countries, even Mexico (see Figure 1).

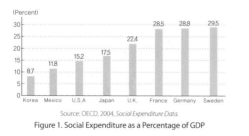

Source: OECD, 2004, Social Expenditure Data.

Figure 1. Social Expenditure as a Percentage of GDP

Over the past 3 years, the health and welfare budget has been 7 percent of the total government budget. The health and welfare budget in 2005 was somewhat lower than previous years because the budget controls for social welfare services (65.9 billion Won) and health promotion funds (23.4 billion Won). The budget which was originally held at the central government level, was transferred to provincial governments (see Figure 2). Regarding Health and Social Welfare Expenditure in 2005, the total expenditure of 8,696 billion won was composed of Social Welfare Services (57.9%), Social Insurance (36.1%), and Health Services (3.7%) (see Figure 3).

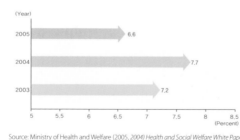

Source: Ministry of Health and Welfare (2005, 2004) Health and Social Welfare White Paper.

Figure 2. Public Health and Welfare Budget Compared to the Total Government's Budget

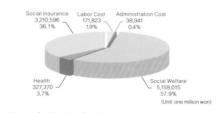

Source: Ministry of Health and Welfare, 2006, 2005 Health and Social Welfare White Paper.

Figure 3. Health and Social Welfare Expenditure (2005)

by gender, men showed higher rates of drinking than women. In addition, the proportion of alcohol drinkers tended to increase with level of education.

The adult smoking rate for males in 2003 was the highest level among OECD countries at 61.8 percent (see Figure 7). This high smoking rate is responsible for approximately one trillion won in social and economic costs associated with premature death, disease, fire, and the effects of secondhand smoke. With regards to the geographical distribution of people smoking at the local level, rates ranged from 29 percent in Ulsan and 29.1 percent in Chungcheongnam-*do*, to 23.6 percent in Jeollanam-*do*.

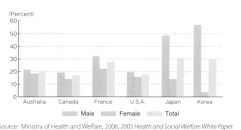

Source: Ministry of Health and Welfare, 2006, *2005 Health and Social Welfare White Paper.*

Figure 7. Adult Smoking Rate by Gender (2003)

Health Insurance

As the National Health Insurance scheme expanded to the national level in July of 1989, every person became eligible to receive health services from the National Health Insurance scheme and the Medical Aid Program. This scheme covers 96.4 percent of the total population (about 47 million), consisting of 27 million industrial workers and 20 million self-employed (see Figure 8). About 1.7 million people (3.6 percent of the total population) who are veterans, disabled, or recipients of the National Basic Livelihood Security scheme, receive coverage from the Medical Aid Program.

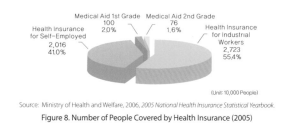

Source: Ministry of Health and Welfare, 2006, *2005 National Health Insurance Statistical Yearbook.*

Figure 8. Number of People Covered by Health Insurance (2005)

With regards to the geographical distribution of the amount of benefits received per person from the National Health Insurance scheme in 2005, the value of benefits ranged from 306.6 won in Ansan-*si*, Gyeonggi-*do* to 608.8 won in Goheung-*gun*, Jeollanam-*do*. Overall, there seemed to be some difference in health insurance utilization between rural and urban areas since rural areas received a greater distribution of benefits than urban areas.

The National Public Pension scheme was introduced in 1988 as a part of an income maintenance program. The scheme targets people who are between 18 and 60 years of age. The purpose of the scheme is to maintain an adequate income level for retired people, while at the same time assisting society in coping with various social risks caused by social and economic changes such as aging, changes in family structure, industrialization, and urbanization. After the introduction of the scheme, beneficiaries gradually expanded, and as of 2006, there were 17.1 million people covered by the scheme (see Figure 9).

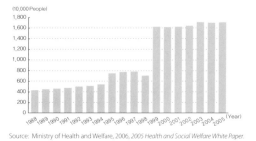

Source: Ministry of Health and Welfare, 2006, *2005 Health and Social Welfare White Paper.*

Figure 9. Number of National Pension Insurants

The National Basic Livelihood Security scheme supports people whose income is below the national poverty line and who are not able to maintain basic necessities. For this, the scheme provides economical, educational, medical, and housing services to the poor to maintain their basic livelihood, while also helping the poor who are able to work to support themselves. In December of 2005, the scheme provided services to 150 million people and 80 million households (see Figure 10). The number of recipients of the National Basic Livelihood Security scheme per 100,000 people ranged from 15,625 people in Eumseong-*gun*, Chungcheongbuk-*do* to 668 people in Yongin-*si*, Gyeonggi-*do*. In particular, Chungcheongnam-*do* showed a relatively higher number of recipients than other provinces and metropolitan cities.

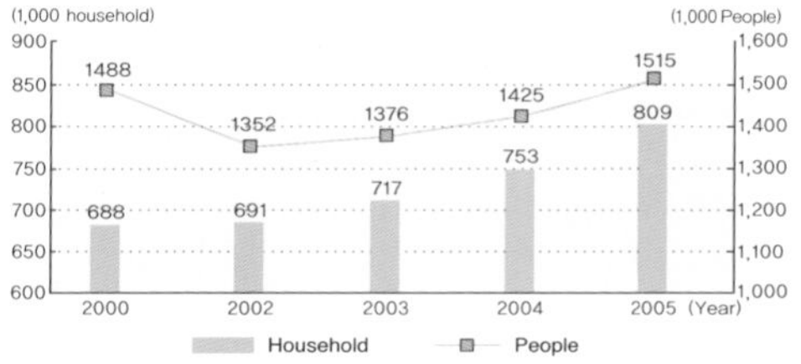

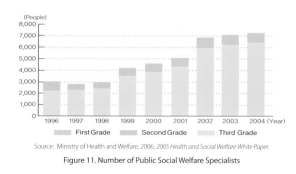

Source: Ministry of Health and Welfare, 2006, *2005 Health and Social Welfare White Paper.*

Figure 10. Number of Recipients of National Basic Livelihood Security

Public social welfare specialists have been placed in local poor areas since 1987 to increase the efficiency and the professionalism of public welfare service delivery systems. In particular, the implementation of the National Basic Livelihood Security Act of 2000 saw the number of public social welfare specialists increase dramatically. Following this implementation, the government hired 1,830 specialists in 2005, which brought the total to 9,920 specialists working at local government offices (see Figure 11). The number of public social welfare specialists per 100,000 people at the si and do levels ranged from a high of 38.42 persons in Jeollanam-*do*, to a low of 7.40 persons in Ulsan-*si*.

(People)

Source: Ministry of Health and Welfare, 2006, *2005 Health and Social Welfare White Paper.*

Figure 11. Number of Public Social Welfare Specialists

Social Welfare Services

Among Korea's social welfare service institutions, senior care facilities have rapidly increased over the past ten years because there has been an increased need for care for the elderly. A portion of this population suffers from chronic diseases requiring long-term institutional care services such as dementia and palsy (see Figure 12). However, there are only 416 long-term care institutions across the nation, and these cover only 0.6 percent of the total elderly population. This is much lower than that of other advanced countries such as France, Germany, and Japan, where coverage is around 5-6 percent of the total elderly population. These figures point to a need for an increase in the number of institutions for the elderly. While the number of institutions for children leveled off during this time period, the number of institutions for the disabled gradually increased.

In terms of geographical distributions, the highest number of institutions and residents were distributed in Gyeonggi-*do*, with 108 institutions and 8,123 residents. At the local level, the number of residents in institutions for the elderly per one thousand people was the highest at 65 residents per one thousand people in Gapyeong-*gun*, Gyeonggi-*do*, and in Yeonsu-*gu*, Incheon. Regarding the number and residents in institutions for the disabled, the greatest number of institutions were distributed in Gyeonggi-*do*, with 46 institutions and 3,335 residents (Map 2-6-2). The highest number of residents per one thousand registered disabled people was in Chungcheongbuk-*do*, with 26.5 residents. Also, Seoul showed the highest number of child welfare facilities (46 facilities) which provided care services for 3,417 children. In the case of the number of institutionalized children per 1,000 children, Jeollanam-*do* showed the highest number, with 3.22 children.

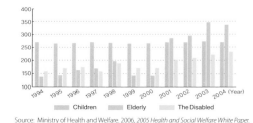

Source: Ministry of Health and Welfare, 2006, *2005 Health and Social Welfare White Paper.*

Figure 12. Number of Social Welfare Service Institutions by Institution Type

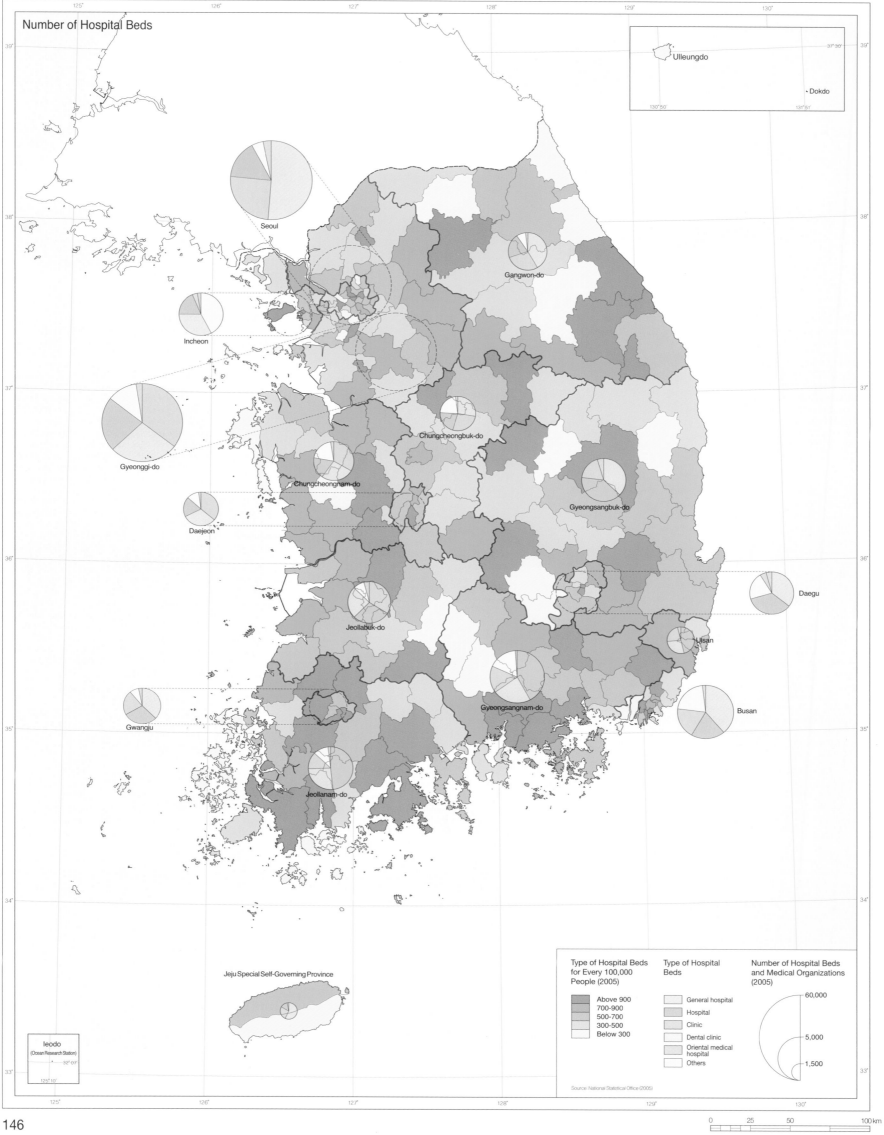

Number of Hospital Beds

Ulleungdo

Dokdo

Seoul

Incheon

Gangwon-do

Gyeonggi-do

Chungcheongbuk-do

Chungcheongnam-do

Daejeon

Gyeongsangbuk-do

Daegu

Jeollabuk-do

Ulsan

Gyeongsangnam-do

Busan

Gwangju

Jeollanam-do

Jeju Special Self-Governing Province

Ieodo
(Ocean Research Station)

Type of Hospital Beds for Every 100,000 People (2005)	Type of Hospital Beds	Number of Hospital Beds and Medical Organizations (2005)
Above 900	General hospital	60,000
700-900	Hospital	
500-700	Clinic	5,000
300-500	Dental clinic	
Below 300	Oriental medical hospital	1,500
	Others	

Source: National Statistical Office (2005)

0   25   50   100km

Alcohol Consumption

By Gender (2006)

By Educational Attainment (2006)

Percentage of the Population (Above 20 years old) that Drinks Alcohol (2006)
- Above 78
- 74-78
- 70-74
- 66-70
- Below 66

- Female
- Male

- University degree or above
- High school grad-diploma or equivalent
- Middle school grad-diploma or equivalent
- Less than elementary school grad-diploma or equivalent

Source: National Statistical Office

Jeju Special Self-Governing Province

Ieodo (Ocean Research Station)

Tobacco Product Use

By Gender (2006)

By Educational Attainment (2006)

Percentage of Tobacco-Smoking Population (2006)
- Above 28.5
- 27.0-28.5
- 25.5-27.0
- 24.0-25.5
- Below 24.0

- Female
- Male

- University degree or above
- High school grad-diploma or equivalent
- Middle school grad-diploma or equivalent
- Less than elementary school grad-diploma or equivalent

Source: National Statistical Office

Jeju Special Self-Governing Province

Ieodo (Ocean Research Station)

Mortality Rate by Etiological Cause

Mortality Rate for Every 1,000 Persons by Etiological Cause (Percent, 2006)
- 2.0
- 1.5
- 1.0
- 0.5
- 0

Crude Death Rate (Percent, 2006)
- Above 10
- 8-10
- 6-8
- 4-6
- Below 4

- Diseases of the alimentary system
- Diseases of the respiratory system
- Diseases of the circulatory system
- Diseases of the digestive system
- Cancer
- Infectious and parasitic diseases

Source: National Statistical Office

Jeju Special Self-Governing Province

Ieodo (Ocean Research Station)

Prevalence Rate of Diseases

Prevalence Rate of Diseases by Age Group (Percent, 2006)
- 55
- 50
- 40
- 30
- 20
- 10
- 0

Prevalence Rate of Diseases by Gender (Percent, 2006)
- 30
- 20
- 10
- 0

- Above 60 years old
- 50-60 years old
- 40-50 years old
- 30-40 years old
- 20-30 years old
- 10-20 years old
- 0-10 years old

- Female
- Male

Prevalence Rate of Diseases (Percent, 2006)
- Above 21.5
- 20.5-21.5
- 19.0-20.5
- 17.5-19.0
- Below 17.5

Source: National Statistical Office

Jeju Special Self-Governing Province

Ieodo (Ocean Research Station)

0   25   50   100 km

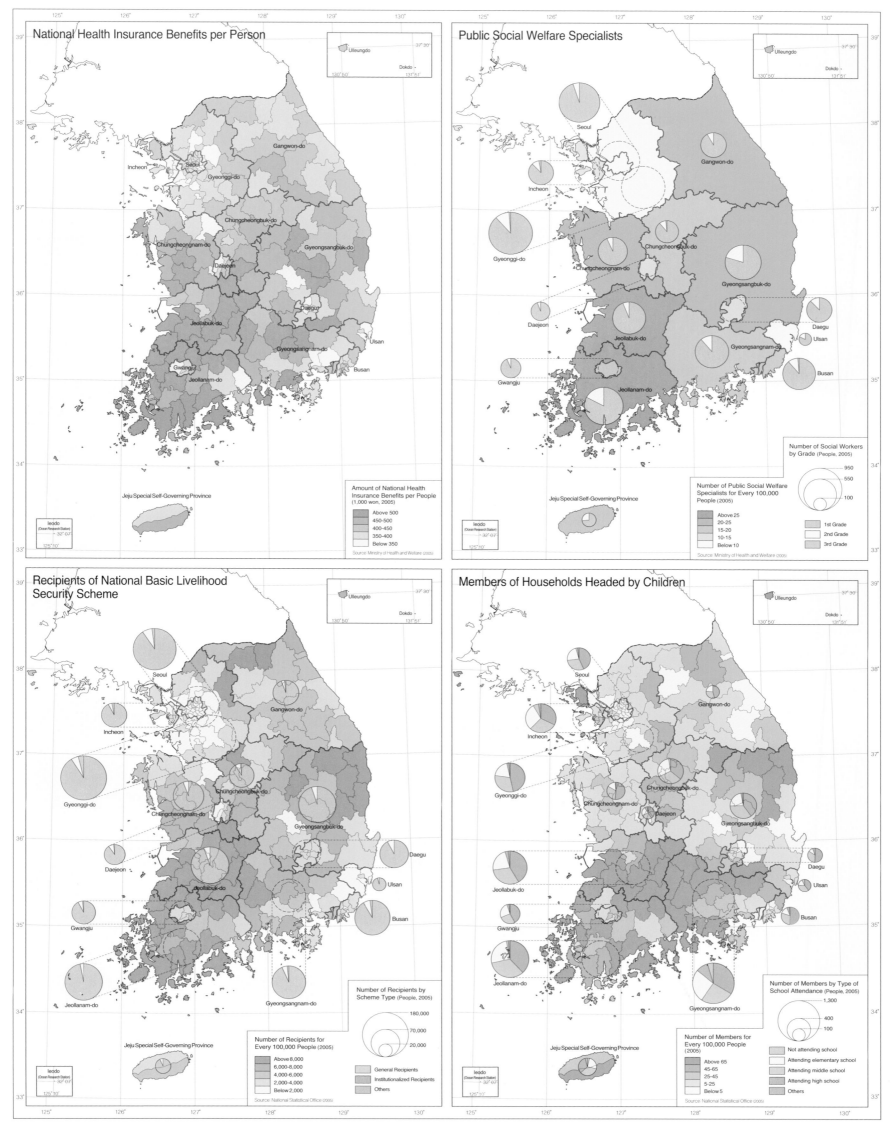

National Health Insurance Benefits per Person

Amount of National Health Insurance Benefits per People (1,000 won, 2005)
- Above 500
- 450-500
- 400-450
- 350-400
- Below 350

Source: Ministry of Health and Welfare (2005)

Public Social Welfare Specialists

Number of Social Workers by Grade (People, 2005)
- 950
- 550
- 100

Number of Public Social Welfare Specialists for Every 100,000 People (2005)
- Above 25
- 20-25
- 15-20
- 10-15
- Below 10

- 1st Grade
- 2nd Grade
- 3rd Grade

Source: Ministry of Health and Welfare (2005)

Recipients of National Basic Livelihood Security Scheme

Number of Recipients by Scheme Type (People, 2005)
- 180,000
- 70,000
- 20,000

Number of Recipients for Every 100,000 People (2005)
- Above 8,000
- 6,000-8,000
- 4,000-6,000
- 2,000-4,000
- Below 2,000

- General Recipients
- Institutionalized Recipients
- Others

Source: National Statistical Office (2005)

Members of Households Headed by Children

Number of Members by Type of School Attendance (People, 2005)
- 1,300
- 400
- 100

Number of Members for Every 100,000 People (2005)
- Above 65
- 45-65
- 25-45
- 5-25
- Below 5

- Not attending school
- Attending elementary school
- Attending middle school
- Attending high school
- Others

Source: National Statistical Office (2005)

0   25   50   100 km

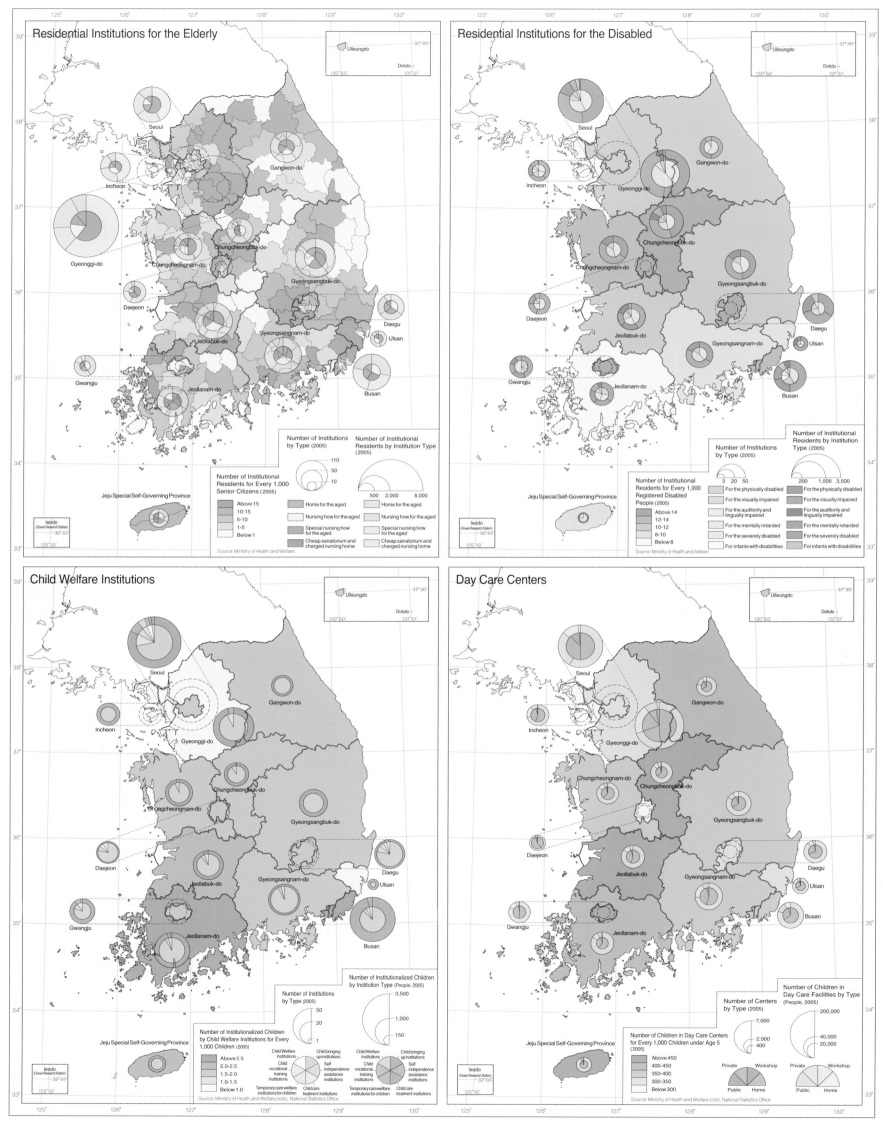

Residential Institutions for the Elderly

Source: Ministry of Health and Welfare

Number of Institutions by Type (2005)
110
50
10

Number of Institutional Residents by Institution Type (2005)
500 2,000 8,000

Number of Institutional Residents for Every 1,000 Senior Citizens (2005)
- Above 15
- 10–15
- 5–10
- 1–5
- Below 1

Home for the aged
Nursing how for the aged
Special nursing how for the aged
Cheap sanatorium and charged nursing home

Home for the aged
Nursing how for the aged
Special nursing how for the aged
Cheap sanatorium and charged nursing home

Jeju Special Self-Governing Province

Ieodo (Ocean Research Station)

Residential Institutions for the Disabled

Source: Ministry of Health and Welfare

Number of Institutions by Type (2005)
3 20 50

Number of Institutional Residents by Institution Type (2005)
200 1,500 3,500

Number of Institutional Residents for Every 1,000 Registered Disabled People (2005)
- Above 14
- 12–14
- 10–12
- 8–10
- Below 8

For the physically disabled
For the visually impaired
For the auditorily and lingually impaired
For the mentally retarded
For the severely disabled
For infants with disabilities

For the physically disabled
For the visually impaired
For the auditorily and lingually impaired
For the mentally retarded
For the severely disabled
For infants with disabilities

Jeju Special Self-Governing Province

Ieodo (Ocean Research Station)

Child Welfare Institutions

Source: Ministry of Health and Welfare 2005, National Statistics Office

Number of Institutions by Type (2005)
50
20
1

Number of Institutionalized Children by Institution Type (People, 2005)
3,500
1,000
150

Number of Institutionalized Children by Child Welfare Institutions for Every 1,000 Children (2005)
- Above 2.5
- 2.0–2.5
- 1.5–2.0
- 1.0–1.5
- Below 1.0

Child Welfare Institutions
Child vocational training institutions
Temporary care welfare institutions for children

Childbringing up institutions
Self independence assistance institutions
Child care treatment institutions

Child Welfare Institutions
Child vocational training institutions
Temporary care welfare institutions for children

Childbringing up institutions
Self independence assistance institutions
Child care treatment institutions

Jeju Special Self-Governing Province

Ieodo (Ocean Research Station)

Day Care Centers

Source: Ministry of Health and Welfare 2005, National Statistics Office

Number of Centers by Type (2005)
7,000
2,000
400

Number of Children in Day Care Facilities by Type (People, 2005)
200,000
40,000
20,000

Number of Children in Day Care Centers for Every 1,000 Children under Age 5 (2005)
- Above 450
- 400–450
- 350–400
- 300–350
- Below 300

Private   Workshop
Public   Home

Private   Workshop
Public   Home

Jeju Special Self-Governing Province

Ieodo (Ocean Research Station)

0 25 50 100 km

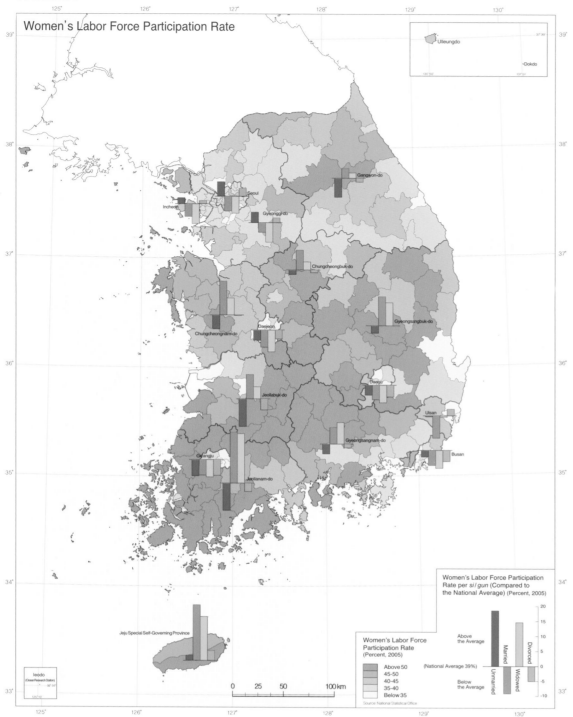

Women's Labor Force Participation Rate

Women's Labor Force Participation Rate per *si / gun* (Compared to the National Average) (Percent, 2005)

Women's Labor Force Participation Rate (Percent, 2005)

Above 50
45-50
40-45
35-40
Below 35

Source: National Statistical Office

0   25   50   100 km

Different cultures around the world have experienced changes in family life. Social participation of Korean women has also changed in response to changes in the Korean society.

Birth and Death of Women

The preference in Korean society for a male child is one form of discrimination against women, and is reflected in the abnormally larger number of newborn male babies. In most countries, the normal sex ratio at birth (defined as the ratio of the number of male births to female births) is between 104 and 106. However, in Korea, the sex ratio at birth has remained quite high (see Figure 1). Although overall the sex ratio at birth has been decreasing over the past 15 years, the ratio still deviated from the norm in 2005 (107.7). In particular, in the lunar Year of the Horse (1990 and 2002) and the Year of the Tiger (1998), considered unlucky years for a female baby to be born, the sex ratio at birth increased noticeably. The sex ratio at birth is greater when the birth order is considered. In 2005, the sex ratio at birth of the first child was 104.8, 106.4 for the second child, 127.7 for the third, and 133.5 for the forth and subsequent children. The ratios for the first two children are within the normal range, but the ratios for the third and successive children were far beyond the normal range (see Figure 2), indicating that illegal medical treatments were taking place to ensure the birth of male children.

With regards to the sex ratio at birth for the first and third child, differences were recorded between cities as well as regions. Relatively low differences in the sex ratio at birth were recorded in Jeollanam-*do* (10%), Jeollabuk-do (10%), and Seoul (11%). In contrast, much greater differences were recorded in Daegu (55%), Ulsan (47%), and Gyeongsangnam-do (47%).

Thus, we can conclude from these results that there still exists a strong preference for a son over a daughter in these latter three regions.

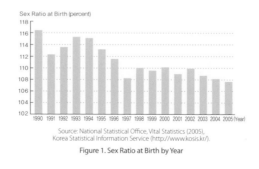

Source: National Statistical Office, Vital Statistics (2005), Korea Statistical Information Service (http://www.kosis.kr/).

Figure 1. Sex Ratio at Birth by Year

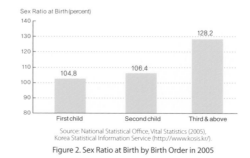

Source: National Statistical Office, Vital Statistics (2005), Korea Statistical Information Service (http://www.kosis.kr/).

Figure 2. Sex Ratio at Birth by Birth Order in 2005

In addition to the preference for a son, the rapidly declining fertility rate is also causing significant social problems. The total fertility rate is the average number of children a woman can have over her full reproductive lifetime (from 15 to 49 years old). A total fertility rate below 2.0 indicates a decrease in population. This decrease will, in the long run, see the working population decrease, which in turn will place a burden on future generations. In 1970, the total fertility rate was 4.53, indicating a woman delivered, on average, more than 4 children. By 2005, this rate had dropped to just 1.08. This drop underlines the urgent need for measures to increase the total fertility rate (see Figure 3). The total fertility rates in large cities such as Busan (0.88), Seoul (0.92), and Daegu (0.99) were low. In contrast, relatively high fertility rates were recorded in the rural areas of Jeollanam-*do* (1.28) and Chungcheongnam-*do* (1.26).

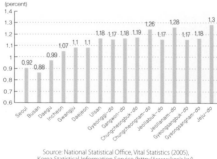

Source: National Statistical Office, Vital Statistics (2005), Korea Statistical Information Service (http://www.kosis.kr/).

Figure 3. Total Fertility Rate by Province in 2005

In addition to major demographic characteristics such as a high sex ratio at birth and a low total fertility rate, Korea is also distinguished by a high sex ratio of death at a certain age. The sex ratio of death is defined as the ratio of the number of male deaths to female deaths. Age-specific mortality rates by sex are very high among the 5 to 9 year-old age group (149 in 2005). This rate has been increasing along with the increase in the average age; there were over 250 in the 40 to 50 year-old age group; there were 5 male deaths for every 2 female deaths in this age group. Compared to the 1995 rate, there has been a reduction, but this relatively high rate is still considered to be cause for concern (see Figure 4).

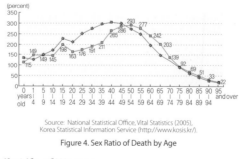

Source: National Statistical Office, Vital Statistics (2005), Korea Statistical Information Service (http://www.kosis.kr/).

Figure 4. Sex Ratio of Death by Age

Family Life of Women

While marriage is a very important event for both women and men, recent statistics show that both young women and men tend to avoid or postpone their marriage. Women may fear that marriage could limit their career, while men may feel pressure to support a family. This trend can be seen in the changes of the mean age at first marriage since 1990. In 1990, a married man's age at the time of his first marriage was 27.8 years, but by 2006, the age had increased to 30.9 years (an increase of 3.1 years). In the case of women, the mean age at the time of first marriage was 24.8 in 1990, but that age increased to 27.8 years by 2006 (an increase of 3 years). This social phenomenon can be explained by the increase of the mean age at first marriage and a decrease in the crude marriage rate (see Figure 5). The crude marriage rate is one of the basic indices of marital status. It refers to the number of marriages occurring during a given year per 1,000 registered population during the same year. The crude marriage rate was 9.3 in 1990, and increased slightly between 1991 and 1992. Despite a spike at 9.4 in 1996, the rate steadily declined, and as of 2006, stood at 6.8.

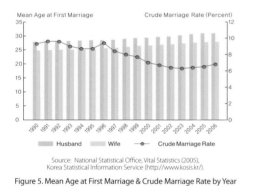

Source: National Statistical Office, Vital Statistics (2005), Korea Statistical Information Service (http://www.kosis.kr/).

Figure 5. Mean Age at First Marriage & Crude Marriage Rate by Year

The Time Use Survey conducted by the Korea National Statistical Office clearly shows the differences in how men and women use their hours in the day. According to the survey results, men spent most of their time engaged in economic activities, while women used their time primarily engaged in housework and family care. These gender specific divisions of work were also present in double-income households. In these households, the husband spent 32 minutes per day for housework, which was about the same amount of time as a husband in a single-income household (31 minutes). However, the wife from a double-income household spent 1 hour and 20 minutes less on economic activities, and 2 hours and 51 minutes more on housework than the husband. Thus, the wife from a double-income household spent 1 hour and 30 minutes more for economic activities and housework than the husband. This division of labor shows that married women still suffer the disadvantage of having to balance a career with household duties. A husband from a double-income household used 51 more minutes per day for leisure time than the wife. However, in the case of families where the husband is the sole wage-earner, the wife had 1 hour and 30 minutes more leisure time than the husband (see Figure 6).

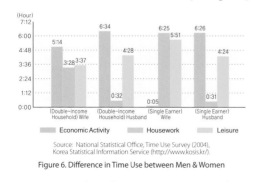

Source: National Statistical Office, Time Use Survey (2004), Korea Statistical Information Service (http://www.kosis.kr/).

Figure 6. Difference in Time Use between Men & Women

In recent years marriages between Korean men and non-Korean women have been increasing, particularly in rural areas; 31,180 such marriages were recorded in 2005. These marriages accounted for almost 10 percent of the total marriages (316,375) of that year. Marriages between Korean women and non-Korean husbands also increased to 3.8 percent, or 11,941

marriages (Korea National Statistical Office Web Site). The majority of foreign husbands were from China (41%) and Japan (31%). Most foreign women married to a Korean husband were from China (65%) and Vietnam (19%). A large number of these women came to Korea with the help of marriage agencies, and did not know much about their future husbands. This situation has led to some of these women suffering from discrimination, cultural differences and language barriers.

Social Participation of Women

With the exception of the 1997-1998 economic crisis, the participation of women in the economic sector has been steadily increasing over the last 40 years. In 1963, only 37 percent of women had careers; this number climbed 13.2 percent to reach a level of 50.2 percent of women in 2006. As for the number of men with careers, the number decreased from 78.4 percent in 1963 to 74 percent in 2006 (a 4.4% decrease). Despite 50.2 percent of women having careers, only a small number of women are highly paid, stable professionals, such as technicians or managers. Most women are service workers with correspondingly low payment and positions. In 2006, the percentage of men who worked as professionals, technicians or managers was 24 percent, while only 19 percent of female workers occupied similar positions in these fields. In the service and sales sectors, as shown in Figure 7, women (36%) occupy a much larger share than men (16%).

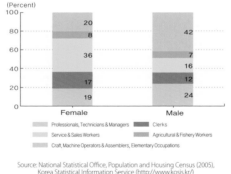

Source: National Statistical Office, Population and Housing Census (2005), Korea Statistical Information Service (http://www.kosis.kr/)

Figure 7. Occupations by Age and Gender (2006)

The increase in the crime rate has raised the public's fear of becoming a victim of crime. In particular, women tend to have a greater fear than males. Twenty-two percent of women answered that they were afraid of crime, and 46 percent answered they were slightly afraid. From these results we can assume that two out of three females have a fear of crime to some degree. However, this is in contrast to the level of fear expressed by men. Only 11 percent of males answered they were afraid of crime, while 36 percent answered they were slightly afraid (Figure 8).

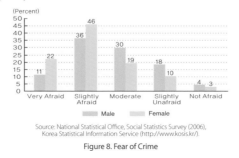

Source: National Statistical Office, Social Statistics Survey (2006), Korea Statistical Information Service (http://www.kosis.kr/).

Figure 8. Fear of Crime

The safety of walking at night is one of the indices which can measure the safety of a society. While 69 percent of Korean

women answered there are certain places where they were afraid of going at night, only 46 percent of men felt this way (see Figure 9).

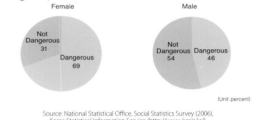

Source: National Statistical Office, Social Statistics Survey (2006), Korea Statistical Information Service (http://www.kosis.kr/).

Figure 9. Safety of Walking at Night: Comparison between Men and Women

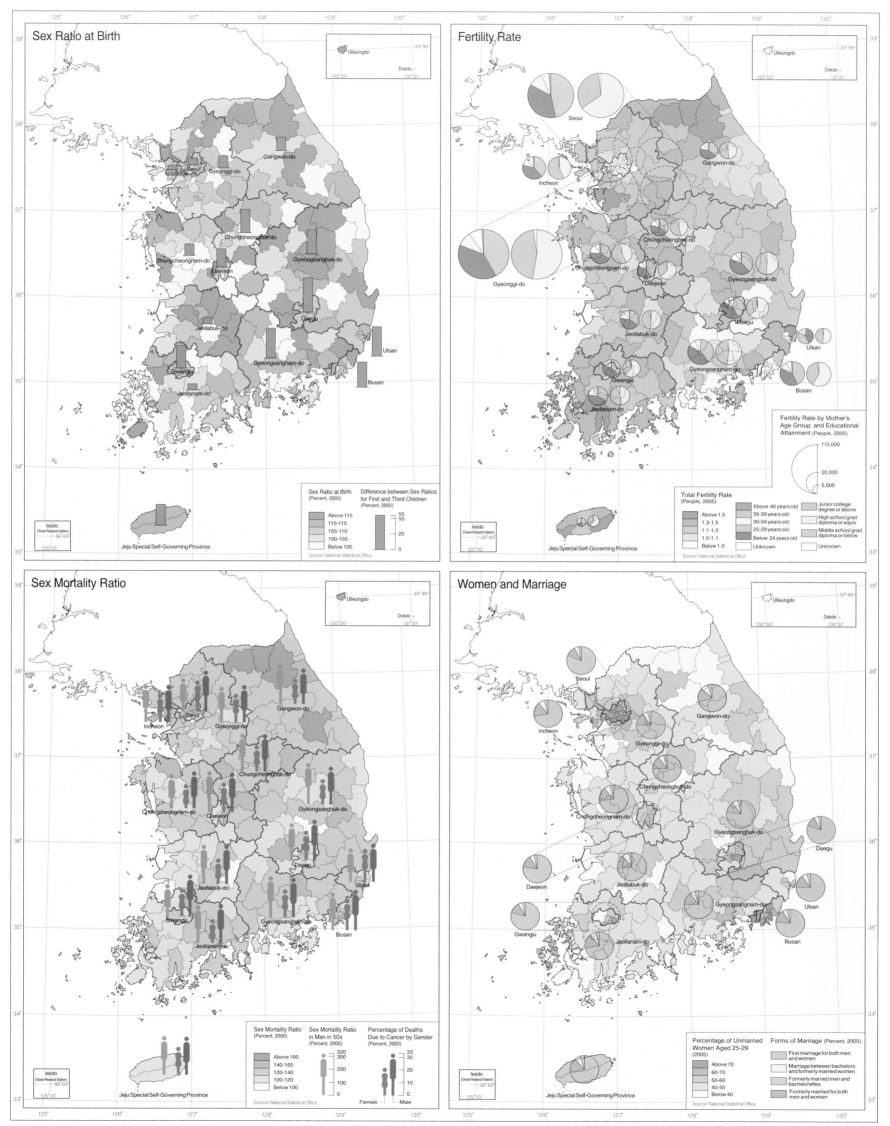

Sex Ratio at Birth

Gangwon-do
Seoul
Incheon
Gyeonggi-do
Chungcheongbuk-do
Chungcheongnam-do
Daejeon
Gyeongsangbuk-do
Jeollabuk-do
Daegu
Ulsan
Gwangju
Gyeongsangnam-do
Busan
Jeollanam-do

Ieodo
(Ocean Research Station)
125°10'
32°07'

Jeju Special Self-Governing Province

Sex Ratio at Birth (Percent, 2005)
Above 115
110-115
105-110
100-105
Below 100

Difference between Sex Ratios for First and Third Children (Percent, 2005)
55
50
25
0

Source: National Statistical Office

Fertility Rate

Ulleungdo
Dokdo

Seoul
Incheon
Gangwon-do
Gyeonggi-do
Chungcheongbuk-do
Chungcheongnam-do
Daejeon
Gyeongsangbuk-do
Jeollabuk-do
Daegu
Ulsan
Gyeongsangnam-do
Gwangju
Busan
Jeollanam-do

Fertility Rate by Mother's Age Group and Educational Attainment (People, 2005)
110,000
20,000
5,500

Ieodo
(Ocean Research Station)
125°10'
32°07'

Jeju Special Self-Governing Province

Total Fertility Rate (People, 2005)
Above 1.5
1.3-1.5
1.1-1.3
1.0-1.1
Below 1.0

Above 40 years old
35-39 years old
30-34 years old
25-29 years old
Below 24 years old
Unknown

Junior college degree or above
High school grad diploma or equiv
Middle school grad diploma or below
Unknown

Source: National Statistical Office

Sex Mortality Ratio

Ulleungdo
Dokdo

Seoul
Incheon
Gyeonggi-do
Gangwon-do
Chungcheongbuk-do
Chungcheongnam-do
Daejeon
Gyeongsangbuk-do
Daegu
Jeollabuk-do
Ulsan
Gwangju
Gyeongsangnam-do
Busan
Jeollanam-do

Ieodo
(Ocean Research Station)
125°10'
32°07'

Jeju Special Self-Governing Province

Sex Mortality Ratio (Percent, 2005)
Above 160
140-160
120-140
100-120
Below 100

Sex Mortality Ratio in Men in 50s (Percent, 2005)
320
300
200
100
0

Percentage of Deaths Due to Cancer by Gender (Percent, 2005)
33
30
20
10
0
Female   Male

Source: National Statistical Office

Women and Marriage

Ulleungdo
Dokdo

Seoul
Incheon
Gangwon-do
Gyeonggi-do
Chungcheongbuk-do
Chungcheongnam-do
Gyeongsangbuk-do
Daejeon
Daegu
Jeollabuk-do
Gyeongsangnam-do
Ulsan
Gwangju
Busan
Jeollanam-do

Ieodo
(Ocean Research Station)
125°10'
32°07'

Jeju Special Self-Governing Province

Percentage of Unmarried Women Aged 25-29 (2005)
Above 70
60-70
50-60
40-50
Below 40

Forms of Marriage (Percent, 2005)
First marriage for both men and women
Marriage between bachelors and formerly married women
Formerly married men and bachelorettes
Formerly married for both men and women

Source: National Statistical Office

0   25   50   100 km

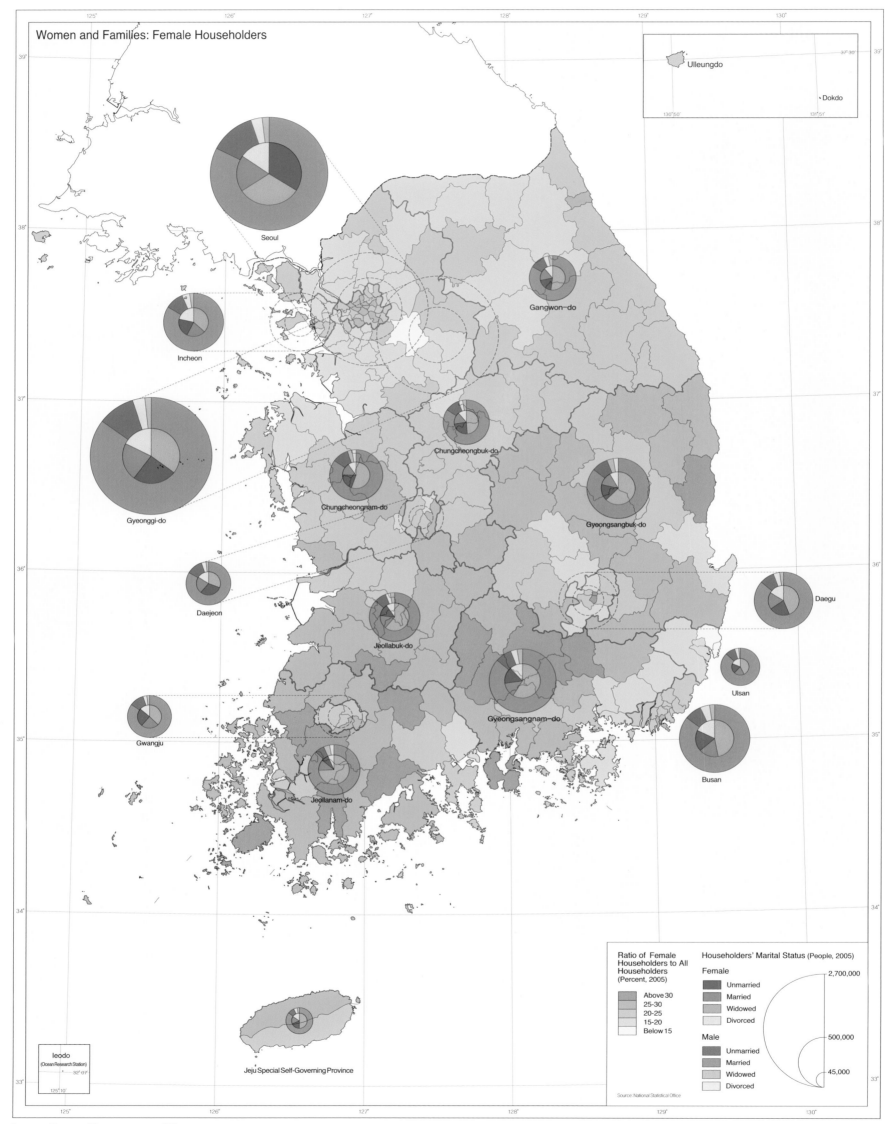

Women and Families: Female Householders

Ulleungdo

Dokdo

Seoul

Incheon

Gangwon-do

Gyeonggi-do

Chungcheongbuk-do

Chungcheongnam-do

Gyeongsangbuk-do

Daejeon

Jeollabuk-do

Daegu

Gyeongsangnam-do

Ulsan

Gwangju

Busan

Jeollanam-do

Ratio of Female
Householders to All
Householders
(Percent, 2005)

Above 30
25-30
20-25
15-20
Below 15

Householders' Marital Status (People, 2005)
Female
Unmarried
Married
Widowed
Divorced

Male
Unmarried
Married
Widowed
Divorced

2,700,000

500,000

45,000

Source: National Statistical Office

Ieodo
(Ocean Research Station)
32° 07'

125° 10'

Jeju Special Self-Governing Province

0   25   50   100 km

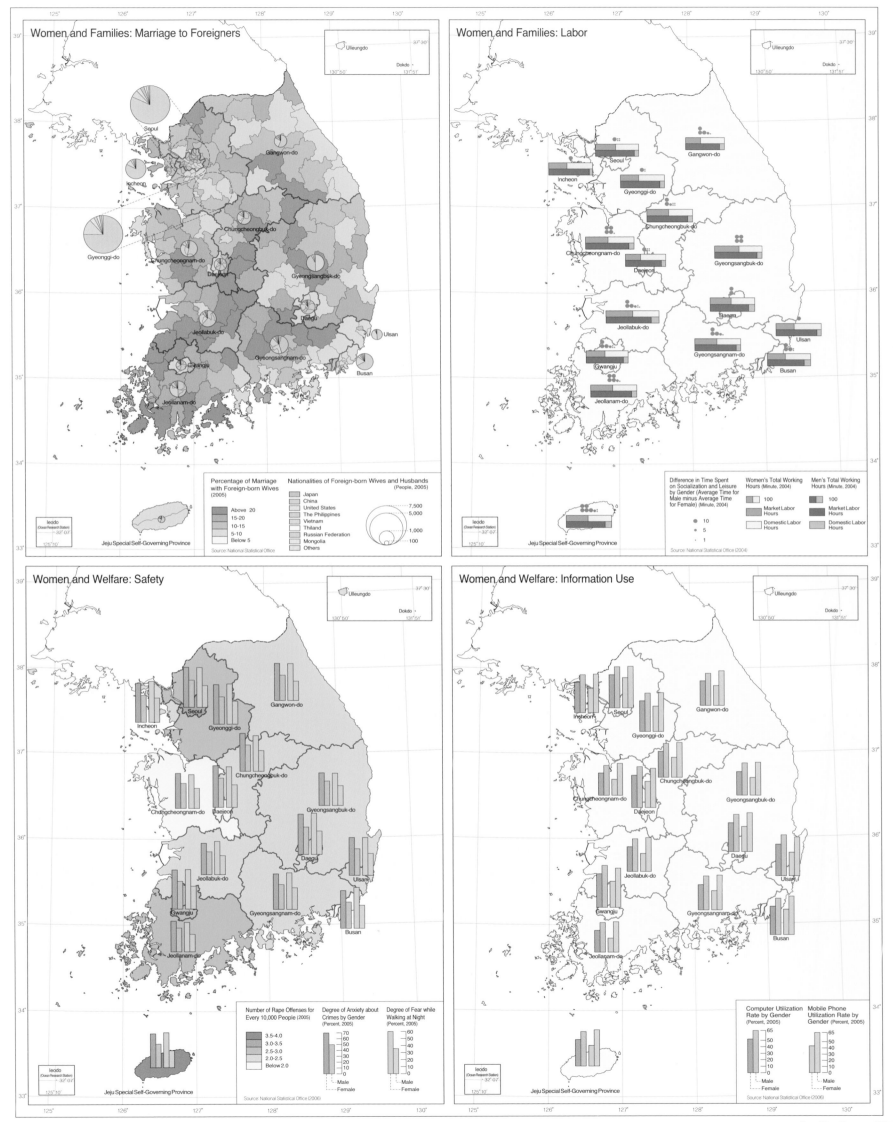

Women and Families: Marriage to Foreigners

Percentage of Marriage with Foreign-born Wives (2005)
- Above 20
- 15-20
- 10-15
- 5-10
- Below 5

Nationalities of Foreign-born Wives and Husbands (People, 2005)
- Japan
- China
- United States
- The Philippines
- Vietnam
- Thailand
- Russian Federation
- Mongolia
- Others

7,500 / 5,000 / 1,000 / 100

Ieodo (Ocean Research Station)
Jeju Special Self-Governing Province

Source: National Statistical Office

Women and Families: Labor

Difference in Time Spent on Socialization and Leisure by Gender (Average Time for Male minus Average Time for Female) (Minute, 2004)
- 10
- 5
- 1

Women's Total Working Hours (Minute, 2004)
- 100
- Market Labor Hours
- Domestic Labor Hours

Men's Total Working Hours (Minute, 2004)
- 100
- Market Labor Hours
- Domestic Labor Hours

Ieodo (Ocean Research Station)
Jeju Special Self-Governing Province

Source: National Statistical Office (2004)

Women and Welfare: Safety

Number of Rape Offenses for Every 10,000 People (2005)
- 3.5-4.0
- 3.0-3.5
- 2.5-3.0
- 2.0-2.5
- Below 2.0

Degree of Anxiety about Crimes by Gender (Percent, 2005)
70 / 60 / 50 / 40 / 30 / 20 / 10 / 0
- Male
- Female

Degree of Fear while Walking at Night (Percent, 2005)
60 / 50 / 40 / 30 / 20 / 10 / 0
- Male
- Female

Ieodo (Ocean Research Station)
Jeju Special Self-Governing Province

Source: National Statistical Office (2006)

Women and Welfare: Information Use

Computer Utilization Rate by Gender (Percent, 2005)
65 / 50 / 40 / 30 / 20 / 10 / 0
- Male
- Female

Mobile Phone Utilization Rate by Gender (Percent, 2005)
65 / 50 / 40 / 30 / 20 / 10 / 0
- Male
- Female

Ieodo (Ocean Research Station)
Jeju Special Self-Governing Province

Source: National Statistical Office (2006)

0　25　50　100 km

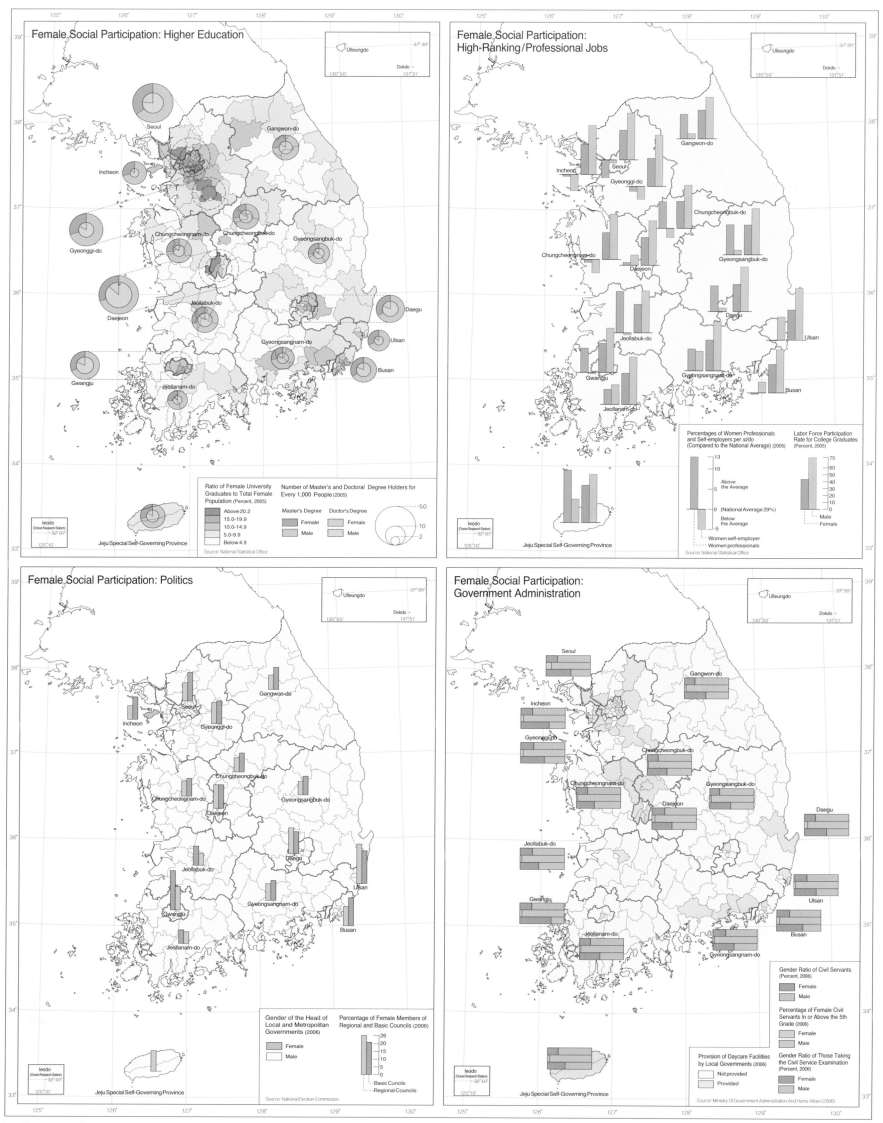

Female Social Participation: Higher Education

Female Social Participation:
High-Ranking/Professional Jobs

Ulleungdo

Dokdo

Seoul
Gangwon-do
Incheon
Gyeonggi-do
Chungcheongnam-do
Chungcheongbuk-do
Gyeongsangbuk-do
Daejeon
Daegu
Ulsan
Gyeongsangnam-do
Jeollabuk-do
Busan
Gwangju
Jeollanam-do

Ratio of Female University Graduates to Total Female Population (Percent, 2005)
Above 20.2
15.0–19.9
10.0–14.9
5.0–9.9
Below 4.9

Number of Master's and Doctoral Degree Holders for Every 1,000 People (2005)
Master's Degree
Female
Male
Doctor's Degree
Female
Male

50
10
2

Ieodo
(Ocean Research Station)
32° 07'
125° 10'

Jeju Special Self-Governing Province

Source: National Statistical Office

Percentages of Women Professionals and Self-employers per si/do (Compared to the National Average) (2005)
13
10
5
Above the Average
0 (National Average 29%)
Below the Average
-5
Women self-employer
Women professionals

Labor Force Participation Rate for College Graduates (Percent, 2005)
75
60
50
40
30
20
10
Male
Female

Source: National Statistical Office

Female Social Participation: Politics

Female Social Participation:
Government Administration

Ulleungdo

Dokdo

Seoul
Gangwon-do
Incheon
Gyeonggi-do
Chungcheongbuk-do
Chungcheongnam-do
Gyeongsangbuk-do
Daejeon
Daegu
Jeollabuk-do
Ulsan
Gwangju
Gyeongsangnam-do
Busan
Jeollanam-do

Gender of the Head of Local and Metropolitan Governments (2006)
Female
Male

Percentage of Female Members of Regional and Basic Councils (2006)
26
20
15
10
5
0
Basic Cuncils
Regional Councils

Ieodo
(Ocean Research Station)
32° 07'
125° 10'

Jeju Special Self-Governing Province

Source: National Election Commission

Gender Ratio of Civil Servants (Percent, 2006)
Female
Male

Percentage of Female Civil Servants In or Above the 5th Grade (2006)
Female
Male

Provision of Daycare Facilities by Local Governments (2006)
Not provided
Provided

Gender Ratio of Those Taking the Civil Service Examination (Percent, 2006)
Female
Male

Source: Ministry Of Government Administration And Home Affairs (2006)

0 25 50   100 km

155

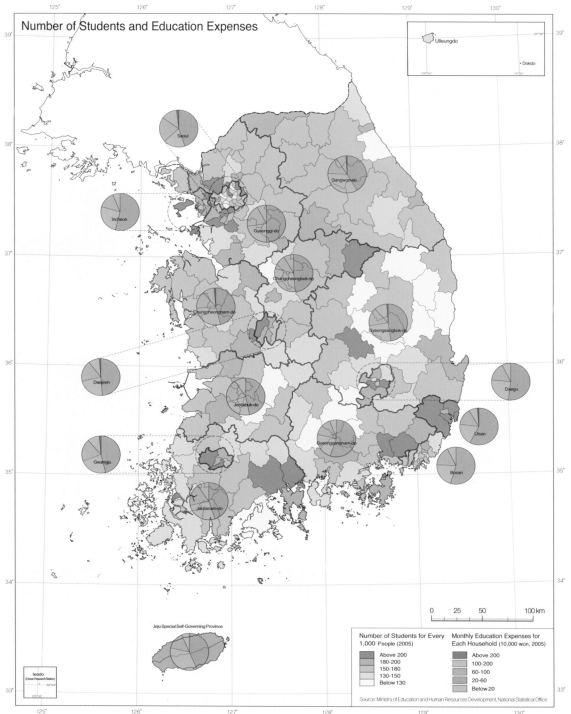

Number of Students and Education Expenses

Number of Students for Every 1,000 People (2005)
- Above 200
- 180-200
- 150-180
- 130-150
- Below 130

Monthly Education Expenses for Each Household (10,000 won, 2005)
- Above 200
- 100-200
- 60-100
- 20-60
- Below 20

Source: Ministry of Education and Human Resources Development, National Statistical Office

As for the age of teachers, the average age of primary school teachers in 2006 was 39.6 years, while that of middle school teachers was 40.1 years; general high school teachers were 40.8 years of age and vocational high school teachers were 42.4. Due to a policy to reduce the number of students in classes in primary schools, the number of primary school teachers in their 20s and 30s rapidly increased. Middle and high school teachers show a similar trend in terms of their age, but overall, high school teachers are older than their counterparts in middle schools, with those in their 40s accounting for the major share. As far as the gender composition is concerned, kindergartens, primary and middle schools show a predominantly high ratio of female teachers, while male counterparts account for a much greater percentage in high schools. Such a gender imbalance of teachers in kindergartens, primary, middle and high schools has emerged as a societal issue. As for kindergartens, female teachers have continuously occupied the vast majority of positions in this field, accounting for 74.6 percent in 1970, and rising steadily to 98.3 percent in 2005.

The academic background of teachers has been significantly enhanced since 2000. Over 80 percent of primary school teachers hold at least a two-year college degree, and more than 13 percent of those teaching in primary schools hold master's degrees. As for middle school teachers, as of 2000 over 95 percent are graduates of four-year universities, and over 23 percent of middle school teachers and over 30 percent of high school teachers have completed graduate school degrees.

Students

The Korean population experienced a rapid growth in the 1960s due to the baby boom after the Korean War, which led to the strong growth of a learned population. The birth control policy launched in the 1970s cut the speed of population growth, but the student registration rate rose swiftly. The school enrollment rate for each academic level in Korea has skyrocketed – a rarity in other countries. In the half century since 1945, the school enrollment rate up to the high school level has been almost 100 percent. Such rapid growth has been attributed to Korea's Confucian emphasis on education. The government has consistently implemented policies to broaden educational opportunities in response to people's needs.

The share of the student population out of Korea's total population can be examined by looking at the number of students per one thousand people. The number of kindergarten students per one thousand is 11.5, that of primary school students is 85.1, and those of middle and high school students 42.5 and 37.3, respectively. Region-wise, the student population is concentrated in the capital regions of Seoul and Gyeonggi-*do* and other major metropolitan areas including Daegu, Gwangju, Daejeon and Ulsan. In addition, it is generally higher in urban areas than rural ones.

The number of students per teacher in 1970 was 13.4 in kindergartens, 56.9 in primary schools, 42.3 in middle schools, and 32.0 in general high schools; these 1970 levels should be compared to the 2005 levels: 17.5, 25.1, 19.4 and 15.1, respectively (15.9 in general high schools). Thanks to the Educational Environment Improvement Project, as well as efforts to reduce the number of students per class, the number of students per teacher has continued to drop.

Regionally, meanwhile, the student distribution rate is generally low in local cities in Chungnam, Jeonbuk, Jeonnam, Gyeongsangbuk-*do*, and mountainous regions. The number of students in capital regions, including Seoul and Gyeonggi-*do*, is still high, meaning that teachers in these regions are responsible for a greater number of students.

The class sizes in primary, middle and high schools sharply dropped thanks to the full implementation in 2001 of the Educational Environment Improvement Project; numbers were reduced to less than 40 students in a single class across all school levels. As for the number of classes, as broken down by class size, 73.6 percent of middle schools and 78.6 percent of high schools have a class size of 31 to 40 students, the most common class size. Middle schools, on average, had denser classes, followed by primary schools and high schools.

Satisfaction levels in educational opportunities are relatively high in seven major cities and Gyeonggi-*do* compared to other provinces. Nevertheless, the difference is not that huge, and students in major cities and other local provinces show almost

Education and the Education Budget

The education system in the Republic of Korea consists of six-year primary schools, three-year middle schools, three-year high schools and four-year universities. Since the late 1950s, six-year primary schooling has been compulsory, and in 2002, economic development and a national aspiration for school education led to free compulsory middle schooling. The Childhood Education Act was promulgated in 2004, and a legal framework guiding the whole educational process from infant education to higher education was put into place. Attempts to make the educational environment no longer uniform, but more liberal and diverse, began in 2005, and included the emergence of independent private high schools. In early 2005, 'Cyber Home Schooling' was adopted nationwide, which enabled free after-school online courses for primary, middle and high school students. As such, a variety of e-learning systems were established. 'After Schools' have been implemented throughout the nation since 2006.

The one-year budget for the Ministry of Education and Human Resources Development continued to increase from 784.7 billion won in 1970, to about two trillion won in 1980, and to 27.438 trillion won in 2005. The Education Ministry's budget was 17.6 percent of the 1970 government budget, and 20.3 percent of the budget in 2005. Most of the educational budget for each city and province is supported by the national budget; 74.6 percent of the educational budget in each local region, city and province comes from the central government, and the remaining 25.4 percent from local revenues. The financial independence rate per region is the highest in Seoul (42.8%) and Gyeonggi-*do* (34.9%), but it is less than 30 percent for the

remaining metropolitan cities and provinces. This indicates that despite the implementation of local autonomy, most of the regional education budget depends on national budgetary support.

Household-wise, pressure on households has grown due to the national emphasis on education and corresponding high expenditures on private education. As such, the average monthly educational expenditure per household has been on the rise since the 1990s. The portion of the cost of education out of all household expenditures continued to grow from 5.3 percent in 2002 to 5.8 percent in 2006. Most households spend 200,000 to 600,000 won for education every month.

Teachers

The number of primary school teachers increased from 101,095 in 1970 to 160,085 in 2005, a growth of 55.7 percent, despite a shrinkage in the number of primary school students. This is a result of the Educational Environment Improvement Project of the 2000s, which drastically cut the number of students for each class. The number of middle school teachers sharply increased from 31,207 in 1970 to 103,835 in 2005. This increase resulted from several factors: the exam waiver to enter middle schools in the 1960s, implementation of compulsory middle school education in the late 1980s, and a policy launched in 2000 to reduce the number of students per class. The number of all high school teachers increased from 19,845 in 1970 to 110,611 in 2005. The number of teachers increased almost nine-fold, from 9,845 in 1970 to 79,158 in general high schools in 2005. The number of teachers in national and public high schools is slightly higher than private schools, but this difference is not statistically significant.

the same levels of satisfaction in their school life, which hints at almost no difference in terms of satisfaction toward educational opportunities and school education in general.

Education Support Environment

A close look at school facilities reveals that the Educational Environment Improvement Project, beginning in 2001, has been carried out successfully in a variety of ways. Continued investment for facility upgrades has greatly enhancing the overall class and educational environment.

As for educational facilities, as of 2005, the area per kindergarten student was 8.8m², and the area per middle and high school student was 21.2m² and 29.0m², respectively (28.9m² for general high schools and 29.3m² for vocational high schools). The school area and the area per teacher in national and public schools were higher than those in private schools. Generally, national and public schools have secured a greater amount of space than private ones. As for primary schools, the severely low birth rate had raised concerns over the possible oversupply of school facilities.

Similar patterns are found in the regional distribution of per-student school areas and building areas. Such areas are small in metropolitan cities, including Seoul and local cities, compared to counties. Overall, there is a stark contrast between the low school area per students in cities and the very high levels in rural areas centered around cities.

The number of books per student in primary, middle and high schools varies a great deal depending on the region. On average, there are 8.3 books per student in Korean primary, middle and high schools: primary (9.6 books), middle (7.7 books), general high (8.3 books), and vocational high schools (9.1 books). The fact that this is higher in counties than metropolitan regions or cities is related to the recent reduction in the number of students in rural areas.

As a consequence of the rapid growth of the IT industry in Korea and the recent considerable investment in IT advancement in education over the past 15 years, the information-enhanced educational environment in primary, middle and high schools has improved enormously since the 1990s. In particular, high schools showed a huge improvement in that the number of students per computer has been reduced from 103.5 in 1991 to just 5.6 in 2005 (see Figure 1).

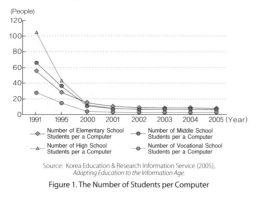

(People)

Source: Korea Education & Research Information Service (2005), *Adapting Education to the Information Age.*

Figure 1. The Number of Students per Computer

Current Status of Each School Level

Pre-schooling is partially paid by the government, but it is not an established public educational institution. Reduction in the number of children due to the low birth rate has led to a smaller number of kindergartens, from 8,329 in 2001 to 8,292 in 2003, and to 8, 275 in 2005. Since 2001, the number of national and public kindergartens has slightly increased, but that of private kindergartens has dropped. Region-wise, rural and fishing areas have many public kindergartens, while small, medium-sized and major cities have many private ones. Most public ones, 98.3 percent, are kindergartens attached to primary schools. In contrast, this rate is very low, 20.9 percent, in island and remote regions. In rural and fishing villages, the enrollment rate in public kindergartens is higher than that of private kindergartens. The rate for private ones is higher in city regions, with the result that opportunities and content in pre-schooling for each region are not equally provided.

As for primary education, the number of primary school students was about 5.74 million in 1970, but this level continuously dropped, falling to 4.02 million in 2005. This large drop was due to industrialization, urbanization and a low birth rate. The number of students was greatly reduced in the 1980s and 1990s; in 1995 the number of primary school students dropped almost 31 percent compared to 1980. Along with the low birth rate resulting from continued population growth control policies up until the 1970s, and the overall population shrinkage due to the emergence of an aging society, the number of students continues to drop. As a result, the number of primary schools, which numbered 5,961 in 1970, continuously dropped from the mid-eighties. However, since 2000, their number began to increase, and as of 2005, there were 5,646 schools. Primary schools are predominantly national and public, so the share of private schools is less than 1.5 percent. This is because primary school education has been made compulsory from an early age, while private school education has been socially regarded as being for the rich.

As for middle school education, the number of middle school students continued to rise, from 1.32 million in 1970, to a peak of 2.78 million in 1985; from then the number dropped continuously. However, numbers began gradually rising again after 2003. In the late 1960s, private schools accounted for more than 50 percent of middle schools, but due to compulsory middle schooling in the mid-1980s, a large part of this enrollment moved to national and public schools.

Meanwhile, like middle schools, the number of general high schools has also increased; from 408 in 1970 to 1,297 in 2003. During this same period, vocational high schools experienced a minor increase from 481 in 1970 to 734 in 2003. Due to an intensified preference for general high schools, the ratio of high school students in general high schools and vocational high schools in 2005 was 71.5 to 28.5. Specialized high schools numbered 92 in 2005; breaking down into 19 alternative schools and 73 specialized vocational schools. Special purpose schools providing specialized education in dedicated fields amounted to 122 schools in nine fields. These included science high schools (17), foreign language high schools (25), art high schools (23), physical education high schools (15) and fisheries high schools (5).

Higher Education (Universities and Graduate schools)

University education in Korea met the country's demand for labor for various industries through quantitative growth during the industrialized period. However, in the knowledge-based society of the 21st century, efforts focusing on university restructuring and specialization are being made to overcome the uniformity of universities and the inefficiencies resulting from overlapping programs.

In 2005, the number of four-year universities nationwide was 232 (173 general, 18 industrial and 33 graduate school universities). The 173 four-year universities are comprised of 10,189 departments and 1,859,629 million students. The number of students, in particular, has increased exponentially (over 30 times previous levels). Two rapid educational expansions, 'The University Open-Door Policy' of the Fifth Republic of South Korea, that is, the government of the country in the 1980s, and the various university diversification reform policies of the Civil Government in the late 1990s have led to this result. The number of registered students in higher education institutions per ten thousand people was 63 in 1970, but increased exponentially up to 742 in 2003. The number of higher education institutions in cities, counties and wards nationwide is 358, which means that each of the 234 cities, counties and wards nationwide has an average of 1.5 higher education institutions. The number of students per professor also shrunk, from 29.9 in 2004 to 28.2 in 2005.

The changes in the number of graduate schools are in line with increases in the number of four-year universities. In 1970, there were 64 graduate schools, but this grew to 1,051 in 2005, showing both a quantitative and qualitative enhancement in higher education. The number of national and public schools in 2005 was 183, while private schools dominated the total with 868, or 82.6 percent. The number of graduate school students was 6,640 in 1970, but also showed an exponential growth as it reached 290,029 in 2005. The number of national and public graduate school students was 86,074 in 2005, and that of private graduate school students was 2.4 times higher at 203,945 students. As for the gender composition in graduate schools, women occupied 45.4 percent of places in 2005, implying almost no difference in the gender ratio. The number of graduate schools slowly rose until the 1980s and then leveled off, while

the number of universities rapidly rose during the 1990s. This can be explained by three factors: the spread of higher education along with a stronger focus on academic achievements, eased regulations in establishing schools on the supply side, and lastly, a soaring enrollment rate due to difficulties for university graduates in gaining employment.

Looking at graduate schools on a regional basis, the number of master's and doctoral courses is predominantly higher in Seoul, while high-skilled talents are fostered mostly in metropolitan areas, such as Seoul and Gyeonggi-*do*. As such, high-skilled labor is concentrated and unbalanced, resulting in severe regional imbalances. Meanwhile, more and more foreign students have chosen to come to Korea to study at higher education institutions thanks to globalization and internationalization. The number of foreign students in Korean universities and graduate schools was 22,624 in 2005. The largest number of students came from China (15,308), followed by Japan (1,267), Vietnam (963), Taiwan (785), the U.S. (773), and Mongolia (539). Chinese students account for 67.7 percent of foreign students, as much as 12 times that of second-ranking Japan.

Enrollment and Employment

The enrollment rate for each school level in Korea has grown at a rapid pace – a rarity in other countries. Throughout half a century of Korea's education history, the enrollment rate has been almost 100 percent at the high school level. This is mostly thanks to Koreans' typical enthusiasm over education. In addition, the government has continuously carried out policies to expand educational opportunities to meet the demands of the people. However, the kindergarten enrollment rate has not grown as greatly because pre-schooling has only recently been included under school education. Daycare centers (or literally "children's houses") previously served as the major pre-schooling institutions.

The primary school enrollment rate for pre-schoolers reached 92.0 percent in 1970 thanks to the government's efforts during the late 1950s. The middle school enrollment rate for primary school students rose from 66.1 percent in 1970 to 95.8 percent in 1980, and reached 99.9 percent in 1996, which is almost a 100 percent enrollment rate. The high school enrollment rate of middle school graduates reached 99.9 percent in 2005. The middle school enrollment rate was almost 100 percent as of 2005 regardless of the region. This is attributable to the elimination of the middle school entrance exam in 1969 and the 1974 high school equalization policy in which the government removed the right of schools to select students and set rates for school fees.

The enrollment rate of high school graduates into higher education institutions was merely 26.9 percent in 1970, though it rose continuously to 36.4 percent in 1985 and to 51.4 percent in 1995. The enrollment rate of general high school graduates into higher education institutions reached a peak of 90.1 percent in 2003, but then went on a gradual decline. The rate for vocational high school graduates reached 49.8 percent in 2002, implying over half of them entered university. Since then, this rate grew rapidly to reach 67.6 percent in 2005. The higher school enrollment rate of female students kept rising after 1970, reaching 50 percent in 1985 and 90.5 percent in 2003, showing no gender difference in entering higher education institutions. In particular, in all educational levels except for vocational high schools, the enrollment rate is almost the same for males and females, a great move toward gender equity in educational opportunities.

As for high school students, most of those not entering high school institutions choose to be employed. The employment rate of high school students was 37.5 percent in 1965 (31.6 percent for those in general schools and 43.4 percent for those in vocational schools), reached 51.0 percent in 1990 and peaked at 72.5 percent in 1997, but has been continuously declining since then. It was 66.1 percent in 2000, but fell further to 52.3 percent in 2005.

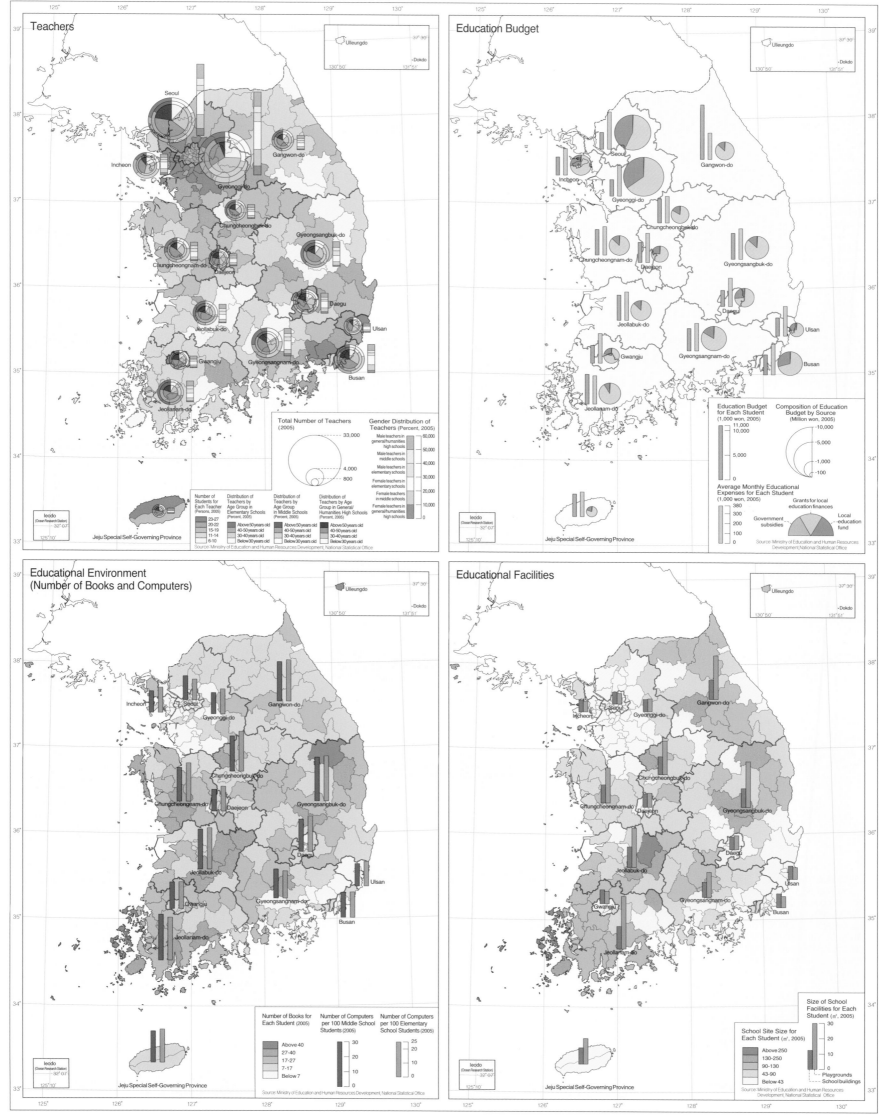

Teachers

Total Number of Teachers (2005)
33,000
4,000
800

Gender Distribution of Teachers (Percent, 2005)
Male teachers in general/humanities high schools
Male teachers in middle schools
Male teachers in elementary schools
Female teachers in elementary schools
Female teachers in middle schools
Female teachers in general/humanities high schools

Number of Students for Each Teacher (Persons, 2005)
23-27
20-22
15-19
11-14
6-10

Distribution of Teachers by Age Group in Elementary Schools (Percent, 2005)
Above 50 years old
40-50 years old
30-40 years old
Below 30 years old

Distribution of Teachers by Age Group in Middle Schools (Percent, 2005)
Above 50 years old
40-50 years old
30-40 years old
Below 30 years old

Distribution of Teachers by Age Group in General/Humanities High Schools (Percent, 2005)
Above 50 years old
40-50 years old
30-40 years old
Below 30 years old

Source: Ministry of Education and Human Resources Development, National Statistical Office

Jeju Special Self-Governing Province
Ieodo (Ocean Research Station)

Education Budget

Education Budget for Each Student (1,000 won, 2005)
11,000
10,000
5,000
0

Composition of Education Budget by Source (Million won, 2005)
10,000
5,000
1,000
100

Average Monthly Educational Expenses for Each Student (1,000 won, 2005)
380
300
200
100
0

Grants for local education finances
Government subsidies
Local education fund

Source: Ministry of Education and Human Resources Development, National Statistical Office

Jeju Special Self-Governing Province
Ieodo (Ocean Research Station)

Educational Environment (Number of Books and Computers)

Number of Books for Each Student (2005)
Above 40
27-40
17-27
7-17
Below 7

Number of Computers per 100 Middle School Students (2005)
30
20
10
0

Number of Computers per 100 Elementary School Students (2005)
25
20
10
0

Source: Ministry of Education and Human Resources Development, National Statistical Office

Jeju Special Self-Governing Province
Ieodo (Ocean Research Station)

Educational Facilities

School Site Size for Each Student (m², 2005)
Above 250
130-250
90-130
43-90
Below 43

Size of School Facilities for Each Student (m², 2005)
30
20
10
0

Playgrounds
School buildings

Source: Ministry of Education and Human Resources Development, National Statistical Office

Jeju Special Self-Governing Province
Ieodo (Ocean Research Station)

0   25   50   100km

Kindergartens

Number of
Kindergartners
per 1,000 People
(2005)

Above 20
15-20
13-15
10-13
Below 10

Number of Teachers
for Each Kindergarten
(2005)

7
6
5
4
3
2
1

Number of Pupils (2005)

100
80
60
40
20
0
Per kindergarten

50
40
30
20
10
0
Per class

Jeju Special Self-Governing Province

Ieodo
(Ocean Research Station)

Source: Ministry of Education and Human Resources Development, National Statistical Office

Elementary Schools

Number of Elementary
School Students per
1,000 People (2005)

Above 100
90-100
80-90
70-80
Below 70

Number of Teachers for
Each Elementary School
(2005)

50
40
30
20
10
0

Number of Elementary School
Students (2005)

1,300
1,200
1,000
800
600
400
200
0
Per school

35
30
20
10
0
Per class

Jeju Special Self-Governing Province

Ieodo
(Ocean Research Station)

Source: Ministry of Education and Human Resources Development, National Statistical Office

Middle Schools

Number of Middle
School Students per
1,000 People (2005)

Above 50
40-50
35-40
30-35
Below 30

Number of Teachers for
Each Middle School
(2005)

55
50
40
30
20
10
0

Number of Middle School
Students (2005)

1,050
1,000
800
600
400
200
0
Per school

40
30
20
10
0
Per class

Jeju Special Self-Governing Province

Ieodo
(Ocean Research Station)

Source: Ministry of Education and Human Resources Development, National Statistical Office

High Schools

Number of High School
Students per 1,000
People (2005)

Above 55
45-55
35-45
25-35
Below 25

Number of Teachers for
Each High School
(2005)

75
60
45
30
15
0

Number of High School
Students (2005)

1,200
900
600
300
0
Per school

35
30
20
10
0
Per class

Jeju Special Self-Governing Province

Ieodo
(Ocean Research Station)

Source: Ministry of Education and Human Resources Development, National Statistical Office

0 25 50   100 km

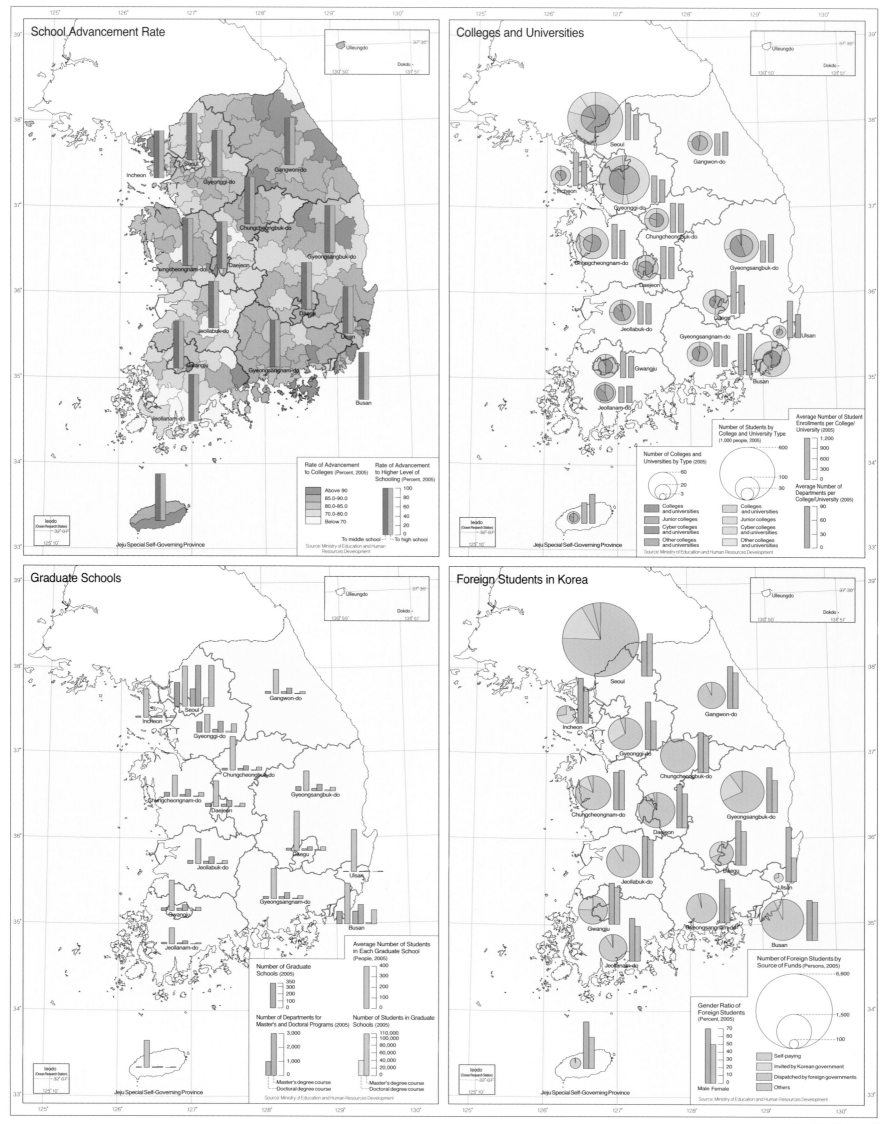

School Advancement Rate

Incheon
Seoul
Gyeonggi-do
Gangwon-do
Chungcheongbuk-do
Chungcheongnam-do
Daejeon
Gyeongsangbuk-do
Jeollabuk-do
Daegu
Ulsan
Gwangju
Gyeongsangnam-do
Jeollanam-do
Busan

Ieodo
(Ocean Research Station)
125° 10′
Jeju Special Self-Governing Province

Ulleungdo
130° 50′
Dokdo
131° 51′
37° 30′

Rate of Advancement
to Colleges (Percent, 2005)

Rate of Advancement
to Higher Level of
Schooling (Percent, 2005)

100
80
60
40
20
0

Above 90
85.0–90.0
80.0–85.0
70.0–80.0
Below 70

To middle school — To high school

Source: Ministry of Education and Human Resources Development

Colleges and Universities

Seoul
Gangwon-do
Incheon
Gyeonggi-do
Chungcheongbuk-do
Chungcheongnam-do
Gyeongsangbuk-do
Daejeon
Jeollabuk-do
Daegu
Gyeongsangnam-do
Ulsan
Gwangju
Busan
Jeollanam-do

Ieodo
(Ocean Research Station)
125° 10′
Jeju Special Self-Governing Province

Ulleungdo
130° 50′
Dokdo
131° 51′
37° 30′

Number of Students by
College and University Type
(1,000 people, 2005)
600
100

Number of Colleges and
Universities by Type (2005)
60
20
3

Average Number of Student
Enrollments per College/
University (2005)
1,200
900
600
300

Average Number of
Departments per
College/University (2005)
90
60
30
0

Colleges
and universities
Cyber colleges
and universities
Other colleges
and universities

Colleges
and universities
Junior colleges
Cyber colleges
and universities
Other colleges
and universities

Source: Ministry of Education and Human Resources Development

Graduate Schools

Seoul
Gangwon-do
Incheon
Gyeonggi-do
Chungcheongbuk-do
Chungcheongnam-do
Gyeongsangbuk-do
Daejeon
Jeollabuk-do
Daegu
Ulsan
Gyeongsangnam-do
Gwangju
Busan
Jeollanam-do

Ieodo
(Ocean Research Station)
125° 10′
Jeju Special Self-Governing Province

Ulleungdo
130° 50′
Dokdo
131° 51′
37° 30′

Average Number of Students
in Each Graduate School
(People, 2005)
400
300
200
100
0

Number of Graduate
Schools (2005)
350
300
250
200
150
100
50
0

Number of Departments for
Master's and Doctoral Programs (2005)
3,000
2,000
1,000

Master's degree course
Doctoral degree course

Number of Students in Graduate
Schools (2005)
110,000
100,000
80,000
60,000
40,000
20,000
0

Master's degree course
Doctoral degree course

Source: Ministry of Education and Human Resources Development

Foreign Students in Korea

Seoul
Gangwon-do
Incheon
Gyeonggi-do
Chungcheongbuk-do
Chungcheongnam-do
Gyeongsangbuk-do
Daejeon
Jeollabuk-do
Daegu
Ulsan
Gwangju
Gyeongsangnam-do
Busan
Jeollanam-do

Ieodo
(Ocean Research Station)
125° 10′
Jeju Special Self-Governing Province

Ulleungdo
130° 50′
Dokdo
131° 51′
37° 30′

Number of Foreign Students by
Source of Funds (Persons, 2005)
6,600
1,500
100

Gender Ratio of
Foreign Students
(Percent, 2005)
70
60
50
40
30
20
10
0
Male Female

Self-paying
Invited by Korean government
Dispatched by foreign governments
Others

Source: Ministry of Education and Human Resources Development

0   25   50   100 km

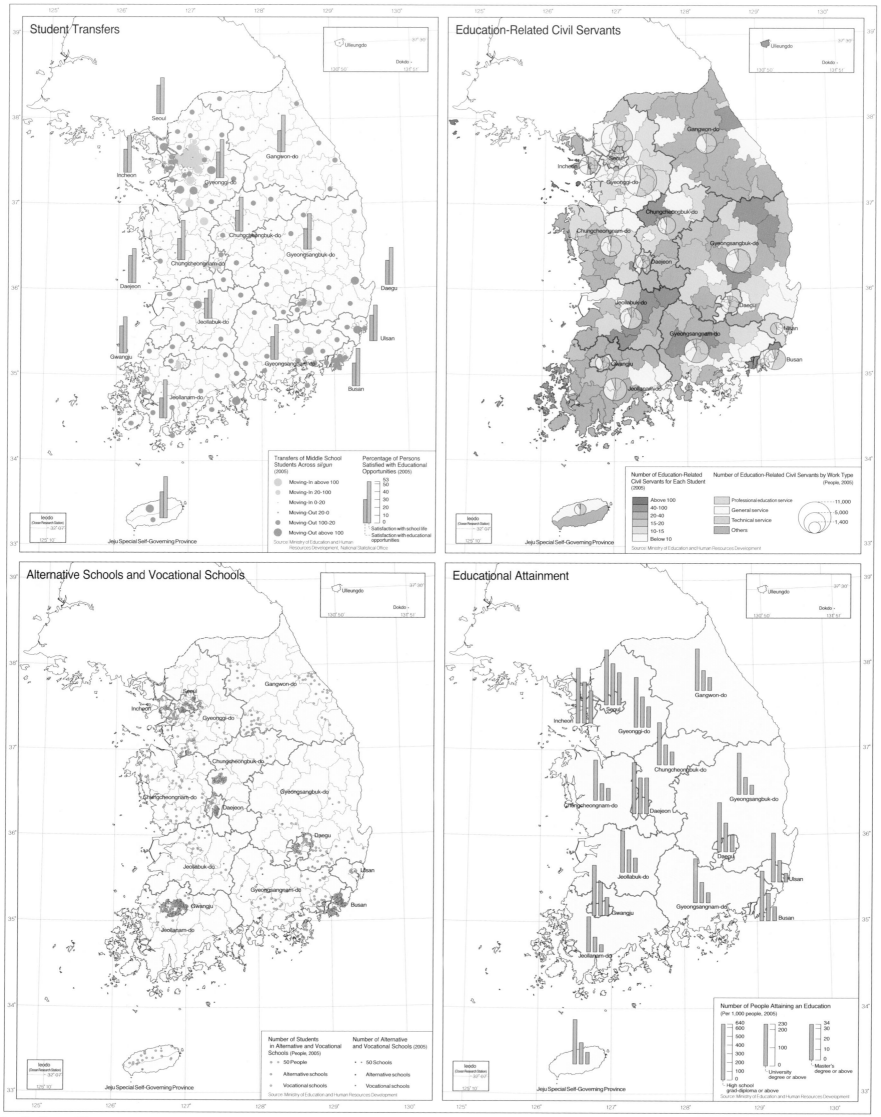

Student Transfers

Transfers of Middle School Students Across *si/gun* (2005)

⚪ Moving-In above 100
⚪ Moving-In 20-100
· Moving-In 0-20
· Moving-Out 20-0
⚫ Moving-Out 100-20
⚫ Moving-Out above 100

Percentage of Persons Satisfied with Educational Opportunities (2005)

53
50
40
30
20
10
0

Satisfaction with school life
Satisfaction with educational opportunities

Source: Ministry of Education and Human Resources Development, National Statistical Office

Education-Related Civil Servants

Number of Education-Related Civil Servants for Each Student (2005)

Above 100
40-100
20-40
15-20
10-15
Below 10

Number of Education-Related Civil Servants by Work Type (People, 2005)

Professional education service
General service
Technical service
Others

11,000
5,000
1,400

Source: Ministry of Education and Human Resources Development

Alternative Schools and Vocational Schools

Number of Students in Alternative and Vocational Schools (People, 2005)

⚬ 50 People
⚫ Alternative schools
⚫ Vocational schools

Number of Alternative and Vocational Schools (2005)

· 50 Schools
· Alternative schools
· Vocational schools

Source: Ministry of Education and Human Resources Development

Educational Attainment

Number of People Attaining an Education (Per 1,000 people, 2005)

640
600
500
400
300
200
100
0

High school grad-diploma or above

230
200

100

University degree or above

34
30
20
10
0

Master's degree or above

Source: Ministry of Education and Human Resources Development

0 25 50   100 km

Korea's Diplomatic Relations

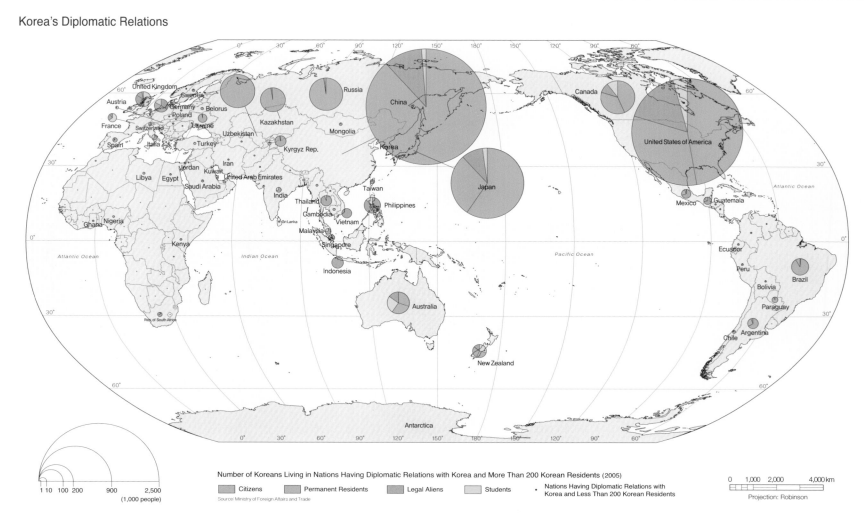

Number of Koreans Living in Nations Having Diplomatic Relations with Korea and More Than 200 Korean Residents (2005)

Citizens	Permanent Residents	Legal Aliens	Students	• Nations Having Diplomatic Relations with Korea and Less Than 200 Korean Residents

Source: Ministry of Foreign Affairs and Trade

1 10 100 200 900 2,500
(1,000 people)

0 1,000 2,000 4,000 km

Projection: Robinson

The maps in this chapter indicate Korea's status within the world from five different points of view.

First, it is important to examine countries which have a diplomatic relationship with Korea, and then also examine Koreans who are currently living in other countries. As of 2005, Korea had diplomatic relationships with 186 countries. In countries like the U.S., Japan and China, where Koreans are living in large numbers, consulates have been established in many locations to assist these people. The living status of Koreans living in foreign countries can be examined by region (see Table 1).

Table 1. Overseas Koreans by Region

(Unit: People)

	2001	2003	2005	Growth Rate (2003-2005)(Percent)
Asia	2,670,723	3,239,904	3,590,411 (54.1%)	10.82
America	2,375,525	2,433,262	2,392,828 (36.1%)	-1.66
Europe	595,073	652,131	640,276 (9.1%)	-1.82
Middle East	7,208	6,559	6,923 (0.1%)	5.55
Africa	5,280	5,095	7,900 (0.1%)	55.05
Total	5,653,809	6,336,951	6,638,338 (100.0%)	4.76

Source: Ministry of Foreign Affairs and Trade (MOFAT), Surveys on Overseas Korean Residents (2005), Ministry of Foreign Affairs and Trade Homepage (MOFAT; http://www.mofat.go.kr).

As of 2005, 54.09 percent of Koreans in foreign countries were living in Asia and 36.5 percent in the U.S. Meanwhile, Europe accounted for 9.65 percent of overseas Koreans, while Africa accounted for just 0.12 percent, and the Middle East only 0.10 percent. The region which has shown the most rapid changes in the Korean population is the African continent; the number of Koreans jumped by 55.05 percent compared to the previous year. In the past, Koreans mostly lived in countries like Japan, China and the U.S., but recently the number of countries in which Koreans have settled down is increasing. This indicates that Koreans are visiting more regions of the world, and that these visits are no longer limited to only a few countries. The Korean population inside the Asian region and the Middle East is showing a gradual and consistent increase. On the other hand, the numbers of Koreans living in the U.S. and Europe are decreasing. The largest group of overseas Koreans are those with foreign residency, followed by persons with foreign citizenship, persons on general visits, and finally, overseas students.

Second, during the 15 years from 1990 to 2005, a variety of changes took place regarding the investment in foreign businesses by Korean companies as well as foreign investment in Korean companies. In 1990, there were 486 cases of foreign companies investing USD 786 million in Korean firms; this climbed to 3,403 cases in 2005, amounting to USD 10.4 billion in investments. This increase was not just limited to the number of cases and amount of investment, but also included an increase in the actual number of countries investing in Korea. In 1990, there were only 23 countries which had invested in Korean businesses, but by 2005 the number had jumped to 56. It is generally believed that the reasons behind such an increase in the total amount of foreign investment in Korean businesses include Korea's successes in developing information technology, well-trained human resources, and the determination of the government to attract foreign investment. Also, Korea is actually quite an attractive location as a potential research and development base, and global corporations which plan to conduct business in the Japanese or Chinese markets are currently considering the Korean market as a test case for their future plans. Yet, although foreign companies have a positive view towards the Korean market, they are also asking the Korean government to dramatically reduce regulations and implement more innovative administrative management, which could considerably improve the environment for future investments. According to certain assessments, while Korea's economy has managed to reach the level of that of an advanced country, customs and regulations hailing from the 'developing country' period still exist, and this potentially prevents foreign companies from freely and actively investing in Korea.

In 1990, Japan (48.1%) and the U.S. (25.9%) accounted for 74 percent of all the investment cases, the largest proportion of foreign companies investing in Korea, in terms of both the total number of cases and the total amount of investment. Other than these two countries, companies from Germany, the United Kingdom, Switzerland, the Netherlands, and France have also been investing in Korea. In 2005, the portion of investment by Japan and the U.S. actually decreased, while investment from China, Pakistan, Nigeria and Mongolia increased. In terms of the total number of investment cases, Japan and the U.S. have dropped since 1995 to 18 percent and 14.6 percent respectively, while China now occupies the top spot at 19.7 percent. In 1990 there was only one case of Chinese investment in Korea, but 2005 saw this number jump to 672. Likewise, investment cases from Germany, the United Kingdom, the Netherlands, France and Russia have also considerably increased.

In 1990, a total of US$ 786 million was invested in Korean businesses, of which 40.4 percent was attributed to the U.S. and 29.9 percent to Japan (these two countries together accounted for 70.3% of the total amount of investment). While Japan's portion was higher than that of the U.S. in terms of the total number of investment cases, the total amount of investment by the U.S. exceeded that of Japan. Germany, the United Kingdom, the Netherlands, France, Switzerland and Singapore invested amounts of over one thousand dollars. In 2005, total investment amounted to USD 10.4 billion, of which 25.8 percent was attributed to the U.S., 22.1 percent to the U.K., 18 percent to Japan, and 11 percent to the Netherlands. These four countries together have invested more than one billion dollars in Korean business. Germany, Singapore and Malaysia have also invested over one hundred million dollars.

Regarding investment by Korean companies into foreign businesses, the number of investment cases jumped from 312 in 1990 to 4,297 in 2005. The total amount of invested funds also increased from USD 945 million in 1990 to USD 6.4 billion in 2005. The number of countries that Korean companies invested money into also jumped from 42 in 1990 to 89 countries in 2005. In 1990, other than the U.S. and Japan, Korean investment was largely limited to Southeast Asian countries such as Indonesia, Malaysia, the Philippines and Thailand. However, investment in Vietnam particularly increased in 2005. Korean companies also started to invest money in countries such as Mongolia, Russia and Cambodia, countries which had not seen any Korean investment in 1990. Compared to the situation in 1990, investment in China, Australia, Japan, Indonesia, India, the Philippines, Singapore, and the U.S. has also significantly increased; China currently accounts for 52.2 percent of Korean overseas investment.

There are several reasons behind such active investment by Korean companies in these particular countries. First, the cost of transportation can be reduced by investing in those countries. Second, by investing in these countries, Korean companies can participate in crucial resource development projects and also secure needed amounts of resources and raw materials. Third, the hiring of low-wage workers in these countries, combined with the easily securable resources and raw materials of the region, mean the price of products can also be considerably lowered. Fourth, Korean companies can develop designs and technology specifically required by the customers in these countries, and therefore increase the volume of sales while simultaneously reducing export costs. Fifth, by investing in these countries companies can also acquire a competitive edge which can help them adapt to changing rival foreign markets. In addition to the above factors, issues like taxes, the environment, governmental regulations, trade barriers, customs, and joint investment usually trigger investments. The decision by companies to build factories in the Southeast Asian region or China concerns the issue of securing raw materials or minimizing labor costs, but if the conditions fit, companies also build factories in advanced countries. Countries that are eager to attract foreign investment usually provide those companies with advantages in taxes, relaxed environmental regulations, and sites for facilities, making such offers very attractive to companies.

Third, the last few decades have seen an increase in the number of foreigners visiting Korea, as well as in the number of Koreans traveling overseas to study. The total number of foreigners who visited Korea for studying amounted to 11,625 in 2001, but jumped almost three-fold to 31,123 by 2006. Foreign students were engaged in a variety of fields of study. In 2001, 6,061 students (52.1%) visited Korea for language studies, 2,861 students (24.6%) came to study in the humanities or social studies fields, and 1,242 students (10.7%) came to study in the natural science or mechanical engineering fields. Additionally, students engaged in miscellaneous studies numbered 1,234 (10.6%), while students involved in artistic or athletic studies and activities numbered 227 (2.0%). However, in 2006, several changes in the number and distribution of foreign students came about. 14,355 (46.1%) students were studying in humanities or social studies, 7,634 (24.5%) students were in language study courses, and 6,022 (19.4%) students were studying natural science or mechanical engineering. Students engaged in miscellaneous studies numbered 1,971 (6.3%), while 1,141 students (3.7%) were engaged in artistic and athletic activities. In 2001, students in language courses occupied the biggest portion of the group, but 2006 saw students studying in the fields of the humanities or social studies occupying the largest portion.

In 2001, 3,565 Japanese students visited Korea, accounting for 30.7 percent of all overseas students visiting Korea. Another huge block of students came from China (3,221, 27.7%), and the U.S. (1,297, 11.2%). The number of students who came from China jumped from 3,211 students in 2001 to 19,160 students in 2006, accounting for 61.6 percent of all foreign students visiting Korea. Japanese students numbered 3,621(11.6%), followed by 1,216 students (3.9%) from the U.S. and 1,179 from Vietnam (3.8%). The increasing number of students from Asian regions is taking place with a corresponding decrease in students from other regions. Recently, 'All Things Korea' has become a prevailing trend in neighboring countries, and this has raised the public's interest in Korean culture. Quite naturally, therefore, the numbers of students from China, Southeast Asia and Central Asia have increased.

Korean students visiting foreign countries for oversea studies totaled 149,938 in 2001, but climbed to 187,436 in 2006, showing an annual 4.6 percent increase. Students who advanced to post-graduate schools accounted for 23.4 percent of the students in 2001, but just 19.3 percent in 2006. Students who entered college accounted for 51 percent of the students in 2001, but by 2006 had dropped to 41.3 percent. On the other hand, language student trainees occupied just 25.6 percent of students studying overseas in 2001, but that number had grown considerably to 40.4 percent by 2006.

In 2001, the number of students (58,457) who went to the U.S. accounted for 39 percent of the entire overseas student group. Students who visited Canada numbered 21,891 (14.6%), China 16,372 (10.9%), Japan 14,925 (10%), and Australia 10,492 (7.0%). In most of these countries, Korean students entered colleges and universities. In the U.S., college students who advanced to graduate schools outnumbered students who did not. In 2006, 57,940 students visited the U.S., amounting for the largest group (30.9%) of Korean students studying overseas. The second largest group consisted of students who visited China (29,102, 15.5%), followed by students in the U.K. (18,845, 10.1%), Australia (16,856, 9.0%), Japan (15,158, 8.1%), and Canada (12,570, 6.7%). Interestingly, although it is a relatively small group, students who visited New Zealand accounted for 73.5 percent of all Korean students enlisted in overseas language courses.

Fourth, the number of Koreans who left the country in 2005 numbered 8,565,560. The vast majority, 57.9 percent, did so for purposes such as religious visits, sightseeing and engagement in artistic activities. 23.4 percent of departees left for foreign countries to attend official functions or to participate in conferences, while 9.9 percent of departees did so to visit acquaintances or to semi-permanently join them. Traveling overseas to engage in research, overseas studies or training, or business opportunities accounted for 5.1 percent of the departees. 3.3 percent of departees were people who had residency status in foreign countries, while 0.3 percent departed for miscellaneous reasons, and 0.08 percent were emigrating. Recently, the foreign exchange rate has dropped, so the number of Koreans leaving the country for sightseeing overseas has naturally increased. The number of departees who visited China was 2,975,466, accounting for 34.7 percent of all departees. Koreans traveling to Japan numbered 1,900,297 (22.2%), while 734,169 Koreans (8.6%) went to the U.S. In addition, major travel destinations included Thailand (664,012, 7.8%), the Philippines (482,928, 5.6%), Vietnam (269,012, 3.1%), Singapore (212,024, 2.5%), Canada (150,536, 1.8%), and the U.K. (117,392, 1.4%). Excluding travelers to the U.S., Canada and the U.K., the majority of the departees went to Southeast Asian countries for sightseeing reasons.

The nature of the 4,776,651 visits by foreigners to Korea can be determined by the type of their visas. Among foreigners who visited Korea, persons who were issued a B-type Visa (Exemption/sightseeing purpose visit) numbered 3,580,037, accounting for 74.9 percent of all visitors. Persons who were issued a C-type Visa (short-term data-collecting, short-term general usage, short-term general visit, short-term employment) accounted for 13.2 percent. Persons who were issued an F-type Visa (visit and joint living, accompaniment, overseas Korean) accounted for 4.4 percent of all visas issued. Persons who were issued a D-type Visa (cultural and artistic visits, overseas studies, industrial training, general training, data-collecting, religious visits, temporary visits, company investment, trades and management) occupied 3.5 percent. Persons who were issued an E-type Visa (professors, foreign language instructor, instruction research, technical consultant, professional employment, art and entertainment, specialized jobs, training and employment) occupied 1.9 percent. Other than these cases, 1.3 percent of foreigners visited Korea for miscellaneous reasons, and of these, 0.7 percent were issued an A-type Visa for diplomatic, and official functions including negotiated agreements. Visitors from Japan numbered 2,421,407 (50.7% of all visitors), followed by 563,351 (11.8%) from China, 385,079 (8.6%) from Taiwan, 381,422 (8.0%) from the U.S., 87,627 (1.8%) from Thailand, and 82,068 (1.7%) from Malaysia. Other than visitors from the U.S., most visitors were Asians from Japan and China who wished to visit Korea for sightseeing purposes because of the aforementioned 'All Things Korean' trend.

Fifth, as of May 1st, 2006, the total number of foreigners who are currently living in Korea numbered 524,345. Among these foreigners, foreign labor workers numbered 251,729, or 48 percent of all foreign residents. Next, there are 90,489 (17.3%) immigrants who came to Korea as a result of international marriages. A total of 38,371 foreigners (7.3%) acquired Korean nationality. According to a survey conducted by the Autonomous Administration Team of the Ministry of Government Administration and Home Affairs (May 2006), 57 percent of foreign residents are male. In the case of foreign workers, 67 percent of them are male, and in case of international marriage-related residents, 84.9 percent are female. Among foreign residents, persons with Chinese nationality account for 46.1 percent of all foreign residents in Korea, while persons with Southeast Asian nationalities account for 23 percent; this is followed by southern Asian (6.3%), American (4.8%), Taiwanese (4.0%), Japanese (3.6%), Mongolian (2.8%), Central Asian (2.4%), and Russian (0.7%). Joseonjok (ethnic Koreans with Chinese nationality) account for 31.7 percent of people with Chinese nationality residing in Korea. These ethnic Korean Chinese ('Joseonjok') account for 55 percent of the foreign resident group of people who acquired Korean nationality, and 41.2 percent of people who came to Korea as a result of an international marriage.

Among foreign workers, workers from Southeast Asia occupy 29.8 percent of the entire group, followed by 'Joseonjok'(28.7%), Chinese workers (14.2%), Southeast Asian workers (8.1%), and Mongolian workers (4.0%). Workers from Southeast Asian regions occupy the biggest portion. Among Southeast Asian workers, 67 percent of them are male. In the case of the ethnic Korean Chinese ('Joseonjok', 51.1 percent are female. The majority of foreigners who came to Korea as a result of international marriages are female and break down by nationality as follows: 'Joseonjok'(42.1), Chinese (20.7), Southeast Asians (18.3), Japanese (8.3), and Southern Asians (1.4). Among these, 55 percent of the ethnic Korean Chinese ('Joseonjok'), 24.7 percent of the Chinese, and 10.6 percent of the Southeast Asians acquired Korean nationality. The majority of international marriages were to people who held Chinese nationality, while foreigners of U.S., Japanese and Taiwanese nationality occupied only 12.4 percent of the entire group. 63.5 percent of foreigners are currently living in areas nearby the capital, such as Seoul, Gyeonggi-*do* and Incheon. Among those regions, Gyeonggi-*do* shows the highest concentration (32.2%), followed by Seoul (148,966, 24.8%), Incheon (33,960, 6.5%), Gyeongsangnam-*do* (28,261, 5.4%), and Gyeongsangbuk-*do* (24,568, 4.7%). 121,518 foreign workers, 48.3 percent of all foreign workers, currently live in the Gyeonggi area. Of those foreign workers, 40,025 (15.9%) live in Seoul, 17,822 (7.1%) live in Incheon, 15,968 (6.3%) in Gyeongsangnam-*do*, 10,456 (4.2%) in Gyeongsangbuk-*do*, and 10,020 (4.0%) in Chungcheongbuk-*do*. In the case of persons who came to Korea as a result of international marriages, 22,331 of them are living in Gyeonggi-do (24.7%), followed by 19,848 (21.9%) in Seoul, 6,869 (7.6%) in Jeollanam-*do*, 6,647 (7.3%) in Incheon, and 5,111 (5.6%) in Gyeongsangnam-*do*. Compared to the capital and adjacent areas, there is a greater concentration in areas where the agricultural population is relatively larger, such as Gangwon-*do* or Jeollanam-*do*.

If we examine foreigners living in cities, or *gun* and *gu* units, eight of those units show more than ten thousand foreign residents, 25 units show between five and ten thousand residents, and 88 units show between one thousand and five thousand foreign residents. 51 percent of all local units show more than one thousand foreigners living inside the unit, while 29 percent of the units record less than 500 foreigners living there. Areas with more than ten thousand foreigners include Ansan-*si*, Gyeonggi-*do* (20,559 people), Hwaseong-*si*, Gyeonggi-*do* (14,970), Yongsan-*gu*, (14,803), Yeongdeungpo-*gu* (14,390), Guro-*gu* (13,499), in Seoul, Siheung-*si* (11,829), Suwon-*si* (11,479), and Seongnam-*si* (10,113) in Gyeonggi-*do*. Areas with less than one hundred foreigners include Gyeongsangbuk-*do*'s Ulleung-*gun* (4), Gyeongsangbuk-*do*'s Yeongyang-*gun* (56), Jeollanam-*do*'s Sinan-*gun* (70), Gyeongsangnam-*do*'s Hadong-*gun* (75), and Chungcheong nam-*do*'s Gyeryong-*si* (93).

From the above figures, we can conclude that the status of Korea in the 21st century looks better than ever. Capital resources, human resources and physical materials are being exchanged between countries in a more active and faster fashion than ever before. As Korea's role in these transactions grows, so will its status. The Korean society is entering a multi-cultural era, and being continually exposed to new ways of living, including ones from foreign countries. In the process, 'their ways of living' and 'their own culture' have also become 'Korean ways of living' and also 'part of Korea's culture.' As a result, the cultural environment of the Korean community has changed. In order to elevate Korea's status within the world, it is important to make sure that the country has competitive power with a sound human resource infrastructure. To do this, it is imperative that Korea's status in the versatile nature of world culture continue to evolve, and that Koreans have an open mind when interacting with other people. Korea is no longer a country of hermits, but should, in fact, continually share its rich culture and heritage with Asia and the entire world. Indeed, Koreans are, not only part of the Asian community, but also part of the global village.

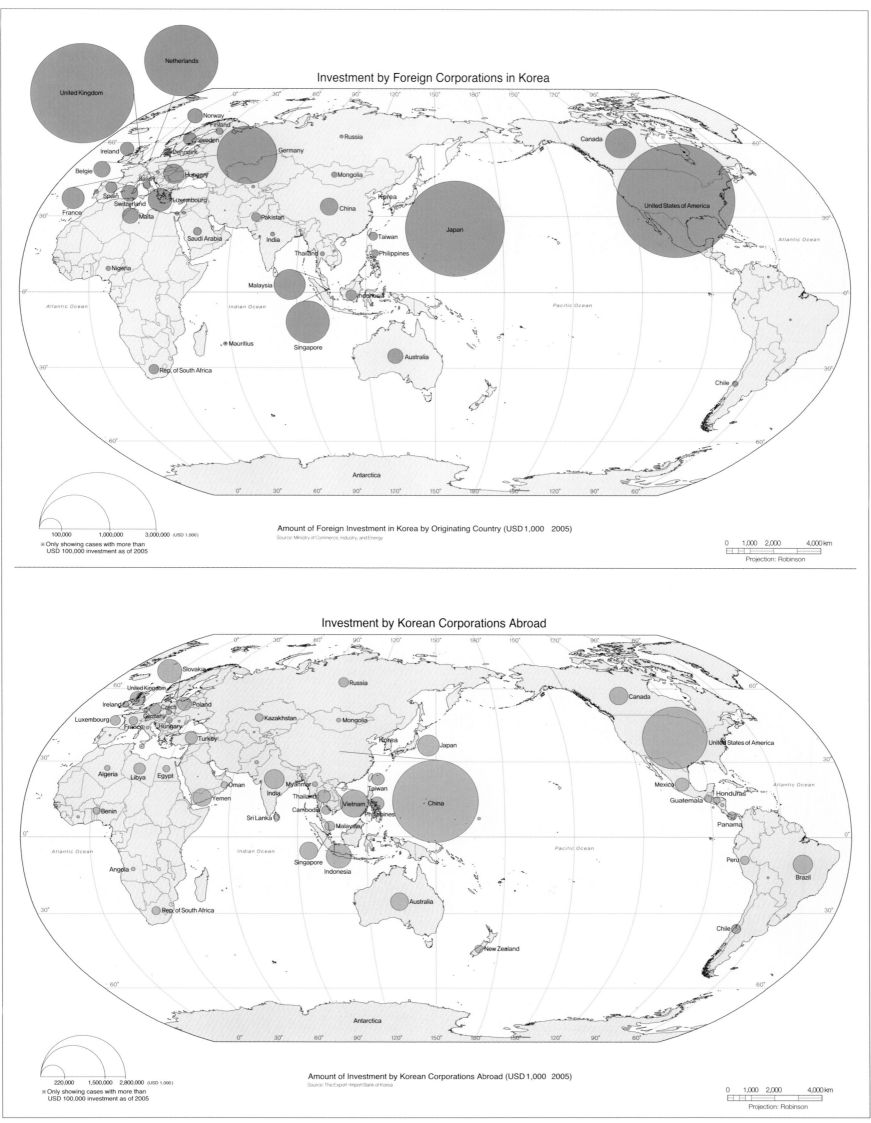

Investment by Foreign Corporations in Korea

Netherlands
United Kingdom
Norway
Finland
Sweden
Ireland
Denmark
Belgie
Italie
Hungary
Germany
Russia
Canada
Spain
Luxembourg
Switzerland
Mongolia
Korea
France
Malta
Pakistan
China
United States of America
Saudi Arabia
India
Taiwan
Japan
Thailand
Philippines
Nigeria
Atlantic Ocean
Malaysia
Indonesia
Mauritius
Singapore
Pacific Ocean
Australia
Rep. of South Africa
Chile
Indian Ocean
Antarctica

100,000   1,000,000   3,000,000 (USD 1,000)

※ Only showing cases with more than
USD 100,000 investment as of 2005

Amount of Foreign Investment in Korea by Originating Country (USD 1,000 2005)
Source: Ministry of Commerce, Industry, and Energy

0   1,000 2,000   4,000 km

Projection: Robinson

Investment by Korean Corporations Abroad

Slovakia
United Kingdom
Czech
Poland
Ireland
Germany
Luxembourg
Hungary
France
Russia
Canada
Kazakhstan
Turkey
Mongolia
Korea
Japan
United States of America
Algeria
Libya
Egypt
Oman
Myanmar
Taiwan
China
Mexico
Honduras
India
Thailand
Yemen
Vietnam
Guatemala
Cambodia
Philippines
Sri Lanka
Malaysia
Panama
Benin
Singapore
Indonesia
Peru
Atlantic Ocean
Pacific Ocean
Brazil
Angola
Rep. of South Africa
Australia
Chile
New Zealand
Antarctica

220,000   1,500,000   2,800,000 (USD 1,000)

※ Only showing cases with more than
USD 100,000 investment as of 2005

Amount of Investment by Korean Corporations Abroad (USD 1,000 2005)
Source: The Export-Import Bank of Korea

0   1,000 2,000   4,000 km

Projection: Robinson

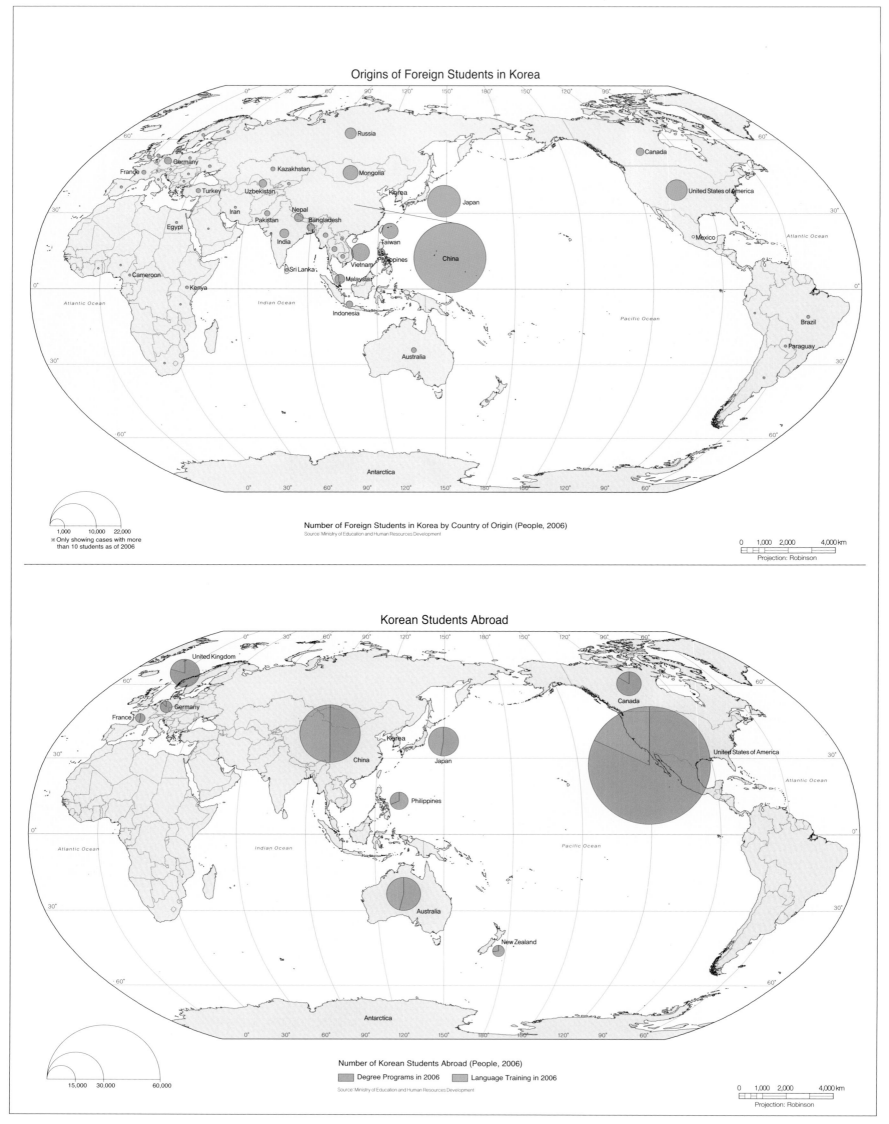

Origins of Foreign Students in Korea

Russia
Germany
France
Turkey
Kazakhstan
Mongolia
Uzbekistan
Korea
Iran
Nepal
Pakistan
Bangladesh
Egypt
India
Taiwan
Sri Lanka
Vietnam
Philippines
China
Japan
Malaysia
Indonesia
Cameroon
Kenya
Canada
United States of America
Mexico
Brazil
Paraguay
Australia
Antarctica

Atlantic Ocean
Indian Ocean
Atlantic Ocean
Pacific Ocean

1,000   10,000   22,000
※ Only showing cases with more
than 10 students as of 2006

Number of Foreign Students in Korea by Country of Origin (People, 2006)
Source: Ministry of Education and Human Resources Development

0   1,000   2,000   4,000 km
Projection: Robinson

Korean Students Abroad

United Kingdom
Germany
France
China
Korea
Japan
Canada
United States of America
Philippines
Australia
New Zealand
Antarctica

Atlantic Ocean
Indian Ocean
Pacific Ocean
Atlantic Ocean

15,000   30,000   60,000

Number of Korean Students Abroad (People, 2006)
■ Degree Programs in 2006   ■ Language Training in 2006
Source: Ministry of Education and Human Resources Development

0   1,000   2,000   4,000 km
Projection: Robinson

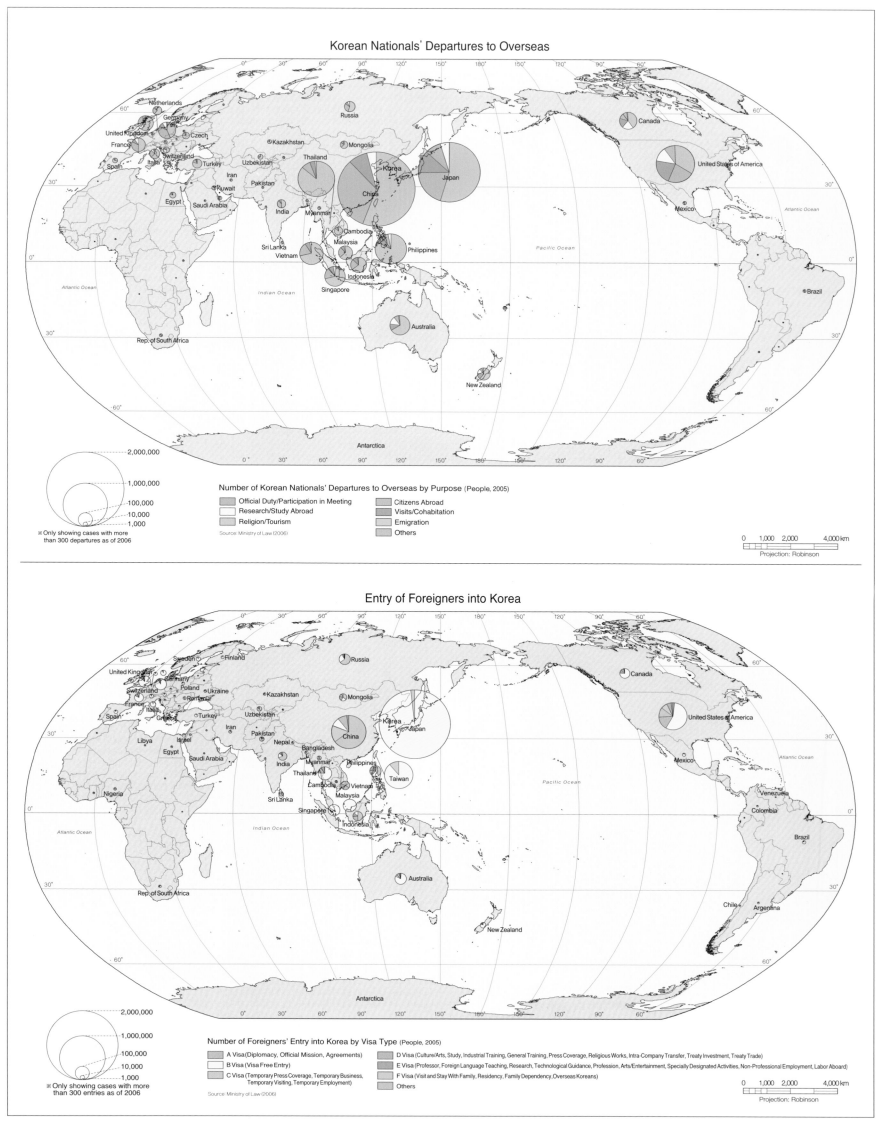

Korean Nationals' Departures to Overseas

Number of Korean Nationals' Departures to Overseas by Purpose (People, 2005)

- Official Duty/Participation in Meeting
- Research/Study Abroad
- Religion/Tourism
- Citizens Abroad
- Visits/Cohabitation
- Emigration
- Others

Source: Ministry of Law (2006)

2,000,000
1,000,000
100,000
10,000
1,000

※ Only showing cases with more than 300 departures as of 2006

0 1,000 2,000 4,000 km

Projection: Robinson

Entry of Foreigners into Korea

Number of Foreigners' Entry into Korea by Visa Type (People, 2005)

- A Visa (Diplomacy, Official Mission, Agreements)
- B Visa (Visa Free Entry)
- C Visa (Temporary Press Coverage, Temporary Business, Temporary Visiting, Temporary Employment)
- D Visa (Culture/Arts, Study, Industrial Training, General Training, Press Coverage, Religious Works, Intra-Company Transfer, Treaty Investment, Treaty Trade)
- E Visa (Professor, Foreign Language Teaching, Research, Technological Guidance, Profession, Arts/Entertainment, Specially Designated Activities, Non-Professional Employment, Labor Aboard)
- F Visa (Visit and Stay With Family, Residency, Family Dependency, Overseas Koreans)
- Others

Source: Ministry of Law (2006)

2,000,000
1,000,000
100,000
10,000
1,000

※ Only showing cases with more than 300 entries as of 2006

0 1,000 2,000 4,000 km

Projection: Robinson

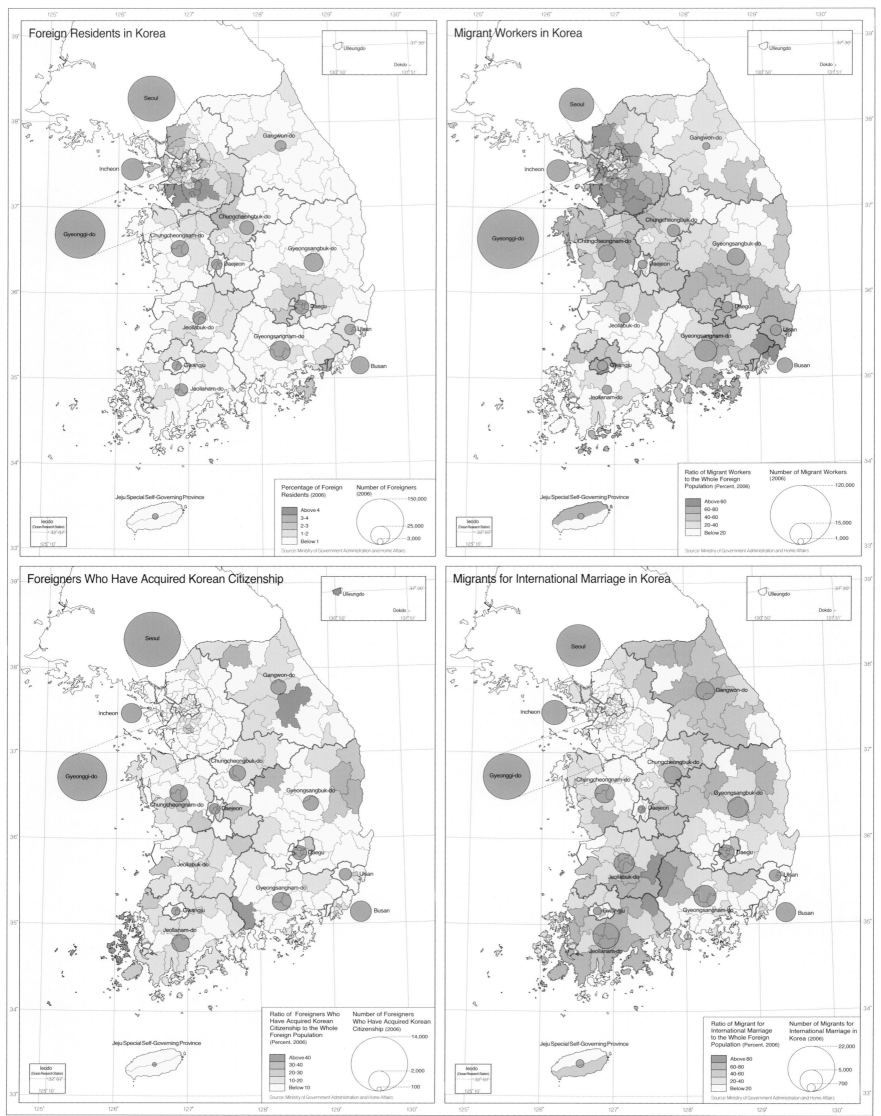

Foreign Residents in Korea

Percentage of Foreign Residents (2006)
- Above 4
- 3-4
- 2-3
- 1-2
- Below 1

Number of Foreigners (2006)
- 150,000
- 25,000
- 3,000

Jeju Special Self-Governing Province

Source: Ministry of Government Administration and Home Affairs

Migrant Workers in Korea

Ratio of Migrant Workers to the Whole Foreign Population (Percent, 2006)
- Above 60
- 60-80
- 40-60
- 20-40
- Below 20

Number of Migrant Workers (2006)
- 120,000
- 15,000
- 1,000

Jeju Special Self-Governing Province

Source: Ministry of Government Administration and Home Affairs

Foreigners Who Have Acquired Korean Citizenship

Ratio of Foreigners Who Have Acquired Korean Citizenship to the Whole Foreign Population (Percent, 2006)
- Above 40
- 30-40
- 20-30
- 10-20
- Below 10

Number of Foreigners Who Have Acquired Korean Citizenship (2006)
- 14,000
- 2,000
- 100

Jeju Special Self-Governing Province

Source: Ministry of Government Administration and Home Affairs

Migrants for International Marriage in Korea

Ratio of Migrant for International Marriage to the Whole Foreign Population (Percent, 2006)
- Above 80
- 60-80
- 40-60
- 20-40
- Below 20

Number of Migrants for International Marriage in Korea (2006)
- 22,000
- 5,000
- 700

Jeju Special Self-Governing Province

Source: Ministry of Government Administration and Home Affairs

0 25 50 100 km

167

National Land and Territory

Image of Korea [2, 3]
This image, which includes Korea and the surrounding countries, was created by pGEOS Ltd., merging and processing the Arirang satellite images from Korea and the Landsat satellite images from the USA.
Source: pGEOS Ltd.

Map of Korea [4]
Source: National Geographic Information Institute, 2006, 1:1,000,000.

Korea and Surrounding Countries [5-1]
Source: National Geographic Information Institute, 2006, 1:3,000,000.

Dokdo [5-2]
Source: National Geographic Information Institute, 1:5,000.

Index Map [6]

Landforms

Topography [38]
Mountain ranges (sanmaek) in Korea are divided into two categories based on their formation. The formation of primary mountain ranges is closely related to tectonic movement, while the secondary mountain ranges have been formed by erosion processes. The mountain ranges belonging to the primary are the Taebaeksanmaek, Nangnimsanmaek, Hamgyeongsanmaek, and Sobaeksanmaek. These mountain ranges have been formed by the asymmetrical uplift and faults during the Cenozoic Era. On the other hand, the secondary mountain ranges were formed by differential erosion processes. The primary mountain ranges are well-defined since they lie along the uplift axes, but the secondary mountain ranges are low and less prominent.

The horizontal profile of the central part of Korea shows that the eastern side of the Taebaeksanmaek is narrow with steep relief, while the western side of the mountain ranges is wide with gentle relief. This overall landform shape is widely believed to have been formed by asymmetrical tectonic movement centered along the Taebaeksanmaek. This tectonic uplift might have begun at the middle of Cenozoic Era after long planation processes during the Mesozoic Era. There are some high altitude (800-1,000m) plateaus located at Gaemagowon and Taebaeksanmaek. These high altitude plateaus are characteristic landforms in northern region of Korea. Baekdugowon, Gaemagowon, Nangnimgowon, Bujeongowon, and Jangjingowon are the names of these representative features.
Elevation data Source: National Imagery and Mapping Agency, U.S. Department of Defense.

Important Landform Areas and Natural Heritage Landforms [40]
Some important landforms are registered and preserved as 'Natural Heritage' in Korea. This map shows the location of such landforms protected by the Korean government. Some selected landforms are visualized to give insights into the geomorphological characteristics of Korea.

① Baekdusan and Lava Plateau
The Baekdusan lava plateau is the widest volcanic landform in Korea, and Baekdusan is a volcanic cone that erupted onto this plateau. The mean elevation of the plateau is about 1,600m, and the peak of Baekdusan is 2,744m tall. The overall shape was formed during the Tertiary in the Cenozoic Era, while the main volcanic cone was formed during the Pleistocene.

② Gilju-Myeongcheon Graben
The most typical graben in Korea lies between Gaemagowon and Chilbosan. The present form was first initiated by fault movement during the Pleistocene, and followed by volcanic eruption. The Chilbosan (1,103m) is raised from the Chilbosan horst which is located at the eastern end of the graben.

③ Chugaryeong Tectonic Valley
This lineament divides the Korean Peninsula into its southern and northern parts. It was formed partially by faulting, but more complex geological processes were also involved, including tectonic and orogenic movement during the Paleozoic and Mesozoic Eras.

④ Punch Bowl (Erosion Basin) in Yanggu-*gun*, Gangwon-*do*
The typical erosion basin in Korea resembles a bowl with only one drainage outlet. The lower part of the basin is granite stock that was easily weathered and eroded, while more resistant metamorphic rocks form the outer rim.

⑤ Ulleungdo
This island is a part of a seamount that is located at 2,200 meters above the ocean floor. The peak of this island is called Seonginbong (984m). The elevation difference between Seonginbong and the base of the seamount is more than 3,000m. Bedrocks forming the island are trachytes, tuffs, and conglomerates.

⑥ Dokdo
Dokdo Island is the tip of undersea volcano complex rising 1,900m above sea floor. It consists of about 80 islands and rocks around two main islands: East Island and West Island. The bedrock consists of volcanic breccia, trachytes, tuffs, and conglomerates.

⑦ Yangsan Fault
The Yangsan fault is the most recent fault in Korea. It runs about 200km starting from Younghae in Yeongdeok-*gun*, passing through Sinkwang-Gyeongju-Eonyang-Yangsan, and ending in the estuary of Nakdonggang.

⑧ Jirisan
Jirisan is a well-known mountain in Korea. This mountain is located at the end of Sobaeksanmaek which has been formed by complex interactions between tectonic uplift and geological difference.

⑨ Dadohae (Many Islands Sea)
The southern and southwestern coasts are widely known for their complex coastal lines and many islands. These complex coastal lines were formed when the eroded surface was submerged by rising sea level.

⑩ Jejudo
Jejudo is the most representative volcanic island in Korea. Significant volcanic eruptions started at the end of the Pliocene. There are many volcanic landforms around a shield volcano (Hallasan) at the center of the island.
Source: Cultural Heritage Administration, Natural Monuments in South and North Korea (http://nature.cha.go.kr).

Slope Angle [41-1]
The slope controls the flow of water on the surface, and is one of the important parameters to determine land uses. Slope was calculated from 20-meter grids of DEM data. The average slope of the Korean Peninsula and its standard deviation are 11.9° and 8.9°, respectively. The figure below illustrates regional average elevation and slope in Korea. The metropolitan area in the west coast shows lower average slope: Jejudo (4.1°), Nampo (4.4°), Seoul (4.4°), Incheon (5.2°), and Gwangju (5.6°). The eastern mountainous area shows steeper slope: Jagang-*do* (16.9°), Gangwon-*do* (15.7°), Hamgyeongnam-*do* (14.8°), and Gyeongsangnam-*do* (12.8°). Significant correlations are found between average elevation and slope. The steepest slope, however, often occurs at the regions of elevations between 500 and 1,000m. Despite higher average elevation of 1,332m, Yanggang-*do*, located in the Gaemagowon, has relatively lower slope (12.3°). Although Korea is mountainous and hilly, slopes are usually gentle and landslide susceptibility is relatively low.

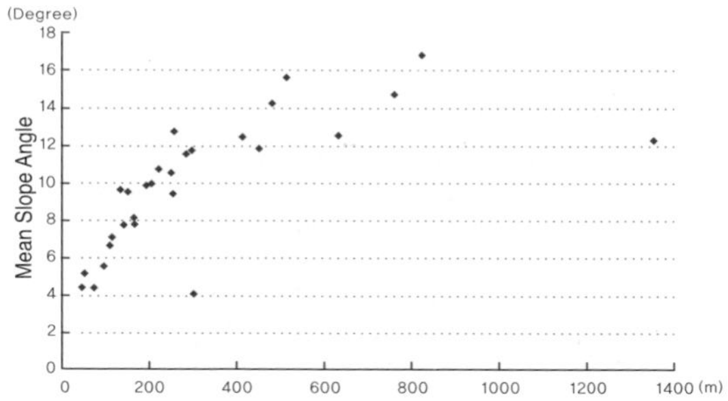

Figure. Relationship between Average Elevation and Average Slope Angle, calculated for Individual Administrative Regions

Relief Energy [41-2]
Relief energy is one of the surface characteristics, and is calculated by the difference in elevation between the highest and lowest points of a defined land surface. Relief energy at a grid resolution of 1km presented on this map was calculated from 20-meter grids of DEM data. The average and standard deviation of relief energy per square kilometer are 335.2m and 438.4m, respectively. Linear relationship between relief energy and elevation is observed.

Lower relief energy values are found at the metropolitan area in the west coast: the volcanic island of Jejudo (44.2m), Seoul (89.0m), Nampo (89.6m), Incheon (109.1m), and Gwangju (121.1m). Higher values of relief energy are found in the eastern mountainous area: Gangwon-*do* (544.2m), Gyeonggi-*do* (489.2m), Jagang-*do* (471.8m), and Hamgyeongnam-*do* (424.8m). However, despite its higher average elevation, relatively lower relief energy values are found at high mountainous regions. Especially, Yanggang-*do*, located in the Gaemagowon, shows low relief energy.

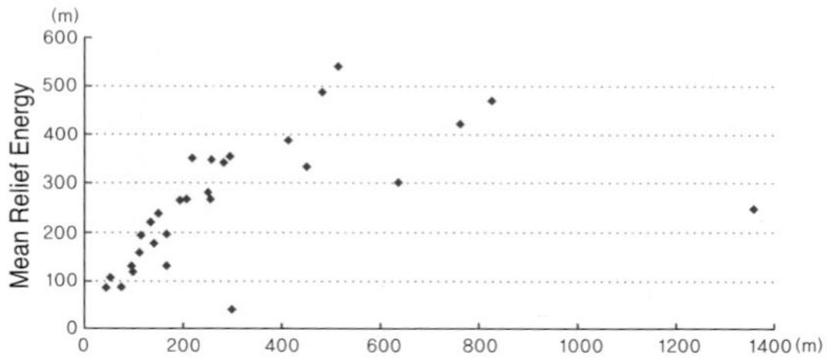

Figure. Relationship between Average Relief Energy and Average Slope Angle, calculated for Individual Administrative Regions

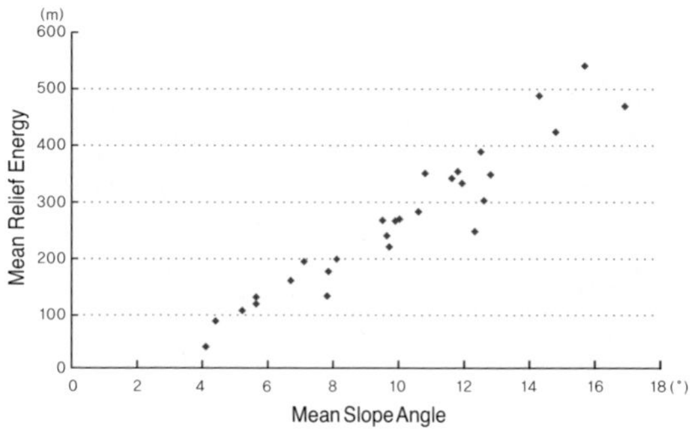

Figure. Relationship between Average Relief Energy and Average Elevation, calculated for Individual Administrative Regions

National Parks and Wetland Protection Areas [41-3]
Since the designation of the Jirisan National Park in 1967, nineteen other areas have been designated as national parks: fifteen national mountain parks, four national maritime or coastal parks, and one national historical park that preserves Korean cultural heritage. National parks cover about 6.6 percent of South Korea with 3,899km² of land, and 2,681km² of maritime and coastal area. The Korea National Parks Authority mapped these twenty national parks in Korea. The map shows the areal extent and other geographical information of these parks.

Korea has been known to have one of the most well-developed tidal flats in the world. In fact, five wetlands in Korea are listed as RAMSAR sites: four inland wetlands and one coastal wetland. The compilation of distribution maps of tidal flats is essential in order to understand the marine environments. The map of protected wetlands was created based on the data from the Ministry of Maritime Affairs and Fisheries. The discrepancy between tidal flat maps and topographic maps is observed since the tidal flat maps are created at low tide, and both maps use a different category.

According to the wetland protection law, wetlands in Korea can be divided into inland wetlands and coastal wetlands. Natural wetlands and lakes are limited in the Korean Peninsula, since tectonic events are rare and there was no glacial activity. Wetlands are also small and scattered. Lagoons often occur along the seashore of the East Sea, and back marshes (back swamps) are common along the midstream of Nakdonggang. The inland wetlands can be divided into river mouth estuaries, river wetlands, floodplains, mountain wetlands, lagoons, paddy field, artificial reservoirs, and natural lakes. Rice paddy fields cover the largest area among different types of wetlands, but their ecological functions are quite limited. Knowledge about ecological functions of other wetland types is still developing.
Source: Ministry of Environment, National Parks Authority, 2006.

Tidal Flats [41-4]
Tidal flats around Korea's southwestern coast account for about 2.5 percent of the territory, but they account for 83 percent of the total area of Korean tidal flats (1,980km²). The tidal flats in Gyeonggi-*do* and Incheon account for 36 percent, and Chungcheongnam-*do*, Jeollabuk-*do*, and Jeollanam-*do* account for 14, 5, and 40 percent, respectively. The tidal flats in Gyeongsangnam-*do*, Busan and Jejudo account for 5 percent. Six seashores in Muan, Jindo, Suncheonman, and three other districts were designated as Tidal Flat Wetland Protection Areas. Sinduri coastal dune, Mundo, Oryukdo and its surrounding environment, and Daeijakdo were designated as Natural Reservation Areas.
Source: Ministry of Maritime Affairs and Fisheries, 2006, unpublished data.

[References]

Koo, B.H. and Kim, G.G., 2001, Classifying and Identifying the Characteristics of Wetlands in Korea: Cases on the Inland Wetlands, *Journal of Korean Society for Environmental Restoration and Revegetation Technology*, 4 (2), 11-25.
National Park Authority, 1997, *Thirty Years History of Korean National Parks*, Seoul: National Park Authority.
Kwon, D.H., 2006, *Geomorphology of Korea*, Seoul : Hanwul Academy.
Kwon, D.H. and Park, H.D., 1993, *Soil Geography*, Seoul: Gyohaksa.
Kwon, S.S., 2005, *Geomorphology of Mass Movements*, Seoul: Darakbang.
Kwon, H.J., 1996, *Korean Geography*, Seoul: Beopmunsa.
Kwon, H.J., 1999, *Geomorphology*, Seoul: Beopmunsa.
Lautensach, H. (translated by Dege, E. and Dege, F.),1988, *Korea: A Geography Nased on the Author's Travels and Literature*, Berlin: Springer-Verlag.
Kim, J.H., 2002, *Geomorphology*, Seoul: Donggeuk University Press.
Park, Y.A. and Kong, W.S., 2001, *Quaternary Environment of Korea*, Seoul: Seoul National University Press.
Pusan Geographical Research Institute (*ed.*), 2006, *Coastal Landforms of Korea*, Pusan: Pusan University Press.
Seo, M.S., 1996, *Karst Landforms in Korea*, Seoul: Segyeojaryosa.
Jang, J.H., 2002, *Granite Erosion Landforms of Korea*, Seoul: Seongshin Woman's University Press.
Cho, H.R., 1987, *Alluvial Plains in Korea*, Seoul: Kyohaksa.
Physical Geography Research Group of Korea, 2003, *Natural Environment and Human*, Seoul: Hanwul.
Geographical Information Research Group of Korea, 2004, *Dictionary of Physical Geography*, Seoul: Hanwul.
Kwon, H.J., 2002, Mountain Range of Korea, *Journal of the Korean Geographical Society*, 35 (3), 389-400.
Kim, N.S. and Lee, M.B., 2004, Landform Classification Using Geomorphometic Analysis, *Journal of the Korean Geomorphological Association*, 11(4), 47-60.
Kim, S.H., 1980, An Introductory Study on the Genesis and Development of the Landform, *Journal of the Korean Geographical Society*, 5, 1-15.
Park, N.S., 1971, Physiographic Provinces of Korea, *Geography*, 6, 1-24.
Park, D.W., 1983, Problems and Future of Geomorphological Studies in Korean, *Journal of Geography*, 10, 27-40.
Park, S.J., 1993, Hydrochemical Research on Characteristics of Chemical Weathering in a Granite Catchment, *Geography*, 28 (1), 1-15.
Park, S.J. and Son, I., 2005, Discussions on the Distribution and Genesis of Mountain Ranges in the Korean Peninsula (I): The Identification of Mountain Ranges using a DEM and Reconsideration of Current Issue on Mountain Range Maps, *Journal of the Korean Geographical Society*, 40 (1), 126-152.
Oh, K.S., 1996, Reflection and Perspective of Geomorphology in Korea, *Journal of the Korean Geographical Society*, 32 (1), 106-127.

Geology

Geologic Map [42]
The geologic map is a special purpose map showing surface and subsurface geological features. It is usually superimposed over a topographic map with major geologic structures, exposed characteristics and ages of rocks. It usually includes a geologic cross-section or a columnar section, depending on the specific purpose. The geologic cross-section is a vertical representation of the subsurface geological features extrapolated using geologic data, often supplemented by coring and geophysical data. The columnar section is also a vertical representation which includes stratigraphy, thickness, fossils, etc. It can also be used to correlate regional stratigraphy in an areal extent. The geologic map has a variety of applications: exploration of natural resources such as coal, presentation of fundamental geologic information for construction, prevention of natural disasters such as landslides, and the basis for mapping soil distribution.

The first geologic map of Korea, scaled at 1:4,000,000, appeared in the book, *Geologische Skizze von Korea* written by the German geologist, Gottsche, in 1886. Since then, geological surveys of Korea have been conducted by the Geological Survey of Korea, founded in 1918. In 1928, the *Geological and Mineral Resources Map of Korea* with a scale of 1:1,000,000 was published and later revised in 1941. Four geologic maps with a scale of 1:200,000 were also published in the period of 1940 and 1945.

The 1:50,000 scaled *Geology of Coalfields in Korea* was issued by the Institute of Fuel and Ore Dressing, established in 1912. In 1946, after the Second World War, the Geological Survey and the Institute of Fuel and Ore Dressing were combined into the Central Geological and Mining Research Institute. This institute was later reorganized as the Central Geological and Mineralogical Research Institute (1949), the Geological Survey of Korea (1961), the Geological and Mineral Institute of Korea (1973), the Korea Research Institute of Geoscience and Mineral Resources (1976), the Korea Institute of Energy and Resources (1981), the Korea Institute of Geology, Mining, and Materials (1991), and finally the Korea Institute of Geoscience and Mineral Resources (2001 to present). Until now, a total of 243 quadrangles with a scale of 1:50,000, covering an areal extent of about 87 percent of South Korea, have been published, including 17 sheets of *Geological Atlas of the Taebaek Mountain Region* published in 1962 used for the exploration of coal, limestone and other natural resources. In 1973, the first set of 1:250,000 scaled geologic maps covering the entire area of South Korea were published, and were revised in the period of 1995 and 2003. In 1981 and 1995, the 1:100,000 scaled Geological Map of Korea was issued by the Korea Institute of Energy and Resources, and the Korea Institute of Geology, Mining, and Materials, respectively.

The Korea Institute of Geology, Mining and Materials published *the Geologic Map of Korea* with a scale of 1:1,000,000 in 1995. The map includes general subsurface geological features and major structural characteristics of the whole Korean Peninsula. It also includes a legend summarizing all the lithostratigraphic units and their geological ages. This map has been simplified by correlating the detailed lithostratigraphic units of 1:50,000 scaled quadrangles to much larger groups, based on large geologic time scales. It is thus widely used for international as well as domestic purposes to understand the general features of Korean geology.

The map of tectonic regions shows tectonic divisions of the Korean Peninsula as large litho-scale masses bounded by significantly large-scale geologic structures. The map shows the structural and lithological characteristics of each tectonic body. In addition, it reveals the origin, evolution, and interrelationship of those litho-scale masses. Some natural phenomena such as volcanic activities or earthquakes are closely related to the dynamics of tectonic segments of the earth's crust. Tectonic segments are large litho-scale masses bounded by big structural breaks. The Korean Peninsula is located at the eastern margin of the Eurasian continent, near the Pacific and Philippine Sea Plates, with the Japanese arc located along the subduction zone. The east-west trending Qinling-Dabie-Sulu collision belt across the Chinese continent extends to the mid-western end of the Korean Peninsula.

Source: Korea Institute of Geology, Mining and Materials,
1995, Geological Map of Korea (1:1,000,000 scale).
Korea Institute of Geoscience and Mineral Resources, 2001,
Tectonic Map of Korea (1:1,000,000 scale).

Gravity Anomaly [44-1]

Gravity survey is based on measuring perturbations in the gravitational field. The gravity anomaly map reflects the spatial distribution of the different density of the earth masses. This map gives information on density and geometric structure of the subsurface geology. The map is generally taken advantages of the implications of tectonic and crustal structure, explorations of natural resources such as oil and mineral deposits, and groundwater.

A gravity anomaly map is made through three main processes: (1) measurements of gravity field at even array of points (one point typically for 4 km×4 km), (2) data correction for the reference station and reduced for earth-tide, free-air, Bouguer, and terrain effects, (3) data compilation and plot represented by the contour lines and color spectra. As a color goes from blue to red, positive gravity anomaly gradually increases. The anomaly may be positive or negative for high or low density mass, respectively. For example, Sobaeksanmaek (Sobaek Mountain Range), south central region of Korea, showing a NE-SW directional trend of negative anomaly in the middle part, can be interpreted as the granitic rocks of low density extend deep into the high density basaltic rocks underneath. A northsouth directional strong positive anomaly can be also interpreted as high density igneous rocks dominate rather than low density sedimentary rocks.

Source: Korea Institute of Geoscience and Mineral Resources, 1996,
1:1,000,000 Scale Bouguer Gravity Anomaly Map of Southern Part of Korea.
Korea Institute of Geoscience and Mineral Resources, 1999-2004,
1:250,000 Scale Bouguer Gravity Anomaly Map of Busan Sheet (5 sheets).

Heat Flow [44-2]

Even though Korea is not usually associated with active thermal activities, it has about 50 hot springs (40-70℃). Recently, geothermal energy has been used for heating and cooling in Korea. If Koreans can discover and develop new sites with low enthalpy geothermal energy (< 90℃), Korea will have a major environmental and economic benefit because geothermal energy offsets air pollution and reduces Korea's dependency on crude oil.

In order to discover new geothermal sites, high heat flow areas should be targeted. Therefore, the heat flow map of Korea will contribute to geothermal energy development.

A total of 359 heat flow values in Korea were used to construct the heat flow map of Korea. The mean geothermal gradient of Korea is 25.1℃/km with the mean heat flow of Korea is 60±11mW/m². High heat flow is present in Asan, Boryeong, Yuseong, Jinan, Uljin, Pohang, Busan, Pocheon, Sokcho, Chungju, and Suanbo. These areas with high flow correspond to the locations of hot springs. Pohang has the highest heat flow (90mW/m²) in Korea. The Pohang area consists of Tertiary rocks (the youngest rocks in Korea): igneous rocks in the lower part of the rocks and unconsolidated mudstones in the upper part. Unconsolidated mudstones probably act as a caprock that prevents the loss of heat.

High heat flow values in the southeastern part of Korea are interpreted to be associated with the faults (Yangsan fault, Miryang fault, Moryang fault, Dongrae fault, and so on) that run NNW-SSE direction. These faults probably act as a conduit for geothermal fluids.

Source: Kim, H.C. and Lee, Y. M., 2007, Heat Flow in Korea, *Journal of Geophysical Research*, 112.

Earthquakes and Epicentral Map [44-3]

The epicentral map shows the distribution of earthquakes that have occurred in the Korean Peninsula since 1905. This map was created to provide information on the earthquake occurrences in and around the Korean Peninsula, and their relation with the existing surface geologic faults. This epicentral map may also provide the information to assist engineers in designing buildings, bridges, highways, and utilities that will withstand earthquakes in Korea. There is no clear relation between earthquake epicenters and known surface geologic faults, which is one of the characteristics of an intraplate earthquake.

Three kinds of data were used to develop the epicentral map. The magnitude and location of earthquakes were compiled and recalculated using the seismological bulletins compiled by the Weather Bureau of Chosun for the period of 1905 to 1942. Data between 1943 and 1977 was from the Seismological Institute of North Korea. The Earthquake Catalogue from the Korea Meteorological Administration (KMA) was used for the data thereafter.

In this map, shallow intraplate earthquakes with the focal depth of earthquakes less than 30km from the surface were used, but deep earthquakes from the East Sea related with plate tectonic between Eurasian and Pacific plates were not included. Focal depth of major earthquakes from waveform modeling was restricted to the upper 10km of the crust in the Korean Peninsula and the Yellow Sea, while in the western East Sea, focal depths were greater than 20km.

Source mechanism study shows that strike-slip faulting with a small amount of thrust component is dominant in and around the Korean Peninsula. The average P-axis from the composite moment tensor component of major earthquakes is almost horizontal and trends ENE-WSW. This stress pattern is very similar to northeastern China, but differs from the eastern East Sea which shows thrust faulting is dominant with a horizontal averaged P-axis trending ESE-WNW. The stress pattern in the eastern East Sea is consistent with the relative motion of the subducting Pacific Plate underneath the Eurasian Plate. This may imply that the collision of the Indian plate gives appreciable effect to the stress field at a level high enough to control the seismicity in and around the Korean Peninsula and in northeast China. However, the seismic activity in this region cannot be independent from the subducting Pacific Plate from the east.

Source: Jun, M.S. and Jeon, J.S., 2001, Early Instrumental Earthquake Data (1905-1942) in Korea, *Korea Society of Economic and Environmental Geology*, 34 (6), 573-581.
Korea Meteorological Administration, 2001, *1978-2000 Earthquake Observation Report*, Seoul: Korea Meteorological Administration, 155p.
Institute of Seismology, DPRK, 1987, *Chosun Earthquake Catalogue*, Pyeongyang: Institute of Seismology, DPRK, 150p.
Korea Meteorological Administration Homepage (http://www.kma.go.kr).

Mohorovic Discontinuity Depth [44-4]

A certain part of the crustal surface of the earth is very unstable, even though most seem to be stable. This kind of instability is derived in general from a deep place rather than a shallow part of the crust. Most earthquakes occur less than several tens of thousands of meters deep which experience a sudden break of equilibrium on the earth's crust. Korea has been located on a relatively stable crust until now, because of being more than a couple of hundred kilometers away from the Circum-Pacific Seismic Belt. Nevertheless, this notion is doubtful, due to the frequent occurrence of seismic activities recently. A mass disaster sometimes occurs in an area which everyone believes is safe and less prepared against disaster. For this reason, it requires a preestimate of instability of the deep crust to understand the depth of deep crust.

The map for the depth of Mohorovicic discontinuity represents the depth of the earth's crust from the subjacent mantle under the Korean Peninsula by using contour lines. The contour interval is 500 meters. The map shows an average depth of about 32km. The shallowest depth of Mohorovicic discontinuity is 20.3km, and the deepest depth is 36.6km.

Source: Korea Institute of Geoscience and Mineral Resources, 2001.
Tectonic Map of Korea (1:1,000,000 scale).

Marine Geological Map [45]

As land geological maps are needed for mineral resource exploration and construction, marine geological maps are useful in providing scientific data for potential areas of marine detrital mineral resources and hazards. Marine geological maps also provide government decision-makers the information tools needed to address pressing societal issues.

Since 1976, Korea Institute of Geoscience and Mineral Resources (KIGAM) has conducted a marine geological and geophysical survey, as a serial project for compiling marine geological maps of Korean Seas. Marine geological maps have been completed in the West Sea (Yellow Sea) and the South Sea, and will be published about the East Sea in 2010. KIGAM's research vessel, *Tamhae 2* weighing 2,000 tons, has been used for this project. It is equipped with a 252 digital multi-channel seismic system, gravitymeter, gradiometer, Chirp profiler, multi-beam echo sounder, deep side scan sonar, and a 10 meter long piston corer.

The marine geological maps of Korean waters consist of a surface sediment distribution map, a bathymetric map, a sediment isopach map, a deep seismic stratigraphic map, a residual magnetic map, and a free-air gravity anomaly map. Here only the surface sediment distribution map of the Yellow and South Sea is presented.

Surface sediments were analyzed and weighed in one-phi interval. The textural parameters, such as mean grain size, standard deviation, skewness, and kurtosis, were calculated according to Folk and Ward's graphic method. The sediment types were classified on the basis of Folk's scheme using relative weight percentages of clay, silt, sand, and gravel fractions.

This surface sediment distribution map is the result of over 20 years of work, compiling data sets of sediment type for each station, seabed morphology, sonograph, and sub-bottom profiling. The Datum used in Jejudo, the Korea Strait and east of 125°E of the Yellow Sea is the Tokyo Datum (1980-1996), and the southern sea of Jejudo, west of 125°E of the Yellow Sea is WGS-84 Datum (1997-2002).

Source: Geological and Mineral Institute of Korea, 1975, Marine Geological Maps of Korean Continental Shelves Series 1. Korea Institute of Energy and Resources, 1981-1990, Marine Geological Maps of Korean Continental Shelves, Series 2 - Series 6.
Korea Institute of Geology, Mining and Materials, 1991-2000, Marine Geological Maps of Korean Continental Shelves, Series 7 - Series 13.
Korea Institute of Geoscience and Mineral Resources, 2001-2004, Marine Geological Maps of Korean Continental Shelves, Series 14 - Series 17.

[References]

Chough, S.K., Kwon, S.T., Ree, J.H. and Choi, D.K., 2000, Tectonic and Sedimentary Evolution of the Korean Peninsula: A Review and New View, *Earth Science Reviews*, 52, 175-235.
Chwae, U., 1998, Does the Imjingang Fold Belt cross the Mid-Korean Peninsula along the Demilitarized Zone (DMZ) as an Extension of the Sulu Balt, China, *Journal of Earth and Planetary Sciences, Nagoya University*, 45, 41-73.
Cluzel, D., 1992, Formation and Tectonic Evolution of Early Mesozoic Intramountain Basins in the Ogacheon Belt (South Korea): A Reappraisal of the Jurassic 'Daebo Orogeny', *Journal of South American Earth Sciences*, 4, 223-235.
Folk, R.L. and Ward, W.C., 1957, Brazos River Bar: A Study in the Significance of Grain-size Parameters, *Journal of Sedimentary Petrology*, 27, 3-27.
Gottsche, O.C., 1886, *Geologische Skizz von Korea*, Sitzungsberichte der Kön Preuss. Akademie der Wissenschaften zu Berlin, xxxvi (G).
Han, W. and Chapman, D.S., 1985, On the Regional Heat Flow around Korea and Reduced Heat Flow, *Journal of Geological Society of Korea*, 21 (2), 74-28.
Han, W., 1979, A preliminary Evaluation of Geothermal Potential of Korea with Emphasis on Geothermometer and Mixing Model, *Journal of Geological Society of Korea*, 15(4), 259-268.
IGSASDPRK (Institute of Geology, State Academy of Sciences, DPR of Korea), 1996, *Geology of Korea*, Pyeongyang: Foreign Languages Books Publishing House, 631p.
Im, J.U., 1995, Geothermal Potential in the Republic of Korea. In: M.L. Gupta and M. Yamano (*eds.*), *Terrestrial Heat Flow and Geothermal Energy in Asia*, 435-467.
Jun, M.S., Jeon, J.S. and Che, L.Y., 1999, Earthquake Mechanism of Korean Peninsula, *Earthquake Engineering Society of Korea*, 3 (2), 58-63.
Kim, J.H., 1996, Mesozoic Tectonics in Korea, *Journal of South American Earth Sciences*, 13, 251-265.
Kim, H.C. and Lee, Y.M., 2007, Heat flow in the Republic of Korea, *Journal of Geophysical Research*, 112, B05413, doi:10.1029/2006JB004266.
Kim, H.C. and Song, Y., 2004, An Analysis of Geothermal Potential in Korea, *Proceedings of the 6th Asian Geothermal Symposium*, Daejeon, Korea, 79-84.
Kim, H.C. and Song, Y., 2005, Characteristics of Geothermal Anomaly in South Korea, *Proceedings World Geothermal Congress*, Antalya, Turkey, 1-5.
Kim, H.C., Lee, S. and Song, M.Y., 2002, Relationship Analysis between Lithology, Geological Time and Geothermal Gradient of South Korea, *Economic and Environmental Geology*, 35 (2), 163-170.
Kim, H.C., Lee, S. and Song, M.Y., 2004, Geological Characteristics and Heat Flow Relationship in South Korea, *Economic and Environmental Geology*, 37 (4), 391-400.
Kim, S.G., 1985, Investigation of Geothermal Sites in Korea, *Journal of the Korean Institute of Mining Geology*, 18 (2), 167-175.
Kim, S.K., 1979, Geodetic and Geophysical Analyses of Gravity Data in Korea, *Journal of the Korean Institute of Mining Geology*, 12, 17-28.
Kim, S.K., 1984, Some Considerations on Heat Flow in Korea, *Journal of the Korean Institute of Mining Geology*, 17 (2), 109-114.
Koo, M.H., Han, U. and Kwon, B.D., 1993, A Study on the Geothermal State around the Kongju Basin, *Journal of Korea Earth Science Society*, 14 (1), 58-66.
Koo, S.B., Im, M.T., Park, Y.S., Im, H.L., Sung, N.H., Go, I.S. and Song, S.Y., 2005, *Regional Geophysical Mapping*, Daejeon: Korea Institute of Geoscience and Mineral Resources, GAA2001004-2005 (5), p. 1-62.
Koo, B.D. and Yang S.Y., 1985, A Study on the Crustal Structure of the Southern Korean Peninsula through Gravity Analysis, *Journal of the Korean Institute of Mining Geology*, 18, 309-320.
Lee, D.S., 1987, *Geology of Korea*, Seoul: Kyohaksa, 514p.
Lee, K.K., Han, U. and Lee, K., 1986, A Study on the Thermal Structure of the Kyeongsang Basin, *Journal of Geological Society of Korea*, 22 (4), 371-379.
Lee, K., 1979, On Isostasy of Korean Peninsula, *Journal of Geological Society of Korea*, 15, 134-140.
Mizutani, H., Baba, K., Kobayashi, N., Chang, C.C., Lee, C.H. and Kang, Y.S., 1970, Heat Flow in Korea, *Tectonophysics*, 10, 183-203.
Park, Y.S., 2006, A Review of Magnetic Exploration in Korea, *Economic and Environmental Geology*, 39 (4), 403-416.
Reedman, A.J. and Um, S.H., 1975, *Geology of Korea*, Daejeon: Korea Institute of Energy and Resources, 139p.
Song, Y., 2004, Recent Activities on Low-temperature Geothermal Development in Korea. *Proceedings of the 6th Asian Geothermal Symposium*, Daejeon, Korea, 13-19.
Song, Y., Kim, H.C. and Lee, S.K., 2006, Geothermal Research and Development in Korea, *Economic and Environmental Geology, 39* (4), 485-494.
Song, Y., Kim, H.C., Yum, B.W. and Ahn, E., 2005, Direct Use Geothermal Development in Korea: Country Update 2000-2004, *Proceedings World Geothermal Congress 2005*, Antalya, Turkey, 1-7.
Yum, B.W., 2000, The Present Status of Korean Geothermal Research and Investigations, *Proceedings World Geothermal Congress 2000*, Kyushu-Tohoku, Japan, 499-504.

Soils

Soil Map [46]

Parent Materials [48-1]

During a field study, morphological and physical characteristics of soil such as parent material, soil texture, topography, soil drainage classes, gravel content, slope, effective soil depth, and the rate of erosion are often used to determine the types and age of a soil. Topography, soil drainage classes, soil texture, effective soil depth, and gravel content not only play important roles in determining soil series, but are significant and fundamental factors for both understanding soil forming processes and analyzing characteristics of farmland.

Soil scientists in Korea classify parent materials into the following categories: acidic rocks, neutral rocks, alkalic rocks, sedimentary rocks, metamorphic rocks, Tertiary deposits, Quaternary deposits, and volcanic ash. Determination of parent material is the first step in conducting a soil survey. A rock may be an assemblage of minerals bound together, or it may be a mass of a single mineral. Thousands of rocks have been identified, but they can be classified into three categories of rock-forming processes: igneous rocks, sedimentary rocks, and metamorphic rocks. Igneous rocks are sub-classified into acidic igneous rocks, neutral igneous rocks, and alkalic igneous rocks. Sedimentary rocks are usually formed from sedimentary deposits that are mechanically transported by water. Sedimentary rocks can be classified by their grain size into shale, sandstone, and conglomerate, and by their mineral content into limestone, zeolite, and diatomite, and by the degree of petrification into hard rocks, and semi-petrified rocks.

Source: National Institute of Agricultural Science and Technology, Korean Rural Development Administration, 1999.

Topography [48-2]

Topography is the configuration of Earth's surface including both natural and human-made features. Geomorphologic classification of topography by characteristic landform or relief is commonly used to identify a type of soil. However, much attention is required to separate landform or relief from physiographical patterns, which consider additional factors that affect vegetation and agricultural condition, such as soil moisture and soil texture. In the case of agricultural lands, surface conditions should be carefully examined. Since topography is a soil-forming factor and controls cross-sectional patterns of a soil, ability to identify various types of topography is required for an accurate soil survey. Researchers should assess how topography affects agricultural activities and land use, as well as to investigate types and the luxuriance of growth of vegetation, and agricultural activities on each landscape. In a soil survey, topography is classified as mountain, lava soil terrace, cinder cone, hill, pediment, alluvial fan, valley, alluvial plain, fluvial plain, and fluvio-marine plain.

Source: National Institute of Agricultural Science and Technology, Korean Rural Development Administration, 1999.

Soil Drainage Class [48-3]

Soil drainage class refers to the frequency and duration of periods of water saturation or partial saturation, which affects runoff, infiltration, permeability, and internal soil drainage (percolation). In this manner, soil drainage classification is based on the moisture index of a soil profile, which is determined by runoff, permeability, and proximity to the ground water table. However, artificial drainage and irrigation are not considered unless they significantly affect soil's morphological characteristics. Soil drainage class description includes somewhat excessively-drained, well-drained, moderately well-drained, somewhat poorly-drained, and poorly-drained. The following table shows morphological characteristics of soil profiles for each soil drainage class.

Source: National Institute of Agricultural Science and Technology, Korean Rural Development Administration, 1999.

Table. Morphological Characteristics of Soil Profile at Each Soil Drainage Class

Class	Morphological Characteristics of Soil Profile	Land Use
Excessively-drained	Free of Mottles (High-relief, Gravel or Sand)	Montane Soil, Riverbed (Sand)
Well-drained	Brown or Yellowish Brown Color, but Free of Grey Mottles (Sandy Loam to Loam)	Most Farmlands
Moderately Well-drained	A Few Grey Mottles in Deep Soil (Primary Soil Color is Brown or Yellowish Brown)	Dry Paddy Fields (Some Farmlands)
Somewhat Poorly-drained	Primary Soil Color is Grey (A Few Brown, Yellowish Brown, and Reddish Brown Mottles)	Semi-dry Paddy Fields
Poorly-drained	Primary Soil Color is Grey or Dark Grey (Yellowish or Reddish Mottles down to 50cm in the Soil)	Paddy Fields
Very Poorly-drained	Dark Grey Color with a Very High Groundwater	Very Wet Paddy Fields

Source: National Honam Agricultural Experimental Station, 2003, *Theory and Practice of Soil Survey*, Suwon: National Honam agricultural Experimental Station (NHAES).

Effective Soil Depth [48-4]

Effective soil depth represents the depth of soil horizons. Areas with deep soil are often found either in the areas with well-weathered bedrock, or in the area where sediments are deposited. Areas with shallow soil represent either poor soil formation or soil removal by erosion. Soil scientists classify soil by effective soil depth into very shallow (< 20㎝), moderate (20-50㎝), and deep (> 100㎝). It is recommended that effective soil depth should be at least 50㎝ for rice paddies or farmlands.

Source: National Institute of Agricultural Science and Technology, Korean Rural Development Administration, 1999.

Gravel Content in Deep Soil [49-1]

The content of gravel in deep soil is strongly associated with root growth, while gravel in top soil is subject to damage by agricultural activities. Higher gravel content (over 35 percent of gravel) impedes the growth of root crops, and reduces the content of water and nutrients in the soil. Soil scientists classify gravel content in soil into the following three categories: below 10 percent (none), between 10 and 35 percent (some), and over 35 percent (plenty).

Source: National Institute of Agricultural Science and Technology, Korean Rural Development Administration, 1999.

Soil Textural Class [49-2]

Soil texture refers to the size and organization of non-organic particles in the soil which range from finest clays to coarser sands (below 2mm in diameter), and is an important attribute that controls soil's physical and chemical characteristics. Soil textural class is one of the sub-categories of Soil Taxonomy, and it classifies soil into the following six categories: sandy, coarse loamy, coarse silty, fine loamy, fine silty, and clay.

There are two methods to determine soil texture: textural analysis in the laboratory and feeling test in the field. Textural analysis in the laboratory uses a soil texture triangle to determine soil texture from the proportions of sand (coarse sand and fine sand), silt, and clay. In the field, the textural class of a soil can be determined by rubbing a mass of wet soil between fingers, but this method requires extensive experience.

Source: National Institute of Agricultural Science and Technology, Korean Rural Development Administration, 1999.

Soil Erodibility [49-3]

Soil erosion can be classified as either natural soil erosion or accelerated erosion. Under normal climate conditions with natural ground cover, soil erosion can often balance out with the rate of soil production. This is called 'natural erosion' or 'geological erosion'. Natural soil erosion includes water erosion caused by rainfall and runoff, wind erosion, glacial erosion caused by flowing ice, stream erosion occurring in channelized water flow, coastal erosion caused by waves and tides, and erosion occurring by transportation. Erosion occurring at a rate that exceeds the rate of natural erosion is called 'accelerated erosion'. Accelerated erosion results from certain human land use practices, such as surface mining, forestry, agriculture, and construction. Additional natural erosion processes, such as water erosion, are responsible for accelerated erosion of the soil.

Soil erosion in Korea is primarily caused by rainfall. Rainsplash detaches earth materials from the surface by the impact of water striking surface and by the force of surface runoff. Wind erosion is found in coastal regions and highlands. The intensity and amount of rainfall, soil type, and the length and steepness of slope determine the degree of soil erosion by rainfall.

Soil erodibility, a useful indicator of soil erosion susceptibility, is an estimate of the ability to resist erosion based on the physical characteristics of each soil. Using soil erodibility, it is easy to identify soil types with high erodibility for a certain slope condition. It is also possible to determine where the eroded soil particles have accumulated.

The map depicts soil erodibility in Korea. Soil erodibility is calculated from weighted averages of soil erodibility for each soil. In this map, soil erodibility is computed by a revised equation which adds gravel content into the existing equation of Universal Soil Loss Equation (USLE). This study converts the conventional unit of ton/hr to the SI unit of mghr MJ^{-1} MM^{-1}, which needs to be multiplied by the conversional factor of 0.13.

The resulting soil erodibility map indicates that lower values are usually found in the headwaters of a river, whereas higher values are commonly found downstream. As a whole, western open field regions show higher soil erodibility than eastern mountainous regions. Lower soil erodibility in the upper reaches of rivers indicate that highly erodible soil particles were already removed and transported by rainfall or gravity from upstream, and deposited in the river downstream. Although soils in Korea have been formed for a long time, they are classified as Inceptisols or Entisols. These soils have relatively shallow soil depths, since they experience severe soil erosion caused by rainfall and steep topography.

Source: National Institute of Agricultural Science and Technology, Korean Rural Development Administration, 2005.

Soil Loss [49-4]

Soil is created by weathering of rocks. Rainfall, temperature, and vegetation play key roles in rock weathering. Korea has favorable conditions for rock weathering, since it is located in the temperate climate zone and has abundant rainfall. However, severe soil erosion often occurs, because most of the rain falls in summer and Korea has relatively steep slopes. Soils in Korea are commonly classified as Inceptisols or Entisols which do not have deep soil development.

Estimated annual total soil loss in Korea is 50 million tons. Twenty seven million tons of soil loss occurs on farmlands which occupy less than 10 percent of the total land area of Korea. The map depicts the annual soil loss from farmlands in Korea. The amount of soil loss is determined by rainfall, soil type, topography, land cover, and soil management practices. The RUSLE (Revised Universal Soil Loss Equation) was used to assess the effects of rainfall erosivity, soil erodibility, and slope length and steepness on the amount of soil loss. In the same manner, the USLE (Universal Soil Loss Equation) was used to determine the effects of crop management.

Higher rainfall erosivities were found in the southern and western coastal regions. The mountain ranges usually contain higher slope length and steepness, but especially high values were found in Pyeongchang in Gangwon-*do*, and Jirisan which divides Gyeongsang-*do* and Jeolla-*do*. Mean annual soil loss is severe in Pyeongchang and Jeongseon in Gangwon-*do*, and Namhae, Geoje, and Goseoung in Gyeongsangnam-*do*. National mean annual soil erosion of farmlands, rice paddies, and forests are 37.7, 1.0, and 3.5 ton/ha, respectively. This study does not create national mean annual soil erosion maps for rice paddies and forests, since soil erosion of these areas are not significant. The following table presents the classification of soil erosion and the total areas within each grade.

Table. Comparison of Soil Loss according to Soil Erosion Grade

Soil Erosion Grade	Slight	Light	Moderate	Heavy	Severe	Extremely Severe
Annual Soil Loss (ton/ha)	0-6	6-11	11-22	22-33	33-50	50<
Area of Farmland (1,000 ha)	126	99	159	82	85	168
OECD Soil Erosion Grade	Tolerable	Low	Moderate	High	Severe	

* 'Farmland' includes orchards, and 'area of farmland' is based on the yearbook of Agricultural Statistics (2004).

Source: National Institute of Agricultural Science and Technology (NIAST), 2005, *An Assessment of Soil Erosion potential*, Suwon: Rural Development Administration (RDA).

Source: National Institute of Agricultural Science and Technology, Korean Rural Development Administration, 2005.

Acidity and Organic Matter Content of Farmland and Rice Paddy Soils [50-1, 2, 3, 4]

Soil testing determines both the amount of soil nutrients essential for plant growth and the existence of any harmful ingredients in the soil. It can be used to make recommendations for the amount and type of fertilizer, timing, and exact location of fertilizer application for optimum plant growth. Furthermore, it can help achieve proper and effective nutrient management of crops. Improper application of fertilizer would be problematic because of the uniqueness of soils and crops. Understanding soil chemistry by measuring the exact content of chemicals in soil is the first step towards maintaining and managing environmentally sound soil.

Soil testing reveals the chemical properties of soil, such as pH, soil organic matter, available phosphoric acid, available silicic acid, substitution cations, and cation exchange capacity. The maps show the acidity and the organic matter content of rice paddies and farmland in Korea. The survey was conducted from 1995 to 2006.

The pH of soil can be an important parameter for crop growth. When a soil's pH is about neutral (6.5-7.0), availability of soil nutrients is at a maximum. As a soil becomes more acidic (pH < 5.5), significant dissolution of manganese and iron from the soil not only impede the crop growth, but also hinder the propagation and function of useful soil microbes. The solubility of cations such as iron and zinc becomes low in the alkaline soils with a pH of greater than 8.0. As a result, crops may suffer a deficiency of these cations. The map indicates that the range of a pH of rice paddy and farmland ranges from less than a pH of 4.5 to above a pH of 6.5. According to Korean Rural Development Administration, National Institute of Agricultural Science and Technology, optimal ranges of pH for rice paddy and farmland are 5.5-6.5 and 6.0-6.5, respectively.

Soil organic matter is an important element in controlling soil fertility. Soil organic matter contains a variety of nutrients, and provides these nutrients to microbes and vegetation. Organic matter in soil enhances soil quality by increasing porosity and permeability. As a result, a soil with abundant organic matter provides the favorable environment for soil microbes to thrive. Soil organic matter content in rice paddy and farmland ranges from below 10g/kg to above 50g/kg. According to Korean Rural Development Administration, National Institute of Agricultural Science and Technology, the optimal ranges of soil organic matter for rice paddy and farmland are 25-30g/kg and 20-30g/kg, respectively.

Source: National Institute of Agricultural Science and Technology, Korean Rural Development Administration, 2006.

Multi-scale Soil Map(1:250,000 Soil Map; 1:50,000 Soil Map; 1:25,000 Soil Drainage Class; 1:5,000 Soil Drainage Class) [51-1, 2, 3, 4]

Soil maps with a variety of scales are currently available to the public in Korea. The following table summarizes soil survey methods at each scale and its application.

Table. Multi-scale Soil Maps in Korea

Division	General Soil Survey	Detailed Soil Survey	Highly Detailed Soil Survey
Scale of Base Map	1:40,000	1:10,000-18,750	1:1,200-5,000
Scale of Soil Map	1:50,000	1:25,000	1:5,000
Minimum Area Presented on Map	6.25ha	1.56ha	10ha
Accuracy and Soil Classification	Aerial Photogrammetry Soil Group and Subgroup	Field Investigation Soil Series and Mapping Units	Analysis of Individual Plots Soil Series and Other Mapping Units, Land Use
Distance between Sampling Points	500-1,000 m	Less than 100m	Less than 50m
Application	Soil Genesis and Distribution of Soil Group Central and Regional Land Use Planning Suitability for Agricultural Land Use	Agricultural Advice at Regional and Local Level Regional Land Use Planning Identification of Major Crop Zone Soil Fertility Management Basic Information for Soil Management	Choice of Crop for Individual Plots Identification of Suitable Crops Selection of Specific Land Management

Source: National Institute of Agricultural science and Technology (NIAST), 2001, Soil Environmental Information System of Korea, Suwon: Rural Development Administration(RDA).

[References]

Agricultural Sciences Institute, 1985, *Soils of Korea with Generalized Soil Map of Pattern of Soil Orders and Suborders of Korea 1:1,000,000*, Suwon: Rural Development Administration (RDA).

Agricultural Sciences Institute, *1992, Korean Soil Survey and Classification*, Suwon: Rural Devel opment Administration (RDA).

National Honam Agricultural Experimental Station, 2003, *Theory and Practice of Soil Survey*, Suwon: National Honam Agricultural Experimental Station (NHAES).

National Institute of Agricultural Science and Technology (NIAST), 1999, *Detailed Soil Survey and Soil Testing Project*, Suwon: Rural Development Administration (RDA).

National Institute of Agricultural Science and Technology (NIAST), 2000, *Taxonomical Classification of the Korean Soil Survey*, Suwon: Rural Development Administration (RDA).

National Institute of Agricultural Science and Technology (NIAST), 2005, *Achievement and Progress of the Korean Soil Survey*, Suwon: Rural Development Administration (RDA).

National Institute of Agricultural Science and Technology (NIAST), 2001, *Soil Environmental Information System of Korea*, Suwon: Rural Development Administration (RDA).

National Institute of Agricultural Science and Technology (NIAST), 2005, *An Assessment of Soil Erosion Potential*, Suwon: Rural Development Administration (RDA).

Climate

Locations of Meteorological Stations and Climographs for Selected Stations [52]

This map represents the location of observation stations and climographs of monthly temperature and precipitation for selected stations in Korea. Korea Meteorological Administration locates in Seoul and there are five regional meteorological offices (Gangneung, Daejeon, Gwangju, Busan, and Jeju), 38 weather stations, and 47 weather observatories in Korea.

Annual Mean Temperature [54-1]

This map is made using climatological normals from 1971 to 2000. Annual mean temperature ranges from 6.4℃ at Daegwallyeong to 16.2℃ at Seogwipo, with the distribution affected by topography and sea. Isolines around the Taebaek and Sobaek Mountains are displaced southward and those around coasts are displaced northward compared to inlands. The climographs represent typical characteristics of a continental climate.

Source: Korea Meteorological Administration, 1971-2000.

Annual Temperature Range [54-2]

This map is made using climatological normals from 1971 to 2000 and isolines at intervals of 1℃. Ranges are lower in the Youngseo area, including Yangpyeong, Hongcheon and Wonju at about 20℃ and the highest in the southwestern coastal area of Jeju. The annual temperature range decreases gradually toward the coast and from north to south.
Source: Korea Meteorological Administration, 1971-2000.

January Mean Temperature [54-3]

January is the coldest month in Korea. This map is made using isolines at intervals of 1℃. The January mean temperature varies from -7 to 6℃ and has larger differences than annual mean temperature although they have similar patterns. Isolines around the Taebaek and Sobaek Mountains are moved southward and those around the coast are curved northward in comparison with the inland area.
Source: Korea Meteorological Administration, 1971-2000.

August Mean Temperature [54-4]

August is the warmest month in Korea. This map is made using climatological normals from 1971 to 2000 and isolines at intervals of 1℃. The August mean temperature ranges from 19 to 26℃ and varies less than annual and January mean temperature across Korea. The temperature in the Taebaek Mountains is lower and that in the coastal zone is higher than in the surrounding areas.
Source: Korea Meteorological Administration, 1971-2000.

Annual Precipitation [55-1]

Annual precipitation ranges from 1,000 to 1,800mm with a large spatial variation. This map is made using climatological normals from 1971 to 2000 and an isoline interval of 100mm. Annual mean precipitation decreases gradually from south to north with some localized maximum and minimum areas. The distribution of precipitation is affected strongly by topography, with large totals over Daegwallyeong, which is on the windward side of the Taebaek Mountains.
Source: Korea Meteorological Administration, 1971-2000.

Annual Snowfall Amount [55-2]

Snow falls from October to March in Korea. This map is made using climatological normals from 1971 to 2000 and an isoline interval of 20cm. Annual snowfall ranges from less than 20 to 240cm with maximum areas over Daegwallyeong, Gangneung, Jeongeup, and Imsil. Minimum areas have virtually no snowfall and are located in the far south. Snowfall distribution follows topography, with large totals over Daegwallyeong, windward of the Taebaek Mountains.
Source: Korea Meteorological Administration, 1971-2000.

Summer Precipitation [55-3]

Summer precipitation is defined as the total of June, July, and August precipitation. This map is made using climatological normals from 1971 to 2000 and an isoline interval of 100mm. The summer precipitation contributes to more than 50 percent of the annual precipitation. Summer precipitation ranges from 500 to 800mm and have a large areal variation.
Source: Korea Meteorological Administration, 1971-2000.

Winter Precipitation [55-4]

Winter precipitation is defined as the total of December, January, and February precipitation. This map is made using climatological normals from 1971 to 2000 and an isoline interval of 20mm. Winter precipitation ranges from 60 to 200mm, with a relatively larger areal variation than in summer. The maximum area over Daegwallyeong is driven by large snowfall totals. The Youngseo and Youngnam areas are very dry during winter.
Source: Korea Meteorological Administration, 1971-2000.

Annual Wind Rose [56-1]

This map shows the annual frequency distribution of wind direction by wind speed categories. The first inner circle represents a speed of less than 0.3 ᵐ/s. Each interval emanating from the circles indicates 5 percent frequency. Wind speed is categorized into four classes, i.e., 0.3-3.3, 3.4-7.9, 8.0-13.8, and higher than 13.9 ᵐ/s. Westerlies ranging from northwesterly to southwesterly prevail because of Korea's latitudinal position with respect to global wind patterns. However, local topographic effects and monsoon flow complicate the wind climatology.
Source: Korea Meteorological Administration, 1971-2000.

Summer Wind Rose [56-2]

This map shows the summer frequency distribution of wind direction by wind speed categories. In summer, southwesterly winds prevail as the clockwise flow around the North Pacific high-pressure system dominates.
Source: Korea Meteorological Administration, 1971-2000.

Winter Wind Rose [56-3]

This map shows the winter frequency distribution of wind direction by wind speed categories. In winter, northwesterly winds prevail as the clockwise flow around the Siberian high-pressure system dominates over the north-central Asian continent.
Source: Korea Meteorological Administration, 1971-2000.

Number of Days with Strong Winds [56-4]

This map shows annual and seasonal distribution of the number of days with strong winds at selected stations. "Days with strong winds" is defined as days with daily maximum wind speed exceeding 13.8 ᵐ/s. Strong winds occur more than 100 days per year over coastal areas such as Ulleungdo, Mokpo, Yeosu, and Busan, and less than 10 days per year in inland areas such as Seoul, Chuncheon and Daejeon.
Source: Korea Meteorological Administration, 1971-2000.

Annual Mean Sea Level Pressure [57-1]

This map uses climatological normals from 1971 to 2000 and an isoline interval of 1hPa. Annual sea level pressure ranges from 1,016 to 1,018hPa

with a very small spatial gradient. The pressures are higher in Daegwallyeong, Namwon, Geochang, Hapcheon, Sancheong, Buyeo, Geumsan, and Cheonan than in the surrounding coast areas.
Source: Korea Meteorological Administration, 1971-2000.

Annual Mean Relative Humidity [57-2]

This map uses climatological normals from 1971 to 2000 and an isoline interval of 5 percent. Annual relative humidity ranges from 65 to 75 percent, with a relatively small difference across Korea. Relative humidity decreases gradually from the west coast areas to the east coast areas.
Source: Korea Meteorological Administration, 1971-2000.

Annual Evaporation [57-3]

This map uses climatological normals from 1971 to 2000 and an isoline interval of 100mm of precipitation equivalent. Annual mean evaporation ranges from 1,000 to 1,300mm. Values are relatively low in the Youngseo and Honam inland areas including Yangpyeong, Hongcheon, Chuncheon, Icheon, Jeongeup, and Imsil, and high in the Yongnam area including Daegu and Andong.
Source: Korea Meteorological Administration, 1971-2000.

Annual Percentage of Sunshine [57-4]

This map uses climatological normals from 1971 to 2000 and an isoline interval of 5 percent. The annual percentage of sunshine ranges from 45 to 60 percent. The value is high at Yeongdeok and Uljin along the eastern coast, and low at Cheorwon and Chuncheon. The minimum is north of Jeju.
Source: Korea Meteorological Administration, 1971-2000.

Date of First Snowfall [58-1]

This map uses daily snowfall data from 1971 to 2000 with an isoline interval of 5 days. The first snow falls in Daegwallyeong around November 5, but at Geoje it occurs near December 30. The mean date of first snowfall in Seoul, Mokpo, and Busan is November 21, November 26, and December 20, respectively.
Source: Korea Meteorological Administration, 1971-2000.

Date of Last Snowfall [58-2]

This map uses daily snowfall data from 1971 to 2000, with an isoline interval of 5 days. The snow stops around February 19 in Geoje and Busan, March 11 in Mokpo, March 21 in Seoul, and April 19 in Daegwallyeong.
Source: Korea Meteorological Administration, 1971-2000.

Date of First Frost [58-3]

This map uses daily frost data from 1971 to 2000 and an isoline interval of 10 days. The first frost occurs earlier over the northern area than in the southern area, and earlier inland than in the coastal area. In Mokpo, the mean date is as late as about November 24 and the mean period susceptible to frost is as short as about 36.6 days. The earliest mean date of the first frost occurs over Daegwallyeong on October 3. Over inland area, the mean date ranges from October 20 to 30.
Source: Korea Meteorological Administration, 1971-2000.

Date of Last Frost [58-4]

The climatological last frost occurs about March 24 in Mokpo, and occurs over Daegwallyeong on May 13. Over inland regions, the date of the last frost ranges from April 10 to 20.
Source: Korea Meteorological Administration, 1971-2000.

Annual Number of Days with Fog [59-1]

The mean annual number of days with fog is mapped using daily data from 1971 to 2000 and a contour interval of 20 days. The annual number of days with fog in Daegwallyeong averages 120 days while over coastal area it is as less as 20 days. The number of days at Seoul and Daejeon is about 40.
Source: Korea Meteorological Administration, 1971-2000.

Annual Number of Days with Frost [59-2]

The mean annual number of days with frost is mapped using daily data from 1971 to 2000 and a contour interval of 25 days. Frost in Daegwallyeong occurs on more than 125 days while in the southern and eastern coastal areas frost occurs on less than 50 days. Despite their inland locations, Seoul, Daegu, and Daejeon show smaller than expected numbers of days with frost due to urban effects.
Source: Korea Meteorological Administration, 1971-2000.

Annual Number of Days with Freezing Temperatures [59-3]

The mean annual number of days with freezing temperatures is mapped using daily data from 1971 to 2000 and a contour interval of 20 days. About 160 days per year have freezing temperatures in Daegwallyeong, with 120 days in Seoul, less than 80 days in the southern coastal area of Korea, and about 20 days in Jeju.
Source: Korea Meteorological Administration, 1971-2000.

Annual Number of Days with Hail [59-4]

The mean annual number of days with hail is mapped using daily data from 1971 to 2000 and a contour interval of 0.4 days. In Korea, May, June, September, and October are the major hail months. The annual mean number of days with hail ranges from about 1.3 in Busan to 2.8 in the western coastal area. The wide range from 1.6 to 2.8 days in Jeju is mainly caused by mountain effects. In Seoul, hail falls on about 2.2 days per year.
Source: Korea Meteorological Administration, 1971-2000.

Tracks of Typhoons [60-1]

A typhoon is defined as a strong tropical cyclone having a wind speed of 33ᵐ/s and above. Tracks of typhoons that influence Korea are aggregated using RSMC(Regional Specialized Meteorological Centre) typhoon track data from 1995 to 2004. Typhoon tracks of June, July, August, and September are indicated by pink dotted, red dotted, solid green and solid blue curves, respectively.
Source: Korea Meteorological Administration, 1971-2000.

Annual Number of Days with Heavy Rainfall [60-2]

The mean annual number of days with heavy rainfall is calculated using daily rainfall data from 1971 to 2000 and a contour interval of 0.5 days. A heavy rainfall day is defined as a day with 80mm or higher precipitation. The mean annual number of days with heavy rainfall ranges from 1-2 days over the central parts of Korea and Daegu to 3-4 days over the southern coastal area, Seoul, and Gyeonggi-do.
Source: Korea Meteorological Administration, 1971-2000.

Extreme Value of Daily Precipitation [60-3]

The extreme value of daily precipitation is defined as the daily maximum value of heavy rainfall at each station. Extreme values are mapped using daily rainfall data from 1971 to 2000 and a contour interval of 80 mm. The climatological mean of heavy rainfall is about 100 to 120mm, while extreme values of heavy rainfall range from 160 to 560mm. More than 500mm occurs over Haenam, 300mm over Busan, 320mm over Seoul, and 160mm over Daegu.
Source: Korea Meteorological Administration, 1971-2000.

Interannual Variation of Mean Temperature and Total Precipitation [61]

Hydrology

River Systems and Watersheds [62]

The distribution of mountain ranges determines the overall pattern of river channels in Korea. Short and steep river channels are common in the east, while rivers flowing into the Yellow and South Sea are relatively long and gentle. Based on the importance to national security, environment, and economy, the Korean River Law classifies rivers into national rivers, 1st order regional rivers, and 2nd order regional rivers.

In 2000, the Korean government designated 82 national rivers into these categories and their total length is 3,066.14km. These national rivers are managed by the Korean central government because of their nationwide environmental and economic importance. Sixty seven 1st order regional rivers with a total length of 1,373.46km are also designated. The provincial governors or mayors manage these rivers, because of region-wide public interest, and environmental and economic importance. There are 3,779 rivers with a total length of 26,088.71km which are designated as 2nd order regional rivers. The provincial governors or mayors also manage these rivers which flow from or to national rivers or 1st order regional rivers.

For the systematic management of rivers and water resources, the Korean government divides land into 21 large-scale basins. Each basin is divided into mid-scale sub-basins, which are further divided into watersheds for various purposes. The total number of sub-basins is 117. These sub-basins are the base unit of information exchange among organization which are involved in the water resource management.

Compared to bigger rivers found in the Asian continent, Korean rivers have relatively shorter channel length and smaller drainage basins. Since about 70 percent of the land area has a slope angle of over 20 percent, the ratio of runoff to rainfall is high. Even for large rivers, such as the Hangang and Nakdonggang, it takes only a few days for the rainwater to reach the sea. Furthermore, the difference in discharge between flooding (June-August) and drought periods is sizable, due to torrential and consistent rainfalls during the Monsoon period.

The Korean Ministry of Construction and Transportation, the Korean Water Resource Corporation (K-water), and other organizations operate several hundred water level gauges to monitor the river discharges. However, due to short records of river discharges, the TANK model that is able to account for the soil moisture was used to estimate the river discharges at 117 sub-basins from 1974 to 2003. In the map, monthly river discharges are the results of summation of the estimated river discharges for each basin. The average annual discharge and runoff ratio for the Hangang Basin are estimated as 16 billion m³ and 57 percent, and 15.7 billion m³ and 56 percent for the Nakdonggang, 7 billion m³ and 57 percent for the Basin, and 2.8 billion and 61 percent for the Yeongsangang Basin. Much like the precipitation, two-thirds of the annual river discharge is concentrated from June to September.
Source: Ministry of Construction and Transportation, 2004, River Statistics of Korea.

Water Usage, Domestic Water Use, Industrial Water Use and Agricultural Water Use [64-1, 2, 3, 4]

The map shows the water use amounts in 2003. The Hangang Basin shows the largest amount of water usage reaching 12 billion m³ per year. It is followed by the Nakdonggang Basin with 9.4 billion m³, the Geumgang Basin with 6.7 billion m³, the Yeongsangang and Seomjingang Basins with a combined total of 5.8 billion m³, and Jejudo with 0.4 billion m³. The primary purpose of water usage in the Hangang Basin is river environment flow, while irrigation water is the top priority in other river basins. Especially in the Yeongsangang and Seomjingang Basins, water usage for agricultural activities reaches up to 76 percent of the total water usage.

Seoul in the Hangang Basin is the largest domestic water consuming area, reaching up to 1.8 billion m³. It is followed by the Anseongcheon basin and the Suyeonggang sub-basin with greater than 0.3 billion m³. Seoul, in the Hangang Basin, is also the largest industrial water consuming area, which reaches up to 0.3 billion m³. Other metropolitan areas, Busan and Deagu, and large-scale industrial complexes, Ulsan and Yeosu-Suncheon region, are the major industrial water consuming areas. The Sapkyocheon Basin is the largest agricultural water consuming area using 0.6 billion m³. Other regions adjacent to the west coast, Anseongcheon, Mangyeonggang, and Dongjingang basins also show large scale agricultural water consumption.
Source: Korea Water Resources Corporation, 2006, Water Resource Plan (2006-2020) Report.

Groundwater Usage [65-1]

Annual groundwater recharge in Korea is estimated at 13-14 billion m³. However, most of the groundwater is discharged as streamflow during the drought season, and poor aquifer conditions are the main obstacle to groundwater development. The amount of sustainable groundwater development, which takes the groundwater recharge rate in a drought year of a 10-year return period into account, is estimated to be about 11.7 billion m^3 per year.

Table. Groundwater Use in 2003

Location	Total		Domestic		Industrial		Agricultural		Others	
	No.of Wells	Pumped Amount (m^3)	No.of Wells	Pumped Amount (m^3)	No.of Wells	Pumped Amount (m^3)	No.of Wells	Pumped Amount (m^3)	No.of Wells	Pumped Amount (m^3)
Total	1,228,290	3,749,300,169	721,396	1,846,592,197	14,077	196,717,995	486,937	1,658,754,902	5,800	47,235,075
Seoul	14,383	38,338,080	10,282	31,439,302	182	1,880,036	3,434	3,575,570	185	1,443,172
Busan	9,580	45,449,030	8,342	35,817,519	337	3,544,222	512	2,760,366	389	3,326,924
Daegu	5,052	31,375,635	3,939	22,967,409	477	5,381,225	601	2,533,632	35	493,370
Incheon	11,446	55,765,729	7,872	31,291,207	257	2,209,812	2,663	18,247,500	654	4,017,210
Gwangju	8,145	24,021,964	6,004	15,344,553	175	1,654,846	1,920	6,742,150	46	280,416
Daejeon	23,892	40,077,993	19,897	30,113,635	366	1,546,412	3,503	8,066,200	126	351,747
Ulsan	4,495	34,233,877	3,394	25,701,936	178	2,341,386	827	5,370,700	96	819,855
Gyeonggi-*do*	165,701	560,294,722	111,989	355,003,607	2,761	35,036,826	48,856	157,823,912	2,095	12,430,378
Gangwon-*do*	85,433	247,580,704	63,415	137,305,711	694	11,312,058	21,075	95,790,988	249	3,171,948
Chungcheong-buk-*do*	146,410	361,702,984	89,703	183,804,813	1,679	18,505,673	54,794	156,771,302	234	2,621,196
Chungcheong-nam-*do*	231,860	486,668,520	133,557	234,977,275	1,182	22,282,059	96,805	227,067,245	316	2,341,942
Jeollabuk-*do*	144,563	333,365,484	68,566	124,749,877	1,272	13,465,015	74,413	192,214,871	312	2,935,721
Jeollanam-*do*	207,618	516,750,500	108,862	151,963,055	810	9,618,548	97,683	351,468,165	263	3,700,732
Gyeongsang-buk-*do*	89,994	401,038,876	46,112	186,455,390	1,554	37,426,815	41,849	170,673,941	479	6,482,730
Gyeongsang-nam-*do*	74,732	441,670,612	37,958	199,174,340	1,653	24,189,824	34,786	215,936,703	335	2,369,746
Jejudo	4,986	130,965,458	1,504	80,482,569	200	6,323,240	3,216	43,711,659	66	447,990

Source: Ministry of Construction and Transportation, 2005, *Groundwater Annual Report of 2004*.

The total usage of groundwater is about 3.7 billion m^3 per year, including 1.8 billion m^3 (49%) for municipal purpose, 1.7 billion m^3 (46%) for irrigation purpose, 0.2 billion m^3 (5%) for industrial purposes, and 0.05 billion m^3 (1%) for other purposes. Gyeonggi-*do*, Chungcheongbuk-*do*, Jeollabuk-*do*, and Jeollanam-*do* are the most active areas for groundwater use, since these regions have relatively well-developed aquifer conditions.

The table shows the annual groundwater use of each provincial administration. The west coast area of Chungcheong-*do* is the most active area for groundwater use, and the ratio of groundwater use to potential amount is higher than 50 percent in the metropolitan areas, such as Gwangju, Busan, and Daegu, while it is relatively low in other areas. In 2003, 3.8 billion m^3 of groundwater was pumped from 1,228,290 wells for domestic, industrial and agricultural use, which excludes the salt groundwater use in Jejudo.

Recently, groundwater dams that intercept the runoff from the aquifer to the river stream or ocean are being constructed. These dams raise the groundwater level and increase the amount of available water, so that it can be easily drawn and used. The Ian Dam was the first of its kind, and now there are 19 groundwater dams nationwide with a total pumping capacity of 321,838m^3/day. From 1994 to 2003, groundwater use increased at the rate of 4.4 percent annually. Prior to 1997, there was a rapid increase of groundwater use, but it remained constant from 1997 to 2002. There has been a tendency to increase groundwater use in 2002 and 2003.

Despite the growing demand for water, new development of water resources is becoming more difficult. Groundwater is drawing more attention from the public as a new and clean water resource. Since groundwater is easily contaminated and its recovery is complicated, use of groundwater should be strictly regulated based on the precise investigation and evaluation of sustainable use, so that it only supplements the surface water at the water deficit area.

Source: Korea Water Resources Corporation, 2006, *Water Resources Plan (2006-2020) Report*.

Drainage Density and River Improvement [65-2]

Due to mountaneous terrains and high concentration of rainfalls in summer, flooding along rivers used to be common in the past. In order to prevent flooding and also to reclaim lands around river channels for agricultural and urban uses, river improvements have been conducted intensively in Korea. This map shows drainage density (km/km²) for individual administrative regions, and also river improvement ratios for national rivers, 1st order regional rivers, and 2nd order regional rivers.

The highest drainage density can be observed in Ulsan, Gwangju, and Seoul, which are all located at relatively flat terrains and their drainage density is over 40 (km/km²). On the other hand, the administrative regions showing low drainage density are Incheon, Gangwon-*do*, Gyeongsang-nam-*do*, and Jeollabuk-*do*. Except Incheon, these regions showing low drainage density are dominant in the mountains.

River improvement practices have commonly straightened channels and built impermeable concrete banks along channels, which have removed the majority of natural fluvial landforms from river channels. Consequently, various negative effects, including the loss of ecological functions of rivers, dry-out of river flows, lowering of groundwater tables, and also water pollutions, are severe, especially in urban areas. In order to overcome these problems, restoration of natural river conditions along already improved river channels has become common practice in recent years.

Source: Ministry of Construction and Transportation, 2004, *River Statistics of Korea*.

Flooding Vulnerability [65-3]

Flooding vulnerability is calculated by the sum of the number of habitual flooding areas which experience flooding every 3 or 4 years and the number of disaster risk areas which are expected to be damaged by landslides and mudflow, and then divided by area in square kilometers.

The number is presented for all administrative regions of *si, gun* and *gu* scale. Since 1980s, a great number of river improvement projects have been conducted to build embankments to protect such vulnerable areas. During the 1st phase (1982-1987), river improvement projects were mainly focused on the national rivers; afterward, during the 2nd phase (1988-1996) and 3rd phase (1999-2004), 1st and 2nd order regional rivers were also improved. In 2003, 870 regions were designated as habitual flooding areas. National Emergency Management Agency has conducted improvement projects for the high disaster risk areas to prevent landslides and mudflow. In 2002, 336 regions were designated as disaster risk areas. Five areas were designated in Seoul and Daegu, 10 in Busan, 1 in Incheon, 6 in Gwangju, 16 in Gyeonggi, 20 in Gangwon-*do*, 38 in Chungcheongbuk-*do*, 25 in Chungcheongnam-*do*, 61 in Jeollabuk-*do*, 45 in Jeollanam-*do*, 41 in Gyeongsangbuk-*do*, 39 in Gyeongsangnam-*do*, and 24 in Jejudo. On the assumption that a larger number of designated areas means higher vulnerability, capital and metropolitan areas are relatively safer than those in the undeveloped regions. The map shows that habitual flooding areas are mainly located in the central part of the Korean Peninsula including the Seoul metropolitan, Gyeonggi-*do* and Gangwon-*do*, while the disaster risk areas are distributed among the inland mountainous regions.

Source: Korea Water Resources Corporation, 2006, *Water Resource Plan (2006-2020) Report*.

Water Shortage [65-4]

This map shows the water shortage regions where water delivery was stopped or limited at least twice during the drought years of 1994, 1995, and 2001. There are 62 administrative regions in this category, which are distributed among the inland areas and the southern areas adjacent to the west coast. Major reason of water shortage problem is the long lasting drought. Insufficient water supply facilities may also contribute to this problem. In this case, the installation of more water intake and supplying facilities as well as new water resources development may relieve the water shortage problem.

Source: Korea Water Resources Corporation, 2006, *Water Resource Plan (2006-2020) Report*.

[Reference]

Korea Water Resources Corporation, 2002, *Guide to Our Rivers*, Daejeon: Korea Water Resources Corporation.
Korea Water Resources Corporation, 2003, *Perspectives on Water Resources Industries in North Korea and Strategies to Collaboration*, Deajeon: Korea Water Resources Corporation.
Korea Water Resources Corporation, 2004, *Dams of Korea*, Daejeon: Korea Water Resource Corporation.
Ministry of Construction and Transportation, Korea Water Resources Corporation, 2004, *River Statistics of Korea*, Daejeon: Ministry of Construction and Transportation.
Ministry of Construction and Transportation, Korea Water Resources Corporation, 2006, *Water Resource Plan (2006-2020) Report*, Daejeon: Ministry of Construction and Transportation.
Ministry of Construction and Transportation, Korea Water Resources Corporation, 2005, *Ground water Annual Report of 2004*, Daejeon: Ministry of Construction and Transportation, Korea Water Resources Corporation.
Ministry of Construction and Transportation, Korea Water Resources Corporation, 2005, *Water and Future*, Daejeon: Ministry of Construction and Transportation, Korea Water Resources Corporation.

Environment

Surface Water Quality [66]

Surface water quality generally depends on the concentration of pollutants and amount of wastewater discharge to a water body. Water quality is now divided into seven categories and is explained with terms of 'very good', 'good', and 'poor' to aid public understanding. The map shows the status of BOD in the major rivers. The classification on the map follows the recent criteria of BOD value.

Continuous monitoring of water quality of a river used for drinking water is mandatory. A nationwide sensor network known as the National Water Environment Information System was built to continuously measure water quality of lakes and rivers. The average BOD value of 2006 was obtained from the information system for water quality. Data for wastewater generation and discharge were obtained the 2006 Environmental Statistics Yearbook. The map gives a better understanding of the general status of the degree of water pollution in rivers.

Source: Ministry of Environment, 2006.

Water Supply System [68-1]

The national map shows the coverage rate divided by small districts, which can give information on degree of service by the water supply system. The map uses the detailed classification of regions to identify the significant differences between large cities and local areas. The coverage rate is calculated by dividing the population served by the total population in the region. The population is expressed using different sizes of human-shaped bars, i.e., 1,000,000, 500,000 and 50,000.

Source: Ministry of Environment, 2005.

Drinking Water Treatment Plants [68-2]

Capacities and locations of water treatment plants are identified to reveal the magnitude of water service in each province. Circles of different sizes are drawn in the location of a plant depending on the daily maximum water capacity. The maximum capacity was divided into less than 1,000, 1,000-5,000, 5,000-10,000, 10,000-50,000, and more than 50,000 ton/day. The classification includes various criteria used in the Ministry of Environment. For instance, turbidity is used as a measure of the success of sand filtration systems. Depending on the capacity of the water treatment plant, i.e., less or more than 5,000 ton/day, different criteria of turbidity are applied. In addition to the capacity of each plant, the total capacity of each province is expressed on the map.

Source: Ministry of Environment, 2005.

Public Sewage Treatment Facilities [68-3]

Wastewater effluents are now considered one of the most valuable water resources in an arid area. The national map shows the sewage service rate divided by small districts, which can give information on the degree of service availability by the sewage system. The map uses the detailed classification of regions to identify the significant differences between large cities and local areas. The coverage rate is calculated by dividing the population covered by the service by total population in the region. The population was expressed using different sizes of human-shaped bars, i.e., 1,000,000, 500,000, and 50,000.

Source: Ministry of Environment, 2005.

Distribution of Wastewater Treatment Plants [68-4]

Wastewater can be categorized by source, i.e., domestic wastewater from household activities, industrial wastewater from various factories, livestock wastewater and excreta from animal farms. The wastewater treatment plants are shown using the classification; there are 79 domestic wastewater treatment plants, 49 wastewater treatment plants for livestock, 49 industrial wastewater treatment plants, and 79 industrial wastewater treatment plants in rural areas.

Source: National Emergency Management Agency, 2005.

Air Quality Management [69-1]

To measure air quality continually, monitoring stations are built by various organizations, including cities and provinces. The data show that all air quality standards are generally met, except that for PM_{10}. The number of violations of the standards is shown by monitoring station.

Source: Institute of Environmental Research, 2005.

Emission and Concentrations: Nitrogen Dioxide [69-2]

The emission per area and concentrations of nitrogen dioxide are shown in the map. Emissions (kg) in 2005 obtained from the National Institute of Environmental Research are tabulated by source type. Emission by district is divided by the district's area in this map. The emission per area of NO_2 was substantial in most metropolitan areas due to the impact of transport vehicles-one of the most typical emission sources. The air quality standards promulgated by the Ministry of Environment in 2001 state that the annual average NO_2 concentration should not exceed 0.05ppm. Emission of NO_2 from each province and the concentrations in major cities are shown.

Source: Institute of Environmental Research, 2005.

Emission and Concentrations: PM_{10} [69-3]

PM_{10} was included in the national air quality standards in 2001 because various hazardous effects by PM_{10} were identified. The emission per area and concentrations of PM_{10} are shown in the map. Emissions (kg) in 2005 obtained from the National Institute of Environmental Research are tabulated by source type. Emission by district is divided by the district's area in this map. The emission per area of PM_{10} displays a great variation. The Gangwon-*do* and Gyeongsang-*do* show low concentrations of PM_{10}. However, the emission per area of PM_{10} is substantial in most metropolitan areas because of the use of transport vehicles (a typical emission source of PM_{10}) is significant in the areas. The air quality standards promulgated by the Ministry of Environment in 2001 state that the annual average PM_{10} concentration should not exceed 70㎍/m². Emission of PM_{10} from each province and the concentrations in major cities are shown.

Source: Institute of Environmental Research, 2005.

Emission and Concentrations: Carbon Monoxide [69-4]

The emission per area and concentrations of CO are shown in the map. Emissions (kg) in 2005 obtained from the National Institute of Environmental Research are tabulated by source type. Emission by district is divided by the district's area in this map. Most locations display concentrations far below the standard. Some places in Gyeonggi-*do* and the southeast coastal area have slightly higher emissions. The air quality standards promulgated by the Ministry of Environment in 2001 state that the 8-hour average CO concentration should not exceed 9 ppm. Emission of CO from each province and the concentrations in major cities are shown.

Source: Institute of Environmental Research, 2005.

Emission of VOC and Ozone Concentrations [69-5]

The emission per area and concentrations of VOC are shown in the map. Emissions (kg) in 2005 obtained from the National Institute of Environmental Research are tabulated by source type. Emission by district is divided by the district's area in this map. The data include emissions from point sources, area sources, and mobile sources. However, emission from natural sources is not included. The emission per area of VOC shows a wide spatial variation. For instance, the emission per area was 0-1 kg/m² in some of Gangwon-*do* province, in contrast to more than 200 kg/m² in metropolitan areas such as Seoul. There is no standard for VOC. Because the VOC react under the sun and generate O_3 as a secondary pollutant, O_3 concentrations are mapped along with emission per area of VOC. The air quality standards promulgated by the Ministry of Environment in 2001 state that the 8-hour average O_3 concentration should not exceed 0.06 ppm. Emission of VOC from each province and O_3 concentrations in major cities are expressed on an annual basis.

Source: Institute of Environmental Research, 2005.

Emission and Concentrations: Sulfur Dioxide [69-6]

The emission per area and concentrations of SO_2 are shown in the map. Emissions (kg) in 2005 obtained from the National Institute of Environmental Research are tabulated by source type. Emission by district is divided by the district's area in this map. The emission per area of SO_2 showed a great variation. Most places emitted less than 1 kg/m² of SO_2. Metropolitan areas or industrial complexes in general emit great amounts of SO_2. The air quality standards promulgated by the Ministry of Environment in 2001 state that the annual average of SO_2 concentration should not exceed 0.02 ppm. Emission of SO_2 from each province and the concentrations in major cities are shown.

Source: Institute of Environmental Research, 2005.

Solid Waste [69-7]

A pie graph was used to express the amount of waste generation. The diameter of the pie increases with increasing generation. The least waste (2,615ton/day) occurred in Jeju-*do*, and the highest generation (46,057ton/day) occurred in Seoul. The disposed waste is classified by source: domestic waste, industrial waste, and specified waste from particular industries. In most places, industrial waste consists of 60-90 percent of the total waste. The emission per area and concentrations of VOC are shown in the map. Generation (kg/day/10,000 people) in 2005 obtained from the National Institute of Environmental Research is tabulated by district. The most crowded area in Korea, Seoul, generated approximately 23 percent of the waste in 2004. The generation in Gongju city of Chungcheongnam-*do* and Suncheon of Jeollanam-*do* was slightly higher than other places.

Source: Ministry of Environment, 2004.

Domestic Waste [69-8]

Generation rates of food waste are shown in the map. Emissions (kg/

day/10,000 people) in 2005 obtained from the National Institute of Environmental Research are tabulated. Food waste consists of almost 44 percent of the total domestic generation in Seoul and the Gyeonggi-*do*. The generation was quite similar in most areas, i.e., 1-3 ton/day/10,000 people. However, it was more than 4 ton/day/10,000 people in metropolitan areas such as Seoul. However, Jincheon-*gun* of Chungcheongbuk-*do* also shows a relatively a high rate of generation because of the industrially-produced food waste, which is five times greater there than domestic portions. Disposal methods of domestic waste are also presented. In most places, recycling and landfill dumping are the major disposal methods.

Source: Ministry of Environment, 2004.

Waste Treatment Facilities [69-9]

The amount of treated waste by the three methods (i.e., landfill, incineration, and recycling/others) in 2004 is shown. Ocean disposal, a popular method employed in past years, has been prohibited. Landfills are now almost at capacity. The public opposes the construction of incinerators because of by-products such as dioxins. Recycling of waste seems to be the most sustainable method for waste management and should be increased.

Source: Ministry of Environment, 2004.

Natural Disasters

Frequency of Natural Disasters and Economic Losses [70-1]

The frequency of natural disasters and economic losses for the past 10 years (1995-2004) by *si, gun*, and *gu* are mapped. The frequency of natural disasters showed regional differences from as few as just one event to as many as 15. When examining the economic losses per person from natural disasters, Gangwon-*do* suffered the most. In Gangwon-*do*, Yangyang-*gun* recorded the highest amount of economic losses caused by natural disasters at 16,538,300won per person. It was followed by Ulleung-*gun* in Gyeongsangbuk-*do* (13,113,200won), Samcheok in Gangwon-*do* (10,299,000won), Goseong-*gun* in Gangwon-*do* (10,222,200won) and Jeongseon-*gun* in Gangwon-*do* (9,857,500won).

Source: National Emergency Management Agency, 1995-2004, 'Annual Report of Natural Disasters'.

Frequency of Natural Disasters: Heavy Rainfall Events, Typhoons, Heavy Snowfall Events [70-2, 3, 4]

The frequency of natural disasters caused by heavy rainfalls, typhoons, and heavy snowfalls for the past 10 years (1995-2004) by *si, gun*, and *gu* are mapped. Heavy rainfalls, which comprises most of the natural disasters, frequently occur in the northern Gyeonggi-*do* and in the Chungcheong-*do*, but are relatively evenly distributed throughout the nation. Typhoons occur most frequently along the southern and eastern coastlines, including Jeju Special Self-Governing Province, which is located on the main typhoon tracks. Heavy snowfall is rare compared to heavy rainfall and typhoons. It usually occurs along the western coastline, with four events at Gongju-*si*, Boryeong-*si*, and Buyeo-*gun* in Chungcheongnam-*do* and in Gochang-*gun* in Jeollabuk-*do*, while it occurred three times in Soecheon-*gun* and Taean-*gun* in Chungcheongnam-*do* and in Gimje-*si* and Jinan-*gun* in Jeollabuk-*do*.

Source: National Emergency Management Agency, 1995-2004, 'Annual Report of Natural Disasters'.

Economic Losses, Deaths and Flooded Areas Caused by Heavy Rainfall Events [72-1, 2, 3]

Economic losses, deaths, and flooded areas caused by heavy rainfall events for the past 10 years (1995-2004) by *si, gun*, and *gu* are mapped. Property damage in northern Gyeonggi-*do* and Gangwon-*do* caused by heavy rainfall was greater than in other regions. Hwacheon-*gun*, Gangwon-*do* had the largest amount of economic losses per person (6,973,300won), followed by Cheorwon-*gun* in Gangwon-*do* (5,163,300 won), Yanggu-*gun* (4,409,300won), Yeoncheon-*gun* in Gyeonggi-*do* (4,326,100won), and Boeun-*gun* in Chungcheongbuk-*do* (2,962,300 won). The most deaths occurred in Gyeonggi-*do*, but were distributed relatively evenly throughout the nation. Within Gyeonggi-*do*, 35 fatalities occurred at Paju-*si*, with 34 in Yangju-*si*, and 28 in Namyangju-*si*. Elsewhere, deaths were extensive in Seogwipo in Jeju (34), and Sancheong-*gun* in Gyeongsangnam-*do* (29). The largest flooded area per administrative district unit caused by heavy rainfall was in Jung-*gu*, Daejeon at 1,045,500m^2 per 1km^2, followed by Gimpo-*si* (340,500m^2) and Paju-*si* (236,700m^2) in Gyeonggi-*do*, Seocheon-*gun* in Chuncheongnam-*do* (201,400m^2) and Ganghwa-*gun* (188,400m^2).

Source: National Emergency Management Agency, 1995-2004, 'Annual Report of Natural Disasters'.

Economic Losses, Deaths and Flooded Areas Caused by Typhoons [72-4, 73-1, 2]

Economic losses, deaths, and flooded areas caused by typhoons for the past 10 years (1995-2004) by *si, gun*, and *gu* are mapped. Economic losses caused by typhoons was greater in Gangwon-*do* and Gyeongsang-*do* than other areas. Yangyang-*gun* in Gangwon-*do* had the most economic losses per person at 16,341,900won, followed by Samcheok-*si* (9,992,300won), Goseong-*gun* (9,941,500won), Jeongseon-*gun* (8,577,600won) in Gangwon-*do* and Yeongyang-*gun* in Gyeongsangbuk-*do* (6,808,200won). Typhoon-related deaths were concentrated in the Yeongdong and southern coastline regions. The most deaths occurred at Gangneung in Gangwon-*do* with 59 -deaths, followed by Gijang-*gun* in Busan (50), Yeosu-*si* in Jeollanam-*do* (50), Tongyeong-*si* in Gyeongsangnam-*do* (48) and Geoje-*si* in Gyeongsangnam-*do* (40). The largest flooded area per administrative district unit caused by typhoons was in Sacheon-*si* in Gyeongsangnam-*do* at 188,200m^2 per 1km^2, followed by Naju-*si* in Jeollanam-*do* (132,700m^2), Changnyeong-*gun* in Gyeongsangnam-*do* (88,200m^2), Yeongam-*gun* in Jeollanam-*do* (87,300m^2) and Miryang-*si* in Gyeongsangnam-*do* (86,900m^2).

Source: National Emergency Management Agency, 1995-2004, 'Annual Report of Natural Disasters'.

Economic Losses, Deaths and Flooded Areas Caused by Typhoon 'Rusa' [73-3, 4]

The property damage, deaths, and flooded areas caused by Typhoon Rusa for the past 10 years (1995-2004) by *si, gun*, and *gu* are mapped. Property damage caused by Rusa occurred most severely in Gangwon-*do*. Property damage per person was highest in Yangyang-*gun* in Gangwon-*do* at 14,779,300won, followed by Goseong-*gun* (8,597,900 won) and Samcheok-*si* (6,617,300won) in Gangwon-*do*, Muju-*gun* in Jeollabuk-*do* (5,798,500won) and Jeongseon-*gun* in Gangwon-*do* (5,343,500won). Deaths were also concentrated in Gangwon-*do*. The most deaths occurred at Gangneung-*si* in Gangwon-*do* with 53, followed by Gimcheon-*si* in Gyeongsangbuk-*do* (26), Samcheok-*si* in Gangwon-*do* (25), Yangyang-*gun* in Gangwon-*do* (23), and Goseong-*gun* in Gangwon-*do* (11). The largest flooded area per administrative district unit caused by the typhoon was in Jeju at 84,700m^2 per 1km^2, followed by Sacheon-*si* in Gyeongsangnam-*do* (83,200m^2), Gwangyang-*si* in Jeollanam-*do* (34,700m^2), Gangseo-*gu* in Busan (20,200m^2), and Jinju-*si* in Gyeongsangnam-*do* (19,000m^2).

Source: National Emergency Management Agency, 1995-2004, 'Annual Report of Natural Disasters'.

Flora and Vegetation

Ecology and Natural Status Map [74]

This map categorizes the preservation value of nature into three levels (first, second, and third), based on the combined evaluation of ecological value, naturality, and visual amenity. This map is compiled by not only vegetation, but also endangered animal species, plant habitats and migration routes, scenic amenity, and biodiversity. According to this map, the first level area, 7,455km^2, is about 7.5 percent of the total land area (100,144km^2) in South Korea, while the second and third levels occupy 39.2 percent and 44.7 percent, respectively. A separate management area which has distinct natural characteristics is about 8.6 percent. This map will provide valuable basic information for administrative and development planning.

Source: Ministry of Environment, 2006, Ecology and Natural Status Map.

Major Tree Species Distribution [76-1]

About 65 percent, 6.4 million m^3 of the Korean Peninsula is covered by forests. A distinct latitudinal zonation of plant communities is easily found from the boreal evergreen coniferous forests in the north to the warm-temperate evergreen broad-leaved forests in the south. Temperate mixed forests are, however, common in Korea. A vertical zonation of plant community often appears within mountains.

Due to significant human intervention from the past, most native forests, *Carpinus laxiflora* forests, have been replaced by oak tree forests including *Quercus acutissma*, Q. *mongolica*, Q. *variabillis*, and *Quercus serrata Thunb*, as well as *Robinia pseudoacacia, Alnus japonica Steud, Prunus sargentii*, and *Styrax japonica*.

Red Pine (*Pinus densiflora*) forests have the largest coverage in Korea. It is not only because the Korean government did not allow any illegal pine tree cutting in the past, but also because pine trees grow relatively well in dry and barren soil. In recent years, its coverage has significantly decreased because of attacks by insects or diseases such as the pine needle gall midge and the pine wilt disease, as well as frequent forest fires.

The Tree Species Distribution map depicts the overall distribution of major tree species across the Korean Peninsula. In 1996, the Korea Forest Research Institute developed the map based on forest vegetation maps at a scale of 1:25,000. Aerial photos were taken between 1986 and 1992, and extensive field surveys were also conducted at the same period.

Source: Korea Forest Service, Korea Forest Research Institute, 1996, Major Tree Species Distribution Map.

Forest Coverage Ratio [76-2]

Forest coverage ratio represents the percentage of the surface covered by forest. The type of tree species, forest structure, succession stages of a forest, and forest management determine the status of forest coverage. Inversely, forest coverage influences not only the growth of forests and forest environments, but also the pattern of land use. The Korean Forest Research Institute has developed a forest coverage ratio map based on digital forest vegetation maps at a scale of 1km × 1km.

Source: Korea Forest Service, Korea Forest Research Institute, 1994, Forest Coverage Map.

Natural Forest and Artificial Forest [76-3]

Forest scientists categorize forests into natural forests and artificial forests according to how the forests were formed. An artificial forest refers to the forest which has undergone significant human intervention, whereas a natural forest is the forest that has evolved and reproduced itself naturally.

Before 1970, the afforestation plan of Korea was designed to recover barren forest soil. After two large-scale artificial forestation-afforestation campaigns, approximately 124,000m^3 of slash-and-burn fields have been turned into artificial forests since 1973. These afforestation plans and activities of the Korean government are considered as one of the most successful afforestation projects in the world in the 20th century. Evergreen coniferous trees, *Pinus koraiensis* and *Pinus rigida*, and deciduous coniferous tree such as *Larix leptolepis* were planted in most artificial forests in the central mountain region, whereas *Cryptomeria japonica* and *Chamaecyparis obtusa* were planted in the south. Currently about 20 percent of the total forests in Korea were established through tree planting.

Although most natural forests in Korea are primarily deciduous forests, it is, however, very rare to find natural and pure deciduous forests, since deciduous tree species are mutually exclusive. In most natural deciduous forests, a canopy consists of oak trees including *Quercus mongolica* and *Quercus acutissma*, as well as *Carpinus laxiflora, Prunus sargentii, Fraxinus rhynchophylla*, maples, birches, Amur trees, elms, *Cornus controversa*, and *Juglans mandshurica. Carpinus cordata, Acer pseudosieboldianum, Styrax obassia* and juvenile stages of deciduous trees are common in the lower level.

During 1986 and 1992, the Korea Forest Research Institute has developed a classification map of natural and artificial forests based on the digital vegetation maps created using aerial photos. A field survey was also conducted to ensure the quality of the maps.

Source: Korea Forest Service, Korea Forest Research Institute, 1996, Natural Forest and Artificial Forest Map.

Naturalized Plants [76-4]

Naturalized plants are species which grow well outside of their natural distribution range and also possess a potential expansion range. They propagate well, and in some cases, they become even more competitive than indigenous species in certain habitats. Distribution maps of Korean naturalized plants have been developed to help government decision-makers manage and control alien plants.

By the end of 2003, about 271 to 287 plants from overseas were growing well in Korea. There was also a sharp increase in the number of naturalized plant species. For example, the current number of naturalized plants expanded to more than double the number of 1980, and increased by more than 100 species in number compared to those of 1995.

A couple of naturalized plants are well known and are presented as an example. The North American species, *Ambrosia artemisiaefolia* var. *elatior* Desc. which is often blamed for causing pollen allergies was introduced around 1968. Another North American naturalized species *Ambrosia trifida* L. was introduced during the early 1970's. *Solanum carolinense* L. and *Eupatorium rugosum* Houtt had been recognized since 1978. Other species had been introduced from other parts of the world, such as *Paspalum distichum* var. *indutum Shin* from tropical Asia introduced in 1994.

Once the naturalized plants occupy the area, they rapidly expand and spread with vigorous regeneration speed and adaptation ability. Therefore, prevention of the arrival and elimination of the alien plant species is the best way of controlling these plants. Although a strict quarantine procedure at ports and national borders is the best way to manage large numbers of people and merchandise, in reality it is quite difficult to control them. Proper methods of control and management of alien plant species should be applied in multiple stages, such as introduction, settlement, and expansion of steps through all available means.

Source: Korea Forest Service, Korea Forest Research Institute, 2002.
Ministry of Environment, National Institute of Environmental Research, 2003.

Land Cover Classification Map (1990s, Highest Level) [77]

A land cover classification map is a thematic map which is widely used for environmental management. The land cover classification map was made using multispectral satellite imageries to depict the physical and ecological status of the earth surface.

Since this map is produced every five years, it is able to detect changes in land cover and spatial structure of the landscape. This map has been used to develop environmental policies, specifically for clean air, clean water, and natural habitat conservation. The estimation of the amount of air pollutants such as isoprene and methane is also possible using the land cover ratio of coniferous forest, rice paddies, and wetland. The classification scheme was prepared to reflect environmental characteristics, land use and spatial planning for sustainable development using three levels of classification such as highest level, middle level, and the most detailed level.

The land cover classification map can be used with other types of maps such as land use map, which were produced not only for environmental purposes but also for regional development. The original source of two maps is vector data extracted from topographic maps which have more detailed information on land use itself, transportation facilities, residential areas, forests, water bodies, wetlands, grasslands, and open lands in general.

The highest level land cover classification contains seven kinds of land cover for Korea. This includes urban-open lands, agriculture lands, forests, grasslands, wetlands, bare lands, and water bodies.

Landsat Thematic Mapper (TM) data is primarily used. Topographic maps with 1:50,000 scale for South Korea, and military maps with 1:50,000 scale for North Korea were used. Aerial photography, high-resolution satellite images, and other TM images were also used. The Ministry of Environment has run the 'Land Cover Classification Map Programme', and prepared the manual of data production specification.

Highest level classification was based on multi-temporal data to remove cloud and seasonal effects. Both supervised and unsupervised classifications were used for all areas. For the georectification, topographic maps were used for South Korea with Trans-Mercator projection with Tokyo datum, and military maps were used for North Korea with converting the Russia 1942 coordinate system to the Trans-Mercator projection with Tokyo datum. Other images were georectified by using an image-to-image method.

Primary datasets for middle level classification include IRS-1C data, Landsat ETM+ data, and digital raster graphics (1:5,000). Stock maps, ecological maps and topographic maps (1:25,000) were also used as ancillary data. Most recently acquired satellite images with minimum cloud contamination were used for an image classification. These data were subdivided into five major basin regions (Seoul metropolitan area, Hangang, Nakdonggang, Geumgang, and Yeongsangang basins).

① Seoul Metropolitan Area and its Vicinity (1990s, Middle Level)
The Land Cover Classification Map for the Seoul Metropolitan area and its vicinity was completed in 2002. Twenty-three classes were plotted. The Metropolitan Seoul and its vicinity showed 7.41 percent of residential areas, 1.34 percent of industrial areas, 0.77 percent of commercial areas, and 1.40 percent of transportation facilities. Large portion of the land is used for residential and industrial purposes reflecting one of the world's highest urbanized environments. A large proportion of forest is protected as Greenbelt by the law, which keeps forest from urban sprawl.

② Hangang Basin (1990s, Middle Level)
The land cover classification map of the Hangang basin (including Seoul Metropolitan Area) was completed in 2002. The Hangang basin showed 23.23 percent of deciduous forest, 27.64 percent of coniferous forest, and 18.18 percent of mixed forest, which acts as a hinterland for the Seoul Metropolitan Area and also as a source of fresh water. Almost 70 percent of the land is preserved as natural forest.

③ Geumgang Basin (1990s, Middle Level)
The land cover classification map of the Geumgang basin was completed in 2004. Twenty-three classes were plotted. The Geumgang basin showed 21.42 percent of rice paddy, 10.86 percent of dry paddy, 16.93 percent of deciduous forest, 23.82 percent of coniferous forest, and 12.68 percent of mixed forest. This basin is one of the largest agricultural regions in Korea. According to the statistics, this basin does not contain many point pollution sources such as industrial parks, but contains a wide variety of non-point pollution sources such as agricultural areas. Industrial and other developed areas are not common in this basin.

④ Nakdonggang Basin (1990s, Middle Level)
In 2003, the land cover classification map of the Nakdonggang basin was completed by compiling 225 classification sheets at a scale of 1:25,000. Twenty-three classes were plotted using IRS-1D and Landsat ETM+ images. Within the Nakdonggang basin, there are many point and non-point pollution sources because the river flows through major cities.

⑤ Yeongsangang Basin (1990s, Middle Level)
In 2004, the map for the Yeongsangang basin was plotted at a scale of 1:25,000. The map has 152 classification sheets. There are many point and large non-point pollution sources within this basin, since Yeongsangang flows through the major agricultural area of Korea.
Source: Ministry of Environment, 2002-2004, Land Cover Classification Map.

Table. Land Cover Classification Scheme for Korea

7 Highest Class (Highest Level)		23 Middle Class (Middle Level)	
Urban Area	100	Residential	110
		Industrial	120
		Commercial	130
		Recreational	140
		Transportation	150
		Public Facility	160
Agricultural Land	200	Rice Paddy	210
		Horticultural Garden	220
		Green House	230
		Orchard	240
		Other Agricultural Area	250
Forest	300	Broadleaf Forest	310
		Coniferous Forest	320
		Mixed Forest	330
Grassland	400	Grassland	410
		Golf Course	420
		Other Grassland	430
Wetland	500	Inland Wetland	510
		Coastal Wetland	520
Bare Ground	600	Mining Field	610
		Other Bare Ground	620
Water	700	Freshwater	710
		Salt Water	720

Source: Ministry of Environment, 2002, Land Cover Classification Map.

[Reference]
Kim, J.M. et al, 1974, *Encyclopedia of Science and Technology, 6, Plant*, Seoul: Hakwonsa.
Kong, W.S., 2006, *Ecosystem of North Korea*, Asian Foundation Research Series, 202, Seoul: Jipmundang.
Kong, W.S., 2007, *Biogeography of Korea*, Seoul: Geobook.
Kong, W.S. and Watts, D., 1993, *The Plant Geography of Korea*, Hague: Kluwer Academic Publishers.
Kim, C.M., 2003, Mapping Forests of South Korea, *ESRI International User Conference Proceedings*, August 7-11, San Diego, California.
Kim, C.M., Rho, D.K. and Jun, E. J., 2004, A Nationwide Forest Mapping using GIS, *Proceedings of the 2004 Summer Meeting of the Korean Forest Society*, 24-25, 2004, Jejudo.
National Institute of Environmental Research, 2003, *Research on the Effects of Alien Plants on Ecosystem and their Management (IV)*, National Institute of Environmental Research Report, South Korea, 123p.
Park S.H., Shin, J.H., Lee, Y.M., Lim, J.H. and Moon, J.S., 2002, Distribution of Naturalized Alien Plants in Korea, *KFRI Research Bulletin*, 193, Korea Forest Research Institute, Seoul: Ukgo Press.
Yim, Y.J. and Cheon, E.S., 1980, Distribution of Naturalized Plants in the Korean Peninsula, *Korean Journal of Botany*, 23, 69-83.

Animals

Distribution of Endangered Wildlife Species [78]
The maps in this chapter show distributions of major wildlife groups including birds, mammals, amphibians, reptiles, fish, and insects. Due to high animal diversity, exhaustive distribution maps of all wildlife are impractical, but maps are included for endemic, rare, and endangered species. Major references used for maps are *National Nature Environment Survey and Endangered Species Distribution Survey* conducted by the Ministry of Environment and National Institute of Environmental Research, and the study of others (see references).

Endangered Mammals [80-1, 2]
Hodgson's bat (*Myotis formosus*) is an endangered species. The largest population inhabits Hampyeong-*gun*, Jeollanam-*do*. New habitats of this species recently have been found in the same region.
The spotted seal (*Phoca largha*) occurs mainly along the coast of the Baengnyeongdo and spend the spring, summer, and autumn for feeding, and return to their breeding grounds in Liodong Bay, China, in the winter. The estimated population size is between 400 and 500 along the coasts of Baengnyeongdo.

The yellow-throated marten (*Martes flavigula*) inhabits high mountains such as Seoraksan, Odaesan, and Jirisan.

The endangered Asiatic black bear (*Ursus thibetanus ussuricus*) was distributed throughout most mountainous regions in the past, but after the 1990s, only a few individuals persist in the region of Jirisan and around the DMZ. A restoration project is going on at Jirisan.
The Siberian musk deer (*Moschus moschiferus*) is an endangered inhabitant of high mountainous areas, but remaining individuals are few and the species is nearly extinct.

The Eurasian flying squirrel (*Pteromys volans*) nests on large dead trees

in mountainous areas, and its population size is currently decreasing due to habitat destruction.

The Amur goral (*Naemorhedus caudatus*) is an endangered species inhabiting the cliffs of high mountains. The total population sizes is between 500 and 600 in the eastern DMZ, Seoraksan, and southern areas of Gangwon-*do*.

Birds [80-3, 4, 82-1, 2]
The black woodpecker (*Dryocopus martius*) is a vulnerable species inhabiting the middle and northern parts of the Korean Peninsula. The white-backed woodpecker (*Dendrocopos leucotos*) and great spotted woodpecker (*Dendrocopos major*) are common inhabitants of hilly and mountainous areas in Korea.

The Eurasian eagle owl (*Bubo bubo*), the largest Korean owl, populates mountain areas, whereas the Eurasian tawny owl (*Strix aluco*) is found in both hilly and mountainous areas. The brown hawk owl (*Ninox scutulata*) occurs both in forests in urban parks, while the collared scops (*Otus lempiji*) and Eurasian scops (*Otus scops*) live in forests, village areas, and parks. All are vulnerable species.

Over 90 percent of the total global population of Baikal teal (*Anas formosa*) annually spend winters in Korea, mainly inhabiting the coasts, lakes, agriculture areas, and reservoirs on western parts of peninsula. It is a vulnerable species.

The swan goose (*Anser cygnoides*) arrives in Korea during the fall from its breeding sites in Siberia and Mongolia. This vulnerable species inhabits estuaries and tidal flats, and often feeds on rice paddies.

During the fall, the bean goose (*Anser fabalis*) arrives in Korea from breeding sites in Siberia or Mongolia. This species inhabits estuaries, tidal flats, and reservoirs, and feed on the paddies. It is a vulnerable species.

The Brent goose (*Branta bernicla*) is a rare winter visitor observed on coastal and agricultural areas of the East Sea and the South Sea.

The red-crowned crane (*Grus japonensis*) and white-naped crane (*Grus vipio*) inhabit agricultural areas, open lands, and estuaries around the DMZ. The hooded crane (*Grus monacha*) inhabits at the Suncheonman.

Permanent breeding populations of golden eagles (*Aquila chrysaetos*) are rare and confined to mountainous regions of Korea, whereas the typical populations found throughout the country are migrating winter visitors.

The Eurasian spoonbill (*Platalea leucorodia*) is a migrating winter visitor locally inhabiting shallow water wetlands such as estuaries, reservoirs, and tidal flats.

Large populations of the black vulture (*Aegypius monachus*) inhabit portions of the DMZ including the Hangang estuary, and the Cheorwon and Yanggu areas, and populations are rarely found in southern parts and Jejudo.

The peregrine falcon (*Falco peregrinus*) is a rare breeding resident along cliff of islands and coastal areas, but may also be found in agricultural areas and open lands in non-breeding seasons.

The total global population of the black-faced spoonbill (*Platalea minor*) is only 1,800. Populations of this species breed on islands on the Yellow Sea of Korea and spend winters in Jejudo, Taiwan, and Hong Kong.

Steller's sea eagle (*Haliaeetus pelagicus*) is a winter visitor distributed all over the country, it is mainly found in coastal areas.

The mute swan (*Cygnus olor*) has the lowest population size of migratory swans recorded in Korea. This species mainly inhabits lagoonal habitats on the East Sea.

The Chinese egret (*Egretta eulophotes*) is a globally endangered species. Populations of this species breed on islands on the Yellow Sea, and inhabit near-coastal areas on the Yellow Sea.

The white-tailed eagle (*Haliaeetus albicilla*) is a rare winter visitor observed along estuaries, rivers, and reservoirs all over the country.

Insects [81-1, 82-3]
The red-spotted Apollo butterfly (*Parnassius bremeri*) was a common species until 1980s, but it is presently endangered with relict populations scattered in low numbers in Gangwon-*do* and Gyeongsangnam-*do*.

Protantigius superans is an endangered butterfly species confined to the mountainous area of northern Gangwon-*do*.

Spindasis takanonsis is an endangered butterfly species found in hilly pine forests with limited distributions in Chungcheong-*do*, and part of Gyeonggi-*do* and Gangwon-*do*.

The longhorn beetle (*Callipogon relictus*) was previously common in Gwangneung in Gyeonggi-*do* and Sogeumgang in Gangwon-*do*, but is now endangered. Only two or three individuals have been reported in Gwangneung since the 1990s.

The dung beetle (*Copris tripartitus*) is an endangered species with scattered distributions in Gyeonggi-*do*, Chungcheongnam-*do*, Gyeongsangbuk-*do*, Gyeongsangnam-*do*, Jeollanam-*do*, and Gangwon-*do*.

The scarab beetle (*Gymnopleurus mopsus*) was broadly distributed all over the country in the past, but this species has not been recently observed.

Formerly, the garden chafer (*Polyphylla laticollis manchurica*) was broadly distributed throughout Seoul, Paju, and Jejudo, but scattered populations now remains only in Chungcheongnam-*do*.

The Chinese stag beetle (*Metopodontus blanchardi*) inhabited the valley around Seogwipo in Jejudo in the past, but now inhabits only Hallasan.

Land Cover Classification Map for Major Drainage Basins

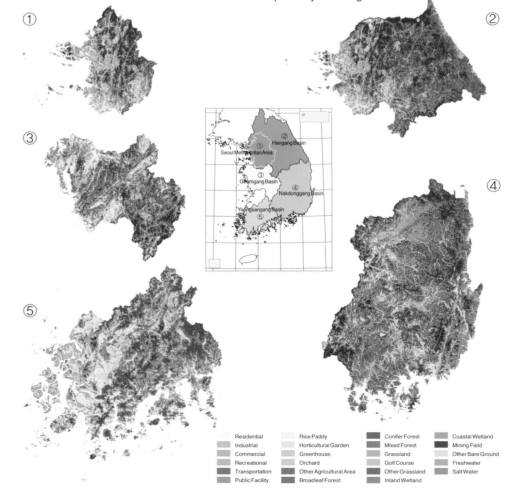

Residential	Rice Paddy	Conifer Forest	Coastal Wetland
Industrial	Horticultural Garden	Mixed Forest	Mining Field
Commercial	Greenhouse	Grassland	Other Bare Ground
Recreational	Orchard	Golf Course	Freshwater
Transportation	Other Agricultural Area	Other Grassland	Salt Water
Public Facility	Broadleaf Forest	Inland Wetland	

Source: Ministry of Environment, 2002-2004, Land Cover Classification Map.

Amphibians and Reptiles [81-2, 3]
The Peking Frog (*Rana plancyi*) is an endangered species observed all over the country, but only in small populations.

The Boreal Digging Frog (*Kaloula borealis*) was widely distributed all over the country in the past, but populations have decreased due to changes in habitat.

The Long-tailed clawed salamander (*Onychodactylus fischeri*) is distributed in mountainous areas over most of the country, but their populations are being seriously affected by road construction and various development projects.

The Cheju Salamander (*Hynobius quelpartensis*) is an endemic inhabitant of Jejudo and southern parts of the Korean Peninsula.

The Mongolian racerunner (*Eremias argus*) is an endangered species found only in sandy agricultural areas and coastal dunes.

Reeve's pond turtle (*Chinemys reevesii*) was widely distributed all over the country in the past, but populations have decreased due to changes in the drainage system.

An endemic Korean subspecies of the collared or many-toothed snake (*Sibynophis collaris*) has a distribution limited to Jejudo only.

The Korean rat snake (*Elaphe schrenckii*) is an endangered species in rapid decline due to habitat destruction and poaching.

Fish [81-4, 82-4, 5, 6, 7, 8, 9]
The sand lamprey (*Lethenteron [Lampetra] reissneri*) is a scientifically valuable endangered species broadly distributed all over the country except Jejudo.

The Siberian sculpin (*Cottus poecilopus*) is an endangered species which mainly inhabits in the Hangang, but small populations remain in the Geumgang, Mangyeonggang, Seomjingang, and Nakdonggang.

The slender shinner (*Pseudopungtungia tenuicorpa*) inhabits swift currents of gravel-bottomed upper streams. Populations have been observed in the Hangang and Imjingang.

The large-headed gudgeon (*Gobiobotia macrocephalus*) is an endemic and endangered inhabitant of swiftly moving currents with gravel bottoms in the upper streams of the Hangang, Imjingang, and Geumgang.

The short-barbeled gudgeon (*Gobiobotia brevibarba*) is an endemic and endangered species found only in the Hangang and Geumgang. Populations have recently declined due to habitat changes.

The Amur stickleback (*Pungitius sinensis sinensis*) is an endangered species inhabiting certain streams flowing into the East Sea.

The Hinsumaja (*Gobiobotia naktongensis*) is an endangered inhabitant of swift currents with sandy bottoms in Nakdonggang, Imjingang, and Geumgang.

The Korean stumpy bullhead (*Pseudobagrus brevicorpus*) is an endemic and endangered species found only in the Nakdonggang.

The Miho spined loach (*Iksookimia choii*) is an endemic and endangered species found only in Geumgang and Mihocheun. Marked decrease of population sizes in those areas are due to water pollution.

The black shinner (*Pseudopungtungia nigra*) is an endemic and endangered species observed in the Geumgang, Mangyeonggang, and Woongcheon.

The bullhead torrent catfish (*Liobagrus obesus*) is an endemic and endangered species with distributions restricted to the Imjingang, Hangang, Anseongcheon, and Sapkyocheon.

The Geumgang minnow (*Moroco kumkangensis*) is an endemic species broadly distributed within the Hangang, but found only in the upper streams of the Geumgang.

The Korean rose bitterling (*Rhodeus uyekii*) inhabits streams that flow into the southern Yellow Sea and the South Sea.

The king spined loach (*Iksookimia longicorpus*) is a common endemic inhabitant of the Seomjingang, Nakdonggang, and streams that flow into the southern East Sea.

The Korean spined loach (*Iksookimia koreensis*) is an endemic species inhabiting the Imjingang, Hangang, Geumgang, and Mangyeonggang as well as the Osypcheon and Maupcheon flowing into the East Sea.

The Korean sawbelly (*Hemiculter eigenmanni*) is an endemic inhabitant of all rivers and streams flowing into the West Sea except for the Imjingang and Hangang.
The Korean splendid dace (*Coreoleuciscus splendidus*) is an endemic inhabitant of most rivers and streams that flow into the East Sea, the Yellow Sea, and the South Sea.

Populations of the Korean spotted barbel (*Hemibarbus mylodon*) were formerly distributed in the upper streams of both the Hangang and Geumgang, but the population in the Geumgang has since disappeared, and only the population within the Hangang remains.

The Korean bitterling (*Acheilognathus signifer*), arctic lamprey (*Lethenteron [Lampetra] japonica*), Siberian sculpin (*Cottus poecilopus*), Amur stickleback (*Pungitius sinensis kaibarae*), Seomjin bitterling (*Acheilognathus somjinensis*), Morejusa (*Microphysogobio koreensis*) are endangered species with limited distributions and low populations.

The Korean bitterling (*Acheilognathus signifer*) is distributed in the Hangang and Imjingang; arctic lamprey (*Lethenteron [Lampetra] japonica*), Amur stickleback (*Pungitius sinensis kaibarae*) is found in streams flowing into the East Sea and Nakdong River; the Siberian sculpin (*Cottus poecilopus*) occurs in streams flowing into the middle portion of the East Sea; the Seomjin bitterling (*Acheilognathus somjinensis*) occurs in the streams of Imsil-*gun*, Jeollabuk-*do*; and Morejusa *(Microphysogobio koreensis)* is found in the Seomjingang and Nakdonggang, and streams that flow into the middle portion of the East Sea.

The greater bitterling (*Acheilognathus majusculus*) is an endemic species in scattered areas of the Seomjingang and Nakdonggang; the Korean bitterling (*Acheilognathus koreensis*), Wakiya's variegated gudgeon (*Sarcocheilichthys variegatus wakiyae*), Mori's rainbow gudgeon (*Sarcocheilichthys nigripinnis morii*), and the Korean rose bitterling (*Rhodeus uyekii*) inhabit streams that flow in the southern portions of the Yellow Sea and the South Sea.

The bitterling (*Acheilognathus yamatsutae*) is an endemic species distributed in all rivers and streams of the country except for those that flow in the East Sea and Seomjingang.

The Korean gudgeon (*Squalidus chankaensis tsuchigae*) is an endemic species inhabiting all rivers and streams between the Mangyeonggang and Nakdonggang, and its relative, the spotted barbel gudgeon (*Squalidus multimaculatus*), is an endemic inhabitant of small streams flowing into the southern East Sea.

The Yalu gudgeon (*Microphysogobio yaluensis*) is an endemic inhabitant of rivers and streams flowing into the Yellow Sea and the South Sea.

Migration Routes of Migratory Birds [83-1]
This map reveals regular pathways of migratory birds. Many migratory birds establish over-wintering sites, breeding sites, and stopover sites on the Korean Peninsula. Shore birds especially those migrating from wintering sites in either Australia or New Zealand to breeding sites in Siberia find sufficient food in the tidal flats of the Yellow Sea in Korea during their migration.

Source: Ministry of Environment, National Institute of Environmental Research, 1999-2006.

Major Wintering and Stopover Sites of Migratory Birds [83-2]
This map shows important wintering sites, and population sizes of winter birds based on the wintering birds monitoring program from 1999 to 2005. Major wintering sites are located at and near the western and southeastern seashores.

There are flyway network sites for conserving the winter birds such as Cranes and Anatidae in East Asia. In Korea, Cheorwon plain, Hangang estuary, Suncheonman, Haipyung plain at Gumi, and Cheonsuman were designated as network sites of Cranes and Anatidae.

This map also shows important stopover sites, and population sizes of shore birds based on the monitor program from 1999 to 2005. Major stopover sites are located at the Yellow Sea. There are East Asia-Pacific Network Sites for conserving the shore birds. Areas along the Dongjingang were designated as network sites of shore birds in Korea.

Source: Ministry of Environment, National Institute of Environmental Research, 1999-2006.

[References]
Kim, I.S., 2000, *Dancing Fishes*, Seoul: Daruenseasang.
Lee, I.K., Kim, G.J., Choi, J.M., Lee, D.W., Choi, D.S. and Yu, J.S., 1994, *Biodiversity of Korea 2000*, Seoul: Mineumsa.
Lee, W.S., Koo, T.H., and Park, J.Y., 2000, *A Field Guide to the Birds of Korean*, Seoul: LG Sanglok Corporation.
Lee, W.O., 2006, *Korean Fishes by Their Characters*, Seoul: Jiseongsa.
Ministry of Environment, 2006, *Green Korea*, Seoul: Ministry of Environment.
Shim, J.H., 2001, *Frogs that Song for a Life*, Seoul: Darumsesang.
Shim, J.H., 2001, *Turtles and Snakes who Dream Green Life*, Seoul: Darumsesang.
Won, C.M. and Smith, K.G., 1999, History and Current Status of Mammals of the Korean Peninsula, *Mammal Review*, 29, 3-33.
Won, C.M. and Yoo, B.H., 2004, Population Dynamics, Seasonal Haul-out Patterns and Conservation of Spotted Seal (*Phoca Largha*) along the Coasts of Bakryoung Island of South Korea, *Oryx*, 38, 109-112.

Ocean

General Chart [84]
This map presents general information necessary for a long-distance navigation rather than a precise description, and communicates marine information. Its scale is less than 1:4 million. A general chart of the coast contains coastline configurations, fishery zones, and administrative borders.

Source: National Oceanographic Research Institute, 2006.

Oceanic Current Chart (Winter) [86-1]
Korean waters are influenced by the Tsushima Warm Current which separates from Kuroshio Current throughout the year. The Tsushima Warm Current is then divided into Yellow Sea Warm Current and East Sea Warm Current between Goto and Jejudo. In winter, the surface current generally moves at 0.5 to 1.0knot, with the slowest mean annual current in the near-shore East Sea. The East Sea Warm Current migrates northward, rotating clockwise near the shores of Sokcho and Geojin in winter. It then retreats southward, making a ring-shaped vortex centered on Wonsan. The Yellow Sea Warm Current flows into the Yellow Sea after passing west of Jejudo and Bohai. On the other side, West Korean Coastal Waters move southward along Korea's west coast, flowing into the East Sea after passing through Jeju Straits and the Straits of Korea. The North Korea Cold Current moves southward across the East Sea to the area of Wonsan at a speed of 0.3 to 0.5knots, where it meets with the East Sea Warm Current near Ulleungdo. From there it flows northeastward to create an eddy current.

Source: National Oceanographic Research Institute, 2006.

Oceanic Current Chart (Spring) [86-2]
Surface currents in spring are generally slower than in winter, at 0.4 to 1.0knot, but velocity increases by more than 0.2knots along the East Sea shoreline. In spring, the East Sea Warm Current rotates clockwise along the Sokcho-*si* and Geojin shores to join with the Tsushima Warm Current south of Ulleungdo, where it moves northeastward. The Yellow Sea Warm Current flows into the Yellow Sea after passing west of Jejudo. It then moves southward, rotating counterclockwise near Gyeongnyeolbiyeoldo. The North Korea Cold Current moves southward across the East Sea to the area of Wonsan at a speed of 0.4 to 0.5knots, where it flows eastward at Ulleungdo northern sea.

Source: National Oceanographic Research Institute, 2006.

Oceanic Current Chart (Summer) [86-3]
Surface current speeds are maximized in summer, generally reaching 0.6 to 1.0knots. The East Sea Warm Current moves northward to Ulleungdo, and then shifts to the northeast. The North Korea Cold Current moves southward at a speed of about 0.4 to 0.5knots, then rotates counterclockwise at Wonsan near the shore and flows back toward the northeast. The Yellow Sea Warm Current migrates northward along Korea's west coast along the shore and then turns southward along the Chinese shore.

Source: National Oceanographic Research Institute, 2006.

Oceanic Current Chart (Autumn) [86-4]
Surface currents in autumn show similar distribution characteristics as in spring, with speed generally around 0.5 to 1.0knot. The East Sea Warm Current flows even farther northward than in spring, creating a counterclockwise vortex near the Wonsan coast before moving southward. The Yellow Sea Warm Current migrates northward near the middle of the Yellow Sea before flowing toward Bohai and turning southward along the shore.

Source: National Oceanographic Research Institute, 2006.

Tide Chart (Flood Current) [87-1]
The flood current moves clockwise, centered on the Korean Peninsula. In the East Sea, the flood current flows southward, and the tidal range is only about 20-30cm. Thus, the tidal current is weak. Along the southern coast, the flood current flows southwestward from 1-2 hours after low tide to 1-2 hours after high tide in Busan offshore, with the highest current speed reaching 50 to 100cm/s. The tidal range of the southern sea is about 1.2m in Busan, and it increases westward, reaching 3m in Wando. Near Heuksando, south of the Yellow Sea, the flood current flows northward until 2-3hours after low tide, and highest current speed reaches 75-125cm/s. In Ongdo, offshore of the West Sea, the flood current flows northward at 0-1 hour after high tide. Flood current inside the gulf tends to flow from northeast to east, at 0-0.5hours after high tide. The tidal range increases northward and reaches 8m near Incheon. The current speed of the West Sea is normally 1-1.5m/s, but reaches 2.5-3m/s between nearshore ports and islands. In Noryang Straits, it reaches approximately 5m/s.

Source: National Oceanographic Research Institute, 2006.

Tide Chart (Ebb Current) [87-2]
An ebb current flows counterclockwise centering on the Korean Peninsula. In the East Sea, the current is weak north of Woolgi, with an ebb current flowing northward. The ebb current turns northeastward beginning about 1-2 hours after high tide until about 1-2 hours after low tide in Busan. Near Heuksando, an ebb current flows south-ward until 2-3 hours after high tide. At Ongdo, the ebb current flows southward within one hour after low tide. The ebb current inside the gulf flows from southwest to west, and flows within a half-hour after high tide.

Source: National Oceanographic Research Institute, 2006.

Water Temperature and Salinity Chart (Summer, Winter) [87-3, 4]
Average water temperature of Korean waters in summer is between 15 and 29℃. The center of the South Sea and Yellow Sea shows higher mean surface temperature than the center of East Sea. Mean summer temperature is lowest near Ulsan. Salinity varies between 26.9 and 33.9g/L, and is higher in the East Sea than in the Yellow Sea; the South Sea has the lowest mean summer salinity. In general, salinity is lower in summer than winter. In the Yellow Sea, because of the abundant freshwater input from inflowing streams, water adjacent to the land has minimum salinity, with increasing values toward the middle. The reason for higher water temperature of the South Sea in winter than the East and Yellow Seas is that the South Sea is influenced by the warm Kuroshio Current moving northward from the tropics. The Kuroshio Current also brings saltier water to the South Sea.

Source: National Fisheries Research & Development Institute, 2006.

Population Distribution and Growth

Population Density [88]
Population density is the most commonly used index in discussing the geographic distribution of a population in relation to land area. Population density is expressed by population size per unit area. The population density of Korea in 2005 was 474.5 persons/km². Administrative units belonging to the first three classes have higher densities than the country's average. Among metropolitan cities and provinces (*do*), Seoul has the highest (16,221/km²), followed by Busan, Gwangju, Daegu, Daejeon, Incheon, and Gyeonggi-*do*, all of which reported more than 1,000/km². At the city (*si*)-county (*gun*)-district (*gu*) level, the highest population density was observed in Yangcheon-*gu* in Seoul (27,256/km²). The geographic center of population is representative of the overall population distribution of a country. It is a mean center of the geographic coordinates of areal units weighted by their population size. Synoptic information can be obtained by mapping the centers of different years. On the map, geographic centers of population are measured for the census years during the period of 1966-2005. The gradual northwestward movement of the geographic centers has been prominent since Korea's independence in 1945, and reflects the fact that the proportion of the Capital Region to the total population has continued to increase.

Source: National Statistical Office, Population and Housing Census (2005), Korean Statistical Information Service (http://www.kosis.kr/).

Population Density (2000, 1990, 1980) [90-1, 2, 3]
The population density of Korea in 2000 was 464 persons/km². Administrative units belonging to the first three classes show higher densities than the country's average. When compared to the 2005 population density map, the 2000 map has a smaller number of areas with a population density below 50 persons/km².

The population density of Korea in 1990 was 437 persons/km^2. When compared to the 2005 and 2000 population density map, the 1990 map has a much smaller number of areas with a population density below 50 persons/km^2.

The population density of Korea in 1980 was 378 persons/km^2. When compared to the 2005 and 2000 population density maps, the 1980 map indicates that many rural areas shifted from higher density classes to the class below 50 persons/km^2 during those 25 years.

Source: National Statistical Office, Population and Housing Census (1980, 1990, 2000), Korean Statistical Information Service (http://www.kosis.kr/).

Population Proximity Index [90-4]

The population proximity index is another measure for the geographical distribution of population. The index refers to a mean distance between adjacent persons with an assumption that people are evenly distributed within a spatial unit. The index can be calculated as:

$$PPI = \sqrt{\text{land area}(m^2)/\text{population}}$$

The population proximity index for all of Korea in 2005 was 45.9m. On the map, administrative units belonging to the first three classes show higher index values than the country's average. Among metropolitan cities and provinces (*do*), Gangwon-*do* showed the highest value (106.5m), while Seoul reported the lowest value (7.9m). At the city (*si*)-county (*gun*)-district (*gu*) level, the highest value was observed in Inje-*gun* in Gangwon-*do* (232m), while Yangcheon-*gu* in Seoul reported the lowest value (6m).

Source: National Statistical Office, Population and Housing Census (2005), Korean Statistical Information Service (http://www.kosis.kr/).

Population Distribution (2005, 1990) [91-1, 2]

One dot represents 1,000 people on the dot density maps. They mirror the population density maps. Comparing the 2005 and 1990 maps, there are three distinguishable patterns. First, the Capital Region has expanded to a large extent and is now linearly connected to the northern part of Chungcheongnam-*do*. Second, outward expansion in other large cities, especially Busan and Daegu, has occurred. Third, rural areas have lost population. This is mainly due to out-migration and an aging population.

Source: National Statistical Office, Population and Housing Census (1990, 2005), Korean Statistical Information Service (http://www.kosis.kr/).

Population Growth Rate (2000-2005, 1995-2000) [91-3, 4]

Population growth is defined as the sum of population increases both by natural means (birth and death) and by social means (migration). Population growth rate refers to how fast population growth has occurred and is calculated as:

$$PGR = \frac{POP_t + POP_0}{POP_0} \times 100$$

Geographical variations of population growth rates reveal the spatiotemporal dynamics of population growth. The overall population growth rate for 2000-2005 was 2.48 percent (annual growth rate was 0.5 percent). The most outstanding pattern on the map is a reconcentration of the population in the Capital Region.

The overall population growth rate for 1995-2000 was 3.42 percent (annual growth rate was 0.7 percent). The map shows that the dominant population growth in the Capital Region has been somewhat alleviated and its spatial variation has been reduced. In particular, the vicinities of Busan and Daegu have grown very fast as suburbanization in the cities has proceeded.

Source: National Statistical Office, Population and Housing Census (1995, 2000, 2005), Korean Statistical Information Service (http://www.kosis.kr/).

[References]
Kim, D.-S., Park, S.-T., and Eun, K.-S., 2002, *The Population of Korea 1*, Daejon: Korea National Statistical Office (in Korean).
Lee, H.-Y., 2003, *Demography: Geographical Interpretation of Population*, Seoul: Bobmunsa (in Korean).

Vital Statistics and Migration

Total Fertility Rate [92]

The total fertility rate (TFR) refers to the average number of children born to a woman over her lifetime (usually aged 15-49). This is a standardized measure widely used to compare fertility rates of different countries or regions in a country. The map shows the spatial variation of TFRs at the city (*si*)-county (*gun*)-district (*gu*) level in 2005. The administrative units belonging to the first three classes report TFRs higher than the national average of 1.08. The spatial distribution of regional TFRs shows a significant geographical variation in the fertility rates. Low TFRs, less than 1, are observed in most areas in Seoul and Busan and in core areas of other major cities; in contrast, high TFRs, those above 1.5, are clustered in some rural areas of northern Gangwon-*do* and Jeollanam-*do*, and in some urban areas such as Hwaseong-*si* in Gyeonggi-*do* and Ulsan.

Source: National Statistical Office, Vital Statistics (2005).

Rate of Natural Increase [94-1]

The rate of natural increase (RNI) refers to the number of births minus deaths per 1,000 persons per year, or the simple difference between the crude birth rate (CBR) and the crude death rate (CDR).

$$RNI = \frac{\text{births minus deaths in a year}}{\text{mid-year population}} \times 1{,}000 = CBR - CDR$$

A map of rates of natural increase can show how much births and deaths contribute to population increase/decrease in a region. The national figure was 5.0 in 2005. The spatial pattern of the RNI is reflective of the CBR and the CDR; urban areas with relatively high CBRs have positive values, but rural areas with relatively high CDRs have negative values. Osan-*si* in Gyeonggi-*do*, Gwangsan-*gu* in Gwangju, Buk-*gu* in Ulsan, and Gumi-*si* in Gyeongsangbuk-*do* reported a rate of higher than 9. In contrast, Cheongdo-*gun* and Uiseong-*gun* in Gyeongsangbuk-*do* and Namhae-*gun* in Gyeongsangnam-*do* showed a rate of lower than -8. The top 5 (1 *myeon* and 4 *dongs*) at the town (*eup*)-township (*myeon*)-neighborhood (*dong*) level reported higher than 20, while the bottom 25 areas (all of them are *myeons*) reported lower than -18.

Source: National Statistical Office, Vital Statistics (2005), Korean Statistical Information Service (http://www.kosis.kr/).

Crude Marriage Rate [94-2]

The crude marriage rate (CMR) refers to the number of marriages per 1,000 persons per year, and is calculated as:

$$CMR = \frac{\text{marrages in a year}}{\text{mid-year population}} \times 1{,}000$$

By mapping regional CMRs, one can explore geographical variations not only of marriage events normalized by population size, but also of future reproduction capacity. In 2005, the CMR of Korea was 6.5. The most distinctive pattern in the geographical distribution of CMRs is a linear clustering of high CMRs from the southwestern part of Seoul to Cheonan-*si* and Asan-*si* in Chungcheongnam-*do*. Other hot spots include Geoje-*si* and Chilgok-*gun*.

Source: National Statistical Office, Vital Statistics (2005), Korean Statistical Information Service (http://www.kosis.kr/).

Gross Number of Migrants [94-3]

The total number of migrants including in- and out-migration across regions provides an overview of regional variation in population movements, the relative importance of in- and out-migration, and the resulting population change across regions. In general, the pattern of migration follows that of the population except in the case of some large numbers of migrants in the south of Seoul. Comparing the in- and out-migration, Counties (*gun*) in Gyeongsangbuk-*do*, Jeollanam-*do*, and Jeollabuk-*do* reveal more out-migrants reflecting a rural-to-urban migration trend; more in-migrants in numerous cities in southern Gyeonggi-*do* reflect the suburbanization of Seoul in that direction.

Source: National Statistical Office, Internal Migration Statistics (2005), Korean Statistical Information Service (http://www.kosis.kr/).

Net Migration Rate [94-4]

The net migration rate is the ratio of in-migrants after subtracting out-migrants to the mid-year population, thus representing the degree of migration effect on the regional population change. The positive or negative sign reflects population increase or decrease, respectively. A positive effect, that is a population increase, is found mostly in the Capital Region and around the metropolitan cities; a negative effect, a population decrease, is found in most of other regions.

Source: National Statistical Office, Internal Migration Statistics (2005), Korean Statistical Information Service (http://www.kosis.kr/).

In-Migration to the Capital Region [95-1]

The number of in-migrants to the Capital Region is about 575,000, and they are widely distributed across regions. The regions which sent over 10 percent of the total in-migrants are Chungcheongnam-*do*, Gangwon-*do*, and Jeollabuk-*do*; just over 2 percent are found in Ulsan and Jeju-*do*. The top 5 sending regions do not include any metropolitan cities, which indicates the dominance of rural-to-urban migration. Also evident are the effects of population size and distance on the flow of inter-regional migration.

Source: National Statistical Office, Internal Migration Statistics (2005), Korean Statistical Information Service (http://www.kosis.kr/).

In-Migration to Busan [95-2]

The number of in-migrants to Busan numbered about 130,000, and some regional biases are found in their distribution. For in-migrants, about 41 percent of the total are from Gyeongsangnam-*do*, followed by about 25 percent from the Capital Region. These are the two dominant in-migration regions. Ulsan and Gyeongsangbuk-*do* are the next group of large in-migration regions, contributing around 8 percent of the total. Overall, Busan shows a regionally biased in-migration flow, receiving in-migrants largely from nearby regions and the Capital Region.

Source: National Statistical Office, Internal Migration Statistics (2005), Korean Statistical Information Service (http://www.kosis.kr/).

In-Migration to Daegu [95-3]

The number of in-migrants to Daegu numbered about 103,000, and their regionally bias distribution is prominent. The role of Daegu as a regional center is clearly revealed in the more than 52 percent of in-migrants drawn from nearby Gyeongsangbuk-*do*. The next highest percentages of in-migrants are from the Capital Region (20 percent), Gyeongsangnam-*do* (10 percent), and Busan (5 percent). Other regions contribute less than 3 percent of the total. The major source regions of in-migrants to Daegu are the nearby regions and the Capital Region.

Source: National Statistical Office, Internal Migration Statistics (2005), Korean Statistical Information Service (http://www.kosis.kr/).

In-Migration to Gwangju [95-4]

The number of in-migrants to Gwangju registered about 88,000, and their distribution is highly biased to certain regions. Gwangju is clearly the regional center, drawing more than 55 percent of its in-migrants from nearby Jeollanam-*do*. The Capital Region, with about 26 percent, is the next most important in-migration source, followed by Jeollabuk-*do* with 8 percent and other regions with less than 2 percent. Gwangju plays the role of regional center while keeping a close relationship with the Capital Region in terms of in-migration flows.

Source: National Statistical Office, Internal Migration Statistics (2005), Korean Statistical Information Service (http://www.kosis.kr/).

In-Migration to Daejeon [95-5]

The number of in-migrants to Daejeon numbered about 98,000, and their distribution is relatively even across regions. Daejeon receives the largest number of in-migrants, 34 percent from the Capital Region, followed by Chungcheongnam-*do*, contributing 28 percent of the total in-migrants. This pattern is the outcome of sharing some business and research functions with the Capital Region. Other migrants come from nearby Chungcheongbuk-*do* (about 11 percent) and Jeollabuk-*do* (about 7 percent).

Source: National Statistical Office, Internal Migration Statistics (2005), Korean Statistical Information Service (http://www.kosis.kr/).

Out-Migration from the Capital Region [95-6]

The number of out-migrants from the Capital Region numbered about 446,000, 130,000 less than the number of in-migrants. While out-migrants are widely distributed across regions, some relatively high percentages are found in Chungcheongnam-*do* (about 17 percent) and Gangwon-*do* (about 12 percent). The relatively even out-migration flows across regions indicate the role of the Capital Region as the national center. Also, the top 5 high percentages are all in provincial regions, which indicates little urban-bias in population movements.

Source: National Statistical Office, Internal Migration Statistics (2005), Korean Statistical Information Service (http://www.kosis.kr/).

Out-Migration from Busan [95-7]

The number of out-migrants from Busan totaled about 168,000, and a regional bias in their distribution. About 41 percent migrate to Gyeongsangnam-*do*, followed by the Capital Region (about 30 percent), amounting to more than 70 percent of the total out-migrants. This is similar to the pattern of in-migration, but the reliance on the two regions is high in out-migration. The out-migration from Busan reflects both the regional hierarchy and geographic contiguity in population movements.

Source: National Statistical Office, Internal Migration Statistics (2005), Korean Statistical Information Service (http://www.kosis.kr/).

Out-Migration from Daegu [95-8]

The number of out-migrants from Daegu numbered about 128,000, and their regional distribution is highly biased. Two regions take more than 73 percent: Gyeongsangbuk-*do*, the highest at 47 percent, followed by the Capital Region at 26 percent of the total out-migrants. Except the nearby Gyeongsangnam-*do* (about 9 percent), all other regions show lower percentages, revealing the regional bias in out-migration flows. Daegu loses most of its migrants to Gyeongsangbuk-*do* and the Capital Region, thus playing dual roles as the regional center as well as the national sub-center for migration.

Source: National Statistical Office, Internal Migration Statistics (2005), Korean Statistical Information Service (http://www.kosis.kr/).

Out-Migration from Gwangju [95-9]

The number of out-migrants from Gwangju reached about 95,000, and their regional distribution is highly biased. Two regions take more than 82 percent: Jeollanam-*do*, with about 46 percent, followed by the Capital Region with about 36 percent of the total out-migrants. Gwangju is similar to Daegu in distribution, but its role as the regional center is somewhat weaker while the relationship with the Capital Region is stronger than that of Daegu. Other regions are less important in receiving out-migrants from Gwangju due to the dominance of the two regions. Similar to Daegu, Gwangju plays roles as the regional center as well as the national sub-center for migration.

Source: National Statistical Office, Internal Migration Statistics (2005), Korean Statistical Information Service (http://www.kosis.kr/).

Out-Migration from Daejeon [95-10]

The number of out-migrants from Daejeon totaled about 95,000, and their regional distribution is relatively even compared to other metropolitan cities. The largest number, about 41 percent of the total migrate to the Capital Region, followed by Chungcheongnam-*do* at about 27 percent, and Chungcheongbuk-*do* at about 9 percent. Thus, the Capital Region is a more important out-migration destination than those of nearby regions. Though there is a heavy pulling effect from the Capital Region, Daejeon still plays the role of regional center, although somewhat weaker than Daegu, Gwangju, and Busan metropolitan cities.

Source: National Statistical Office, Internal Migration Statistics (2005), Korean Statistical Information Service (http://www.kosis.kr/).

[References]
Gu, J.-H., 2002, *Theory and Practice in Demographic Statistics*, Seoul: Kyousa (in Korean).
Kim, D.-S., Park, S.-T., and Eun, K.-S., 2002, *The Population of Korea 1*, Daejeon: Korea National Statistical Office (in Korean)
Min, G.-S., Wu, S.-I., Jung, I.-S., Choi, J.-S., 2004, *The Transition of Korea from the Perspective of Statistics*, Daejeon: Korea National Statistical Office (in Korean)
Lee, H.-Y., 2003, *Demography: Geographical Interpretation of Population*, Seoul: Bobmunsa (in Korean)
United Nations, 2007, *World Population Prospects*: The 2006 Revision.

Population Structure

Classification of the Population Pyramid [96]

The population pyramid, which shows the age distribution of a specific year, is considered the most effective way to draw out general information about socioeconomic and demographic characteristics of a given society. From the population pyramid, historical changes in population during the last 100 years can be recognized all at once. That is, through the population pyramid the variations in population by age and sex can be observed, which are caused by war, migration and changes in fertility/mortality rates. With economic development and modernization underway, the shapes of national population pyramids have changed over the last 40 years due to the continuous decline in fertility rates. Also, the shapes of the population pyramids for individual cities and counties show strong differences because of massive migrations of populations from rural areas to cities and the differences in labor force demands according to the economic base of each region.

Source: National Statistical Office, Population and Housing Census (2005), Korean Statistical Information Service (http://www.kosis.kr/).

Sex Ratio [98-1]

The gender ratio, the most basic population description with direct comparison to actual fertility levels, is defined as the number of males per 100 females. In the 2005 census, the gender ratio was 99.53, indicating that there are 99.53 males for every 100 females. The national gender ratio follows a natural trend, whereas the ratios in cities and rural areas show a big difference driven by social influences, especially inward-outward migration. The ratios of neighborhoods (*dong*) and towns (*eup*) are 99.8 and 101.1 respectively, showing similar ratios of men and women, but in townships (*myeon*) the ratio is 96.5, indicating a surplus of women. Meanwhile, for gender ratios based on age, the

ratios among the younger age groups, particularly of a marriageable age, between myeon and dong areas show the greatest differences. This phenomenon can be interpreted as a result of the outward migration of young women from rural areas to cities.
Source: National Statistical Office, Population and Housing Census (2005), Korean Statistical Information Service (http://www.kosis.kr/).

Median Age [98-2]
The median age is well reflective of the urban-rural divide; a low age in urban areas and a high age in rural areas. In 2005, the lowest median ages are found in Gumi-*si* in Gyeongsangbuk-*do*, Yeongtong-*gu* (Suwon-*si*), Osan-*si*, and Ansan-*si* in Gyeonggi-*do*, Yuseong-*gu* in Daejeon, Gwangsan-*gu* in Gwangju, Heungdeok-*gu* (Cheongju-*si*) in Chungcheongbuk-*do*, and Cheonan-*si* in Chungcheongnam-*do*. There are 96 areas at the town (*eup*)-township (*myeon*)-neighborhood (*dong*) level reporting a median age of less than 30. Higher values are mostly distributed in many counties (*gun*) in Gyeongsangbuk-*do* (Uiseong-*gun*, Gunwi-*gun*, Yeongyang-*gun*, and Yecheon-*gun*), Gyeongsangnam-*do* (Hapcheon-*gun* and Uiryeong-*gun*), Jeollabuk-*do* (Imsil-*gun*), and Jeollanam-*do* (Goheung-*gun* and Sinan-*gun*). There are 171 areas (170 *myeons* and 1 *dong*) at the town (*eup*)-township (*myeon*)-neighborhood (*dong*) level reporting median ages higher than 60.
Source: National Statistical Office, Population and Housing Census (2005), Korean Statistical Information Service (http://www.kosis.kr/).

Total Dependency Ratio [98-3]
The relationship between the population of youth and elderly groups, which are comprised mostly of nonproductive consumers, and the population of working age group is very important in economic terms. Therefore, the dependency ratio can be applied as an index of a country's economic structure. The total dependency ratio means the proportion of the nonproductive population to the productive population. Hence, the productive population, the population of working age in the 15-64 age group, is defined simply by the age range regardless of actual participation in economic activities. In 1960, the total dependency ratio was 86, but this ratio has gradually decreased as the birth rate has declined due to economic development and national family planning. The total dependency ratio dropped considerably from 84 in 1970 to 60.5 in 1980, and the steady decline continued, reaching 52.1 in 1985, 40.6 in 1995 and 39.7 in 2005.

There are some counties (*gun*) reporting more than a ratio of 80, such as Imsil-*gun* and Sunchang-*gun* in Jeollabuk-*do*, and Boseong-*gun*, Jangheung-*gun*, Goheung-*gun* and Gokseong-*gun* in Jeollanam-*do*. In contrast, some districts (*gu*) in Seoul, such as Gangnam-*gu*, Gwanak-*gu*, Seocho-*gu*, Gwangjin-*gu*, Dongjak-*gu* and Songpa-*gu* reported less than 30. The top 10 areas (all of them being *myeons*) at the town (*eup*)-township (*myeon*)-neighborhood (*dong*) level overpassed a ratio of 120, while the bottom 13 areas (12 *dongs* and 1 *myeon*) reported less than 18.
Source: National Statistical Office, Population and Housing Census (2005), Korean Statistical Information Service (http://www.kosis.kr/).

Population Structure by Industry [98-4]
The ratio of the population working in traditional industries in Korea has declined and ratio of people working in newer industries such as business services, personal services, education, and public services has increased. This shift displays a gradual change from hardware-based industries to software-based industries. When the industrial structures of specific cities and provinces are compared, cities like Seoul, Busan, Gwangju, and Daejeon have a relatively high proportion of workers in higher-level industries, indicating tertiary economization. On the other hand, provinces like Chungcheongnam-*do* and Jeollanam-*do* show a relatively higher proportion of the population engaged in the agriculture, forestry or fisheries industries.
Source: National Statistical Office, Population and Housing Census (2005), Korean Statistical Information Service (http://www.kosis.kr/).

Graduates from Four-Year or Higher College Programs [99-1]
The number of graduates from four-year or higher college programs is a barometer of the cultural level and qualitative characteristics of the population. The portion of the population with academic backgrounds at the university level or higher was about 10,496,000 (34.3 percent) in 2005. Seoul shares 30 percent of the total graduates from a four-year or higher college program, and cities like Seongnam-*si* and Goyang-*si* have about 2 million graduates. Some remote mountainous counties in the Jeolla and Gyeongsang Regions have no more than 1,000 graduates. The difference in the higher education level among regions is very severe.
Source: National Statistical Office, Population and Housing Census (2005), Korean Statistical Information Service (http://www.kosis.kr/).

Average Years of Schooling [99-2]
A society's average education level and its distribution are regarded as very important indexes to estimate the level of welfare and qualitative characteristics of the society. The average years of schooling was computed from a target population of age 30 and above, and was 11.01 years in 2005, corresponding to the second year of high school. However, there has been a steady increase from 9.67 years in 1995 and 10.24 years in 2000. When the average years of schooling for the population of age 6 and older are compared between counties and cities, Seocho-*gu* and Gangnam-*gu* in Seoul show a little bit more than 13 years, and the other districts (*gu*) in Seoul show at least 11 years. However, in the case of the inland rural areas of the Jeolla and Gyeongsang Regions, the average years of schooling reach only 6-7 years.
Source: National Statistical Office, Population and Housing Census (2005), Korean Statistical Information Service (http://www.kosis.kr/).

International Marriages [99-3]
The ratio of international marriages in 2005 in Korea was about 13.6 percent, meaning approximately 13 out of every 100 Koreans married a foreigner that year. In agricultural areas, the international marriage rate reaches up to 27.4 percent, which means about one out of four couples in these areas are multi-national. Hence, it can be concluded that Korea has entered into a multi-ethnic and multi-cultural phase.
Source: National Statistical Office, Vital Statistics (2005), Korean Statistical Information Service (http://www.kosis.kr/).

Composition of Religious Population [99-4]
Among the religious ratios of individual cities and counties, Busan had the highest ratio, with 58.6 percent of its population, while the religious ratios for Seoul and Ulsan exceeded 55 percent. However, the Gwangju metropolitan area, Gangwon-*do*, Chungcheongbuk-*do*, and Jeollanam-*do* showed ratios of 49 percent, which are much lower than the average for the whole nation. Protestants are mostly distributed in major metropolitan cities, Chungcheongnam-*do*, Jeollabuk-*do*, and Jeollanam-*do*, and Catholics are located in the Capital Region and major cities in the provinces (*do*), Buddhists are largely based in Daegu, Gyeongsangbuk-*do*, Busan, and Gyeongsangnam-*do*.
Source: National Statistical Office, Population and Housing Census (2005), Korean Statistical Information Service (http://www.kosis.kr/).

[References]
Kim, D.-S., Park, S.-T., and Eun, K.-S., 2002, *The Population of Korea 1*, Daejeon: Korea National Statistical Office (in Korean)
Kim, D.-S., Park, S.-T., and Eun, K.-S., 2002, *The Population of Korea 2*, Daejeon: Korea National Statistical Office (in Korean)
Lee, H.-Y., 2003, *Demography: Geographical Interpretation of Population*, Seoul: Bobmunsa (in Korean)
Peters, G. L. and Larkin, R.P., 2002, *Population Geography: Problem, Concepts and Prospects*, 7th ed., Dubuque, Iowa: Kendall/Hunt.
Weeks, J.R., 2002, *Population: An Introduction to Concept and Issues*, 8th ed., Belmont: Wadsworth Publishing.

Household and Housing

Average Number of People per Household [100]
The average number of people per household is defined as the average number of members who constitute a family or household, and is computed by dividing the total population by the total number of households. In the spatial distribution of the average number of people per household, we can understand the spatial differentiation of the size of the household. In 2005, the average number of people per household nationwide was 2.88, which means about three members constituted a family. The regions with above-the-national average number of people per household are the Capital Region and the metropolitan cities such as Busan, Daejeon, Daegu, and Gwangju, while the areas with below-the-average number are traditionally rural areas.
Source: National Statistical Office, Population and Housing Census (2005), Korean Statistical Information Service (http://www.kosis.kr/).

Percent Change in the Number of Households (2000-2005) [102-1]
The percent change in the number of households explores the changes in the total number of household from 2000 to 2005, and is defined as the rate of change in household numbers between 2000 and 2005. In general, changes in household numbers have a similar pattern to those of population, except some different spatial patterns due to social and institutional situations (i.e., trends toward a nuclear family and one-person households). The changing rate of the number of households nationally is about an 11.1 percent increase. In general, the absolute number of the total population increased during this period, but with different changes in rates by region. That is, there is a higher increase in the rate of the number of households in metropolitan cities and the Capital Region, while a relatively lower increase in the rate or a decrease in the rate in rural areas.
Source: National Statistical Office, Population and Housing Census (2000, 2005), Korean Statistical Information Service (http://www.kosis.kr/).

One-Generation Households [102-2]
The rate of one-generation households as an index to explore household constitution by generation can be defined by dividing the number of one-generation households by the total number of households. As Korea's societal structure has changed along with the trend toward nuclear families, the rate of one-generation households has increased recently. The rate of one-generation households nationally is 16.2 percent, and in terms of the rate, neighborhoods (*dong*) and towns (*eup*) account for 14.1 percent and 19.4 percent, respectively, while townships (*myeon*) account for 28.8 percent. In terms of regional distribution, the regions with below-national average rates (less than 15 percent) are metropolitan cities and the Capital Region, while other regions have relatively higher rates.
Source: National Statistical Office, Population and Housing Census (2005), Korean Statistical Information Service (http://www.kosis.kr/).

Two-Generation Households [102-3]
The rate of two-generation households is the index used to explore household composition by generation, and is defined as the ratio of the number of two-generation households to the total number of households. The two-generation household type covers married couples with children, with a national rate of 55.4 percent. In terms of regional distribution, neighborhoods (*dong*) and towns (*eup*) have 58 percent and 52 percent, respectively, while townships (*myeon*) are at 35 percent. The rate of two-generation households is higher in metropolitan cities and the Capital Region, while lower in rural areas. These patterns are opposite to the rate of one-generation households in spatial distribution between urban and rural areas.
Source: National Statistical Office, Population and Housing Census (2005), Korean Statistical Information Service (http://www.kosis.kr/).

One-Person Households [102-4]
The rate of one-person households is defined as the rate of the number of one-person households in proportion to the total number of households. In terms of household composition by generation, the proportion of one-person households is the second highest (the two-generation households is the highest), and with the trend of the nuclear family and an individual-centered society, the importance of a one-person households is increasing. The national rate of one-person households is 20.0 percent, and the rates in neighborhoods (*dong*) and towns (*eup*) are 19.1 percent and 19.2 percent, respectively, which are similar to the national rate, while in townships (*myeon*) the rate is 26.2 percent, which is higher than the national rate. In the spatial distribution, there are fewer one-person households in metropolitan cities and the Capital Region, and more in rural areas, especially in the rural regions of Gyeongsangnam-*do*.
Source: National Statistical Office, Population and Housing Census (2005), Korean Statistical Information Service (http://www.kosis.kr/).

Apartment-Resident Households [103-1]
The rate of apartment-resident households explores the characteristics of living quarters, and is calculated by dividing the number of households residing in apartments by the total number of households. The rate of apartment-resident households has rapidly increased, and in 2005 the national rate was 41.7 percent, which is similar to the rate of one-person households (44.5 percent). In terms of regional patterns, in neighborhoods (*dong*) and towns (*eup*) the rates are 46.1 percent, 41.1 percent, respectively, while in townships (*myeon*) the rate is 11.8 percent, which explains concentrations of apartment-resident households in urban regions. In terms of spatial distribution, there are higher rates in metropolitan cities and the Capital Region.
Source: National Statistical Office, Population and Housing Census (2005), Korean Statistical Information Service (http://www.kosis.kr/).

Average Number of Rooms per Household [103-2]
The average number of rooms per household as a residential characteristic is the average number of rooms which can be occupied by household members. The average number of rooms by nation is 3.6. It is higher than the average number of people per household (2.88), which means there is more than one room per each member of a household. In the regional pattern, the average number in neighborhoods (*dong*) and towns (*eup*) are 3.6 and 3.8, respectively, while in townships (*myeon*) it is 3.9, which indicates a greater availability of rooms in rural regions. In terms of spatial distribution, there is no difference between urban and rural areas, and some counties (*gun*) have a higher number of rooms available.
Source: National Statistical Office, Population and Housing Census (2005), Korean Statistical Information Service (http://www.kosis.kr/).

Housing Supply Rate [103-3]
The housing supply rate is an index used to explore how many housing units are available to the residential population, and is defined by dividing the number of houses by the number of households, and then multiplying it by 100. It is especially important to understand the spatial distribution of the rate of housing supply, in that it shows the degree of spatial mismatch in the housing supply. In particular, an imbalance between residential distribution and housing supply can indicate demographic and social problems. If the rate of housing supply is 100, it shows a balance between housing supply and demand, and if the rate is less than 100, it means there is a shortage of housing stock, while any number above 100 means an excess in the availability of housing supply. The national rate is 105.9 percent, which shows an excess in housing supply. In terms of regional patterns, in neighborhoods (*dong*) the rate is 98.7 percent (a shortage), and in towns (*eup*) and townships (*myeon*), the rates are 123.9 percent and 146.5 percent, respectively, which shows a balance or slight excess in the availability of housing, and explains the spatial mismatch. In terms of spatial distribution, there is a lower rate of housing supply in metropolitan cities and the Capital Region, and a higher rate in the other regions.
Source: National Statistical Office, Population and Housing Census (2005), Korean Statistical Information Service (http://www.kosis.kr/).

Housing Construction [103-4]
The rate of growth of housing units since 2000 is derived by dividing housing units built since 2000 by the total number of houses. The total number of houses in 2005 was about twelve million units (non-residential and vacant housing units are excluded), and among them, 46 percent were built in the 1990s, while 22 percent were built since 2000, while the remaining 32 percent were built before 1990. In terms of housing units built since 2000, in neighborhoods (*dong*) and towns (*eup*) the numbers are 22.7 percent and 23.7 percent respectively, (similar to the national rate), while in townships (*myeon*) the rate is 17.3 percent (lower than the national rate). This indicates a concentration of recently-built homes in the urban regions. In terms of spatial distribution, there are a greater number of housing units supplied since 2000 in metropolitan cities and the Capital Region.
Source: National Statistical Office, Population and Housing Census (2005), Korean Statistical Information Service (http://www.kosis.kr/).

[References]
Gu, J.-H., 2002, *Theory and Practice in Demographic Statistics*, Seoul: Kyousa (in Korean).
Kwon, T.-S. and Kim, D.-S., 2002, *Understanding of Population*, Seoul: Seoul National University Press (in Korean).
Lee, H.-Y., 2003, *Demography: Geographical Interpretation of Population*, Seoul: Bobmunsa (in Korean).
Youn, J.-H., 2002, *The Housing in Korea*, Daejeon: Korea National Statistical Office (in Korean).

Culture and Tourism

World Cultural Heritage [104]
This map shows the number and geographic distribution of cultural heritage sites as representative indicators of cultural resources. Korea is home to 10 UNESCO World Cultural Heritage Sites, which include Changdeokgung (Jongno-*gu* in Seoul), Jongmyo (Jongno-*gu* in Seoul), Hwaseong Fortress (Suwon-*si* in Gyeonggi-*do*), Tripitaka Koreana at Haeinsa Temple (Hapcheon-*gun* in Gyeongsangnam-*do*), Bulguksa Temple (Gyeongju-*si* in Gyeongsangbuk-*do*), Seokguram Grotto (Gyeongju-*si* in Gyeongsangbuk-*do*), Gyeongju Historic Areas (Gyeongju-*si* in Gyeongsangbuk-*do*), Ganghwa Dolmen Sites (Ganghwa-*gun* in Incheon), Gochang Dolmen Sites (Gochang-*gun* in Jeollabuk-*do*), and Hwasun Dolmen Sites (Hwasun-*gun* in Jeollanam-*do*). 50 percent of Korean sites are concentrated in Gyeongju and Seoul: the former used to be the capital city of the ancient Silla Kingdom, and the latter was the capital city during the Joseon Dynasty.
Source: Cultural Heritage Administration; Cultural Heritage Information Center (http://info.cha.go.kr/).

Cultural Heritage: National Treasures [106-1]
National Treasures refer to rare and significant heritage-related items of value in terms of human culture, and are more valuable and fewer in number than Treasures. Korea has slightly more than 300 National Treasures among its State-designated Treasures (as of 2005), and each metropolitan city or province (*do*) possesses about 19 on average. On the map, a location having multiple treasures, such as the National Museum of Korea, is marked with only one point. The geographical pattern of National Treasures consists of several spatial clusters. Nearly half of all National Treasures (147) are located in Seoul, the capital city since the Joseon Dynasty,

17 percent (53) are in Gyeongsangbuk-*do*, which contains Gyeongju-*si*, and 9 percent (27) are in Chungcheongnam-*do*, which contains Gongju-*si* and Buyeo-*gun*. By contrast, National Treasures are rarely found in areas located far away from past capitals such as Jeju-*do* (0 percent), Jeollabuk-*do* (2 percent), and Gangwon-*do* (7 percent).

Source: Cultural Heritage Administration, 2006, *Yearbook of Koran Cultural Heritages*; Cultural Heritage Information Center (http://info.cha.go.kr/).

Cultural Heritage: Treasures [106-2]

Treasures refer to tangible cultural heritage items of importance, such as historic architecture, ancient books and documents, paintings, sculptures, handicrafts, archeological materials and armory items. Although Treasures may not be significant for a period or are not as unique as National Treasures, they are designated as Treasures as long as they are worthy of notice. There are more than 1,400 Treasures in Korea (as of 2005), and each metropolitan city or province (*do*) possesses about 88 on average. One the map, a location with multiple treasures, such as the National Museum of Korea, is marked with only one point. The geographical distribution of Treasures shows a much weaker spatial concentration compared to that of National Treasures. Treasures are found most frequently in Seoul (436, 29 percent), followed by Gyeongsangbuk-*do* (265, 18 percent), Gyeonggi-*do* (155, 10 percent), and Jeollanam-*do* (137, 9 percent). Gyeonggi-*do* and Jeollanam-*do* have relatively more Treasures than National Treasures, which are found in higher numbers in Chungcheongnam-*do*. Treasures are found the least in Jeju-*do* (4, 0.2 percent) and Gangwon-*do* (54, 4 percent).

Source: Cultural Heritage Administration, 2006, *Yearbook of Koran Cultural Heritages*; Cultural Heritage Information Center (http://info.cha.go.kr/).

Cultural Heritage: Historic Sites [106-3]

Historic Sites refer to places and facilities of great historic and academic value: for example, prehistoric sites, fortresses, ancient tombs, kiln sites, dolmens, temple sites and shell mounds. Korea has 458 State-designated Cultural Heritage Historic Sites (as of 2005), and each metropolitan city or province (*do*) possesses about 29 on average. The geographical distribution of Historic Sites shows that most of them are located in Gyeongsangbuk-*do* (96, 21 percent), which includes Gyeongju-*si*. Seoul (69, 15 percent) has the second most Historic Sites, followed by Gyeonggi-*do* (58, 13 percent). The fewest Historic Sites are found in Jeju-*do* (5, 1 percent) and Gangwon-*do* (13, 3 percent).

Source: Cultural Heritage Administration, 2006, *Yearbook of Koran Cultural Heritages*; Cultural Heritage Information Center (http://info.cha.go.kr/).

Cultural Heritage: Natural Monuments [106-4]

Natural Monuments refer to animals, plants, minerals, caves, geological features, biological products and special natural phenomena, carrying great historic, cultural, scientific, aesthetic or academic value, through which the history of a nation and or the secrets to the creation of the earth can be identified or revealed. Even though the total number of Natural Monuments is about 460, the ones identifiable on a map number only about 330 as of 2005. Based on this figure, each metropolitan city or province (*do*) can be said to possess about 21 on average. Unlike National Treasures, Treasures, and Historic Sites, Natural Monuments are heritage items or sites with a natural property, and therefore are affected more by natural environmental conditions than by historical or cultural factors. In this regard, the geographical distribution of Natural Monuments shows that the majority of them are located in Gyeongsangbuk-*do* (58, 18 percent), followed by Jeollanam-*do* (45, 14 percent), Jeju-*do* (39, 12 percent), Gyeongsangnam-*do* (38, 11 percent), and Gangwon-*do* (37, 11 percent). Jeju-*do* and Gangwon-*do* rank relatively higher in terms of Natural Monuments compared to their ranks in terms of National Treasures, Treasures, and Historic Sites. By contrast, Seoul has the lowest number of Natural Treasures (10, 3 percent).

Source: Cultural Heritage Administration, 2006, *Yearbook of Koran Cultural Heritages*; Cultural Heritage Information Center (http://info.cha.go.kr/).

Employment in Cultural Industries [107-1]

Cultural industries include those that generate publications, comics, films, animation, and digital education and information services. Cultural industries are highly concentrated in Seoul (64.4 percent of total cultural industry employees reside here), followed by Gyeonggi-*do* (10.2 percent), Busan (4 percent), and Daegu (3 percent). Such distinct spatial concentrations in the metropolitan cities are due to the strong locational preferences of cultural industries to areas with highly-skilled human resources, cultural resources, and consumers. Seoul shows an even stronger centrality in employment in such sub-sectors as digital education and information services (91 percent) and animation (85 percent).

Source: Ministry of Culture and Tourism, 2006, *Statistics of Cultural Industries* (as of 2005).

Local Festivals [107-2]

Local festivals allow us to identify the characteristics of cultures, industries, and tourist attractions of a region. As of 2006, there were a total of 725 festivals held across the nation. The city hosting the largest number of local festivals was Busan (60), followed by Jeju-*si* (27) in Jeju-*do*, Daegu (26), Incheon (20), Ulsan (20), Gangneung-*si* (19) in Gangwon-*do*, Seogwipo-*si* (18) in Jeju-*do*, and Seoul (15). Except for the metropolitan cities, festivals are held in regions with rich culture and tourism resources such as Jeju-*si* and Seogwipo-*si* in Jeju-*do*, and Gangneung-*si* in Gangwon-*do*. Festivals are sub-divided into four categories in terms of their purpose and nature: culture/art, tourism/specialty, traditional/folk, and other festivals. Tourism/specialty festivals, which aim to promote and market tourism and special products, are the most popular type and account for 310 out of the total 725 festivals. Culture/art festivals rank as the second largest type (237). County (*gun*)-level festivals are mostly characterized as tourism and specialty festivals. This implies that local festivals are used as a means for stimulating the local economy through regional natural tourism resources and specialty marketing.

Source: Each Administrative Unit, Survey on Local Festivals (2006); Korean Culture and Tourism Institute.

Special Tourist Zones and Tourist Resorts [107-3]

Special Tourist Zones are areas designated to intensively develop tourist-friendly services, including legal services, high-grade services, and public information, in order to attract foreign tourists. Large shopping districts in Seoul, such as Jongno, Dongdaemun Fashion Town, Myeongdong, Namdaemun, and Bukchang, and the U.S. Army bases and their surrounding shopping districts such as Itaewon, Dongducheon, and Songtan (Pyeongtaek-*si*), focus on foreign tourists. The remaining 17 Special Tourist Zones, except Gyeongju, are mainly dependent on natural features such as mountains, hot springs, and valleys. Tourist resorts comprehensively develop various facilities to serve tourists' needs associated with sightseeing and recreation. Twelve tourist resorts, except Gyeongju Bomun Tourist Resort and Andong, where cultural attractions are the major tourist draws, have been designated owing to their natural landscapes, such as the sea, mountains, and hot springs. Five tourist resorts out of 14 are located in Gangwon-*do*, which has beautiful natural landscapes.

Source: Ministry of Culture and Tourism, Designation of Special Tourist Zones and Tourist Resorts (2006); Korean Culture and Tourism Institute.

Designated Tourist Attractions [107-4]

Designated tourist attractions are areas designated by law that provide natural or cultural tourist attractions with basic facilities established for tourists. In 2006, Korea had a total of 225 designated tourist attractions, distributed relatively evenly across the nation. Gangwon-*do*, with its natural landscape, has 39 designated tourist attractions, the most of any region. Jeju-*do*, with its unique landscape, has 19 designated tourist attractions, which are numerous when considering its small size. By contrast, Gyeonggi-*do* has a relatively small number of sites with only 14, and major metropolitan cities such as Seoul, Daegu, Incheon, Gwangju, Daejeon, and Ulsan have no attractions.

Source: Ministry of Culture and Tourism, Designation of Tourist Attractions (2006); Korean Culture and Tourism Institute.

[References]
Korea National Statistical Office,2005, *Social Indicators in Korea*, Daejeon: Korea National Statistical Office (in Korean).
Ministry of Culture and Tourism, Korea Culture & Tourism Policy Institute, 2006, *Survey Report on Cultural Enjoyment*, Seoul: Ministry of Culture and Tourism (in Korean)

Urban and Rural Settlements

Urban and Rural Areas [108]

A categorical map for 3,573 areal units at the lowest administrative level, the *eup-myeon-dong* level with three administrative categories presents the distribution of urban and rural areas. The sizes are quite different, though; *dong*s are small and the other two categories are much larger. Thus, *dongs* are the most urbanized and characterized by a much higher population density; *myeon*s are the least urbanized, and *eup*s are in-between. Among the 3,573 areal units, 2,163 are *dongs*, 210 are *eup*s, and 1,200 are *myeon*s. *Dongs* contain 81.5 percent of the total population, whereas 8.3 percent live in *eups* and 10.2 percent reside in *myeon*s. If *dongs* and *eups* are regarded as urban areas, 89.8 percent of the population reside in urban areas.

Source: National Statistical Office, Korean Classification of Administrative Districts (As of December, 31, 2005).

Urbanization Rate [110-1]

Urbanization rates refer to the proportion of a population who live in urban areas. The statistics vary according to how urban areas are defined; whether only neighborhoods (*dong*) comprise urban areas, or whether neighborhoods (*dong*) and towns (*eup*) are collectively included. The nationwide urbanization rate in 2005 was 81.5 percent when only *dong*s were considered, but 89.8 percent when *eups* were also included in the calculation. The map shows percentages of people residing in a *dong* or an *eup* at the city (*si*)-county (*gun*)-district (*gu*) level. All the districts (*gu*) in the 7 metropolitan cities of Seoul, Busan, Daegue, Incheon, Gwangju, Daejeon, and Ulsan, consist of dongs only. All the counties (*gun*) are composed of *eups* and *myeon*s. Before the introduction of the concept of an urban-rural integrative city in the mid-1990s, all the cities were composed of *dongs*. However, most cities (*si*) currently employ *eups* and *myeon*s, as do some metropolitan cities such as Busan, Daegu, Incheon, and Ulsan due to the annexation of adjacent *guns*. As a result, the urbanization rate varies not only county by county, but city by city.

Source: National Statistical Office, Population and Housing Census (2005), Korean Statistical Information Service (http://www.kosis.kr/).

Daytime Population Index [110-2]

The daytime population index refers to the ratio of daytime to nighttime population in an area by percentage. An index value of more than 100 means that the daytime population in a given area is larger than the nighttime population and thus indicates that the area has more commuting inflows than out-flows. At the city (*si*)-county (*gun*)-district (*gu*) level, there are some areas with an index value of higher than 200 in 2005; Jung-*gu* (353.9) and Jongno-*gu* (251) in Seoul, and Gangseo-*gu* (213.3) in Busan. The fact that the areas with high scores in the Daytime Population Index are mostly districts (*gu*) in the major metropolitan cities indicates that the higher the centrality of employment, the higher the Daytime Population Index. In contrast, some districts (*gu*) in the metropolitan cities including Dobong-*gu*, Jungnang-*gu*, Gangbuk-*gu* and Eunpyeong-*gu* in Seoul, Buk-*gu* in Busan, and Jung-*gu* in Ulsan reported an index value of less than 80.

Source: National Statistical Office, Population and Housing Census (2005), Korean Statistical Information Service (http://www.kosis.kr/).

Land-Value Variation Rate [110-3]

Land-value variation rates can be used to explore where a transition from rurality to urbanity happens, mainly because a growing demand for urban land use usually results in land-value growth. An annual land-value variation rate refers to a percent change calculated by comparing land-values on the first and the last days in a year. The land-value variation rate in 2005 was 5.0 percent nationwide. Yeongi-*gun* reported the highest rate (27.7 percent), followed by its neighbors, Gongju-*si* (17.7 percent) and Yuseong-*gu* (10.2 percent) in Daejeon. This is mainly due to high expectations for the construction of the Multifunctional Administrative City and related property speculation.

Source: Koran Land Corporation, Survey on Land-Value Variation Rates (2005), Onnara Real Estate Information Portal (http://www.onnara.go.kr).

Construction of New Concept Cities for Balanced National Development [110-4]

Since the mid-2000s, the Korean government has established a construction plan for various new concept cities throughout the nation to alleviate the uneven development monopolizing the Capital Region. The new concept cities include the Multifunctional Administrative City (Sejong Special Autonomous City), Innovation Cities, and Enterprise Cities. The Multifunctional Administrative City, anchored by the relocation of administrative institutions from the Capital Region, has been designed to become a self-sufficient city that undertakes multiple functions such as education, culture, and welfare. It will be located in parts of Yeongi-*gun* and Gongju-*si* in Chungcheongnam-*do* and construction is expected to be finished by 2012. Innovation Cities, backed by the relocation of public agencies mainly from the Capital Region, are designed to become new focal points for regional growth. The development plans for 11 Innovation Cities have been approved to be finished by 2012; Busan (Nam-*gu*, Yeongdo-*gu*, and Haeundae-*gu*), Daegu (Dong-*gu*), Gwangju-Jeonnam (Naju-*si*), Ulsan (Jung-*gu*), Gangwon (Wonju-*si*), Chungbuk (Jincheon-*gun* and Eumseong-*gun*), Chungnam (Yeongi-*gun* and Gongju-*si*), Jeonbuk (Jeonju-*si* and Wanju-*gun*), Gyeongbuk (Gimcheon-*si*), Gyeongnam (Jinju-*si*), and Jeju (Seogwipo-*si*). An Enterprise City is a new city designed to facilitate private sector investment into the regional economy by providing various types of initiatives for city construction and urban development. At present, 6 Enterprise Cities have been selected, with construction expected to be finished by the mid-2010s. The selected areas are located in Muan in Jeollanam-*do*, Muju in Jeollabuk-*do*, Wonju in Gangwon-*do*, Chungju in Chungcheongbuk-*do*, Taean in Chungcheongnam-*do*, and Yeongam-Haenam in Jeollanam-*do*.

Source: Multifunctional Administrative City Construction Agency; Ministry of Construction and Transportation.

Periodical Markets [111-1]

In rural areas, periodical markets are dominant because these areas do not provide sufficient customers required for the establishment of permanent markets. Thus, the geographical distribution is well reflective of rural locales. This map shows the number of periodical markets per 100,000 persons at the city (*si*)-county (*gun*)-district (*gu*) level. The four core areas, above 15, include Injae-*gun* (15.6) in Gangwon-*do*, Cheongsong-*gun* (19.2) in Gyeongsangbuk-*do*, Sancheong-*gun* (21.2) in Gyeongsangnam-*do*, and Jinan-*gun* (23.0) in Jeollabuk-*do*. Around these areas, four rural regions can be identified: the first three guns function as pivotal areas in the provinces that they belong to; the last one is connected to Muju-*gun* (15.0) and Imsil-*gun* (14.6) in the same province, and stretches out to Yeongdong-*gun* (14.8) and Boeun-*gun* (12.8) in Chungcheongbuk-*do*, creating a huge rural region.

Source: Korean Institute for Urban Public Administration, 2005, *Korean Regional Statistics Annual*.

Digital Divide between Urban and Rural Areas [111-2]

The digital divide has been a focus for discussing the difference between urban and rural areas. The percentage of internet line-owned households signifies a level of information advancement. The nationwide percentage in 2000 was 21.4 but geographical variation was prominent: 14 out of the top 18 areas reporting over 30 percent at the city (*si*)-county (*gun*)-district (*gu*) level are districts in the metropolitan cities; in contrast, bottom 86 areas, mostly rural counties, reported less than 10 percent.

Source: National Statistical Office, Population and Housing Census (2000), Korean Statistical Information Service (http://www.kosis.kr/).

Urban Population Distribution (2005) & (1990) [111-3, 4]

The urban system in a country can be most easily described when urban locations and their population sizes are given simultaneously on a map. The 1990 map displays a central place system before the concept of an urban-rural integrative city was introduced, including not only urban centers, but also central places (*eups*) located in counties (*guns*). If those *eups* were integrated into adjacent urban centers to make up an urban-rural integrative city, they do not show up in the 2005 map.

When the 2005 map is compared to the 1990 map, one can see the geographical expansion of the Capital Region and the growth of port cities in the Southeastern Industrial Belt. The two urban agglomerations have increasingly been connected along the Seoul-Busan axis. Recently, the Jeonju-Gwangju-Mokpo connection in the Jeolla Region has developed into another urban growth axis. Many inland cities which are either natural-resource rich or traditional administrative centers have declined to a large extent.

Source: National Statistical Office, Population and Housing Census (1990, 2005), Korean Statistical Information Service (http://www.kosis.kr/).

Commuting Patterns in Major Regions [112]

Commuting patterns provide crucial information on spatial interaction and regional linkages. The flow maps, based on the number of inter-areal commuters measure the amount and direction at the city (*si*)-county (*gun*)-district (*gu*) level. Commuting flows were classified into three groups, 10,000-20,000, 20,000-30,000, and over 30,000, with ones less than 10,000 commuters being excluded to avoid complexity. Commuting flows occurring across the regional boundaries were also ignored.

In the Capital Region, intra-urban commuting flows within Seoul are predominant. The largest destinations among 25 districts (*gu*) in Seoul include Gangnam-*gu* (542,689 persons), Jung-*gu* (345,998 persons), Jongno-*gu* (267,073 persons), Seocho-*gu* (265,961 persons), and Yeongdeungpo-*gu* (248,334 persons). In-flows to Jung-*gu* come mostly from the northern districts, while the origins of commuters to Gangnam-*gu* tend to be scattered over the city. The largest commuting flows to Gangnam-*gu* come from Songpa-*gu* (40,914 persons), Gwanak-*gu* (30,124 persons), Seocho-*gu* (29,102 persons), Gangjin-*gu* (21,745 persons), and Dongjak-*gu* (20,105 persons). Significant commuting flows are also found from Gangseo-*gu* and Yangcheon-*gu* to Yeongdeungpo-*gu*. Within Incheon, more than 20,000 commuters from each of Nam-*gu* and Yeonsu-*gu* head for Namgdong-*gu*, which is the largest destination within Incheon. Commuting linkages between Seoul and urban areas in Gyeonggi-*do* are also significant. The largest origins in terms of commuting toward Seoul include Seongnam-*si* (141,393 persons), Goyang-*si* (139,515 persons), and Bucheon-*si* (104,706 persons). The largest commuting flows include ones from Seongnam-*si* to Gangnam-*gu* (43,446 persons) and to Seocho-*gu* (20,874 persons), and from Yongin-*si* to Gangnam-*gu* (22,075 persons). Out-flows from Goyang-*si* tend to disperse across Seoul. Commuting flows between the cities in Gyeonggi-*do* are also significant. There are enormous commuting flows from Suwon-*si* to Hwaseong-*si* (52,015 persons) and Yongin-*si* (35,789 persons), from Ansan-*si* to Siheung-*si* (32,315 persons), and from Yongin-*si* to Seongnam-*si* (30,638 persons). This means that some satellite cities in the Capital Region have closer relationships with each other than they do to Seoul, and a hierarchical structure among those cities has formed.

In the Gyeongsang Region, the most prominent commuting flows within Busan are found between Buk-*gu*, a densely populated residential area, and Sasang-*gu*, possessing a large-scale industrial complex. In Gyeongsangnam-*do*, the largest commuting flow is found between Masan-*si*, a traditional regional center, to Changwon-*si*, a new industrial core. In Daegu, the dominant pattern is a convergence of the commuting flows from various parts of the city into the traditional CBD in Jung-*gu*. However, the largest commuting flow within Daegu is one from Dong-*gu* to Buk-*gu* (22,207 persons). A counter-commuting also occurs in the region from Suseong-*gu* in Deagu to Gyeongsan-*si* (22,824 persons). In Ulsan, the largest flows are from Jung-*gu* to Nam-*gu*, and another from the inner city to the outer industrial areas. In Gyeongsangbuk-*do*, there is a significant commuting flow from residential Chilgok-*gun* to industrial Gumi-*si*.

In the Jeolla Region, there are 4 different sub-zones in terms of commuting flows. The first and second largest commuting flows are from Buk-*gu* to Gwangsan-*gu*, and from Buk-*gu* to Dong-*gu* within Gwangju. The largest flow in Jeollabuk-*do* is from Jeonju-*si* to Wanju-*gun*. In the Gwangyang Bay region, the largest commuting flow is from Suncheon-*si* to Gwangyang-*si*. The major commuting out-flows from Mokpo-*si* are bound for Muan-*gun*, the provincial capital, and Yeongam-*gun*, where an industrial complex is located.

As for the Chungcheong Region, the largest flows within Daejeon are observed between Seo-*gu* and Yuseong-*gu*. However, in-flows to Seo-*gu*, which possesses the city hall, are also large. Overall, there are various commuting linkages among 5 districts in Daejeon without a dominate destination. In Chungcheongbuk-*do*, the largest flow is from Cheongju-*si* to Cheongwon-*gun*, while it is from Cheonan-*si* to Asan-*si* in Chungcheongnam-*do*.

Source: National Statistical Office, Population and Housing Census (2005),
Korean Statistical Information Service (http://www.kosis.kr/).

Land-Value Distributions in Large Cites [113]

The spatial distribution of land-values is believed to expose the most important aspect of the internal urban structure, since land-values is reflective of urban functional regionalization and nodal structures. To visualize the land value distribution, the maximum land value for each areal unit was used. In most cases, the highest value came from commercial landuse, but in cases where commercial landuse was rare, the highest land value was obtained from either residential or industrial districts.

In Seoul, the highest land value is found in Chungmuro 1 (il)-*ga-dong*. This shows that Seoul is still a uni-centric city in terms of land-value distribution, even though many commentators maintain that Seoul has been fragmented mainly due to the emergence of Gangnam as another central business district (CBD).

The highest land-value in Busan is found in Bujeon-*dong* in Busanjin-gu. However, some areas in the traditional core, such as Nampo-*dong* and Gwangbok-*dong*, also show very high land-values. Also, second-tier land-value districts are scattered around, which is indicative of the city's poly-centricity, heavily influenced by topographical features.

In Daegu, all the districts assigned to the highest category are located in the traditional core in Jung-*gu*, including the highest land-values spot, Dong-seongro 2 (i)-*ga-dong*. From the core, land-values concentrically fall, which is indicative of the city's uni-centricity.

As for Incheon, Bupyeong-*dong* in Bupyeong-*gu* recorded the highest land value, followed by Guwol-*dong* in Namdong-*gu*, Samsan-*dong* in Bupyeong-*gu*, Juan-*dong* in Nam-*gu*, and Nae-*dong* and Inhyeon-*dong* in Jung-*gu*. This indicates that the internal structure of Incheon has increasingly become multi-nucleated.

The location of the highest land-value in Gwangju is found in Chungjangno 2 (i)-*ga-dong*, the central location of the CBD. Along the west-east axis from the traditional CBD to the newly developing sub-center, the Sangmu district, high land-values are distributed in a linear fashion. However, recently developed residential areas also show relatively high land-values. From the west-east axis, a concentric pattern emerges. All these land-value patterns hint at many things concerning the city's urban structure: a relatively weak industrial base has made residential functions more important in the city; the development of sub-centers has been limited, and residential differentiation has not been deployed to a large extent.

In Daejeon, the area with the highest land value is located in Eunhaeng-*dong* in Jung-*gu*. Some *dongs* in Jung-*gu* (Seonhwa-*dong* and Daeheung-*dong*) and Dong-*gu* (Jung-*dong*) showed a high land value. From theses areas to the outskirts of the city, land-values concentrically fall. However, in the top 10 *dong*s, some in Seo-*gu* (Dunsan-*dong* and Yongmun-*dong*) and Yuseong-*gu* (Bongmyeong-*dong*, Banseok-*dong*, and Jijok-*dong*) are included, indicating a primitive form of multi-nucleation.
As for Ulsan, the highest land value is found in Samsan-*dong*, and nearby areas in Jung-*gu* (Seongnam-*dong* and Okgyo-*dong*) and Nam-*gu* (Dall-*dong* and Sinjeong-*dong*) also report a high landvalue. From this nucleus outward, land-values drop sharply. Even though some places in Eonyang-*eup* and Beomseo-*eup* in Ulju-*gun* report a relatively high land-value, Ulsan still remains uni-central.

Source: Korean Association of Property Appraisals,
Officially Assessed Reference Land Price (2005)

[Reference]
Nam, Y.-W., 2007, *Spatial Structure of the City*, Seoul: Bobmunsa (in Korea).
Kim, I. and Park, S.-J., eds., 2006, *Urban Geography and Urbanology*, Seoul: Purungil (in Korean).
Kim, D.-S., Park, S.-T. and Eun, K.-S., 2002, *The Population of Korea 2*, Daejeon: Korea National Statistical Office (in Korea).
Korean Urban Geographical Society, ed., 1999, *The Korean Cities*, Seoul: Bobmunsa (in Korean).
Kwon, Y.-W., et al., 1998, *Understanding Cities*, Seoul: Pakyoungsa (in Korean).

Regional Economic Indicators

Gross Regional Domestic Product [114]

This represents *per capita* Gross Regional Domestic Product in order to interpret sense of the proportion of GRDP to the total population. In addition, the map illustrates GRDP at current prices by considering the proportion of each industry sector and the inter-relationship between industry sectors. Each region's GRDP is classified into five industry sectors; i) agriculture, forestry and fisheries; ii) chemical and plastic goods and the textile; iii) steel and machinery; iv) electric and electronics; v) personal care goods and other goods.

Source: National Statistical Office, Regional Income Statistics (2004),
National Statistics Information Service (http://www.kosis.kr).

Total Establishments and Total Employees [116]

This map represents total establishments and total employees by basic administrative area. The number of establishments tends to be in proportion to the number of employees. Considering the fact that regional economic indicators are scarce, these indicators are important when examining the reality of regional economies. In general, the proportion of the number of establishments and employees tends to be high in large metropolitan areas and major industrial cities, but low in rural areas. On this map, the number of total establishments by region is expressed on the map, the number of total employees by region is provided in the form of a circle.

Financial Independence Ratio and Revenues [117-1]

A region's financial independence ratio and revenues are two of the most critical indicators widely used to understand the characteristics of a local administration and a regional economy. In general, GRDP and the financial independence ratio have a positive inter-relationship. Also, the financial independence ratio and revenues are closely associated with each other. In this context, a region in which the ratio of financial independence is high tends to be represented by high revenues.

Source: National Statistical Office, Financial Independence Ratio and Revenues (2004),
National Statistics Information Service (http://www.kosis.kr).

Gross Value-Added and Net Production [117-2]

Gross Value-Added (GVA) is one of the major indicators that presents regional accounts in relation to GRDP. This represents value-drawn intermediary consumption from total output. A region's GVA number tends to grow in proportion to value-added in-production activities. Like GVA, net production is also a major indicator that presents regional accounts in relation to gross regional domestic product. This represents value-drawn intermediary consumption from the gross regional domestic product. In general, a region's net production tends to become high in proportion to its GVA.

Source: National Statistical Office, Regional Income Statistics (2004),
National Statistics Information Service (http://www.kosis.kr).

Amount of Exports [117-3]

In an era of economic globalization, trade-related indicators, particularly the amount of exports, are used in order to measure the competitiveness and dynamics of a regional economy. It can be said that the higher the amount of exports from a region, the higher the international competitiveness of its local firms. This map demonstrates the absolute amount of exports by region, together with the relative proportion of exports by region. The five export sectors are classified as follows; i) agriculture, forestry and fisheries; ii) chemical and plastic goods and the textiles; iii) steel and machinery; iv) electric and electronics; v) personal care goods and other goods.

Source: Korea International Trade Association, 2005, *Statistics on International Trade.*

Amount of R&D Investment [117-4]

The amount of R&D investment is one of the most conventional indicators used to measure regional scientific and technological capabilities. It is widely accepted that the larger the proportion of R&D investment in a region, the better its R&D infrastructure, thus reflecting relatively high technological capabilities for the region. This map illustrates the proportion of R&D investment by the type of R&D institutions by region.

Source: Korea Ministry of Science & Technology, 2004, *Science & Technology Yearbook.*

Industrial Property Rights [117-5]

This map displays the number and ratio of industrial property rights by region. In addition, industrial property rights are represented by type in the form of a pie graph. Industrial property rights can be classified into four types: a patent, a patent on a new device, a design, and a registered trademark.

Source: The Korean Intellectual Property Office, 2005, Statistics on Knowledge Property Right.

Amount of Imports [117-6]

Together with the amount of exports, the amount of imports by region is also regarded as a basic unit of measurement used to identify the degree of globalization in a regional economy. Supposing the amount of exports is more than the amount of imports. This can mean that a regional economy has a good base of economic power and regional income. The five industry sectors are classified as follows; i) agriculture, forestry and fisheries; ii) chemical and plastic goods and the textiles; iii) steel and machinery; iv) electric and electronics; v) personal care goods and other goods. This map demonstrates the absolute amount of imports by region, together with the relative proportion of imports by region. The five industry sectors used are classified as follows; i) agriculture, forestry and fisheries; ii) chemical and plastic goods and the textiles; iii) steel and machinery; iv) electric and electronics; v) personal care goods and other goods.

Source: Korea International Trade Association, 2005, *Statistics on International Trade.*

Industrial Infrastructure and Energy

Establishments and Employees in Industrial Complexes [118]

The development of industrial complexes, which has played a significant role in the Korean industrialization process, was initiated with the construction of the Ulsan Industrial Complex in the 1960s. Industrial complex construction has been utilized as a method of industrial location policy in many countries worldwide. In Korea, industrial complexes can be classified into three types, the national industrial complex, the local industrial complex and the agro-industrial complex, depending on who designates and develops the complexes. Since the existence of an industrial complex in a region implies a foundation of value-added industrial production for the region, the distribution and geography of production is significant when exploring the regional characteristics and inter-regional differences among economic structures.

The map displays the employment distribution of industrial complexes at the basic autonomous administration levels in Korea called *si* (city), *gun* (county) and *gu* (sub-level administration in the metropolitan city), as well as the establishment numbers of three different types of industrial complexes at metropolitan city and *do* (province levels). Concerning employment distribution, concentration takes place along the major transportation routes of the Gyeongbu axis from the Southeast Seaboard Industrial Zone, the Honam axis, and in Gangwon-*do*, Chungcheongnam-*do* and Chungcheongbuk-*do* near the Capital Region, which also have a relatively higher share of employment. However, for establishments, the Capital Region has the highest share of national industrial complexes, and is followed only by the metropolitan cities and provinces in the Gyeongsang-*do* region.

Source: Korea Industrial Complex Corporation, 2005, *Statistics of Industrial Complexes in Korea.*

Location of Industrial Complexes [120-1]

The actual location of industrial complexes at the level of *si*, *gun* and *gu* can give an insight to the situation and foundation of the regional economies. The map shows the actual location of three different types of industrial complexes. The national industrial complexes at the central government level tend to be concentrated in the regions of the Capital, the Southeast Seaboard Industrial Zone, and in Gyeongsangbuk-*do* and Gumi-*si*, whereas the local industrial complexes at the provincial level, whose locations are similar to the national ones, are more spatially dispersed. The agro-industrial complexes are the most dispersed across the entire territory.

Source: Korea Industrial Complex Corporation, 2005, *Statistics of Industrial Complexes in Korea.*

Area and Number of Industrial Complexes [120-2]

The area and number of industrial complexes in a regional economy, are significant. The map shows the area of industrial complexes at the level of *si*, *gun* and *gu*, as well as the numbers of three different types of industrial complexes at the level of the metropolitan city and *do*. Regions with national industrial complexes tend to have a larger area, whereas most metropolitan cities, including Seoul and Incheon, are likely to have fewer industrial complexes. However, most *dos* have more complexes due to the large number of agro-industrial complexes. In contrast, Gyeonggi-*do* in the Capital Region has a comparatively larger number of local industrial complexes.

Source: Korea Industrial Complex Corporation, 2005, Statistics of Industrial Complexes in Korea.

Output and Export Values of Industrial Complexes [120-3]

Output and export values reflect the significance of the industrial complex for the host regions. The map spatially describes the output values of industrial complexes at the *si*, *gun* and *gu* levels, as well as export values at the metropolitan city and *do* levels. The spatial distribution of output, like that of area, tends to mirror the location of national industrial complexes, which implies importance for industrial production and export Gyeongsangbuk-*do* Ulsan, Chungcheongnam-*do*, and Gyeongsangnam-*do* have the largest shares of industrial export, respectively, whereas the metropolitan cities tend to have relatively smaller shares.

Source: Korea Industrial Complex Corpforation, 2005, Statistics of Industrial Complexes in Korea.

Operation Rates of Industrial Complexes [120-4]

In addition to the location, the operation rate of an industrial complex must be considered when examining its role in promoting a regional economy. However, extra caution needs to be taken because the calculation of the operation rate is different for each type of industrial complex. The calculation of the operation rate for different types is as follows:

- operation rate for national industrial complexes: (quarterly real output value/quarterly normal output capacity)×100

- operation rate for local industrial complexes: (quarterly number of operating establishments/quarterly number of tenant-contracted establishments)×100

- operation rate for agro-industrial complexes: (quarterly number of operating establishments/quarterly number of construction-completed establishments)×100

The map shows the average of three different operation rates at the *si*, *gun* and *gu* levels. The spatial pattern of the rates, which can be translated as actual utilization rates of industrial complexes, is highly differentiated.

Source: Korea Industrial Complex Corporation, Industrial Complexes in Korea (2005),
Industry-University-Research Integrated Information Network (http://www.e-cluster.net).

Land Use of Key National Industrial Complexes [121-1]

The land use of industrial complexes consists of both industrial use and support facility use. Given its purpose, industrial use takes a lion's share of the land. Nowadays, however, land use has become increasingly diversified due to the growth of energy-centered industrial complexes and the pursuit of industrial complex value. The share of industrial use is highest in the Onsan and Gwangju High-Tech Complexes, whereas the share of green zones is highest in the Banweol and Daebul Complexes. In the meantime, the share dedicated to power a facility zone is remarkably high in the Osong Complex, whereas the share comprising a public facility zone is highest in the Paju Complex. In general, the land use of newly designated complexes tends to be diversified away from industry-dominant use.

Source: Korea Energy Economics Institute (2005).

Industrial Divisions of Key National Industrial Complexes [121-2]

The national industrial complex, an engine of regional economic growth, has played a role in Korea's industrialization process. The production structure of each complex is likely to reflect the characteristics of its corresponding regional economy, and are therefore highly differentiated. The industrial division occupying the largest share of industrial complex property encompasses oil, coke, chemical and plastic products, followed by metal and mechanical products. On the contrary, light industries such as food and beverage, sewing, leather and shoe products, and timber, paper and printed products have very small shares. In addition, the share of non-manufacturing use is also among the smallest. By complex, almost all (96%) of the Changwon Complex property is taken up by metal and mechanical products, whereas in the Yeosu Complex, oil, coke, chemical and plastic products account for 96% of the property. The Ulsan and Gunsan Complexes tend to have larger shares dedicated to automobile and transportation equipment, whereas the Gumi and Gwangju Complexes reserve larger shares for computer, electrical and medical equipment. Finally, the entire Seoul Digital Complex is uniquely taken up by non-manufacturing production.

Source: Korea Industrial Complex Corporation, Industrial Complexes in Korea (2005), Industry-University-Research Integrated Information Network (http://www.e-cluster.net).

Overseas Energy Import [121-3]

The energy self-sufficiency in Korea is only around 3%, requiring the import of almost all of the nation's energy needs. Therefore, the mapping of two major imported energies, crude oil and LNG, can provide significant insight into the global spatial dependence for national energy consumption. There is very high dependency of crude oil from the Middle East, and only quite recently some diversification of imports from Southeast Asia and South America. Meanwhile, the LNG import pattern is spatially more diversified, including Qatar as well as Southeast Asia and Australia.

Source: Korea Energy Economics Institute, 2005, *Annual Statistics of Regional Energy*.

Total Energy Consumption [122-1]

Energy is produced mainly through the use of coal, oil, natural gas and, hydraulic and atomic power. Therefore, Energy consumption is usually estimated by the use of these sources. The map spatially describes the total energy consumption at the metropolitan city and do levels based on the calculation of Ton of Oil Equivalent (TOE) or other varied energy sources. Total energy consumption is highest in Jeollanam-*do*, followed by Chungcheongnam-*do* and Gyeongsangbuk-*do*. The Capital Region and metropolitan cities tend to have higher consumption of oil, whereas regions with atomic power plants consume more atomic energy.

Source: Korea Energy Economics Institute, 2005, *Annual Statistics of Regional Energy*.

Energy Consumption by Source: Manufacturing Sector [122-2]

The manufacturing sector takes a larger share of total energy consumption than any other sector. The map shows the spatial pattern of energy consumption by source in the manufacturing sector at the metropolitan city and do levels. Total consumption in this sector is the largest in Jeollanam-*do* followed by Ulsan and Gyeongsangbuk-*do*. In many regions, oil is the most common source of energy for the manufacturing sector.

Source: Korea Energy Economics Institute, 2005, *Annual Statistics of Regional Energy*.

Energy Consumption by Source: Domestic and Commercial Sectors [122-3]

The domestic and commercial sectors account for the second largest share of energy consumption second to manufacturing. The map shows the spatial pattern of energy consumption by source in the domestic and commercial sectors at the metropolitan city and *do* levels. Unlike the manufacturing sector, consumption levels are in proportion to population size. Areas such as Seoul have higher consumption levels.

Source: Korean Energy Management Corporation, New and Renewable Energies (2006), Korea New and Renewable Energy Center (http://www.knrec.or.kr).

Production of New Renewable Energy [122-4]

New renewable energy can be generated by transforming either existing fossil fuels or renewable energies including solar radiation, water, subterranean heat, precipitation, and bio-organisms. This type of energy consists of eight renewable energies, as well as 3 new energies, fuel cell, coal liquefaction gas and hydrogen. The map shows the production levels of new renewable energies at the metropolitan city and do levels. Jeollanam-*do*, Gyeonggi-*do* and Ulsan are the largest producers, with waste energy accounting for the largest share of production compared to all other energy types.

Source: Korea Energy Economics Institute, 2005, *Annual Statistics of Regional Energy*.

Electric Power Production by Type [123-1]

Power production at the metropolitan city and do levels can give insight into the energy foundation of regional economies. The map provides the spatial pattern of regional electric power production facilities consisting of thermoelectric, hydroelectric and atomic power sources. Atomic power plays a paramount role in Busan, Jeollanam-*do* and Gyeongsangbuk-*do*, which all have atomic power stations. Chungcheongbuk-*do* has the largest share of hydroelectric power, whereas in most other regions thermoelectric power exclusively accounts for the largest share of the regional power production.

Source: Korean Electric Power Corporation, 2005, *Statistics of Electric Power in Korea*.

Electricity Consumption by Category of User [123-2]

Electricity is consumed for various purposes by homes, services and manufacturing. The map shows the consumption patterns for the domestic, public, and service sectors, the primary sector, and the mining and manufacturing sectors at the metropolitan city and *do* levels. The total consumption level is highest in Gyeonggi-*do*, followed by Seoul and Gyeongsangbuk-*do*. In terms of usage, Seoul tends to have higher consumption rates for the service sector, whereas most other regions to have higher consumption levels for manufacturing.

Source: Korea Energy Economics Institute, 2005, *Annual Statistics of Regional Energy*.

Oil Consumption by Product Type [123-3]

Imported oil is usually processed into different products before being finally consumed. The map shows the pattern of oil consumption by product types such as gasoline, kerosene, light oil, bunker C oil and naphtha at the metropolitan city and do levels. Overall, naphtha accounts for the largest share of oil consumption. In regional term, Jeollanam-*do* ranks first, followed by Ulsan and Chungcheongnam-*do*, in oil product consumption.

Source: Korea Energy Economics Institute, 2005, *Annual Statistics of Regional Energy*.

City Gas Establishments and Gas Supply [123-4]

In 2005, about 70% of city gas was consumed in the domestic and commercial sectors, which indicates its significance in people's everyday lives. The map shows the spatial pattern of city gas establishments and their gas supply at the metropolitan city and do levels. The spatial distribution of the establishments and the gas supply is largely determined by both population distribution and the characteristics of the city gas supply system. There is a spatial concentration of establishments and gas supply in the Capital Region.

Source: Korea City Gas Association (2006).

[References]
Cho, Hye-Young, 2002, "The current Conditions of Industrial Complexes and Policy Tasks in Korea, "*Industrial Location*, 9 (in Korean).
Ryu, Seung-Han, 2005, "The Classification of Industrial Complexes and Policy Tasks," *Industrial Location*, 19 (in Korean).
Kim, In-Jung, 2005, "Establishing Designation-Development-Management Governance for Industrial Complexes," *Industrial Location*, 19 (in Korean)

Agriculture and Mining

Ratio of Cultivated Land and People Engaged in Agriculture [124]

The map shows the current ratio of cultivated land in use and persons engaged in agriculture, which are the most fundamental and essential elements of the primary sector. The choropleth map displays the nation's ratio of cultivated land (area of cultivated land/area of the entire nation) by *si* and *gun*. Likewise, the dot map displays the population involved in agriculture by *si* and *gun*. Korea has consistently experienced a decrease in the area of cultivated land since the beginning of full-scale industrialization across the nation. The map is intended to show the regional differences on the basis of higher and lower ratios. The distribution of the agricultural population is also presented to help identify those areas where the ratio of agriculture is high.

Source: National Agricultural Products Quality Management Service, Cultivated Land Area (2005), Agricultural Statistics Information (http://www.naqs.go.kr/). Korea National Statistical Office, Basic Agricultural Statistics Survey (2005), Korea Statistical Information Service (http://www.kosis.kr/).

Rice Production [126-1]

Rice is not only the most consumed of all food crops in Korea, but is also a representative food crop. Although rice consumption per capita has continuously dropped in Korea, it still remains the staple food of the nation and is accordingly granted the most significance. The nation's rice production (unit: tons) is displayed by *si* and *gun* so that regional differences can be seen.

Source: Ministry of Agriculture & Forestry, 2005, *Agriculture & Forestry Statistical Yearbook*. National Agricultural Products Quality Management Service, Crop Product (2005), Agricultural Statistics Information (http://www.naqs.go.kr/).

Certified Areas Using Environmentally Friendly Agricultural Techniques [126-2]

People's growing concern with healthy eating has led to an increase in the adoption of environmentally-friendly agricultural techniques used by farmers. Agriculture has long been the foundation of Korean life, which means that it is important to pay continuous attention to its basic practices. At the same time, it is also crucial to reflect the impact of contemporary concerns. Thus, information concerning environmentally-friendly agricultural techniques is added here. The choropleth map shows the certified areas (unit: ha) employing environmentally-friendly agricultural techniques in addition to their distribution by *si* (cities) and *guns* (towns).

Source: Ministry of Agriculture & Forestry, 2005, *Agriculture & Forestry Statistical Yearbook*. National Agricultural Products Quality Management Service, Crop Product (2005), Agricultural Statistics Information (http://www.naqs.go.kr/). National Agricultural Products Quality Management Service, Crop Cultivation Area (2005), Agricultural Statistics Information (http://www.naqs.go.kr/).

Types of Environmentally Friendly Agricultural Techniques [126-3]

The public's interest in healthy living has manifested itself in the form of environmentally-friendly techniques being used in the field of agriculture. The types of environmentally-friendly agricultural techniques employed in metropolitan cities and provinces are classified into organic, pesticide-free, and low-pesticide techniques, each of which is presented by area (unit: ha).

There are four kinds of products according to the certification system of environmentally-friendly agricultural products. Organic agricultural products are grown without the application of organic and/or synthetic pesticides or chemical fertilizers for longer than the transition period (three years for perennial crops and two years for all other crops). The transition to organic crops should be made without the application of organic and/or synthetic pesticides or chemical fertilizers for a year or longer. Pesticide-free crops should be grown without the application of organic and/or synthetic pesticides, and an application of no more than one-third of the recommended amount of chemical fertilizers. Finally, low-pesticide crops should meet the following requirements: one-half or less of the recommended amount of chemical fertilizers should be used; pesticides should be sprayed fewer than half the number of times prescribed in the "Criteria of Safe Applications of Pesticides;" no herbicides should be used; and residual pesticide use should be less than half the "Allowable Standard for Residual Pesticides in Agricultural Products" as dictated by the Korea Food and Drug Administration. The map groups agricultural products into three types by including the transition to organic crops in the organic category.

Source: Ministry of Agriculture & Forestry, 2005, *Agriculture & Forestry Statistical Yearbook*. National Agricultural Products Quality Management Service, Crop Product (2005), Agricultural Statistics Information (http://www.naqs.go.kr/). National Agricultural Products Quality Management Service, Crop Cultivation Area (2005), Agricultural Statistics Information (http://www.naqs.go.kr/).

Harvested Areas: Vegetable Production [126-4]

Vegetables play a critical role in Korean's dietary pattern along with food crops and fruits. Vegetables are categorized into leafy, fruit, root, and seasoning vegetables, the categorization of which is too detailed to be displayed on a map. Thus, the total harvested area of vegetables is taken into account along with the production of major vegetables closely related to Korean's everyday dietary intake. These vegetables include Chinese cabbage (leafy vegetables), radishes (root vegetables), and red peppers, leeks, onions and garlic (seasoning vegetables). The total harvested area (unit: ha) of vegetables is shown on the choropleth map by metropolitan cities and provinces, and their production (unit: tons) is displayed by category in the pie chart.

Source: Ministry of Agriculture & Forestry, 2005, *Agriculture & Forestry Statistical Yearbook*. National Agricultural Products Quality Management Service, Crop Product (2005), Agricultural Statistics Information (http://www.naqs.go.kr/). National Agricultural Products Quality Management Service, Crop Cultivation Area (2005), Agricultural Statistics Information (http://www.naqs.go.kr/).

Harvested Areas: Barley Production [126-5]

In the past, the government promoted the consumption of barley due to a shortage of rice. Recently, people's desire for a healthier lifestyle has driven the consumption of various kinds of food crops, including barley, higher. Among these food crops, rice and barley are marked on a map as their consumption levels are the highest. Barley includes barley, naked barley, beer barley, and wheat. The total harvested area (unit: ha) of barley is displayed on the choropleth map, and the production (unit: tons) of barley is displayed by variety in the pie chart.

Source: National Agricultural Products Quality Management Service, Certified Quality Environment-Friendly Agricultural Products-Provincial-(2005), Agricultural Statistics Information (www.enviagro.go.kr).

Harvested Areas: Fruit Production [126-6]

Rising income levels and more diversified consumption habits have resulted in changes to the pattern of dietary intake, which in turn have caused an ongoing increase in the consumption ratio of fruit. Supported by advancements in many different farming techniques, along with increasing consumption, fruit consumption is now on an upward path.

Fruits are categorized into pears, apples, peaches, grapes, tangerines, persimmons, and others according to the amount produced. The total harvested area (unit: ha) of fruit is displayed on a choropleth map, and the production (unit: tons) of fruit is displayed by type in the pie chart.

Source: National Agricultural Products Quality Management Service, Environment-Friendly Agricultural Product Certification (2005), Agricultural Statistics Information (www.enviagro.go.kr).

Livestock Farms [127-1]

In recent years the nation's dietary intake has become more diversified, which has led to an increase in the consumption of meat. Although the kinds of livestock that farms raise have become more diverse, the number of livestock farmers has continued to drop, with small variations among the kinds of livestock raised. However the number of livestock raised per farmer is on the rise. Included in the livestock statistics are Korean beef cattle, milk cows, horses, pigs, sheep, deer, dogs, goats, rabbits, chickens, geese, turkeys, and bees. Farmers who raise Korean beef cattle, milk cows, pigs, and chickens are included as the variables given that their stock has close relationship to average everyday consumption patterns. The numbers are shown on the choropleth map by *si* and by *gun*.

Source: National Agricultural Products Quality Management Service, Livestock Statistics (2005), Agricultural Statistics Information (http://www.naqs.go.kr/).

Cattle Farming [127-2]

Regarded as the base of the livestock industry, Korean beef cattle and milk cows are marked on this map. From recent statistics, it is apparent that the number of farmers who raise five head of Korean beef cattle or less has decreased, and those who raise 40 or more head has increased. The number of cattle farms is indicated on the choropleth map to show the regional differences in 2005. The number of Korean beef cattle and milk cows is displayed on the pie chart.

The milk cow industry is included in the map and graph because it demonstrates clear differences in terms of regional distribution. Most cows are intensively raised in areas in Gyeonggi-*do*, Chungcheongnam-*do* and Gyeongsangbuk-*do* that are accessible to big cities, an important vantage point for distribution.

Source: National Agricultural Products Quality Management Service, Livestock Statistics (2005), Agricultural Statistics Information (http://www.naqs.go.kr/).

Forest Land Area and Forest Growing Stock [127-3]

Although forestry accounts for the smallest proportion of output in terms of the number of people engaged in the industry and the amount, it does perform important economic functions. Forestry produces a variety of forest products and serves the public good by promoting land preservation, the cultivation of riverheads, forest recreation, the protection of wild animals, the supply of oxygen, and the purification of the air. Thanks to the "Green Revolution" that began in 1973, Korea has successfully preserved its forests to a certain degree. Forest land area and forest growing stock, which are the basics of forestry, are examined here. Forest land area is displayed on the choropleth map by metropolitan cities and provinces, and the forest growing stock is displayed via a bar graph.

Source: Korea Forest Service, 2005, *Statistical Yearbook of Forest*.

Value and Volume of the Fishing Industry [127-4]

The fishing industry is categorized into sea fishing, shallow sea culture, inland fishing, and ocean fishing. As management conditions have grown worse due to many factors, including the opening of the market, the government has decided to promote the stable production, supply, and export of high-grade, cultured marine products to protect domestic fisheries. The total value of sea fishing, shallow sea culture, and inland fishing, which make up domestic fishing, is displayed on the choropleth map. Volume is displayed in the pie chart and shows regional differences.

Source: Ministry of Maritime Affairs & Fisheries, 2005, *Statistical Yearbook of Ministry of Maritime Affairs & Fisheries*.

Mines [127-5]

This map shows locations where major mineral resources (gold, silver, lead, zinc, iron, titanium iron, scale-like graphite, talcum, zeolites) are currently being exploited in Korea.

Source: Ministry of Commerce, Industry and Energy·Korea Resources Corporation, 2005, Mineral Reserves of Korea.

Production of Mineral Resources [127-6]
This map shows total production quantity per type of major mineral resource produced in Korea (limestone, silex, kaolinite, talcum, silica, ophiolite, iron, titanium, and zeolites) by province.
Source: Ministry of Commerce, Industry and Energy-Korea Resources Corporation, 2005, *Mineral Reserves of Korea.*

Imported Amount of Mineral Resources by Type [127-7]
This map shows the countries Korea imports mineral resources (over USD 15 million), and the types and amounts per country.
Source: Ministry of Commerce, Industry and Energy-Korea Institute of Geoscience and Mineral Resources, 2005, *Supply-demand Statistics of Mineral Commodities.*

[References]
Kwon, YYoung-Kun, 2006, Understanding of Agriculture & Rural Community, Pakyoungryul.
Kown, Hyuck-jae, 2004, Geography of Korea, Bubmunsa.
Kim, Chul-sang, 2006, Trend of Forest Economy, Korea Forest Research Institute.
Jeong, Young-il, 2006, Choice of Korea Agriculture on transition stage, Pakyoungsa.
Ju, Rin-won, 2006, Statistics of Forest Resource & Forest Product Supply-demand, Korea Forest Research Institute.
Hyong, Kie-joo, 1993, Agricultural Geography, Bobmunsa.

Manufacturing

Manufacturing Employees and Output [128]
This map depicts the overall situation of Korean manufacturing. Manufacturing employment and output are mapped according to the major regional districts. Korean manufacturing employment and output have traditionally been concentrated in the Capital region, Seoul, Incheon, and Gyeonggi-*do*, and the Southeastern part of Korea. Recently, however, manufacturing industries have spread out from the Capital region to Chungcheong-*do*, resulting in the Seoul-Busan diagonal manufacturing belt formation.
Source: National Statistical Office, 2007, Census on Basic *Characteristics of Establishments, Business Enterprise, Korea Statistical information Service.*

Employees by Gender [130-1]
The share of female employment is growing in the metropolitan areas, and this is one of the major characteristics of Korean manufacturing. Female employment is still relatively low in comparison to the global standard. Globally the share of female employment has been growing at a rapid rate recently.
Source: National Statistical Office, 2007, *Census on Basic Characteristics of Establishments, Business Enterprise, Korea Statistical Information Service.*

Labor Productivity and Value-added Products [130-2]
One of the economic advantages resulting from industrial activities is the generation of value-added products. This map shows the national distribution of the manufacturing of value-added products. The pattern looks very similar to the distribution of manufacturing outputs. The metropolitan areas such as Seoul, Gyeonggi-*do*, Daegu, and Ulsan, however, depict higher manufacturing levels of value-added products. These areas are the hometowns of large firms, implying the existence of a discrepancy in value-added production between large and small-to-medium sized firms in Korea. Labor productivity is a basic indicator of the efficiency and outcome of manufacturing activities. This map shows the national distribution of manufacturing labor productivity. Compared to the spatial distribution of manufacturing employment, metropolitan areas and their vicinities, where small firms are concentrated, have lower labor productivity levels than non-metropolitan areas.
Source: National Statistical Office, 2007, Census on Basic Characteristics of Establishments, *Business Enterprise, Korea Statistical Information Service.*

Employees by Job Type [130-3]
In this post-Fordist era, flexibility in manufacturing employment has been a dominant feature. One of the major characteristics lies in the growth of flexible employment. This map shows the national distribution of manufacturing employment by job type, i.e., production, clerical, managerial, and dispatched employment. The share of production employees is growing, while clerical and managerial employees are decreasing outside the metropolitan areas. The share of dispatched employees, on the other hand, is growing in the metropolitan areas, and flexible workers are flourishing in the urban setting.
Source: National Statistical Office, 2007, Census on Basic *Characteristics of Establishments, Business Enterprise, Korea Statistical Information Service.*

Manufacturing R&D Investment [130-4]
Manufacturing R&D investment is an important indicator of the potential for long-term development and competitiveness. Manufacturing R&D investment tends to be concentrated in the national economic control centers, largely because R&D investment is highly value-added and employees in R&D activities tend to reside in metropolitan areas. In Korea, manufacturing R&D investment is concentrated in the Capital region.
Source: National Statistical Office, Research institute & researchers & technical (2005), Korea Statistical Information Service (http://www.kosis.kr).

Construction [130-5]
The construction industry serves as a leading indicator of national economic vitality. The sector includes not only housing, but also important physical infrastructure such as highways, railways, bridges, and other buildings. This map depicts the national distribution of employees in the construction industry. Most of the employees are concentrated in the capital region, reflecting the fact that regionally-based construction companies have grown, and they have relocated their headquarters to the Capital region in the process.
Source: National Statistical Office, Construction Industries Statistics (2005), Korea Statistical Information Service (http://www.kosis.kr).

Housing Construction by Type [130-6]
This map is closely related to the quality of life in Korea vis-à-vis housing type. It classifies housing into apartment buildings, detached houses, row houses, and multiplex houses. Even though the overall pattern of distribution is similar to that of the population, multiplex houses are concentrated in the metropolitan region, suggesting that residential density and quality are inferior at this level. The predominance of apartment buildings all over the nation has given Korea the nickname "The Republic of Apartment Buildings."
Source: National Statistical Office, Housing Construction Statistics (2005), (http://www.kosis.kr), Korea Statistical Information Service (http://www.kosis.kr).

[References]
Korea Association of Information & Telecommunication, 2006, *Statistical Yearbook of Information & Telecommunication Industries,* Korea Association of Information & Telecommunication.
Korea Development Institute, 2004, *Economic Structural changes and Job Creation in Korea,* Korea Development Institute.

Motor Vehicles [131-1]
This map shows the employment and output of motor vehicles, one of the top 5 industries in Korea. The motor vehicle assembly industries are concentrated in the cities of Gyeonggi-*do* and Chungcheong-*do*, and Ulsan, the "motor city" of Korea. Suppliers for the major assemblers are distributed all over the country. The common characteristic of the Korean motor vehicle industries is the tendency to locate in port cities, as the growth of the motor vehicle industry has been led through exports.
Source: National Statistical Office, 2007, Census on Basic *Characteristics of Establishments, Business Enterprise, Korea Statistical Information Service.*

Apparel and Clothing [131-2]
This map shows the employment and outputs of the apparel and clothing industry, one of the top 5 industries in Korea. The traditional location for the apparel & clothing industry has been Daegu. Recently, firms are locating in Seoul and Gyeonggi-*do*, reflecting industry-specific requirements such as information for exports and for changing consumers' tastes and trends. Also, the overall size of the firms in Daegu is smaller and less competitive.
Source: National Statistical Office, 2007, Census on Basic Characteristics of Establishments, *Business Enterprise, Korea Statistical Information Service.*

Ship Building [131-3]
This map shows the employment and output of the ship building industry, one of the top 5 industries in Korea. For a long time, the ship building industry was solely located in the Southeastern part of Korea, Gyeongsangnam-*do* and Gyeongsangbuk-*do*. Recently, however, the Daebul National Industrial Complex located in Jeollanam-*do*, where suppliers to the Gyeongsangbuk-*do* headquarters are located, has shown rapid growth.
Source: National Statistical Office, 2007, Census on Basic Characteristics of Establishments, *Business Enterprise, Korea Statistical Information Service.*

Steel and Metal [131-4]
This map shows the employment and output of the steel and metal industry, one of the top 5 industries in Korea. The Korean steel & metal industry has developed in line with the locations of major iron works: namely in Pohang-*si*, Gwangyang-*si*, and Dangjin-*gun*. As a result, steel and metal industry facilities are distributed throughout Gyeongsangbuk-*do*, Jeollanam-*do*, and Gyeonggi-*do*.
Source: National Statistical Office, 2007, Census on Basic Characteristics of Establishments, *Business Enterprise, Korea Statistical Information Service.*

Service Industry

Employees and Establishments in the Service Industry [132]
The overall geographic pattern of the service industry can be captured in a map representing the employment and number of establishments in the service industry, including Wholesale and Retail Trade, Hotels and Restaurants, Transportation, Real Estate and Renting, Business Services, Recreational, Cultural and Sporting Activities, Repair and Personal Services, and Household Services. Excluded here are such service categories as Public Administration, Military, Education, Health and Social Work, which are dealt with in another Public Affairs section.
Source: National Statistical Office, 2006, *Census on Basic Characteristics of Establishments, Business Enterprise, Korea Statistical Information Service.*

Amount of Sales: Wholesale and Retail Trade [134-1]
Wholesale and retail trades, generally called commercial activities, account for the highest proportion of the service industry. An examination of annual sales by large metropolitan cities and provinces allows for a comparison of the location and activities of wholesale and retail trade across regions. Large cities, including Seoul, show higher wholesale trade than retail amounts by a ratio of 5 to 2. Other regions, however, reveal similar wholesale and retail amounts, or a slightly higher total for the wholesale trade, which reflects the centrality of large cities in wholesale under Korea's hierarchical urban systems.
Source: National Statistical Office, 2006, *Census on Basic Characteristics of Establishments, Business Enterprise, Korea Statistical Information Service.*

Number of Retail Establishments per 1,000 People [134-2]
Retail trade is closely related to the everyday needs of people, and is the most common source of self-employment. This map, based on the number of establishments per 1,000 people, shows that while large metropolitan cities such as Seoul, Busan, Daegu, and Gwangju. have somewhat more establishments in relation to population size, retail trade establishments are more widely and evenly distributed across regions.
Source: National Statistical Office, 2006, *Census on Basic Characteristics of Establishments, Business Enterprise, Korea Statistical Information Service.*

Large-sized General Retail Stores [134-3]
Retail trade establishments has recently become larger in size and more comprehensive in terms of items available for purchase. Large-sized discount stores have newly sprung up all over Korea, while traditional markets have been in decline. The purpose of this map is to understand the distribution of large-sized general retail stores, such as department stores and large-sized discount stores, across regions. As expected, department stores tend to be concentrated in large cities. Large retail stores (the official term for large discount stores) are somewhat diffused compared to department stores. Such a spatial pattern is the result of large retail stores carrying similar daily convenience and necessity goods as those carried in traditional markets.
Source: National Statistical Office, 2006, *Census on Basic Characteristics of Establishments, Business Enterprise, Korea Statistical Information Service.*

Hotels and Restaurants [134-4]
Hotels and restaurants are as easily found as retail trade establishments. On this dot map, each dot represents a certain number of establishments. Hotels and restaurants are widely distributed across regions, but the concentration in large metropolitan cities and the Capital Region is a little bit higher than that of retail trade.
Source: National Statistical Office, 2006, *Census on Basic Characteristics of Establishments, Business Enterprise, Korea Statistical Information Service.*

Banking [134-5]
Banking is central among financial service activities along with insurance and securities. Banks include general banks as well as credit unions, which appear in significant proportions in local financial markets. Banks are money-handling service organizations for individual customers, so excluded here are development banks and export-import banks. Credit unions are financial institutions that make loans to members, and funds come from the customer savings deposits. Credit unions operating on a small scale show a relatively even distribution, whereas banks are highly concentrated in large metropolitan cities such as Seoul, Busan, Daegu, Gwangju, and Daejeon.
Source: National Statistical Office, 2006, *Census on Basic Characteristics of Establishments, Business Enterprise, Korea Statistical Information Service.*

Insurance [134-6]
Insurance, an important financial service both as a consumer service and as a producer service, has taken the lead in the growing service industry. Insurance is largely subdivided into life insurance, including personal pensions, personal accident insurance, and non-life insurance, including insurance against loss or property damage from accident or fire, and insurance against debt through the guaranteeing of payments. Life insurance excludes national pension, government employee pension, military pension, and teacher pension. These pensions are public rather than individual in character, and are thus categorized as separate pension fund service activities. Insurance establishments are highly concentrated in Seoul and only a few other large metropolitan cities.
Source: National Statistical Office, 2006, *Census on Basic Characteristics of Establishments, Business Enterprise, Korea Statistical Information Service.*

Securities Intermediation and Insurance Agencies [134-7]
Securities Intermediation and Insurance Agencies have increased their relative importance in financial service activities, and this increase is positively evaluated in the transition toward a service economy. Securities Intermediation is most often associated with securities companies, which intermediate securities trading. Insurance intermediation includes agencies dealing in life insurance or insurance for loss which contract, intermediate, or recommend insurance for insurance companies. This map, presenting the branch offices of securities companies and agencies for insurance companies in dots, allows for an examination of the regional pattern of the newly-growing financial service activities. Securities intermediation tends to concentrate in large metropolitan cities more so than any other financial activities; Seoul is prominent in its concentration. Insurance agencies reveal a somewhat diffused pattern all over the country.
Source: National Statistical Office, 2006, *Census on Basic Characteristics of Establishments, Business Enterprise, Korea Statistical Information Service.*

Transportation Services Establishments [134-8]
Transportation service is related to all spatial movements of people and goods, and encompasses such diverse activities as land transport, water transport, air transport, travel, and storage. The number of establishments dealing in transportation services are concentrated in the Capital region, the southeast region ranging from Pohang-*si*, Yeocheon-*si*, to Gwangyang-*si*, and the major cities of the inland provinces. Also noticeable is the concentration in the southeastern part of the Capital Region and around the Asan Bay area.
Source: National Statistical Office, 2006, *Census on Basic Characteristics of Establishments, Business Enterprise, Korea Statistical Information Service.*

Employees in Transportation Services [134-9]
Transportation service facilitates the interregional movement of people and goods, and expands the commuter zone boundary. Recently, transportation services, including parcel delivery, have grown rapidly. This map, based on employment numbers, provides a more comprehensive picture not readily reflected by the number of establishments. The overall pattern is similar to that of establishments, but a somewhat diffused pattern is noticeable along with a relatively high concentration in mid-sized cities such as Cheonan-*si*, Cheongju-*si*, Jeonju-*si*, Masan-*si*, Gangneung-*si*, Yeosu-*si* & Gwangyang-*si*, Pohang-*si*, and Jinju-*si*.
Source: National Statistical Office, 2006, *Census on Basic Characteristics of Establishments, Business Enterprise, Korea Statistical Information Service.*

Business Services Establishments [135-1]
Service activities are divided into producer and consumer services according to user. Business services are one of the representative producer services along with banking and insurance services. Included in this category are information processing and other computer related activities, research and development, professional scientific and technical services, and business support services. These activities have been increasing in importance as information technology has lead industrial development. A highly concentrated pattern is noticeable in a few large cities, and there are 7 to 8 clusters around the dense center of Seoul.
Source: National Statistical Office, 2006, Census on Basic Characteristics of Establishments, *Business Enterprise, Korea Statistical Information Service.*

Employees in Business Services [135-2]
Based on the number of employed personnel, this map reveals an almost identical distribution pattern to that of the number of business services establishments. Clusters however are more prominent in large, industrial cities such as Seoul, Busan, Daegu, Ulsan, Pohang-*si*, Gumi-*si*, and Changwon-*si*, and in mid-sized cities such as Cheongju-*si*, and Jeonju-*si*.
Source: National Statistical Office, 2006, Census on Basic Characteristics of Establishments, *Business Enterprise, Korea Statistical Information Service.*

Personal Services Establishments [135-3]
Personal services, or typical consumer services, are necessary to maintain everyday individual lives. Included in this category are repair, barbershop-beauty parlor, sewage and refuse disposal, and sanitation activities. Religious organizations and organizations of membership and trade unions are

also included in this category, but they are excluded in mapping due to their different characteristics. The distribution of the four personal service activities reveals a spatial concentration in Seoul and other large cities, but to a lesser degree than that of business services.

Source: National Statistical Office, 2006, Census on Basic Characteristics of Establishments, Business Enterprise, Korea Statistical Information Service.

Communication Services Establishments [135-4]

Communication services have recently become one of the primary growing industries with the development of information and communication technology. Included are postal, wired and wireless communication, such as telephone and mobile phone, and value-added communication services such as computer internet. Facilitating spatial interaction, communication services have regional patterns close to, and a bit diffused from transportation services.

Source: National Statistical Office, 2006, *Census on Basic Characteristics of Establishments, Business Enterprise*, Korea Statistical Information Service.

Employees in Communication Services [135-5]

The complete regional picture of certain industrial sectors needs to be examined both in terms of the number of establishments and employed personnel due to the diverse employment size of establishments. This map, based on the number of people employed in communication services, does not reveal any significant difference from the distribution pattern of establishments. This implies that communication services are less diverse in establishment employment size than in transportation services.

Source: National Statistical Office, 2006, *Census on Basic Characteristics of Establishments, Business Enterprise*, Korea Statistical Information Service.

Employees in Personal Services [135-6]

This map, based on the number of personnel employed in personal services, closely follows the pattern of the number of establishments, to the point where it is difficult to distinguish between them. In other words, personal services operate at similar but smaller scales.

Source: National Statistical Office, 2006, Census on Basic Characteristics of Establishments, Business Enterprise, Korea Statistical Information Service.

Transportation and Communication

Transportation Networks [136]

This map shows Korea's main road and railroad networks, the location of airports and trading ports, and the country's transportation structure. In terms of road transportation, its directions are oriented along the north-south axis, especially the Seoul-Busan axis, rather than along the east-west axis. Road transportation, such as expressways and national highways formed higher, dense networks as the importance of motor transportation in Korea has grown. Railway transportation encompasses networks of high speed railway and other railway transportation. Airports and trading ports are linked to main road networks of transportation.

Source: Ministry of Construction and Transportation, Highway Statistics (2005), Korea Transport Database (http://www.ktdb.go.kr).

Number of Flights by Domestic Air Route [138-1]

This map shows flights by airport domestic air routes in order to examine air transportation demand. The Gimpo-Jeju line accounts for 25 percent of total flights by domestic air route. Jeju *Int'l Airport* has 12 of the total 27 domestic air routes.

Source: Korea Tourism Organization (2005). Ministry of Construction and Transportation, Aviation Statistics (2005), Korea Transport Database (http://www.ktdb.go.kr).

Length of Roadway by Road Rank [138-2]

Road ranks in Korea are classified by expressway, national highway, provincial way and city-country road. As the main components of national road networks, expressways and national highways are linked to principal cities, designated ports, airports, national industrial complexes, and tourist resorts. Provincial ways compose main regional road networks which run from provincial governments to city halls and county offices, as well as from airports, seaports, railway stations, expressways, national highways and provincial ways within each province. City-county roads link administrative organizations in local counties.

Source: Ministry of Construction and Transportation, 2006, *Yearbook of Road Statistics*.

Traffic by Road [138-3]

In terms of passenger and freight traffic by road transportation by metropolitan city and province, the Seoul metropolitan area has the highest share. In particular, Seoul accounts for 45 percent of total passenger traffic, most of which is concentrated in the Seoul metropolitan area. Compared to passenger traffic, freight traffic shows lower variation then passenger traffic at the national level. Notably, freight traffic in the Gwangju metropolitan area, Gangwon-*do*, Gyeongsangbuk-*do* and Jeollabuk-*do* is relatively lower than other in metropolitan areas and provinces.

Source: Ministry of Construction and Transportation, Highway Statistics (2005), Korea Transport Database (http://www.ktdb.go.kr).

Seaports Traffic [138-4]

Seaports are located where ships can come, go, and moor safely. The scale of a seaport can be determined by its volume of freight, type of freight, number of passengers, topographical features, linkage of land and sea transportation, and the expansion and improvement of facilities due to an increase of passengers and freight, to name but a few. The largest seaports in Korea are Busan Port (149 vessels), Ulsan Port (94 vessels), Incheon Port(78 vessels) and Gwangyang Port (71 vessels). Seaports larger in functional size are Busan Port (219 million RT), Gwangyang Port (172 million RT), Ulsan Port (161 million RT) and Incheon Port (115 million RT).

Source: Ministry of Construction and Transportation, 2005, Ministry of Construction and Transportation Statistics Annual Report, Ministry of Construction and Transportation, Maritimes Statistics (2005), Korea Transport Database (http://www.ktdb.go.kr).

Freight by Seaports and Type of Goods [138-5]

By port and by item, machinery (19 million RT), fuel (6 million RT) and food and beverage (5 million RT) are imported to Busan Port. Machinery (27 million RT) is the main export from Busan Port. In the case of Incheon Port, fuel (36 million RT) and steel material (8 million RT) are imported and machinery (7 million RT) is exported. At Ulsan Port, the main import and export item is fuel (imports of 73 million RT; exports of 36 million RT). With respect to Gwangyang Port, import items are fuel (49 million RT) and iron ore (26 million RT), and export items are fuel (23 million RT) and steel material (10 million RT).

Source: Ministry of Construction and Transportation, Maritimes Statistics (2005), Korea Transport Database (http://www.ktdb.go.kr).

Traffic by Railway [138-6]

With respect to passenger traffic by railway, the Gyeongbu and Honam lines account for 60.4 percent and 6 percent of the total, respectively. However, other lines share an extremely small portion. As a result, the freight traffic in Korea is considerably uneven. In terms of freight traffic, the Yeongdong line has a high share (21.2% of the total), followed by the Gyeongbu line (20.7%), the Goedong line (13.9%) and the Nambu line (11.1%). The southeast region has a high share of the proportion of freight traffic because there is a high demand for transportation due to the development of heavy industry in the region.

Source: Ministry of Construction and Transportation, Railway Statistics (2005), Korea Transport Database (http://www.ktdb.go.kr).

Information and Communication Networks [139-1]

This map shows important networks of main internet service providers in Korea. The main internet network is the high capacity transmission line which makes high-speed internet possible. The primary line for internet service with large scale transmission capacities distributes to metropolitan cities and major cities from the nexus of the starting point, Seoul.

Source: National Internet Development Agency of Korea, Internet Usage Statistics (2006), Internet Statistics Information System (http://isis.nida.or.kr).

Diffusion of Personal Computers and Internet Service [139-2]

Personal computers in Korea were first developed in Korea in 1981. Korea Telecom (KT corporation) opened commercial internet service in 1994. In 2006, the rate of diffusion for personal computers and internet services was about 79 percent and 78 percent, respectively. There is little gap by region in terms of the diffusion of personal computers and internet services.

Source: National Internet Development Agency of Korea, Internet Usage Statistics (2006), Internet (http://isis.nida.or.kr).

Wireless Internet Use Ratio and Average Duration per Week of Using Wireless Internet [139-3]

With the increasing importance of the internet, the inconvenience of immobility associated with cabled internet service is the main constraint on internet use. Since 1998, internet services to mobile telephone have been set up, and the wireless internet use rate has increased along with the growth in use of notebook computers and PDAs. Examining the wireless internet use rate and the average duration of use per week by region, there is little difference by region. However, in the average duration of use per week, Jeollanam-*do*, Jeju Special self-governing, Gangwon-*do* and Daegu have higher wireless use rates than other cities and provinces.

Source: National Internet Development Agency of Korea, Internet Usage Statistics (2006), Internet Statistics Information System (http://isis.nida.or.kr).

Information and Communication Services [139-4]

Information and telecommunication services are divided into facilities-based telecommunications service, specific telecommunications service, value added communication service and broadcasting service. Of these services, the facilities based telecommunications service deals with the installation of the electronic telecommunication service. This category can be divided into telephone service, telex service, telecommunication facility rent service, telephone service, telex service, and assigned radio frequency-based service. It is used as the index which represents the establishment of basic telecommunication infrastructure in a particular region. Value added communication service provides improved value-added communication services such as circuit switching, code conversion, data signaling rate conversion, the accumulation of information, transmission, media exchange, calculation processing, and the creation of databases. In Korea, facilities based telecommunications services and the value added communication services are considerably concentrated in the Seoul metropolitan area.

Source: Ministry of Information and Communication, 2004, *Statistical Yearbook of Information and Communication*.

Labor

Employment Rate [140-1]

This map shows the employment rate by gender and age group. It was produced to estimate and compare employment rates per *si* and *do* for populations aged 15 and above by gender and age group. When briefly examined, the distribution pattern by area shows that employment is high in areas including Jeju Special Self-Governing Province, Gyeongsangbuk-*do*, Jeollanam-*do*, and Chungcheongnam-*do*, with the metropolitan area showing a high employment rate for young people.

Source: National Statistical Office, Economically Active Population Survey (2005), Korea Statistical Information Service (http://www.kosis.kr/).

Unemployment Rate [140-2]

This map shows the unemployment rate by gender and age group. It was produced to estimate and compare the unemployment rate per *si* and *do* by gender and age group. When briefly examined, the distribution pattern by area shows that the unemployment rate is relatively higher in large cities, but lower in urban-rural areas, with the proportion of unemployed young people to all unemployed people being the lowest in Busan and Incheon.

Source: National Statistical Office, Economically Active Population Survey (2005), Korea Statistical Information Service (http://www.kosis.kr/).

Labor Force Participation Rate (LFPR) by Gender [142-1]

This map shows the LFPR per *si* and *do* and by gender. It was produced to estimate and compare the size of the population, out of all those aged 15 years or older, participating in economic activities per *si* and *do* by dividing the LFPR for 2006 per *si* and *do* by the total population and classifying it according to gender. As for the LFPR per *si* and *do*, Jeju Special Self-Governing Province showed the highest level for both men and women, followed by Seoul, Chungcheongnam-*do*, Jeollanam-*do*, Gyeongsangbuk-*do*, and Gyeongsangnam-*do*, which saw an above-average LFPR for both sexes. Daegu showed an above-average LFPR for women, and Incheon, Gyeonggi-*do*, and Ulsan showed an above-average LFPR for men.

Source: National Statistical Office, Economically Active Population Survey (2005), Korea Statistical Information Service (http://www.kosis.kr/).

Labor Force Participation Rate (LFPR) by Age Group and Educational Attainment [142-2]

This map indicates LFPR by age group and educational attainment. It was produced to estimate and compare the level of aging and the increase in educational attainment by classifying the LFPR for 2005 per *si* and *do* by age group and educational attainment and deriving the ratio of the economically active population. The distribution pattern by area shows that the LFPR is highest on Jeju Special Self-Governing Province. As for the LFPR for young people (ages 15-29), it is high in the metropolitan areas (Seoul, Incheon, and Gyeonggi-*do*). The LFPR for the middle-aged and the highly educated groups (university degree or above) is high in Gyeongsangnam-*do*, Gyeongsangbuk-*do*, and Jeollanam-*do*.

Source: National Statistical Office, Economically Active Population Survey (2005), Korea Statistical Information Service (http://www.kosis.kr/).

Employment by Gender, Age Group and Educational Attainment [142-3]

This map shows employment by gender, age group, and educational attainment. It was produced to estimate and compare the proportion of employed people to the entire population per *si* and *do* by these three attributes. The distribution pattern by area shows that the proportion of employed women to all employed people is relatively low in Ulsan, Incheon, and Gyeonggi-*do*. The proportion of employed young people to all employed people is high in large cities excluding Busan and Gyeonggi-*do*. The employment rate of highly educated people (university degree or above) is low in more urbanized rural areas.

Source: National Statistical Office, Economically Active Population Survey (2005), Korea Statistical Information Service (http://www.kosis.kr/).

Employment by Industry and Occupation [142-4]

This map shows employment by industry and occupation. It was produced to estimate and to compare employment by industry and occupation per *si* and *do* by these main attributes. When briefly examined, the distribution pattern by area shows that employment in manufacturing is high in Ulsan, Incheon, Gyeongsangnam-*do*, and Daegu, while employment in agriculture, forestry, and fishery is relatively high in urban-rural areas excluding Gyeonggi-*do*, and employment in the service industry is high in other areas including Seoul and Gyeonggi-*do*. As for each occupation, employment in production and manufacturing is high in Ulsan and Incheon, whereas employment in the service industry is high in Seoul, Gyeonggi-*do*, and Gwangju.

Source: National Statistical Office, Economically Active Population Survey (2005), Korea Statistical Information Service (http://www.kosis.kr/).

Turnover Rate of Workers at Businesses Employing Five or More Workers [143-1]

This map shows the turnover rate of workers at all businesses, including the turnover rate by gender. It was produced to estimate and compare the turnover rate of workers at businesses and that of workers by gender per *si* and *do* by indicating the turnover rate of workers at businesses consisting of five or more workers in terms of the number of all employed people and by gender per *si* and *do*. When briefly examined, the distribution pattern by area shows that the turnover rate of workers is relatively higher in Chungcheongbuk-*do*, Seoul, and Gyeonggi-*do*.

Source: Ministry of Labor (MOLAB; http://www.molab.go.kr), Monthly Labor Statistical Database (2005), Korea Statistical Information Service (http://www.kosis.kr/).

Working Hours of Workers at Businesses Employing Five or More Workers [143-2]

This map shows the monthly working hours of workers at businesses and the proportion of overtime working hours by gender. It was produced to indicate the total working hours and overtime working hours of workers at businesses employing five or more workers per si and *do* and to estimate and compare the working hours of workers at businesses by gender per *si* and *do*. The distribution pattern by area shows that working hours are relatively longer in Chungcheongnam-*do*, Chungcheongbuk-*do*, and Gyeongsangnam-*do*, but are the shortest in Seoul.

Source: Ministry of Labor (MOLAB; http://www.molab.go.kr), Monthly Labor Statistical Database (2005), Korea Statistical Information Service (http://www.kosis.kr/).

Monthly Salary of Workers at Businesses Employing Five or More Workers [143-3]

This map shows the monthly salary of all workers at businesses, including comparison by gender. It was produced to estimate and to compare workers' wage income per *si* and *do* by indicating the total monthly salary of workers at businesses employing five or more workers by gender per *si* and *do*. The distribution pattern by area shows that the monthly salary is the highest in Seoul and Ulsan. In comparing genders, women workers' monthly salary is the lowest in Ulsan and Jeollanam-*do* when compare to the monthly salaries of their male counterparts.

Source: Ministry of Labor (MOLAB; http://www.molab.go.kr), Monthly Labor Statistical Database (2005), Korea Statistical Information Service (http://www.kosis.kr/).

Employment by Work Status [143-4]

This map indicates the proportion of wage workers and the composition of employment by work status. It was produced to estimate and to compare the relative proportion of employment by work status per *si* and *do* by showing the proportion of wage workers to all employed people and the composition of employment by work status. When briefly examined, the distribution pattern by area shows that the proportion of wage workers is high in Gyeonggi-*do*, Gangwon-*do*, and most cities, while that of self-employed people is high in more urbanized rural areas.

Source: National Statistical Office, Economically Active Population Survey (2005), Korea Statistical Information Service (http://www.kosis.kr/).

Public Health and Social Welfare

Number of Health Professionals [144]

This map shows the number of health professionals for every 100,000 people per *si* and *gun*, in addition to the number of health professionals by type including doctors, dentists, traditional Asian doctors, nurses, and pharmacists per *si* and *do*. Understanding the number of health professionals for every 100,000 people per *si* and *gun* and the number of health professionals by type are useful for grasping health and medical resources and used as important basic data when establishing and evaluating health and medical plans. When briefly examined, the distribution pattern by area shows that the number of health professionals for every 100,000 people is higher in the metropolitan area, Jeollanam-*do*, and Chungcheongnam-*do*. As for the number of health professionals by type, the proportion of doctors to other health professionals is high in the metropolitan area and Busan.

Source: National Statistical Office, 2005, *Korea Statistical Yearbook*.

Number of Hospital Beds [146]

This map shows the number of hospital beds for every 100,000 people per *si* and *gun*, the number of hospital beds by hospital type, and the number of medical organizations by hospital type per *si* and *do*. Together with statistics on health and health professionals, statistics on health and medical facilities are useful data when examining health and medical resources. As for Korea, most medical facilities, including medical organizations and hospital beds, belong to the civilian sector and medical resources are most heavily found in cities. While the government has endeavored to expand public medical facilities, in addition to implementing national medical insurance, some farming and fishing communities still lack adequate hospital beds and are provided with medical services that are relatively poorer than those available in cities. Such a tendency is indicated in this map, where large cities, including the metropolitan area and main regional cities, have many hospital beds per 100,000 people, with Seoul and Busan showing a higher ratio of general hospitals.

Source: National Statistical Office, 2005, *Korea Statistical Yearbook*.

Alcohol Consumption [147-1]

This map shows the ratio of alcohol drinkers, the ratio of alcohol drinkers by gender, and the ratio of alcohol drinkers by educational attainment per *si* and *do*. The ratio of alcohol drinkers to the total population was studied because the ratio of alcohol drinkers is rising in importance as illness and death due to alcohol consumption are increasing. When briefly examined, the distribution pattern by area shows that the ratio of alcohol drinkers is higher in Seoul, Gyeonggi-*do*, and Ulsan, but does not exhibit noticeable regional differences in terms of the ratio of alcohol drinkers by gender and educational attainment.

Source: National Statistical Office, Social Statistics Survey (2006), Korea Statistical Information Service (http://www.kosis.kr/).

Tobacco Product Use [147-2]

This map shows the ratio of the tobacco-smoking population, the ratio of the tobacco-smoking population by gender, and the ratio of the tobacco-smoking population by educational attainment per *si* and *do*. The ratio of the tobacco-smoking population to the total population is rising in importance because smoking is known to be harmful to personal health, and causes losses to society and the economy through early death, illness, fire, and second-hand smoke. In particular, the smoking rate for adult males in Korea is the highest among all member states of the Organization for Economic Cooperation and Development (OECD), thus requiring a smoking prevention and cessation policy on a national level. When briefly examined, the distribution pattern by area shows that the ratio of tobacco-smoking population is relatively higher in Chungcheongbuk-*do* and Ulsan, but does not exhibit noticeable regional differences in terms of the ratio of the tobacco-smoking population by gender and educational attainment.

Source: National Statistical Office, Social Statistics Survey (2006), Korea Statistical Information Service (http://www.kosis.kr/).

Mortality Rate by Etiological Cause [147-3]

This map shows the crude death rate and mortality rate for 1,000 people by etiological cause per *si* and *do*. An index based on the fact that the relative number of total deaths and the composition of etiological causes change as a nation's health level rises, mortality rate by etiological cause is known to be high in countries with poor health conditions with prevalent epidemics and parasitic illnesses, but low in developed nations where chronic illnesses and accidents are prevalent. This map shows mortality by etiological cause, with a focus on illnesses. When briefly examined, the distribution pattern by area shows that the crude death rate is relatively low in urban areas such as Seoul, Gyeonggi-*do*, Daegu, Daejeon, Gwangju, Busan, Incheon, and Ulsan, but high in rural areas.

Source: National Statistical Office, Vital Statistics (2006), Korea Statistical Information Service (http://www.kosis.kr/).

Prevalence Rate of Diseases [147-4]

This map shows the prevalence rate of diseases by gender and age group per *si* and *do*. The prevalence rate of diseases is an index calculated by dividing the number of current patients by the entire population, regardless of the time at which illnesses occurred. Here, current patients include: a) children who are too ill to engage in normal childhood activities and need hospitalization or medication, b) students and workers who are too ill to study or work, c) housewives and other workers who are too ill to study or work, and d) long-term patients and people suffering from other disorders. When briefly examined, the distribution pattern by area shows that the prevalence rate is lower in Seoul, Gyeonggi-*do*, Daejeon, and Ulsan.

Source: National Statistical Office, Social Statistics Survey (2006), Korea Statistical Information Service (http://www.kosis.kr/).

National Health Insurance Benefits per Person [148-1]

This map shows the amount of national health insurance benefits by person per *si* and *gun*. An institutional plan is directed at the entire population and intended to disperse the illness risk of economically viable people along with making possible mutual aid and income redistribution. The amount of national health insurance benefits indicates the average amount paid to each person from among the population covered by national health insurance. When briefly examined, the distribution pattern by area shows that the amount of national health insurance benefits by person is lower in large cities such as Seoul, Gyeonggi-*do*, Incheon, Daegu, Busan, Ulsan, Gwangju, and Daejeon.

Source: Ministry of Health and Welfare (MOHW), 2005, *National Health Insurance Statistical Yearbook*.

Public Social Welfare Specialists [148-2]

This map shows the number of public social welfare specialists and the ratio of social workers by grade per *si* and *do*. Public social welfare specialists began to be dispatched to towns, districts, and blocks in 1987 to implement social welfare efficiently and professionally for recipients of the National Basic Livelihood Security Scheme, children, senior citizens, and the disabled. within the social welfare dissemination system, they serve as the first channel of public welfare policy and community welfare services. When briefly examined, the distribution pattern by area shows that the number of public social welfare specialists for every 100,000 people is low in Seoul, Gyeonggi-*do*, Incheon, Ulsan, and Busan, but high in Jeollanam-*do* and Jeollabuk-*do*. The ratio of social workers rated at the highest grade to all social workers is the highest in Seoul.

Source: Ministry of Health and Welfare (MOHW), 2005, *Yearbook of Health and Social Welfare Statistics*.

Recipients of National Basic Livelihood Security Scheme [148-3]

This map shows the number of recipients of the National Basic Livelihood Security Scheme for every 100,000 people per *si* and *gun* and the number of these recipients by type per *si* and *do*. An index indicating the number of people who receive benefits from the National Basic Livelihood Security Scheme, which is a part of the welfare policy that strengthens the state's responsibility to low-income groups. The number of recipients of the National Basic Livelihood Security Scheme is used to measure the number of absolute poor who need state protection, to provide them with benefits from the National Basic Livelihood Security Scheme, and to afford them comprehensive self-reliance and self-support services. When briefly examined, the distribution pattern by area shows that the number of recipients of the National Basic Livelihood Security Scheme for every 100,000 people is low in Seoul, Gyeonggi-*do*, Incheon, Ulsan, Busan, Chungcheongbuk-*do*, and Chungcheongnam-*do*, and relatively high in rural areas such as Jeollanam-*do*, Jeollabuk-*do*, and northern Gyeongsangbuk-*do*.

Source: National Statistical Office, 2005, *Korea Statistical Yearbook*.

Members of Households Headed by Children [148-4]

This map shows the number of members of households headed by children for every 100,000 people per *si* and *gun* and the number of members of households headed by children who are attending school per *si* and *do*. Children aged 20 or below indicated on the map are responsible for the livelihood of their respective households due to problems in families such as the deaths or illness of parents. Children who head households are designated as children in need of protection and provided with livelihood, medical support, and educational support so that they may lead stable lives and continue schooling. When briefly examined, the distribution pattern by area shows that the number of members of households headed by children for every 100,000 people is high in rural areas such as Jeollabuk-*do*, south-western Jeollanam-*do*, northwestern Gyeongsangnam-*do*, and northern Gyeongsangbuk-*do*, but relatively low in urban areas such as Seoul, Gyeonggi-*do*, Chungcheongnam-*do*, Daegu, Ulsan, and Busan.

Source: National Statistical Office, 2005, *Korea Statistical Yearbook*.

Residential Institutions for the Elderly [149-1]

This map shows the number of residents by institutions for the elderly for every 1,000 senior citizens per *si* and *gun* and the number of residents by institution type and the number of institution per *si* and *do*. With the lengthening of the average lifespan and the consequent increase in the number of senior citizens, these citizens' diverse requirements for welfare have increased. In addition, to secure the livelihood of low-income senior citizens, the government accommodates and protects these citizens in welfare facilities for senior citizens, thus providing support, including relief and protection, to senior citizens who cannot lead normal social lives. The number of institutions for the elderly and of residents can be used as data to measure these citizens' needs for social welfare and for providing appropriate support.

Source: Ministry of Health and Welfare (MOHW), Social Welfare Institution for the Elderly (2005), Korea Statistical Information Service (http://www.kosis.kr/).

Residential Institutions for the Disabled [149-2]

This map shows the number of residents by welfare institution for the disabled, the number of residents by institution type, and the number of institution-by-institution type for every 1,000 registered disabled people per *si* and *do*. Social welfare institution can provide the disabled with counseling, treatment, education, training, and recuperation necessary for rehabilitation. Services are provided through long-term or short-term visits. Social welfare institutions for the disabled are being asked to expand, to strengthen their functions, and to improve their services so that they may meet changes in social conditions and the increasing demands of the disabled for social welfare services. The social importance of data on such institutions has, in turn, increased. When briefly examined, the distribution pattern by area shows that Chungcheongbuk-*do* and Chungcheongnam-*do* have a larger number of residents in the facilities for the disabled for every 1,000 registered disabled people.

Source: Ministry of Health and Welfare (MOHW), 2005, *Yearbook of Health and Social Welfare Statistics*.

Child Welfare Institutions [149-3]

This map shows the number of institutionalized children by child welfare facilities, the number of institutionalized children by facility type, and the number of such facilities by facility type for every 1,000 children per *si* and *do*. Child welfare facilities protect runaway children, abandoned children, lost children, teenage mothers, and children who have suffered from abuse and neglect, and therefore need protection. They provide support such as relief and protection so that children may grow and develop in a healthy manner. When briefly examined, the distribution pattern by area shows that the number of institutionalized children by child welfare facility for every 1,000 children is relatively high in Jeollabuk-*do* and Jeollanam-*do*, but relatively low in Gyeonggi-*do*, Incheon, and Ulsan.

Source: Ministry of Health and Welfare (MOHW), 2005, *Yearbook of Health and Social Welfare Statistics*. National Statistical Office, Vital Statistics (2006), Korea Statistical Information Service (http://www.kosis.kr/).

Day Care Centers [149-4]

This map shows the number of children in day care facilities, the number of children in day care facilities by facility type, and the number of such facilities by facility type for every 1,000 children per *si* and *do*. Day care facilities that protect and raise children have emerged as main focal points of social welfare policies and projects since the 1990s to meet the increasing demand and to help working parents maintain their livelihood and families. However, the ratio of national and public day care facilities to all day care facilities was 5.2 percent as of 2006, indicating that the majority of day care facilities are private. Quality day care service must be provided to secure the public interest. When briefly examined, the distribution pattern by area shows that the number of children accommodated by day care facilities for every 1,000 children is relatively high in Jeollabuk-*do* and Chungcheongbuk-*do*, but relatively low in Seoul, Gyeonggi-*do*, Incheon, and Ulsan.

Source: Ministry of Health and Welfare (MOHW), 2005, Yearbook *of Health and Social Welfare Statistics*. National Statistical Office, Vital Statistics (2006), Korea Statistical Information Service (http://www.kosis.kr/).

[References]

Ministry of Health and Welfare, 2006, 2005 Health and Social Welfare White Paper (in Korean).

Ministry of Health and Welfare, School of public Health at Seoul National University, 2006, *Current Status of, and Future Development plan for, Health and Welfare Statistic*, Ministry of Health and Welfare (in Korean).

National Statistical Office, 2006, *Social Indicators in Korea*, National Statistical Office (in Korean).

Women

Women's LFPR [150]

This map analyzes women's LFPR (labor force participation rate). Women's LFPR is the most basic index of women's social participation. It shows that, because women's economic activities are heavily affected by their marital status and the existence of children, burdens such as domestic labor, childrearing, and care for senior citizens must be shared by the entire family, and supported by society and the state to raise women's participation in economic activities qualitatively and quantitatively. Women's LFPR drops drastically after marriage and childbirth, and, to show this, LFPR is compared according to marital status: single, married, widowed, and divorced. The national distribution shows that women's LFPR is high in rural districts, but low in small to medium cities. As for LFPR by marital status and area, the LFPR of unmarried women is high in Seoul, Incheon, and Gyeonggi-*do*, which have a developed service industry. The LFPR of married women is higher in Jeollanam-*do*, Chungcheongnam-*do*, and Jeju Special Self-Governing Province, where agriculture is prominent.

Source: National Statistical Office, Population and Housing Census (2005), Korea Statistical Information Service (http://www.kosis.kr/).

Sex Ratio at Birth [152-1]

This map shows regional differences in the sex ratio at birth. In particular, the sex ratio becomes highly unbalanced for third-born children, which shows that the Korean preference for sons is still strong. While the sex ratio in the normal range is 104-106, Korea exhibits a high sex ratio nationally, which becomes especially high in particular years (years of the horse, dragon, and tiger according to the traditional Asian calendar) and in particular areas (Gyeongsangnam-*do*, Gyeongsangbuk-*do*, and Ulsan). Though the number of children per family has decreased to one or fewer, the sex ratio is higher for children born later (second and third children), thus showing that people choose to have sons. As for the sex ratio at birth per *si, gun,* and *gu*, it is generally high in Gyeongsangbuk-*do*, with Seongju-*gun* and Goryeong-*gun* the highest (152). When compared per *si* and *do*, the sex ratio of third children is the highest in Daegu (162) and the lowest in Incheon (113). Nevertheless, even the ratio for Incheon is above the normal range of the sex ratio, again clearly showing Koreans' preference for sons.

Source: National Statistical Office, Vital Statistics (2005), Korea Statistical Information Service (http://www.kosis.kr/).

Fertility Rate [152-2]

This map shows that, with a drastic fall in the total fertility rate (TFR), low fertility has become a national problem. The TFR of large cities such as Seoul and Busan is especially low, having reached 0.76 in Jongno-*gu*, Seoul. The TFR is the highest in Yeongam-*gun*, Jeollanam-*do* (1.59). As for the age distribution of new mothers, mothers' ages are generally higher in large cities but lower in rural districts. In Seoul, new mothers in their 20s account for 42 percent and those in their 30s constituted 57 percent of first-time mothers; in Chungcheongnam-*do*, the figures are 57 percent and 42 percent, respectively.

Source: National Statistical Office, Vital Statistics (2005), Korea Statistical Information Service (http://www.kosis.kr/).

Sex Mortality Ratio [152-3]

This map compares sexes in deaths, indicates the high mortality rate of men in their 50s, and reflects gender differences in causes of deaths. The national sex mortality ratio is 100 or above, with only two areas with a figure below 100: Gwacheon-*gun*, Gyeonggi-*do*; and Gunwi-*gun*, Gyeongsangbuk-*do*. In terms of areas, the sex ratio of people in their 50s, whose sex mortality ratio is the highest, is the highest in Gyeongsangbuk-*do* (321) and the lowest in Gwangju (247). When the sex mortality ratio is 300 or above, it means three men die for every one woman's death. The ratio of deaths due to cancer is the highest for men in Seoul (33 percent) and the lowest for women in

Jeollanam-*do* and Chungcheongnam-*do* (19 percent).
Source: National Statistical Office, Vital Statistics (2005), Korea Statistical Information Service (http://www.kosis.kr/).

Women and Marriage [152-4]

This map shows that when the ratios of unmarried women aged 25-29 per *si* and *do* are compared, the proportion of unmarried women in this age group is generally high, especially in large cities. In addition, with a decrease in a first marriage for both men and women, other forms of marriage are increasing and there are regional differences as well. As for women aged 25-29, those unmarried reach 59 percent, which means that 3 out of 5 are unmarried. The ratio of unmarried women is generally high in large cities, the highest in Gangnam-*gu*, Seoul (81 percent), with 4 out of 5 women of marriageable age unmarried, and the lowest in Hwacheon-*gun*, Gangwon-*do* (23 percent). As for forms of marriage, the ratio of first marriage for both men and women is highest in Seoul (80.4 percent) and the ratio of remarriage is highest in Incheon (17.4 percent). The ratio of marriage between bachelors and formerly married women is higher in all areas than that between formerly married men and bachelorettes.
Source: National Statistical Office, Vital Statistics (2005), Korea Statistical Information Service (http://www.kosis.kr/).
National Statistical Office, Population and Housing Census (2005), Korea Statistical Information Service (http://www.kosis.kr/).

Women and Families: Female Householders [153]

This map shows that increasingly more householders are women, a phenomenon removed from the typical nuclear family (consisting of father, mother, and children) in industrial societies. The causes of this increase in women householders are considerably different between urban and rural areas. Continuously increasing, the ratio of women householders to all householders is the highest in Uiryeong-*gun*, Gyeongsangnam-*do* (35.6 percent) and the lowest in Buk-*gu*, Ulsan (11.1 percent). As for householders' marital status, women householders are more likely to be unmarried than male householders nationwide, with the ratio of unmarried women householders the highest in Seoul (34 percent) and the ratio of unmarried male householders the lowest in Jeollanam-*do* (6 percent). The ratio of widowed women householders is the highest in Jeollanam-*do* (74 percent) and the lowest in Seoul (32 percent). Generally, women householders in large cities are more likely to be unmarried, while those in rural districts are more likely to have been widowed.
Source: National Statistical Office, Population and Housing Census (2005), Korea Statistical Information Service (http://www.kosis.kr/).

Women and Families: Marriage to Foreigners [154-1]

This map first examines the ratio of foreigner's residences in Korea, then compares the nationalities of foreign-born wives and husbands by area. The ratio of Korean men's marriages to foreign-born wives is generally higher in rural districts than in cities. In particular, it is the highest in Sancheong-*gun*, Gyeongsangnam-*do* (33.0 percent) and the lowest in Seocho-*gu*, Seoul (4.8 percent). There are also differences in the nationalities of foreign-born wives and husbands: the former are mainly from China, Vietnam, and Japan (in descending order), and the latter are mainly from China, the United States, and Japan (in descending order).
Source: National Statistical Office, Vital Statistics (2005), Korea Statistical Information Service (http://www.kosis.kr/).
National Statistical Office, Population and Housing Census (2005), Korea Statistical Information Service (http://www.kosis.kr/).

Women and Families: Labor [154-2]

This map shows gender differences in the use of time. It classifies gender differences by the time spent on socialization and leisure per area, and shows that women's total working hours are longer, with domestic labor hours (household management and taking care of the family) and market labor hours (work) differentiated between the sexes. The time spent on socialization and leisure is higher for men in all areas. Gender differences are the greatest on Jeju Special Self-Governing Province (57 minutes) and the lowest in Incheon (10 minutes). Total working hours, which combine domestic labor hours and market labor hours, are longer for women in all areas, reaching the highest level for women in Jeollanam-*do* (411 minutes/day). The group with the shortest working hours consists of men in Busan (209 minutes). Domestic labor hours are the shortest for men in Incheon (25 minutes/day), and the longest for women in Ulsan (209 minutes/day).
Source: National Statistical Office, Time Use Survey (2004), Korea Statistical Information Service (http://www.kosis.kr/).

Women and Welfare: Safety [154-3]

This map compares the number of actual crimes and people's fear of crime per si and do to determine the safety of daily life. According to the map, women are much more fearful of crime. This is true in all areas. When only women are examined, the fear of crime is the highest in Seoul (72.1 percent) and the lowest in Jeollabuk-*do* (40.5 percent). The difference between the sexes in the fear of crime is the least in Jeollanam-*do* (12.2 percent) and the greatest in Seoul (22.8 percent).
Source: National Statistical Office, Social Statistics Survey (2006), Korea Statistical Information Service (http://www.kosis.kr/).

Women and Welfare: Information Use [154-4]

This map compares gender differences in the possession and use of computers and mobile phones, both of which are prevalent in Korea. The computer utilization rate is generally higher for men, with the highest group consisting of men in Gwangju (64 percent) and the lowest group consisting of men in Jeollanam-*do* (33 percent). The mobile phone utilization rate, likewise, is generally higher for men, with the highest group consisting of men in Seoul (68.4 percent) and the lowest group consisting of women in Gyeongsangnam-*do* (31.2 percent). As for women only, the highest group consists of those in Seoul (49.8 percent).
Source: National Statistical Office, Social Statistics Survey (2006), Korea Statistical Information Service (http://www.kosis.kr/).

Female Social Participation: Higher Education [155-1]

This map shows that, amidst increasing women's participation in education, women's participation in higher education per area has yet to rise. When compared, the ratio of women university graduates per area is high in large cities, but low in rural districts. The ratio is the highest in Gangnam-*gu* and Seocho-*gu*, Seoul (32 percent) and the lowest in Gokseong-*gun*, Goheung-*gun*, and Sinan-*gun*, Jeollanam-*do* (1.7 percent). As for the number of master's degree holders per 1,000 people, Daejeon is the highest (33 per 1,000 men) when only men are examined, while Seoul is the highest (17 per 1,000 women) when only women are examined.
Source: National Statistical Office, Population and Housing Census (2005), Korea Statistical Information Service (http://www.kosis.kr/).

Female Social Participation: High-Ranking Professional Jobs [155-2]

This map shows that, despite women's increasing social participation, the social status of women has yet to rise. As for social participation by occupation, the ratios of women professionals and entrepreneurs are low, and the LFPR of women with university degrees is lower than that of other OECD member states, signifying that highly educated women still cannot participate in society actively. The ratio of women professionals is 38.6 percent nationwide, with that for Jeju Special Self-Governing Province the highest, exhibiting a pure difference of 9 percentage points, and that for Seoul the lowest, exhibiting a reverse difference of 7.9 percentage points. The ratio of self-employed women, likewise, is the highest in Jeju Special Self-Governing Province (35.0 percent) and the lowest in Incheon (25.3 percent).
Source: National Statistical Office, Economically Active Population Survey (2005), Korea Statistical Information Service (http://www.kosis.kr/).

Female Social Participation: Politics [155-3]

This map compares the ratio of women members of local governments and metropolitan councils per *si* and *do* to measure women's participation in politics. As for local governments in *si, gun,* and *gu* by gender, women head them in only three areas – Songpa-*gu* in Seoul; Jung-*gu* in Daegu; and Jung-*gu* in Incheon-out of 230 areas. The ratio of women members of regional councils is 12.1 percent nationwide, with Ulsan the highest (26.3 percent) and Incheon and Gyeongsangbuk-*do* the lowest (9.1 percent). The ratio of women members of basic councils is 15.1 percent nationwide, with Gwangju the highest (26.5 percent) and Jeollanam-*do* the lowest (9.1 percent).
Source: National Election Commission, The 4th Local Election (2006), Electoral Information System (http://www.nec.go.kr/sinfo/).

Female Social Participation: Government Administration [155-4]

This map compares women's participation in civil service and daycare facilities per *si* and *do* in order to grasp women's participation in civil service. As for the ratio of female civil servants, the national average is 26.5 percent, which means that approximately one out of four civil servants is a woman. This ratio is the highest in Gyeonggi-*do* (29.5 percent) and the lowest in Gyeongsangbuk-*do* (23.0 percent). The ratio of female civil servants at or above the 5th grade is considerably lower, amounting to a national average of 5.9 percent. This ratio is the highest in Seoul (12.1 percent) and the lowest in Chungcheongnam-*do* (2.5 percent). On the other hand, the ratio of women who take the civil service examination is considerably high, amounting to a national average of 50.5 percent. This ratio is the highest in Gwangju (71 percent) and the lowest in Jeju Special Self-Governing Province (39.8 percent).
Source: Ministry of Government Administration and Home Affairs (MOGAHA; http://www.mogaha.go.kr), 2006, *Statistics on Female Civil Servants in Local Governments.*

Education

Number of Students and Education Expenses [156]

This map shows the number of students for every 1,000 people per *si* and *gun* and education expenses for each household per *si* and *gun*. Because the simple regional distribution of the student population only shows the size, it is impossible to know the proportion of the student population to the total population per area. This map uses the ratio of the student population to the total population as an index to show the size of, and regional differences in, the student population. As a result, it is possible to understand the distribution of student population sizes and to confirm the actual proportion of the student population to the regional population. Here, the number of students designates the sum of students in institutions from kindergartens to high schools. This map also shows regional differences in education expenses per household by using the average monthly education expense per household. The average monthly education expenses per household can be an important index of Korean households' economic power and education expenses alike.
Source: Ministry of Education and Human Resources Development (MOE & HRD; http://www.moe.go.kr).
National Statistical Office, Population and Housing Census (2005), Korea Statistical Information Service (http://www.kosis.kr/).

Teachers [158-1]

This map shows the number of students for each teacher per *gun*, the distribution of teachers by age group (primary schools, middle schools, general/humanities high schools, vocational schools) per *si* and *do*, and the gender distribution of teachers per *si* and *do*. To understand the differences in regional educational conditions for teachers, it shows the average number of students per teacher, teachers' age, and teacher gender distribution. Because the quality of education depends on the number of students assigned to each teacher, that number is the most widely used education-related index. In addition, the physical condition of teachers, who are the main disseminators of education, are likewise important for the provision of quality education. To confirm this, the map uses teachers' age as an important index. Because it considerably affects teachers' educational activities, the gender composition of teachers is yet another important index for understanding Korea's educational environment.
Source: Ministry of Education and Human Resources Development (MOE & HRD; http://www.moe.go.kr). National Statistical Office, Population and Housing Census (2005), Korea Statistical Information Service (http://www.kosis.kr/).

Education Budget [158-2]

This map shows the education budget for each student per *si* and *do*, the average monthly educational expenses for each student per *si* and *do*, and the composition of the education budget per *si* and *do*. It shows Korea's education budget and the regional distribution and characteristics of education expenses per student. Representing the education expenses that the state uses to provide education, the education budget per student is the total education budget divided by the total number of students in each *si* and *do*. To measure regional differences, this map also shows the educational budget for each student per area. In addition, it classifies the education budget into categories to explain the composition of the budget, and presents regional differences in the composition of the education budget. On an individual level, the average monthly education expenses for a student become an important index of educational activities. Therefore, it is possible to understand state and individual expenses when the regional distribution of the government's education budget and an individual student's education expenses are compared. It is possible to understand the composition of financial resources for local education budgets since the introduction of local governments. In addition, the degree of the local education budget's dependence on state financial resources can be analyzed.
Source: Ministry of Education and Human Resources Development (MOE & HRD; http://www.moe.go.kr).

Educational Environment (Number of Books and Computers) [158-3]

This map shows the number of books for each student per *si* and *gun*, computers for each primary school student per *si* and *do*, and computers for each middle school student per *si* and *do*. It indicates regional differences in the educational environment through the number of books and computers. The school education support environment includes various facilities, equipment, and books. Especially representative of education quality is the library holding index. Also, the degree of information access within education institutions is well represented by the degree of the dissemination of computers. While the number of students for each computer is generally used as an index here, because regional differences are slight, the number of computers for each student, which is derived by dividing the total number of computers in primary and middle schools per *si* and *do* by the total number of students, is used as an index.
Source: Ministry of Education and Human Resources Development (MOE & HRD; http://www.moe.go.kr).
National Statistical Office, Population and Housing Census (2005), Korea Statistical Information Service (http://www.kosis.kr/).

Educational Facilities [158-4]

This map shows the areas of the campus for each student per *si* and *gun*, the school buildings for each student per *si* and *do*, and sports arenas for each student per *si* and *do*. It shows the regional distribution of the area of educational facilities, school buildings, and sports arenas for each student. One important variable that explains the school education environment is educational facilities, and the area of school facilities reflects the quality of the physical environment of schools. From among them, the area of the campus (unit: 1m²) is useful for grasping the spatial size of schools, but the area of the buildings where students' actual school activities take place is a better index than the area of the campus and/or the area of the entire school building. In addition, the area of the sports arena is an important index for the existence and scale of space for outdoor activities, including physical education activities for students.
Source: Ministry of Education and Human Resources Development (MOE & HRD; http://www.moe.go.kr). National Statistical Office, Population and Housing Census (2005), Korea Statistical Information Service (http://www.kosis.kr/).

Kindergartens [159-1]

Elementary Schools [159-2]

Middle Schools [159-3]

High Schools [159-4]

These maps show the numbers of kindergartens, elementary/middle/high schools per 1,000 people per *si* and *gun*, of teachers for each kindergarten and school per *si* and *do*, and of pupils for each kindergarten and school and for each class per *si* and *do*. They show regional differences in kindergarten, elementary, and secondary education. To illustrate regional differences in education, they show the distribution of the number of students per 1,000 people, teachers and students for each kindergarten and school, and students for each class. The number of teachers and pupils per kindergarten and school, and of pupils per class are important indices for understanding the condition of kindergarten, elementary, and secondary education. However, here, simple indices such as the numbers of teachers, kindergartens, schools and pupils are not used. The numbers of kindergarteners and schools per 1,000 people better reflect regional population structures. The three indices of the number of teachers per kindergarten/school, pupils per kindergarten/school, and pupils per class have been selected more easily to display regional differences in these schools' physical environment.
Source: Ministry of Education and Human Resources Development (MOE & HRD; http://www.moe.go.kr).
National Statistical Office, Population and Housing Census (2005), Korea Statistical Information Service (http://www.kosis.kr/).

School Advancement Rate [160-1]

This map shows the rate at which students continue on to universities per *si* and *gun*, to middle schools per *si* and *do*, and to high schools per *si* and *do*. Briefly, it shows regional differences in Korean students' advancement rate to middle schools, high schools, and universities. Index reflects various factors including the state's advancement and educational policy, vocational policy, educational opportunities, and vocational preferences. In particular, while the rates of advancement from kindergartens, primary schools, and middle schools are nearly 100 percent in Korea, the rates of advancement to high school and universities clearly show social, class, and regional differences in Korean society. Thus, the distribution of these latter rates is used to measure regional differences in educational opportunities and accomplishments.
Source: Ministry of Education and Human Resources Development

(MOE & HRD; http://www.moe.go.kr).
National Statistical Office, Population and Housing Census (2005),
Korea Statistical Information Service (http://www.kosis.kr/).

Colleges and Universities [160-2]
This map shows the number of universities by type per *si* and *do*, students by university type per *si* and *do*, and students and departments for each university per *si* and *do*. It shows regional differences in college education. To understand the quantity and quality of college education, factors have been selected as important indices of university or higher education. They include the number of four-year universities, departments, students, and sex ratio in terms of various regions, the number of universities per *si* and *do*, college students per *si* and *do*, students per university, and departments per university. In addition, indices have been established to understand the number of faculty members, departments, and students per region.
Source: Ministry of Education and Human Resources Development
(MOE & HRD; http://www.moe.go.kr).
National Statistical Office, Population and Housing Census (2005),
Korea Statistical Information Service (http://www.kosis.kr/).

Graduate Schools [160-3]
This map shows the number of graduate schools per *si* and *do*, graduate students (male/female) per *si* and *do*, departments (master's/doctoral programs) in each graduate school per *si* and *do*, and students in each graduate school per *si* and *do*. It also shows regional differences in graduate schools. The number of graduate schools per *si* and *do*, graduate students per *si* and *do*, and students in each graduate school per si and do are useful indices for understanding qualitative and quantitative differences in the conditions of graduate education. The more students there are in a graduate school, the larger the school is. The number of departments in a graduate school reflects the diversity of majors offered, and serves as an index of the school's professionalization and specialization. The number of students in a graduate school also serves as an index of the regional distribution of large graduate schools, and is especially useful for pinpointing the locations of large graduate schools. The number of departments in a graduate school serves as an index of the diversity of graduate education; the larger this index is, the more majors are offered, which means that higher education is more professionalized. The regional distribution of this index shows the locations of graduate schools with diverse majors. However, the drawback is that areas with graduate schools that only offer specialized majors exhibit a low value, thus making it difficult to adequately reflect their degree of specialization.
Source: Ministry of Education and Human Resources Development
(MOE & HRD; http://www.moe.go.kr).
National Statistical Office, Population and Housing Census (2005),
Korea Statistical Information Service (http://www.kosis.kr/).

Foreign Students in Korea [160-4]
This map shows the number of foreign students in Korea by type per *si* and *do* and the total number of these students in Korea per *si* and *do*. It reveals the distribution of foreign students in Korea. To examine the characteristics of foreign students, this map shows the number of such students, their sex ratio, and their financial sources vis-à-vis their education expenses by area. As an index of the size of the influx of foreign students, the total number of these students by area shows which areas host the greatest number of foreign students. The financial sources of foreign students' education expenses show the range of such students hosted by Korea, given foreign support, and student exchange abroad. They can also be classified into self-payment, invitation by the Korean government or university, support from the students' home countries, and others. These indices in turn show what the Korean government and universities must do, and how active they must be, to competitively engage in student exchange with other countries. In addition, the sex ratio of foreign students in Korea shows which areas host more male or female students.
Source: Ministry of Education and Human Resources Development
(MOE & HRD; http://www.moe.go.kr). National Statistical Office,
Population and Housing Census (2005),
Korea Statistical Information Service (http://www.kosis.kr/).

Student Transfers [161-1]
This map shows middle school students' transfers per *si* and *gun*, Koreans' satisfaction with educational opportunities per *si* and *do*, and Korean middle school students' satisfaction with school life per *si* and *do*. It displays areas where middle school student populations and transfers are concentrated through an examination of student transfers, and explains them in terms of regional differences in educational conditions. Student transfers can be measured by the number of transferring students, with the difference between incoming and outgoing students used to determine areas with significant numbers of student transfers. It is also possible to understand which areas are considered to have many educational advantages. In addition, student transfers can be explained through variables such as the amount of expected educational advantage, quality of educational services, satisfaction with educational opportunities, and satisfaction with school life. Here, the reasons for transfers are sought out through educational opportunities and satisfaction with school life. With "0" representing a balance between incoming and outgoing students, this map indicates student transfers above and below the boundary and shows which is more prevalent. In addition, it compares the degree of satisfaction with educational opportunities and with school life as an indication of the reasons behind student transfers.
Source: Ministry of Education and Human Resources Development
(MOE & HRD; http://www.moe.go.kr). National Statistical Office,
Population and Housing Census (2005),
Korea Statistical Information Service (http://www.kosis.kr/).

Education-Related Civil Servants [161-2]
This map shows the number of education-related civil servants for each student per *si* and *gun*, and the composition of these civil servants by work status per *si* and *do*. It presents regional differences in the educational services support environment through the distribution of education-related civil servants and their number for each student per *si* and *gun*. To evaluate the quality of educational services, it is necessary to measure the number of administrative service personnel who support teachers' activities in educational institutions. The map displays the number of civil servants who systematically support education. For this goal, the index of the number of education-related civil servants per 1,000 students is used. By examining regional differences in this index through choropleth maps, it is possible to indicate regional differences in educational services. In addition, the work status of education-related civil servants makes it possible to identify the types of education support services.
Source: Ministry of Education and Human Resources Development
(MOE & HRD; http://www.moe.go.kr). National Statistical Office,
Population and Housing Census (2005),
Korea Statistical Information Service (http://www.kosis.kr/).

Alternative Schools and Vocational Schools [161-3]
This map shows the distribution of alternative and vocational schools per *si* and *gun*. It thereby displays the regional distribution of specialized education in Korea. It is important to understand alternative and vocational schools, which perform special educational functions despite their differences from regular school education. By indicating the national distribution of these specialized schools, it is possible to identify areas where specialized education is offered, and to explain them in terms of their regional characteristics.
Source: Ministry of Education and Human Resources Development
(MOE & HRD; http://www.moe.go.kr). National Statistical Office,
Population and Housing Census (2005),
Korea Statistical Information Service (http://www.kosis.kr/).

Educational Attainment [161-4]
This map shows the number of master's/doctoral degree holders per 1,000 people per *si* and *do*, bachelor's degree holders per 1,000 people per *si* and *do*, and high school graduates per 1,000 people per *si* and *do*. It displays regional differences in levels of Koreans' education and Koreans' qualitative (educational) characteristics by indicating the regional distribution of population vis-à-vis educational attainment. Examining this regional distribution helps to understand populational characteristics and distribution vis-à-vis people's highest educational attainment.
Source: Ministry of Education and Human Resources Development
(MOE & HRD; http://www.moe.go.kr).
National Statistical Office, Population and Housing Census (2005),
Korea Statistical Information Service (http://www.kosis.kr/).

Korea in the World

Korea's Diplomatic Relations [162]
This map shows the nations with which Korea has diplomatic relations and the number of Koreans living in those countries. It was produced to estimate Korea's place in the world by displaying the nation's diplomatic network, and to understand the degree of these countries' exchanges with Korea by investigating the number of Koreans living in them. Whether a nation has diplomatic relations with Korea and the number of Koreans living in it can both be indices of the degree of the country's exchange with Korea. By classifying Korean residents in these nations according to citizens, permanent residents, legal aliens, or students, the map depicts the qualitative characteristics of Korea's exchange with these countries.
Source: Ministry of Foreign Affairs and Trade (MOFAT),
Surveys on Overseas Korean Residents (2005),
Ministry of Foreign Affairs and Trade Homepage (MOFAT; http://www.mofat.go.kr).

Investment by Foreign Corporations in Korea [164-1]
This map shows the distribution of foreign corporate investment in Korea in 1990 and 2005. It was created to show the number and amount (unit: US$ 1,000) of foreign corporate investment in Korea, and to estimate the position of the Korean market in the world. In particular, by comparing data for 1990 and 2005, thereby indicating changes in foreign corporate investment in Korea, it is possible to estimate the future competitiveness of the Korean economy. Considering the quickly changing world economic environment, data on changes in foreign corporate investment in Korea in 1990 and 2005 makes it possible to estimate Korea's position in the world economic order.
Source: Ministry of Commerce, Industry, and Energy (MOCIE; http://www.mocie.go.kr),
Statistics on Foreign Investment in Korea (1990, 2005), Ministry of Commerce,
Industry, and Energy Homepage (http:// www.mocoe.go.kr).

Investment by Korean Corporations Abroad [164-2]
This map indicates Korean corporations' investments abroad. It indicates changes in the number and amount (unit: US$ 1,000) of Korean corporate investment abroad to grasp these corporations' competitiveness and position in the world economic environment. Considering the quickly changing world economic situation, the comparison of data on Korean corporate investment abroad in 1990 and 2005 makes it possible to estimate these corporations' competitiveness and, as such, the position of the Korean economy in the world.
Source: Korea Eximbank (The Export-Import Bank of Korea),
Economic Development Cooperation Fund (EDCF) Annual Report (1990, 2005),
Korea Eximbank Homepage (http://www.koreaexim.go.kr/kr/).

Origins of Foreign Students in Korea [165-1]
This map shows the number of foreign students in Korea in 2001 and 2006. It reflects the degree to which the nation has constructed infrastructures to publicize Korea worldwide by classifying foreign students in Korea according to their countries of origin and majors of study. This is significant because Korea must foster competitive human resources to be competitive in the future and to train talented foreign experts who are amicable to Korea. Both of these goals will help to publicize Korea and to improve the nation's image around the globe. Based on 2001 and 2006 data, the map indicates changes in foreign students in Korea by country of origin, program, and time by classifying these students according to categories including degree programs (science and engineering, humanities and social sciences, arts and physical education) and language training.
Source: Ministry of Education and Human Resources Development (MOE & HRD),
2006 Statistics on Foreign Students in Korea (2006),
Ministry of Education and Human Resources Development (http://www.moe.go.kr).

Korean Students Abroad [165-2]
This map shows the distribution of Korean students abroad in 2001 and 2006. It indicates Korean students abroad and changes in numbers of Korean students abroad for these two time periods per country and major of study. This is significant because in order to raise national competitiveness in the future, Korea must foster talented experts and, in particular, those qualified to work in the changing global environment. Moreover, it indicates changes by classifying students according to categories, including degree programs (undergraduate programs, graduate programs) and language training.
Source: Ministry of Education and Human Resources Development (MOE & HRD)
2006 Statistics on Korean students abroad (2006),
Ministry of Education and Human Resources Development (http://www.moe.go.kr).

Korean Nationals' Departures to Overseas [166-1]
This map shows the departures of Korean citizens. Based on 2005 data from the Korean Immigration Service, it shows for what purposes and for which nations Koreans departed. This is significant because it displays the degree of civilian exchange between Korean nationals and foreigners, which plays a key role in cross-cultural understanding. As for departures from Korea, the purposes of departure (religion/tourism/art/official duty/participation in meetings/visits/cohabitation/research/study abroad/training/ employment/ citizens abroad/emigration/others) recorded on departure cards were classified according to destinations.
Source: Korea Immigration Service (KIS), 2005, 2006, Yearbook of Departures and Arrivals.

Entry of Foreigners into Korea [166-2]
This map shows foreigners' entry into Korea. Its purpose is to indicate how many foreigners from which countries come to Korea for what purposes. This is significant because foreigners' visits to Korea serve as an opportunity to publicize the culture and history of the country through direct exchange. Based on such exchange, the degree to which Korean culture and history are disseminated worldwide can be estimated. Foreigners' purposes of entry are classified according to the visa types issued by the Korean government and are indicated on the map.
Source: Korea Immigration Service (KIS), 2005, 2006, Yearbook of Departures and Arrivals.

Foreign Residents in Korea [167-1]
This map shows the number of foreigners who are living in Korea. Within the increasing cultural diversification in this age of internationalization, foreigners residing in Korea represent an opportunity for Koreans to broaden their understanding of foreign places and cultures. In addition, this map indicates the ratio of foreigners living in Korea per *si* and *gun* based on the number of registered population according to 2006 data.
Source: Ministry of Government Administration and Home Affairs
(MOGAHA; http://www.mogaha.go.kr), Surveys on Foreign Residents in Korea (2006).

Migrant Workers in Korea [167-2]
This map shows the number of migrant workers in Korea. Based on 2006 data, it shows the influx of migrant workers per *si* and *gun*. With the active international and spatial division of labor in this age of globalization, Korea, like many other countries, has seen a large influx of migrant workers. By indicating how many workers from which countries have come to Korea, it is possible to spatially grasp the degree of influx of migrant workers into the country. To do so, this map also indicates the ratio of migrant workers per si and gun based on the number of foreigners living in the country according to 2006 data, thus making it possible to confirm regional differences in the influx of migrant workers.
Source: Ministry of Government Administration and Home Affairs
(MOGAHA; http://www.mogaha.go.kr), Surveys on Foreign Residents in Korea (2006).

Foreigners Who Have Acquired Korean Citizenship [167-3]
This map shows the number of foreigners in Korea who have acquired Korean citizenship. This is significant because the number of foreigners who have acquired Korean citizenship is an index of the degree of cultural diversification in Korean society, which is largely and historically exclusionist due to its strong, age-old cultural homogeneity. In addition, it indicates the ratio of foreigners who have acquired Korean nationality per *si* and *gun*, thus making it possible to confirm regional differences in the number of people who have acquired Korean citizenship.
Source: Ministry of Government Administration and Home Affairs
(MOGAHA; http://www.mogaha.go.kr), Surveys on Foreign Residents in Korea (2006).

Migrants for International Marriage in Korea [167-4]
This map shows the number of migrants who entered Korea for international marriage. More specifically, it shows the number of foreigners who have migrated to Korea for international marriage per si and gun based on 2006 data. Today, the number of foreigners who come to Korea for marriage is increasing, with widespread arranged marriages between foreigners and rural or low-income Korean men who are older than the traditional optimal marriageable age. The purpose of this map is to examine how many foreigners from which nations have become members of Korean society through international marriage. In addition, it indicates the ratio of foreigners who have come to Korea for international marriage per *si* and *gun* based on the number of foreigners living in the country according to 2006 data, thus making it possible to confirm regional differences in international marriage rates.
Source: Ministry of Government Administration and Home Affairs
(MOGAHA; http://www.mogaha.go.kr), Surveys on Foreign Residents in Korea (2006).

1:500,000 INDEX

1:500,000 INDEX

1:500,000 INDEX

Peninsula/Islands/Island

Temple

Expressway/Interchange